Litigating Animal Law Disputes

A Complete Guide for Lawyers

JOAN SCHAFFNER
AND JULIE FERSHTMAN
EDITORS

TORT TRIAL & INSURANCE PRACTICE SECTION

Defending Liberty
Pursuing Justice

Cover design by ABA Publishing.

Printed in the United States of America
09 08 07 06 05 5 4 3 2 1

Library of Congress Cataloging-in-Publication Data

Litigating animal law disputes / [editors] Julie I. Fershtman and Joan E. Schaffner.
p. cm.
Includes index.
ISBN-13: 978-1-60442-001-2
ISBN-10: 1-60442-001-4
1. Domestic animals--Law and legislation--United States. I. Fershtman, Julie I. II. Schaffner, Joan E.

KF390.5.A5L58 2009
346.7304'7--dc22

2009005557

Discounts are available for books ordered in bulk. Special consideration is given to state bars, CLE programs, and other bar-related organizations. Inquire at Book Publishing, ABA Publishing, American Bar Association, 321 North Clark Street, Chicago, Illinois 60654-7598.

www.ababooks.org

TABLE OF CONTENTS

ABOUT THE EDITORS

Joan E. Schaffner is an Associate Professor of Law at the George Washington University Law School in Washington, D.C. She received her B.S. in mechanical engineering and J.D. from the University of Southern California and her M.S. in mechanical engineering from the Massachusetts Institute of Technology. She worked at the law firm of Irell & Manella in Los Angeles, California, and clerked for the Honorable Mariana Pfaelzer in the Central District of California before coming to GW.

Professor Schaffner teaches Civil Procedure, Remedies, and Sexuality and the Law, and writes in these areas as well. She is the faculty advisor to Lambda Law, the GLBT student organization at GW, and is faculty advisor and editor-in-chief of the *American Intellectual Property Law Association Quarterly Journal.*

Professor Schaffner directs the GW Animal Law Program, which consists of the GW Animal Welfare Project, a pro bono effort of faculty and students devoted to researching and improving animal welfare laws in the District of Columbia; teaches seminars in animal law; and is the faculty advisor to a student chapter of the Animal Legal Defense Fund (SALDF). Additionally, Professor Schaffner has testified on behalf of non-breed-specific dangerous dog laws and has presented on animal law panels at conferences worldwide. She is active in various organizations, holding the offices of Chair-Elect (8/08), Publications Chair, and Editor of the newsletter of the ABA Tort Trial and Insurance Practice Section (TIPS) Animal Law Committee, Founding Chair of the Association of American Law Schools Section on Animal Law, and consumer member for the District of Columbia Board of Veterinary Medicine. She was recently selected as a Fellow of the Oxford Centre for Animal Ethics.

Professor Schaffner is a volunteer for Washington Humane Society, fosters feline families, and is committed to saving the lives of homeless animals. She lives with many felines; Jackie, a Jack Russell; and Rocky, a brilliant African Grey parrot.

Julie I. Fershtman is Of Counsel to the Farmington Hills, Michigan, law firm of Zausmer, Kaufman, August, Caldwell & Tayler, P.C., where she practices in the areas of insurance defense, insurance coverage, business litigation, and equine law. With experience handling cases involving equine liability, animal sales, and animal insurance coverage, she has tried cases successfully before juries in three states and has been admitted to practice as *pro hac vice* counsel in state and federal courts in 12 states.

Fershtman is an officer of the State Bar of Michigan and is on track to become its president in 2011. She is also a Vice-Chair of the TIPS Animal Law Committee and a Fellow of the American Bar Foundation.

The ABA/YLD's *Barrister Magazine* profiled her as one of "21 Young Lawyers Leading Us into the 21st Century" in 1995. In 2007, *Crain's Detroit Business* magazine named her one of "Metro Detroit's Most Influential Women," and in 1996, *Crain's Detroit Business* honored her as one of "40 Outstanding Business Leaders Under 40." She was named by *Law & Politics* magazine as a Michigan "Super Lawyer" in 2008.

She is the author of the books *Equine Law & Horse Sense* (Horses & The Law Publishing, 1996) and *More Equine Law & Horse Sense* (Horses & The Law Publishing, 2000) and has written over 185 published articles on equine law. She has lectured at seminars, conventions, universities, and continuing education conferences in 26 states. Her equine law practice has been profiled in such publications as the *Houston Chronicle* and the *Chicago Tribune*, and she has been quoted on liability issues in such publications as the *New York Times*.

Fershtman volunteers her time to serve on boards and to assist numerous nonprofit associations throughout the country that involve equine activities, youth, and land conservation. She received the national Partner in Safety Award from the Certified Horsemanship Association in 1997, the Outstanding Achievement Award from the American Riding Instructor Certification Program in 1998, and the Catalyst Award from the Michigan Horse Council in 2002.

She is a 1983 graduate of Emory College and a 1986 graduate of Emory Law School. Her Web site is available at http://www.equinelaw.net.

ABOUT THE CONTRIBUTORS

Zandra Anderson is a practicing Houston trial attorney who represents dog owners and their dogs (and other animals including cats, horses, ferrets, and geese) in a variety of animal law matters. She has represented owners all over Texas in dangerous dog determinations, felony dog attack cases, dog-bite cases, cruelty matters, ownership issues, contractual matters, kennel name infringement issues, kennel club issues, and liability issues regarding veterinarians, breeders, kennels, dog trainers, pet sitters, and rescue organizations. She consults to municipalities, governmental agencies, city councils, animal control, attorneys, veterinarians, and rescue organizations, and has participated in writing state animal laws and many city ordinances. Anderson actively works to ensure that owners' rights are fairly represented in both state and local laws and that laws do not discriminate against breeds of dogs. She is the author of the *Texas Dog Law Manual (and Kitties, Too)*, which is a compilation of Texas laws regarding dogs and cats. She originated the first Texas Dog Law Seminar (2006–2008) and was the key speaker. She lectures on dog law throughout the state and is a frequent guest at dog shows, at rescue events, and on television and radio programs regarding animal-related issues. Additionally, she has written for various publications regarding animal issues.

Anderson is a member of the College of the State Bar of Texas and its Animal Law Section. She is licensed in both Texas and Colorado, and is Legal Counsel to Spindletop Refuge, a no-kill dog rescue in Texas dedicated to the responsible placement of abandoned and abused dogs, particularly American pit bull terriers. She resides with her two dogs, Zeus and Zena, in Hilshire Village, Texas (a municipality in Houston), where she is on the City Council. She is particularly proud that Zeus has earned his Canine Good Citizen title from the American Kennel Club, and she is currently working with Zena to achieve the same.

Katherine C. Bloomquist, of Bloomquist Law Firm, LLC, practices in the areas of corporate, business litigation, employment, and equine law.

She has litigated in diverse matters including equine, employment, and commercial. Her litigation experience involves jury trials, court trials, appeals, arbitrations, and alternative dispute resolution proceedings. She has managed litigation as an in-house corporate attorney, handling diverse corporate and transactional matters. Reported cases include *Gross v. Victoria Station Farms* (578 N.W.2d 757 (1998)). She recently litigated precedent-setting equine cases in Texas Federal Court, California Federal Court, and the Minnesota Supreme Court.

Bloomquist is a recognized leader in equine law. She is a frequent speaker at the National Equine Law Conference in Kentucky and the equine law conference in California. In 2005 she was the first speaker on equine law at the American Bar Association in Chicago, and is presently the subcommittee chair for Equine Law of the Animal Law Committee of the Tort Trial and Insurance Practice Section (TIPS) of the American Bar Association. Bloomquist was the 2005–2007 chair of the Animal Law Section of the Minnesota State Bar and chaired the first-ever Animal Law Conference sponsored by the Minnesota State Bar Association in 2006. Additionally, Bloomquist has published numerous articles in the area of equine law.

Bloomquist is a member of the Animal Law Committee of the American Bar Association, a Council Member of the Animal Law Section, and Chair of the Committee on Equine Law of the Minnesota Bar Association. She is also a member of the Hennepin County Bar Association. Bloomquist was admitted in 1989 to the Minnesota Bar, the U.S. District for Minnesota, and the Eighth Circuit Court of Appeals.

She received her B.A. in 1986 from the University of Minnesota and her J.D. from the University of Oregon School of Law in 1989.

Dana M. Campbell is an attorney for the Criminal Justice Program of the Animal Legal Defense Fund (ALDF), a national nonprofit organization of attorneys dedicated to enforcing and enhancing laws affecting the welfare of animals. She is also an adjunct professor of Animal Law at Cornell Law School in Ithaca, New York. Previously, she taught Animal Law as an adjunct professor at Lewis & Clark Law School in Portland, Oregon, and Vermont Law School.

In addition, she has presented nearly 60 lectures on assorted animal law topics across the United States and Canada, including at the New York County District Attorney's Office; numerous law schools and humane societies; the Washington, Oregon, and New York State Bar Associations; and the National Animal Control Officer's Association. Campbell has advised the Delaware and New Jersey Governors' Task Forces on Animal

Welfare, as well as the Oregon Zoo. She is the author of the *Legal Advocates' Manual for Animal Abuse Criminal Cases*, and has been the source for numerous television, radio, and print media interviews.

Prior to her animal law career, Campbell was a deputy district attorney both in Oregon and in Maui, Hawaii, and successfully tried hundreds of criminal cases, specializing in animal cruelty and neglect, domestic violence, and child sexual assault cases. She was a founding member of the Maui County Domestic Violence Task Force, has received training on witness interview techniques from the FBI, and taught police officer refresher courses in evidence collection and courtroom techniques.

Campbell earned her B.S. at Oregon State University and her J.D. at Lewis & Clark Law School. She is licensed to practice law in New York, Oregon, Hawaii, and Washington.

She and her family share their home with two rescued dogs.

Gregory M. Dennis practices law in Overland Park, Kansas. He is Legal Counsel for the Kansas and Missouri veterinary medical associations and represents veterinarians in those states. He is a charter member and past president of the American Veterinary Medical Law Association and was Editor of the AVMLA's *Newsletter* from 1993 to 2004. Dennis has written and spoken extensively on numerous and diverse legal matters, both within and without the United States, pertaining to the practice of veterinary medicine. He is a coeditor of the *Veterinary Report* for the Animal Legal Reports Service. Dennis has also served on two American Veterinary Medical Association Task Forces, the Model Veterinary Practice Act Task Force, and the Legal Status of Animals Task Force.

Julie I. Fershtman is Of Counsel to the Farmington Hills, Michigan, law firm of Zausmer, Kaufman, August, Caldwell & Tayler, P.C., where she practices in the areas of insurance defense, insurance coverage, business litigation, and equine law. With experience handling cases involving equine liability, animal sales, and animal insurance coverage, she has tried cases successfully before juries in three states and has been admitted to practice as *pro hac vice* counsel in state and federal courts in 12 states.

Fershtman is an officer of the State Bar of Michigan and is on track to become its president in 2011. She is also a Vice-Chair of the TIPS Animal Law Committee and a Fellow of the American Bar Foundation.

The ABA/YLD's *Barrister Magazine* profiled her as one of "21 Young Lawyers Leading Us into the 21st Century" in 1995. In 2007, *Crain's Detroit Business* magazine named her one of "Metro Detroit's Most Influential Women," and in 1996, *Crain's Detroit Business* honored her as one of "40

Outstanding Business Leaders Under 40." She was named by *Law & Politics* magazine as a Michigan "Super Lawyer" in 2008.

She is the author of the books *Equine Law & Horse Sense* (Horses & The Law Publishing, 1996) and *More Equine Law & Horse Sense* (Horses & The Law Publishing, 2000) and has written over 185 published articles on equine law. She has lectured at seminars, conventions, universities, and continuing education conferences in 26 states. Her equine law practice has been profiled in such publications as the *Houston Chronicle* and the *Chicago Tribune*, and she has been quoted on liability issues in such publications as the *New York Times*.

Fershtman volunteers her time to serve on boards and to assist numerous nonprofit associations throughout the country that involve equine activities, youth, and land conservation. She received the national Partner in Safety Award from the Certified Horsemanship Association in 1997, the Outstanding Achievement Award from the American Riding Instructor Certification Program in 1998, and the Catalyst Award from the Michigan Horse Council in 2002.

She is a 1983 graduate of Emory College and a 1986 graduate of Emory Law School. Her Web site is available at http://www.equinelaw.net.

Pamela D. Frasch is Assistant Dean, Animal Law Program, and Executive Director of the Center for Animal Law Studies (CALS) at Lewis & Clark Law School in Portland, Oregon. CALS is an academic animal law program with a focus on research, scholarship, and experiential education. CALS is dedicated to

- Training law students and lawyers for careers as leaders in animal law and public policy;
- Conducting, supporting, and promoting rigorous, independent legal research that advances the field of animal law; and
- Developing innovative recommendations and legal strategies relating to animal law within administrative, legislative, litigation, and other settings.

Previously, Frasch was General Counsel for the Animal Legal Defense Fund, a national nonprofit animal protection law organization that seeks to protect the lives and advance the interests of animals through the legal system. In 1996, Frasch created the ALDF Criminal Justice Program, which has since assisted law enforcement and animal advocates in investigating and prosecuting thousands of animal abuse and neglect cases nationwide.

In addition to her duties with CALS, Frasch is coauthor of the first American legal casebook in the field, *Animal Law, Cases and Materials*, now in its third edition (Carolina Academic Press, 2006), and the forthcoming *Animal Law in a Nutshell* (Thomson West, 2010). She has taught survey and advanced courses in animal law at Lewis & Clark Law School since 1998.

Frasch is a frequent speaker on issues of animal law and is the principal author of Oregon's first felony anticruelty law. She has authored or coauthored many articles and book chapters in the field, and has been recognized by the Humane Society of the United States and the Oregon Humane Society for her contributions.

Barbara J. Gislason is internationally recognized as a pioneer in the practice area of animal law. A graduate of Carleton College and William Mitchell College of Law, she is an American Bar Foundation Fellow and a Super Lawyer. In 2003, she was the founding chair of the Minnesota State Bar Association Animal Law Committee, and later, Section.

She brought animal law to the American Bar Association (ABA) in 2004 by the unanimous vote of the ABA's prestigious Tort Trial and Insurance Practice Section (TIPS) Council. When the Animal Law Committee was created, Gislason was appointed its first Chair. This is the only Animal Law Committee in the ABA and its scope is broad, ranging from equine, family, endangered species, and criminal law to torts and insurance law. She gathered the best and brightest animal lawyers from four continents, and under her stewardship, the Committee earned TIPS Innovation Awards two years in a row.

While chairing the ABA-TIPS Animal Law Committee for two years, she created and served as editor-in-chief of the Animal Law Committee Newsletter and has published articles in this newsletter and in ABA-TIPS's *The Brief*, *TortSource*, and *Tort Trial & Insurance Law Journal*.

When Hurricane Katrina devastated the Gulf Coast in the fall of 2005, Gislason expanded her ABA efforts and she was selected as the TIPS Liaison to the ABA Special Committee on Disaster Response and Preparedness, and later, also selected as Liaison for the ABA Family Law Section. She created and directed the ABA-TIPS Animal Disaster Relief Network, and created and convened the ABA-TIPS Select Legal Panel on Emergency Management regarding animals, which fast-tracked model language on hold periods. This has been sponsored by the ABA-TIPS, co-sponsored by the ABA Special Committee on Disaster Response and Preparedness, and is now pending before the ABA House of Delegates.

Gislason was appointed the ABA-TIPS Advisor to the National Conference of Commissioners on Uniform State Laws regarding the Uniform Emergency Volunteer Health Practitioners Act. There, she was influential in having veterinarians included in the Act and drafted model language concerning them. Gislason serves on the Project Advisory Committee for the Regional Institute for Community Policing, the U.S. Department of Homeland Security Animal Rescue and Restore Project, and the U.S. Department of Homeland Security National Response Plan Revision Animals Work Group. She is also featured in *Left Behind Without a Choice*, a Hurricane Katrina Rescue Film.

Gislason has spoken at national conferences and annual meetings including the Humane Society of the United States, the Lewis & Clark Animal Law Conference, the ALDF Harvard University Animal Law Legal Conference, the ABA Annual Meeting, and the American Veterinary Medical Law Association Annual Meeting. She also spoke at the Ceoladeo National Park in Bharaptur, India, and is scheduled to speak at the first International Animal Law Conference in Canada, called "The Animal Within the Sphere of Humans' Needs Conference," at the University of Quebec in Montreal (UQAM).

Gislason's contribution to animal law was acknowledged in the *New York Times*. She was featured in the *ABA Journal*, *Minnesota Law & Politics*, the *Maddie's Fund Newsletter*, the book *Rescued: Saving Animals from Disaster*, and in the online publication *On the Issues Magazine*. Dr. Phil McGraw called her the "top animal advocate attorney in the country" on the *Dr. Phil* show. Recently, she became one of the co-hosts for the Legal TIPS program on Legal Talk Network.

Gislason is in private practice, with law offices in Minneapolis and Fridley, Minnesota. She handles a broad range of animal law cases, including contract formation and interpretation, tort claims (including veterinary malpractice and business defamation), custody and ownership disputes, harassment, dangerous dog proceedings, zoning violations, and more. See her Web site at http://www.animalattorneyonline.com.

Stacy L. Kelly is a litigation and appellate attorney practicing in Houston, Texas. Having received her B.S. from the University of Texas at Austin, Kelly continued her education by receiving her J.D. from South Texas College of Law. Kelly is a member of the American Bar Association and the State Bar of Texas. She is an associate editor of the Animal Law Section Newsletter for the American Bar Association and Treasurer of the State Bar of Texas Animal Law Section. Kelly is licensed to practice law in the State of Texas, Fifth Circuit Court of Appeals, and the United

States Supreme Court. She speaks frequently on fiduciary relationships and duties and on the creation of animal trusts. Kelly is a member of the Advisory Board for the Houston Society for the Prevention of Cruelty to Animals and is the proud mother of dogs Turbo and Choctaw, and cats Peta, Mondavi, and Boo, all rescues.

Gary C. Norman is the 2008 recipient of the Edward F. Shea, Jr. Award for Professionalism, presented by the Maryland State Bar Association, and presently serves as a staff attorney at the Department of Health and Human Services at the Centers for Medicare and Medicaid Services. Licensed in Ohio and Maryland, he is the founder and principal of Norman Access and Conflict Resolution Consultants Group. The firm provides mediation and arbitration services on a range of issues, animal law and policy services, wills and estate administration, disability law and policy, services regarding elder access issues, and transactional matters.

In addition to those achievements, Norman is an American Marshall Memorial Fellow with the German Marshall Fund of the United States and was recently accepted as a member of the Fulbright Scholar Senior Specialist Roster. He serves on various boards of advocacy nonprofits, including the National Council for the Support of Disability Issues (of which he is the former Vice President, Legal Chair, and Spokesperson). In the summer of 2007, he completed a one-year term as a Fellow of the Leadership Academy of the Maryland State Bar Association and coauthored the report that the Leadership Academy of 2007 issued as part of its larger project on youth violence prevention (available at http://www.msba.org/sec_comm/committees/leadership/). As a follow-up to the Leadership Academy, Norman was appointed to the Special Committee of Editorial Advisory, which establishes policy for and helps to edit the *Maryland Bar Journal*.

He also serves on the Animal Law Section of the Maryland State Bar Association and is the CEO and president of the Maryland Area Guide Dog Users, Inc. Under Norman's direction, MAGDU has developed the first series of one-day substantive technical assistance conferences of its kind in the dog guide advocacy community, the Canine Partnership Series, to be held through 2009.

Norman dedicates his chapter to his soon-to-be-retiring guide dog, Langer, and in memory of his mother, Mary Ann Norman.

Joan E. Schaffner is an Associate Professor of Law at the George Washington University Law School in Washington, D.C. She received her B.S. in mechanical engineering and J.D. from the University of Southern

California and her M.S. in mechanical engineering from the Massachusetts Institute of Technology. She worked at the law firm of Irell & Manella in Los Angeles, California, and clerked for the Honorable Mariana Pfaelzer in the Central District of California before coming to GW.

Professor Schaffner teaches Civil Procedure, Remedies, and Sexuality and the Law, and writes in these areas as well. She is the faculty advisor to Lambda Law, the GLBT student organization at GW, and is faculty advisor and editor-in-chief of the *American Intellectual Property Law Association Quarterly Journal*.

Professor Schaffner directs the GW Animal Law Program, which consists of the GW Animal Welfare Project, a pro bono effort of faculty and students devoted to researching and improving animal welfare laws in the District of Columbia; teaches seminars in animal law; and is the faculty advisor to a student chapter of the Animal Legal Defense Fund (SALDF). Additionally, Professor Schaffner has testified on behalf of non-breed-specific dangerous dog laws and has presented on animal law panels at conferences worldwide. She is active in various organizations, holding the offices of Chair-Elect (8/08), Publications Chair, and Editor of the newsletter of the ABA Tort Trial and Insurance Practice Section (TIPS) Animal Law Committee, Founding Chair of the Association of American Law Schools Section on Animal Law, and consumer member for the District of Columbia Board of Veterinary Medicine. She was recently selected as a Fellow of the Oxford Centre for Animal Ethics.

Professor Schaffner is a volunteer for Washington Humane Society, fosters feline families, and is committed to saving the lives of homeless animals. She lives with many felines; Jackie, a Jack Russell; and Rocky, a brilliant African Grey parrot.

PREFACE

Animal Law: A Significant Journey

BARBARA J. GISLASON

I want to realize brotherhood or identity not merely with the beings called human, but I want to realize identity with all life, even with such things as crawl upon earth.

—Mahatma Gandhi

The ocean of life is never still. The waves line up to advance in time. We, as humans, come forward and consider the idea of Animal Law, the emergence of a new field.

In addition to commercial interests, Animal Law is impacted by a conversation between lawyers about how to treat, interact with, and think about animals. The exchange is like a morality tale all dressed up in lofty language. Beneath the rhetoric are simple questions about how animals belong in the world, and what humans are willing to offer.

Discerning which case is an Animal Law case requires perhaps an arbitrary entry point to begin the inquiry. Ask about the circumstances of the animal's birth, and how the animal lived and died. Ask about what the animal's owner expected. Ask if the animal hurt a human; or the human, an animal. If the answers are relevant to the claims in your case, you may have an Animal Law case.

Animal Law has, of course, a focus on animals. There are complex interdisciplinary aspects to it with Animal Law pioneers borrowing a little from here, a little from there, and proclaiming a new field.

The seeds of the field were planted throughout human history. Particularly large seeds were planted as long ago as 1760 BC. Under the Code of Hammurabi in ancient Babylon, veterinary surgeons were paid more if they cured, rather than killed, an ass or an ox.

Unusual seeds were planted in the 16th century French ecclesiastical courts where animals, including pigs, were (in effect) prosecuted and punished for crimes. A magnificent seed was embedded in the Constitution of India in 1949. Citizens were to protect and improve the natural environment as a fundamental duty, and to have compassion for living creatures. Future seeds were described in 1999, when the European Commission issued a directive calling for the ban on conventional battery cages for laying hens beginning in 2012.

The First Wave of the organized Animal Law field in the West came in the 1970s and 1980s. It was propelled by philosophers and lawyers who imagined the idea of animal rights through an open heart and a willingness to see. Why did they come forward?

Consider an animal, any animal. Let us choose a donkey—simple in nature, yet stubborn and willful. Come face to face with this donkey who is suffering, and know the depths of pain. Failure to see it is a kind of blindness, not of sight, but of the inner eye.

The donkey may be touched and smelled. There is the dampness and matting of the coat, the sense of lingering mold in the tissue, the recognition of a living emblem of decay, decomposition, and loss of a simple servant who asks little but who often lifts the burdens of daily life.

With the assessment of this suffering, an observer was tempted to order a personal halo and proclaim, "I am the virtuous one," as compared to the "other" who caused the donkey's suffering. But the observer's attitude of superiority neither helps the donkey nor the observer carrying the yoke of anger, and through identification with the animal, pain.

The donkey might be better served if judgment was withheld, and forgiveness and kindness extended in its place that reached the heart of the "other." For the observer, there may also be the need for a cleansing through the natural purification of tears.

In writing this preface, I began with more lawyer-like drafts with traditional legal analysis, models, footnotes, and hypotheticals. Wanting to skip trace history, I broke time into landmark moments, like 17th-century philosopher and scientist René Descartes's pronouncement that animals were more like machines unable to experience pain like humans do, and 20th-century primatologist Jane Goodall's decision to give her research subjects names, not numbers. I mentioned living lawyers, like David Favre, Joyce Tischler, Raj Panjwani, Kristina Hancock, Jim Carr, and Sarah Babcock, and their contributions.

I thought about my own roots and how ideas captured in memorized language have represented templates for me that enhance my strength and conviction to act. One template gave me direction when I had my own unique role to play in the creation and advancement of Animal Law in state and national bar associations. It was a poem derived from an 1854 communication in the Lushootseed language from Chief Seattle to Governor Stevens, and it says in part:

> . . . I have seen a thousand rotting buffaloes on the prairie,
> left by the white man who shot them from a passing train.
> I am a savage and I do not understand how the smoking
> iron horse can be more important than the buffalo
> that we kill only to stay alive.
>
> Where is man without the beasts?
> If all the beasts were gone, men would die
> from a great loneliness of spirit.
> For whatever happens to the beasts, soon happens to man.
> All things are connected.
>
> This we know.
> The Earth does not belong to man -
> man belongs to the Earth.
> This we know . . .
>
> Man did not weave the web of life -
> he is merely a strand in it.
> Whatever he does to the web,
> he does to himself . . .

I memorized these words long after I saw my first "Silent Spring" in North Dakota (Rachel Carson's expression), over farmlands covered with DDT. Chief Seattle's ideas were already part of me when I saw my second "Silent Spring" upon the legendary Yangtze River in China, devoid of fish or fowl.

Perhaps, because I had the absolute conviction of a witness to unnatural phenomena, it was possible for me to succeed in asking the Tort Trial and Insurance Practice Section (TIPS) of the American Bar Association (ABA) to create an Animal Law Committee in 2004.

This watershed event took place when only a handful of Animal Law Sections existed in individual states. There were no such committees at all in the ABA, and the subject matter was highly controversial. TIPS, by unanimously embracing the creation of the Animal Law Committee, representatively established Animal Law as a mainstream practice area in the country, even the world.

I sought to better understand what was inside and outside of the practice area of Animal Law as I participated in propelling the field forward, and began using images. Think of a river coming into existence because of the confluence of tributaries. Thus, the tributaries of Equine Law, with a transactional focus, and Animal Welfare and Animal Rights Law, with a humane focus, would each flow into the river of Animal Law, as would Wildlife and Endangered Species Law.

From the bottom of the river would rise matter that had been buried, or lurked beneath the surface. Now the river would float weighty matters, tossed from shore to shore, like, "Is there a humane way to proceed with transgenetic research through the use of cloned animals?" "Why do we pretend to be serious about ourselves, in this place in time, when the very little part of ourselves that is transformative does not know it is there?"

Then, in continuing with my struggle to define Animal Law, I thought about the equitable doctrine, "there is no wrong without a remedy," and explained how this doctrine is effectively an emperor with no clothes in the practice area of Animal Law because most animals lack value and are therefore worthless. I made up examples for why this was true, draping and undraping the emperor. It was an interesting exercise in creative writing, but the examples did no more than show that because most animals lack economic value, there must be some other way to value them in order to achieve a just result. The struggle concerning the value and valuation of animals is to the Second Wave of Animal Law as personhood was to the First.

I, of course, included in my drafts of this preface how the First Wave of what we now call Animal Law was influenced by philosopher Peter Singer, the author of *Animal Liberation*, first published in 1975, as well as Animal Rights lawyers who emerged in the 1980s. They were concerned about subjects like standing, anticruelty, and of course, personhood.

The Second Wave came in this new millennium, where it was particularly influenced by law school courses, case books, and law reviews, and the formation and evolution of bar associations, including the momentous inclusion of Animal Law in the ABA in 2004, the largest professional organization in the world.

Then I tried to explain, though not very satisfactorily, how Animal Law is like a horizontal line, called Animal Law, cutting across countless vertical lines, which are established practice areas. Every time the horizontal line crosses a vertical line, there is an intersection. If all these intersections were added together, you could say that you had a pretty good model for what Animal Law is. Also, in expanding the idea of the horizontal line being Animal Law, you could see how what happened at one horizontal intersection could have a trickle-over (as opposed to trickle-down) impact on the next intersection.

Then, I made up all kinds of examples of what these intersections would look like and how the trickle-over effect would work, wanting to be comprehensive, but discovering no short and effective way to explain it. I will point out that now, most Trusts and Estates lawyers can engage in estate planning that allows people to leave property to or for *live* animal property, that Family lawyers are beginning to think about animals' best interests and their vulnerability to domestic abuse, and Emergency Management lawyers now often include veterinarians and companion animals in preparedness and response plans. These things are happening because of the intersection of Animal Law with these established fields.

But the more I worked on this intersection model, I could see that it could not begin to describe the complexity of this emerging field. So, I thought about quantum physics and what is known as the Heisenberg uncertainty principle wherein it is possible to measure the position or the momentum of a particle, but not both. Ah, dualism. I decided that I would simply think of the well-established areas of legal practice, like real estate, as a particle, and the field of Animal Law as a wave, while being uncertain if just the opposite or both were true.

And so, let us shake it up. Animal Law is like a river, with its tributaries helping to define it and important matters rising to the top, bouncing from shore to shore, century by century. It is like the cumulative intersections of Animal Law with other practice areas, and it is interdisciplinary, while the disciplines themselves change. Aspects of it are like particles and yet it is a powerful wave influenced by social movements, like the First Wave of Animal Law was. It is all of the above, and yet, I have not captured it.

As I said before, I did make the effort to write a more traditional preface. The only problem was that I was trying to do too much, while somehow leaving out the essence of what Animal Law is.

Then, I thought about Mahatma Gandhi and why I chose his words for the lead quote of this preface. He was in my mind last year as I walked where he walked in his homeland of India, and I thought about his influence on India's remarkable constitution. I came face to face with the suffering donkey and stood there stroking and stroking him, knowing I was learning truths about life that were incubating in my brain. The challenge was to bring them forth.

And so, in the present time, I put away my computer, hid my notes, and imagined I was writing to you with Gandhi beside me. Picturing his presence took me to a deeper place where my ego—that wants to flaunt itself—was quieted.

There is room in this book for some soul searching, I decided, because the pioneers in this field who are contributing to this book are developing and defining Animal Law through logic, trial and error, and inspiration. Besides, soul searching is best done by being in the moment, not entangled by footnotes.

It has been said that all great writing is, at its core, an argument with God. This would make legal writing a part of this conversation. In bringing Animal Law to the American Bar Association, I did my level best to present the reasons the field needed to be embraced in the most conventional of ways.

I pointed out how Animal Law interfaced with more than 30 committees, like Space Law and Transportation Law, in TIPS alone. But while the case for bringing Animal Law into the fold and thereby mainstreaming Animal Law into the biggest and most powerful law association in the world was a conservative one, the mission statement for the committee was not. It called for the best and brightest lawyers in the world to bring a paradigm shift that brought humane concerns to the table.

On the day the creation of the Animal Law Committee was realized, the TIPS Council recognized they had done something momentous. Though I was not in the room when the vote was passed, I was later told, "It was like a love-in in there!" In my mind, and no one can tell me differently, forces more powerful than I can understand were present.

My experience at the helm of the committee, and for those who succeeded me, is that it felt like we were being helped in ways we did not understand because everywhere we turned, red lights changed to green. Other groups, no matter how different they seemed from us, and even how initially distasteful the idea of Animal Law was to them, were turning around and willing to talk to us and cosponsor programs, including controversial ones.

We were on the home page of the American Bar Association for our groundbreaking program at Duke Law School on bioengineering. It is the kind of program that would have seemed impossible, even now, as the panelists could have been expected to refuse to sit down together. Not only are improbable people engaging in a conversation about what change is possible, but Michel Bastarache of the Supreme Court of Canada participated in it.

It is my belief that the ABA-TIPS Animal Law Committee's intention to work cooperatively and without judgment, while holding the subject of animals dear, was necessary to create these opportunities. I think about Norman Vincent Peale and his ideas about how to win friends and influence people. It is through our connections to both people and animals that the paradigm shift is occurring.

In our lives, we have heard much self-congratulatory talk about the great civilization we have, and we point to buildings, structures, inventions, and even mathematical formulas for tangible proof. But, it is perhaps in the smaller things that civilization lies, like in the universal truths told through the eyes of a donkey.

We are better people if we can reach into the genuine part of ourselves to understand and care about the animal "other," even those that have a displeasing appearance. If we can love the "other" as human or animal, then we can look into our own flawed nature and love ourselves.

Now we return to the ocean. Animal Law is the wave, and I ask you, with no instructions, to gain the top of that wave. Tell those behind you where we are going and chart the course. Expect to be surprised. But also, when the wave is too much, get off and bask in the sunlight, next to a whole donkey.

ACKNOWLEDGMENTS

This book is the brainchild of ABA-TIPS Animal Law Committee Founding Chair Barbara Gislason. The coeditors, Julie Fershtman and Joan Schaffner, are honored to have been chosen by Barbara to make the idea a reality. Since the scope of the text is broad, the editors brought together experienced practitioners in each substantive area of the law to draft the individual chapters and provide insight into how best to handle animal-related cases. The author(s) of each chapter is individually noted. The editors wish to thank each of the authors for their willingness to share their knowledge, time, and valuable insight: Zandra Anderson, Katherine Bloomquist, Dana Campbell, Greg Dennis, Pamela Frasch, Stacy Kelly, and Gary Norman. Brief biographies of each author are included at the beginning of this book. Moreover, the ABA publication staff, especially Rick Paszkiet, have been very helpful and supportive while we developed this book over the past two years.

Finally, we wish to thank the ABA Tort Trial and Insurance Practice Section for recognizing the importance of this emerging area of the law by approving the creation of the Animal Law Committee and supporting our activities and publications.

CHAPTER 1

Introduction

JOAN E. SCHAFFNER

JULIE I. FERSHTMAN

I. Overview

Issues surrounding animals and the law have gained widespread interest in the past few years. In 2005, when Hurricane Katrina struck the Gulf Coast, thousands of people were forced to flee without their companion animals or risk death by remaining at home to protect them. Many animals, left homeless, were rescued and shipped throughout the country to await reunification with their owners or to find new homes. Myriad legal issues followed, including questions of proper holding periods, transfer of ownership, and liability of rescuers. Congress passed legislation requiring that states include animals in their emergency evacuation plans in order to receive federal funding to support such plans.

Early in 2007, contaminated pet food affecting many of the most popular brands led to the death of hundreds of animals and the recall of thousands of bags and cans of pet food sold over a period of several weeks. Numerous legal issues following this episode have raised questions of liability and proper remedy for the loss of one's companion animal. Later in the year, NFL quarterback Michael Vick was charged with animal fighting, a felony under federal law and in many states, and the huge underground enterprise in animal fighting was exposed to a horrified public. Hotelier Leona Helmsley passed away in 2007 and gained notoriety by leaving $12 million in trust to her beloved white Maltese, Trouble. Late in the year, a large puppy mill enterprise was exposed in which over a thousand dogs were rescued from deplorable circumstances of alleged cruelty and neglect. These highly publicized events and tragedies reflect only a small part of the policy and law that governs our relationship with animals.

A 2007–2008 study by the American Pet Products Manufacturers Association (APPMA) estimates there are 153.7 million pet dogs and cats in U.S. households,[1] and almost nine in ten pet owners consider their pets members of the family.[2] The average annual veterinary expense per pet was $366.[3] We use animals not only for companionship and service, but for food and clothing, for research and entertainment. Nearly 10 billion animals are raised and killed for food annually in the United States,[4] and in 2004 more than a million reportable warm-blooded animals were used by American labs.[5] In the U.S. equine industry alone, there are 9.2 million horses, according to the American Horse Council. The Council reports that the equine industry has a $39 billion direct economic effect on the U.S. economy.[6] The law regulates our use of and relationship with these animals and is developing dramatically as human society alters its views of its relationship to nonhumans.

II. "Animal Law"

Animal law is gaining widespread interest within law schools and among practicing lawyers. More than 95 law schools have a class on animal law.[7] Over 130 law schools have a student chapter of the Animal Legal Defense Fund.[8] In June 2008, the American Association of Law Schools approved the establishment of a Section on Animal Law. There are now five journals that are devoted to animal law—*Animal Law Review* (Lewis & Clark), *Journal of Animal Law* (Michigan State), *Journal of International Wildlife Law and Policy* (Whittier), *Journal of Animal Law & Ethics* (University of Pennsylvania), and *Stanford Journal of Animal Law & Policy*. In 2006, Carolina Academic Press published the third edition of the casebook *Animal Law,* by Sonia Waisman, Pamela Frasch, and Bruce Wagman; a new casebook, *Animal Law, Welfare, Interests and Rights,* by David Favre, was just released in 2008 by Wolters Kluwer.

The practicing bar has embraced this area of the law as a legitimate and growing area of practice by creating committees or sections devoted to animal law. Currently 16 state bars and the Bar of the District of Columbia have sections or committees devoted to animal law.[9] Another 12 regional bar sections or committees of animal law exist.[10] Perhaps most significant, the American Bar Association's Tort Trial and Insurance Practice Section established an Animal Law Committee in 2005, which has been extremely active since its inception.

So, what exactly *is* "animal law"? All law is animal law. Animal law cuts across virtually every substantive area of the law, including tort, contract, property, family, taxation, trust and estates, insurance, criminal, administrative, international, and environmental. On the one hand, because companion animals are now so common in the United States and they are often considered family members, lawyers are now finding themselves confronted with "animal law" cases more frequently and require guidance. On the other hand, because of the continued growth in business industries involving animals, such as the dog show and horse show industries, the demand is greater than ever for lawyers to serve these businesses on the many legal issues they confront. This book is designed to provide such guidance.

III. Litigating Animal Law Disputes

Entitled *Litigating Animal Law Disputes*, this book focuses on the numerous legal issues that arise for people with animals and people affected by animals that may result in litigation. Whether it be the divorcing couple with a dispute over who should have "custody" of the family cat, the owner who boards a dog at a kennel and returns to find the dog ill, the elderly woman who wants to provide for her pet parrot after her death, the owner of a horse in a dispute with a boarding stable, the prosecutor confronted with a person arrested for cruelly beating an animal, or the veterinarian who is sued by the owners of a dog under his care, the legal issues are varied and numerous.

The authors assume that the reader has a basic understanding of the relevant substantive area of the law—for example, contracts, wills, and malpractice—and address the unique questions that arise when an animal is involved in the case. The following questions, which cross several substantive legal areas, are typical:

- What losses are compensable for the death of one's pet, and how should those losses be valued?
- What types of evidence must be secured at the scene of an animal neglect incident?
- How may a prosecutor most effectively utilize veterinary forensics in proving a case?
- How does the law define "service animal," and what protections are available to the disabled person with a dog guide?
- What is the potential liability for equine activity sponsors should a rider fall from a horse?

- How do animal insurance policies differ from the traditional human insurance policies?

These are but a very few of the many questions that may confront the lawyer with a client who owns an animal or a prosecutor who is assigned an "animal" case.

Each chapter of this book is designed to provide a basic understanding of the animal-related issues that arise within that area of the law. The bulk of the legal issues derive from state law. While each state's law cannot be addressed specifically, or in great detail, the authors discuss the law most common throughout the states and provide suggestions on what to look for in determining the unique characteristics in your state. Many of the chapters also include appendices with sample documents typical of those an attorney may need to draft in the area of interest. Thus, for example, sample pleadings, discovery documents, jury instructions, and trust agreements are provided so that the reader need not reinvent the wheel. The goal is to provide an easily accessible text for busy practitioners to quickly identify the unique issues that may arise in their animal law case and how they might address them.

This book does not address the law that is unique to animals because such cases are typically handled by animal law attorneys with highly specialized expertise in the area. Thus, for example, cases arising under the Endangered Species Act or the Marine Mammal Protection Act, or administrative law cases involving the Animal Welfare Act, are not within the scope of this text.

One final note: The area of animal law is not only a newly emerging field of law, it also raises many controversial issues concerning how animals should be treated by humans. For example, the range of philosophical views on humans' relation to animals is broad—from Descartes's belief that "man is the master of all and has the right to subject animals to his will" to Tom Regan's and Peter Singer's beliefs that animals have rights in their own right. Even within the animal advocacy community, advocates debate "animal welfare" versus "animal rights" and whether animals should be deemed "property" under the law. Furthermore, the terminology to refer to animals and their human counterparts also can be controversial. For example, advocates debate whether "pets" should be referred to as "companion animals" or whether their owners should consider themselves "guardians." This book does not address these debates nor take sides within the debates. Rather, the goal of this text is to provide an "objective" (to the extent possible) discussion of the current legal landscape as it concerns animal-related legal issues and to use terminology that reflects the current state of the law.

The editors hope you find this text useful.

Notes

1. American Pet Prods. Mfrs. Ass'n, 2007–2008 APPMA Nat'l Pet Owners Survey 7 (2007) (72 million dogs and 81.7 million cats).
2. HarrisInteractive, The Harris Poll, Pets Are "Members of the Family" and Two-Thirds of Pet Owners Buy Their Pets Holiday Presents (Dec. 4, 2007), *available at* http://www.harrisinteractive.com/harris_poll/index.asp?PID=840.
3. American Veterinary Medical Association, 2007 U.S. Pet Ownership & Demographics Sourcebook (2007), *available at* http://www.avma.org/reference/marketstats/sourcebook.asp.
4. Erin Williams & Margo DeMello, Why Animals Matter 22 (2007).
5. *Id.* at 180. The Animal Welfare Act excludes mice, rats, birds, reptiles, and amphibians from protection, although they compose approximately 90 percent of all animals used in labs, and thus they are not reportable to the USDA. Consequently, the number of all animals used in labs is likely over 10 million. *Id.*
6. American Horse Council, National Impact of the Horse Industry (2005), *available at* http://www.horsecouncil.org.
7. Animal Legal Defense Fund, Animal Law Courses, *available at* http://aldf.org/article.php?id=445 (last visited Jan. 1, 2009).
8. Animal Legal Defense Fund, SALDF Chapters, *available at* http://aldf.org/article.php?id=446 (last visited Jan. 1, 2009).
9. Animal Legal Defense Fund, Bar Association Animal Law Sections and Committees, *available at* http://aldf.org/article.php?id=277 (last visited Jan. 1, 2009).
10. *Id.*

CHAPTER 2

Negligence and Tort Law

JULIE I. FERSHTMAN

I. Introduction

Tort cases probably compose the greatest volume of animal-related litigation. Few statutes exist that are specifically designed to regulate or control liabilities involving animals. The overwhelming majority of cases involve the application of a variety of common-law theories as to claims and defenses.

Animal law practitioners, whether representing plaintiffs or defendants in these cases, bring a valuable perspective to virtually all aspects of the litigation. These practitioners often have a unique understanding and appreciation of the subject matter and are better able to analyze the claims and defenses; they have better knowledge of available legal resources; they bring depth and focus to the briefs they draft and the advocacy they present in court; they often can select expert witnesses with superior qualifications; they can better challenge the knowledge and credentials of the opposing expert; they can simplify the case for the judge and jury.

This section explores several common-law and statutory tort theories as well as defenses and offers suggestions for effective advocacy when handling these cases.

II. Basic Elements

Black's Law Dictionary (5th ed.) defines negligence, in part, as follows:

> Negligence is the failure to use such care as a reasonably prudent and careful person would use under similar circumstances; it is the doing of some act which a person of ordinary prudence would not have done under the circumstances or failure to do what a person of ordinary prudence would have done under similar circumstances. Conduct which falls below the standard established by law for the protection of others against unreasonable risk of harm; it is a departure from the conduct expectable of a reasonably prudent person under like circumstances.

The tort of negligence has four elements: duty, breach, proximate cause, and damages. A highly authoritative treatise, *Prosser and Keeton on the Law of Torts*, briefly explains these elements in the following way:[1]

1. A duty, or obligation, recognized by the law, requiring the person to conform to a certain standard of conduct for the protection of others against unreasonable risks.
2. A failure on the person's part to conform to the standard required: a breach of the duty. These two elements go to make up what the courts usually have called negligence; but the term quite frequently is applied to the second alone. Thus, it may be said that the defendant was negligent, but is not liable because he was under no duty to the plaintiff not to be.
3. A reasonably close causal connection between the conduct and the resulting injury. This is what is commonly known as "legal

cause," or "proximate cause," and which includes the notion of cause in fact.[2]

4. Actual loss or damage resulting to the interests of another. Since the action for negligence developed chiefly out of the old form of action on the case, it retained the rule of that action, that proof of damage was an essential part of the plaintiff's case.

III. *Theories of Liability*

A. Common Law

1. *Animal's "Vicious or Dangerous Propensities"*

In cases involving animal-inflicted injuries, liability can exist under a general theory of common-law negligence where the animal had "vicious or dangerous" propensities of which the owner, keeper, or handler knew but failed to take appropriate protective action.[3] However, this common-law theory could be inapplicable if the jurisdiction has a dog-bite statute and the incident at issue falls within that law.

For cases involving "vicious or dangerous propensities," the key elements that the plaintiff must prove typically are

1. The animal had "vicious or dangerous" propensities abnormal to its class;
2. The injury resulted from the animal's "vicious or dangerous" propensities; and
3. The animal's owner or keeper knew or had reason to know of these propensities but failed to take appropriate corrective action.

Black's Law Dictionary has defined "vicious propensities" as "a propensity or tendency of the animal to do any act which might endanger the safety of a person and property of others in a given situation. A propensity or tendency of animal to do any act which might endanger the safety of persons or property of others in a given situation." One case noted that the animal's behavior should be such that "a reasonable person of ordinary prudence [should] foresee harm to the person or property of others."[4]

Some factual settings involving the "vicious or dangerous propensity" rule are

- Attacks by animals on pets belonging to others;[5]
- Riders thrown from horses;[6]

- Bites inflicted by animals, such as a stallion, to someone approaching its stall;[7]
- People injured by runaway horses pulling a wagon;[8]
- People injured when a dog ran into the back of their legs, knocking them off balance and causing them to fall;[9] and
- People injured from a cat's bite or scratch.[10]

One court established a few criteria to determine whether the defendant should have anticipated that his or her dog would attack and injure others:

- The dog was of a particular breed, in that case a German shepherd.
- The dog had been trained as a watchdog.
- The dog was actually kept as a watchdog.
- The dog was kept chained.
- The dog was large, weighing between 80 and 100 pounds.
- The dog stood 5½ feet tall on its hind legs.[11]

Other factors that have been considered to determine whether the animal had dangerous propensities that the owner knew or should have known include the following:

- The animal at issue suffered from an injury or disease that rendered it more irritable, such as a cat afflicted with a painful kidney ailment.[12]
- The animal had been abused or mistreated.[13]
- The owner warned others about the animal before the incident, such as a warning to people to "stay away" from the animal.[14]
- The animal had a well-known reputation for being ill-tempered.[15]
- The dog was kept muzzled and restrained.[16]
- The animal had attacked people before, such as a delivery person.[17]
- The premises where the animal was maintained had a "beware of dog" sign on the premises.[18]
- The dog owner admitted that the dog was vicious.[19]

Defense counsel, with appropriate factual support, can raise several arguments to oppose application of the "vicious or dangerous" propensity rule to the case. They can argue, for example:

- The complained-of behavior on part of the animal does not qualify as a "vicious or dangerous propensity."[20] For example, a cat's tendency to scratch or bite at play has been found to not necessarily equate with a propensity to attack people.[21]
- The animal has shown no prior "vicious or dangerous" propensities.[22]
- Past behavior, such as merely barking at the garbage collector, does not evidence a dangerous propensity.[23]
- The owner or keeper was unaware of an alleged propensity on part of the animal.[24]
- The animal's breed or type does not automatically evidence a dangerous propensity.[25]

Counsel for the plaintiff have incentive to assert that the determination of whether an animal was, in fact, dangerous[26] or whether the animal's owner or keeper knew of dangerous propensities is best left to the trier of fact to determine.[27] In some cases, plaintiffs have asserted that they need not prove the defendant actually knew of a dangerous propensity, but, rather, it was sufficient for the plaintiff to merely prove that the defendant *should have known* of the animal's propensity to harm others.[28]

Depending on the facts of the particular matter, expert testimony might be of little use in establishing knowledge of dangerous tendencies. It has been argued that the standard of knowledge of such propensities is judged subjectively by what the owner or keeper knew, as opposed to an objective standard.

2. *Negligent Supervision or Instruction*

Cases have been brought against professionals, particularly in the equine industry, asserting negligent instruction or supervision of the rider or handler.[29] This is especially likely in states without equine activity liability statutes, or in cases where these statutes are inapplicable for some reason.

3. *Gross Negligence and Willful and Wanton Misconduct*

With particularly egregious facts, theories of gross negligence and wanton and willful misconduct could potentially apply. These theories are more likely to be asserted in cases where

- The conduct at issue exceeded a mere negligence standard because of particularly aggravating factors on part of the defendant, such as deliberately allowing a dog to attack a human or animal.

- A liability release agreement existed between the parties, but the jurisdiction prevents such documents from barring claims of gross negligence or willful and wanton misconduct.
- An applicable equine activity liability act bars liability except for claims of egregious wrongdoing, such as gross negligence or willful and wanton misconduct.
- The claim involves an especially strong element of emotional injury.

In *Hawkins v. Ranch Rudolph, Inc.*,[30] the plaintiff was injured during a trail ride on a rented horse, and his lawsuit alleged gross negligence. Though the facts were disputed, the plaintiff claimed that the defendant's trail guide "bolted" her horse into a "fast or full-out run," causing his rented horse to take off, after which time the saddle slipped and he fell. Although the trial court dismissed the case based on a release and the state equine activity liability statute, the appellate court reversed. It noted that issues of fact existed as to whether the trail guide's actions amounted to grossly negligent conduct.

In another case, the court found issues of fact under the "willful and wanton misconduct" exception of the Texas Equine Activity Liability Act.[31] There, the plaintiff alleged that the defendant and its employees knew, but failed to warn, of a stallion's aggressive history.

4. *Premises Liability*

Premises liability is rarely asserted in claims that relate strictly to an animal's propensities. In a case that related to the animal owner's failure to control or restrain the animal, the court declined to apply the theory of premises liability.[32] However, in a setting where a business patron was injured from a dog bite on the premises, while the patron was lawfully on the property, a premises liability theory could potentially succeed.[33]

5. *Strict Liability*

The theory of strict liability is typically asserted in matters involving (1) injuries inflicted by wild, as opposed to domesticated, animals and (2) injuries inflicted by animals where the animal's keeper or handler knew of the animal's vicious or dangerous propensities.

In cases involving wild animals, the *Restatement (Second) of Torts*, for example, provides that the possessor of a wild animal is liable for harm the animal causes to another, even though the possessor has exercised the utmost care to confine the animal or prevent it from doing harm.[34] In a case involving strict liability related to wild animals, it is immaterial that the animal owner was unaware of the animal's prior propensity to cause harm to others or that the owner exercised reasonable care in the keeping and confinement of the animal.[35] For example, the owner or keeper of a bear was found to have accepted the risk that people approaching it could be injured.[36]

Where domesticated animals are alleged to have inflicted injuries, a legal presumption has been found to exist that these types of animals, such as horses, do not have vicious or dangerous propensities as would a wild animal.[37] In one strict liability case, the court held that a domesticated cat, which rubbed against plaintiff's legs, did not present an unreasonable risk of harm.[38] However, the theory of strict liability has been applied when the domestic animal has a vicious propensity.[39]

6. *Products Liability*

Depending on the jurisdiction, litigation involving defective products can be brought under several possible theories that include breach of warranty, negligence, and strict liability.[40]

Product liability cases have been brought against animal-related product manufacturers. The most publicized in recent years has been litigation against Menu Foods, a manufacturer and distributor of pet foods that were blamed in the deaths of numerous pets across the country.[41]

The case of *Moreland v. Weaver Leather Goods*[42] involved a company that was sued for allegedly manufacturing a defective saddle. While using the saddle, the plaintiff, a trick rider, was dragged from her horse and injured. She claimed that a part of the saddle, an off-billet, breached the implied warranty of fitness for a particular purpose. She also sued for products liability and failure to warn. The court dismissed her case, finding insufficient evidence that the saddle was defective when it left the manufacturer or that it was unreasonably dangerous. In addition, the facts showed that the plaintiff had used the saddle for five months before the incident, without a problem.

7. *Trespass of Animal*

Unless a state statute imposes liability on the owner or keeper of an animal that runs loose and trespasses onto property of another,[43] basic common-law principles will apply. One court held that a dog's caretaker was not liable when the dog escaped and injured a motorcyclist because of the caretaker's reliance on an invisible fence that had been used to contain the dog, and no evidence existed that the invisible fence was malfunctioning on the day of the incident or that the dog had a tendency to attack people or chase motorcycles.[44]

8. *Res Ipsa Loquitur*

Res ipsa loquitur is Latin for "the thing speaks for itself." States may apply their own standards to determine liability under this legal theory. However, at common law, res ipsa loquitur has been utilized in negligence cases where

- The harm would not ordinarily have occurred without someone's negligence;
- The instrumentality that caused the harm was under the exclusive control of the defendant at the time of the alleged negligent act; and
- No reasonable explanation can be given as to how the harm occurred.

Although the theory of res ipsa loquitur is rarely asserted, it has been occasionally found to apply to animal-related cases. In century-old cases, for example, courts held that horses that are well broken and kept under control do not break away and injure others, thereby allowing the injured party to sue under a res ipsa loquitur theory.[45]

9. *Attractive Nuisance*

The attractive nuisance doctrine is generally designed to offer some potential recourse for injured child trespassers. An attractive nuisance is a potentially dangerous item or condition of the land that, by its features, tends to lure unsuspecting children who might not perceive or appreciate the hazard posed by the item. *Restatement (Second) of Torts* Section 339 is often quoted as setting forth the attractive nuisance doctrine.[46]

The majority view appears to be that animals do not qualify as an attractive nuisance.[47] For example, the doctrine has been held inapplicable to dogs.[48] In another case, however, the court declined to find a German shepherd an attractive nuisance but recognized that a dog, with appropriate facts, might qualify if it posed foreseeable dangers to others.[49] Cases have found the doctrine inapplicable to horses[50] and mules.[51] One court expressed doubts that the doctrine could apply to "horses, cattle, hogs, sheep, and chickens" as they would not qualify as "artificial conditions" of the land.[52]

10. *Negligence Per Se*

A violation of a statute or ordinance could potentially constitute negligence per se, or, to a lesser degree, the statutory violation could serve as evidence of negligence. Typically, the plaintiff will need to prove that the statute or ordinance at issue was intended to protect people like the plaintiff against the type of harm at issue. For example, a few cases have held that "leash law" statutes were intended to prevent dog bites.[53]

B. Statutory

1. Strict Liability and Dog-Bite Statutes

Under the common law, a plaintiff needed to establish that the dog was vicious or had a propensity for viciousness of which the owner or keeper was aware—known as the "one-bite rule." About half of the states have abolished this traditional rule through legislation governing liability for dog bites.[54] Consequently, counsel handling dog-bite cases, whether representing plaintiffs or defendants, should evaluate whether the state where the incident occurred follows the common law or, instead, has an applicable statute.

Although the statutes differ, they often provide for the following:

- The animal owner and sometimes, depending on the law, the animal keeper, is strictly liable for injuries inflicted by the dog without regard to whether the dog previously exhibited vicious behavior.
- The injured person must not have been a trespasser and, instead, must have been injured in a location where he or she was lawfully permitted to be.
- If the injured person provoked the animal, he or she cannot recover.

The defense of assumption of risk is typically inapplicable in defense of a case brought under a dog-bite statute.[55]

Although these statutes usually, by their terms, specify that they apply to injuries inflicted by dogs, courts have held that they do not implicitly extend to injuries inflicted by cats.[56]

Counsel evaluating dog-bite liability cases should pay particular attention to the history and propensities of the dog at issue. If the dog has, for example, attacked or bitten others and the owner was aware of the problem, liability is stronger. In addition, the key defense of provocation should be examined. If provocation by the injured person played a significant role in causing the incident, then the case or claim is weaker, but counsel will need to determine whether the animal responded in a reasonable manner to the provocation. Finally, the location of the incident is important; if the injured party truly qualified as a trespasser at the time of the incident, this will weaken or possibly eliminate liability.[57]

2. *Animal Running at Large Statutes*

Loose or trespassing livestock have generated considerable litigation, and the state-by-state variations can be significant. Areas of high population density—typically in the Eastern United States—tend to follow the "fence in" rule that obligates animal owners and/or keepers to keep their livestock off of the roadways and attaches liability in some fashion when the animals escape, whether under theories of negligence or strict liability. By comparison, other states, typically in the Western United States, have abandoned the "fence in" rule in favor of an open range or "fence out" rule.

Over the years, cases involving loose livestock have involved several different factual settings and theories including the following:

- *Defective fences.* Liability has been predicted on situations in which the stable's fences were not properly maintained, causing horses to escape on several occasions.[58]
- *Open gates.* Negligence cases have been brought after horses escaped from gates that were left open.[59]
- *Negligence per se by violation of statute, code, or ordinance.* In some states, liability could potentially be predicated on the defendant's failure to comply with fencing statutes.[60] However, this is not absolute and other states differ.
- *Inference of negligence—"res ipsa loquitur."* Some states have allowed liability in loose livestock cases to be inferred under the legal doctrine of res ipsa loquitur.[61]

Several possible defenses, depending on the facts and applicable law, potentially apply to loose livestock claims depending on the facts and law:

- The animal was in an "open range" district, which imposes no absolute duty to fence it in.[62]
- A third party should bear responsibility for the incident.[63]
- The defendant exercised *reasonable care* in the care, keeping, and confinement of the animal(s) at issue and therefore cannot be liable.
- The causal connection between the defendant's complained-of acts and the incident or injuries of the claimant is insufficient.
- Damages were caused by comparative negligence or contributory negligence of the claimant.
- There is no basis for legal action under the statute asserted.

Some statutes impose liability on the "owner" of the loose animal, but counsel should carefully read the statutory definitions and applicable case law to determine which individuals or entities can be targeted in litigation.[64]

The common law might impose liability on the keeper of the animal who was, arguably, in the best position to prevent its escape. Over the years, however, counsel have engaged in creative strategies in an attempt to expand the list of potential defendants in loose livestock cases to include municipalities[65] and police officers, with mixed results.[66]

3. *Equine Activity Liability Statutes*

As of March 2008, 46 states—all but California, Maryland, Nevada, and New York—have passed some form of an equine activity liability law. Most of these laws state that if an equine activity "participant" is injured while he or she is "engaging in an equine activity," he or she cannot bring a claim against an "equine activity sponsor," "equine professional," and "another person" if the injury was the proximate result of an "inherent risk of equine activity." Most, *but not all*, of these statutes follow a general pattern in which they allow an "equine activity sponsor," "equine professional," or possibly others referenced in the laws to be sued if they perform any of the following acts and the act was the proximate cause of injury, death, or damage:

- Provide faulty tack or equipment that somehow causes injury, death, or damage to the equine activity participant.[67]
- Fail to determine the participant's ability to safely manage the horse based on the participant's actual abilities or representations of his or her abilities.[68]
- Own, lease, or have lawful use of land or facilities that have a dangerous latent condition but for which no conspicuous warning signs were posted.[69]

Some laws have exceptions that may allow liability for "gross negligence," "willful and wanton misconduct," or intentional wrongdoing.[70] A small number of the equine activity liability acts *appear* to include an exception related to claims alleging ordinary negligence. States with such language include Florida, Kentucky, Michigan, Missouri, Nebraska, New Jersey, New Mexico, North Carolina, Utah, and Virginia.

These statutes can furnish grounds for liability. Counsel representing plaintiffs can cite specific provisions of the law that defendants allegedly violated, such as providing a horse that was equipped with a faulty bridle that broke during the ride, caused the horse to become uncontrollable and to bolt, and caused injuries to the plaintiff.

Equine activity liability statutes also offer defendants grounds to seek dismissal of litigation. Several states have dismissed litigation involving persons injured while riding, handling, or being near horses based on these statutes.[71]

Counsel should pay particular attention to requirements, if any, in these laws for sign posting and contracts. Many of these laws require certain categories of individuals and businesses, especially "equine professionals" or "equine activity sponsors," to post "warning" signs. Kentucky's law requires this language:

WARNING

> Under Kentucky law, a farm animal activity sponsor, farm animal professional, or other person does not have the duty to eliminate all risks of injury of participation in farm animal activities. There are inherent risks of injury that you voluntarily accept if you participate in farm animal activities.

Several equine activity liability acts require "equine professionals" and sometimes "equine activity sponsors" to include certain language in their contracts and liability releases. Some of these laws condition the entitlement to immunities on compliance with the sign and warning language requirements.[72] Courts have found that average horse owners are not necessarily subject to signage requirements because they do not qualify as "equine activity sponsors or "equine professionals."[73]

Liability waivers and releases could potentially bar liabilities under equine activity liability acts, but counsel will find that states differ. Some prevent waivers that seek to bar such liabilities.[74] Others have enforced releases and dismissed claims under equine activity liability statutes.[75]

4. *Federal Tort Claims Act*

The Federal Tort Claims Act[76] can serve as a basis for liability. This statute provides a limited waiver of the federal government's sovereign immunity when its employees are negligent within the scope of their employment. The act provides that suits can be brought against the federal government only "under circumstances where the United States, if a private person, would be liable to the claimant in accordance with the law of the place where the act or omission occurred."[77] Governmental liability is determined "in accordance with the law of the place where the [allegedly tortious] act or omission occurred."[78]

In one case involving a camper who was killed by a bear at a federal park, the court found that the lawsuit against the federal government was barred by the Federal Tort Claims Act.[79] In another case, however, the plaintiff mink farmer prevailed against the government when government planes flew low over his land and frightened the female mink, causing the offspring to be destroyed.[80]

5. *Civil Rights Laws and Section 1983*

Section 1983 of the Civil Rights Act of 1871 allows citizens to sue persons who, under color of state law, violated the plaintiff's rights under the Constitution or certain federal laws.[81] Section 1983 actions can be brought against state officials in their personal capacity, but not in their official capacity. City and county and other nonstate officials can be sued in their official capacity, which allows damages to be obtained from the governmental entity, and in their personal capacity.

To prevail, the plaintiff must prove that the official's conduct violated clearly established statutory or constitutional rights of which a reasonable official should have known. If the official was mistaken about the law but had no reason to know that his or her actions were improper, or if the official acted under a law later declared unconstitutional, no liability would be found. Courts have required persons bringing actions under this statute to show significant harm as well as improper conduct.

Cases brought against municipal or state authorities who killed dogs without proper justification have succeeded and the defense of qualified immunity rejected. In a recent California case, for example,[82] the plaintiffs, members of a motorcycle club that was subjected to a police search, sued police officers under Section 1983. The plaintiffs alleged that the police violated their rights under the Fourth Amendment by shooting and killing dogs owned by club members without justification. Because the police officers knew in advance that the dogs were on the property and would be present during the search, the court emphasized, the defendants had an opportunity to develop a strategy for the searches and the defendants should have been aware of the fact that "any reasonable officer [should know] that the Fourth Amendment forbids the killing of a person's dog."[83] The court affirmed the denial of the defendants' qualified immunity defense.

IV. Defenses

A. Reasonable Care Exercised by Defendant

The fact that the defendant exercised reasonable care in his or her keeping and restraint of the animal can defeat claims of negligence. Counsel will need a thorough review of the facts to establish the defense.

Over the years, some cases have evaluated the following circumstances and found that they supported no negligence on the part of the defendant:

- The dog was restrained in such a manner as to keep it chained with a circumference that would not reach a public sidewalk.[84]
- The owner posted appropriate warning signs, such as a "beware of dog" sign.[85]

Testimony of a qualified expert witness, in some cases, can be necessary to prove that the defendant exercised reasonable care in the keeping, control, and/or restraint of the animal.

B. Assumption of Risk

The elements of assumption of risk have been set forth as (1) a risk of harm to plaintiff caused by defendant's conduct or property; (2) the plaintiff's actual knowledge of the particular risk and appreciation of its magnitude; and (3) the plaintiff's voluntary choice to accept the risk given the circumstances.[86]

Where allowed in the jurisdiction, assumption of risk can be an important and powerful defense in animal-inflicted injury cases. The success of the defense will depend on the particular facts. In equestrian liability litigation, assumption of risk is frequently raised as a defense in states such as California and New York that have not passed equine activity liability legislation.[87] However, where the plaintiff equestrian has insignificant riding experience, and where the plaintiff can prove that the incident did not result from an assumed risk, the court might refuse to apply the defense.[88]

Assumption of risk is typically not a defense against claims and cases brought under state dog-bite statutes. In a case involving an equine activity liability statute, one court cited assumption of risk as being a viable defense and a basis for dismissal of the litigation.[89]

Assumption of risk in the occupational setting is sometimes known as the "Firefighter's Rule" and, when applicable, can be a complete defense to personal injury actions by injured employees. In *Adams v. Lewis*,[90] the issue was whether defendant could assert the "Veterinarian's Rule," a variant of the Firefighter's Rule related to occupational primary assumption of risk, to bar the claims of an experienced animal behaviorist and trainer who was bitten by the plaintiff's dog whom he was hired to train. Dismissing the action, the court noted that the California legislature did not intend statutory strict liability claims to prevent the assumption of the risk defense. In addition, the court found that the Veterinarian's Rule, like the Firefighter's Rule, could bar personal injury claims arising out of conditions a person is expected to confront on the job. Although the plaintiff was an animal behavior specialist and not a veterinarian, the court nevertheless extended the doctrine to him.

In other occupational settings, such as where a professional horse trainer or farrier is hired, the defense of assumption of risk has seen some success where it supports dismissal of the case[91] but the defense has not succeeded in other cases.[92]

These defenses have, on occasion, been rejected. In one case, the City of New York could not assert the defense where it was sued by a mounted patrol officer who asserted violations of state labor laws when the city allegedly provided a police horse known to be unsafe.[93] In another case, the court found that the riding instructor, by creating an especially rigorous jumping course, improperly elevated the risks such that the plaintiff's fall was not the result of an assumed risk.[94]

C. Comparative and Contributory Negligence

Comparative negligence and/or contributory negligence, depending on the jurisdiction, are common defenses in animal tort litigation. Some states have abolished contributory negligence altogether. Arizona, for example, adopted the Uniform Contribution Among Tortfeasors Act and abolished contributory negligence as an absolute defense.[95] Some states, such as California and Florida, have adopted a system of pure comparative negligence.[96] Other states prevent plaintiffs from recovering damages if their negligence is greater than that of the defendants.[97]

Contributory negligence, in states that consider it, requires a showing that the injured person failed to exercise reasonable care for his or her own safety that an ordinary and prudent person would exercise under similar circumstances. For example:

- An experienced horseman was found contributorily negligent by approaching a stallion from the rear within kicking distance without watching the stallion.[98]
- The animal handler's act of picking up the dog to protect it from an attack by the defendant's dog was not found to be contributory negligence.[99]
- No contributory negligence was found when a plaintiff was unaware of "beware of dog" signs or of dangerous propensities of the animal at issue.[100]

D. Waivers, Releases of Liability, and Exculpatory Agreements

Most states nationwide have enforced waivers and releases of liability. Common animal-related settings in which these exculpatory agreements have been used include bailment settings such as dog and horse boarding facilities as well as animal training contracts, equestrian events, and horseback riding rental and instruction agreements.[101] These documents have been utilized and enforced in animal bailment settings.[102]

Sometimes liability releases are analyzed under general legal principles of express assumption of risk.[103] Express assumption of risk occurs in cases where the plaintiff expressly contracts with another to accept certain risks and to refrain from suing for any future injuries that may be caused by that person's negligence. In this connection, the *Restatement (Second) of Torts* states that "[a] plaintiff who by contract or otherwise expressly agrees to accept a risk of harm arising from the defendant's negligent or reckless conduct cannot recover for such harm, unless the agreement is invalid as contrary to public policy."[104]

Counsel would be wise to carefully scrutinize the language found in all liability releases at issue in the case. Numerous grounds have been cited for *refusal* to enforce liability releases. Here are a few of them:

- An applicable state statute forbids enforcement of the release document.[105]
- The document had faulty or incomplete drafting that failed to comply with the state requirements.[106]
- The release language was inconspicuous because, for example, the type size was too small or its language was buried within a large document.[107]
- Evidence existed of fraud in the document or in its execution.[108]
- At the time of the accident, the one attempting to rely on the release had violated a statute or public duty.[109]
- The court believed that a general public policy within the particular state forbids enforcement of the waiver or release.[110]
- The court found insufficient evidence of a bargained-for exchange between the parties, making it unfair to enforce the release.[111]
- There were perceived faults in the execution of the instrument, such as an underage signer.[112]
- Parent was found legally unable to waive claim of his or her minor child who took part in the activity and was injured.[113]
- The release could not waive the loss of consortium claim of a spouse who did not sign the release.[114]

- The signer was given an inadequate opportunity to read or understand the document before signing it.[115]

E. Sovereign Immunity

Principles of sovereign immunity or official immunity can override traditional concepts of strict liability for dog bites inflicted by police dogs. In *Hyatt v. Anoka Police Department*,[116] a police dog bit the plaintiff, whose husband was avoiding arrest. She sued the police department and city under a theory of strict liability. The court dismissed the action, noting that a police department was not a legal entity that could be subject to civil liability. It also held that actions involving police dogs were barred by the principle of vicarious official immunity but not by statutory immunity.

In *Audette v. Commonwealth*,[117] a drug-sniffing dog bit a police officer during a vehicle search at the police station. The officer sued under a strict liability theory. Without evidence that the dog's owner or keeper knew of any prior vicious or dangerous propensities of the dog, however, the court found that sovereign immunity precluded the imposition of strict liability and dismissed the action.

In a case involving allegations of unreasonable killings of dogs during the exercise of police functions, the court denied qualified immunity. In *San Jose Charter of Hells Angels Motorcycle Club v. City of San Jose*,[118] police officers searched a motorcycle club that had guard dogs on the property and shot and killed dogs owned by members of the club. The members sued, alleging that the police violated the Fourth Amendment. The court refused to allow the defendant officers to raise qualified immunity as a defense.

V. Intentional Torts

A. Practical Considerations in Bringing Intentional Tort Claims

Plaintiff's counsel should be aware of possible negative consequences of invoking these theories in litigation. Most significantly, policies of liability insurance, such as homeowners policies and commercial liability policies, specifically exclude coverage for allegations of "intentional" misconduct on part of an insured party. Counsel seeking to preserve insurance coverage should consider whether these theories should be dropped and negligence theories maintained instead.

Also, plaintiff's counsel should be aware of the possibility that the defendant's liability insurer might institute declaratory judgment proceedings designed to look beyond the pleadings to find that the conduct pled in the litigation is really one of an "excluded" intentional act.

B. Intentional Infliction of Emotional Distress

Intentional infliction of emotional distress can serve as an independent cause of action. One court recognized, citing the *Restatement (Second) of Torts*:

> One who by extreme and outrageous conduct . . . causes severe emotional distress to another is subject to liability for such emotional distress, and if bodily harm [to the other] results from it, for such bodily harm. The defendant must not merely have acted in a negligent or even in an intentional way. Rather, the defendant's conduct typically must be "so outrageous in character, and so extreme in degree, as to go beyond all possible bounds of decency and to be regarded as atrocious and utterly intolerable in a civilized society.[119]

Claims of this nature typically do not require a direct physical injury to the plaintiff as a result of the allegedly wrongful actions.

In the small number of animal-related cases in which this theory has succeeded, damages can be substantial. For example, in *Burgess v. Taylor*,[120] an appellate court in Kentucky upheld an award of $126,000 in damages for intentional infliction of emotional distress. In that case, the plaintiff became too ill to care for her two horses and placed them with the defendants for care and keeping, with the understanding that no board fees would be paid. Instead of keeping the horses, however, the defendants sold them to a slaughter buyer for $1,000, then lied to the plaintiff about the horses' whereabouts. Also, in *LaPorte v. Associated Independents*,[121] emotional distress damages were awarded when a garbage collector threw a can at a leashed dog, killing the dog.

Far more frequently, however, trial and appellate courts have dismissed cases alleging intentional infliction of emotional distress, usually finding that no right exists under applicable state law to sue for intentional or negligent infliction of emotional distress resulting from injury to property, such as a pet. For example, despite egregious facts, this was the holding in *Pantelopoulos v. Pantelopoulos*.[122] In that case, a restraining order in a contentious divorce proceeding denied the plaintiff access to her former residence, where her dog lived. The defendant, the ex-husband, vacated the premises and abandoned the dog, where it died of starvation and dehydration. Courts in other states have similarly held that intentional and negligent infliction of emotional distress claims cannot be maintained over the loss of a house pet.[123]

Counsel representing defendants in these cases can, where applicable, bring motions to dismiss on the basis that prevailing law does not permit such claims. Other defenses can be brought on the basis that the conduct at issue does not rise to the "extreme and outrageous" level that is typically required for these cases to prevail.

VI. Litigation

A. Early Case Considerations

Counsel should give special consideration to these factual matters that are unique to animal-related cases:

- If the case involves an animal that your client will seek to recover in the litigation, such as through a claim of replevin, consider giving appropriate notice to the opposing party not to sell, change, move, or dispose of the animal. Depending on state law, it might be necessary to seek an injunction or temporary restraining order that is designed to restore the status quo for a period of time and to prevent the opposing party from doing any of these things.
- If the case involves bailment issues, such as the loss of horses in a barn fire, consider whether it is appropriate to seek an independent inspection of the fire scene to evaluate possible causes of the fire and, potentially, liability of the facility owner or management for negligence.[124]
- If the dispute involves custody of the animal, but the animal is boarded in a facility or stable, applicable state agister's lien law might give the stable a lien on the animal, and the removal of the animal could be in violation of the facility's lien rights.[125]
- Obtain and carefully review copies of all written contracts between the parties, especially liability waivers and releases.
- Look for any written communications between the parties to determine whether they could have established a "course of dealing."

B. Statutes of Limitation

As the statute of limitations is examined, keep in mind that applicable state law can vary considerably on the allowable time frame for bringing litigation. For tort claims, the statute of limitations can vary considerably on a state-by-state basis. Some statutes provide a two-year statute of limitations for certain tort claims.[126] Other state laws provide a four-year statute of limitations for tort claims.[127] Some are five years.[128] A few are six years.[129] Counsel are encouraged to examine the applicable state law carefully.

C. Discovery

Because of the myriad of discovery tools available to counsel, the question confronting counsel will be the appropriate method and the timing of discovery. Typically, discovery will involve interrogatories, document requests, requests for admission, subpoenas for documents and/or testimony, and depositions.

1. Depositions

Clients sometimes prefer that counsel avoid the expense of taking depositions. Frankly, in most cases the client cannot afford *not* to take depositions. They can be beneficial for several reasons: (1) They allow counsel to receive spontaneous answers from the witness, not always the rehearsed answers from counsel; (2) they allow counsel to make judgments on the credibility of the witness; (3) they allow counsel to assess whether the witness will be accepted by a jury or, instead, show clear bias; (4) compared to interrogatories, which counsel and opposing parties sometimes take an inordinate time to answer, the deposition proceeds at a mutually agreeable date and time.

Depositions of the following persons are especially worth considering:

- Opposing parties
- Friendly witnesses whose availability for trial is uncertain
- Adverse or hostile witnesses
- The opposing party's expert witnesses
- Your expert witnesses (if their availability for trial is uncertain)

Consider taking a videotaped deposition. These depositions offer several advantages, such as allowing you to confront a witness at trial with inconsistent videotaped deposition testimony. Also, if the deponent proves to be unavailable for trial, and the video is available, chances are good that it can be used as evidence and played in whole or in part before a jury. The obvious downside is the added expenses these depositions pose.

Make sure you are familiar with deposition protocol in your jurisdiction, such as stipulations.

2. *Interrogatories*

Interrogatories can be an extremely important discovery tool. Unlike a deposition, where the witness provides spontaneous answers, the interrogatories can ask a party to review sources and gather information such as names of treating doctors, employers, and prior addresses.

On the negative side, interrogatory answers are typically drafted by counsel, which means that they will likely be combined with objections and carefully crafted answers, sometimes perceived as evasive. Strategically, it might benefit counsel to draft interrogatories that are designed to gather certain basic details, such as "name all witnesses to the incident" while leaving other questions, such as "explain how you believe my client is liable" for the deposition. Also, be sure to check applicable court rules for limitations, if any, on the number of interrogatories that can be served.

With animal-related injury cases, needed information can generally include:

- All prior owners of the animal
- All prior keepers of the animal
- All veterinarians who attended the animal
- The animal's health history
- The animal's training and utilization
- All trainers of the animal
- Sophistication and experience level of the animal's typical handlers or riders
- Any prior complaints, incidents, or citations involving the animal
- Any prior incidents where people or other animals were injured, or even threatened, while near, or riding, the animal
- Warning signs posted, if any, regarding the animal

Sample sets of interrogatories are in Appendices D and E for consideration by counsel representing plaintiffs and defendants.

3. *Document Requests*

In any type of lawsuit, documents are often very valuable evidence. Documents can have a dramatic effect on witnesses, when confronted with them. For example, exculpatory language in a dog-boarding contract can be powerful enough to dismiss litigation if the evidence is clear that the signer knowingly executed it. More and more jurisdictions have adopted mandatory disclosure rules, such as Federal Rule of Civil Procedure 26(a)(1). These rules mandate each party to produce, early on in the litigation, documents to the opposing side. Examples include (1) disclosure of names and contact information for people "likely to have discoverable information" and (2) disclosure of the contents of any insurance agreement that might satisfy a judgment in the litigation.

Where the jurisdiction does not make discovery of this nature mandatory, document requests can be developed and submitted to opposing counsel, often early in the case, seeking production of several documents and things, such as

- All medical records or veterinary records involving the individual or animal
- Tax returns (if the case includes a wage loss claim)[130]
- All expert witness reports
- All documents received from any key witnesses

4. Subpoenas

Subpoenas are notices, typically to nonparties, to compel their attendance at a deposition. Subpoenas can also request the production of documents either in addition to or instead of a deposition. The Federal Rules of Civil Procedure[131] and sometimes local court rules provide penalties for those who fail to obey a subpoena.

5. Requests for Admission

A request for admission is a discovery tool in which a party asks another party to admit or deny the truth of a key fact.[132] Requests for admission can also ask an opposing party to admit that a specified document is genuine. The effect is that an admission from the opposing party, when the request for admission is clearly and succinctly set forth, can help narrow the issues in the litigation. When an opposing party has admitted a material fact, the request for admission can assist in developing trial strategy or in drafting a motion for partial or complete summary judgment.

Denials of a request to admit must fairly meet the substance of the request. Applicable court rules might allow the answering party to neither admit nor deny, if the party cannot truthfully do either. In this instance, the rules typically require that the party at least try to make reasonable inquiry into the matter.

If the party propounding the request for admission believes that an objection is inappropriate or that an answer is evasive, he or she typically may petition the court to determine the sufficiency of the responses. Federal Rule of Civil Procedure 37 addresses motions of this type.

6. Expert Witnesses

Expert witnesses are sometimes utilized in animal liability cases. As you evaluate possible experts, and as you consider a strategy for cross-examination of the opposing party's expert, be sure to gather information on the expert's credentials, training, work experience, advertisements (if any), prior testimony, and publications.

D. Proving Damages

Chapter 9, "Remedies in Animal-Related Litigation," addresses several types of damage theories.

1. Injured People

Elements of damages for cases involving injuries to or death of an injured human can generally include, but are not limited to, the following:

- Medical expenses
- Present and future pain and suffering or mental anguish
- Loss of earning capacity
- Lost wages
- Disfigurement
- Aggravation of preexisting injury
- Loss of consortium
- Prenatal injuries
- Expenses reasonably and proximately related to the injury and incident

2. Injured Animals[133]

Where the animal's market value is at issue in the litigation, counsel can consider the following and its impact on establishing or diminishing value:

- Breed
- Purchase price
- Pedigree
- Scarcity or abundancy of animals with similar bloodlines
- Age, health, and condition
- Show or race record
- Produce record of breeding animals, such as stud fee, past stud fee earnings, and quality and sale prices of offspring
- Temperament
- Extent of training and training expenses
- Recent purchase offers
- Value of comparable animals in the marketplace
- Cost of obtaining replacement animal

Occasionally, the animal might have no fair market value. This might merit an award of nominal damages, but some courts will consider the animal's actual value to the owner and sometimes even its sentimental value.[134] A dog's usefulness can be considered in assessing its value, such as a service animal used to help disabled people.[135]

E. Trial Strategy

Animal law practitioners can sometimes bring unique presentations into court. For example, in an attempt to demonstrate that the animal is normally docile, it might be appropriate to ask the court to bring the animal in the courtroom before the jury.[136]

APPENDIX A

Checklist for Evaluation of a Loose Livestock Case

When confronted with a case involving a collision between loose livestock and a motorist, here are several questions that counsel for both plaintiffs and defendants can consider in investigating the claims and defenses:

- ❑ The accident's date, time, and location
- ❑ Name and addresses of owner(s), lessor(s), or lessee(s) of the loose animal(s)
- ❑ Names and addresses of owners and keepers of the animal(s) involved
- ❑ Names and addresses of the owners of the land from which the animal(s) escaped
- ❑ If defective fencing is at issue, whether the fencing was joined with a neighboring landowner (such as a common fence), and the names and addresses of the adjoining land owners
- ❑ Names and addresses of all persons charged with maintaining the animal (such as pasturing, feeding, and exercising)
- ❑ Names and addresses of the last known person(s) with access to the facility and/or fencing at issue

- ❑ Information regarding the animal(s) (type, size, color, weight, path taken before collision)
- ❑ Quality of confinement (fences, gates, latches, stalls, electrified wires and chargers, dates fences constructed and repaired before incident, inspection schedules of the fencing, if any, etc.); photographs of several areas and/or video are very helpful
- ❑ Local ordinances regarding fencing quality and type (fence heights, materials, etc.)
- ❑ Police report, if any
- ❑ Signage, if any, in the area of the collision (examples: speed limit, open range district warning sign, etc.)
- ❑ Details regarding the sequence of events before and after the collision (examples: time of animal's escape; efforts to recapture; evidence of avoidance maneuvers, if any, by driver, etc.)
- ❑ Autopsy and toxicology reports of injured plaintiff, if applicable
- ❑ Motor vehicle speed limit in roadway where injured person or motorist proceeded
- ❑ Driver's history and conduct at time of the incident (speed; experience; driving record; intoxication level, if any, etc.)
- ❑ Weather report for the area and information regarding outdoor lighting, if any
- ❑ Information regarding prior escapes of animals from the potential defendant's facility or pastures

APPENDIX B

Sample Complaint in an Equestrian Personal Injury Case

IN THE CIRCUIT COURT OF THE
1ST JUDICIAL CIRCUIT
IN HORSE COUNTY, FLORIDA
GENERAL JURISDICTION DIVISION
CASE NO. ______________________

PETER G. PLAINTIFF AND POLLY
PLAINTIFF, individually, and as parents
and natural guardians of PIPER
PLAINTIFF, a minor,

Plaintiffs,

vs.

BIG BUSINESS, INC., a Florida
Corporation for Profit; and DAVID
DEFENDANT and DEBBIE DEFENDANT,

Defendants.

Complaint for Damages

Plaintiffs, by and through undersigned counsel, sue the Defendants and allege as follows:

1. This is an action for damages in excess of $50,000.00, exclusive of interest and costs, and otherwise within the jurisdiction of this Court.
2. At all times material, the Plaintiffs, PETER PLAINTIFF and POLLY PLAINTIFF, have been and are residents of Horse County, Florida, and are otherwise *sui juris*.
3. At all times material, the Plaintiffs, PETER G. PLAINTIFF and POLLY PLAINTIFF, were and are the parents and natural guardians of PIPER PLAINTIFF, a minor.
4. At all times material, the Defendant, BIG BUSINESS, INC., was a Florida corporation for profit, engaged in the operation of horse stables and associated equine activities for commercial gain, with its principal place of business located at 12345 Recreation Street in Pleasantville, Florida, and was authorized to do and was doing business in Horse County, Florida.
5. At all times material, Defendants, DAVID and DEBBIE DEFENDANT, were residents of Horse County, Florida, who were engaged in the operation of horse stables and associated equine activities for commercial gain.
6. On or about September 9, 2009, due to the joint and/or several and/or combined negligence of the Defendants, PIPER PLAINTIFF, a minor, was thrown from a horse on the Defendants'

premises located at 12345 Recreation Street in Pleasantville, Florida, and sustained serious and permanent physical injury.

Count I: Negligence of Big Business, Inc.

Plaintiffs reallege and readopt Paragraphs 1 through 6 as though fully set forth herein, and alternatively and concurrently further allege:

7. At all times material, BIG BUSINESS, INC., possessed, owned, operated, managed, and/or controlled horse stables located at 12345 Recreation Street in Pleasantville, Florida.
8. At all times material, BIG BUSINESS, INC., conducted equine activities for profit at the above location.
9. At all times material, BIG BUSINESS, INC., had a duty to maintain and operate its stables and conduct any equine activities associated with it in a safe, reasonable, and prudent manner for the benefit of their business invitees and patrons, including the minor Plaintiff, PIPER PLAINTIFF, who was owed the highest duty of care.
10. At all times material, BIG BUSINESS, INC., breached its duty of care and was negligent and careless, and demonstrated a willful and wanton disregard for the safety of PIPER PLAINTIFF in ways which included, but were not limited to, the following:

    a. Failing to maintain horseback riding equipment and/or tack in good and safe condition and repair;
    b. Failing to provide necessary horseback riding equipment and/or providing horseback riding equipment to the minor Plaintiff which the Defendant knew or should have known was defective, and/or inadequate, and unsafe for use;
    c. Failing to adequately supervise and instruct the minor Plaintiff as she rode horseback;
    d. Failing to select an adequately and appropriately trained and safe horse for the minor Plaintiff to ride;
    e. Selecting a horse for the Plaintiff to ride which the Defendant knew or should have known to possess dangerous propensities that rendered the animal unsafe for the minor Plaintiff;
    f. Failing to provide the minor Plaintiff with adequate and appropriate instruction and guidance to permit her to safely ride the horse selected for her;
    g. Failing to make reasonable and prudent efforts to determine the ability of the minor Plaintiff to safely engage in the sub-

ject equine activity and to safely ride and manage the particular horse selected for her;

h. Failing to maintain the premises and its equipment in a reasonably safe condition for the equine activities being conducted thereon;

i. Failing to hire, retain, and train competent and reasonably skilled personnel;

j. Failing to adopt reasonable policies, practices, and procedures for the safe pursuit of equine activities on the premises;

k. Failing to provide adequate warning of dangerous conditions on the premises and/or associated with the equine activities being conducted thereon;

l. Failing to remedy and/or warn of dangerous, latent conditions arising from the premises or its equipment which the Defendant knew or should have known to exist;

m. Otherwise failing to operate its facilities in a safe, reasonable, and prudent manner; and

n. Other acts of negligence as determined through discovery.

11. Defendant, BIG BUSINESS, INC., is directly and/or vicariously liable for the negligent acts or omissions of its agents, employees, or apparent agents.
12. As a direct and proximate result of the above mentioned negligence of the Defendant, BIG BUSINESS, INC., the minor Plaintiff, PIPER PLAINTIFF, was injured in and about her head, body, and extremities, experienced pain and suffering therefrom, and sustained disability, scarring, disfigurement, physical impairment, mental anguish, aggravation of preexisting conditions, the loss of capacity for the enjoyment of life, the loss of earning capacity and income in the future, and all other elements of damages allowed under Florida law. Said damages are permanent and continuing in nature, and Plaintiff will suffer these losses and impairments in the future.
13. As a further direct and proximate result of the above-mentioned negligence of Defendant, BIG BUSINESS, INC., Plaintiffs, PETER PLAINTIFF and POLLY PLAINTIFF, have incurred medical expenses related to the treatment and care of PIPER PLAINTIFF's injuries and will continue to incur such expenses in the future.

WHEREFORE, Plaintiffs, PETER PLAINTIFF and POLLY PLAINTIFF, individually, and as parents and natural guardians of PIPER PLAINTIFF, demand judgment against the Defendant, BIG BUSINESS, INC., for damages in excess of this Court's minimal jurisdictional limits, as well as prejudgment and postjudgment interest and costs as allowed by law, and a trial by jury of all issues so triable.

Count II: Negligence of David Defendant and Debbie Defendant

Plaintiffs reallege and readopt paragraphs 1 through 13 as though fully set forth herein, and alternatively and concurrently further allege:

14. At all times material, DAVID DEFENDANT and DEBBIE DEFENDANT possessed, owned, operated, managed, and/or controlled horse stables located at 12345 Recreation Street in Pleasantville, Florida.
15. At all times material, DAVID DEFENDANT and DEBBIE DEFENDANT conducted equine activities for profit at the above location.
16. At all times material, DAVID DEFENDANT and DEBBIE DEFENDANT had a duty to maintain and operate their stables and conduct any equine activities associated with it in a safe, reasonable, and prudent manner for the benefit of their business invitees and patrons, including the minor Plaintiff, PIPER PLAINTIFF.
17. At all times material, DAVID DEFENDANT and DEBBIE DEFENDANT breached their duty of care, and were negligent and careless, and demonstrated a willful and wanton disregard for the safety of PIPER PLAINTIFF in ways which included, but were not limited to, the following:

    a. Failing to maintain horseback riding equipment and/or tack in good and safe condition and repair;
    b. Failing to provide necessary horseback riding equipment and/or providing horseback riding equipment to the minor Plaintiff which the Defendants knew or should have known was defective, and/or inadequate, and unsafe for use;
    c. Failing to adequately supervise and instruct the minor Plaintiff as she rode horseback;
    d. Failing to select an adequately and appropriately trained and safe horse for the minor Plaintiff to ride;
    e. Selecting a horse for the Plaintiff to ride which the Defendants knew or should have known to possess dangerous propensities that rendered the animal unsafe for the minor Plaintiff;
    f. Failing to provide the minor Plaintiff with adequate and appropriate instruction and guidance to permit her to safely ride the horse selected for her;

g. Failing to make reasonable and prudent efforts to determine the ability of the minor Plaintiff to safely engage in the subject equine activity and to safely ride and manage the particular horse selected for her;
h. Failing to maintain the premises and its equipment in a reasonably safe condition for the equine activities being conducted thereon;
i. Failing to hire, retain, and train competent and reasonably skilled personnel;
j. Failing to adopt reasonable policies, practices, and procedures for the safe pursuit of equine activities on the premises;
k. Failing to provide adequate warning of dangerous conditions on the premises and/or associated with the equine activities being conducted thereon;
l. Failing to remedy and/or warn of dangerous, latent conditions arising from the premises or its equipment which the Defendants knew or should have known to exist;
m. Otherwise failing to operate its facilities in a safe, reasonable, and prudent manner; and
n. Other acts of negligence as determined through discovery.

18. Defendants, DAVID DEFENDANT and DEBBIE DEFENDANT, are directly and/or vicariously liable for the negligent acts or omissions of their agents, employees, or apparent agents.
19. As a direct and proximate result of the above-mentioned negligence of the Defendants, DAVID DEFENDANT and DEBBIE DEFENDANT, the minor Plaintiff, PIPER PLAINTIFF, was injured in and about her head, body, and extremities, experienced pain and suffering therefrom, and sustained disability, scarring, disfigurement, physical impairment, mental anguish, aggravation of preexisting conditions, the loss of capacity for the enjoyment of life, the loss of earning capacity and income in the future, and all other elements of damages allowed under Florida law. Said damages are permanent and continuing in nature, and Plaintiff will suffer these losses and impairments in the future.
20. As a further direct and proximate result of the above-mentioned negligence of Defendants, DAVID DEFENDANT and DEBBIE DEFENDANT, Plaintiffs, PETER PLAINTIFF and POLLY PLAINTIFF, have incurred medical expenses related to the treatment and care of PIPER PLAINTIFF's injuries and will continue to incur such expenses in the future.

WHEREFORE, Plaintiffs, PETER PLAINTIFF and POLLY PLAINTIFF, individually, and as parents and natural guardians of PIPER PLAINTIFF, demand judgment against Defendants, DAVID DEFENDANT and DEBBIE DEFENDANT, for damages in excess of this Court's minimal jurisdictional limits, as well as prejudgment and postjudgment interest and costs as allowed by law, and a trial by jury of all issues so triable.

Count III: Loss of Services, Society, and Consortium

Plaintiffs reallege and readopt paragraphs 1 through 20 as though fully set forth herein, and alternatively and concurrently further allege:

21. As a further direct and proximate result of the joint and/or several negligence of BIG BUSINESS, INC., and/or DAVID DEFENDANT, and/or DEBBIE DEFENDANT, as outlined in the preceding paragraphs, Plaintiffs, PETER PLAINTIFF and POLLY PLAINTIFF, have lost in the past and will lose in the future the companionship, society, love, affection, services, earning ability, attention and solace of their seriously and permanently injured and disabled daughter, PIPER PLAINTIFF.

WHEREFORE, plaintiffs PETER AND POLLY PLAINTIFF demand judgment against BIG BUSINESS, INC., and/or DAVID DEFENDANT, and/or DEBBIE DEFENDANT for damages in excess of this Court's minimal jurisdictional limits, as well as prejudgment and postjudgment interest and costs as allowed by law, and a trial by jury on all issues so triable.

Respectfully submitted,

GOOD, BETTER, BEST, P.L.C.

By:____________________

Carry Professional
Attorney for Plaintiffs
9876 Shiny Street
Sunny, Florida 33333
Phone: (305) 555-1212

Dated: January 1, 2010

APPENDIX C

Sample Affirmative Defenses in an Equine-Related Personal Injury Case

Affirmative Defenses

Defendants John and Jane Doe d/b/a SWEETBRIAR FARM state that they will or may rely on the following defenses if applicable and if supported by facts to be determined through discovery:

A. Plaintiffs' Complaint fails to state a claim upon which relief can be granted.
B. Plaintiffs' Complaint is barred, in whole or in part, since any damages alleged were proximately caused by the culpable acts of others over whom these Defendants have no control and for whom these Defendants cannot be held accountable.
C. Plaintiffs' Complaint is barred, in whole or in part, since Defendants took all reasonable precautions and measures and exercised the required degree of care.
D. Plaintiffs' Complaint is barred, in whole or in part, due to the sole, comparative, or contributory negligence of Plaintiffs, or either of them individually.
E. Plaintiffs' Complaint is barred, in whole or in part, because Plaintiffs have failed to mitigate their damages.
F. Plaintiffs' Complaint is barred, in whole or in part, since the horse at issue did not, to Defendant's knowledge, information, and belief, have a history of exhibiting prior "vicious or dangerous" conduct.
G. Plaintiffs' Complaint is barred since Plaintiff's Complaint fails to plead a cause of action under the ________ Equine Activity Liability Act, [citation], which is the Plaintiff's exclusive remedy for such an equine-related action.
H. Plaintiffs' Complaint is barred, in whole or in part, since Plaintiff assumed the inherent risks of equine activities and the incident at issue arose from an "inherent risk of an equine activity," within the meaning of the ________ Equine Activity Liability Act, [citation].

I. Defendants claim all rights, privileges, and immunities available under the _______ Equine Activity Liability Act [citation].
J. Plaintiff's Complaint is barred, in whole or in part, since it fails to state legally cognizable duties breached by this Defendant.
K. Defendants reserve the right to amend their answer to plead further and other affirmative defenses after a reasonable opportunity for discovery.

APPENDIX D

Sample Plaintiff's Interrogatories to Defendant in a Personal Injury Case

STATE OF ______________________
IN THE CIRCUIT COURT FOR THE COUNTY OF _____________

The Honorable _____________
Civil Action No. ____________

_______________,

Plaintiff,

vs.

_______________,

Defendant.

Laura Lawyer
Attorney for Plaintiff
555 Recovery Road
Money, MI 48888
Telephone: (800) 555-2221

Adam Attorney
Attorney for Defendant
3000 Dismissal Drive
Money, MI 48888
Telephone: (800) 555-3331

Plaintiff's First Set of Interrogatories to Defendant

Introduction

Pursuant to Rules 26 and 33 of the Rules of Civil Procedure for ____________, plaintiff propounds the following interrogatories to defendants. Pursuant to Section IV (c) of Corrected Case Management Order Number 1, plaintiffs are serving a single set of interrogatories. Not all of the interrogatories are propounded on behalf of, or at the request of, the plaintiff, including the discovery coordinators. As contemplated by Corrected Case Management Order No. 1, the consolidated set of Interrogatories encompasses the individual general discovery requests of the plaintiff. These consolidated interrogatories are intended to minimize the need for duplicative discovery and the need to file separate interrogatories. Each interrogatory incorporates the following Definitions and Instructions.

Definitions

Unless specifically indicated otherwise, the following definitions are applicable throughout these interrogatories (including in this Definitions section) and are incorporated into each specific interrogatory. The definitions shall be limited, if at all, only to the extent necessary to avoid a nonsensical meaning of any interrogatory.

1. "Claimant" means a demand or assertion, whether oral or written, formal or informal, by any person upon ____________ for actual or potential monetary payment or the actual or potential undertaking or cessation of action.
2. "Claimant" means any person who, singly or in combination with other persons, has filed, made, or asserted one or more claims, potential claims, or suits against __________.
3. "Communication" means, without limitation, any oral, written, or electronic transmission of information, demands, or questions, including but not limited to conversations, meetings, discussions, telephone calls, telegrams, telecopies, telexes, seminars, conferences, writings, letters, messages, notes, or memoranda.
4. "Complaint" means the complaint or amended complaint filed in this case.
5. "Defendants" means the defendants in the complaint and all their predecessors in interest, successors in interest, directors, officers, employees, agents, representatives, and others known to you to have acted on their respective behalfs.

6. "Document" means each and every form in which information is kept, however produced, reproduced, or stored, in your actual or constructive possession, custody, or control, or of which you have knowledge of its existence, and whether prepared, published, or released by you or by any other person or entity, including but not limited to letters, reports, agreements, correspondence, intra-office or inter-office correspondence, telegrams, minutes or records of meetings, reports or summaries of investigations, expressions or statements of policy, opinions or reports of consultants, lists, drafts, revisions, invoices, receipts, original and preliminary notes, preliminary sketches, records, ledgers, contracts, bills of lading, bills, inventories, financial data, maps, memoranda, accounting and financial records, diaries, journals, calendars, statements, work papers, videotapes, photographs, pamphlets, brochures, advertisements, trade letters, press releases, drawings, recaps, maps, tables, articles, summaries of conversations, computer cards, tapes, disks, and other means of electronically or magnetically maintained information, and printouts. "Document" includes, without limitation, all originals and nonidentical copies. "Document" includes a copy of the original when the original is not in your possession, custody, or control, and every nonidentical copy of the original.
7. "Identify" when used with respect to documents means that you are required, for each and every document, to

   a. State its exact name and title;
   b. State the date of the document and all other serial or identifying numbers thereon;
   c. State its general subject matter;
   d. Describe the document by type, e.g., a letter, newspaper, memorandum, etc.;
   e. Provide the information required by Definition No. 15 for each person who participated in the creation of the document;
   f. Provide the information required by Definition No. 15 for each addressee, if any, of the document or any copy; and
   g. Specify the location of any file or files where the document, or any copy thereof, is normally or presently kept, and provide the information.

   In lieu of identifying a document, the particular document may be referred to and produced.

8. "Identify" when used with respect to a person means that you are required to

   a. State his, her, or its full name;
   b. State the last known residence and business address, last known employer, job title, and job description of any natural person or, if other than a natural person:

      (1) the full name and address of the entity's principal place of business and state of incorporation; and
      (2) the name, last known address, place of employment, and employer of each natural person employed or representing such entity, having knowledge of or with whom communications have been had relating to the subject matter of the interrogatory; and

   c. State all of the person's positions, titles, job descriptions, and periods of employment, if any, with ____________ or any other entity of which you are aware.

9. "Identify" with respect to a communication means that you are required to

   a. Identify every person participating in or present during the communications;
   b. State the place where the communication was made;
   c. State the date the communication was made;
   d. State the substance and subject matter of the communication; and
   e. State the method and manner by which the communication was accomplished.

10. "Person" means any entity of any description that has a separate identity, recognized in law or in fact to have legal rights and obligations. This term includes, but is not limited to, any natural person, corporation, partnership, joint venture, association, company, group, organization, trust, estate, business, or governmental entity or agency (public or private). Any reference to a person that is not a natural person includes its present and former officers, executives, partners, directors, trustees, employees, attorneys, agents, representatives, and all other persons acting or purporting to act on behalf of the person, and also its subsidiaries, affiliates, divisions, predecessors, and successors in interest.

11. "Plaintiff" means the plaintiff in the complaint.
12. "Relating to" or "relates to" means consisting of, referring to, describing, discussing, reflecting, citing, pertaining to, regarding, evidencing, concerning, summarizing, or analyzing, whether directly or indirectly, the matter discussed.
13. "Response activity" means all actions taken, considered, planned, or prepared by or for in response to
    a. Any proposed, drafted, or filed version of any judicial or administrative order, settlement agreement, or decree entered upon consent, which order, agreement, or decree relates in any way, directly or indirectly, to any environmental claim, injury to the environment, or hazardous material or waste;
    b. Any release of a hazardous material or waste;
    c. Any proposal, inquiry, or direction from any environmental or natural resources governmental authority which relates directly or indirectly to any environmental claim, injury to the environment, or hazardous material or waste; or
    d. Any claim by any private person which relates directly or indirectly to any environmental claim, injury to the environment, or hazardous material or waste.
14. "Site" means any specific physical location or premises.

Instructions

1. Unless otherwise stated, each interrogatory refers to the time period from _____ until the present.
2. Unless the text clearly requires otherwise, you shall interpret
    a. The singular form of a word to include the plural and vice versa;
    b. The conjunctive "and" to include the disjunctive "or" and vice versa; all pronouns to apply to the male, female, and neutral genders;
    c. The word "any" to include the word "all" and vice versa; and
    d. The past tense of a word to include the present tense and vice versa.
3. If you assert that an interrogatory is objectionable, state your objection clearly and specifically identify which parts of the interrogatory or the responses it requires are objectionable and why.
4. If you assert that part of an interrogatory is objectionable, respond to those remaining parts of the interrogatory to which you do not object.

5. If you choose to respond to an interrogatory by producing documents, clearly indicate to which interrogatory and subparagraph the documents are responsive. If you have already produced documents which are responsive to an interrogatory, describe the documents and the interrogatory and subparagraph to which they respond.
6. If you cannot answer any portion of any of the following interrogatories in full, after exercising due diligence to secure the information to do so, so state, and answer to the extent possible, specifying your inability to answer the remainder, and stating whatever information or knowledge you have concerning the unanswered portions.
7. If you claim a privilege as a ground for failing to answer any interrogatory, respond to a part of each such interrogatory that, in your view, does not contain allegedly privileged communications. For each interrogatory, or portion thereof, for which you claim a privilege, describe the factual basis for your claim of privilege in sufficient detail to permit adjudication of the validity of that claim, including without limitation, the following:

   a. A brief description of the type of document or communication;
   b. The date of the document or communication;
   c. The name, title, and job description of the transmitter of the document or communication;
   d. The name, title, and job description of the person to whom the document or communication was addressed;
   e. The name, title, and job description of each person who has received or had access to the document or communication;
   f. A brief description of the subject matter of the document or communication; and
   g. The nature of the privilege claimed.

8. If _______________ at any time had possession or control of a document responsive to these interrogatories and if such document has been lost, destroyed, or purged or is not presently in your possession or control, then (a) identify the document; (b) state the date of its loss, destruction, purge, or separation from your possession or control; (c) state the circumstances surrounding its loss, destruction, purge, or separation from your possession or control; and (d) state its present or last known location, including the name, address, and telephone number of each person believed to have possession of such document.

Interrogatories

INTERROGATORY NO. 1: For each and every witness listed on the defendant's witness list, please provide the following:

a. His or her full complete name;
b. His or her present or last known address and telephone number;
c. Any and all opinions, lay or expert, which the witness intends to offer at the time of trial;
d. If the witness is an expert witness, please provide a copy of his or her curriculum vitae;
e. Whether the witnesses are related any way to either the defendants or any other individuals listed on the defendants' witness list and if so, whom;
f. Whether the witness has been a witness or party to a lawsuit and if so the name and address of the court in which the case was pending;
g. Whether the defendants or their counsel have obtained a written statement from said witness, and if so, whether the defendants will produce the same without a Motion to Compel.

INTERROGATORY NO. 2: As to each and every affirmative defense set forth by the defendants in their answer to Plaintiff's First Amended Complaint, please state as follows:

a. Each and every witness intended to be called as a witness in support of said affirmative defense;
b. Each and every fact known to the defendants or said witnesses, which supports the defense.

INTERROGATORY NO. 3: Please state the inherent risk of the activity of horseback riding as referred to by the defendants in their answer to the complaint.

INTERROGATORY NO. 4: Please state the name and address of the owner, trainer, breeder, and veterinarian of the subject horse.

INTERROGATORY NO. 5: Please state any and all veterinarian care and treatment provided to the horse from which the plaintiff fell in the ten years prior to this incident.

INTERROGATORY NO. 6: Please state the name, address, and telephone number of any individual to whom medical treatment has been rendered or for which an incident report was filled out, where the incident or inquiry was caused as a result of a fall or injury with a horse utilized at by defendants.

INTERROGATORY NO. 7: Please state the process by which the defendants undertook to determine the qualifications of individuals to assist in the Handicapped Rider program.

INTERROGATORY NO. 8: Please state the process by which the defendants determined the competency of individuals to assist with its riding program.

INTERROGATORY NO. 9: Please state all factual evidence in support of the defendants' claim that the plaintiff was comparatively negligent.

INTERROGATORY NO. 10: Please state all medical information about the plaintiff contained in the medical file as referred to in Defendants' Answers, Paragraph 4 of the First Amended Complaint.

INTERROGATORY NO. 11: Please state the name and address of each of the individuals present at the time of the plaintiff's incident and who they were employed by at the time of this incident, as well as their present or last known address.

INTERROGATORY NO. 12: Please state what facts the defendants rely upon in support of its statement in Answer to Plaintiff's Paragraph 6 of the First Amended Complaint that "it acted reasonably at all times."

INTERROGATORY NO. 13: Pursuant to Court Rule ___, please state each and every fact defendants rely upon in support of its Answer to Paragraph 9, 10, and 11 of the Plaintiff's Complaint.

By: ______________________

Laura Lawyer
Attorney for Plaintiff
555 Recovery Rd.
Money, MI 48888
Telephone: (800) 555-2221

APPENDIX E

Sample Defendant's Interrogatories to Plaintiff in an Equestrian Personal Injury Case

STATE OF ______________

IN THE CIRCUIT COURT FOR THE COUNTY OF __________

WIFE PLAINTIFF and HUSBAND PLAINTIFF, Plaintiffs, vs. DEFENDANT COMPANY, a __________ corporation, Defendants.	The Honorable ______________ Civil Action No. ______________

Defendants' First Set of Interrogatories

DEFENDANT COMPANY, a ________ corporation, by and through its attorney, for its First Set of Interrogatories and Request for Production of Documents to Plaintiffs, pursuant to Court Rules ________, requests that both plaintiffs answer the following Interrogatories and produce the following documents within twenty-eight (28) days from the date of service hereof.

Preliminary Instructions and Definitions

For purposes of these Interrogatories and Requests for Production of Documents served by the defendants, the following definitions and instructions shall apply:

A. All information is to be divulged that is in the possession of the plaintiffs, their attorneys, consultants, investigators, agents, or other representatives of the plaintiffs and their attorneys.

B. Where an individual Interrogatory calls for an answer which involves more than one part, each part of the answer should be clearly set out so that it is understandable.

C. These Interrogatories are to be regarded as continuing and you are instructed to provide, by way of supplementary answers thereto, such additional information as may hereafter be obtained by you or any person on your behalf which will augment or otherwise modify any not given to these Interrogatories answers.

D. "You" or "plaintiffs" refers to ___________ and their attorneys, consultants, investigators, agents, or other representatives or persons who may have these interrogatory answers.

E. "Complaint" refers to the plaintiffs' Complaint in the instant case.

F. "Document" shall have its customary broad meaning and shall include, without limitation, the following items, whether printed, recorded, or reproduced by any other mechanical process, or written or produced by hand, including but not limited to letters, writings, correspondence, photographs, memoranda, drawings, notes, transcripts, contracts, agreements, telegrams, books, magazines, advertisements, statements, notices, reports, diaries, logs, calendars, videos, movies, audiotapes, CDs, diskettes, or materials similar to any of the foregoing.

Interrogatories

INTERROGATORY NO. 1: Please identify by name, address, and telephone number, and (if also available) business address and business telephone number, all persons with knowledge of the facts which allegedly constitute the plaintiffs' claim against the named defendants.

INTERROGATORY NO. 2: Have plaintiffs ever been known by any other names? If your answer is "yes" for either or both plaintiffs, please state all other name(s) by which either or both plaintiffs have been known and the inclusive dates in which they have been known by those names.

INTERROGATORY NO. 3: With respect to all physicians, osteopaths, chiropractors, psychotherapists, therapists, social workers, or other licensed medical and/or psychological practitioners who have examined, treated, or attended plaintiff for the injuries alleged in the Complaint:

a. Identify each such person, including their respective name(s), business name(s), address(es), and telephone number(s);

b. State the date(s) and period(s) this plaintiff was under the care of each such person identified in answer to Interrogatory No. 3(a), above;
c. Describe the nature of the treatment given by each such person identified in answer to Interrogatory No. 3(a), above;
d. As to those persons listed above who only conducted an examination of this plaintiff, identify each person and the date of each examination; and
e. Attach to your answers to these Interrogatories copies of all reports, statements, bills, or other documents given to you or received by you from each of the persons referenced in answer to Interrogatory Nos. 3(a) through 3(d) above.

INTERROGATORY NO. 4: If plaintiff, WIFE PLAINTIFF, received treatment from a hospital, clinic, or other institution for the injuries complained of in the Complaint, please state:

a. The name of the hospital or institution rendering treatment;
b. The name(s) of all professionals who treated this plaintiff at such hospital or institution;
c. Nature of treatment received;
d. Date(s) in which this plaintiff received treatment; and
e. Attach to your answers to these Interrogatories copies of all reports, statements, bills, or other documents given to you or received by you from each of the persons, facilities, or institutions referenced in answer to Interrogatory Nos. 4(a) through 4(d) above.

INTERROGATORY NO. 5: With respect to the medical insurance applicable to both individual named plaintiffs, please state:

a. Name(s) and addresses of each medical insurer from August 1, 1993, to the present;
b. With respect to each insurer identified in answer to Interrogatory No. 5(a) above, identify all policy numbers or policy reference numbers applicable (e.g., group insurance numbers, etc.); and
c. Time period(s) during which benefits were paid and amounts paid.

INTERROGATORY NO. 6: With respect to plaintiff, WIFE PLAINTIFF, employment for the last ten (10) years, please state:

a. Name(s) and addresses of the plaintiff's employer(s) with whom this plaintiff worked;
b. Name of this plaintiff's immediate supervisor(s) at each such place of employment identified above, for the last ten (10) years; and
c. Plaintiff's job titles at each such place of employment identified above for the last ten (10) years.

INTERROGATORY NO. 7: Have either or both plaintiffs ever ridden horses before the date of the incident in this case? If your answer is "yes," for each plaintiff please state:

a. Name and address of each facility where horse(s) were ridden by each plaintiff;
b. Dates in which horses were ridden (if specific dates are unknown, then approximate month and year will be sufficient, together with the number of rides during the specified period); and
c. Names of all persons who accompanied each plaintiff in rides referenced above (including but not limited to friends, relatives, riding instructors, etc.) and dates of accompaniment.

INTERROGATORY NO. 8: With respect to each person you will or may call as a witness at the trial of this action, either in person or by deposition, please state:

a. Name, address, and telephone number;
b. A synopsis of the expected testimony of each witness identified above; and
c. Attach to your answers to these Interrogatories copies of all documents given to or received by you from any person(s) referenced in response to Interrogatory No. 8, above, regarding this lawsuit.

INTERROGATORY NO. 9: Please state the name, address, and telephone number of each person who is expected to be called as an expert witness on behalf of the plaintiffs, or either of them, at trial, together with the subject matter on which the expert is expected to testify.

INTERROGATORY NO. 10: Please state whether each plaintiff was ever involved in any other incidents or accidents involving horses resulting in an injury, either before or after the incident at issue in this lawsuit. If your answer is "yes" for either or both plaintiffs, please state:

a. Date(s) and place(s) of incident(s) or accident(s);
b. Description of incident(s) or accident(s);
c. Nature of injury/injuries received; and
d. Identity and address of any doctor, hospital, clinic, or other medical institution that treated either plaintiff or both.

INTERROGATORY NO. 11: With respect to paragraph 13(A) of the Complaint, in which you allege that the defendant "failed to provide a safely prepared horse and saddle for the plaintiff, WIFE PLAINTIFF, to ride," please state:

a. All facts upon which you will rely in support of these allegations;
b. All eyewitnesses, lay witnesses, and/or expert witnesses (including name, address, and telephone number, and if also available, business address and business telephone number) upon which you will rely in support of these allegations;
c. All documents of any kind upon which you will rely in support of these allegations;
d. Attach to your answers to these Interrogatories copies of all documents referenced in answer to Interrogatory Nos. 11(a) through 11(c) above.

INTERROGATORY NO. 12: With respect to paragraph 13(B) of the Complaint, in which you allege that the defendant "failed to properly train its staff on the proper way to prepare a horse for business invitee," please state:

a. All facts upon which you will rely in support of these allegations;
b. All eyewitnesses, lay witnesses, and/or expert witnesses (including name, address, and telephone number, and if also available, business address and business telephone number) upon which you will rely in support of these allegations;
c. All documents of any kind upon which you will rely in support of these allegations;
d. Attach to your answers to these Interrogatories copies of all documents referenced in answer to Interrogatory Nos. 12(a) through 12(c) above.

INTERROGATORY NO. 13: With respect to paragraph 13(C) of the Complaint, in which you allege that the defendant "failed to use a proper way to fix a saddle to a horse so it will not come loose and fall off," please state:

a. All facts upon which you will rely in support of these allegations;
b. All eyewitnesses, lay witnesses, and/or expert witnesses (including name, address, and telephone number, and if also available, business address and business telephone number) upon which you will rely in support of these allegations;
c. All documents of any kind upon which you will rely in support of these allegations;
d. Attach to your answers to these Interrogatories copies of all documents referenced in answer to Interrogatory Nos. 13(a) through 13(c) above.

INTERROGATORY NO. 14: State whether any of the medical or hospital expenses or charges, expenses of rehabilitation services, loss of earnings, loss of earning capacity, or other economic loss that you claim to have incurred as a result of the incident described in the Complaint have been or will be paid by anyone on your behalf, and if so give the name and address of the person or organization, stating further whether or not that past or prospective payment will result in their obtaining an interest by way of subrogation, statutory or contractual lien, or otherwise.

Request for Production of Documents

Pursuant to __________ Court Rules ________, defendants request that the following documents and things be produced for inspection and copying within twenty-eight (28) days from the time this request is served on you. Theses items may be produced by mailing or hand-delivering them within the time permitted by court rule to: ________________________ __________. Clear and complete copies of documents may be served in place of originals.

1. All documents which plaintiffs will or may introduce into evidence at the trial of this matter.
2. Copies of all snapshots or photographs taken of plaintiffs which depict the injuries plaintiffs allege they received from the defendants' facility in August 1993.
3. Copies of all income tax returns filed by each of the plaintiffs for the years ____, ____, and ____, including: Form 1040, Schedule C, and copies of all W-2s for each specified year.

[Attorney signature]

APPENDIX F

Sample Complaint in a Breach of Bailment and Negligence Case Arising from a Boarded Horse That Became Loose and Died*

COMMONWEALTH OF KENTUCKY
JESSAMINE CIRCUIT COURT
CIVIL ACTION NO. 00-00000-AB

RIVERVIEW RANCH, INC.,

Plaintiff,

vs.

RELIABLE NATIONAL INSURANCE COMPANY,
ED EMPLOYEE, WARD WORKER,
DONALD DEFENDANT, AND DEBBIE DEFENDANT,

Defendants.

Complaint

Plaintiff, RIVERVIEW RANCH, INC., by counsel, for its Complaint against the Defendants, RELIABLE NATIONAL INSURANCE COMPANY, ED EMPLOYEE, WARD WORKER, DONALD DEFENDANT, and DEBBIE DEFENDANT, states as follows:

**The applicable law required that the insurer also be named as a plaintiff.*

Parties

1. Plaintiff, Riverview Ranch, Inc., at all relevant times was a Kentucky corporation, wholly owned by Oliver Owner, with its principal place of business at 27 Jockey Drive, Turfway, Jessamine County, Kentucky, and engaged in the business of breeding and boarding Thoroughbred horses for profit.
2. Defendant, Reliable National Insurance Company, was at all relevant times a foreign Corporation authorized to do business and to write insurance policies in the Commonwealth of Kentucky; Joseph S. Smith, 1111 Avenue of the Americas, New York, NY, is the agent for service of process of Reliable National Insurance Company, and is authorized to accept service for and on the behalf of Reliable National Insurance Company.
3. Defendants, Ed Employee and Ward Worker, at all relevant times were residents of Jessamine County, Kentucky, on information and belief residing at or about 222 Keeneland Court, Bluegrass, Kentucky, and employees of Defendants, Donald Defendant and Debbie Defendant.
4. Defendants, Donald Defendant and Debbie Defendant, at all relevant times were residents of Jessamine County, Kentucky, on information and belief residing at or about 222 Keeneland Court, Bluegrass, Kentucky, and were the owners of said property.

Factual Basis to All Counts

5. On or about April 4, 2009, Plaintiff, Riverview Ranch, Inc., was the owner of the 1986 Thoroughbred Mare named "SAND PIPER."
6. On or about April 4, 2009, Plaintiff, Riverview Ranch, Inc., was a lawful tenant for agricultural purposes of certain pastures on the farm property of Defendants, Donald Defendant and Debbie Defendant, located at or about 222 Keeneland Court, Bluegrass, Kentucky. On or about April 4, 2009, Plaintiff, Riverview Ranch, Inc., together with other Thoroughbred horses, had lawfully located Sand Piper in one of said pastures.
7. On or about April 4, 2009, Defendants, Ed Employee and Ward Worker, while in the employment of Defendants, Donald Defendant and Debbie Defendant, and in the course and scope of their employment with Defendants, entered into the pasture of the property leased by the Plaintiff, Riverview Ranch, Inc., from Defendants Donald Defendant and Debbie Defendant, in which

Sand Piper was located, for the purposes of removing a downed tree and/or other related tree work on or about the property of Defendants, Donald Defendant and Debbie Defendant.

8. On or about April 4, 2009, Defendants, Ed Employee and Ward Worker, during the course of performing their duties for Defendants, Donald Defendant and Debbie Defendant, described in numerical paragraph 7 hereof, negligently, carelessly, maliciously, oppressively, intentionally, wantonly, willfully, and recklessly disregarded the evidence fact of Sand Piper's presence in the pasture and left a previously latched and secured gate to the pasture unlatched and unsecured, which directly and proximately resulted in Sand Piper being permitted to leave the security of the pasture and entering onto Keeneland Court, Bluegrass, Kentucky, where a motor vehicle subsequently struck and killed Sand Piper. Defendants Ed Employee and Ward Worker's actions described herein were the direct and proximate cause of Sand Piper's death.
9. At all relevant times hereto, Defendants, Ed Employee and Ward Worker, and their employees in the course and scope of their employment with Defendants, Donald Defendant and Debbie Defendant, were an insured of Defendant, Reliable National Insurance Company. At all relevant times, Plaintiff, Riverview Ranch, Inc., was also an insured of Defendant, Reliable National Insurance Company.
10. Plaintiff, Riverview Ranch, Inc., at all relevant times has fully complied with all requests for relevant veterinary medical information, evidence of fair market value, and other requests for information made by Defendant, Reliable National Insurance Company.
11. Defendant, Reliable National Insurance Company, has received all reasonable and necessary proof as to the losses and damages to Plaintiff, Riverview Ranch, Inc., by reason of the death of Sand Piper, and the liability of Defendants, Ed Employee and Ward Worker, Donald Defendant and Debbie Defendant, for the death of Sand Piper.

Count I

12. Plaintiff, Riverview Ranch, Inc., incorporates and realleges the allegations set forth in numerical paragraphs 1 through 11 hereof as if fully set forth at length herein.
13. As a direct and proximate result of the careless, reckless, negligent, malicious, oppressive, intentional, wanton, willful actions

and conduct of Defendants, Donald Defendant and Debbie Defendant, referred to in numerical paragraph 8 hereof, Plaintiff, Riverview Farm, Inc., has suffered losses and damages in an amount in excess of the minimal jurisdictional limits of this Court.

14. Defendants, Ed Employee and Ward Worker, as employers of Defendants, Donald Defendant and Debbie Defendant, at the relevant times, as respondent superiors, are directly and proximately responsible for the negligent, careless, intentional, willful, wanton, and reckless conduct and actions of Defendants, Ed Employee and Ward Worker, referred to herein, and the losses and damages suffered by Plaintiff, Riverview Ranch, Inc., which are in excess of the minimal jurisdictional limits of this Court.

Count II

15. Plaintiff, Riverview Ranch, Inc., incorporates and realleges the allegations set forth in numerical paragraphs 1 through 14 hereof as if fully set forth at length herein.
16. Defendant, Reliable National Insurance Company, and its employees and agents, in violation of Ky. Rev. Stat. 304.12-230 *et seq.* and applicable law and administrative regulations, have breached their duty to the Plaintiff, Riverview Ranch, Inc., without limitation in the following respects:

    a. Defendant, Reliable National Insurance Company, has intentionally and deliberately failed and refused to timely negotiate with the Plaintiff, Riverview Ranch, Inc., to pay insurance benefits to which it was and is entitled at a time when the Defendant, Reliable National Insurance Company, knew Plaintiff, Riverview Ranch, Inc., was and is entitled to such benefits.
    b. Defendant, Reliable National Insurance Company, has failed to acknowledge and act reasonably and promptly with respect to the Plaintiff, Riverview Ranch, Inc.'s claim.
    c. Defendant, Reliable National Insurance Company, has failed to confirm in writing its obligation for Plaintiff, Riverview Ranch, Inc.'s claim.
    d. Defendant, Reliable National Insurance Company, has failed to make a proposal in good faith to settle and resolve Plaintiff, Riverview Ranch, Inc.'s claim.
    e. Defendant, Reliable National Insurance Company, has compelled the Plaintiff, Riverview Ranch, Inc., to institute this

action by failing and refusing to make any reasonable proposal to settle and resolve Plaintiff, Riverview Ranch, Inc.'s claim.

f. Defendant, Reliable National Insurance Company, has intentionally and deliberately delayed making a reasonable proposal to settle and resolve Plaintiff, Riverview Ranch, Inc.'s claim.

g. Defendant, Reliable National Insurance Company, has failed and refused to provide any reasonable explanation for its failure to make a reasonable proposal to settle and resolve Plaintiff, Riverview Ranch, Inc.'s claim.

17. As a direct and proximate result and cause of the action and conduct of Defendants, Reliable National Insurance Company, Ed Employee and Ward Worker, Donald Defendant and Debbie Defendant, described herein, Plaintiff, Riverview Ranch, Inc., has suffered and will suffer mental pain and anguish and economic losses and hardships and attorney fees and costs in an amount in excess of the minimal jurisdictional limits of this Court.

Count III

18. Plaintiff, Riverview Ranch, Inc., incorporates and realleges the allegations set forth above in numerical paragraphs 1 through 17 above, as if fully set forth at length herein.
19. Defendant, Reliable National Insurance Company, and its employees and agents, in violation of Ky. Rev. Stat. 367, the Kentucky Consumer Protection Act, have breached their duty of fair dealing and good faith owed to the Plaintiff, Riverview Ranch, Inc., without limitation, in the following respects:

a. Defendant, Reliable National Insurance Company, has intentionally and deliberately failed and refused to timely negotiate with the Plaintiff, Riverview Ranch, Inc., to pay insurance benefits to which it was and is entitled at a time when the Defendant, Reliable National Insurance Company, knew Plaintiff, Riverview Ranch, Inc., was and is entitled to such benefits.

b. Defendant, Reliable National Insurance Company, has failed to acknowledge and act reasonably and promptly with respect to Plaintiff, Riverview Ranch, Inc.'s claim.

c. Defendant, Reliable National Insurance Company, has failed to confirm in writing its obligation for Plaintiff, Riverview Ranch, Inc.'s claim.
d. Defendant, Reliable National Insurance Company, has failed to make a proposal in good faith to settle and resolve Plaintiff, Riverview Ranch, Inc.'s claim.
e. Defendant, Reliable National Insurance Company, has compelled the Plaintiff, Riverview Ranch, Inc., to institute this action by failing and refusing to make any reasonable proposal to settle and resolve Plaintiff, Riverview Ranch, Inc.'s claim.
f. Defendant, Reliable National Insurance Company, has intentionally and deliberately delayed making a reasonable proposal to settle and resolve Plaintiff, Riverview Ranch, Inc.'s claim.
g. Defendant, Reliable National Insurance Company, has failed and refused to provide any reasonable explanation for its failure to make a reasonable proposal to settle and resolve Plaintiff, Riverview Ranch, Inc.'s claim.

20. As a direct and proximate result of the actions and conduct of the Defendant, Reliable National Insurance Company, its employees and agents described herein, Plaintiff, Riverview Ranch, Inc., has suffered and will suffer mental pain and anguish, and economic losses and hardships, and attorney fees and costs in an amount in excess of the minimal jurisdictional limits of this Court.

Count IV

21. Plaintiff, Riverview Ranch, Inc., incorporates and realleges the allegations set forth above in numerical paragraphs 1 through 20 above, as if fully set forth at length herein.
22. Defendant, Reliable National Insurance Company, and its employees have acted toward Plaintiff, Riverview Ranch, Inc., with a conscious, malicious, and oppressive disregard of Plaintiff, Riverview Ranch, Inc.'s rights, with intent to vex, injure, and/or annoy Plaintiff, Riverview Ranch, Inc., such as to constitute oppression, fraud, or malice thereby entitling Plaintiff, Riverview Ranch, Inc., to an award of punitive damages against Defendant, Reliable National Insurance Company.

Count V

23. Plaintiff, Riverview Ranch, Inc., incorporates and realleges the allegations set forth above in numerical paragraphs 1 through 22 above, as if fully set forth at length herein.
24. The actions and conduct of Defendants, Ed Employee and Ward Worker, described herein entitle Plaintiff, Riverview Ranch, Inc., to an award of punitive damages against Defendants, Ed Employee and Ward Worker.

WHEREFORE, Riverview Ranch, Inc., respectfully requests the following Relief:

1. For Judgment for Plaintiff, Riverview Ranch, Inc., against Defendants, Donald Defendant and Debbie Defendant, for compensatory damages in an amount in excess of the jurisdictional limits of this Court sufficient to compensate Plaintiff, Riverview Ranch, Inc., for the losses and damages it has sustained by reason of Defendants, Donald Defendant and Debbie Defendant's actions and conduct in solely, directly and proximately causing the death of Sand Piper referred to herein.
2. For Judgment in favor of Plaintiff, Riverview Ranch, Inc., against the Defendants, Ed Employee and Ward Worker, for punitive damages based on the conduct and actions of said Defendants, Ed Employee and Ward Worker, described herein.
3. For Judgment in favor of Plaintiff, Riverview Ranch, Inc., against Defendant, Reliable National Insurance Company, for compensatory and punitive damages as allowed by law for violations of Ky. Rev. Stat. 304.12-230 and Ky. Rev. Stat. 367 and applicable laws and its actions and conduct as determined by the trier of the facts.
4. For Judgment in favor of Plaintiff, Riverview Ranch, Inc., against Defendant, Reliable National Insurance Company, for Plaintiff, Riverview Ranch, Inc.'s reasonable costs and attorney fees herein incurred.
5. For prejudgment and postjudgment interest on all Judgments herein.
6. For trial by jury on all issues so triable.
7. For such other relief as Plaintiff, Riverview Ranch, Inc., may be properly entitled to.

[Attorney signature]

APPENDIX G

Sample Answer to Complaint in a Breach of Bailment and Negligence Case Arising from a Boarded Horse That Became Loose and Died

COMMONWEALTH OF KENTUCKY
JESSAMINE CIRCUIT COURT
CIVIL ACTION NO. 00-00000-AB

RIVERVIEW RANCH, INC.,

Plaintiff,

vs.

RELIABLE NATIONAL
INSURANCE COMPANY,
ED EMPLOYEE, WARD WORKER,
DONALD DEFENDANT, AND DEBBIE DEFENDANT,

Defendants.

Answer to Complaint

Defendants, RELIABLE NATIONAL INSURANCE COMPANY, DONALD DEFENDANT, and DEBBIE DEFENDANT (collectively the "Defendants"), by counsel, and for their Answer to the Complaint of the Plaintiff, RIVERVIEW RANCH, INC. (hereinafter referred to as "Plaintiff"), state as follows:

First Defense

1. The Defendants are without knowledge or information sufficient to form a belief as to the allegations contained in numerical paragraph 1 of the Complaint and therefore deny said allegations.

2. The Defendants admit the allegations contained in numerical paragraph 2 of the Complaint.
3. The Defendants admit the allegations contained in numerical paragraph 3 of the Complaint.
4. The Defendants admit the allegations contained in numerical paragraph 4 of the Complaint.
5. The Defendants are without knowledge or information sufficient to form a belief as to the truthfulness of the allegations contained in numerical paragraph 5 of the Complaint and therefore deny those allegations.
6. Upon information and belief, the Defendants admit the allegations contained in numerical paragraph 6 of the Complaint.
7. The Defendants admit the allegations contained in numerical paragraph 7 of the Complaint.
8. The Defendants admit so much of the allegations contained in numerical paragraph 8 of the Complaint as allege that in the course of his employment, Ed Employee was negligent, and that his negligence was a substantial factor in the mare SAND PIPER getting out of the paddock in which it was kept and being fatally injured, but the Defendants expressly deny all of the remaining allegations of numerical paragraph 8 of the Complaint, including any allegation that: Ward Worker left the gate referenced therein unlatched or unsecured; any of the Defendants other than Ward Worker were negligent in any way; and any of the Defendants or their agents acted maliciously, oppressively, intentionally, wantonly, willfully, and/or recklessly.
9. The Defendants admit the allegations contained in numerical paragraph 9 of the Complaint.
10. The Defendants deny the allegations contained in numerical paragraph 10 of the Complaint.
11. The Defendants deny the allegations contained in numerical paragraph 11 of the Complaint.
12. The Defendants restate and reiterate their previous responses to the allegations realleged in numerical paragraph 12 of the Complaint.
13. The Defendants admit only so much of the allegations contained in numerical paragraph 13 of the Complaint as allege ordinary negligence on the part of Ward Worker, but the Defendants deny all the remaining allegations in said numerical paragraph and expressly deny the characterization of their conduct in said numerical paragraph and the allegation concerning the amount of the Plaintiff's alleged damages.

14. The Defendants admit so much of the allegations contained in numerical paragraph 14 of the Complaint as allege that the Defendants were the employers of Ed Employee and Ward Worker on or about April 21, 2009, but the Defendants expressly deny the remaining allegations contained in said numerical paragraph.
15. The Defendants restate and reiterate their previous responses to the allegations realleged in numerical paragraph 15 of the Complaint.
16. The Defendants deny the allegations contained in numerical paragraph 16 of the Complaint, including all subparts of said numerical paragraph.
17. The Defendants deny the allegations contained in numerical paragraph 17 of the Complaint.
18. The Defendants restate and reiterate their previous responses to the allegations realleged in numerical paragraph 18 of the Complaint.
19. The Defendants deny the allegations contained in numerical paragraph 19 of the Complaint, including all subparts of said numerical paragraph.
20. The Defendants deny the allegations contained in numerical paragraph 20 of the Complaint.
21. The Defendants restate and reiterate their previous responses to the allegations realleged in numerical paragraph 21 of the Complaint.
22. The Defendants deny the allegations contained in numerical paragraph 22 of the Complaint.
23. The Defendants restate and reiterate their previous responses to the allegations realleged in numerical paragraph 23 of the Complaint.
24. The Defendants deny the allegations contained in numerical paragraph 24 of the Complaint.
25. The Defendants deny any allegation contained in the Complaint which is not expressly admitted herein.

Second Defense

The Complaint fails to state a claim against the Defendants upon which relief can be granted.

Third Defense

The Defendants acted in good faith with regard to the facts and circumstances alleged in the Complaint.

Fourth Defense

If the Plaintiff has been damaged as alleged in the Complaint, which allegation is hereby specifically denied, then said damage is a result of the negligence of persons or entities other than the Defendants and their agents.

Fifth Defense

If the Plaintiff has been damaged as alleged in the Complaint, which allegation is hereby expressly denied, then said damages are a result of the Plaintiff's own negligent, grossly negligent, reckless, intentional, or other conduct.

Sixth Defense

The Plaintiff has failed to provide the Defendants with certain information and records regarding Plaintiff's alleged loss, and said failure is a complete or partial bar to the claims that the Plaintiff has asserted in its Complaint.

Seventh Defense

The Defendants rely on the Kentucky Constitution and the United States Constitution to bar in whole or in part the Plaintiff's claim for punitive damages.

Eighth Defense

The Plaintiff has failed to state a claim under Kentucky's Consumer Protection Act because, inter alia, the goods or services involved were not purchased primarily for personal, family, or household purposes.

WHEREFORE, the Defendants pray this Court for the following relief:

1. That Plaintiff's Complaint be dismissed and held for naught.
2. For all recoverable costs and fees, including any reasonable attorneys' fees.
3. That the Plaintiff's claims based on Ky. Rev. Stat. 304.12-230 *et. seq.* and Ky. Rev. Stat. Chapter 367 be bifurcated, prepared, and tried separately from the underlying negligence claim.
4. For all other relief, legal or equitable, to which they may appear entitled.

[Attorney Signature]

APPENDIX H

Sample Complaint in a Dog-Bite Case

STATE OF MICHIGAN
IN THE CIRCUIT COURT FOR THE COUNTY OF WAYNE

MARY MINOR, a minor,
by her Next Friend, NANCY FRIEND,

Plaintiff,

vs.

DANA DEFENDANT,

Defendant.

Complaint

NOW COMES the above-named Plaintiff, MARY MINOR, a minor, by her Next Friend, NANCY FRIEND, by and through attorneys, and for her cause of action against the Defendant herein, state as follows:

1. That Plaintiff, Mary Minor, resides with her mother Nancy Friend, in the City of Rochester, County of Oakland, State of Michigan.
2. That the Defendant, Dana Defendant, is a resident of the City of Detroit, County of Wayne, State of Michigan.
3. That on or about February 2, 2009, the Defendant, Dana Defendant, did own, maintain, keep, and/or harbor a dog or dogs upon the premises owned by Defendant located at 1234 Vicious St., in the City of Detroit, County of Wayne, State of Michigan.
4. That on or about February 2, 2009, minor Plaintiff, Mary Minor, was sitting on the couch in the aforementioned premises, when she was suddenly and unexpectedly attacked and bitten, without provocation, by the Defendant's dog.

5. That pursuant to the Statutes of the State of Michigan and specifically the Michigan Dog Bite Statute, the Defendant is liable to your Plaintiff for the damages sustained in the aforedescribed incident.
6. That furthermore, by virtue of the Statutes of the State of Michigan, and the principles of the Common Law, it was the duty of the Defendant to keep said dog under control at all times.
7. That notwithstanding said duties owed, and in negligent breach of same, the Defendant:

   a. Failed to keep her dog under control at all relevant times;
   b. Harbored a dog with actually or constructively known violent, aggressive, dangerous, and vicious propensities;
   c. Otherwise breached her duties owed under the circumstances.

8. That as a direct and proximate result of the negligence of the Defendant herein, as aforesaid, your minor Plaintiff, Mary Minor, sustained serious personal injuries, including but not limited to a large laceration of the lip resulting in permanent scarring, which injuries have caused and in the future will continue to cause great pain, suffering, fright, shock, mental anguish, suffering, disability, disfigurement, embarrassment, humiliation, mortification, and loss or impairment of social and/or recreational pleasures and activities, and loss or impairment of wages and/or earning capacity.
9. That in the event that it is discovered that your minor Plaintiff was suffering from a preexisting condition, whether congenital or caused by disease, injury or trauma, it is further alleged that said injuries caused by the negligence of the Defendant herein aggravated said condition.

WHEREFORE, your minor Plaintiff, Mary Minor, by her Next Friend, Nancy Friend, prays for damages against the Defendant herein in a sum exceeding Twenty-Five Thousand ($25,000.00) Dollars, together with interest, costs, and attorney fees.

[Attorney signature]

APPENDIX I

Sample Answer and Defenses in a Dog-Bite Case

STATE OF MICHIGAN
IN THE CIRCUIT COURT FOR THE COUNTY OF WAYNE

MARY MINOR, a minor,
by her Next Friend, NANCY FRIEND,

Plaintiff,

vs.

DANA DEFENDANT,

Defendant.

Answer to Complaint

Defendant DANA DEFENDANT, by her attorney, for her Answer to the plaintiff's Complaint, states as follows:

1. Defendant neither admits nor denies the allegations as she is without sufficient knowledge and information to form a belief as to the truth thereof but holds plaintiff to her proofs.
2. Admitted.
3. Defendant admits only that she had a dog at her residence at the cited address on the date referred to in paragraph 3.
4. Defendant denies the allegations as they are false.
5. Defendant denies the allegations as they are false.
6. Defendant neither admits nor denies the allegations contained in paragraph 6 with respect to alleged "duties" and the referenced statutes as they state conclusions of law, not allegations of fact, and therefore require no answer. Further, Defendant submits that

any statutes or regulations, should they apply to the incident at issue in this case, speak for themselves. Defendant denies that she was negligent or legally liable in any way, as any such allegations are false.

7. Defendant neither admits nor denies the allegations contained in paragraph 7 with respect to alleged "duties" owed and the alleged "negligent breach" by defendant as they state conclusions of law, not allegations of fact, and therefore require no answer. Defendant denies the remaining allegations in paragraph 7, including subparts a through c, as they are false.
8. Defendant neither admits nor denies the allegations contained in paragraph 8 with respect to "as a direct and proximate result of the negligence of the Defendant" as they state conclusions of law, not allegations of fact, and therefore require no answer. Further answering paragraph 8, Defendant neither admits nor denies all of the allegations in regard to plaintiff Mary Minor's alleged damages as Defendant is presently without sufficient knowledge and information to form a belief as to the truth thereof but leaves Plaintiff to her proofs. Defendant denies that she has any legal responsibility for any and all alleged damages as such allegations are false.
9. Defendant neither admits nor denies the allegations in paragraph 9 as they are not statements of fact but, rather, a statement of intention on part of the Plaintiff and/or her counsel as to the potential for aggravation of preexisting injuries. However, Defendant denies the allegations contained in paragraph 9 with respect to "the negligence of the Defendant herein" as they are false. Further answering paragraph 9, Defendant neither admits nor denies all of the allegations in regard to Plaintiff Mary Minor's alleged damages and conditions as Defendant is without sufficient knowledge and information to form a belief as to the truth thereof but leaves Plaintiff to her proofs. Defendant denies that she has any legal responsibility for any and all alleged damages as such allegations are false.

WHEREFORE, Defendant respectfully requests that this Honorable Court dismiss the Plaintiff's Complaint in its entirety with prejudice and that defendant be awarded her court costs and attorney fees.

Affirmative Defenses

In further answer and by way of affirmative defense, Defendant Dana Defendant, by her attorney, states that she will or may rely on the following defenses, if applicable and if supported by facts to be determined through discovery:

A. Plaintiff has failed to state a claim upon which relief can be granted.
B. Plaintiff's Complaint is barred, in whole or in part, since Plaintiff Mary Minor provoked the Defendant's dog, intentionally or unintentionally.
C. Plaintiff's Complaint is barred, in whole or in part, since the proximate cause of Plaintiff Mary Minor's injuries, if any, was the conduct and/or wrongdoing of Mary Minor, and not the Defendant.
D. Plaintiff's Complaint is barred, in whole or in part, since damages alleged in the Complaint were proximately caused by the sole or comparative negligence, or the intervening culpable acts or omissions of Plaintiff Mary Minor.
E. Plaintiff's Complaint is barred, in whole or in part, since Defendant breached no duty to the Plaintiff, contrary to the allegations in the Complaint.
F. Plaintiffs' Complaint is barred, in whole or in part, because Plaintiff Mary Minor has failed to mitigate her damages.
G. Plaintiff's Complaint is barred, in whole or in part, since the liability for economic loss, including lost wages, impairment of earning capacity, and hospital and medical expenses sought by Plaintiff are to be reduced by that portion paid or payable by a collateral source, pursuant to [statute].
H. Defendant reserves the right to amend her answer to plead further and other affirmative defenses after a reasonable opportunity for investigation and discovery.

WHEREFORE, Defendant respectfully requests that this Honorable Court dismiss the Plaintiff's Complaint in its entirety with prejudice and that defendant be awarded her court costs and attorney fees.

Demand for Trial by Jury

Pursuant to Court Rule ________, Dana Defendant hereby gives notice of her demand for a trial by jury of all issues so triable in this action.

[Attorney signature]

Notes

1. Prosser and Keeton on the Law of Torts §§ 164–165 (5th ed. 1984).
2. *See, e.g.*, O'Mara v. City of New York, 819 N.Y.S.2d 263 (N.Y. Ct. App. 2006) (dismissing a mounted police officer's suit against the city for its alleged failure to provide a helmet because helmet was not found to be a substantial cause of the incident and plaintiff's expert conceded that injuries could occur even with one); Smith v. Jett Hill Farm, 579 N.E.2d 295 (Ohio Ct. App. 1989) (finding a genuine issue of proximate cause in case where deliveryman tripped over a chain tied to dog); Whitefield v. Stewart, 577 P.2d 1295 (Okla. 1978) (stating that plaintiff might not have been bitten by defendant's monkey but instead may have cut her finger on sharp projections on a chain link fence when she withdrew her hand after petting the monkey through the fence).
3. Heath v. Fruzia, 123 P.2d 560 (Cal. Ct. App. 1942).
4. Hillier v. Noble, 458 A.2d 1101, 1104 (Vt. 1983).
5. Marshall v. Darmody-Latham, 783 N.Y.S.2d 738 (N.Y. Ct. App. 2004) (dog attacked).
6. Berneathy v. Pursley, 832 S.W.2d 524 (Mo. Ct. App. 1992); Appel v. Charles Heinsohn, Inc., 458 N.Y.S.2d 619 (N.Y. Ct. App. 1983); Pearce v. Shanks, 266 S.E.2d 353 (Ga. Ct. App. 1980).
7. Kinley v. Bierly, 876 A.2d 419 (Pa. Super. 2005) (plaintiff, bitten by defendant's stallion, argued that stallions, by their very nature, are unpredictable and therefore have "vicious propensities." Court rejected this theory and found that horse owners are not responsible for vicious acts "unless the owners have knowledge that [the horses] are likely to break away from their normal domestic nature and become vicious." 876 A.2d at 422.); Vigue v. Noyes, 550 P.2d 234 (Ariz. 1976); Robidoux v. Busch, 400 S.W.2d 631 (Mo. Ct. App. 1966) (finding no liability for injury caused by miniature horses pulling a wagon because they had no known tendency to bolt and run away).
8. Robidoux v. Busch, 400 S.W.2d 631 (Mo. Ct. App. 1966) (injury from wagon pulled by miniature horses that had no known tendency to bolt and run away).
9. Northon v. Schultz, 279 P.2d 103 (Cal. Ct. App. 1955).
10. Rickrode v. Wistinghausen, 340 N.W.2d 83 (Mich. Ct. App. 1983); Clark v. Brings, 169 N.W.2d 407 (Minn. 1969).
11. Radoff v. Hunter, 323 P.2d 202, 204 (Cal. Ct. App. 1958).
12. Rickrode v. Wistinghausen, 340 N.W.2d 83 (Mich. Ct. App. 1983).
13. Denil v. Coopersmith, 343 N.W.2d 136 (Wisc. Ct. App. 1983) (finding the fact that the dog had never been exercised and was kept on a short chain could potentially evidence that dog could develop dangerous propensities); Richmond v. Knowles, 265 A.2d 53 (Del. Super. 1970) (fact that dog was kept on a chain and ordered to attack people who entered the area could evidence that the animal developed vicious propensities).

14. Richmond v. Knowles, 265 A.2d 53 (Del. Super. 1970) (discussing a dog owner known to warn children, including the plaintiff in that case, to stay away from the dog).
15. Sink v. Moore, 148 S.E.2d 265 (N.C. 1966) (attempting to introduce testimony that dog at issue was well known to be ill-tempered); Butts v. Houston, 86 S.E. 473 (W. Va. 1915) (finding that because horse had a reputation for being vicious, an inference was made that defendant was aware of such behavior before the plaintiff was injured).
16. Russell v. Lepre, 470 N.Y.S.2d 430 (N.Y. Ct. App. 1984).
17. Warwick v. Mulvey, 127 N.W.2d 433 (S.D. 1964).
18. Dargen v. King, 742 P.2d 72 (Or. Ct. App. 1987).
19. Swerdfeger v. Krueger, 358 P.2d 479 (Colo. 1960).
20. Kaplan v. C Lazy U Ranch, 615 F. Supp. 234 (D. Colo. 1985) (a horse's tendency to "bloat" or expand its chest while being saddled and the cinch tightened was not deemed to be a "dangerous propensity"); Timpanaro v. Topping Riding Sch., 575 N.Y.S.2d 933 (N.Y. Ct. App. 1991) (holding that a horse's well-known propensity to be a difficult loader in the horse trailer was not found to be a "dangerous propensity").
21. Ray v. Young, 572 S.E.2d 216 (N.C. Ct. App. 2002).
22. *See, e.g.*, Kinley v. Bierly, 876 A.2d 419, 422 (Pa. Super. 2005) (horses do not have "vicious or dangerous" propensities merely by virtue of being a stallion); Marshall v. Darmody-Latham, 783 N.Y.S.2d 738 (N.Y. Ct. App. Div. 2004) (case dismissed involving attack by defendant's bulldog on plaintiff's dog because no proof was shown that the bulldog was involved in prior incidents); Mason v. Komlo, 1990 Ohio App LEXIS 1214 (Ohio Ct. App. 1993); Berneathy v. Pursley, 832 S.W.2d 524 (Mo. Ct. App. 1992) (horse throwing a rider on one occasion does not prove it was not "well broken"); Beers v. Elebash, 589 N.Y.S.2d 325 (New York 1992); Landes v. HE Farms, Inc., 564 N.Y.S.2d 151, 169 A.D.2d 446 (N.Y. 1991); McNish v. Gilbert, 361 S.E.2d 231 (Ga. Ct. App. 1987); Appel v. Charles Heinsohn, Inc., 458 N.Y.S.2d 619, 91 A.D.2d 1029 (1983) (finding there was no proof that horse which threw plaintiff on one occasion manifested "vicious propensities" in the past); Groh v. Hasencamp, 407 So. 2d 949 (Fla. Ct. App. 1981); Hojem v. Kelly, 606 P.2d 275 (Wash. 1980); Allen v. Green Acres Farm, 396 F. Supp. 442 (N.D. Ill. 1975); Finneran v. Wood, 241 A.2d 579 (Md. Ct. App. 1968).
23. Herring v. Cunningham, 507 So. 2d 1324 (Ala. 1987).
24. For example, in Whitcanock v. Nelson, 400 N.E.2d 998 (Ill. Ct. App. 1980), the failure to prove knowledge on behalf of the owner could warrant dismissal of the case.
25. DeVaul v. Carvigo, Inc., 526 N.Y.S.2d 483 (N.Y. 1988); Wignes v. Bottger, 518 N.Y.S.2d 936 (N.Y. Ct. App. 1987) (holding that cat who bit plaintiff when plaintiff attempted to hold it by the scruff of the neck displayed a natural reaction and did not demonstrate a "vicious propensity").
26. Miller v. Snipes, 183 S.E.2d 270 (N.C. Ct. App. 1971).

27. Doe v. Barnett, 251 N.E.2d 688 (Ind. Ct. App. 1969); Cowan v. Sullivan, 199 So. 2d 500 (Fla. Ct. App. 1967).
28. *See* DeRobertis v. Randazzo, 462 A.2d 1260 (N.J. 1983); Hamby v. Haskins, 630 S.W.2d 37 (Ark. 1982).
29. Miller v. Foster, 686 So. 2d 783 (Fla. Ct. App. 1997); Galardi v. Seahorse Riding Club, 16 Cal. Ct. App. 4th 817 (Cal. Ct. App. 1993); Tan v. Goddard, 13 Cal. App. 4th 1528 (Cal. Ct. App. 1993).
30. Hawkins v. Ranch Rudolph, Inc., No. 254771, 2005 WL 2372008 (Mich. Ct. App. 9/27/2005).
31. Johnson v. Smith, 88 S.W.3d 729 (Tex. Ct. App. 2002).
32. Mercer v. Fritts, 676 P.2d 150 (Kan. Ct. App. 1984).
33. In Burke v. Fischer, 182 S.W.2d 638 (Ky. 1944), for example, the plaintiff was bitten by a watchdog at the defendant's produce farm and brought such a claim.
34. Restatement (Second) of Torts § 507(1) (1965).
35. Am. Jur. 2d *Animals* § 62, at 427 (2007); Poznanski *ex rel.* Poznanski v. Horvath, 788 N.E.2d 1255 (Ind. 2003). For more information on liability related to wild animals, see Annotation, *Owner's or Keeper's Liability for Personal Injury or Death Inflicted by Wild Animal*, 21 A.L.R.3d 603 (1968).
36. Mangum v. Brownlee, 75 P.2d 174 (Okla. 1938).
37. *See* Speiser, The American Law of Torts § 21.52, at 489 (1993); Groh v. Hasencamp, 407 So. 2d 949 (Fl. 1981); Moessinger v. Johnson, 292 So. 2d 606 (Fla. Ct. App. 1974) (finding that a horse is not presumed to be dangerous).
38. Boyer v. Seal, 534 So. 2d 30 (La. Ct. App. 1988), *aff'd*, 553 So. 2d 827 (La. 1989).
39. Marshall v. Ranne, 511 S.W.2d 25 (Tex. 1974) (stating liability for domestic animals with a vicious propensity must be based on strict liability).
40. *See, e.g.*, Restatement (Second) of Torts § 402A (1965) (strict liability).
41. *See* Jeff Cereghino, *The Menu Foods Pet Food Recall Utilizing Class Action/ Mass Tort Procedures to Assist Damaged Pet Owners*, ABA-TIPS Animal Law Comm. Newsletter, Spring 2008, at 16.
42. Moreland v. Weaver Leather Goods, 13 Fed. Appx. 329 (6th Cir. 2001).
43. *See* Section III.B.2 of this chapter, regarding loose livestock statutes.
44. *See* Stout v. Bartholomew, 544 S.E.2d 653 (Va. 2001).
45. *See, e.g.*, Rosenberg v. Dahl, 172 S.W. 113 (Ky. 1915); Gorsuch v. Swan, 69 S.W. 1113 (Tenn. 1902); Hart v. Wash. Park Club, 41 N.E. 620 (Ill. 1895).
46. Zukatis v. Perry, 682 A.2d 964 (Vt. 1996).
47. For more information, see Annotation, *Animals as Attractive Nuisance*, 64 A.L.R.3d 1065 (1975).
48. Hampton v. Hammons, 743 P.2d 1053 (Okla. 1987); Dykes v. Alexander, 411 S.W.2d 47 (Ky. 1967).
49. Rolen v. Md. Cas. Co., 240 So. 2d 42 (La. Ct. App. 1970).
50. *See, e.g.*, Pullan v. Steinmetz, 16 P.3d 1245 (Utah 2000); Dyches v. Alexander, Ky., 411 S.W.2d 47 (Ky. 1967); N. Hardin Developers, Inc. v. Corkran,

839 S.W.2d 258 (Ky. 1992); Hall v. Edlefson, 498 S.W.2d 514 (Tex. Ct. App. 1973) (holding Shetland pony from which the plaintiff child fell was not an attractive nuisance).

51. Brady v. Skinner, 646 P.2d 310 (Ariz. Ct. App. 1982).
52. N. Hardin Developers, Inc. v. Corkran, 839 S.W.2d 258, 261 (Ky. 1992).
53. *See, e.g.*, Miller v. Hurst, 448 A.2d 614 (Pa. Super. 1982); Butler v. Frieden, 158 S.E.2d 121 (Va. 1967).
54. States with dog-bite statutes are Alabama, ALA. CODE § 3-6-1; ARIZ. REV. STAT. §§ 11-1020 *et seq.*; CAL. REV. STAT. §§ 3342 *et seq.*; CONN. STAT. § 22-357; DEL. STAT. tit. 7 § 1711; FLA. REV. STAT. § 767.04; CODE GA. ANN. § 51-2-7; HAW. REV. STAT. § 142-75; 510 ILL. COMP. STAT. 5/16; IND. STAT. § 15-5-12-1; IOWA STAT. § 351.28; LA. STAT. ANN. art. 2321; ME. REV. STAT. ANN. § 3961; MASS. ANN. LAWS ch. 140 § 155; MICH. COMP. LAWS § 287.351; MINN. STAT. ANN. § 347.22; MONT. STAT. § 27-1-715; NEB. REV. STAT. §§ 54-601 *et seq.*; N.H. REV. STAT. ANN. § 466:19; N.J. STAT. § 4:19-16; OHIO REV. CODE ANN. § 955.28; OKLA. STAT. vol. 4 § 42.1; PENN. STAT. tit. 3 § 459-502; R.I. GEN. LAWS § 4-13-17; S.C. CODE ANN. § 47-3-110; UTAH CODE ANN. § 18-1-1; WASH. REV. CODE. § 16.08.040; WISC. STAT. ANN. § 174.02.
55. *See, e.g.*, Massey v. Colaric, 725 P.2d 1099 (Ariz. 1986); Pulley v. Malek, 495 N.E.2d 402 (Ohio Ct. App. 1986).
56. Jackson v. Mateus, 70 P.3d 78 (Utah 2003); Clark v. Brings, 169 N.W.2d 407 (Minn. 1969).
57. For more information, see Annotation, *Modern Status of Rule of Absolute or Strict Liability for Dogbite*, 51 A.L.R.4TH 446 (1987).
58. Petersheim v. Corum, 815 N.E.2d 1132 (Ohio Ct. App. 2004); Kelley v. Barrett, 897 P.2d 289 (Okla. 1995).
59. Atkins v. Stratmeyer, 600 N.W.2d 891 (S.D. 1999); Toole v. Dupuis, 735 So. 2d 582 (Fla. Ct. App. 1999).
60. *See* Inendi v. Workman, 899 P.2d 1085 (Mont. 1995) (negligence per se when the property owner's fencing failed to comply with statutory fencing requirements). *But cf.* Harlow v. Hayes, 991 S.W.2d 745 (Tex. 1999) (fencing standards in the Texas Agricultural Code *did not* establish the defendant's standard of care).
61. Honeycutt v. State Farm Fire & Cas. Co., 890 So. 2d 756 (La. Ct. App. 2004); Granger v. Guillory, 819 So. 2d 477 (La. Ct. App. 2002).
62. *See, e.g.*, Moreland v. Adams, 143 Idaho 687, 153 P.3d 558 (Idaho Ct. App. 2007) (dismissing a lawsuit involving a car that collided with a loose calf pursuant to Idaho "open range" statute); Anderson v. Two Dot Ranch, 49 P.3d 1011 (Wyo. 2002); Willis v. Cloud, 758 So. 2d 835, 837 (La. Ct. App. 2000), *writ denied*, 760 So. 2d 347 (La. 2000); Gibbs v. Jackson, 990 S.W.2d 745 (Tex. 1999).
63. Kallage v. Alvidrez, 969 P.2d 743 (Colo. Ct. App. 1998) (finding liability of county's snowplow operator who filled a cattle guard with snow and allowed cattle to escape onto highway); Butcher v. White's Iowa Inst., 541

N.W.2d 262 (Iowa Ct. App. 1995) (stating defendant stable owner could rebut presumption of negligence in animals' escape by proving that a truck driver broke the defendant's pasture fencing).

64. Supchak v. Pruitt, 503 S.E.2d 581 (Ga. Ct. App. 1998) (holding that merely having temporary custody of livestock was not tantamount to "ownership" for loose livestock law).
65. Malloy v. Colchester, 858 A.2d 813 (Conn. Ct. App. 2004) (injured motorist's litigation against town, city councilman, zoning officer, and animal control officer arising out of collision with loose horse failed).
66. Larreau v. DeLara, 2004 WL 2339481 (Neb. Ct. App. 2004) (finding litigation against county and deputy sheriff after collision with a loose horse on a highway); White v. City of Waldo, 659 So. 2d 707 (Fla. Ct. App. 1995) (finding sovereign immunity might not protect municipality for police officer allegedly chasing loose horse at night along highway).
67. *See, e.g.*, Snider v. Fort Madison Rodeo Corp., 2002 WL 570890 (Iowa Ct. App. 2002); Svacha v. Waldens Creek Saddle Club, 60 S.W.3d 851 (Tenn. Ct. App. 2001); Kangas v. Perry, 620 N.W.2d 429 (Wisc. Ct. App. 2000); Riehl v. B & B Livery, Inc., 944 P.2d 642 (Colo. Ct. App. 1997), *rev'd*, 960 P.2d 134 (Colo. 1998); Young v. Brandt, 485 S.E.2d 519 (Ga. Ct. App. 1997); Easterling v. English Riding Stables, Inc., 1994 U.S. Dist. LEXIS 3470, 1994 WL 10155 (E.D. La. 1994); Day v. Snowmass Stables, Inc., 810 F. Supp. 289 (D. Colo. 1993); Patrick v. Sferra, 855 P.2d 320 (Wash. Ct. App. 1993).
68. *See, e.g.*, Mettler v. Nellis, 695 N.W.2d 861 (Wisc. Ct. App. 2005); Barritt v. Lowe, 669 N.W.2d 189 (Wisc. Ct. App. 2003); Fielder v. Acad. Riding Stables, 49 P.3d 349 (Colo. Ct. App. 2002); Powers v. Mukpo, 2000 WL 33170940 (Mass. Super. Ct. 10/2/2000); Willeck v. Mroteck, 616 N.W.2d 526, 235 Wisc. 2d 278 (Wisc. Ct. App. 2000); Adams v. Hare, 536 S.E.2d 284 (Ga. Ct. App. 2000); Hendricks v. JAFI, Inc., 1999 Mass. Super. LEXIS 44, 1999 WL 1336069 (1/20/99); Riehl v. B & B Livery, Inc., 944 P.2d 642 (Colo. Ct. App. 1997), *rev'd*, 960 P.2d 134 (Colo. 1998); Young v. Brandt, 485 S.E.2d 519 (Ga. Ct. App. 1997); Muller v. English, 472 S.E.2d 448 (Ga. Ct. App. 1996); Cave v. Davey Crockett Stables, No. 03A01-9504-CV-00131 (Tenn. Ct. App. 1995); Easterling v. English Riding Stables, Inc., 1994 U.S. Dist. LEXIS 3470, 1994 WL 10155 (E.D. La. 1994).
69. *See, e.g.*, Allison v. Johnson, 2001 WL 589384 (Ohio Ct. App. 2001); Nielson v. AT&T Corp., 597 N.W.2d 434 (S.D. 7/28/1999); Muller v. English, 472 S.E.2d 448 (Ga. Ct. App. 1996).
70. *See, e.g.*, Geman v. McLaury, 698 N.W.2d 132 (Wisc. Ct. App. 2005); Snider v. Fort Madison Rodeo Corp., 2002 WL 570890 (Iowa Ct. App. 2002); Svacha v. Waldens Creek Saddle Club, 60 S.W.3d 851 (Tenn. Ct. App. 2001); Adams v. Hare, 536 S.E.2d 284 (Ga. Ct. App. 2000); Lessman v. Rhodes, 721 N.E.2d 178 (Ill. Ct. App. 1999); Riehl v. B & B Livery, Inc., 960 P.2d 134 (Colo. 1998), *rev'g* 944 P.2d 642 (Colo. Ct. App. 1997); Faul v. Trahan, 718 So. 2d 1081 (La. Ct. App. 1998); Gaurtreau v. Washington, 672 So. 2d

262 (La. Ct. App. 1996); Muller v. English, 472 S.E.2d 448 (Ga. Ct. App. 1996); Cave v. Davey Crockett Stables, No. 03A01-9504-CV-00131 (Tenn. Ct. App. 1995); Patrick v. Sferra, 855 P.2d 320 (Wash. Ct. App. 1993).

71. Little v. Needham, 2007 WL 1844692 (Tex. Ct. App. 2007); McGuire v. Jewett, 2007 WL 1810529 (Ohio Ct. App. 6/22/2007); Gamble v. Peyton, 182 S.W.3d 1 (Tex. Ct. App. 2005); Snider v. Fort Madison Rodeo Corp., 2002 WL 570890 (Iowa Ct. App. 2/20/2002); Svacha v. Waldens Creek Saddle Club, 60 S.W.3d 851 (Tenn. Ct. App. 2001); Allison v. Johnson, 2001 WL 589384 (Ohio Ct. App. 6/2/2001); Culver v. Samuels, 37 P.3d 535 (Colo. Ct. App. 2001); Wiederkehr v. Brent, 248 Ga. Ct. App. 645, 548 S.E.2d 402 (Ga. Ct. App. 2001); Kangas v. Perry, 620 N.W.2d 429 (Wisc. Ct. App. 2000); Adams v. Hare, 536 S.E.2d 284 (Ga. Ct. App. 2000); Street v. Darwin Ranch, 75 F. Supp. 2d 1296 (D. Wyo. 1999); Amburgey v. Sauder, 238 Mich. Ct. App. 228 (Mich. Ct. App. 1999); Lessman v. Rhodes, 721 N.E.2d 178 (Ill. Ct. App. 1999); Cooperman v. David, 23 F. Supp. 2d 1315 (D. Wyo. 1998), *aff'd*, 214 F.3d 1162 (10th Cir. 2000); Faul v. Trahan, 718 So. 2d 1081 (La. Ct. App. 1998); Young v. Brandt, 485 S.E.2d 519 (Ga. Ct. App. 1997); Gaurtreau v. Washington, 672 So. 2d 262 (La. Ct. App. 1996); Muller v. English, 472 S.E.2d 448 (Ga. Ct. App. 1996); Patrick v. Sferra, 855 P.2d 320 (Wash. Ct. App. 1993).

72. Laws with these provisions can be found, for example, in Alabama, Georgia, Indiana, Kentucky, Louisiana, Mississippi, North Carolina, and South Carolina. Georgia's law, for example, states in part: "Failure to comply with the requirements concerning warning signs and notices provided in this Code section shall prevent an equine activity sponsor or equine professional from invoking the privileges of immunity provided by this chapter." GA. CODE ANN. § 4-12-4(c).

73. *See, e.g.*, Wiederkehr v. Brent, 548 S.E.2d 402 (Ga. Ct. App. 2001); Gaurtreau v. Washington, 672 So. 2d 262 (La. Ct. App. 1996).

74. Berlangieri v. Running Elk Corp., 76 P.3d 1098 (N.M. 2003); Teles v. Big Rock Stables, L.P., 419 F. Supp. 2d 1003 (E.D. Tenn. 2006).

75. *See* Terrill v. Stacy, 2006 WL 473799 (Mich. Ct. App. 2/28/2006); Raveson v. Walt Disney World, 793 So. 2d 1171 (Fla. Ct. App. 2001); Street v. Darwin Ranch, 75 F. Supp. 2d 1296 (D. Wyo. 1999); B & B Livery, Inc. v. Riehl, 960 P.2d 134, 136 (Colo. 1998).

76. 28 U.S.C. §§ 1291 *et seq.*

77. 28 U.S.C. § 1346(b).

78. *Id.*

79. Martin v. United States, 546 F.2d 1355 (9th Cir. 1976), *cert. denied*, 432 U.S. 906 (1976).

80. Leisy v. United States, 102 F. Supp. 789 (D. Minn. 1952).

81. 42 U.S.C. § 1983.

82. San Jose Charter of the Hells Angels Motorcycle Club v. City of San Jose, 402 F.3d 962 (Cal. Ct. App. 2005).

83. *Id.* at 977.
84. Alfano v. Stutsman, 471 N.E.2d 1143 (Ind. Ct. App. 1984).
85. *Id.*
86. Gonzales v. Arizona Pub. Serv. Co., 775 P.2d 1148, 1153 (Ariz. Ct. App. 1989).
87. Kirkland v. Hall, 38 A.D.3d 497, 832 N.Y.S.2d 232 (N.Y. Ct. App. 2007); Dalton v. Adirondack Saddle Tours, Inc., 40 A.D.3d 1169, 839 N.Y.S.2d 303 (N.Y. Ct. App. 2007); Joseph v. N.Y. Racing Ass'n, 28 A.D.3d 105, 809 N.Y.S.2d 526 (N.Y. Ct. App. 2006); Tilson v. Russo, 2006 WL 1703632 (N.Y. Ct. App. 6/22/2006); Thompson v. Sprouse, 2006 WL 1232999 (Cal. Ct. App. May 9, 2006); Cooperman v. David, 214 F.3d 1162 (10th Cir. 2000); Kinara v. Jamaica Bay Acad., 783 N.Y.S.2d 636 (N.Y. Ct. App. 2004). In Knight v. Jewett, 834 P.2d 696 (Cal. 1992), the court recognized that in an appropriate case, primary assumption of risk could remain a total bar to the plaintiff's cause of action.
88. *See, e.g.*, Lipari v. Babylon Riding Ctr., Inc., 796 N.Y.S.2d 632 (N.Y. Ct. App. 2005).
89. Young v. Brandt, 485 S.E.2d 519 (Ga. Ct. App. 1997) (noting that "when injuries have arisen from the risks identified in [the statute], in most cases, the plaintiff should be found to have assumed the risk, as a matter of law, even when defendants are not asserting the immunity" under the equine activity liability statute).
90. Adams v. Lewis, No. G031197, 2004 WL 2192336 (Cal. Ct. App. 9/30/2004).
91. Adams v. Hare, 2000 WL 802946 (Ga. Ct. App. 6/23/2000) (dismissing professional horse trainer's suit due to assumption of risk and state equine activity liability act); Shelly v. Stepp, 73 Cal. Rptr. 2d 323 (Cal. Ct. App. 1998) (holding race horse exercise rider "assumed the risk of injury" when injured on the track); Hardin v. Christy, 462 N.E.2d 256 (Ind. Ct. App. 1984) (holding horse trainer attacked by a horse assumed the risk of injury).
92. *See, e.g.*, Hiller v. Huyck, 1996 WL 45178 (Minn. Ct. App. 1996) (finding issues of fact when professional horseshoer injured while shoeing a horse because evidence was raised that the owner knew, but never warned, that the horse was a known "kicker").
93. Campbell v. City of N.Y., 819 N.Y.S.2d 294 (N.Y. Ct. App. 2006).
94. Galardi v. Seahorse Riding Club, 20 Cal. Rptr. 2d (Cal. 1993).
95. Ariz. Rev. Stat. §§ 12-2501 *et seq.*
96. Li v. Yellow Cab Co., 119 Cal. Rptr. 858 (Cal. 1975); Fla. Stat. § 768.81(2).
97. Colo. Rev. Stat. § 13-21-111.
98. Hebert v. Md. Cas. Co., 366 So. 2d 1044 (La. Ct. App. 1978).
99. Litzkuhn v. Clark, 339 P.2d 389 (Ariz. 1959).
100. Pisciotta v. Parisi, 547 N.Y.S.2d 352 (N.Y. Ct. App. 1989).

101. Cases in which releases have been held to be enforceable in animal and equine settings include Markowitz v. Bainbridge, 2007 WL 959906 (Ohio Ct. App. Mar. 30, 2007); Anderson v. Four Seasons Equestrian Ctr., Inc., 852 N.E.2d 576 (Ind. Ct. App. 2006); Salazar v. Riverdale Riding Corp., 701 N.Y.S.2d 878, 183 Misc. 2d 145 (N.Y. Super. Ct. 1999); Street v. Darwin Ranch, 75 F. Supp. 2d 1296 (D. Wyo. 1999); B & B Livery, Inc. v. Riehl, 960 P.2d 134 (Colo. 1998); Swierkosz v. Starved Rock Stables, 607 N.E.2d 280 (Ill. Ct. App. 1993); Guido v. Koopman, 2 Cal. Rptr. 2d 437, Cal. Ct. App. 4th 837 (Cal. Ct. App. 1991).
102. Exculpatory agreements have been enforced in bailment settings. *See, e.g.*, Anson v. Les Bois Race Track, Inc., 939 P.2d 1382 (Idaho 1997) (race-track release); Norton v. Jim Phillips Horse Transportation, Inc., 901 F.2d 821 (10th Cir. 1989) (equine transportation contract); Rutter v. Arlington Park Jockey Club, 510 F.2d 1065 (7th Cir. 1975) (stall application).
103. *See, e.g.*, Schmidt v. United States, 912 P.2d 871, 874 (Okla. 1996).
104. Restatement (Second) of Torts § 496B (1965).
105. *See, e.g.*, Brancati v. Bar U Farm, 583 N.Y.S.2d 660 (N.Y. Ct. App. 1992) (finding New York General Obligations Law, § 5-326, which forbids enforceability of releases used by places of "public recreation or amusement," rendered release in trail ride operation unenforceable); Filson v. Cold River Trail Rides, Inc., 661 N.Y.S.2d 841, 242 A.D.2d 775 (N.Y. Ct. App. 1997) (same).
106. Cases include Park-Childs v. Mrotek's, Inc., 578 N.W.2d 210 (Wisc. Ct. App. 1998); Bothell v. Two Point Acres, Inc., 965 P.2d 47 (Ariz. Ct. App. 1998); O'Connell v. Walt Disney World Co., 413 So. 2d 444 (Fla. Ct. App. 1982); Reckleben v. Boca Underwater Servs., 673 So. 2d 185 (Fla. Ct. App. 1996); Thompson v. Otterbein Coll., 1996 Ohio App. LEXIS 389 (Ohio Ct. App. 1996); Wright v. Loon Mountain Recreation Corp., 663 A.2d 1340 (N.H. 1995); Tanker v. N. Crest Equestrian Ctr., 621 N.E.2d 589 (Ohio Ct. App. 1993); Rickey v. Houston Health Club, 863 S.W.2d 148 (Tex. Ct. App. 1993); Reuther v. S. Cross Club, 785 F. Supp. 1339 (S.D. Ind. 1992); Weiner v. Mt. Airy Lodge, Inc., 719 F. Supp. 342 (M.D. Pa. 1989); Celli v. Sports Car Club of Am., Inc., 29 Cal. App. 3d 511, 105 Cal. Rptr. 904 (Cal. 1972); Ferrell v. S. Nev. Off Road Enthusiasts, Ltd., 147 Cal. App. 3d 309, 195 Cal. Rptr. 2d 90 (Cal. Ct. App. 1983); Jones v. Walt Disney World Co., 409 F. Supp. 526 (W.D. N.Y. 1976).
107. Conservatorship of Link v. Nat'l Ass'n for Stock Car Auto Racing, 158 Cal. App. 3d 138, 205 Cal. Rptr. 513 (Cal. 1984); Baker v. Seattle, 484 P.2d 405 (Wash. 1991).
108. Merten v. Nathan, 108 Wisc. 2d 205, 321 N.W.2d 1173 (Wisc. 1982); Palmquist v. Mercer, 43 Cal. 2d 92 (Cal. 1954).
109. *See* Powers v. Mukpo, 2000 WL 33170940 (Mass. Super. Court 10/2/2000) (holding the defendant horseback riding instructor violated statute

requiring instructor licensing); Lee v. Sun Valley Co., 695 P.2d 361, 107 Idaho 976 (Idaho 1984) (discussing a statute requiring outfitter license). For a good discussion of how courts evaluate whether an exculpatory agreement violates public policy, see also Tunkl v. Regents of Univ. of Cal., 383 P.2d 441 (Cal. 1963).

110. Reardon v. Windswept Farm L.L.C., 280 Conn. 153, 905 A.2d 1156 (Conn. 2006) (holding an exculpatory agreement "violates public policy and is not in the public interest"); Mettler v. Nellis, 695 N.W.2d 861 (Wis. Ct. App. 2005); Coughlin v. T.M.H. Int'l Attractions, 895 F. Supp. 159 (W.D. Ky. 1995) (stating Kentucky's general public interest in not enforcing waivers and releases); Hiett v. Lake Barcroft Cmty. Ass'n, Inc., 418 S.E.2d 894 (Va. 1992).
111. Morganteen v. Cowboy Adventures, Inc., 949 P.2d 552 (Ariz. Ct. App. 1997); Fedor v. Mawehu Council, Boy Scouts of Am., 143 A.2d 466 (Conn. 1958).
112. Dilallo v. Riding Safely, Inc., 687 So. 2d 353 (Fla. Ct. App. 1996); Smoky, Inc. v. McCray, 396 S.E.2d 794 (Ga. Ct. App. 1990).
113. Meyer v. Naperville Manner, 634 N.E.2d 411 (Ill. Ct. App. 1994); Rogers v. Donelson-Hermitage Chamber of Commerce, 807 S.W.2d 242 (Tenn. Ct. App. 1990); Fedor v. Mawehu Council, Boy Scouts of Am., 143 A.2d 466 (Conn. 1958). *But cf.* Brooks v. Timberline Tours, Inc., 127 F.3d 1273 (10th Cir. 1997) (Colorado) (holding where a parent executed snowmobile tour provider's release, and a wrongful death case was barred as a result).
114. Hardy v. St. Clair, 739 A.2d 368 (Me. 1999); Arnold v. Shawano County Agric. Soc'y, 330 N.W.2d 773 (Wisc. 1983). *But cf.* Grbac v. Reading Fair Co., 521 F. Supp. 1351 (W.D. Pa. 1981), *aff'd*, 688 F.2d 215 (3rd Cir. 1981) (enforcing a racetrack's release to bar a spouse's claims).
115. Eder v. Lake Geneva Raceway, 523 N.W.2d 429 (Wisc. Ct. App. 1994); Kushner v. McGinnis, 194 N.E. 106 (Mass. 1935) (discussing amusement park admission ticket that was torn quickly after it was presented). *But cf.* Del Raso v. United States, 244 F.3d 567 (7th Cir. 2001) (North Carolina law) (enforcing a release even though the plaintiff who signed it claimed that he spent only about "two seconds" glancing at it before signing).
116. Hyatt v. Anoka Police Dep't, 700 N.W.2d 502 (Minn. Ct. App. 2005).
117. Audette v. Commonwealth, 829 N.E.2d 248 (Mass. Ct. App. 2005).
118. San Jose Charter of the Hells Angels Motorcycle Club v. City of San Jose, 402 F.3d 962 (Cal. Ct. App. 2005).
119. Miller v. Willbanks, 8 S.W.3d 607, 614 (Tenn. 1999), quoting RESTATEMENT (SECOND) OF TORTS § 46, cmt. d (1965).
120. Burgess v. Taylor, 44 S.W.3d 806 (Ky. Ct. App. 2001).
121. LaPorte v. Assoc. Indeps., 163 So. 2d 267 (Fla. 1964).
122. Pantelopoulos v. Pantelopoulos, 869 A.2d 280 (Conn. Super. Ct. 2005).
123. *See also* Myers v. City of Hartford, 853 A.2d 621 (Conn. Ct. App. 2004) (dismissing a claim against a municipality for wrongfully euthanizing

a dog because Connecticut law, CONN. GEN. STAT. § 22-350, considered dogs "property"); Schrage v. Hatzlacha Cab Corp., 788 N.Y.S.2d 4 (N.Y. Ct. App. 2004) (holding defendant taxicab company whose driver ran into and killed the dog not liable for plaintiff's emotional injury because state law considered pets personal property); Carbasho v. Musulin, 618 S.E.2d 368 (W. Va. Ct. App. 2005); Koester v. VCA Animal Hosp., 627 N.W.2d 5 (Mich. Ct. App. 2001).

124. For example, in Barrister Farm v. Upson Downs Farm, 2006 WL 259608 (Ky. Ct. App. 2/10/2006), a breach of bailment case involving the demise of plaintiff's horses in a fire at a racetrack, the issue arose as to whether the track unlawfully engaged in spoliation of evidence when it cleared the fire site, thereby preventing plaintiff from conducting an independent investigation.
125. Several states have agister's lien laws that allow the keeper of the animals a lien and give the facilities the right to insist on continued possession until paid in full. *See, e.g.*, IOWA CODE ch. 579; MICH. COMP. LAWS § 570.185; NEV. STAT. tit. 9, ch. 108.540.
126. *E.g.*, ALA. CODE § 6-2-38; ARIZ. REV. STAT. ANN. § 12-542; CAL. CIV. PROC. CODE § 335.1; COLO. REV. STAT. § 13-80-101; MASS. GEN. LAWS ch. 260 §§ 2A & 4.
127. *E.g.*, FLA. STAT. § 95.11(3) (a) (2005).
128. *E.g.*, MO. REV. STAT. § 516.120(4) (2006).
129. Minnesota, for example, has a six-year statute of limitations. *See* MINN. STAT. § 541.05, subdiv. 2 (2004).
130. The party can also be asked to complete an IRS Form 4506, which is a Request for Copy of Tax Form.
131. *See* FED. R. CIV. P. 45.
132. *See, e.g.*, FED. R. CIV. P. 36.
133. For more information, see Annotation, *Measure and Elements of Damages, in Action Other Than One Against a Carrier, for Conversion, Injury, Loss, or Destruction of Livestock*, 79 A.L.R.2D 677 (1961); Annotation, *Measure, Elements, and Amount of Damages for Killing or Injuring a Cat*, 8 A.L.R.4TH 1287 (1981).
134. Anzalone v. Kragness, 826 N.E.2d 472 (Ill. Ct. App. 2005) (discussing damages and considering the value of the dog to its owner and not merely the animal's fair market value).
135. Carbasho v. Musulin, 618 S.E.2d 368 (W. Va. 2005).
136. *See, e.g.*, Arnold v. Laird, 621 P.2d 138 (Wash. Ct. App. 1980); Burns v. Janes, 398 A.2d 1125 (R.I. Ct. App. 1979).

CHAPTER 3

Ownership, Custody, and Keeping of Animals

STACY L. KELLY

- **I. Introduction: Animals as Personal Property**
- **II. Owner or Guardian**
- **III. Custody and Possession of Animals**
  - A. In the Event of Separation or Divorce
    - *1. Custody*
    - *2. Visitation*
    - *3. Damages Clause*
  - B. Lost and Found Animals
  - C. Abandoned Animals
    - *1. Generally*
    - *2. In Cases of Emergency or Disaster*
  - D. Seized Animals
- **IV. Planning for the Continued Care of Pets**
  - A. Power of Attorney
  - B. Bequest in a Will
    - *1. Unconditional Bequest*
    - *2. Conditional Bequest*
    - *3. Pet Trusts*
  - C. Inter Vivos Pet Trusts
    - *1. Statutory Pet Trusts*
    - *2. Factors to Consider in Creating Pet Trusts*
      - a. Select and Designate Trustee
      - b. Select and Designate Caregiver
      - c. Identify Animals
      - d. Identify Standards of Care and Living

I. Introduction: Animals as Personal Property

There are two types of property, real or personal. Real property is defined as land erected or growing upon or affixed to the land, and personal property is, effectively, what is not real property. Throughout the United States, animals are treated as personal property in the eyes of the law.

This classification of animals as personal property has a long history, and can be traced back to 2100 BC.[1] The tradition of classifying animals as property impacts how animal lawyers, animal owners, and animal advocates approach the protection of nonhuman interests. It is notable that notwithstanding these legal classifications, many Americans consider animals to be family members.

II. Owner or Guardian

Although people have title to animals as personal property, some animal advocates prefer to call the title holder "Guardian" rather than "Owner." The idea is that the term "guardian" more accurately reflects the legal obligations that humans should have with respect to animals. There are currently 17 laws including city codes, county ordinances, and one state statute that include the designation of citizens and professionals as "guardians."[2]

A person who owns property has rights under the United States Constitution not to be deprived of that property without due process of law. Guardians do not own the property that is the subject of the guardianship. A guardian has limited or temporary possession of the animal as a trustee. The trustee then has responsibilities for the benefit of the animal ward.[3]

The idea is that a "guardian" has enforceable rights and obligations different from an owner's. This means that a guardian is more accountable to the public interest than an owner is.

The relationship of guardian and ward is historically a fiduciary relationship[4] that requires the utmost duty of loyalty on the part of the guardian to work for the ward to the exclusion of all personal gain.[5] In theory, applying guardianship principles to animal guardians results in the requirement that the guardians use ordinary care and diligence in serving as the guardian of the animal.[6] What constitutes the use of ordinary care and diligence will be determined in developing jurisprudence.

The grounds for which a guardian can be removed may be specified by statute.[7] Typically, the enumerated grounds for removal are exclusive. Simply put, inclusion of enumerated grounds precludes removal for reasons not enumerated.[8]

It is unclear whether the adoption of the term "guardian" in these city codes, county ordinances, and one state statute will alter the relationship between people and animals. Some of the jurisdictions, like Boulder, Colorado, have completely replaced the term "owner" with the term "guardian." Others, like Berkeley, California, did not replace the term but rather changed the term "owner" to "pet owner/guardian." The only state that has addressed this issue, Rhode Island, created a definition for "guardian" and uses the word interchangeably with "owner."

Although the terminology in some laws has been altered to include the word "guardian," this change is not intended to affect substantive provisions of the law. For example, the change is not intended to affect the actual title to the animal. The human is still the owner of the animal. The intent behind the change in terminology is to promote personal responsibility rather than to alter the legal relationship of owners and animals by granting animals any special rights or social role. It is for this reason that these laws passed, many times without much debate or public resistance.

If animal guardians are held to the same standard as other guardians under the law, it is possible the animals could be removed from a "guardian" when the guardian fails to fulfill mandated obligations. It remains to be seen what effect ever increasing guardian laws will have on the legal status of animals as personal property.

Notwithstanding the above, it is not known what will happen to an animal that is in the possession of a guardian who moves to a residence where guardianship rights and responsibilities are not recognized. In reviewing the legislative history, public discussions, and debates on these various laws, there appears to have been no consideration given to the issue. In all likelihood, the "guardian" role would disappear, and the obligations of a title holder of property would resume.

III. Custody and Possession of Animals

A. In the Event of Separation or Divorce

If one examines cases over the last few decades, it is obvious that the courts are using less property language and more custody and visitation language in making property determinations as if pets were family members. Emerging language used by the courts reflects child custody language, however inadvertently. For example, in *Raymond v. Lachmann*, the Court found "it best for all concerned that, given his limited life expectancy, Lovey, who is now almost ten years old, remain where he has lived, prospered, loved and been loved for the past four years."[9] This use of language could signal future trends.

The award of the family pet following a separation or divorce is a question courts seem reluctant to address. Generally, pets stay in the home where the children primarily live.[10] When the splitting couple does not have children, the courts are less consistent, but typically treat pets like any other marital personal property.

In *Bennett v. Bennett*,[11] the parties stipulated to all issues in the final judgment of dissolution of their marriage except which party would receive possession of the dog, "Roddy." After a hearing, the trial judge awarded possession of the dog to the husband and gave the wife visitation every other weekend and every other Christmas. Following that decision, the case became even more highly contested. The Florida appellate court determined that this procedural history demonstrated the morass in which a trial court could find itself when extending the right to visit personal property, and discussed enforcement problems. The court determined that the trial court lacked the authority to order dog visitation, and that the dog was subject to the equitable distribution process. The tone of the decision is reflected as follows. "Our courts are overwhelmed with the supervision of custody, visitation and support matters related to the protection of our children. We cannot undertake the same responsibility as to animals."[12]

Likewise, a Texas divorce court refused to appoint the husband as managing conservator of Bonnie Lou, the family dog.[13] The trial court gave possession of the dog to the wife. The husband agreed that his wife could have custody of the dog if he could have reasonable visitation and be named managing conservator. The appellate court held that "[a] dog, for all its admirable and unique qualities, is not a human being and is not treated in the law as such."[14] A dog is simply owned personal property.[15] These cases illustrate how lawyers are challenging the manner in which pets have traditionally been awarded by the courts. Because of the perception that courts will not help them, some people are attempting to form binding contractual obligations concerning their animals. A prenuptial agreement or cohabitation agreement is one form of a contract.[16] Parties can agree on the dates and times of access as well as the standard of care expected. It has yet to be tested whether courts will enforce these contractual obligations in the absence of claims of fraud, forgery, or undue influence, relating to the execution of the contract. The case law is developing on whether courts will enforce language in a prenuptial agreement that they would not permit in a marital termination agreement. The next sections discuss what some lawyers believe will likely be enforceable.

1. *Custody*

If a prenuptial agreement indicates what party is awarded custody, which is effectively an award of personal property, the agreement is more likely to be enforceable than if there is a visitation clause. If a separating or divorcing couple is each determined to share time with their pet, one possible solution is to continue joint ownership and leave it at that.[17] A court may well enforce a provision that requires both of the owners to contribute to the cost of the care for a pet as long as the provision is clear.[18] The courts may not enforce an agreement that pertains to residence and access.[19]

2. *Visitation*

It's fairly well known how a divorce court will utilize the best interest test to determine where children should live.[20] This is not the way it works for the family pet.[21] Although that pet may be a "member of the family" to one or more of the parties, to a judge, the pet may be just another piece of property.[22]

More and more divorce decrees are requiring that the family pet stay with the children of the marriage. As the children move from parent to parent, so does the family pet. Courts are not as likely, however, to make rulings on the access rights of divorcing adults.[23]

3. *Damages Clause*

The courts treat a prenuptial agreement as an enforceable contract consistent with public policy. If the parties have arranged for visitation in their prenuptial agreement, they should consider including a liquidated damages clause. Since courts are reluctant to get involved with visitation disputes regarding pets, a damages clause can be beneficial.

B. Lost and Found Animals

With respect to lost animals, at least one court has held that where the finder of a lost animal provided care and shelter for a reasonably extensive period of time and made every reasonable effort to find the animal's owner, the finder will be awarded possession of the animal against the original owner.[24] In *Morgan v. Kroupa*, a five-year-old dog named Boy broke free of his collar, ran away, and became lost.[25] Two weeks later, Boy was found by a woman who took the dog in.[26] The finder made a report to the local humane society, posted printed notices around town, and broadcast her finding of Boy on local radio stations.[27]

Although Boy's original owner lived in the same town, he claimed he had been unable to locate the dog for more than one year after the dog became lost.[28] During that year, the finder took care of the dog, fed, and sheltered it.[29]

A year later, a friend of the original owner told him that he had seen Boy at a house down the road.[30] The original owner drove to the house, and left with Boy.[31] The finder brought an action to recover Boy.[32] Determining that the finder diligently attempted to locate Boy's owner and responsibly sheltered and cared for Boy for over a year, the trial court awarded her possession.[33]

Some states have enacted laws governing the disposition of lost property.[34] It is unclear whether any of these codes would apply when the "lost property" is a companion animal.[35] Two states specifically exclude animals from their provisions, in part perhaps because the legislature considered the term "animal" to be a commercial animal rather than a cat or dog.[36] In any event, no state has enacted provisions that specifically cover the issue of a lost dog. Thus, it may be argued that the traditional common law rule of original ownership applies, rather than lost property law.[37]

Some states actually mention the term "stray dog" or "stray beast" in their dog statutes. A Hawaiian statute requires that "[e]very person who takes into the person's possession any stray dog shall immediately notify the animal control officer and release the dog to the animal control officer upon demand."[38] If the dog has tags, the animal control agency then notifies the owner in writing.[39] The owner then has 24 hours from the time notice is given to reclaim the dog.[40] If the owner does not reclaim the dog, or the owner of the dog cannot be identified, the animal shelter retains the dog for nine days.[41] After nine days, the dog can be sold or destroyed.[42]

Unlike Hawaii, Massachusetts law does not require the finder of a stray beast to take that stray beast to animal control or an animal shelter.[43] Rather, the finder, if said finder wants compensation for expenses for caring for the animal, must post or advertise the finding of the stray beast.[44] If the owner appears within three months and pays all reasonable expenses, the owner shall have the restitution of the beast.[45] Like Massachusetts, Wisconsin requires the finder of the stray to attempt to locate the owner.[46] The finder has seven days to notify the owner.[47] If the owner is not known, the finder shall file a notice with the county clerk within ten days of finding the stray.[48] If the finder fails to file the notice, he shall be liable in double the amount of damages sustained by the owner of the stray.[49]

C. Abandoned Animals

1. *Generally*

When an animal is abandoned, the original owner is deemed to have relinquished custody of the animal to the appropriate government authority, such as the county animal shelter.[50] Whether an owner has abandoned an animal is not always obvious. Abandonment is defined as "a virtual throwing away without regard as to who may take over or carry on."[51] Evidence of abandonment must be "direct, affirmative or reasonably beget the exclusive inference of throwing away."[52]

Most states have laws governing the abandonment of animals by the owner.[53] Usually these statutes cover situations in which the owner leaves the animal at a veterinarian, kennel, or similar facility.[54] If an owner does not collect the animal and pay for the services within a certain number of days, the animal is considered abandoned.[55] Before a veterinarian, kennel, or similar facility can gain title to the abandoned animal, certain duties must be fulfilled.[56] Most statutes require that the owner be notified that the owner can take possession of the animal by paying for the services.[57] If the owner does not respond, the facility must then turn the animal over to the local shelter and notify the owner.[58] A facility that does not comply with a state statute can be liable to the owner for expenses incurred.[59]

2. *In Cases of Emergency or Disaster*

In the aftermath of Hurricane Katrina it became apparent that difficulties exist in determining whether an animal is considered lost or abandoned. As Katrina was bearing down on Louisiana, some owners left their pets at home intending on returning within days.[60] Others took their pets to local kennels or shelters for safety.[61] When the owners could not return to recover their pets, many animal organizations took possession of these animals and subsequently found other families to adopt the animals.[62] Now courts in North Carolina, Florida, and Texas have stepped in to determine where the pets belong.[63] As demonstrated previously, determination of whether the pet was abandoned or lost will certainly affect the outcome.

D. Seized Animals

Dogs, and to a lesser extent cats, may be subject to the state's police powers. If there is a violation of animal welfare laws or if an animal is alleged to be dangerous, officials can remove the animal from the home without the owner's consent.[64] The owner is entitled to due process.[65] At a minimum, due process requires that the owner be given notice and the opportunity to be heard prior to the destruction (or sometimes even seizure) of an animal.[66] Normally the removal of an animal from the owner's home does not, by itself, result in transfer of ownership of the animal.[67]

IV. Planning for the Continued Care of Pets

What will happen to a person's pet when he or she becomes incapacitated or dies? The continued care of pets upon the owner's death or incapacity can be addressed in a power of attorney, last will and testament, and/or a trust document. For a person concerned with the continued care of their pets, it is important to make provisions for their pet in their estate planning documents.

A. Power of Attorney

A power of attorney is an instrument in writing whereby one person, the principal, appoints another person as his agent and confers authority to perform certain specified acts or kinds of acts on behalf of the principal.[68] The principal can appoint an agent and give that agent the specific authority to take possession of the principal's pet(s) in the event of the principal's incapacity. In the power of attorney, the principal can also authorize the agent to take all steps necessary to care for the pet including but not limited to expending funds for the care of the pet(s).

The owner should consider including special instructions pertaining to his or her pet(s) in the owner's durable power of attorney.[69] These instructions should authorize the agent to care for the pet and to spend the owner's money on the pets' care (day-to-day, veterinarian, etc.).[70] The owner may also wish to grant the agent the power to place the pet with a long-term caregiver.[71] The following is sample language to include in a durable power of attorney:

> In the event that the Principal is unable to provide for the care of the Principal's pets, the Agent is authorized to: (1) take possession and custody of the pets [OPTION: or provide possession and custody of the pet to the Trustee of the [INTER VIVOS TRUST]]; and (2) expend or otherwise utilize such amounts of the Principal's funds or other property as may be necessary or advisable to provide for the health, care, and welfare of the pets, including (but not limited to) food, veterinary care and/or insurance, toys and other recreational activities, and temporary boarding and/or pet-sitting fees. In exercising such authority, it is intended that the Agent will maintain the pets in the same standard of health, care, and welfare as the Principal provided. [OPTIONAL: Unless medically or physically impracticable, the Agent shall permit the Principal to have as much contact with the pets as the Principal did before becoming incapacitated.] For the purposes of this instrument, any such actions by the Agent taken for the benefit of the Principal's pets shall be considered taken for the benefit of the Principal.

B. Bequest in a Will

A bequest placed in a will for the care of a person's pet is an uncomplicated way to help protect the pet after the owner's death. A bequest can take several forms. It can be a specific sum, a percentage of a person's estate, or the remainder of a person's estate after expenses and gifts to other beneficiaries. In addition, the bequest can be a conditional bequest or an unconditional bequest.

1. *Unconditional Bequest*

An unconditional bequest is one in which the testator gifts his or her pet(s) and a sum of money to an individual. There is no mechanism to ensure that the testator's intent will be fulfilled, as there is no person directly charged with ascertaining that the animal is receiving proper care, so this technique should only be used if the testator trusts the beneficiary who will receive the pet to properly care for the pet.[72] The following is sample language to create an unconditional bequest:

> I leave [description of pets] and [amount of money adequate for animal's care] to [name of individual to care for pets]. If [such pets] do not survive me by [survival period], this provision of my will is of no effect.

2. *Conditional Bequest*

A conditional bequest is one in which the testator gifts his or her pet(s) and a sum of money to an individual conditioned on that individual providing for the proper care of the pet(s). Creating a conditional gift in a will is a much simpler method than creating a pet trust, but a bequest may not provide the testator with the necessary legal protections.

One method to alleviate this concern is to designate another person to receive the original gift of money if the pets are not receiving proper care. This provides the testator with the knowledge that someone is policing the caretaker. But if the potential gift-over amount is small or the alternate taker does not live close enough to the caregiver to make firsthand observations of the animal, the alternate caretaker may lose interest. In these situations, creating a legally binding pet trust may be the best solution.

The owner should expressly state what happens to the gift if all of the pets predecease the owner.[73] In the absence of express language, the caregiver would still receive a condition subsequent gift but not one based on a condition precedent.[74] The following is sample language to create a conditional bequest:

> I hereby give my pet, [NAME OF PETS], [DESCRIPTION OF PETS], to [NAME OF CARETAKER], and the sum of $________, which shall be expended for the care of my pets during their remaining lifetimes; provided, however, that this gift shall lapse if my pets are not living at the time of distribution according to this provision *or* if [NAME OF CARETAKER] does not undertake to

use the funds gifted herein for the care of my pets. [OPTIONAL: This provision is intended to be a gift subject to a condition precedent, and I do *not* intend to impose any trust upon the beneficiary herein, under common law or statute.] If [such pets] do not survive me by [survival period], this provision of my will is of no effect.

3. *Pet Trusts*[75]

A pet trust is a legal technique an owner may use to ensure that a pet receives proper care after the owner dies. The pet owner creates the trust either in his or her will (a testamentary trust) or in a trust document (inter vivos trust). By the terms of either type of trust, the pet owner gives his or her pets and enough money for the care of the pets to a trustee who is under a duty to make arrangements for the proper care of the pets according to the standards outlined in the trust.

The owner must initially determine whether to create a testamentary trust or an inter vivos trust. A testamentary trust is the less expensive option because the trust does not take effect until the testator dies and his or her will is declared valid by a court ("probating the will"). However, there may not be funds available to care for the pet during the gap between when the owner dies and his or her will is probated.

C. Inter Vivos Pet Trusts

A recent and growing trend in animal law is for states to enact statutes specifically authorizing trusts for pets. Prior to these statutes, attempts to create a trust for one's pet failed because the actual beneficiary was not a human or because of the application of the rule against perpetuities.

A pet trust is a legally sanctioned arrangement providing for the care and maintenance of one or more pets in the event of the settlor's disability or death. The "settlor" is the person who creates the trust. By the terms of the trust, the settlor gives his or her pet(s) and enough money for its care to a trustee who is under a duty to make arrangements for the proper care of the pet according to the standards outlined in the trust by the settlor.

One benefit to providing for a pet's care through the vehicle of an inter vivos trust as opposed to a testamentary trust is that an inter vivos trust can provide for a pet's care immediately and, therefore, applies not only if the pet owner dies, but also if the pet owner becomes ill or incapacitated. That is because an inter vivos trust is in effect during the pet owner's life. Many times a long delay occurs between the death of a testator and the probating of his or her will. This delay can hinder the ability of a caretaker to provide for the ongoing care of the testator's pet(s).

One drawback is that the inter vivos trust has start-up costs and administration expenses. Not only is a separate trust document needed to create an inter vivos trust, but the trust must be funded to become effective. Many clients do not want to create and fund a trust while they are alive. The inter vivos trust, could, however, be nominally funded in the beginning. The settler could then provide for additional funding at his or her death. Additional funding could come from a nonprobate asset, such as a bank account or a life insurance policy naming the trust as the beneficiary or as the payee on death.

1. *Statutory Pet Trusts*

A trend in animal law is for states to enact statutes specifically authorizing trusts for pets. Prior to these statutes, attempts to create a trust in which the pet was the beneficiary failed because the actual beneficiary was not a human or because of the application of the rule against perpetuities.

In 1990, the National Conference of Commissioners on Uniform State Laws added a section to the Uniform Probate Code to validate "a trust for the care of a designated domestic or pet animal and the animal's offspring."[76] This provision, as amended in 1993, provides as follows:

> **§ 2-907. Honorary Trusts; Trusts for Pets.**
>
> (a) [Honorary Trust.] Subject to subsection (c), if (i) a trust is for a specific lawful noncharitable purpose or for lawful noncharitable purposes to be selected by the trustee and (ii) there is no definite or definitely ascertainable beneficiary designated, the trust may be performed by the trustee for [21] years but no longer, whether or not the terms of the trust contemplate a longer duration. [Notes to the Uniform Probate Code state that "the figure '21' is bracketed to indicate that an enacting state may select a different figure."]
>
> (b) [Trust for Pets.] Subject to this subsection and subsection (c), a trust for the care of a designated domestic or pet animal is valid. The trust terminates when no living animal is covered by the trust. A governing instrument must be liberally construed to bring the transfer within this subsection, to presume against the merely precatory or honorary nature of the disposition, and to carry out the general intent of the transferor. Extrinsic evidence is admissible in determining the transferor's intent.
>
> (c) [Additional Provisions Applicable to Honorary Trusts and Trusts for Pets.] In addition to the provisions of subsection (a) or

(b), a trust covered by either of those subsections is subject to the following provisions:

(1) Except as expressly provided otherwise in the trust instrument, no portion of the principal or income may be converted to the use of the trustee or to any use other than for the trust's purposes or for the benefit of a covered animal.

(2) Upon termination, the trustee shall transfer the unexpended trust property in the following order:

(i) as directed in the trust instrument;

(ii) if the trust was created in a nonresiduary clause in the transferor's will or in a codicil to the transferor's will, under the residuary clause in the transferor's will; and

(iii) if no taker is produced by the application of subparagraph (i) or (ii), to the transferor's heirs under Section 2-711.

(3) For the purposes of Section 2-707, the residuary clause is treated as creating a future interest under the terms of a trust.

(4) The intended use of the principal or income can be enforced by an individual designated for that purpose in the trust instrument or, if none, by an individual appointed by a court upon application to it by an individual.

(5) Except as ordered by the court or required by the trust instrument, no filing, report, registration, periodic accounting, separate maintenance of funds, appointment, or fee is required by reason of the existence of the fiduciary relationship of the trustee.

(6) A court may reduce the amount of the property transferred, if it determines that that amount substantially exceeds the amount required for the intended use. The amount of the reduction, if any, passes as unexpended trust property under subsection (c)(2).

(7) If no trustee is designated or no designated trustee is willing or able to serve, a court shall name a trustee. A court may order the transfer of the property to another trustee, if required

> to assure that the intended use is carried out and if no successor trustee is designated in the trust instrument or if no designated successor trustee agrees to serve or is able to serve. A court may also make such other orders and determinations as shall be advisable to carry out the intent of the transferor and the purpose of this section.

At least ten states have enacted this provision, including Alaska, Arizona, Colorado, Hawaii, Illinois, Michigan, Montana, North Carolina, South Dakota, and Utah.[77] In addition, several other states have used the UPC provision as a model for their own enabling legislation.[78]

Likewise, the Uniform Trust Code added a section in 2000 that provides that a "trust may be created to provide for the care of an animal alive during the settlor's lifetime."[79] This provision reads as follows:

> **§ 408. Trust for Care of Animal.**
>
> (a) A trust may be created to provide for the care of an animal alive during the settlor's lifetime. The trust terminates upon the death of the animal or, if the trust was created to provide for the care of more than one animal alive during the settlor's lifetime, upon the death of the last surviving animal.
>
> (b) A trust authorized by this section may be enforced by a person appointed in the terms of the trust or, if no person is so appointed, by a person appointed by the court. A person having an interest in the welfare of the animal may request the court to appoint a person to enforce the trust or to remove a person appointed.
>
> (c) Property of a trust authorized by this section may be applied only to its intended use, except to the extent the court determines that the value of the trust property exceeds the amount required for the intended use. Except as otherwise provided in the terms of the trust, property not required for the intended use must be distributed to the settlor, if then living, otherwise to the settlor's successors in interest.

At least 18 jurisdictions have already adopted this provision: Alabama, Arkansas, the District of Columbia, Florida, Kansas, Maine, Missouri, Nebraska, New Hampshire, New Mexico, North Dakota, Ohio, Oregon, Pennsylvania, South Carolina, Tennessee, Virginia, and Wyoming.[80]

Many other states have developed their own statutes, often using the uniform provisions as models. These states include Florida, Idaho, Indiana, Iowa, Nevada, New Jersey, New York, Rhode Island, Texas, and Washington.[81] Although many of the pet statutes are titled Honorary Trust for Pets, only one state, Wisconsin, has an unenforceable pet trust statute.[82] In other words, in this state, the trust is merely honorary.[83] There are about 12 states remaining that have not yet legislatively authorized pet trusts. Some of these states are in the process of enacting pet trust statutes.

2. *Factors to Consider in Creating Pet Trusts*

A. Select and Designate Trustee[84]

The pet owner needs to select the trustee with care and check with the trustee before making a nomination. The trustee, whether individual or corporate, must be willing to administer the property for the benefit of the animal and to expend the time and effort necessary to deal with trust administration matters. Trustee commissions are set by state statute, or the pet owner can specify a set stipend for the trustee in the trust instrument. Note that corporate trustees typically charge a higher fee for their services. The pet owner should name alternate trustees should the named trustee be unable to serve until the trust terminates. In addition, an alternate trustee may have standing to remove the original trustee from office should the original trustee cease to administer the trust for the benefit of the pets.

B. Select and Designate Caregiver[85]

The pet owner should select a caregiver for the animal. Depending on the terms of the pet trust statute, the caregiver may have standing to enforce the trust if the trustee fails to carry out its terms. Thus, the caregiver should be sufficiently savvy to understand the basic functioning of a trust and his or her enforcement rights.

It is of utmost importance that the pet owner locate a caregiver who is willing and able to care for the animal in a manner that the owner finds acceptable. The prospective caregiver should be questioned before being named to make certain the caregiver will assume the potentially burdensome obligation of caring for the pet, especially when the pet is in need of medical care or requires special attention as it ages. The pet and the prospective caregiver should meet and spend quality time together to make sure they, and the caregiver's family, get along harmoniously with each other.

The pet owner should name several alternate caregivers should the owner's first choice be unable to serve for the duration of the lives of the pets. To prevent the pets from ending up homeless, the owner should authorize the trustee to select a good home for the pets if none of the named individuals are willing or able to accept the animal. The trustee should not, however, have the authority to appoint him or herself as the caregiver as such an appointment would eliminate the checks and balances aspect of separating the caregiver from the money provider. However, in some cases, the pet owner has the utmost trust in the person selected to be trustee and wants that same person to be the caregiver. If this is the case, it should be specified in the trust document.

If the pet owner is unable to name a caregiver and does not want to leave the selection up to the trustee, the pet owner could appoint several individuals, such as veterinarians, family members, and friends, to an animal care panel that is charged with the responsibility of locating a suitable caregiver. The panel could use various means to locate a proper caregiver, such as advertising in a local newspaper and consulting with local animal welfare organizations. The panel would interview the prospective caregivers and select the person it felt would provide the best care for the pets under the terms of the trust.

c. Identify Animals[86]

The pet owner may want to identify the animals that are to receive care under the trust. If this step is not taken, an unscrupulous caregiver could replace a deceased, lost, or stolen animal with a replacement so that the caregiver may continue to receive benefits. For example, there is a report that "[a] trust was established for a black cat to be cared for by its deceased owner's maid. Inconsistencies in the reported age of the pet tipped off authorities to fact that the maid was on her third black cat, the original long since having died."[87]

The pet owner may use a variety of methods to identify the animal. A relatively simple and inexpensive method is for the trust to contain a detailed description of the animal including any unique characteristics such as blotches of colored fur and scars. Veterinarian records and pictures of the animal would also be helpful. A professional could tattoo the pet with an alphanumeric identifier. A tattoo, however, could later cause problems for the pet because a pet thief could mutilate the pet to remove the tattoo, such as cutting off an ear or leg, if the pet's primary function is breeding. A more sophisticated procedure is for the pet owner to have a microchip implanted in the animal. The trustee can then have the animal scanned to verify that the animal the caregiver is minding is the same animal. Of course, an enterprising caregiver could surgically remove the microchip and have it implanted in another physically similar animal. The best, albeit expensive, method to assure identification is for the trustee to retain a sample of the animal's DNA before turning the animal over to the caregiver and then to run periodic comparisons between the retained sample and new samples from the animal.

A pet owner, however, may be less concerned with providing for the animals owned at the time of the will execution or creation of the inter vivos trust, but rather want to arrange for the care of the animals actually owned at time of death. "It would be onerous for [the owner] to execute a new trust instrument or will whenever a new animal joins the family."[88] In this situation, the owner may wish to describe the animals as a class instead of by individual name or specific description. For example, a testamentary trust could state that the beneficiaries of the pet trust are all the companion animals owned by the testator at the time of his or her death.

D. Identify Standards of Care and Living[89]

The owner should specify the type of care the caregiver is to give the animals and the expenses for which the caregiver can expect reimbursement from the trust. Typical expenses include food, housing, grooming, medical care, and burial or cremation fees. The pet owner may also want to include more detailed instructions. Alternatively, the owner may leave the specifics of the type of care to the discretion of the trustee. If the pet owner elects to do so, the pet owner should seriously consider providing the caregiver with general guidelines to both (1) avoid claims that the caregiver is expending an unreasonable amount on the animals and (2) prevent the caregiver from expending excessive funds. For example, in the case of *In re Rogers*,[90] the court determined that the caregiver was acting in an unreasonable manner when he purchased an automobile to transport the dog while stating that it was a matter of opinion whether the purchase of a washing machine to launder the dog's bed clothing was reasonable.

E. Establish Duties and Powers of Trustee

i. Inspection of Animal[91] The owner should require the trustee to make regular inspections of the animals to determine their physical and psychological condition. The inspections should be at random times so the caregiver does not provide the animal with extra food, medical care, or attention merely because the caregiver knows the trustee is coming. The inspections should take place in the caregiver's home so the trustee may observe firsthand the environment in which the animal is being kept.

ii. Liability Insurance Depending on the assets available to fund the pet trust, the owner should consider providing funds for the caretaker to purchase liability insurance. Thus, in the event the pets cause damage to a third party or property, the caretaker will not be personally liable.

iii. Health Insurance More and more pet owners are purchasing health insurance for their pets.[92] Again, depending on the assets available, the pet owner can make provisions for the trustee to purchase health insurance for the owners pet(s).

iv. Accounting As with traditional trusts, it is a prudent practice for the settlor to require the trustee to provide annual accountings to the caregiver. This will decrease the likelihood of malfeasance by the trustee.

F. Calculate Amount Needed to Fund Trust[93]

The pet owner should carefully compute the amount of property necessary to care for each animal and to provide additional payments, if any, for the caregiver and the trustee. Many factors will go into this decision, such as the number of animals, the type of animals, the animals' life expectancies,[94] the standard of living the owner wishes to provide for the animals, and the need for potentially expensive medical treatment. Adequate funds also should be included to provide the animals with proper care, be it with an animal-sitter or at a professional boarding business, when the caregiver is on vacation, out of town on business, receiving care in a hospital, or otherwise temporarily unable to personally provide for the animals.

The size of the pet owner's estate must also be considered. If the owner's estate is relatively large, the owner could transfer sufficient property so the trustee could make payments primarily from the income and use the principal only for emergencies. On the other hand, if the owner's estate is small, the owner may wish to transfer a lesser amount and anticipate that the trustee will supplement income with principal invasions as necessary. The pet owner must avoid transferring an unreasonably large amount of money or other property to the trust because such a gift is likely to encourage heirs and remainder beneficiaries of the owner's will to contest the arrangement.

Unhappy remainder beneficiaries and heirs could allege that the use of property to care for specific animals is a capricious use of funds and an inefficient use of valuable resources. Consequently, they could urge that enforcement of arrangements for the care of a pet after the owner's death are against public policy and that the policy favoring freedom of property disposition at death is counterbalanced by the desire to avoid the frivolous use of property for animal care when the needs of humans are considered more important. This argument has not been successful. In fact no case has been located where this was the basis for a court holding that the gift for the animals was ineffective.[95] There are, however, several instances where courts determined that the pet owner left excessive funds for the care of the animals and reduced the gift to a more reasonable amount.[96]

The pet owner should determine the amount that is reasonable for the care of the animals and fund the trust accordingly. Even if the owner has no desire to benefit family members, friends, or charities until the demise of the animals, if the owner leaves his or her entire estate for the animals' benefit, the will may be contested. It is often a good idea to state expressly in the trust that if a court determines that excess funds were placed into the trust, that they pass to a certain person or charity that in the pet owner's opinion would be very unlikely to ever make a claim that the funds were excessive. Thus, an incentive to contest the amount is removed.

G. Specify Distribution Method[97]

The owner should specify how the trustee is to make disbursements from the trust. The simplest method is for the owner to direct the trustee to pay the caregiver a fixed sum each month regardless of the actual care expenses. If the care expenses are less than the distribution, the caregiver enjoys a windfall for his or her efforts. If the care expenses are greater than the distribution, the caregiver absorbs the cost. The caregiver may, however, be unable or unwilling to make expenditures in excess of the fixed distribution that are necessary for the animal. Thus, the owner should permit the trustee to reimburse the caregiver for out-of-pocket expenses exceeding the normal distribution.

Alternatively, the owner could provide only for reimbursement of expenses. The caregiver would submit receipts for expenses associated with the animals on a periodic basis. The trustee would review the expenses in light of the level of care the pet owner specified and reimburse the caregiver if the expenses are appropriate. Although this method may be in line with the owner's intent, the pet owner must realize that there will be additional administrative costs and an increased burden on the caregiver to retain and submit receipts.

H. Determine Distributions for Beneficiary/Caretaker[98]

The owner should determine whether the trustee should make distributions to the caregiver above and beyond the amount established for the animal's care. An owner may believe that the addition of the animals to the caregiver's family is sufficient, especially if the trustee will reimburse the caregiver for all reasonable care expenses. On the other hand, the animals may impose a burden on the caregiver and thus additional distributions may be appropriate to encourage the caregiver to continue to care for the animals. In addition, the caregiver may feel more duty-bound to provide good care if the caregiver is receiving additional distributions contingent on providing the animal with appropriate care.

I. Determine Trustee Compensation

The trust instrument may provide a clause that specifies trustee compensation for the trustee's services. Otherwise, trust compensation is set by state statute. The owner should consider the size of his or her estate in setting the amount of compensation. The compensation could be a set amount to be paid monthly or annually or the compensation could be a percentage of the income and distributions.

J. Consider Requiring a Bond

Another method to protect the assets of the trust for the continued care of the pet beneficiaries is to require the trustee to post a surety bond. The bond amount should be directly proportional to the size of the trust. The pet owner can allow the premium payments for the bond to be paid from the trust assets. While a bond provides protection, it is an annual expense to the trust and may use up too much of the trust's funds. In most cases, clients will want a provision waiving bond requirements.

K. Consider Including Exculpatory Clauses

The trust instrument may contain a clause that purports to relieve the trustee from liability for certain described types of conduct or limits the trustee's responsibilities to the maintenance of a standard of care less than ordinary or reasonable care.[99] The settlor could limit the trustee's liability for any act other than the trustee's own bad faith. Or the settlor could limit liability of the trustee to only the trustee's willful default or gross negligence. These clauses are called immunity or exculpatory clauses because they attempt to relieve the trustee from duties or liabilities that would otherwise be imposed.[100]

L. Specify Duration of Trust

Before state pet trust statutes were enacted, animals could not be beneficiaries of trusts because of the rule against perpetuities, which states that no property can continue in trust longer than lives in being plus 21 years. Only a human life could be a life in being, for purposes of this rule. Most pet trust statutes allow the trusts to continue for the lives of the animal beneficiaries, so this rule does not apply. However, several states still have pet trust statutes with 21-year limitations; and in those states, special planning is needed for animals, such as horses and birds, that may live longer than 21 years. One option at the end of the 21-year term is to leave the animals and remaining funds to an animal sanctuary that cares for the species of animal involved. For example, a horse could be left to a sanctuary that cares for horses (along with the remaining trust funds) when the trust terminates.

M. Provide Instructions for Disposition of Animal at Death[101]

The pet owner may want to include instructions for the final disposition of the animal when the animal dies. The will of one pet owner is reported as containing the following provision: "[U]pon the death of my pets they are to be embalmed and their caskets to be placed in a Wilbert Vault at Pine Ridge Cemetery."[102] The owner may want the animal to be buried in a pet cemetery or cremated with the ashes either distributed or placed in an urn. The cost for a pet burial ranges from $250 to $1,000 while pet cremations are significantly less expensive.

N. Select and Designate Remainder Beneficiary[103]

The pet owner should clearly designate a remainder beneficiary to take any remaining trust property upon the death of all the pet beneficiaries. Otherwise, court involvement will be necessary with the most likely result being a resulting trust for the benefit of the owner's successors in interest.[104] The pet owner must be cautioned not to leave the remaining trust property to the caregiver because the caregiver would then lack a financial motive to care for the animal and thus might accelerate its death to gain immediate access to the trust corpus. The pet owner may also want to authorize the trustee to terminate the trust before the death of all of the pet beneficiaries, "if the remaining principal is small and suitable arrangements have been made for the care of the animals."[105]

A general trust rule is that a trustee has a duty to balance the interests of the life beneficiaries with the interests of the remainderman. Most clients want to create a trust for the care of their animals, and the selection of the remainderman is an afterthought and not of great importance to them. Therefore an important provision to add to the trust is that the interest of the animals has priority over the interest of the remainderman, so that all of the funds in the trust can be used for the animals without balancing the interests of the animals with the interest of the remainderman.

The pet owner may wish to consider naming a charity that benefits animals as the remainder beneficiary. "Hopefully the charity would want to assure the well-being of the animals and an added advantage is that the Attorney General would be involved to investigate if any misappropriation of funds by the trustee occurred."[106] The pet owner must precisely state the legal name and location of the intended charitable beneficiary so the trustee will not have difficulty ascertaining the appropriate recipient of the remainder gift.

3. *Options for Pet Owners Residing in States with No Pet Trust Statute*

A. TRUST FOR HUMAN BENEFICIARY WITH PET CARE AUTHORIZED

For clients in states that do not yet have a state pet trust statute, the pet owner can create a testamentary or inter vivos trust with a human beneficiary, and direct the trustee of the trust to make distributions to cover the costs of care of companion animals, on the theory that such payments benefit the human beneficiary. The human beneficiary could be the caregiver of the animals.

B. USE OF A PET TRUST STATUTE OF ANOTHER STATE

Another method for pet owners residing in states that do not yet have a pet trust statute is to create an inter vivos trust using the statute of a state that does have a pet trust statute. For example, Connecticut has not yet enacted a pet trust statute, but Connecticut residents could create a pet trust and provide that it is to be governed by the New York pet trust statute. Jurisdictional requirements would have to be met, such as having a trustee residing in New York and keeping a bank account in New York.

D. Euthanasia of Pet upon Death of Owner

Sometimes the testator will include a provision in his or her will that authorizes the executor or administrator to euthanize the testator's pets after the testator dies. In one case, *In re Capers Estate*, the court refused to allow the executors to fulfill the euthanasia provision.[107] Capers's will directed her executors to arrange for her two Irish setters, Brickland and Sunny Birch, to "be destroyed in a humane manner."[108]

The executors filed for a declaratory judgment to have the court determine their rights and duties by reason of the aforementioned clause in the will.[109] The court recognized that if the executors had carried out the provisions of the will, "they would have followed an inhumane course of action from which there is no appeal" and would have established a precedent with which the court was in disagreement.[110]

In analyzing Capers's intent, the court concluded that she was "deeply interested in the humane care and treatment of animals."[111] The court also found that Capers "feared that either [her Irish setters] would grieve for her or that no one would afford them the same affection and kindness that they received during her life."[112] After considering the testimony of the veterinarian who cared for Capers's dogs, the court concluded that Capers's fears were unfounded.[113] Finding no reason for carrying out the literal provision of the will, the court concluded that Capers's intent would be better served if Brickland and Sunny Birch were placed in a good home "where they are given the same care and attention that [Capers] bestowed on them."[114]

The court then analyzed whether the pet-destruction provision was against public policy, and found that there is "no question of the strength of the public sentiment in favor of preserving the lives of these animals."[115] The court found that to destroy Brickland and Sunny Birch "would be an act of gross inhumanity."[116] Because the court invalidated the provision in Capers's will, the residuary clause was invoked.[117] Based on the residuary clause, Brickland and Sunny Birch went to the Western Pennsylvania Humane Society, which had been caring for the animals for almost two years.[118]

V. Bailment Agreements

A. Bailment Defined

Blackstone defined a bailment as "a delivery of goods in trust, upon a contract expressed or implied, that the trust shall be faithfully executed on the part of the bailee."[119] The person delivering the property is the bailor.[120] The person receiving the property is the bailee.[121] A bailment can exist only for personal property; it cannot exist for real property.[122]

People enter into bailment agreements every day, sometimes without the realization that a legal relationship has been formed.[123] The significance of bailment as a cause of action is often overlooked. Possibly this is because bailment overlaps with other areas of the law such as contract, tort, and property law.[124] Some common examples of bailment of animals include horses rented to riders, male animals rented out for stud fees, dogs dropped off at the groomers for the day, animals boarded at kennels, and, in some instances, animals treated by a veterinarian.

B. Types of Bailment[125]

For many years, bailments have been divided into categories, based on the purpose of the bailment.[126] American law has traditionally divided bailments into three categories: bailments for the benefit of the bailor, bailments for the benefit of the bailee, and bailments that are mutually beneficial to the bailor and the bailee.[127] Bailments that are for the sole benefit of the bailor or the bailee are called gratuitous bailments because one party receives a benefit from the bailment relationship as a gratuity of the other party.[128] Alternatively, bailments where the relationship is mutually beneficial to the bailor and bailee are sometimes called lucrative bailments or bailments for hire.[129] Mutually beneficial bailments include the performance of a service upon the delivered property[130] in exchange for consideration, and the payment of consideration in exchange for use of the delivered property.[131] The situation in which a veterinarian would be part of a bailment relationship falls into the category of mutually beneficial bailments: the animal owner (the bailor) delivers the animal to the veterinarian (the bailee) for veterinary services to be performed upon the animal, in exchange for payment for the service rendered.

When a bailment is for hire, and the bailee is hired to provide services upon a piece of property, the bailee has a legal duty to provide those services. If the bailee must only care for the bailed property, such as boarding an animal in a kennel, the bailee is under a duty to use ordinary diligence in providing that care and would be liable for ordinary neglect.[132] The standard of ordinary diligence, also called "reasonable care," is best described as the same level of care that a person would provide to their own property under similar circumstances.[133] Thus, reasonable care in the boarding of a dog at the kennel would include feeding and watering the animal, providing it with exercise, and securing medical attention if needed. The bailee would be liable if he neglected to provide this level of ordinary care.

However, if the bailee purports to have specialized skill or knowledge in the service he is hired to provide, he is bound to exercise that skill or knowledge, and will be held liable if he fails to do so.[134] Furthermore, when a bailee is hired for his specialized skill, the bailor is compensating the bailee for "both his labor and his judgment. [The bailee] ought not to undertake the work, if he cannot succeed; and he should know whether he can or not."[135]

C. Elements of Bailment[136]

A bailor can sue the bailee for a breach of the bailment if the property (e.g., the animal) was damaged or not returned.[137] The bailor must first make a prima facie showing that the terms of the bailment were not met.[138] To make this showing, the bailor must establish that the animal was delivered to the bailee, that he demanded the return of the animal, and that the animal was either not returned or was returned in a damaged condition.[139] If the bailee had sole, actual, and physical possession of the animal, there is a presumption that the bailee was negligent, meaning that the court will assume that the bailee did not meet the requisite standard of care.[140]

D. Bailee's Defense[141]

The presumption of negligence is rebuttable, or vanishing. If the bailee produces a reason for the breach of the bailment, other than his failure to use a reasonable standard of care, the presumption that the bailee was negligent will be overcome and the burden of production will shift back to the bailor to prove the elements of negligence.[142] In some jurisdictions the presumption is rebuttable only if the bailee proves the actual cause of the injury or loss of the property.[143] It is important to note that the burden of proof of all facts relevant to the cause of action remains with the bailor at all times; the presumption merely shifts the burden of production to the bailee after the bailor makes a prima facie showing.[144] If the bailee fails to overcome the presumption, the bailor will be entitled to judgment as a matter of law.[145]

E. Bailment and Pets

Because of a pet's status as property, bailment is a possible and logical cause of action in cases of injury or death to the pet during entrustment to a groomer, boarding or breeding facility, or a veterinarian. It is important to note that the entrustment of animals to veterinarians may or may not constitute bailment, depending upon the jurisdiction.[146]

There is currently a split between the courts on whether to apply human medical malpractice principles to veterinary injury cases.[147] An Ohio court refused to apply a human medical malpractice cause of action in a case of injury to a horse by a veterinarian.[148] In *Southall v. Gabel*, the horse was injured during transport following surgery, not from the surgery itself.[149] The court found this distinction to be controlling, and held that the action is "based on negligence for the transporting rather than malpractice."[150] The court further stated that "the very essence of 'malpractice' is the patient-physician relationship."[151]

Veterinary physicians' training and education is, however, parallel to human physicians: undergraduate college, medical college, residency and clinical rotations, and finally receipt of the doctor of medicine title.[152] It is because of these similarities that many courts align their veterinary jurisprudence with human medical jurisprudence, adopting malpractice as a valid cause of action.[153] In *Williamson v. Prida*, a racehorse developed thrombosis after several weeks of receiving oxytetracycline injections, and the owners sued the veterinarian for malpractice.[154] As in medical malpractice cases, the California appellate court applied the rule that "a doctor must exercise the degree of skill or care usual in the profession, and will not be held liable for untoward consequences in the absence of a want of such reasonable care and skill."[155] In several other jurisdictions, the courts have also applied malpractice standards to veterinarians.[156]

On the other hand, a Pennsylvania court created a common law cause of action for veterinarian malpractice.[157] In *Price v. Brown*, an English bulldog died after surgery to correct a prolapsed urethra.[158] The court specifically refused to apply a bailment standard because the dog died as a result of the surgery.[159] The court instead held that "professional negligence concepts also extend to veterinary medicine."[160]

For plaintiffs, a claim based on bailment is a more attractive option than veterinarian malpractice because expert witnesses are not required. Both veterinarian malpractice and traditional negligence place the burden of proof on the plaintiff, making bailment a better option because there the burden of proof is on the defendant to explain what happened to the animal.[161]

The case of *David v. Lose*[162] is an example of the traditional application of the theory of bailment. The plaintiff delivered his mare to defendant's stable for breeding purposes and was charged a stud fee, thereby creating a bailment.[163] While in the defendant's stable, the mare suffered a broken leg.[164] The plaintiff sued the stable owner for breach of the bailment contract, due to the bailee's failure to return the mare in an undamaged condition.[165] Because the bailee could not show how the damage occurred, he had to affirmatively prove that he took reasonable precautions to prevent damage from occurring and that he had not acted unreasonably in any way.[166] The bailee failed to meet that burden and was found liable for breach of the bailment contract.[167]

F. Damages

For a discussion on damages see Chapter 9, "Remedies in Animal-Related Litigation."

APPENDIX A[168]

Sample Testamentary Animal Trust

ARTICLE [ ]
[*name of animal*] TRUST

A. Conditions of Creation

This trust is to be created upon the conditions stated in Article [ ].

B. Governing Law

This trust is to be governed by [*name of state*] law unless this Article provides to the contrary.

C. Trustees

I appoint [*primary trustee*] as the trustee of this trust. If [*primary trustee*] is unwilling or unable to serve, I appoint [*alternate trustee*] as trustee.

D. Bond

No bond shall be required of any trustee named in this Article.

E. Trustee Compensation

The trustee shall be entitled to reasonable compensation from the trust for serving as trustee.
[*or*]
No trustee shall be entitled to compensation for serving as trustee.

F. Beneficiaries of Trust

The beneficiaries are all of the companion animals owned by the testator at the time of the testator's death. If no such animals survive the testator, then no trust shall be created under this Article.

G. Proper Care

The trustee shall find a good caregiver for the animals.
[*or*]
I appoint [*name of Caregiver, name of alternate caregiver*]. The trustee shall visit [*Caregiver*]'s home at least [*monthly*] [*quarterly*] [*annually*] to make certain [*animal*] is receiving proper care. Proper care means [*description of care including, for example, requirement of regular visits to a veterinarian*]. If in the trustee's sole discretion [*animal*] is not receiving proper care as defined above, trustee shall immediately remove [*animal*] from the Caregiver's possession and deliver the animal to the alternate caregiver.

H. Distribution of Trust Property While [Animal] is Alive

1. Care of [Animal]

The trustee shall distribute [*amount*] to the caregiver each [*month*] [*year*] provided the Caregiver is taking proper care of [*animal*] as defined in Section G of this Article.
[*or*]

The trustee shall reimburse [*Caregiver*] for all reasonable expenses [*Caregiver*] incurs in the proper care of [*animal*] as defined in Section G of this Article. Reasonable expenses include, but are not limited to, [*food, housing, grooming, medical care, and burial or cremation fees.*]

[2. Caregiver Compensation]

The trustee [*shall*] [*may*] pay [*dollar amount*] to trustee on a [*monthly*] [*annual*] basis provided [*Caregiver*] is taking proper care of [*animal*] as defined in Section G of this Article.

[3. Liability Insurance]

The trustee [*shall*] [*may*] use trust property to purchase liability insurance to protect the trust, the trustee, and [*Caregiver*] from damage [*animal*] causes to property or persons.

[4. Offspring of [Animal]]

The trustee [*shall*] [*may*] [*shall not*] use trust property to reimburse [*Caregiver*] for expenses associated with any offspring of [*animal*].

[5. Excess Principal]

If a court determines that this trust contains excess property and orders the trustee to distribute that property other than as described above, then that excess shall be distributed under Subsection (I) as if this trust were terminating to [*name of remainder beneficiary*].

I. Termination of Trust

This trust terminates upon the death of [*the last to die of testator's animals*]. [*consider including how death of animal is to be proven, e.g., death certificate from a vet*] [*consider having trust also terminate when animal is deemed "lost"—require evidence to prove loss of pet, e.g., copies of police reports, ads in newspapers seeking the pet's return, copies of posters placed in the community*] [If the trust is created in one of the few states that has a 21-year limitation, then state:] This trust terminates upon the earlier of (1) the death of [the last to die of testator's animals] or (2) 21 years from the date of the creation of this trust.

J. Distribution of Property upon Trust Termination

Upon the termination of this trust all remaining trust property shall pass to [*remainder beneficiary*] if [*he*] [*she*] is alive at the time of trust termination, or to a charity [*if such charitable organization is in existence at the time of trust termination*]. If [*remainder beneficiary*] is not alive at the time of trust termination, all remaining trust property shall pass to [*alternate remainder beneficiary*] if [*he*] [*she*] is alive at the time of trust termination. [*continue in like manner for additional alternates*]

K. Principal and Income

The trustee shall have the discretion to credit a receipt or charge an expenditure to income or principal or partly to each in any manner which the trustee determines to be reasonable and equitable.

L. Trustee Powers

The trustee shall have all powers granted to trustees under [*name of state*] law.
[*or*]
The trustee shall have the following powers: [*enumerate trustee powers*]

M. Exculpatory Clause

The trustee shall not be liable for any loss, cost, damage, or expense sustained through any error of judgment or in any other manner except for and as a result of a trustee's own bad faith or gross negligence.

APPENDIX B

Sample Inter Vivos Animal Trust

Trust Agreement

The Settlor hereby gives all of [his/her] pets, and the sum of [AMOUNT OF CARETAKING FUNDS] to the Trustee of the [NAME OF TRUST] (the "Trust"), to be administered and distributed as follows:

A. *Trustee.* [NAME OF INITIAL TRUSTEE] shall serve as initial Trustee; but in the event that [NAME OF INITIAL TRUSTEE] is unable or unwilling to serve, [NAME OF SUCCESSOR TRUSTEE] shall serve as successor Trustee. In the event that both of the above-named parties are unable or unwilling to serve, the successor Trustee shall be appointed by [*consider listing a panel of persons consisting of a veterinarian and officers of a local animal rescue charity*], or if such panel is unable or unwilling to do so, by a court of competent jurisdiction. The Trustee may resign by providing 30 days' written notice thereof to the alternate trustee, or any other party appointed by the court to enforce this Trust. Except as otherwise provided herein, the Trustee shall have all the rights, powers, duties, and obligations of a trustee under applicable law.

B. *Caregiver*. [CAREGIVER] shall serve as initial CAREGIVER; but in the event that [CAREGIVER] is unable or unwilling to serve, [NAME OF SUCCESSOR CAREGIVER] shall serve as successor CAREGIVER. In the event that both of the above-named parties are unable or unwilling to serve, the Trustee shall name a CAREGIVER. Notwithstanding the foregoing, in no event shall the Trustee serve as CAREGIVER.

C. *Beneficiaries*. All of the companion animals owned by the settlor at any time during the existence of this trust are the beneficiaries of this trust. The settlor will maintain records describing each such animal and give such information to the trustee from time to time. Such description may include [*description of pet, identifying markings, tattoos, chips, or DNA records*].

D. *Standard of Care*. Proper care means [*description of care including, for example, requirement of regular visits to a veterinarian*].

E. *Trustee Powers and Duties*. The trustee shall have all powers granted to trustees under [NAME OF STATE] law. [*or*] The trustee shall have the following powers: [*enumerate trustee powers*]

1. *Inspection*. The trustee shall visit [CAREGIVER]'s home at least [*monthly*] [*quarterly*] [*annually*] to make certain the beneficiaries are receiving proper care. If in the trustee's sole discretion any one or more of the beneficiaries is not receiving proper care as defined above, trustee shall immediately remove such beneficiaries from the caregiver's possession and deliver the animals to the alternate caregiver.
2. *Liability Insurance*. The Trustee [*shall*] [*may*] use trust property to purchase liability insurance to protect the trust, the trustee, and [*caregiver*] from damage [*animal*] causes to property or persons.
3. *Health Insurance*. The Trustee [shall] [may] use trust property to purchase health insurance to protect the health of the beneficiaries.

4. *Accounting*. The Trustee [shall] [may] provide an accounting at least annually to the [CAREGIVER]. The accounting shall include the original or copies of all documents, receipts, vouchers, and exhibits necessary to substantiate all receipts and disbursements from the inception of the Trust through the date that the accounting is actually finalized.

F. *Expenditures and Distributions*. During the term of the Trust, the Trustee shall be entitled to expend such sums of net income, and if necessary, principal, as the Trustee determines to be necessary or advisable for the health, care, and welfare of the beneficiaries, including (but not limited to) food, veterinary care and/or insurance, toys and other recreational activities, and temporary boarding and/or pet-sitting fees. In exercising such discretion, it is intended that the Trustee will maintain the beneficiaries in the same standard of health, care, and welfare as the Settlor provided. The Trustee is also authorized to pay, or reimburse to the Trustee, any income taxes attributable to the Trust and other necessary expenses associated with the administration and distribution thereof. [OPTION: In addition to the foregoing, the Trustee is authorized to receive compensation in the amount of $______ per year.] [OPTION: In addition to the foregoing, the Trustee shall pay compensation to [CAREGIVER] in the amount of $______ per year.]

G. *Bond*. The Trustee shall obtain a surety bond in amount equal to the value of the Trust. The Trustee is to provide proof of the surety bond to the [CAREGIVER] upon request by the [CAREGIVER]. The Trustee shall utilize assets of the Trust to pay the premiums on the surety bond. [*or*] No bond shall be required of any trustee named in this Trust.

H. *Liability*. No Trustee hereunder shall be liable for any loss or depreciation in value of the properties of this Trust, except such loss as is attributable to gross negligence, a willful breach of trust or bad faith on the part of the Trustee, and no Trustee shall be accountable or held liable for any act or omission of any agent of the Trustee, if the Trustee has used good faith and ordinary care in the selection of such agent, and in such event, any liability shall be solely that of the agent. Any successor Trustee is relieved of any duty to examine the acts of any prior fiduciary, or to require an accounting therefrom, and shall be responsible only for those assets actually delivered to the Trustee.

I. *Termination and Final Distribution*. The Trust shall terminate upon the earlier of the following: (a) the net value of the Trust assets (other than the value of the beneficiaries) decreases to less than

$______; or (b) the death of the last to die of the beneficiaries. If termination of the Trust occurs because of the death of the last to die of the beneficiaries, the Trustee shall, at the expense of the Trust, provide for the respectful and proper disposition of the remains of the beneficiaries, pay any remaining debts and expenses of the Trust, and then distribute the remaining assets of the Trust to [NAME OF REMAINDER BENEFICIARY] provided, however, that if [NAME OF REMAINDER BENEFICIARY] does not then qualify as an organization exempt from federal income taxes under Section 501(c)(3) of the Internal Revenue Code, then the Trustee shall select an appropriate tax-exempt organization that provides for the care of similar pets to receive such distribution.

[*If the trust is created in one of the few states that has a 21-year limitation, then state:*] This trust terminates upon the earlier of (1) the death of the last to die of testator's animals or (2) 21 years from the date of the creation of this trust. If there are any beneficiaries alive at the time of termination, the Trustee shall distribute the remaining assets of the Trust to the Trustee, who shall hold such assets outright and free of trust, but conditioned on providing for the continued health, welfare, and care of the beneficiaries.

J. *Applicable Law.* This Trust is established by the Settlor and accepted by the Trustee under the laws of the State of [NAME OF STATE], and in particular, [CITATION TO PET TRUST STATUTE], and all questions concerning its validity and construction shall be determined under [NAME OF STATE] law, regardless of any change in the situs of the Trust.

APPENDIX C

Sample Bailment Complaint

PLAINTIFF'S ORIGINAL PETITION
TO THE HONORABLE COURT:

______________ [*Name*], plaintiff, complains of ___________ [*name*], defendant, and for cause of action shows:

I.

[Party Allegations, Plead the Parties]

II.

At all times mentioned defendant was in the business of __________ [*type of business, e.g., operating a boarding facility, veterinarian, groomer, sitter*], located at __________ [*address*].

III.

On or about ________ [*date*], plaintiff delivered ________ [*describe animal(s)*] to defendant's care at ___________ [*location of bailment, e.g., defendant's place of business*] pursuant to _____________ [*an oral or a written*] agreement specifying that ________________ [*terms of agreement, e.g., plaintiff would pay defendant $50 per day to board plaintiff's pet*]. [A copy of this agreement is attached as Exhibit A and incorporated by reference for all purposes.]

IV.

On __________ [*date*], the ___________ [*bailed item, e.g., pet*] was delivered to defendant in good condition [*add detail as necessary*].

V.

On __________ [*date*], plaintiff arrived at ______________ [*location of bailment, e.g., defendant's place of business*] to take possession of ______________ [*describe animal(s)*]. Defendant refused to deliver ____________ [*describe animal(s)*] to plaintiff.

VI.

Immediately prior to its delivery to defendant the ____________ [*describe animal(s)*] had a fair market value of $________, in ___________ County, ___________ [*state*].

WHEREFORE, plaintiff requests that defendant be cited to appear and answer, and that on final trial, plaintiff have:

1. Judgment against defendant for a sum within the jurisdictional limits of the Court.

2. Prejudgment interest and postjudgment interest as provided by law.
3. Costs of suit.
4. Such other and further relief to which plaintiff may be justly entitled.

Respectfully submitted,

____________________________ *firm name*
By: __________________________ *signature*
___________________________ *typed name*
______________________________ *address*
____________________________ *telephone*
____________________________ *facsimile*
__________________________ *state bar i.d.*
Attorney for __________________________

APPENDIX D

Sample Requests for Production to Defendant

REQUEST FOR PRODUCTION 1: Please produce any and all documents referring or relating to [*bailed item, e.g., pet*].

REQUEST FOR PRODUCTION 2: Please produce any and all documents referring or relating to Plaintiff between April 2009 and the present.

REQUEST FOR PRODUCTION 3: Please produce any and all documents referring or relating to any and all treatment [*bailed item, e.g., pet*] received at VETERINARY HOSPITAL between May 3, 2009, and May 7, 2009.

REQUEST FOR PRODUCTION 4: Please produce any and all documents referring or relating to any communication between You and Plaintiff from April 2009 to the present.

REQUEST FOR PRODUCTION 5: Please produce any and all documents referring or relating to any communication between You and any third party regarding [*bailed item, e.g., pet*] from April 2009 to the present.

APPENDIX E

Sample Interrogatories to Defendant

INTERROGATORY 1: Please identify, by stating the name, address, and telephone number, of each Person who treated [*bailed item, e.g., pet*] at VETERINARY HOSPITAL in [*date*].

INTERROGATORY 2: For each Person identified in Your response to Interrogatory No. 1, please state the date on that each Person treated [*bailed item, e.g., pet*] at VETERINARY HOSPITAL in [*date*].

INTERROGATORY 3: Please identify all diagnostic tests You performed on [*bailed item, e.g., pet*], or any of [*bailed item, e.g., pet*]'s bodily fluids between May 3, 2009, and May 5, 2009. For the purposes of this Interrogatory, the term "identify" shall mean to state the nature of the test performed, the date and time on which the test was performed, the result of the test performed, and the name of the Person who conducted the test.

INTERROGATORY 4: Please identify, by stating the name, address, and telephone number, each person who had contact with [*bailed item, e.g., pet*] at BOARDING FACILITY in [*date*].

INTERROGATORY 5: Please identify, by stating the name, address, and telephone number, each person who had dominion and control over [*bailed item, e.g., pet*] during the period of May 3, 2009, through May 7, 2009, while [*bailed item, e.g., pet*] was located at BOARDING FACILITY.

APPENDIX F

Sample Requests for Admissions to Defendant

REQUEST FOR ADMISSION 1: Please admit that [*bailed item, e.g., pet*] died while in Your custody and control on May 5, 2009.

REQUEST FOR ADMISSION 2: Please admit that on May 3, 2009, Plaintiff placed [*bailed item, e.g., pet*] in Your custody and control for treatment.

REQUEST FOR ADMISSION 3: Please admit that on May 4, 2009, You did not perform any blood tests on [*bailed item, e.g., pet*] to determine if he had any infections.

REQUEST FOR ADMISSION 4: Please admit that the original of the post-operative instructions attached hereto as Exhibit A is genuine.

REQUEST FOR ADMISSION 5: Please admit that on May 5, 2009, You knew [*bailed item, e.g., pet*] was Plaintiff's dog and that Plaintiff claimed ownership of and title to [*bailed item, e.g., pet*].

REQUEST FOR ADMISSION 6: Please admit that You lost custody and control of [*bailed item, e.g., pet*] between May 3, 2009, and May 7, 2009.

APPENDIX G

Sample Questions for Plaintiff's Expert Deposition

Q: Have you reviewed the relevant medical records in this matter?

Q: And what can you tell me on the issues of causation?

Q: So you have a pretty good picture in time of what was going on?

Q: Is the declaration of [*date*] a true and accurate compilation of your opinions in this case?

Q: You executed the declaration under penalty of perjury, correct?

Q: In paragraph 1 you identified that you were retained to determine if the defendants met the recognized standard of care for veterinary treatment in [*state*]; is that correct?

Q: And whether the failure to meet the standard of care may have caused or contributed to [*name of dog*]'s death; is that true?

Q: And in your various veterinary practices here in [*state*], [*Doctor's name*], have you performed [*identify treatment*]?

Q: Turning your attention to paragraph 6 of your declaration, you indicated in the last paragraph—last sentence of paragraph 6, "By failing to run a presurgical blood panel and urinalysis, [*Doctor's name*] did not meet the standard of care." Do you read that there?

Q: Was there any resultant consequence of failing to run presurgical blood panel or urinalysis?

Q: Is the degree of skill required to perform a [*identify treatment*] on a dog more or less involved than performing a surgical procedure, say, to do a [*identify treatment*]?

Q: Have you observed in the course of practicing in [*state*] as a veterinarian that training is being offered on the job in [*identify treatment*]?

Q: And has that training been offered to unlicensed veterinary technicians, in your observations?

Q: In paragraph 8 you speak about the drugs—"drugs or medications that are prescribed by unqualified personnel may cause injury or death to an animal patient." Were there any drugs or medicines prescribed by unqualified personnel in this case?

Q: Do you have any opinions in this case that drugs or medicines prescribed by unqualified personnel injured [*name of dog*]?

Q: "By allowing an unregistered lay assistant to prescribe drugs used in anesthesia for [*name of dog*], [*Doctor's name*] did not meet the standard of care." What are the specific facts that you are aware of that an unregistered lay assistant prescribed drugs used in anesthesia for [*name of dog*]?

Q: Was there injury to [*name of dog*] from allowing an unregistered lay assistant to prescribe drugs used in anesthesia?

Q: When you use the terms "drug miscalculation" or "technical error," are you referring specifically to the administration of drugs?

Q: And is it your opinion that [*name of dog*] was injured by a drug miscalculation or technical error in the administration of drugs?

Q: Is it medically probable that [*name of dog*] was injured by a drug miscalculation or a technical error made in the administration of drugs?

Q: Is a medical possibility, in the abstract, in your opinion, less likely than a medical probability?

Q: But you are not willing to use the term "within a reasonable medical probability"?

Q: What is it that makes it possibly likely that there was a drug miscalculation or technical error in the administration of a drug used in anesthesia for [*name of dog*]?

Q: Is it your opinion that [*name of dog*] was in a shock situation?

Q: When did the shock situation first manifest itself?

Q: And what is the basis for your adoption of the opinion that [*name of dog*] was in a shock situation?

Q: When did the first evidence of a shock situation manifest in [*name of dog*]?

Q: How much time elapsed between the dog's collapse and the emergency physician's notes?

Q: What medicine or medicines trigger the shocklike symptoms that you have identified?

Q: Did [*name of dog*] have aspiration pneumonia?

Q: Is that something that normally you would be able to find on a necropsy report?

Q: Based upon your review of the necropsy report and the inflammatory response, can you conclude to a medical probability that [*name of dog*] had aspiration pneumonia?

Q: Is it your opinion that [*name of dog*] had aspiration pneumonia?

Q: Would the signs consistent with aspiration pneumonia be attributable to other conditions as well?

Q: What other conditions?

Q: When would you expect a reaction in an animal after the administration of anesthesia, if indeed, during the course of the administration of anesthesia, water, dental debris, or bacteria were introduced and allowed to fill [*name of dog*]'s lungs?

Q: What would be the soonest time you would expect a manifestation of symptoms?

Q: What would account for the difference in time between a few minutes and several hours?

Q: You have a few minutes as the earliest you would find it. What would be the outside end of that?

Notes

1. Katie J. L. Scott, *Bailment and Veterinary Malpractice: Doctrine Exclusivity, or Not?*, 55 Hastings L. J. 1009 (March, 2004).
2. Boulder, Colo. (July 12, 2000); Berkeley, Cal. (Feb. 27, 2001), BMC Chapter 10; West Hollywood, Cal. (Feb. 19, 2001); Rhode Island (July 5, 2001), R.I. Stat. § 4-1-1-39; Sherwood, Ark. (Sept. 24, 2001); Menomonee Falls, Wis. (Mar. 11, 2002); Amherst, Mass. (Apr. 24, 2002); Woodstock, N.Y. (2003), Art. II § 14-6; San Francisco, Cal. (Jan. 13, 2003); Marin County, Cal. (all 28 cities) (Dec., 2003); Sebastopol, Cal. (Dec. 2003); Wanaque, N.J. (May 10, 2004); Albany, Cal. (June 7, 2004); St. Louis, Mo. (Aug. 9, 2004); Bloomington, Ind. (Dec. 21, 2005); Santa Clara County, Cal. (Apr. 25, 2006), Title B, Div. B-31-1; and Imperial Beach, Cal. (July 19, 2006).
3. Doran v. Hibernia Sav. & Loan Soc'y, 80 Cal. App. 2d 790, 793, 182 P.2d 630, 631 (1st Dist. 1947).
4. *See, e.g.*, Vos v. Farm Bureau Life Ins. Co., 667 N.W.2d 36 (Iowa 2003); *In re Estate of Karmey*, 468 Mich. 68, 658 N.W.2d 796 (Mich. 2003); Van Noy v. State Farm Mut. Auto. Ins. Co., 142 Wash. 2d 784, 16 P.3d 574 (Wash. 2001); Matlock v. Simpson, 902 S.W.2d 384 (Tenn. 1995); People v. Rhodus, 870 P.2d 470 (Colo. 1994).
5. *See, e.g.*, Shoen v. SAC Holding Corp., 137 P.3d 1171 (Nev. 2006); Zastrow v. Journal Commc'ns, Inc., 291 Wis. 2d 426, 718 N.W.2d 51, 38 Empl.

Benefits Cas. 2843, 2006 WI 72 (Wis. 2006); Sherwood v. Danbury Hosp., 278 Conn. 163, 896 A.2d 777 (Conn. 2006); Hodges v. Callaway, 279 Ga. 789, 621 S.E.2d 428, 05 FCDR 3202 (Ga. 2005).

6. *See, e.g.*, *In re Okla. Unif. Jury Instructions for Juvenile Cases*, 116 P.3d 119, 2005 OK 12 (Okla. 2005); Hoverson v. Hoverson, 216 Minn. 237, 12 N.W.2d 497 (Minn. 1943).
7. *In re Guardianship of Lloyd*, 8 Ohio App. 2d 223, 32 Ohio Op. 2d 128, 197 N.E.2d 377 (8th Dist. Cuyahoga County 1964); *In re Reid's Estate*, 1956 OK 64, 294 P.2d 544 (Okla. 1956).
8. *In re Estate of Davis*, 758 S.W.2d 461 (Mo. Ct. App. W.D. 1988).
9. 264 A.D.2d 340, 341 (N.Y. Sup. Ct. 1st Div. 1999).
10. Jane Porter, *Custody Battles over Pets Look Like a Dogfight*, HARTFORD COURANT, Oct. 1, 2006.
11. 655 So. 2d 109 (Fla. App. 1 Dist. Jan. 19, 1995).
12. *Id.* at 110–11.
13. Arrington v. Arrington, 613 S.W.2d 565 (Tex. Civ. App. Fort Worth 1981, no writ).
14. *Id.* at 569.
15. *Id.*
16. *See, e.g.*, Montoya v. Montoya, 280 Conn. 605, 909 A.2d 947 (Conn. 2006); Gamache v. Smurro, 904 A.2d 91, 2006 VT 67 (Vt. 2006); Jangula v. Jangula, 706 N.W.2d 85, 2005 ND 203 (N.D. 2005); Lashkajani v. Lashkajani, 911 So. 2d 1154, 30 Fla. L. Weekly S496 (Fla. 2005); Stoner v. Stoner, 572 Pa. 665, 819 A.2d 529 (Pa. 2003).
17. Lee Borden, Visitation with Pets After Divorce (2007), *available at* http://divorceinfo.com/petvisitation.htm.
18. *Id.*
19. *Id.*
20. *Id.*
21. *Id.*
22. *Id.*
23. *See* Bennett v. Bennett, 655 So. 2d 109 (Fla. App. 1 Dist. 1995) note 23 (28).
24. Morgan v. Kroupa, 167 Vt. 99, 702 A.2d 630 (1997).
25. *Id.*
26. *Id.*
27. *Id.*
28. *Id.*
29. *Id.*
30. *Id.*
31. *Id.*
32. *Id.*
33. *Id.*
34. Rebecca F. Wisch, *Summary of State Lost Property Statutes*, MICH. ST. U.C.L. (2006), *available at* http://www.animallaw.info/articles/ovuslost

dogpropertystatutes.htm (citing CAL. CIV. CODE §§ 2080–2082 (Lost and Unclaimed Property); CONN. GEN. STAT. § 50-1-14 (Lost and Unclaimed Property); FLA. STAT. § 705.101–19 (Lost or Abandoned Property); 765 ILL. COMP. STAT. 1020/0.01–36 (Estrays and Lost Property Act); IOWA CODE § 556F.1 (Lost Property); ME. REV. STAT. tit. 33, §§ 1051–1060 (Lost Goods and Stray Beasts); MASS. GEN. LAWS ch. 134, §§ 1–7 (Lost Goods and Stray Beasts); MICH. COMP. LAWS § 434.21–29 (Lost Property); MO. REV. STAT. § 447.010–721 (Lost and Unclaimed Property); MONT. CODE ANN. § 70-5-101–107 (Rights and Duties of Finders Generally); N.Y. PERS. PROP. LAW §§ 251–258 (Lost and Found Property); N. D. CENT. CODE § 60-01-34–42 (Deposits—General Provisions); OKLA. STAT. ANN. §§ 511–518 (Finders of Lost Goods.); OR. REV. STAT. § 98.005–.040 (Lost, Unordered and Unclaimed Property); S. D. CODIFIED LAWS § 43-41-1–10 (Lost and Found Property); VT. STAT. ANN. tit. 27, §§ 1101–1110 (Lost Property); WASH. REV. CODE § 63.21.010–900 (Lost and Found Property); WIS. STAT. § 170.01–12 (Strays and Lost Chattels)).

35. *Id.*
36. *Id.* (citing N.Y. Pers. Prop. Law §§ 251–258; S. D. CODIFIED LAWS 43-41-1–10).
37. *Id.*
38. HAW. REV. STAT. § 143-10.
39. *Id.*
40. *Id.*
41. *Id.*
42. *Id.*
43. MASS. GEN. LAWS ch. 134, §§ 1–7.
44. MASS. GEN. LAWS ch. 134, § 2.
45. MASS. GEN. LAWS ch. 134, § 3.
46. WIS. STAT. § 170.02.
47. *Id.*
48. *Id.*
49. *Id.*
50. Rebecca J. Huss, *Separation, Custody and Estate Planning Issues Related to Companion Animals*, 74 U. COLO. L. REV. 181, 206 (2003).
51. Long v. Noah's Lost Ark, Inc., 814 N.E.2d 555 (7th Dist. Mahoning County 2004).
52. *Id.*
53. Patricia A. Bolen, *Lost and Found: Human Societies' Rights and Obligations Regarding Companion Animal Ownership*, MICH. ST. U.C.L. (2005), *available at* http://www.animallaw.info/articles/dduspetadoption.htm.
54. *Id.*
55. *Id.*
56. *Id.*
57. *Id.*

58. *Id.*
59. *Id.*
60. Patrick Johnson, *Lost in Katrina and in New Homes—Whose Pet Now*, CHRISTIAN SCI. MONITOR, July 21, 2006, *available at* http://www.csmonitor.com/2006/0721/p01s03-ussc.html.
61. *Id.*
62. *Id.*
63. *Id.*
64. Huss, *Separation, Custody and Estate Planning*, *supra* note 50, at 210.
65. *Id.* (citing Porter v. DiBlasio, 93 F.3d 301, 307 (7th Cir. 1996) (holding Wisconsin must provide an animal owner notice and an opportunity for a hearing prior to permanently terminating a person's interest in a seized animal)); *see also* Phillips v. San Luis Obispo County Dep't Regulation, 183 Cal. App. 3d 372, 376, 228 Cal. Rptr. 101 (2d Dist. 1986) (due process requires dog owners have an opportunity to be heard prior to the destruction of the dog, unless a need for prompt government action exists).
66. *Id.*
67. *Id.*
68. Hardy v. Robinson, 170 S.W.3d 777, 780 (Tex. App. Waco 2005, no pet.); D.D.B. Interior Contracting Inc. v. Trends Urban Renewal Ass'n, Ltd., 176 N.J. 164, 821 A.2d 1135 (N.J., May 12, 2003).
69. GERRY W. BEYER, ESTATE PLANNING FOR NON-HUMAN FAMILY MEMBERS (2008), http://www.professorbeyer.com/Articles/Pet_Trusts_01-14-2008.pdf [hereinafter BEYER, ESTATE PLANNING].
70. *Id.*
71. *Id.* (citing *See Providing for Your Pet's Future Without You*, 69 TEX. B.J. 1025 (2006)).
72. BEYER, ESTATE PLANNING, *supra* note 69.
73. *Id.*
74. *Id.* citing (*In re Andrews's Will*, 228 N.Y.S.2d 591, 594 (Sup. Ct. 1962) (holding that the beneficiary received the legacy even though the pet died before the testator because the condition was subsequent)).
75. *See* Appendix F.
76. BEYER, ESTATE PLANNING, *supra* note 69, (citing UNIF. PROB. CODE § 2-907, cmt. (1990)).
77. *Id.*
78. *Id.*
79. *Id.* (citing UNIF. TRUST CODE § 408 (2000)).
80. *Id.*
81. *Id.*
82. *Id.*
83. *Id.*
84. Portions of this section are reprinted by permission from BEYER, ESTATE PLANNING, *supra* note 69.

85. *Id.*
86. *Id.*
87. Torri Still, *This Attorney Is for the Birds*, RECORDER (San Francisco), Mar. 22, 1999, at 4.
88. Frances Carlisle & Paul Franken, *Drafting Trusts for Animals*, N.Y.L.J., Nov. 13, 1997, at 1.
89. Portions of this section are reprinted by permission from BEYER, ESTATE PLANNING, *supra* note 69.
90. 412 P.2d 710, 710–11 (Ariz. 1966).
91. This section is reprinted with permission from BEYER, ESTATE PLANNING, *supra* note 69.
92. *See* Jason Hulott, *The Importance of Pet Insurance*, EZINEARTICLES.COM, July 4, 2007, *available at* http://ezinearticles.com/?The-Importance-Of-Pet-Insurance&id=631776.
93. This section is reprinted with permission from BEYER, ESTATE PLANNING, *supra* note 69.
94. *See* Estate Planning for Pets, How Long Will My Pet Live?, http://estateplanningforpets.org/faq2.htm (sets out the life expectances for various breeds of dogs, cats, parrots, reptiles, amphibians, rodents, and some exotics).
95. *See generally* 2 AUSTIN WALKMAN SCOTT & WILLIAM FRANKLIN FRATCHER, THE LAW OF TRUSTS § 124.3, at 244 (4th ed. 1987) (concluding that even though there is no direct benefit to a living person, "it would seem that there is nothing rising to the dignity of public policy to prevent the carrying out of the [pet owner's] purpose"); Edward C. Halbach, Jr., *The 1999 Joseph Trachtman Lecture—Uniform Acts, Restatements and Other Trends in American Trust Law at Century's End*, 25 ACTEC Notes 101, 107 (1999) (discussing trust purposes that are contrary to public policy without mentioning trusts for the care of specific animals).
96. *See, e.g.*, *In re Templeton Estate*, 4 Pa. Fiduc. Rep. 2d 172, 175 (Orphans' Ct. 1984) (applying "inherent power to reduce the amount involved . . . to an amount which is sufficient to accomplish [the owner's] purpose"); *In re Lyon Estate*, 67 Pa. D. & C.2d 474, 482–83 (C.P. Orphans' Ct. 1974) (reducing the amount left for the animal's care based on the supposition that the owner mistook how much money would be needed to care for the animals); *see also* UNIF. PROB. CODE § 2-907(c)(6) (1993) (authorizing the court to reduce amount if it "substantially exceeds the amount required" to care for the animal).
97. This section is reprinted with permission from BEYER, ESTATE PLANNING, *supra* note 69.
98. *Id.*
99. G. BOGERT & G. BOGERT, LAW OF TRUSTS AND TRUSTEES, § 542, at 187 (1993).
100. *Id.*

101. *Id.*
102. *The Last Laugh—Wills With a Sense of Humor*, Fam. Advoc., Summer 1981, at 60, 62.
103. This section is reprinted with permission from Beyer, Estate Planning, *supra* note 69.
104. *See* Willett v. Willett, 247 S.W. 739, 741 (Ky. 1923) (noting that the pet owner neglected to provide for the distribution of the remaining trust property upon the pet's death and thus the property would pass through intestate succession).
105. Carlisle & Franken, *supra* note 88.
106. *Id.*
107. 34 Pa. D. & C.2d 121, 15 Pa. Fiduc. Rep. 150 (Orphans' Ct. 1964).
108. *Id.* at 122.
109. *Id.*
110. *Id.* at 125.
111. *Id.*
112. *Id.* at 126.
113. *Id.*
114. *Id.* at 129–30.
115. *Id.* at 130.
116. *Id.* at 133.
117. *Id.*
118. *Id.*
119. William Blackstone, 2 Commentaries on the Laws of England 452 (1st ed. 1765–69).
120. Armistead M. Dobie, Handbook on the Law of Bailments and Carriers § 1, at 2 (1914).
121. *Id.*
122. *Id.* § 9, at 20.
123. A. Darby Dickerson, *Bailor Beware: Limitations and Exclusions of Liability in Commercial Bailments*, 41 Vand. L. Rev. 130 (1988).
124. *Id.*
125. This section is reprinted from Katie J. L. Scott, *Bailment and Veterinary Malpractice: Doctrine Exclusivity, or Not?*, 55 Hastings L.J. 1009 (March, 2004) [hereinafter Scott, *Bailment and Veterinary Malpractice*], by permission of Katie J. L. Scott and the University of California, Hastings College of Law.
126. Edwin C. Goddard, Outlines of the Law of Bailments and Carriers § 12, at 5 (1904) (bailments were first divided into categories in Roman law, and those divisions heavily influenced English legal writers).
127. 8A Am. Jur. 2d *Bailments* § 7 (1997). Justice Story was first to divide bailments into these three categories in his treatise, *Commentaries on Bailments*. See Goddard, *supra* note 126, § 12, at 5 (citing Joseph Story, Commentaries on Bailments (1832)).
128. 8A Am. Jur. 2d *Bailments* § 7.

129. *Id.*
130. This subcategory of mutually beneficial bailments is also called "hired services about a thing" or "locatio operis faciendi." *See* Dobie, *supra* note 120, § 58, at 129.
131. *Id.*
132. Joseph Story, Commentaries on the Law of Bailments with Illustrations from the Civil and the Foreign Law § 23, at 27 (James Schouler rev. corrected enlarged, Little, Brown, and Co., 9th ed. 1878) (1836).
133. Goddard, *supra* note 126, § 16, at 9.
134. Story, *supra* note 132, § 431, at 392.
135. *Id.* at 393.
136. This section is reprinted with permission from Scott, *Bailment and Veterinary Malpractice*, *supra* note 125.
137. 8A Am. Jur. 2d *Bailments* § 240 (1997).
138. *Id.* § 244.
139. *See, e.g.*, Inter-Ocean (Free Zone), Inc. v. Manaure Lines, Inc. "Manana V," 615 F. Supp. 710, 716 (S.D. Fla. 1985); Price v. Brown, 680 A.2d 1149, 1152 (Pa. 1996); Sky Aviation Corp. v. Colt, 475 P.2d 301, 304 (Wyo. 1970).
140. 8A Am. Jur. 2d *Bailments* § 233.
141. This section is reprinted with permission from Scott, *Bailment and Veterinary Malpractice*, *supra* note 125.
142. *See, e.g.*, Leake & Nelson Co. v. W. J. Megin, Inc., 111 A.2d 559, 560–61 (Conn. 1955); Vece v. Vanacore, 198 A.2d 728, 730–31 (Conn. Cir. Ct. 1963); Value Rent-A-Car, Inc. v. Collection Chevrolet, Inc., 570 So. 2d 1376, 1377–78 (Fla. Dist. Ct. App. 1990).
143. 8A Am. Jur. 2d *Bailments* § 234.
144. *Id.* § 244.
145. Alamo Airways, Inc. v. Benum, 374 P.2d 684, 686 (Nev. 1962); Sky Aviation, 475 P.2d at 304.
146. *See, e.g.*, Price v. Brown, 680 A.2d 1149, 1154 (Pa. 1996).
147. Kim Eileen Bell, *Nelson v. State Board of Veterinary Medicine: The Commonwealth Court Carves a Sharper Definition of Veterinary Malpractice*, 16 Widener L.J. 473 (2007), *available at* http://www.animallaw.info/articles/arus16widenerlj473.htm.
148. Southall v. Gabel, 277 N.E.2d 230 (Ohio Ct. App. 1971).
149. *Id.*
150. *Id.* at 233.
151. *Id.* at 232.
152. Bell, *supra* note 147.
153. *Id.*
154. 89 Cal. Rptr. 2d 868 (1999).
155. *Id.* at 1424–25.
156. Bell, *supra* note 147 (citing McGee v. Smith, 102 S.W.3d 725 (Tex. App. Fort Worth 2003, no pet.); McAdams v. Cunayn, 2006 WL 2623324, (96 Ark. App. 118); Phillips v. Baus, 2007 WL 1976219, (Conn. Super. May 24,

2007); Spilotro v. Hugi, 417 N.E.2d 1066 (1981); Ullman v. Duffus, 2005 WL 3047433, (Ohio App. 10 Dist. Nov. 15, 2005)).

157. Price v. Brown, 680 A.2d 1149, 1154 (Pa. 1996).
158. *Id.*
159. *Id.*
160. *Id.* at 222.
161. *See, e.g.*, Price v. Brown, 680 A.2d 1149, 1154 (Pa. 1996).
162. 7 Ohio St. 2d 97, 36 Ohio Op. 2d 81, 218 N.E.2d 442, 444 (1966).
163. *Id.*
164. *Id.*
165. *Id.*
166. *Id.* at 445.
167. *Id.*
168. This section is reprinted with permission from BEYER, ESTATE PLANNING, *supra* note 69.

CHAPTER 4

Veterinary Malpractice

GREGORY M. DENNIS

I. Overview

A. Veterinary Law—Generally

In recent years with expanding interest in what is generally referred to as "animal law," and an increasing number of law schools offering such courses,[1] there has been corresponding expansion in what is the legal responsibility of veterinarians toward their clients and patients. Further, what establishes a violation of those responsibilities; when may a veterinarian be sued for malpractice; and what damages might be recoverable if a veterinarian has committed malpractice?

B. Brief History of Veterinary Malpractice Law

Veterinary malpractice lawsuits, or what now would be recognized as such, are neither a recent phenomenon nor confined to the last few decades. In American law, references to veterinary (farrier[2]) malpractice lawsuits can be detected as early as 1809.[3] Justice Oliver Wendell Holmes Jr., in his massive work *The Common Law* (1881),[4] refers to *Marshall's Case* from England in 1441,[5] an action against a farrier who so negligently treated and carelessly applied medicines that a horse died.[6] Other early American cases involving or referring to veterinary (farrier) malpractice actions can be found in Alabama,[7] Hawaii,[8] Indiana,[9] Iowa,[10] Massachusetts,[11] Maine,[12] Nebraska,[13] New York,[14] Ohio,[15] Pennsylvania,[16] and Wisconsin.[17]

C. Veterinarian-Client-Patient Relationship

The starting point for any consideration or defense in a veterinary malpractice lawsuit is the "veterinarian-client-patient relationship"[18] (VCPR), which virtually all states have fully or substantially adopted either by statute or regulation and which federal agencies also have adopted or adhere to.

Unlike the professional relationship in human medicine, which is bipartite (doctor and human patient), in veterinary medicine the professional relationship is *tri*partite (veterinarian, animal patient, and human client).

A common statutory and regulatory definition of the VCPR is as follows:

> (1) The veterinarian has assumed the responsibility for making medical judgments regarding the health of the animal or animals and the need for medical treatment, and the client, owner, or other caretaker has agreed to follow the instruction of the veterinarian;
>
> (2) there is sufficient knowledge of the animal or animals by the veterinarian to initiate at least a general or preliminary diagnosis of the medical condition of the animal or animals. This means that the veterinarian has recently seen [and] [or[19]] is personally acquainted with the keeping and care of the animal or animals by virtue of an examination of the animal or animals, or by medically appropriate and timely visits to the premises where the animal or animals are kept, or both; and
>
> (3) the practicing veterinarian is readily available for follow-up in case of adverse reactions or failure of the regimen of therapy.[20]

Attorneys bringing or defending a veterinary malpractice action should identify how the state in which the lawsuit is brought defines the veterinarian-client-patient relationship, for if the parameters of a VCPR are not present, then a professional malpractice action might not exist against a particular veterinarian or some nonprofessional malpractice claim might be involved.

II. Types of Claims Asserted against Veterinarians

In actions arising from injury to or death of an animal, besides professional malpractice claims,[21] veterinarians have also been sued for ordinary negligence,[22] negligence *per se*,[23] breach of contract (written and oral), breach of fiduciary duty, bailment,[24] conversion,[25] trespass to chattel, products liability, breach of express warranties, breach of implied warranties,[26] violation of consumer protection laws, intentional misrepresentation or fraud, negligent misrepresentation, intentional or negligent infliction of emotional distress, outrage, violation of civil rights under 42 U.S.C. § 1983,[27] and others.[28] This chapter, however, will principally focus on professional malpractice actions against veterinarians: "veterinary malpractice."

A. Legal Standard of Care Applicable to Other Professionals Also Applies to Veterinarians

As one American court has noted, "veterinary" means "relating to, or constituting a branch of science and art dealing with the prevention, cure or alleviation of disease in animals."[29] More extensive and encompassing definitions of "veterinary medicine" or the "practice of veterinary medicine" is found in each state's veterinary practice act.[30]

Those states that have considered if veterinarians should be subject to the same standard of care as human medical professionals have held they should be.[31] Some courts have concluded that veterinary and medical malpractice standards of care are indistinguishable.[32]

Indicative of applying human medical professional standards of care to veterinarians is *Price v. Brown*,[33] where the Pennsylvania Supreme Court said:

> As to a cause of action based on the negligence of a veterinarian in the performance of his/her professional duties or services, we note at the outset that malpractice claims have traditionally arisen in the context of services provided by the legal and medical professions. Similar to the practice of law or medicine, the vocation of veterinary medicine involves specialized education, knowledge, and skills. We conclude, therefore, that professional negligence concepts also extend to veterinary medicine.[34]

In *Pruitt v. Box*,[35] a Texas court of appeals questioned, but did not disagree with, another Texas court of appeals' decision[36] that had applied the human malpractice standards to veterinary medicine actions:

> We are not convinced that the standard applicable to medical malpractice on human beings should be applied to veterinary malpractice cases in light of Texas law relegating animals to personal property status [*e.g.*, Tex. Prop. Code Ann. § 42.002(a)(10)(A), 42.002(a)(11)]. Generally, a claim of professional malpractice

is based in negligence [*e.g., Cosgrove v. Grimes*, 774 S.W.2d 662, 664 (Tex. 1989)]. The elements of a cause of action for negligence are well established. They are: (1) a legal duty owed by one person to another; (2) a breach of that duty; (3) the breach was an actual cause of injury; and (4) actual injury [*e.g., Colvin v. Red Steel Co.*, 682 S.W.2d 243, 245 (Tex. 1984)]. Accordingly, the more appropriate standard [for veterinary malpractice] may be, as in other professional malpractice cases where money or personal property is at stake, a general negligence standard utilizing a standard of care applicable to a professional of ordinary skill and care in similar communities. At least one other jurisdiction has applied this standard to veterinary malpractice cases [*e.g., Williams v. Reynolds*, 45 N.C. App. 655, 263 S.E.2d 853 (1980)]. For the purposes of our disposition of this case, however, we need not decide which standard to apply because we find that the issue of causation is dispositive and would be so under either the causation standard articulated for medical malpractice cases, or under the general "but for" or "actual" causation associated with general negligence.[37]

B. Required Elements for Veterinary Malpractice

Generally, to make a prima facie case of veterinary malpractice, the plaintiff must establish

1. The *existence of a legal duty* to be performed by the defendant-veterinarian in favor of the plaintiff client;
2. A breach or *violation of the legal duty* by the veterinarian;
3. That the breach or *violation* of the legal duty *caused* the animal's injury or death;[38] and
4. That the plaintiff sustained or incurred *damages* as a result of the defendant-veterinarian's breach of the legal duty it owed to the plaintiff-client.[39]

Alternatively stated, the plaintiff must establish

1. The act or omission of the veterinarian that failed to meet the requisite veterinary medical standard of care;
2. That the veterinarian's act or omission was *performed negligently*;
3. That the veterinarian's negligently performed act or omission *caused* the plaintiff-client's injuries; and
4. That as a *result* thereof, the plaintiff was *damaged*.[40]

The burden of proof to establish these elements is on the plaintiff.[41]

Even if a veterinarian committed malpractice, there can be no recovery if the animal owner has not sustained any damages.[42] Finally, a veterinarian is not excused from having committed malpractice by the fact that he or she performed the services for free.[43]

1. *Negligence on the Veterinarian's Part Is* Not *Presumed*

Mere proof that a veterinarian made a mistake is not sufficient in and of itself to establish veterinary malpractice.[44] In other words, negligence on the part of a veterinarian is never presumed, and may not be inferred merely from a lack of success or an adverse result from treatment.[45]

2. *Veterinarians Have a Wide Range of Discretion in Exercising Veterinary Medical Judgments*

Veterinarians enjoy a wide range of discretion in exercising veterinary medical judgments, and they cannot be found negligent unless it is shown that their course of treatment was clearly contrary to treatments generally recognized as correct by the veterinary profession. Reflective of this is the following utterance of the Alabama Supreme Court in *Turner v. Benhart*,[46] whereby the court held that the fact that the veterinarian had treated a horse by other than the preferred method, where there was more than one treatment method possible, did not mean the veterinarian had committed malpractice:

> The law does not require a veterinarian to be infallible in his treatment of an animal. This Court has recently reaffirmed the "medical judgment rule," the principle that a physician is not liable for malpractice when he chooses a recognized method of treatment, even though other experts testify that they would have chosen an alternative method of treatment.[47]

Proceeding:

> [The plaintiff's veterinary expert witness] testified that the most preferred method of administering a bicarbonate of soda solution is through an intravenous solution and that the next most preferred method would be nasogastric[[48]], or a tube to the stomach. [The plaintiff's expert also] testified that he did not believe that he would use the method utilized by [the defendant veterinarian] because the horse had received sedatives and was lying down. This testimony does not state that the actions taken by

> [the defendant veterinarian] were not recognized and accepted practices in the veterinary profession, or that the actions fell below the appropriate standard of care [for a veterinarian]. [The plaintiff's expert] merely testified that he did not believe that he would have taken such action.[49]

Concluding:

> None of the plaintiff's experts expressly stated that the actions taken by [the defendant veterinarian] fell below the standard of care owed by the defendant [veterinarian] under the circumstances.[50]

C. Standing to Maintain a Veterinary Malpractice Action

A person or entity that owns an animal has standing[51] to bring and maintain a malpractice suit against a veterinarian.[52] Also, a person or entity who holds an economic interest in an animal might have standing to assert a claim.[53] Without a statutory enactment, an animal, either directly or through a guardian, cannot maintain such a suit or be a coplaintiff.[54] Finally, with most states now recognizing pet trusts, a question might arise as to whether the individual or the trust is the "owner" to sue for malpractice.[55]

D. Comparative Fault and Contributory Negligence

Like other negligence actions, a possible question or defense in a veterinary malpractice action is whether the plaintiff has comparative fault or contributory negligence. There are some appellate decisions that have considered this.

Mazella v. Fairfield Equine Associates, P.C.,[56] was a personal injury lawsuit alleging that the veterinarian had failed to diagnose that a riding horse was suffering from equine protozoal myeloencephalitis[57] (EPM) and failed to warn of the danger of the horse collapsing if ridden. While being ridden by the plaintiff, the horse's hindquarters gave way and the horse collapsed on the plaintiff. As a result, the plaintiff suffered serious and permanent injuries.

The veterinarian moved for summary judgment, contending he had no duty to warn the plaintiff of dangers associated with riding horses as she was a horse trainer and riding instructor already knowledgeable of such dangers. The trial court denied summary judgment by noting that

> the heightened risk of injury due to undetected disabling disease in a riding horse is not within "those commonly appreciated

> risks which are inherent in and arise out of the sport generally and flow from such participation" [citation omitted]. Clearly [the plaintiff], a professional in the field, was acutely aware of the inherent risks. A jury may find she was unaware of the additional risk of collapse due to EPM, and that [the veterinarian], having superior knowledge, did in fact have a duty to warn.[58]

Further:

> That [the plaintiff] was an experienced horsewoman does not absolve [the veterinarian], with his superior professional knowledge, of his responsibility to provide reasonable veterinary care, to detect EPM, if indeed it was present, and warn her of this enhanced and extraordinary risk of injury.[59]

Though denying the veterinarian summary judgment, the court ruled the veterinarian would be permitted to show at trial that the plaintiff had contributory negligence for her injuries.[60]

Anderson v. Blackfoot Livestock Commission[61] was a negligence action against a livestock company from which a hog owner had purchased animals and a private veterinarian who inspected animals at the facility before they were placed for sale. The plaintiff had bought hogs and had placed them in a pen with other hogs he owned. A few days later, his animals started to become ill and several died. The animals were diagnosed with hog cholera. The plaintiff sued, and prevailed at trial, asserting the defendants either failed to administer a hog serum inoculation to some of the sold hogs or they improperly inoculated them with the result that the herd became infected with hog cholera. At trial, the defendants asserted the hogs must have contracted cholera from another source; not from the livestock company. In refusing to accept this contention, the Idaho Supreme Court noted the question of proximate causation is almost always for the jury to decide and that this rule was derived from cases that negligence, contributory negligence, and proximate cause are jury questions unless the proof was so clear that different minds cannot reasonably draw a different conclusion.[62]

Breece v. Ragan[63] entailed a claim against a veterinarian who, in order to vaccinate nearly 60 head of cattle, placed all of them in a pen. The cattle became frightened by the needle and many piled upon each other with six being trampled to death. The cattle owner asserted the veterinarian had been negligent to continue to vaccinate the cattle by the procedure he had employed. The veterinarian countered that the owner had been contributorily negligent by retaining his father and another man to place the cattle in the pen. In rejecting the veterinarian's defense, the court said:

> The evidence is undisputed, and virtually conclusive, to the effect that *all* that [the plaintiff's father] did was to assist in the assembling of the cattle in the barn. [The veterinarian] alone, by his own testimony, was the *only* person inside the pen where the cattle were being vaccinated. Neither [the plaintiff's father] nor [the other man] ever entered the pen. Neither of them did anything whatever to cause the cattle to become frightened or to mill about and climb on top of each other, which was the proximate and effective cause of their being killed. The only negligence, if any it was, that [the plaintiff's father] and [the other man] were guilty of, was in placing the cattle in the barn. But that was not what caused the damage, according to all of the testimony.[64]

Finally, *Barlett v. MacRae*[65] was a product strict liability wrongful death action against a veterinarian for dispensing poisonous dye that was accidentally ingested by the plaintiff's decedent. The jury found the veterinarian 30 percent at fault and the decedent 70 percent at fault. The Oregon Court of Appeals affirmed.

E. *Res Ipsa Loquitur*

Like in other professional malpractice actions, courts commonly do not favor the *res ipsa loquitur* doctrine and apply it only if a plaintiff is clearly able to establish the doctrine's applicability to the particular complained-of act or omission.[66] For instance, in *Brockett v. Abbe*[67] a veterinarian told a client his cow was not pregnant and the animal was sold for $170. Later it was determined the cow was pregnant when the veterinarian examined her and if this had been known, the animal could have been sold at a higher price. The trial court applied *res ipsa loquitur* and entered judgment for the cow's previous owner. On appeal, the judgment was reversed because as a matter of law, *res ipsa loquitur* does not apply in cases involving diagnosis and scientific treatment.[68] Traditionally, most courts have said the doctrine does not apply when the facts show no more than a mistake in diagnosis.[69] Finally, since a veterinarian normally undertakes to exercise the skill and care common to the profession, a mistaken diagnosis alone is usually not enough to show the necessary lack of skill or care.[70]

Durkin v. Equine Clinics, Inc.[71] concerned a racehorse that died ten minutes after an injection of Butazolidin (phenylbutazone). The trial court refused to give a *res ipsa loquitur* instruction. The plaintiffs' argument on appeal that the trial judge had erred by not so instructing the jury was rejected by the appellate court. In explaining its decision, the appellate court said:

> As with malpractice cases involving human patients, no presumption or inference of negligence arises merely because the medical treatment culminates in a bad result. The question in this case involved a reaction to certain types and dosages of drugs and the possible cause of such a reaction. An adverse reaction to medication may have many possible causes. Therefore, this was not an appropriate case for an instruction on *res ipsa loquitur*.[72]

Hight v. Dublin Veterinary Clinic[73] entailed the death of a goat following surgery to remove its horns. The appellate court agreed with the trial court that with regard to the administration of anesthetics, *res ipsa loquitur* did not apply.[74]

In *Williamson v. Prida*,[75] a California appellate court refused to apply *res ipsa loquitur* where the plaintiffs had argued that since their race horse had developed a thrombosis after three injections of oxytetracycline by the veterinarian, he must have been negligent. The court declined to apply the doctrine because even the plaintiffs' veterinary expert had testified that thrombosis can occur in the absence of negligence.

Res ipsa loquitur was successfully invoked in *Safford Animal Hospital v. Blain*[76] against a veterinarian when a cow escaped from the veterinary practice and injured a neighbor. However, *Safford* was not a veterinary malpractice action but, rather, an ordinary negligence claim for personal injuries.

III. Requirement of Expert Testimony to Establish Veterinary Malpractice

Generally, in malpractice lawsuits the plaintiff must have an expert witness testify that the defendant committed professional malpractice.[77] In other words, to establish a veterinary malpractice claim, a plaintiff is required to present expert testimony establishing the appropriate standard of care and that the defendant's breach of that standard caused the animal's injury or death.[78] Such "standard" is a matter peculiarly within an expert's knowledge; it presents the basic issue in a malpractice case and can be proved only by the expert's testimony unless the complained-of act or omission would be within the common knowledge of lay people.[79] Also, causation must be established within a reasonable veterinary medical probability based on competent veterinary expert testimony.[80] When death occurs, consideration should be given promptly to having a postmortem (necropsy[81]) examination because, if not, the absence of a postmortem report might prevent the animal owner from recovering in later litigation.[82]

Other than with the possible exception of a small claims proceeding[83] a litigant may not state at trial what its expert veterinary witness said. Rather, like with any other witness, expert witnesses must testify in person at trial or, if allowed, by their deposition testimony being read or played to the jury.

A plaintiff also may not offer an unsworn letter[84] from a veterinarian or veterinary medical records lacking evidentiary foundation.[85] Like any expert opinions, such evidence must be in a form (testimony, deposition, affidavit, declaration) that is admissible under the rules of evidence.

Many states now have statutes requiring at the time of filing a medical malpractice lawsuit or within a certain time thereafter, the plaintiff file an affidavit from an expert stating that the defendant deviated from the standard of care, how the defendant deviated, and that the deviation caused the plaintiff's injuries.[86] Close attention should be given to whether such medical malpractice procedure statutes include or apply to veterinarians.[87]

The following cases reflect veterinary malpractice cases concerning expert issues:

- *Diakakis v. Western Reserve Veterinary Hospital*[88]—where a plaintiff does not provide an affidavit from a veterinary expert indicating what the standard of veterinary care is, that the defendant-veterinarian breached that standard, and how that breach caused the animal's injury or death, then in the absence of such an opposing affidavit, an affidavit from the defendant-veterinarian that he or she complied with the applicable standard of veterinary care would be sufficient to entitle the veterinarian to summary judgment. A defendant-veterinarian is competent to testify as an expert about the applicable standard of care.
- *Petrosian v. Connor*[89]—a plaintiff may call the defendant-veterinarian and designate him or her as the plaintiff's expert witness to establish the required elements for malpractice of what is the standard of care and that the defendant's complained-of acts or omissions caused the animal's injury or death.[90]
- *Kenney v. Lesser*[91]—a university veterinary professor who was board-certified in anesthesiology was qualified to testify as an expert witness against veterinarians in private practice about the

standard of care for anesthesiology even though the professor did not practice in a private clinical setting.

- *Pruitt v. Box*[92]—reversal of a trial court's summary judgment for a veterinarian, wherein the appellate court ruled that the affidavit of the veterinarian's expert did not negate the veterinarian's act as having caused a horse's death. Also, the expert's affidavit contained sufficient information to present a jury question of whether the veterinarian's act had caused the horse's death.
- *Williamson v. Prida*[93]—plaintiffs failed to present any evidence on the standard of care for a veterinarian when their expert witness (also a veterinarian) only testified "that he 'didn't agree with' the use of oxytetracycline for noninfected scratches [on race horses], 'couldn't see the reason,' and thought it was 'overzealous'" for the defendant-veterinarian to have so treated a race horse.
- *DeCurtis-Slifkin v. Kolbert*[94]—plaintiff's dog was neutered by a veterinarian in the afternoon and discharged to the plaintiff. Later that evening, at home, the dog bit the plaintiff. The plaintiff brought suit alleging the veterinarian had been negligent in discharging the dog as it was still under the effects of the anesthesia administered during the surgery. The veterinarian moved for summary judgment, presenting an affidavit from his expert veterinarian witness that the defendant had conducted himself in accordance with acceptable veterinary practice. The plaintiff did not have any evidence from an expert witness to the contrary. The veterinarian's summary judgment motion granted.
- *Downing v. Gully*[95]—appellate ruled that a plaintiff had to present testimony from a veterinarian establishing what the standard of veterinary care was and that the defendant-veterinarian had not met that standard. In *Downing* the defendant-veterinarian moved for summary judgment and presented an affidavit that he had met the required standard. The plaintiff did not offer any affidavit to counter the defendant's contention that he had met the standard of care. The appellate court affirmed summary judgment for the defendant-veterinarian.
- *Price v. Brown*[96]—rejected an attempt to avoid the general requirement that in a malpractice action the plaintiff must have expert testimony that the defendant-veterinarian committed malpractice. The plaintiff had delivered her dog to a veterinarian for surgery to correct a prolapsed urethra. The surgery was performed but the dog died two days later. Apparently, the plaintiff had not been able to find an expert who would testify that the vet-

erinarian had committed malpractice. The plaintiff then sued the veterinarian for breach of a bailment agreement contending that the veterinarian had breached the agreement by not monitoring the dog's postoperative condition and by not returning the dog in good health. The Pennsylvania Supreme Court found that the substance of the plaintiff's claim sounded in professional malpractice rather than bailment: "The allegations relating to the professional services rendered by [the veterinarian] cannot be deliberately exercised from the complaint as if the veterinarian's services were no different from those offered by a kennel operator or dog groomer. There are significant differences between surgical services provided by a veterinarian and grooming or caretaking services."[97]

- *Zimmerman v. Robertson*[98]—court rejected argument that unlike in human medical malpractice actions, expert testimony should not be required to establish a veterinarian's negligence: "Since juries composed of laymen are normally incompetent to pass judgment on [such] questions . . . it has been held in the great majority of malpractice cases that there can be no finding of negligence in the absence of expert testimony to support it."[99]
- *Chicago, I. & L. Railway Co. v. Blankenship*[100]—action for death of cattle that had allegedly contracted a disease because of the defendant's negligence. The plaintiff was not allowed to testify about statements his veterinarian had purportedly made to him about the nature of the disease from which the cattle had died. Such testimony was hearsay and, therefore, not admissible. Incredibly, one of the plaintiff's "veterinarians was in the courtroom, but he was not called [as a witness]. The jury should have heard from him as to the [cattle's] ailment."[101]

Occasionally, questions may arise whether a person who is not a veterinarian may testify as an expert witness in a malpractice action or in a suit involving injury to or disease in an animal. Times have greatly changed since the Indiana Supreme Court in 1837 rejected an argument that the trial court had erred in not requiring a veterinary expert witness because "[w]e have scarcely any veterinary surgeons in our country."[102]

Reflective of requiring *veterinary* experts, and not others, to testify on *veterinary* standard of care and causation is *Sumner v. Bridge*.[103] The case concerned the death of an acutely ill cat. The cat owner identified two individuals, both of whom had bachelor of science degrees in animal science, to testify that the veterinarian deviated from the standard of veterinary care. In granting a summary judgment for the veterinarian, the trial court recited:

> Kansas law recognizes a requirement of expert veterinary testimony involving animal diseases. For example, in *Mo. Pac. Ry. Co. v. Finley*, 38 Kan. 550, Syl. ¶ 5, 16 Pac. 951 (1888), the [Kansas] Supreme Court held that a person who was not a veterinarian, but who had read extensively and heard testimony of experts regarding diseases of cattle, was *not* competent as an expert to testify on the causation of diseases in animals.
>
> "Where a person has been educated in a particular profession as a physician, surgeon, or veterinarian, he is presumed to understand thoroughly the questions pertaining to his profession; but a person not a member of those professions, who has read extensively from books and heard the testimony of experts in court in regard to the diseases of men or cattle, is *not* considered an expert concerning the same." (Italics supplied.) 38 Kan. at 561, 16 Pac. at 957.
>
> Likewise, in *Rouse v. Youard*, 1 Kan. App. 270, Syl. ¶ 3, 41 Pac. 426 (1895), the [Kansas] Court of Appeals held that a witness who was not a veterinarian was *not* competent to testify as an expert as to a disease with which certain cattle had been afflicted by the fact that he had some experience in observing the treatment of diseases in livestock by veterinarians, in handling stock, and had read about diseases among animals.
>
> "A medical man may give his opinion as to the cause of disease or death. So a veterinary surgeon may give his opinion as to what cause produced diseases in animals, and whether the disease is contagious, and how the disease may become communicated to other animals, and also as to what disease an animal died of; and may found his opinion on his own observation or on the symptoms described by other witnesses. As a physician, surgeon or veterinarian is presumed to understand thoroughly the questions pertaining to his profession, he is allowed to give his opinion respecting any subject that comes within his profession. But persons not acquainted with the science of medicine, surgery, or veterinary, who may have had some experience in observing the treatment of diseases by physicians or operations performed by a surgeon, or in the handling of stock and in reading accounts

> of different diseases among animals, are *not* supposed to be possessed of the necessary qualifications of an expert; and *it was error to permit these witnesses to give in evidence their opinions as to the disease the cattle were affected with and from which they died*. It was competent for these witnesses to state the symptoms that they noticed in the cattle, the conduct of the animals, and all the conditions that were observable when they first discovered the cattle were sick, the appearance of the animals and length of time that occurred before death, and the appearance on the post mortem." (Italics supplied.) 1 Kan. App. at 276–77, 41 Pac. at 428–29.
>
> Consequently, the plaintiff's designation of non-veterinarians . . . to testify as "expert" witnesses against the defendant [veterinarian] is not permissible under Kansas law.[104]

In *Gross v. Victoria Station Farms*,[105] the defendant, a horse stable, had affidavits from four veterinarians stating that a horse's lameness had not been caused by an event at the stable but, rather, was attributable to a previous surgery. The horse owner did not have a veterinarian for its expert witness but an individual who held an M.S. in geology and a Ph.D. in biology/systematics and ecology and was the owner of a horse who supposedly had an ailment similar to plaintiff's horse. The plaintiff's expert had also published many articles on horses; however, none on diagnosing equine lameness. Additionally, the plaintiff's proposed expert had founded the Equine Studies Institute "to promote higher education in horsemanship through attention to the nature and the needs of horses" and was the Institute's director.

The Minnesota Supreme Court, in affirming the trial court's decision that declared the plaintiff's designated expert witness was not qualified to testify, said:

> We have previously applied a deferential standard of review to cases involving animal experts. *Kastner v. Wermerskirschen* involved the sale of chickens allegedly infected with a disease. [In that case, the] defendant's proffered expert testified that he was a "chicken hatchery operator and pullet raiser of 25 years' experience, a student at 15 to 20 diagnostic clinics and lectures by veterinarians schooled in chicken diseases, and a performer of chicken autopsies covering several years, and that he had read literature in the field of chicken diseases." Because animal care is often in the hands of lay people, "a lower standard of qualification [applies] to witnesses giving opinion testimony on

such matters than is generally applied to expert witnesses offering testimony as to the diseases and ailments of humans." We based this decision on precedent holding that a "formal education in animal diseases is not necessary to qualify a witness as an expert." Yet, this precedent does "not hold that a so called lay expert witness who is qualified to diagnose the presence of an animal disease necessarily qualifies also as an expert in the causation and onset of that animal disease." We therefore held that the district court did not abuse its discretion when it concluded that the expert was not qualified to offer an opinion as to the cause and onset of the chicken disease.

The case now before us is remarkably similar to *Kastner*. [The plaintiff's witness] has an extensive amount of experience with horses, but the record does not support that she has the necessary qualifications to meet the higher standard required to offer her opinion on the causation and onset of [the horse's] current lameness. The lengthy medical history of [the horse's] lameness before the November 1993 accident [at the defendant's facility] underscores the complex nature of [the horse's] current lameness and the need for competent expert opinions on the causation of such lameness. The record indicates that [plaintiff's witness] had no experience in diagnosing equine lameness. Her background does not include any veterinary science studies, and her work and research has focused only on horse evolution and conformation rather than equine lameness diagnosis. Moreover, because we apply a deferential standard to evidentiary rulings, we cannot say that the district court abused its discretion in excluding [the plaintiff's witness's] opinion.[106]

In conclusion, the Minnesota Supreme Court commented:

"Where a question involves obscure and abstruse medical factors such that the ordinary layman cannot reasonably possess well founded knowledge of the matter and could only indulge in speculation in making a finding, there must be expert testimony, based upon an adequate factual foundation that the thing alleged to have caused the result not only might have caused it but in fact did cause it."[107]

The ordinary layperson is not versed in horse lameness or horse anatomy and therefore could not decide whether the November

> 1993 accident [at defendant's facility] caused [the horse's] current lameness. Expert testimony on causation was required before [the plaintiff] could recover damages on his claims for negligence, breach of contract, and conversion. We affirm that part of the court of appeals' decision requiring [the plaintiff] to submit expert testimony on causation. Because the district court did not abuse its discretion in excluding [the plaintiff's witness's] opinion and [the plaintiff] offered no evidence of causation, we conclude that summary judgment for [the defendant] was appropriate.[108]

In *Purina Mills, Inc. v. Odell*,[109] an intermediate Texas appellate court held that a trial court had erred in allowing testimony from two veterinarians retained by a farmer because their opinions were scientifically unreliable. The plaintiff alleged that the feed manufacturer sold him feed that was contaminated by metal fragments, causing traumatic *reticulo pericarditis* (hardware disease) in 11 of his animals and would cause future injury to his remaining stock. There was no dispute that the feed contained metal fragments. The plaintiff's attending veterinarian, and another veterinarian retained for the case, both testified the metal fragments in the feed caused the hardware disease and would likely result in the disease developing in the rest or most of the remainder of the plaintiff's animals. In accepting the defendant's argument that the veterinarians' testimony should not have been permitted by the trial court because the expressed opinions were not scientifically reliable, the intermediate Texas appellate court noted that "[t]o be reliable, the underlying scientific technique or principle must be grounded in the methods and procedures of science; otherwise, it is no more than a subjective belief or unsupported speculation of no assistance to the trier of fact."[110]

The Texas appellate court observed that neither veterinarian had conducted any tests to exclude other potential causes for the presence of hardware disease. The court noted that both veterinarians had acknowledged that the presence of metal in the animals might have come from other sources beside the defendant's feed. The court also commented:

> [T]he evidence does not reveal how much of the feed was contaminated with metal or to what degree. [The veterinarians] did not take random representative samples of all the Purina feed furnished to Odell. [The veterinarians] postulated that because Odell fed his herd Purina feed, because some of the feed contained metal, and because some of the cows sustained injuries consistent with hardware disease, the contaminated feed must be

> the source of the injury to all of the cows. This kind of reasoning cannot suffice where several possible causes might produce the same effect.[111]

Further:

> [N]either [veterinarian] conducted a methodological or technical study of all the cattle or representative samples of the feed. Neither [veterinarian] presented any testimony regarding their respective rate of error analysis.[112]

Concluding:

> Scientifically unreliable evidence is of no assistance to the trier of fact and is inadmissible. With the exception of their testimony from personal knowledge gained from examining and diagnosing specific cows, [both veterinarians'] testimony lacked a reliable foundation, and it was an abuse of the trial court's discretion to admit the testimony in evidence.

Finally, a court may not ignore uncontroverted testimony from a veterinary expert. For instance, *Augillard v. Madura*[113] concerned a dispute regarding the ownership of a dog between a Louisianan and a Texan in which a veterinary epidemiologist gave uncontradicted conclusive testimony and DNA that the dog was the Louisianan's. However, despite this uncontroverted testimony, the trial judge ruled for the Texan. In reversing the judgment, the Texas Court of Appeals stated, "the trial court erred by choosing to disregard that evidence, which was conclusive of the vital fact of the dog's ownership."[114]

A. *Daubert* and Veterinary Expert Witnesses

Today, there are many federal and state veterinary malpractice decisions or actions entailing a veterinarian testifying as an expert witness, applying the United States Supreme Court ruling in *Daubert v. Merrell Dow Pharmaceuticals, Inc.*[115]—scientifically reliable; grounded in science's methods and procedures; a body of known facts or ideas inferred from such facts or accepted as true on good grounds. For instance:

- *Brooks v. Goettl*[116]—plaintiff's veterinary expert allowed to testify in a malpractice action.

- *State v. Bowman*[117]—veterinarian's testimony allowed; rejecting suggestion his testimony was novel.
- *Twyman v. GHK Corp.*[118]—alleged groundwater contamination injuring cattle; applying *Daubert*, the trial court erred in allowing the plaintiffs' veterinary expert to testify as he was not aware of any scientific literature that supported a synergism theory with respect to components involved in the case and their effect upon animals; nor was the expert aware of anyone else advancing such a theory. Additionally, there was no evidence the theory had been subjected to peer review and it was an entirely new theory.
- *Schafersman v. Agland Coop*[119]—on first appeal, reversal of trial court's decision to exclude veterinarian's testimony because it did not meet the "generally accepted" *Frye* standard,[120] with trial court directed upon the retrial to consider if the testimony was admissible under *Daubert*. On remand the trial court excluded the veterinarian's testimony under *Daubert*, and on the second appeal the Nebraska Supreme Court upheld the exclusion.
- *Courtaulds Fibers, Inc. v. Long*[121]—whether *Frye* or *Daubert* standards applied, veterinary toxicologist's testimony was admissible on the cause of the death of horses.
- *Jahn v. Equine Services, Inc.*[122]—Kentucky district court erred by excluding the plaintiff's expert veterinary report without a hearing as the record before the court was not sufficient to make a proper *Daubert* determination on the admissibility of the plaintiff's veterinary expert witnesses as to the postoperative cause of the death of the plaintiff's horse.
- *Carpenter v. Land O'Lakes, Inc.*[123]—contaminated dairy feed action; defendants' *Daubert* challenge of the plaintiffs' three veterinary experts rejected.
- *Stover v. Eagle Products, Inc.*[124]—applying *Daubert* and striking a veterinary toxicologist's affidavit that differed from his deposition testimony; summary judgment for defendant.

B. Expert Testimony Must Indicate Not Only Professional Error, but That Error Caused Injury

It is not enough for the plaintiff's expert witness to say the veterinarian committed an error in his or her treatment of an animal. The expert must go further and testify that such professional error *caused the injury to the animal*. For example:

- *Lewis v. Hendrickson*[125]—"In order to establish negligence by a veterinarian, a party must show 'that the injury complained of was caused by doing of a particular thing that a veterinarian of ordinary skill, care and diligence would not have done under like or similar circumstances, or by the failure or omission to do some particular thing that such veterinarian would have done under like or similar circumstances.'"
- *Austin v. State*[126]—dog owner's claim for malpractice against a state veterinary teaching hospital denied where the owner's expert stated he could not testify that any of the defendant's deviations from the standard of veterinary care that the expert had identified had been the proximate cause of the dog's death.
- *Schwartz. v. Neil Anderson, D.V.M. & Kansas State University Veterinary Medical Hospital*[127]—as plaintiffs' expert witness was willing to say only that veterinarian's purported error "may have" or "might have possibly" caused the death of the animal, but was not willing to say to a degree of reasonable veterinary medical certainty that the veterinarian's purported error caused the death of the animal, the plaintiffs' case for veterinary malpractice had to be dismissed.[128]
- *Janovski v. Greer*[129]—veterinarian's alleged negligent care of a boarded dog was *not* shown to have caused the dog's death even though, when picked up from the veterinary clinic, the dog was dirty and thin. The evidence revealed the dog was elderly and had a history of health problems. Further, stress-induced diarrhea was common among boarded dogs. Also the owner had been treating the dog with human medications without consulting a veterinarian and it was undetermined when the dog's fatal condition had been contracted.
- *Moreland v. Lowdermilk*[130]—experts in equine medicine disagreed on the proper course of treatment for thromboembolic colic and disagreed on how a horse with the illness should be treated. The veterinarian, therefore, could not be held to have committed malpractice in exercising his judgment to use one course of treatment as opposed to another. Also, evidence suggested the horse could have died of an infestation of parasites, as the owner had not been properly and timely in having the horse dewormed.
- *Katz v. Spindel*[131]—where veterinarian's expert witness testified that circumstances besides the veterinarian's alleged improper deworming procedures might have caused the death of a horse and the owner presented no evidence to rule out these other possible causes of death, the veterinarian could not be found liable.

- *Nikolic v. Seidenberg*[132]—exculpatory clause in animal shelter's pet adoption contract absolving animal shelter from having provided a sick animal did not extend to include a veterinarian who had negligently treated an adopted animal.

C. Common-Knowledge Exception

As in medical malpractice actions,[133] courts recognize the common-knowledge exception to the need for expert testimony in veterinary malpractice lawsuits. A well-recognized exception to the general rule is that expert testimony is required in a professional malpractice action to establish that the professional was negligent.[134] As succinctly stated in *Prosser and Keeton on the Law of Torts*:

> Where the matter is regarded as within the common knowledge of laymen, as where a surgeon saws off the wrong leg, or there is injury to a part of the body not within the operative field, it is often held that the jury may infer negligence without the aid of expert testimony.[135]

Reflective of the common-knowledge exception is *Durocher v. Rochester Equine Clinic*,[136] where the defendant-veterinarian had operated on the wrong horse—a mare instead of a stallion. Expert testimony was not required as the jury, by its common knowledge, could determine whether operating on the wrong horse was a negligent act.

In *Mathew v. Jerome L. Klinger, D.V.M., P.C.*,[137] an owner brought her dog, which was crying and making noises, to a clinic, reporting that the animal had gotten into some garbage and been chewing on bones. The attending veterinarian did not x-ray the dog's throat, esophagus, or stomach to see if it might have swallowed something. A necropsy done by another veterinarian found a chicken bone that had perforated the dog's esophagus and caused its death. The trial court ruled, and the appellate court agreed, that it had not been necessary for the plaintiff to present expert testimony where the "very nature of the acts complained of bespeaks improper treatment and malpractice. . . . No expert is necessary to explain that a veterinarian should x-ray a dog's throat, esophagus and stomach if she suspects that the dog has swallowed something."[138]

Carter v. Louisiana State University[139] was a malpractice action brought by the owner of a registered quarter horse against a veterinarian at a veterinary college for loss of the horse's tail. The horse had been admitted for a stomach disorder and diarrhea. At the hospital, the horse's tail was covered with a plastic protective sleeve that was bound with a strip of adhesive tape by a student who was under the veterinarian's control and supervision. The adhesive tape was wrapped too tight, causing gangrene and, thereby, necessitating amputation of the horse's tail. The Louisiana Supreme Court noted that since horses being treated for stomach disorders do not ordinarily lose their tails, an inference of negligence arose against the veterinarian.[140]

Ullmann v. Duffus[141] was an avian malpractice action in which the owner alleged the veterinarian had provided a medication that was poisonous to birds. The owner also asserted she did not need an expert because of the common-knowledge exception. In declaring that the exception was not available to the plaintiff and that she did need a veterinary expert, the appellate court said, "Despite appellant's protestations to the contrary, the standard of care required of a veterinarian prescribing medication in the course of treatment is not within the common experience and understanding of laypersons."[142]

In *Collins v. Newman*,[143] an animal owner argued that she did not need an expert affidavit as required by a Georgia statute, when a veterinarian had left a instrument inside a dog during a spaying procedure. The Georgia Court of Appeals, while acknowledging that where malpractice would be obvious to a layman such an action could be presented to a jury, ruled nonetheless that a plaintiff was still required to provide an affidavit from an expert witness or suffer dismissal of its action:

> Notwithstanding the fact that there is a "judicially created rule" dispensing with the expert-evidence requirement in cases of "clear and palpable" professional negligence, . . . [Ga. Code Ann.] § 9-11-9.1 supersedes this rule, so that even in cases of "clear and palpable" professional negligence it is still necessary that the plaintiff file an expert affidavit contemporaneously with the filing of the complaint. Accordingly, the trial court correctly dismissed [the plaintiff's] claim for professional negligence due to her failure to file an expert affidavit.[144]

Similarly, *Hamilton v. Thompson*[145] was a small claims collection action in which the client counterclaimed alleging the veterinarian's assistant had misread an ultrasound and diagnosed pregnancies in horses that were not correct.[146] While a small claims proceeding, the action was still required to be dismissed because the client had not filed an affidavit or "certificate of review" from a veterinary expert at the commencement of the action that the treating veterinarian had committed malpractice.

Somewhat related to there being no need for an expert witness is *Safford Animal Hospital v. Blain*,[147] where a cow escaped from a veterinary hospital. While loose, the animal ran into and injured the veterinarian's neighbor who was trying to help the veterinarian to capture the cow. The veterinarian was found liable, not by the standard of care in a professional malpractice action but rather by the *ordinary* standard of care that applies to any owner or keeper of a domestic animal that injures another person.

A similar result to *Safford Animal Hospital* may be seen in *Elephant, Inc. v. Hartford Accident & Indemnity Co.*,[148] where a veterinarian boarding an elephant that was being used for a Republican congressional candidate placed it in a pen immediately adjacent to where poison was stored. The elephant was able to reach and eat the poison and died. According to the appellate court, it was clear from the record that the veterinarian had been negligent in placing the elephant in a stall from which it could easily reach a lethal dose of poison; he had a duty "of *ordinary* care which was expected of a prudent man," and the veterinarian's conduct was the failure "to exercise *ordinary* care required of him."[149]

D. Professional versus Ordinary Negligence

There are important reasons to determine if the claims, or at least some of them, against a veterinarian are for *professional* or *ordinary* negligence. Besides a possibly shorter statute of limitations to lodge a *professional* malpractice action is the question of whether a veterinary expert is needed to prosecute the lawsuit and, in some states, even to be able to file the lawsuit in the first place. Generally, if the claim is one of ordinary negligence, an expert witness should not be needed. However, for professional negligence a veterinary expert will be needed unless the veterinarian's negligence should fall within the confines of the common-knowledge exception.

For instance, *Moses v. Richardson*[150] was an action against a veterinarian for injuries to a horse from a treadmill. The veterinarian argued that the trial court should have required the plaintiff to present expert testimony on the standard of care applicable to veterinarians. The appellate court held that the trial court was correct by not requiring expert testimony because the action was one for *ordinary*, rather than professional, negligence. According to the appellate court:

> If a horse were injured on a treadmill at a training facility, expert medical testimony would not be required to prove negligence. The result should not be different merely because the treadmill here was used in a veterinary hospital. In other words, the acts of [the veterinarian] are not matters peculiarly within the knowledge of veterinary professionals.[151]

E. Reading Veterinary Books or Texts Alone Is Not Sufficient

A plaintiff cannot try to circumvent the need for a veterinary expert witness by reading or presenting to the jury, as substantive evidence, veterinary texts, articles, or Internet sites, unless a competent witness has testified that the text is a reputable and standard authority in veterinary medicine.[152]

IV. Additional Considerations

A. Statute of Limitations[153]

In considering statutes of limitations for veterinary malpractice claims initially two questions must be answered. *First*, in the state in question, is a "veterinarian" within a statutory definition of a "health care provider"[154] to enjoy the benefit of a shorter statute of limitations[155] or statute of repose that many states have provided for health care providers?[156] Sometimes, this can have a converse effect of cutting off a veterinary malpractice suit before a medical malpractice claim would be negated.[157]

Second, does the claim pertain to a single animal, a few animals, or a herd? If the last, courts have struggled and taken different views of when the statute of limitations is deemed to have commenced.

Even when a state has the same time period for commencing a medical malpractice action as a veterinary malpractice action, the state might command that a medical malpractice action is deemed to have commenced from the date of the alleged wrongful act or omission, even though the plaintiff did not discover until later that malpractice happened, whereas for a veterinary malpractice suit, it might allow for the statute of limitations to commence from the discovery of the malpractice.[158]

In *Berres v. Anderson*,[159] the Minnesota Court of Appeals ruled that the statute of limitations on a veterinary malpractice claim was to be measured from when the veterinarian ceased treatment on a herd rather than on a particular animal. The veterinarian in *Berres* had suspected that a heifer in a herd had Johne's disease[160] and treated that animal. The veterinarian never reported this belief to the state board of health. The plaintiffs sued, alleging the veterinarian also failed to take appropriate measures to confirm, treat, and prevent the spread of Johne's disease among other animals in the herd. In ruling that the plaintiffs' action was not barred by Minnesota's two-year statute of limitations for veterinary malpractice, the Minnesota Court of Appeals distinguished veterinary medicine from human medicine:

> Regardless of when the heifer [with Johne's disease] was treated the [plaintiffs] claim that the statute of limitations started to run when treatment of Johne's disease ceased in the entire herd, not just the individual suspect animal. We agree. The practice of veterinary medicine differs from human medicine in that individual animals in a herd may be disposed of to prevent the spread of disease within that herd and to protect the economic interests of the dairy herd owner. The "patient" is the entire herd and treatment of the dairy herd does not cease when treatment of an infected animal ceases.[161]

Finally, a veterinarian's failure to timely plead the statute of limitations may permit an otherwise stale claim to proceed.[162]

B. Long-Arm Jurisdiction over Out-of-State Veterinarians

In bringing or defending against a veterinary malpractice action, consideration might need to be given to whether an out-of-state veterinarian is subject to a state's long-arm jurisdiction. In other words, both a state's long-arm statute and constitutional due process "minimum contact" standards must be examined. There are some cases that have addressed whether an out-of-state veterinarian has subjected himself or herself to a state's long-arm jurisdiction.

Ammon v. Kaplow[163] was an action brought in Kansas by citizens of that state against a horse seller and a veterinarian in New York state. The New York veterinarian was the seller's veterinarian, who did a prepurchase examination on the horse and declared that the animal was sound. The New York veterinarian was held subject to suit in Kansas because he had entered into a prepurchase contract with Kansans, had telephone communications with the Kansans' veterinarian, mailed a letter and x-rays of the horse to the Kansas veterinarian, and mailed his bill to Kansas, and the Kansans sent a check from Kansas to the veterinarian. Also, the New York veterinarian had issued an equine soundness certificate that listed Kansas as the destination state and declared that the horse complied with the entrance requirements for Kansas.[164]

Hiwassse Stables, Inc. v. Cunningham[165] concluded that Florida veterinarians who had examined a horse in their home state that was to be and was sent to North Carolina were not subject to suit in North Carolina. Similarly, *Threlkeld v. Colorado*[166] ruled that Montanans who had communicated with and had their horse treated at Colorado State University did not have long-arm jurisdiction to maintain suit against the university in Montana. A like result may be seen in *Bartusch v. Oregon State Board of Higher Education*,[167] dismissing a Washington state resident's attempt to sue the Oregon State University College of Veterinary Medicine teaching hospital for veterinary malpractice.

Finally, in suing or defending an out-of-state veterinarian, consideration should be given to whether the in-state veterinary practice act addresses out-of-state veterinarians rendering veterinary services. A growing number of states are enacting statutes or promulgating regulations about when an out-of-state veterinarian providing veterinary telemedicine, telemedical, or e-medicine will or will not be considered practicing in the state.[168]

C. Governmental Immunity

Most American veterinary colleges operate a teaching hospital where animals receive care and treatment. In considering an action against a veterinary school's teaching hospital or a staff member, it will need to be determined if the facility is a state institution that is covered by a state tort claims act.[169] If so, is the act one that declares the state immune from civil liability unless it has provided that it may be sued for specific types of claims, or is the act one where the state may be sued like any private individual or entity unless the act identifies specific exceptions from liability? Further, if suit is possible, can it be filed in a state court or must it be filed in a state court of claims[170] or initially tendered to a particular state entity before suit can be commenced? Can suit be filed against the state employee only and not just against the state? If so, can the suit proceed in a state court or must it still be filed before a court of claims or some other government entity?[171] Also, what is the time period in which a claim must be lodged with the state claims court or presented to a particular state entity?

Indicative of how state tort claim acts or waiver of sovereign immunity might impact prosecuting a malpractice claim against a state veterinary teaching hospital is *State v. Hartsough*,[172] involving owners of a llama asserting a claim for malpractice against the state university's veterinary hospital, a veterinarian, and a veterinary student. The defendants argued they could not be sued because of state governmental immunity. The plaintiff asserted she could sue for malpractice because the state had enacted a law waiving sovereign immunity for state hospitals. The Colorado Supreme Court, reversing its Court of Appeals,[173] ruled while the state had waived sovereign immunity, that waiver concerned only hospitals that treated humans, not animals. Consequently, the state university's veterinary hospital, the treating veterinarian, and the student enjoyed governmental immunity and the plaintiff's case had to be dismissed.

D. Veterinary Good Samaritan Laws

If a veterinary malpractice case involves an emergency situation, state laws should be explored to see if there is a Good Samaritan law that may preclude a malpractice action where a veterinarian has acted in good faith or require a higher level of negligence, such as gross, to prevail.[174] Some laws protect the conduct of veterinary employees when a veterinarian is absent from the clinic or hospital, while other veterinary Good Samaritan laws include treatment of humans.[175] Whether a veterinary Good Samaritan law applies in a given situation is, in the first instance, a question of law to be resolved by the trial judge.[176]

Hoffa v. Bimes[177] concerned a horse that was brought to a veterinary clinic from a training facility late at night. Initially, the first veterinarian who saw the horse thought it had colic. However, when the horse did not respond to standard treatment, the first veterinarian called in another veterinarian to assist. Attempts to diagnose why the animal had abdominal pain led to the second veterinarian performing an abdominal tap—a needle inserted into the abdominal cavity to extract fluids that could be analyzed to determine the cause of the horse's clinical signs. About 3:30 A.M. the horse was transported to the University of Pennsylvania for surgery.[178] It was later discovered that during the abdominal tap the needle had pierced the horse's small intestine, allowing fluids to leak into the abdominal cavity and infection to develop, which, according to the plaintiff, caused the horse's death a year later.

The veterinarians in *Hoffa* asserted they had been confronted with an emergency and, therefore, could not be held liable under Pennsylvania's Veterinary Immunity Act (Good Samaritan law) unless their conduct was *grossly* negligent. While the Veterinary Immunity Act did not define "emergency," "emergency care," or an "emergency situation," the Pennsylvania court defined veterinary emergencies as "life-threatening situations allowing a decision-maker (veterinary doctor) the flexibility to act based upon information received or garnered upon an examination of the animal to make medically sound decisions regarding treatment."[179] Therefore:

> [A]pplying the facts to the applicable law, we hold that [the veterinarian] was confronted with an emergency medical condition

> necessitating, first, a medical examination, and, second, such treatment as might be required to stabilize the medical condition or for the transfer of the animal to another medical facility should a diagnosis show that care and/or treatment was beyond the doctor's or the facility's capacity to administer on site. Herein, [the veterinarian] acted with all deliberate speed and medical acumen to examine the horse and conclude that it needed treatment that could only be provided by a veterinary hospital in another county.[180]

E. Informed Consent and Owner Consent

One type of a malpractice claim is that a professional did not fully and properly inform the patient or client of the various types of treatment and care available and/or that the professional did not properly inform the client or patient of the risks associated with each such treatment and/or care approach. Consequently, the client's or patient's consent to the suggested or recommended treatment was not an "informed consent" and, therefore, the professional committed an act or omission of negligence.[181] As one court succinctly stated, "Informed consent is part of and necessary to a veterinarian's duty of care."[182]

While there is little doubt the doctrine applies to veterinarians,[183] it might have a particular impact upon those veterinarians who practice, suggest, or recommend to a client an alternative, complementary, or holistic approach to the care and treatment of an animal.[184]

Lawrence v. Big Creek Veterinary Hosp., L.L.C.[185] concerned an agricultural male horse who had its teeth cleaned and floated by a veterinarian. Before the procedure, the veterinarian sedated the horse with xylazine,[186] acepromazine,[187] and Torbugesic.[188] The acepromazine manufacturer's product insert warned not to use or be very cautious of using the product on males. Five days after the procedure, the owner noticed that her animal had a persistent erection (priapism[189]). According to the treating veterinarian, after cleaning and floating the horse's teeth, he saw the penis retract back into its sheath. After the horse's penis had to be partially amputated (partial phallectomy[190]), the owner sued, alleging the attending veterinarian had failed to obtain informed consent before administering acepromazine.

Veterinary experts for both sides agreed that if the penis had retracted after the dental cleaning and floating, then the persistent erection noticed by the owner five days later would not have been caused by the acepromazine administered by the veterinarian. After concluding the informed consent doctrine does apply to veterinarians, the Ohio court declared:

> Based upon failure to inform [the horse owner] of the potential risks associated with administering acepromazine to a male horse, *inter alia*, [the plaintiff's veterinary expert] testified that [the veterinarian] failed to comply with the applicable standards of veterinary care demanded of practicing Ohio veterinarians, possessing similar education, training and experience, and practicing veterinary medicine under like or similar circumstances. The informed consent doctrine is not codified in Ohio. However, such practice is clearly indicative of the veterinarian's duty of care. This is an evidentiary issue that goes directly to the standard of care in a malpractice case. Finally, we note that experts should also be able to testify regarding this standard, as it goes to the central issue of compliance with professional conduct. Informed consent is part of and necessary to a veterinarian's duty of care.
>
> In this case, there were warnings and risks associated with the drug and included in the packaging by the manufacturer. [The male horse] was not used for stud but agrarian purpose, he was the means to the farmer's livelihood. The veterinary field, according to the [plaintiff's] expert, requires, pursuant to their code of conduct, that prior to treatment of animals, owners of livestock be informed as to the risk of that treatment. The owner of livestock is entitled to know the risk of harm to his property before he consents to administering drugs rendering the livestock commercially useless. Veterinary malpractice is similar to that of doctors; the professional qualifications and licensure is of similar rigor, due to the current and historical importance of farming and agriculture to our society and our food supply.[191]

Despite its comments on the veterinary informed consent, the Ohio intermediate appellate court concluded that as the plaintiff's expert was not willing to say the attending veterinarian could not have seen the penis retract on the day of treatment, there was not sufficient evidence by which he could be found liable.[192]

Whether the informed consent doctrine[193] in human medicine is precisely appropriate in *veterinary* medicine is becoming a matter of discussion and debate. Reflective of this debate is a decision by the American Veterinary Medical Association's Executive Board in November 2007 to no longer use the term "informed consent" in its publications but, rather, "*owner* consent."[194] The reason for the AVMA's decision was because in human medicine, unlike veterinary medicine, the cost[195] of the medical procedure or endeavor is not a part of consent in human medicine.[196]

Finally, like in human medicine, consent for treatment generally is not required in an emergency situation.[197]

V. Special Issues

A. Liability for the Transmission of Zoonotic[198] or Parasitic Diseases from Animals to Humans

Lawsuits have been filed by plaintiffs against veterinarians and others alleging they contracted a zoonotic disease[199] from an animal or that they were injured because of contracting a zoonotic illness that a veterinarian[200] or a vendor[201] had the duty to warn about such a risk.[202]

Zoonotic transmission happens when diseases are transmitted from animals to humans.[203] Human exposure can happen through various methods such as by air (aerosol), orally, or direct transmission. Contraction of rabies is the best example of direct transmission from animal to human.[204] Another example of direct transmission is a cat scratch that might transmit bartonellosis,[205] or "cat scratch fever," to a human.[206]

Sloan v. Canadian Valley Animal Clinic, Inc.[207] is an example of a personal injury action brought against a practice arising from an individual contracting brucellosis.[208] The clinic argued that the individual had not timely commenced her action because she had known for more than two years (the statute of limitations in Oklahoma) that she was ill. However, it was not until her third hospitalization that she obtained the correct diagnosis of brucellosis. Additionally, the Oklahoma court commented that it was reasonable for the plaintiff not to have sooner thought about brucellosis because that disease "does not occur with regularity or to the extent that it is usual and expected result of working with cattle; in fact, fewer than 200 cases of brucellosis are diagnosed each year in the United States."[209]

In 2005, the Center for Food Security and Public Health at Iowa State University reported that outbreaks of zoonotic diseases appeared to be on the rise at veterinary practices.[210] The report noted that pregnant clients may "be at greater risk of the consequences of zoonotic disease such as toxoplasmosis,[211] cat scratch fever, psittacosis[212] or brucellosis."[213] According to the report, "[h]aving current knowledge and information for vulnerable clients or staff will provide them with resources to make informed decisions and avoid potential risks."[214]

Who has the duty to warn about zoonotic diseases—physicians or veterinarians? The former, who are to detect and treat diseases in humans, or the latter, who are to detect and treat diseases in animals?

Osburn v. Anchor Laboratories, Inc.[215] is a personal injury action from Texas that suggests a veterinarian's role is to treat animals, rather than the human conditions or diseases that he or she has no duty to treat. *Osburn* concerned a cowboy who developed leukemia by coming into contact with veterinary chloramphenicol. The cowboy sued the manufacturer. While not a zoonotic parasitic disease case, the manufacturer contended that the veterinarian who had prescribed the chloramphenicol had an obligation to warn the plaintiff about the potential risk to humans from coming into contact with veterinary chloramphenicol. In rejecting the manufacturer's contention, the Fifth Circuit Court of Appeals stated:

> Although a veterinarian receives training in pharmacology, his "patients" are animals rather than humans. A veterinarian, therefore, can be expected to have knowledge of the particular susceptibilities of the *animals* he treats, or of *animals* generally, but not of those of persons, by definition not under his care, either in general or who happen to obtain from the veterinarian a prescription drug to be used in treatment of an animal. Hence, it may have been reasonable for Rachelle [manufacturer] to expect [the veterinarian] to have particular expertise and knowledge concerning the dangers *to animals* involved in the use of chloramphenicol and thus to communicate those dangers to persons who will directly administer the drug to an animal. But it seems unreasonable to expect a veterinarian . . . to have the medical expertise necessary to make him in all instances a "learned intermediary" with regard to dangers to *humans* who are exposed to a drug in the process of administering it to animals. At least this is so where, as here, the drug is properly dispensed for subsequent use by animal owners away from the direct supervision of the prescribing veterinarian.[216]

The Fifth Circuit though, added the following caveat in a footnote:

> The situation here is perhaps distinct from one where a veterinarian personally administers a drug to an animal, and a danger exists to persons expected to come into contact with the animal. In this latter context, the veterinarian at least controls exposure to the drug by his patient, the animal. The veterinarian then has only to communicate dangers running from the animal he

> treated to the persons exposed to the animal. We likewise do not speak to the situation where an employee of the veterinarian comes into contact with the drug while administering it to animals in the course of his employment pursuant to the prescription and under the general supervision of the veterinarian. The type of cases mentioned in this footnote are not before us, and we intimate no view as to any of them.[217]

Osburn might be read to suggest that a veterinarian, trained in animal, rather than human, medicine, has a duty only to warn about potential harm to animals, not of potential harm to humans.

A similar view may be suggested by *Garrelts v. SmithKline Beecham*,[218] which involved United States Department of Agriculture, Animal and Plant Health Inspection Services (APHIS) regulations (under the federal Virus-Serum-Toxin Act) that preempted state law tort claims for injuries to animals against animal vaccine manufacturers who had properly manufactured their vaccines per APHIS's regulations.[219] However, such regulations did not preempt state law tort claims for *human* injury.

B. Liability for Transmission of Diseases between Animals

More common than contraction of a zoonotic disease by a human are claims when a veterinarian failed to detect or warn of a disease in an animal or herd with the result that those animals come into contact with other animals that then contract the disease.[220]

Dorking Genetics v. U.S.[221] involved an American cattle seller who retained a private veterinarian for a buyer to inspect cattle that were to be shipped to Zimbabwe. The veterinarian's test for bovine leukosis[222] was negative. However, the veterinarian knew three other animals in the herd had previously tested positive. The veterinarian prepared a health certificate incorporating specific Zimbabwean requirements for the cattle, including a statement that the cattle had not come from a herd with a history of bovine leukosis. In moving for dismissal, the veterinarian argued he had not been retained by the buyer but rather by the seller and, therefore, owed no duty to the buyer. The trial court agreed and dismissed the action. However, the Second Circuit Court of Appeals reversed, noting that under New York law,[223] a person who issued a report might be liable to a third party if that party could show (1) awareness that the report was to be used for a particular purpose; (2) reliance by the known party in furtherance of that purpose; and (3) some conduct by the defendant linking it to the party and evincing the defendant's understanding of their reliance.[224]

Stratmeyer v. U.S.[225] affirmed a trial court's grant of summary judgment in favor of the United States where a cattle lessee asserted that a USDA veterinarian had been negligent in not quarantining all of a herd of cattle after three of the cattle had tested positive for brucellosis. The USDA veterinarian, while quarantining the three animals that had a positive reaction for brucellosis, released the other cattle. Later, the released animals were shipped to the plaintiff's ranch and mixed with the plaintiff's existing herd. Subsequently, when brucellosis was detected in the plaintiff's herd, all of his cattle had to be destroyed. The plaintiff contended the USDA veterinarian had been negligent in failing to quarantine the herd. The USDA veterinarian did not know the herd was going to be shipped to the plaintiff. The trial and appellate courts ruled that the USDA veterinarian had not owed any special duty to the plaintiff:

> "When the government's duty is owed to the public at large, there is no governmental liability for negligence." To recover under a theory of negligence when the liability of a government entity is at issue, therefore, the plaintiff must show that the duty of care running from the government defendant to the plaintiff is not an obligation to the public at large, but rather an obligation to the plaintiff as a particular individual. "Liability to an individual for damages will not lie when the government entity owed a duty to the public as a whole, unless the plaintiff can show a special duty or relationship which would entitle one to recovery."[226]

Concluding:

> [I]t is clear that the animal health and brucellosis statutes were enacted pursuant to the police power of the state to safeguard the public health and welfare of the citizens. . . .[227]

In *Hubbard v. State*,[228] blood tests conducted at a state veterinary diagnostic laboratory resulted in a report that five of the plaintiff's 226 cattle herd were positive for anaplasmosis,[229] a highly contagious and infectious disease. As a result, the state veterinarian quarantined the entire herd as being infected with the disease. Later tests were inconsistent for the five suspected animals; one week the animals would be positive, the next week they were not. Blood samples were then sent to another diagnostic laboratory. When those results came back differently from the state laboratory, the state veterinarian lifted the quarantine. The cattle owner sued the State of Iowa, alleging it had been negligent in failing to use recognized and appropriate tests, use skilled diagnostic specialists in veterinary medicine, carry out tests in accordance with recognized procedures, and discover discrepancies in the tests. The state argued, and the Iowa court agreed, that the essence of the plaintiff's claim action was not for negligence but, rather, misrepresentation. While the Iowa Tort Claim Act permitted a negligence claim against the state, it did not allow for a misrepresentation action.[230]

Greives v. Greenwood,[231] while recognizing that a cattle breeder had a claim against a veterinarian for negligent inoculation of two cows that resulted in the entire herd being labeled suspect or reactors to brucellosis, the damages that the cattle breeder could recover were limited:

> Where damages are allowed for injury to or loss of cows, damages cannot also be allowed for the loss of unborn calves carried by them, since unborn calves have no market value and a separate allowance for them would amount to double damages.
>
> The basic measure of damages is generally the market value of the animal, if there is a market value, immediately prior to the [veterinarian's negligent] act.[232]

Fitch v. Prather[233] raised the question of whether a veterinarian treating animals on one property has a duty to inform a sometime client on an adjoining property of an infectious disease that had been detected on the first property. In *Fitch*, a veterinarian had discovered equine infectious anemia in a horse. He did not tell the neighbor because he believed it would have been a violation of this responsibility to his client on the basis that such information was privileged and confidential.[234] Subsequently, six horses on the adjoining property were diagnosed with the same disease. The trial court granted the veterinarian summary judgment. However, given an undeveloped evidentiary record, the Louisiana Supreme Court reversed. The court was not able to answer the question of whether the veterinarian had a duty to inform the neighbor, whom he sometimes did work for, of the presence of the infectious disease on an adjoining property.

Finally, *Carter v. State*[235] was a malpractice action for the death of a cow due to a malignant edema[236] that allegedly resulted from the insertion of a blood needle to draw a sample for a brucellosis test without the veterinarian participating in a federal-state program or taking proper sanitary precautions. According to the Illinois Court of Claims, the alleged facts made out a claim for negligence against the state.

C. Client Injuries from Animals under Treatment

Generally, once a veterinarian takes control of an animal for examination or treatment, he or she has the duty to control that animal until it is returned to the client's possession.[237] "One of the most frequent—and potentially most serious—sources of malpractice claims is injury to clients who assist veterinarians by restraining their own animals during examination or treatment."[238]

One writer on this subject has noted:

> Perhaps the greatest risk of human injury is from harm caused by the animals that the veterinarian has undertaken to treat. Frequently, animals attack their owners or other people. The treating veterinarian may be subject to liability for such animal attacks under a number of circumstances. The veterinarian may have allegedly failed to take reasonable precautions to protect the animal's owner from bites, kicks, or other injuries from the animal during or following treatment. In a recurring factual pattern, the owner is present and often assisting the veterinarian in restraining or calming the animal during treatment when it suddenly bites or kicks the owner. The risk of human injury in such situations is facilitated by the practice of some veterinarians to permit animal owners to assist the veterinarian in managing and controlling the animal during treatment.[239]

Continuing:

> Potential negligence might include the decision to allow the owner to be in contact with the animal during treatment, the failure to warn the owner of the dangers that might arise both during and following treatment, and the failure to use safety measures such as muzzles and sedation. Claims might also be based on the veterinarian's failure to inform the owner or other appropriate individuals about a characteristic or condition of an animal that might pose a danger to the plaintiff. A strong argument can be made, for example, that a veterinarian has a duty to warn owners who

> keep wild animals as pets, such as ferrets, of the dangers that such animals might pose to them and to members of their families. Or the veterinarian might fail to warn a pet owner about the effects of medication on the temperament of the animal or might release an animal too soon after treatment.[240]

Additionally, such claims can be determined on the basis of *ordinary* negligence, not malpractice,[241] therefore negating the animal owner's need for an expert witness.

While the better practice would be for a veterinarian not to permit his or her client to restrain an animal while it is being examined or treated, it is possible for a veterinarian to defend by asserting the client already knew of its animal's propensities or inclinations and, therefore, the veterinarian had no duty to warn or to prevent the client from restraining the animal. Further, that even if the veterinarian had fault, so too did the client and, consequently, comparative fault or negligence applies.[242]

There is always a case that presents the exception to prove the rule. For instance, in *Branks v. Kern*,[243] the pet owner and a veterinary assistant were holding a cat, the assistant let go once, reheld, then let go a second time, at which point the cat bit the owner. In finding for the veterinarian, the North Carolina Supreme Court declared, "[The owner] was in as good a position as the veterinarian to appreciate the danger that the cat would try to bite someone in his immediate vicinity."[244]

As the owner already knew of the danger[245] that the cat might bite, there was no liability on the part of the veterinarian.[246] When an employee of a veterinarian is injured by an animal, their injury will probably be covered by workers' compensation.[247]

Finally, depending upon the jurisdiction, assumption of risk might still be a complete bar, partial defense, or considered an aspect of comparative fault in response to a client's personal injury action against a veterinarian. For instance, *Molinari v. Tuskegee University*[248] involved a veterinary student who sued for personal injuries after being kicked by a cow during a surgical procedure. The university and the teaching professor contended, among other things, that the student's action was barred by assumption of risk. In Alabama this doctrine is a form of contributory fault that is an absolute bar to recovery for personal injuries.[249] Generally, there are two elements necessary for assumption of risk. *First*, the plaintiff knew and appreciated the danger that the animal was harmful. *Second*, the plaintiff voluntarily consented to bear the risk posed by that danger. In *Molinari*, there was conflicting evidence on the second factor and, consequently, neither the university nor the veterinary professor was entitled to summary judgment on their assumption of risk defense.[250]

D. Extralabel or Off-Label Use of Drugs

When an animal or animals are injured or die from a drug or biologic while under the care of a veterinarian, the question should be asked and examined if the drug[251] or biologic provided was adverse or toxic to that sex[252] or species[253] and/or if the attending veterinarian used the drug or biologic in a manner other than provided for in the manufacturer's directions and instructions (so-called "extralabel" or "off-label" use). There are extensive federal[254] and state regulations governing such use, particularly for food animals. If a violation of a pertinent federal or state regulation exists, then a claim of negligence *per se* might exist if that violation caused the animal's injury or death.[255]

Durkin v. Equine Clinics, Inc.[256] was a case in which a veterinarian chose to administer twice the manufacturer's maximum recommended dosage of Butazolidin to a race horse. Ten minutes after administration the horse collapsed and died. The trial court refused to give an instruction to the jury on a veterinarian administering medications contrary to the manufacturer's label directions. The appellate court noted that the fact the veterinarian had administered twice the recommended dosage was crucial evidence for the plaintiffs to be able to establish their case and the veterinarian's liability. Consequently, the appellate court held that it was extremely prejudicial to the plaintiffs and error for the trial court not to have instructed the jury that in determining whether the veterinarian was negligent and whether that negligence caused the race horse's death, it could consider the fact that the veterinarian had failed to follow the manufacturer's recommended dosage.[257]

In *Ruden v. Hansen*,[258] a veterinarian was found liable after he had vaccinated pregnant gilts with modified live cholera vaccine contrary to the manufacturer's label directions.

In *Kohler v. Orrville Veterinary Clinic*,[259] where a veterinarian had allegedly administered bovine virus diarrhea (BVD) vaccine to dairy cows, which manufacturer's labeling warned against giving it to pregnant cows, the appellate court upheld the trial court's decision not to give a negligence *per se* instruction to the jury because the plaintiffs were not entitled to such a charge. The appellate court explained its ruling by saying:

> Negligence *per se* is a violation of a specific requirement of law or ordinance, the only fact for determination for the jury being the

commission or omission of the specific act inhibited or required. Clearly, in Ohio, there is no specific requirement of law or ordinance regarding vaccinations in violation of manufacturer's warnings which, if violated, would constitute negligence *per se*.[260]

Anderson v. Blackfoot Livestock Commission Co.[261] was a negligence action against a livestock company and a private veterinarian who conducted inspections at the company to detect diseased animals and to inoculate them. The plaintiff was a hog owner who was successful at trial in establishing liability against both of the defendants. Part of the plaintiff's case was that the defendants had violated state laws and regulations pertaining to animal health and that those violations had caused diseased animals to pass through the livestock company and be bought by the plaintiff. In upholding the trial court's decision to give a negligence *per se* instruction,[262] the Idaho Supreme Court stated that regulations and orders enacted by administrative authorities pursuant to statutory authority had the force and effect of law and that the evidence showed not only that the subject administrative regulations were relevant but that by violating those regulations the defendants had caused the plaintiff's damages. Concluding, the court declared that when the veterinarian "undertook the task of vaccinating plaintiff's hogs, he was under a duty to comply with the regulatory requirements. Failure to comply with the regulations constitutes negligence *per se*."[263]

Finally, *Bartlett v. MacRae*[264] was a wrongful death action against a veterinarian for dispensing poisonous cattle dye in an improperly labeled container, whereupon the poison was accidentally drunk by the plaintiff's decedent. The plaintiff argued the veterinarian had violated a provision of the Oregon Hazardous Substance Act and, therefore, was negligent *per se*. The trial court granted the veterinarian a directed verdict on this contention. In agreeing with the trial court's decision, the Oregon Court of Appeals noted that the veterinarian was licensed in Washington state, that his only office was in Washington, and that the plaintiff had presented no evidence that the defendant had distributed the cattle dye in Oregon or done anything in Oregon. Consequently, the Oregon law could not be asserted against the Washington veterinarian in attempt to contend he had been negligent *per se*.[265]

VI. Damages Recoverable in Veterinary Malpractice Actions[266]

Discussed in Chapter 9 are types of damages that might be recoverable for the loss of or injury to an animal.[267] According to one court, "The only effective difference between malpractice actions involving veterinarians and physicians is, that as to the measure of damages where an animal has been treated, there would be no component for an award of pain and suffering. Because an animal is personal property, the value of the property lost or damages would be the measure of damages."[268] This is too sweeping a generalization.

In synopsis, the following types of damages, depending on the claim, evidence, and/or jurisdiction, might be recoverable in a veterinary malpractice action:

1. The market value of the animal by a comparison of the difference between its value immediately before injury or death and afterward.[269] Valuation might also be affected by whether the animal is pregnant or was used for breeding.
2. Replacement damages; the financial expenses to replace the animal with another comparable animal.[270]
3. Expenses for hiring or obtaining a substitute animal.
4. Veterinary expenses,[271] including past and anticipated future veterinary expenses.
5. Lost income, time, costs, and inconvenience spent caring for an injured or diseased animal.
6. Expenses for keeping and feeding the animal during the time of recuperation.
7. Loss of breeding fees.
8. Loss of offspring.[272]
9. Disposal, burial, or cremation expenses.[273]
10. Medical expenses, lost income, and other economic and noneconomic damages to an individual who has been injured by an animal under the control of a veterinarian,[274] failure to warn about dangers posed by the animal's condition,[275] or as a result of the veterinarian's failure to warn about the risk of transmission of a zoonotic disease from the animal to the individual.
11. Wrongful death[276] arising from injuries inflicted by an animal under the control of a veterinarian or as a result of the veterinarian's failure to warn about the risk of transmission of a zoonotic disease from the animal to the individual.
12. Punitive or exemplary damages arising from gross negligence and/or willful, wanton, malicious, intentional, or vindictive infliction of injuries.[277]
13. Emotional pain and suffering and/or loss of companionship damages.[278]
14. Negligent or improper disposal of animal's remains.[279]

VII. Conclusion

Numerous legal claims have been asserted against veterinarians and their practices for injury or death of an animal. However, when all the dust is cleared, most cases come down to the requirements of establishing, though expert testimony, what the standard of veterinary care is; how the veterinarian's treatment or care did or did not deviate from that standard; how the veterinarian's treatment or care did or did not injure the animal; and how the plaintiff was or was not damaged.

VIII. Pleadings and Discovery

24B AM. JUR. PLEADINGS & PRACTICE FORMS ANNOTATED, *Veterinarians* §§ 16–18.1 (1999).

Bruce A. Wagman & Jayne M. DeYoung, *Actions Involving Injuries to Animals*, 90 AM. JUR. PROOF OF FACT 3D 1, §§ 35–37 (2006).

Sam A. Mackie, *Veterinary Malpractice*, 32 AM. JUR. PROOF OF FACTS 3D 351, § 13 (1995).[280]

Notes

1. While much has been made in recent years of American law schools offering animal law courses, the tradition of American veterinary colleges providing a legal course to their students seems to well precede law schools. For instance, a common text used in American veterinary colleges after World War I was Henry Bixby Hemenway, *Essentials of Veterinary Law* (T. H. Flood & Co. 1916). *See also* WILLIAM FRANKLIN FRATCHER, CASES AND MATERIALS ON VETERINARY JURISPRUDENCE: COLLECTED AND ANNOTATED FOR THE USE OF STUDENTS IN THE SCHOOL OF VETERINARY MEDICINE, UNIVERSITY OF MISSOURI (Univ. of Mo. 1951).
2. While today "farrier" is generally understood to refer to a person who makes, fits, and remodels horseshoes (D. C. BLOOD, V. P. STUDDERT & C. C. GAY, SAUNDERS COMPREHENSIVE VETERINARY DICTIONARY 683 [Elsevier Ltd. 3rd ed. 2007]), in earlier times, particularly before the advent of state veterinary licensing laws in the second half of the 19th century, "farrier" could also mean a person who treated illnesses or injuries of animals. *See, e.g.*, ROBERT H. DUNLOP & DAVID J. WILLIAMS, VETERINARY MEDICINE: AN ILLUSTRATED HISTORY 235 (Mosby-Year Book, Inc. 1996) ("After the first horseshoes were invented, the veterinary art was practiced by farriers, who originally were mainly shoers of horses. Farriery was an 'occupation' rather than a profession. Much later it became the stepping stone to the veterinary art.").
3. Thorne v. Deas, 4 N.Y. (Johns.) 84 (1809) (a nonveterinary case wherein the New York court referred to an English decision from the reign of Elizabeth I, to wit: "The case of *Powtuary v. Walton*, cited from 1 *Roll. Ab.* 10 [pl. 5 (39

Eliz.), YLS MS. G. R29.9, fo. 239v; abridged in HLS MS. 2069, fo. 277; 1 Rolle Abr. 10, line 1 (1597)] (*See also* 1 *Vin*. 277, 1 *Danv*. 32, pl. 5) was that of a farrier, who undertook to cure a horse, and did so negligently, that the horse died; and it was said, 'that an action would lie, without alleging a consideration, for the *negligence* is the cause of the action, not the *assumpit*.'").

4. Oliver Wendell Holmes, Jr., The Common Law (Barnes & Noble 2004).
5. Y. B. Hil. 19 Hen. VI, fo. 49, pl. 5; BL MS. Harley 4557, fo. 212 (C.P.). *See also* J. H. Baker & S. F. C. Milsom, Sources of English Legal History: Private Law to 1750, at 367–69 (Butterworths 1986).
6. "A carpenter need not go to work upon another man's house at all, but if he accepts the other's confidence and intermeddles, he cannot stop at will and leave the roof open to weather. *So in the case of the farrier, when he has taken charge of a horse, he could not stop at the critical moment and leave the consequences to fortune*" (emphasis added). Holmes, *supra* note 4, *Lecture 7—Contract History* n. 279/1, citing 19 Henry VI, 49, pl. 5, ad fin. Newton, C. J., for this case involving a farrier.
7. Staples v. Steed, 167 Ala. 241, 52 So. 646, 647 (1910). *See also* Latham v. Elrod, 6 Ala. App. 456, 60 So. 428 (1912) (making clear that, like in human medicine, the rendering of gratuitous services by a veterinarian was no excuse to claim of malpractice).
8. Cook v. Dayton, 8 Haw. 8, 10 (Hawai'i Kingdom 1889).
9. Schwartz v. Ostimer, 4 Ind. 109 (1853); Conner v. Winton, 7 Ind. 523 (1856), *appeal after remand*, 8 Ind. 315 (1856). *See generally* House v. Fort, 4 (Ind.) Blackf. 293, 1837 WL 1830, at *2 (1837) (defendant objected to a witness's opinion testimony about the condition of a horse because the witness was not a veterinarian. The Indiana Supreme Court rejected the defendant's argument because then in Indiana "[w]e have scarcely any veterinary surgeons in our country, and the opinions of men of such knowledge as this witness appears to have, must be admitted in cases like the present.").
10. Morrison v. Altig, 134 N.W. 529 (Iowa), *rev'd on reh'g*, 157 Iowa 265, 138 N.W. 510 (1912) (if a veterinary student, in treating a horse, held himself out as a competent veterinarian, then he would be held to the standards of professional care applicable to a veterinarian regardless of whether or not he was paid for his services).
11. Eastman v. Sanborn, 85 Mass. 594 (1862) (defendant who hired horse and returned it ill defended on the basis that the horse did not die as a result of his mishandling but, rather, that a veterinarian who later treated the horse had done so improperly and the horse had died because of the veterinarian's negligence).
12. Williams v. Gilman, 71 Me. 21, 1880 WL 4062 (1880). *See also* Stover v. Inhabitants of Bluehill, 51 Me. 439 (1863).
13. Barney v. Pinkham, 29 Neb. 350, 45 N.W. 694 (1890), *appeal after remand*, 37 Neb. 664, 56 N.W. 323 (1893) (holding that a "veterinary surgeon impliedly engages and is bound to use, in the performance of his duties in his employment, such reasonable skill, diligence, and attention as may be ordinarily

expected of persons in that profession. He does not contract to use the highest degree of skill, nor an extraordinary amount of diligence, but to exercise a reasonable degree of knowledge, diligence, and attention.").

14. Boom v. Reed, 52 N.Y. St. Rep. 777, 69 Hun. 426, 23 N.Y.S. 421, 422 (1893) (successful counterclaim to veterinary surgeon's suit for unpaid bill).
15. While not precisely a veterinary malpractice action, Brown v. State, 26 Ohio St. 176, 178–79 (1875), was a criminal case that can best be described as a veterinary Munchausen syndrome by proxy in which the veterinarian injected horses with substances that would make them sick. His idea, or hope, was that the owners would then have him treat their horses so he could collect a fee.
16. Zell v. Arnold, 2 Pen. & W. 292 (Pa. 1830) (stating "In all cases where the action is not on the contract, but for the breach of a collateral duty, the gist is a personal tort; as where a smith pricks a horse in shoeing, *or a farrier kills him by bad medicine or neglect* . . ." (emphasis added)).
17. Kuhen v. Wilson, 13 Wis. 104 (1860).
18. Some states say "veterinary" rather than "veterinarian."
19. Some states at this point use the conjunctive "and" while other states use a disjunctive "or."
20. *See, e.g.*, KAN. STAT. ANN. § 47-816(n). *See also* Model Veterinary Practice Act § 2(22), 2008–2009 AVMA MEMBERSHIP DIRECTORY & RESOURCE MANUAL 293 (Am. Veterinary Med. Ass'n, 57th ed. 2008).
21. *See, e.g.*, Rowland v. Harrison, 320 Md. 223, 577 A.2d 51 (1990); Turner v. Sinha, 65 Ohio App. 3d 30, 582 N.E.2d 1018 (12th Dist. 1989); Massa v. Dep't of Registration & Educ., 116 Ill. 2d 376, 107 Ill. Dec. 661, 507 N.E.2d 814 (1987); Southall v. Gabel, 28 Ohio App. 2d 295, 277 N.E.2d 230 (10th Dist. 1971), *appeal after remand*, 33 Ohio Misc. 194, 293 N.E.2d 891 (Franklin County Mun. 1972); Breece v. Ragan, 234 Mo. App. 1093, 138 S.W.2d 758 (K.C. 1940).
22. *See, e.g.*, Smith v. Kerns, 281 Mont. 114, 931 P.2d 717, 719 (1997).
23. *See, e.g.*, Mark Samson, *A Potpourri of Issues in Veterinary Regulatory and Malpractice Law: "Per Se" Negligence—A Bridge Between Regulation and Negligence*, Am. Veterinary Med. Law Ass'n meeting (Pittsburgh, Penn. July 1995). *See generally* RESTATEMENT (SECOND) OF TORTS § 286: When Standard of Conduct Defined by Legislation or Regulation Will Be Adopted & § 288: When Standard of Conduct Defined by Legislation or Regulation Will Not Be Adopted.
24. *See generally* Katie J. L. Scott, *Bailment and Veterinary Malpractice: Doctrinal Exclusivity, or Not?*, 55 HASTINGS L. J. 1009 (2004). This law journal article's comments on Price v. Brown, 545 Pa. 216, 680 A.2d 1149 (1996), were criticized in Hoffa v. Bimes, 2008 Pa. Super. 181. ¶ 17, fn. 3, 954 A.2d 1241, 1249, fn. 3 (2008): "The point missed by the law review article and [the plaintiff] is the fact that Price equated the practice of veterinary medicine with services provided by the legal and other medical professions because each involved specialized education, knowledge, and skills. This

distinguishes the veterinarian from the above-referenced 'mechanic' or 'dry cleaner,' which opens the door for the conclusion that professional negligence concepts also extend to veterinary medicine. Price, [545 Pa.] at 222, 680 A.2d at 1152. [The plaintiff] has not provided this Court with any persuasive argument to distinguish Price from the case at bar."

25. *E.g.*, Freedeen v. Stride, 269 Or. 369, 375, 525 P.2d 166, 170 (1974) (*en banc*).
26. *See, e.g.*, Ullmann v. Duffus, 2005 Ohio 6060, ¶ 25 (App. 10th Dist. 2005), *appeal denied*, 109 Ohio St. 3d 1406, 845 N.E.2d 523, *reh'g denied*, 109 Ohio St. 3d 1498, 848 N.E.2d 859 (2006).
27. *E.g.*, Zinn v. City of Ocean Springs, 928 So. 2d 915 (Miss. App. 2006) (private veterinarian accompanied animal control officers to plaintiff's residence where diseased cats were found. After seizure, the veterinarian found that many of the felines had numerous and chronic health problems. The plaintiff brought a 42 U.S.C. § 1983 suit alleging, among other things, that the veterinarian had "misdiagnosed her cats, and caused her stress and humiliation." 928 So. 2d at 921. Trial court's dismissal of suit affirmed on appeal.).
28. *See, e.g.*, Anzalone v. Kragness, 356 Ill. App. 3d 365, 826 N.E.2d 472 (1st Dist. 2005) (veterinarian sued for breach of bailment, breach of fiduciary duty, negligence, and intentional infliction of emotional distress); Haverstock v. Hoge, 2003 WL 1788787, at *2 (Cal. App. 4th Dist. 2003) (claims of strict products liability, breach of expressed and implied warranties, intentional and negligent misrepresentation, malpractice and breach of an oral agreement); Price v. Brown, 545 Pa. Super. 216, 680 A.2d 1149 (1996) (owner of dog that died during surgery could not sue the veterinarian for breach of bailment but, rather, had to sue for professional negligence).
29. Neasbitt v. Warren, 22 S.W.3d 107, 111 fn. 7 (Tex. App. Ft. Worth 2000), *appeal after remand*, 105 S.W.3d 113 (Tex. App. Ft. Worth 2003), citing Webster's Third New Int'l Dictionary 2548 (1981). *See generally* Brown v. Ga. State Bd. of Veterinary Med., 134 Ga. App. 574, 575–76, 215 S.E.2d 332, 333–34 (1975).
30. Reflective of the common elements running through state veterinary practice act definitions is the American Veterinary Medical Association's definition of the "practice of veterinary medicine":

    > (a) To diagnose, treat, correct, change, alleviate, or prevent animal disease, illness, pain, deformity, defect, injury, or other physical, dental, or mental conditions by any method or mode, including:
    >
    > i. the prescription, dispensing, administration, or application of any drug, medicine, biologic, apparatus, anesthetic, or other therapeutic or diagnostic, substance or medical or surgical technique, or

ii. the use of complementary, alternative, and integrative therapies, or
iii. the use of any manual or mechanical procedure for reproductive management, or
iv. the rendering of advice or recommendation by any means including telephonic and other electronic communications with regard to any of the above.

(b) To represent, directly or indirectly, publicly or privately, an ability and willingness to do an act described in subsection 19(a).
(c) To use any title, words, abbreviations, or letters in a manner or under circumstances that induce the belief that the person using the term is qualified to do any act described in subsection 19(a).

AVMA Model Veterinary Practice Act § 19 (Revised 2007), *available at* http://www.avma.org/issues/policy/mvpa.asp. *See also* A.V.M.A. Model Veterinary Practice Act § 23 (rev. ed. 2007): "'Veterinary medicine' means all branches and specialties included within the practice of veterinary medicine." *See generally* Donald M. Zupanec, Annotation, *Validity, Construction, and Effect of Statutes or Regulations Governing the Practice of Veterinary Medicine*, 8 A.L.R.4TH 223 (1981).

31. *E.g.*, Lauderbaugh v. Gellasch, 2008 Ohio 6500, ¶ 7 (Ohio App. 8th Dist. 2008) (similar elements); Ullmann v. Duffus, 2005 Ohio 6060, ¶ 14 (10th Dist. App. 2005), *appeal denied*, 109 Ohio St. 3d 1406, 845 N.E.2d 523, *reh'g denied*, 109 Ohio St. 3d 1498, 848 N.E.2d 859 (2006); Downing v. Gully, 915 S.W.2d 181, 183 (Tex. App. Ft. Worth 1996); Williamson v. Prida, 75 Cal. App. 4th 1417, 1424–25, 89 Cal. Rptr. 2d 868, 872 (2nd Dist. 1999); Fackler v. Genetzky, 257 Neb. 130, 595 N.W.2d 884 (1999), *appeal after remand*, 263 Neb. 68, 638 N.W.2d 521 (2002); Ladnier v. Norwood, 616 F. Supp. 940 (E.D. La. 1985), *aff'd*, 781 F.2d 490, 492 (5th Cir. 1986); Restrepo v. State, 146 Misc. 2d 349, 550 N.Y.S.2d 536 (1989), *aff'd*, 179 App. Div. 2d 804, 580 N.Y.S.2d 874 (1992); Turner v. Sinha, 65 Ohio App. 3d 30, 582 N.E.2d 1018 (1989); Spilotro v. Hugi, 93 Ill. App. 3d 837, 49 Ill. Dec. 239, 417 N.E.2d 1066, 1070 (1981); Bartlett v. MacRae, 54 Or. App. 516, 635 P.2d 666 (1981); Dyress v. Caraway, 190 So. 2d 666, 668 (La. App. 2nd Cir. 1966); Storozuk v. W. A. Butler Co., 3 Ohio Misc. 60, 31 Ohio Op. 2d 91, 203 N.E.2d 511, 512–13 (1964); Bekkemo v. Erickson, 186 Minn. 108, 110, 112, 242 N.W. 617, 618–19 (1932); Barney v. Pinkham, 29 Neb. 350, 45 N.W. 694 (1890), *appeal after remand*, 37 Neb. 664, 56 N.W. 323 (1893); Conkey v. Carpenter, 106 Mich. 1, 4–5, 63 N.W. 990, 991 (1885).
32. *E.g.*, Mazella v. Fairfield Equine Assocs., P.C., 2005 WL 2452908, at *3 (S.D.N.Y. 2005) (Connecticut law).
33. 545 Pa. 216, 680 A.2d 1149 (1996), *rev'g* Price v. Brown, Super. 68, 651 A.2d 548 (1994).

34. *Id.* at 222, 680 A.2d at 1152.
35. 984 S.W.2d 709 (Tex. App. El Paso 1999).
36. Downing v. Gully, 915 S.W.2d 181 (Tex. App. Ft. Worth 1996).
37. *Pruitt*, 984 S.W.2d at 711.
38. *See, e.g.*, Block v. State, 53 Ill. Ct. Cl. 128 (2000) (veterinary malpractice and breach of oral contract action against the state arising from treatment of a foal at the University of Illinois Teaching Veterinary Hospital dismissed, for various reasons, including because the plaintiffs did not show the administered drug was the proximate cause of the animal's death).
39. Fackler v. Genetzky, 257 Neb. 130, 136, 595 N.W.2d 884, 889–90 (1999), *appeal after remand*, 263 Neb. 68, 638 N.W.2d 521 (2002).
40. *See, e.g.*, Ronald W. Eades, *Jury Instructions on Medical Issues, in* VETERINARIANS 7–20, at 7–35 to 7–37 (Matthew Bender & Co., Inc, 6th ed. 2004); Hohenstein v. Dodds, 215 Minn. 348, 351–52, 10 N.W. 236, 238 (1943). *See generally* Kippenberger v. Bd. of Registration in Vet. Med., 448 Mass. 1035, 1036–37, 864 N.E.2d 515, 518 (2007); McGee v. Smith, 107 S.W.3d 725, 727 (Tex. App. Ft. Worth 2003); Pruitt v. Box, 984 S.W.2d 709 (Tex. App. El Paso 1999); Berres v. Anderson, 561 N.W.2d 919, 924 (Minn. App. 1997); Downing v. Gully, 915 S.W.2d 181, 184 (Tex. App. Ft. Worth 1996).
41. Fackler v. Gentzky, 257 Neb. 130, 136, 595 N.W.2d 884, 889–90 (1999), *appeal after remand*, 263 Neb. 68, 638 N.W.2d 521 (2002).
42. *See, e.g.*, Peltier v. McCartan, 2005 Ohio 3901, ¶ 9, (App. 3rd Dist. 2005).
43. *E.g.*, Latham v. Elrod, 6 Ala. App. 456, 60 So. 428 (1912).
44. *See, e.g.*, Mires v. Evans, 1986 WL 8117, at *11 (E.D. Pa. 1986) (as "with medical malpractice cases involving human patients, no presumption or inference of negligence arises merely because the medical treatment of a racehorse yields a bad result. Durkin v. Equine Clinics, Inc., 313 Pa. Super. 75, 79–80, 459 A.2d 417, 419 (1983) [*aff'd* 376 Pa. Super. 557, 546 A. 2d 665 (1988), *appeal denied*, 524 Pa. 608, 569 A.2d 1367 (1989)]."); Brockett v. Abbe, 3 Conn. Cir. Ct. 12, 16, 206 A.2d 447, 449 (1964) (mere proof that a veterinarian's diagnosis later turned out to be wrong is not sufficient to support a malpractice judgment).
45. *E.g.*, Sumner v. Bridge, 2005 WL 2414718, at *4 (Reno County, Kan. 2005).
46. 527 So. 2d 717 (Ala. 1988).
47. *Id.* at 718, citing James v. Woolley, 523 So. 2d 110 (Ala. 1988).
48. "Nasogastric: pertaining to the nasal cavity and the stomach." SAUNDERS COMPREHENSIVE VETERINARY DICTIONARY, *supra* note 2, at 1210.
49. *Turner*, 527 So. 2d at 718.
50. *Id.* at 718. *See also* Williamson v. Prida, 75 Cal. App. 4th 1417, 1426–27, 89 Cal. Rptr. 2d 868, 873 (2nd Dist. 1999) (stating: "'[T]he fact that another [veterinarian] might have elected to treat the case differently or use methods other than those employed by the defendant does not of itself establish negligence.' [Citation omitted.] The merits of this rule [are] illustrated by the facts of this case. [The plaintiff's veterinary expert witness],

who was not a race-track veterinarian, could not see a reason for giving the Oxytetracycline [injections]. Other veterinarians, who did work at race tracks, testified that the [defendant's] treatment was appropriate as a preventive treatment for horses with scratches [that] were to race in the near future. This disagreement does not establish the standard of care [for a veterinarian], or a violation thereof.").

51. Standing: A party's right to make a legal claim or seek judicial enforcement of a duty or right. BLACK'S LAW DICTIONARY 1413 (7th ed. 1999). *See generally* Gregory M. Dennis, *Cry "Havoc!" and Let Slip the Dogs of Law: Veterinarians, Microchips, Lost, Stolen & Escaped Animals, Cremation and Pet Cemeteries*, Am. Veterinary Med. Law Ass'n meeting (New Orleans, La., July 20, 2008); Bruce A. Wagman & Jayne M. DeYoung, *Actions Involving Injuries to Animals*, 90 AM. JUR. PROOF OF FACTS 3D 1, § 17: Ownership, pp. 41–43 (2006).
52. Grabowicz-Kretunski v. ASPCA, 20 Misc. 3d 132(A), 867 N.Y.S.2d 374 (2008); Peloquin v. Calcasieu Parish Police Jury, 367 So. 2d 1246 (La. App. 3rd Cir.), *appeal after remand*, 378 So. 2d 560 (La. App. 3rd Cir. 1979).
53. Alaimo v. Racetrack at Evangeline Downs, Inc., 893 So. 2d 190, 195–96 (La. App. 3rd Cir. 2005) (horse breeder could assert claim for percentage of winnings horse could have had).
54. *See* McAdams v. Faulk, 2002 Ark. App. LEXIS 258, 2002 WL 700956, at *2 (2002), *appeal after remand*, 96 Ark. App. 118, 239 S.W.3d 17 (2006) (while an owner could maintain a veterinary malpractice action, his deceased dog could not); Veale v. Furness, 2007 WL 54820, *report & recommendation adopted* 2007 U.S. Dist. LEXIS 9276, 2007 WL 465405 (D.N.H. 2007) (deceased dog could not assert a federal civil rights action against a veterinarian for violation of constitutional rights); Oberschlake v. Veterinary Assocs. Animal Hosp., 151 Ohio App. 3d 741, 785 N.E.2d 811 (2nd Dist. 2003) (not allowing a claim by a dog for its pain and suffering brought by his owners as "pet guardians"); Wolverton v. Young, 131 Wash. App. 1020, 2006 Wash. App. LEXIS 78, at *28, 2006 WL 165734, at *10 (2006) (individual could not file a lawsuit making a claim for animals as the individual lacked next friend status to sue on behalf of the animals); Pickford v. Masion, 124 Wash. App. 257, 98 P.3d 1232 (2004) (suit brought by plaintiffs for themselves and as guardians for their dog; suit dismissed as Washington state did not recognize a cause of action for destruction of a companion relationship with a dog); Ramey v. Collins, 2000 Ohio App. LEXIS 2540, 2000 WL 776932 (4th Dist.), *appeal denied*, 90 Ohio St. 3d 1428, 736 N.E.2d 25 (2000) (veterinary malpractice action holding a dog owner had no First Amendment constitutional right of freedom of association with its dog; stating "'[f]reedom of association' only pertains to association with humans, not with animals"); City of Akron v. Tipton, 53 Ohio Misc. 2d 18, 21, 559 N.E.2d 1385, 1388 (Akron Mun. 1989) (a dog does not have a constitutional fundamental right to travel); Cetacean

Cmty. v. Bush, 386 F.3d 1169, 1178 (9th Cir. 2004) (whales, dolphins, and porpoises did not have legal standing to sue under the Endangered Species Act, Marine Mammal Protection Act, National Environmental Policy Act and the Administrative Procedure Act; stating "[a]nimals are not authorized to sue in their own names to protect themselves"); Hawksbill Sea Turtle v. Fed. Emergency Mgmt. Agency, 126 F.3d 461, 466, fn. 2 (3rd Cir. 1997) (from Virgin Islands, sea turtles and tree boa snakes did not have legal standing to sue under the Endangered Species Act; stating "[i]f Congress 'intended to take the extraordinary step of authorizing animals . . . to sue, they could, and should, have said so plainly'"); Citizens to End Animal Suffering & Exploitation, Inc. v. New England Aquarium, 836 F. Supp. 45 (D. Mass. 1993) (dolphin did not have legal standing to bring a lawsuit under either the U.S. Constitution or the Marine Mammal Protection Act, nor does Fed. R. Civ. P. 17(b), defining who is a "party" who can file a lawsuit in federal court, apply to nonhuman forms of life); Falls Mills Assocs., Ltd. v. Maruzo, 13 Conn. App. 119, 534 A.2d 912 (1987) (tenants in landlord eviction action moved to join their dog as a necessary party and to appoint a guardian *ad litem* for their dog; the trial court denied the motion and the appellate court said "[t]his 'issue' will be afforded no discussion," calling it frivolous); Int'l Primate Prot. League v. Inst. for Behavioral Research, Inc., 799 F.2d 934 (4th Cir. 1986), *cert. denied*, 481 U.S. 1004, *reh'g denied*, 482 U.S. 909 (1987) (from Maryland, dismissed complaint brought by individuals as guardians for laboratory animals). *But see In re* Estate of Callan, Jr. (Shelby County, Tenn. D-2252, Mar. 20, 2007) (probate court appointed a guardian *ad litem* for a dog that had been owned by the decedent "not as an advocate for the dog, but . . . to determine what is best for the dog's welfare"); Palila v. Haw. Dep't of Land & Natural Res., 852 F.2d 1106, 1107 (9th Cir. 1988) ("[a]s an endangered species under the Endangered Species Act . . . the bird, a member of the Hawaiian honeycreeper family . . . has legal status and wings its way into federal court as a plaintiff in its own right"); Jones v. Butz, 374 F. Supp. 1284 (S.D.N.Y.), *aff'd*, 419 U.S. 806 (1974) (lawsuit challenging provisions of the federal Humane Slaughter Act, brought by the plaintiff "as next friend and guardian for all livestock now and hereafter awaiting slaughter in the United States"); Jones v. Beame, 86 Misc. 2d 832, 382 N.Y.S.2d 1004 (1976), *rev'd & dismissed*, 56 App. Div. 2d 778, 392 N.Y.S.2d 444 (1977), *aff'd*, 45 N.Y.2d 402, 408 N.Y.S.2d 449, 380 N.E.2d 277 (1978) (lawsuit initially allowed to proceed through a plaintiff "as guardian for all animals now confined in" New York City zoos, subsequently dismissed for other reasons). *See generally* Richard L. Cupp, Jr., *A Dubious Grail: Seeking Tort Law Expansion and Limited Personhood as Stepping Stones Toward Abolishing Animals' Property Status*, 60 SMU L. Rev. 3 (2007); Gregory M. Dennis, *Legal Implications of Guardianship & Personhood of Animals for Veterinary Medicine* (Wash.,

D.C., Am. Veterinary Med. Ass'n convention, Lab. Animal Med., July 16, 2007); *It's Official: In Austria, a Chimp Is Not a Person* (MSNBC.com Jan. 15, 2008), *available at* http://www.msnbc.msn.com/id/22670956/.

55. *See, e.g.*, FED. R. CIV. P. 17(a): "*Real Party in Interest*. Every action shall be prosecuted in the name of the real party in interest. An executor, administrator, guardian, bailee, *trustee of an express trust*, ..." (emphasis added).
56. 2005 WL 2452908 (S.D.N.Y. 2005).
57. "Equine protozoal myeloencephalitis (EPM) presents with focal and multifocal signs of neurologic disease involving the brain, brain stem and or spinal cord. It is caused most commonly by *Sarcocystis neurona* but occasionally by *Neospora caninum* or the closely related *N. hughesi*. The definitive host for *S. neurona* in North America is the North American possum *Didelphis virginiana* and in South America *D. marsupialis* and *D. albiventris*. The disease is more common in the summer, may be acute or chronic, and there is great variation in clinical signs due to the ability of the organism to infect both white and gray matter at multiple sites in the central nervous system." SAUNDERS COMPREHENSIVE VETERINARY DICTIONARY, *supra* note 2, at 1195.
58. *Mazella*, 2005 WL 2452908, at *5.
59. *Id.* at *5.
60. *Id.* at *6.
61. 85 Idaho 64, 375 P.2d 704 (1962).
62. *Id.* at 74–75, 375 P.2d at 710.
63. 234 Mo. App. 1093, 138 S.W.2d 758 (K.C. 1940).
64. 138 S.W.2d at 759 (emphasis in original).
65. 54 Or. App. 516, 635 P.2d 666 (1981).
66. *See, e.g.*, Mires v. Evans, 1986 WL 8117, at *12 (E.D. Pa. 1986). *See generally* James M. Rose, *Res Ipsa Loquitur (Humor) Rights a Goldfish Can Carp About*, 33 Westchester Bar J. 61 (Spring–Summer, 2006).
67. 3 Conn. Cir. Ct. 12, 206 A.2d 447 (1964).
68. *Id.* at 15, 206 A.2d at 449.
69. *Id. See also* Dyress v. Caraway, 190 So. 2d 666, 669 (La. App. 2nd Cir. 1966).
70. *Brockett*, 3 Conn. Cir. Ct. at 15–16, 206 A.2d at 449.
71. 313 Pa. Super. 75, 459 A.2d 417 (1983), *aff'd*, 376 Pa. Super. 557, 546 A. 2d 665 (1988), *appeal denied*, 524 Pa. 608, 569 A.2d 1367 (1989).
72. *Durkin*, 313 Pa. Super. at 79–80, 459 A.2d at 419, citing Ragan v. Steen, 229 Pa. Super. 515, 331 A.2d 724 (1974).
73. 22 S.W.3d 614 (Tex. App. Eastland 2000).
74. *Id.* at 623, citing Downing v. Gully, 915 S.W.2d 181, 185 (Tex. App. Ft. Worth 1996).
75. 75 Cal. App. 4th 1417, 89 Cal. Rptr. 2d 868 (2nd Dist. 1999). The California Court of Appeal, Second District, omitted its discussion of the *res ipsa loquitur* from its published decision.

76. 119 Ariz. 296, 298–99, 580 P.2d 757, 759–60 (App. 1978).
77. *See, e.g.*, Brockett v. Abbe, 3 Conn. Cir. Ct. 12, 16, 206 A.2d 447, 449 (1964) (since a cow owner failed to offer any expert evidence as to what method or means the veterinarian should have used to determine the presence or absence of pregnancy, the judgment for the animal owner could not stand). *See generally* Joseph H. King, Jr., *The Standard of Care for Veterinarians in Medical Malpractice Claims*, 58 TENN. L. REV. 1, 41–50 (1990); Paul Baker, *Giving Evidence in Court Appearances*, Vol. 77, No. 12 AUSTRALIAN VETERINARY J. 826 (Dec. 1999).
78. *E.g.*, Petrosian v. Connor, 2004 WL 837997, at *3 (Cal. App. 4th Dist. 2004).
79. *Id.*
80. *Id.*
81. "Necropsy [necroscopy]: Examination of a body after death. See also Autopsy." SAUNDERS COMPREHENSIVE VETERINARY DICTIONARY, *supra* note 2, at 1214.
82. *See, e.g.*, Hudson v. McDaniel, 1989 WL 1650, at *4 (Ohio App. 9th Dist. 1989).
83. *E.g.*, Lewis v. Hendrickson, 2003 Ohio 3756 (App. 4th Dist. 2003) (by statute in Ohio, the rules of evidence do not apply in a small claims action. Therefore it was permissible for the plaintiff to testify about what other veterinarians had told her about the defendant-veterinarian's treatment of her dog, even though in other courts such testimony would have been inadmissible hearsay.). *See also* Lauderbaugh v. Gellasch, 2006 Ohio 2877, 2006 WL 1555471 (App. 8th Dist. 2006) (same).
84. *See* Lauderbaugh v. Gellasch, 2006 Ohio 2877, ¶¶ 16–17 (App. 8th Dist. 2006), *appeal after remand*, 2008 Ohio 650 (App. 8th Dist. 2008) (as Ohio's rules of evidence did not apply to small claims cases, small claims judge erred in not allowing the plaintiff to read into evidence a notarized letter from a veterinarian).
85. *E.g.*, Diakakis v. W. Reserve Veterinary Hosp., 2006 Ohio 201, ¶ 22 (App. 11th Dist. 2006).
86. *See, e.g.*, Hamilton v. Thompson, 23 P.3d 114, 115, fn. 2 (Colo. 2001) (*en banc*) (small claims case where a client, by counterclaim, alleged veterinary malpractice. The client did not file a "certificate of review" required by Colo. Rev. Stat. § 13-20-602, which certificate must show that the person claiming malpractice has consulted with an expert who has experience in the area of alleged negligent conduct and that the expert has concluded that the claim is meritorious.).
87. *E.g.*, Gilreath v. Ohio State Univ. Veterinary Hosp., 2002 Ohio 5408, ¶¶ 79–87 (Cl. Ct. 2002) (rejected contention by a dog owner that an affidavit of a defense veterinary expert did not comply with an Ohio statute (OHIO REV. CODE § 2743.43) setting forth the requirements of an expert's affidavit in a medical malpractice action as the statute did not apply to

veterinary malpractice claims (Ohio Rev. Code 2305.11[D][3]–defining "medical claim")); Lakeshore Animal Hosp. v. Sutton, 1989 WL 78582, at *2 (Ohio App. 11th Dist. 1989) (same).

88. 2006 Ohio 201, ¶ 15 (11th Dist. 2006).
89. 2004 WL 837997, at *3 (Cal. App. 4th Dist. 2004).
90. While the trial court allowed the plaintiff to call the defendant as its expert witness during the plaintiff's case, not surprisingly, the defendant's testimony did not show that he had violated the standard of care nor that his acts or omissions had caused the animal's injuries. *Id.* at *2.
91. 281 App. Div. 2d 853, 722 N.Y.S.2d 302 (2001).
92. 984 S.W.2d 709 (Tex App. El Paso 1999).
93. 75 Cal. App. 4th 1417, 1426–27, 89 Cal. Rptr. 2d 868, 873 (2nd Dist. 1999).
94. 248 App. Div. 2d 428, 668 N.Y.S.2d 949 (1998).
95. 915 S.W.2d 181 (Tex. App. Ft. Worth 1996).
96. 545 Pa. 216, 680 A.2d 1149 (1996).
97. *Id.*, 680 A.2d at 1153.
98. 254 Mont. 105, 854 P.2d 338 (1993).
99. *Id.* at 108, 854 P.2d at 339–40.
100. 77 Ind. App. 225, 127 N.E. 209 (1920).
101. *Id.*, 127 N.E. at 211.
102. House v. Fort, 4 Blackf. (Ind.) 293 (1837); Gilmore v. Brost, 39 Minn. 190, ¶ 1, 39 N.W. 139 (1888) (expert witness testified in a case involving the death of a mare, had been "a practicing physician and surgeon, *which fact by itself would render him equipped to some degree and knowledge necessary to answer the questions*" (emphasis added)). *But see* Wozny v. Godsil, 474 So. 2d 1078, 1080 (Ala. 1985) (veterinarian was not competent to be an expert witness in a *medical* malpractice action).
103. 2005 WL 2414718 (Reno County, Kan. May 10, 2005).
104. *Id.* at **3–4. *See also* Petrosian v. Connor, 2004 WL 837997, at *7 (Cal. App. 4th Dist. 2004) (upheld a trial court's decision not to allow a horse trainer, who was not a veterinarian, to testify as an expert witness on standard of care and causation against a veterinarian in a malpractice action).
105. 578 N.W.2d 757 (Minn. 1998), *rev'g in part and aff'g in part* Gross v. Victoria Station Farms, Inc., 1997 WL 471388 (Minn. App. 1997).
106. *Id.* at 761–62 (quoting Kastner v. Wermerskirschen, 295 Minn. 391, 392–395, 205 N.W.2d 336, 337–339 (1973)).
107. *Id.* at 762 (quoting Bernloehr v. Central Livestock Order Buying Co., 296 Minn. 222, 225, 208 N.W.2d 753, 755 (1973)).
108. *Id.* at 762. *See generally* Lott v. C & W Trucking, Inc., 15 F. Supp. 2d 1167, 1171 (S.D. Miss. 1997).
109. 948 S.W.2d 927 (Tex. App. Texarkana 1997).
110. *Id.* at 933.
111. *Id.* at 934.
112. *Id.*

113. 257 S.W.3d 494 (Tex. App. Austin 2008).
114. *Augillard* was one of many lawsuits that arose from relocation of animals after Hurricane Katrina. *See also* Webb v. Amtower, 178 P.3d 80 (Table), 2008 Kan. App. Unpub. LEXIS 253, 2008 WL 713728 (2008).
115. 509 U.S. 579 (1993).
116. 2006 WL 3691000, at **4–5 (W.D. Tex. 2006).
117. 321 Mont. 176, 186–87, ¶¶ 37–43, 89 P.3d 986, 993–94 (2004).
118. 2004 OK Civ. App. 53, ¶ 32, 93 P.3d 51, ¶ 32, 58 (2004).
119. 262 Neb. 215, 631 N.W.2d 862 (2001), *appeal after remand*, 268 Neb. 138, 681 N.W.2d 47 (2004).
120. Frye v. United States, 54 U.S. App. D.C. 46, 293 F. 1013 (1923).
121. 779 So. 2d 198, 202 (Ala. 2000).
122. 233 F.3d 382, 393 (6th Cir. 2000).
123. 976 F. Supp. 968, 972 (D. Or. 1997).
124. 1996 WL 172972, at **6–10 (D. Kan. 1996).
125. 2003 Ohio 3756, at ¶ 14 (App. 4th Dist. 2003) (quoting Turner v. Sinha, 65 Ohio App. 3d 30, 35, 582 N.E.2d 1018 (1989)).
126. 54 Ill. Ct. Cl. 375 (2002).
127. Riley County, Kan., 94-C-170.
128. In *Schwartz, id.*, there was an indication that the animal owner, upon the advice of a physician, had ceased giving a medication to the animal that had been prescribed by the veterinarian. Further, there was testimony the owner gave the animal other drugs that had been recommended by the physician. Also, there was testimony that laboratory personnel at a human hospital were testing blood samples from the animal that had been drawn by the owner. *Question*: The unlawful practice of veterinary medicine by a physician? *See* Kimberly v. Ledbetter, 183 Kan. 644, 331 P.2d 307 (1958) (a wrongful death action against a veterinarian who negligently performed an abortion on a woman was allowed to proceed).
129. 588 So. 2d 885 (Ala. 1991).
130. 709 F. Supp. 722 (W.D. La. 1989).
131. 260 So. 2d 766 (La. App. 4th Cir. 1972).
132. 242 Ill. App. 3d 96, 610 N.E.2d 177 (1993).
133. *See generally* Joseph H. King, Jr., *The Common Knowledge Exception to the Expert Testimony Requirement for Establishing the Standard of Care in Medical Malpractice*, 59 ALA. L. REV. 51 (2007).
134. *See generally* Joseph H. King, Jr., *The Standard of Care for Veterinarians in Medical Malpractice Claims*, 58 TENN. L. REV. 1, 46–50 (1990).
135. PROSSER AND KEETON ON THE LAW OF TORTS § 32, at 189 (5th ed. 1984).
136. 137 N.H. 532, 629 A.2d 827, 829 (1993).
137. 179 Misc. 2d 609, 686 N.Y.S.2d 549 (1998).
138. *Id.* at 610, 686 N.Y.S.2d at 550 (citing Restrepo v. State, 146 Misc. 2d 349, 355, 550 N.Y.S.2d 536, 541 (Cl. Ct. 1989), *aff'd*, 179 App. Div. 2d 804, 580 N.Y.S.2d 874 (1992)).

139. 520 So. 2d 383 (La. 1988).
140. *See* Morrison v. Altig, 157 Iowa 265, 138 N.W. 510 (1912) (veterinary student requested by the owner of a horse to treat the animal informed the owner he was reluctant to do so because he had not yet completed his education. If the student had held himself out to the owner as being a competent veterinarian, he would be bound to bring to the treatment of the horse that degree of learning, care, and skill of a competent veterinarian.).
141. 2005 Ohio 6060 (10th Dist. App. 2005), *appeal denied*, 109 Ohio St. 3d 1406, 845 N.E.2d 523, *reh'g denied*, 109 Ohio St. 3d 1498, 848 N.E.2d 859 (2006).
142. *Id.* at ¶ 19.
143. 237 Ga. App. 861, 517 S.E.2d 100 (1999).
144. *Id.*, 517 S.E.2d at 102 (citations omitted).
145. 23 P.3d 114 (Colo. 2001) (*en banc*).
146. *See, e.g.*, Peltier v. McCartan, 2005 Ohio 3901, ¶ 9 (App. 3rd Dist. 2005) (plaintiffs alleged that veterinarian misread ultrasounds of alpacas, saying they were pregnant when they were not. As the plaintiffs had not sustained any damages, summary judgment for the veterinarian was warranted.).
147. 119 Ariz. 296, 580 P.2d 757 (App. 1978).
148. 216 So. 2d 837 (La. App. 1st Cir. 1968), *appeal after remand*, 239 So. 2d 692 (La. App. 1st Cir. 1970).
149. 239 So. 2d at 694 (emphasis added).
150. 2001 WL 1513764 (Cal. App. 4th Dist. 2001).
151. *Id.* at *3.
152. *E.g.*, Yi v. State Bd. of Veterinary Medicine, 960 A.2d 864, 2008 (Pa. Commw. Ct. 2008) (error for licensing board to have derived factual findings from treatises and Internet sites that were not in the record); Washburn v. Cuddihy, 74 Mass. (Gray) 430, 431 (1857) (trial court did not commit error in refusing to allow defense counsel "to read works or medical or veterinary practice to the jury"). *See also* Legg v. Drake, 1 Ohio St. 286, 288–89 (1853).
153. *See generally* Harold W. Hannah, *Bars to Malpractice Action: Statutes of Limitations and Res Judicata*, 217 (5), J.A.V.M.A. 656 (Sept. 1, 2000).
154. *See, e.g.*, Sherman v. Kissinger, 146 Wash. App. 855, 867, ¶ 21, 195 P.3d 539, 545 ¶ 21 (2008) (the Washington Medical Malpractice Act "applies only to human health care, and does not apply to veterinarians or veterinary clinics"); DeMercado v. Superior Court, 148 Cal. App. 4th 711, 716, 55 Cal. Rptr. 3d 889, 892 (4th Dist. 2007) (veterinarian did not come within California's health care provider statute of limitations nor within a statute requiring a plaintiff to seek leave of the court to make a punitive damage claim in a medical malpractice suit); Neasbitt v. Warren, 22 S.W.3d 107, 111 (Tex. App. Ft. Worth 2000), *appeal after remand*, 105 S.W.3d 113 (Tex. App. Ft. Worth 2003) (veterinarians are not covered by the Texas Medi-

cal Liability & Insurance Improvement Act and, therefore, the requirements for initiating and maintaining a medical malpractice action are not required for a veterinary malpractice suit). *See also* Williams v. Neutercorp, 1995 WL 231140, at *3 (Tex. App. Houston 1995).

155. *E.g.*, Williamson v. Prida, 75 Cal. App. 4th 1417, 1425, 89 Cal. Rptr. 2d 868, 872 (2nd Dist. 1999); Haverstock v. Hoge, 2003 WL 1788787, at *2 (Cal. App. 4th Dist. 2003). *See also* Ratusch v. Attas, 3 Misc. 3d 763, 765, 777 N.Y.S.2d 880, 883 (2004). *Contra* Hitchcock v. Conklin, 107 Ohio App. 3d 850, 669 N.E.2d 562 (10th Dist. 1995); Southall v. Gabel, 28 Ohio App. 2d 295, 277 N.E.2d 230 (10th Dist. 1971), *appeal after remand*, 33 Ohio Misc. 194, 293 N.E.2d 891 (Mun. 1972); Lakeshore Animal Hosp. v. Sutton, 1989 WL 78582, at *2 (Ohio App. 11th Dist. 1989). *See generally* Harold W. Hannah, *Bars to Malpractice Action: Statutes of Limitations and Res Judicata*, 217 (5) J.A.V.M.A. 656 (Sept. 1, 2000).
156. *E.g.*, Ark. Code Ann. § 16-114-203: *Limitations*, veterinarians are covered by Arkansas's two-year medical malpractice statute of limitations. By contrast, however, in Kansas that state omits veterinarians from its definition of a "health care provider." *"Health Care Provider" Defined*, Kan. Stat. Ann. § 60-513d. Arkansas's statute of limitations is one year if a foreign object has been left in a patient or from the date the object should have been reasonably discovered. *E.g.*, Ark. Code Ann. § 16-114-203(d).
157. *E.g.*, Ratusch v. Attas, 3 Misc. 3d 763, 764–65, 777 N.Y.S.2d 880, 882–83 (2004) (qualification of medical malpractice statute of limitations allowed suit to be filed after the running of a 30-month time period, in the event of a later discovery of a foreign object left in a patient, did not apply to a veterinary malpractice action).
158. *E.g.*, Indiana permits two years for malpractice actions against physicians and veterinarians. For physicians, that time is measured from the date of the alleged negligent act or omission. Ind. Code Ann. § 34-11-2-3 and 34-18-7-1(b). However, for veterinarians it can be measured from a later time of when the client knew or reasonably should have known that a negligent act or omission had happened. Ind. Code Ann. § 34-11-2-4(2).
159. 561 N.W.2d 919 (Minn. App. 1997).
160. "Johne's disease: a specific, infectious disease of cattle, sheep and goats caused by Mycobacterium *avium* subspecies *paratuberulosis*. In cattle it is characterized by chronic diarrhea and thickening and corrugation of the intestinal wall. In all species there is progressive wasting." Saunders Comprehensive Veterinary Dictionary, *supra* note 2, at 999.
161. *Berres*, 561 N.W.2d at 923.
162. *E.g.*, Lobrillo v. Brokken, 837 So. 2d 1059, 1060–61 (Fla. App. 3rd Dist. 2002).
163. 468 F. Supp. 1304 (D. Kan. 1979).
164. *Id.* at 1313.
165. 135 N.C. App. 24, 519 S.E.2d 317 (1991).

166. 303 Mont. 432, 16 P.3d 359 (2000).
167. 131 Wash. App. 298, 126 P.3d 840 (2006).
168. *See, e.g.*, Mo. Rev. Stat. § 340.217: *Practice across state lines. See also* Ala. Code Ann. § 34-29-61(14)(f) (the practice of veterinary medicine includes providing "veterinary medical services to a client or patient in [Alabama], through telephonic, electronic, or other means, regardless of the location of the veterinarian, shall constitute the practice of veterinary medicine in this state and shall require licensure within this state and a veterinarian-client-patient relationship must be established"); Ala. Code Ann. § 34-29-76(8); Idaho Code Ann. § 54-2103(34) ("'Practice of veterinary medicine' in this state, through telephonic, electronic, or other means, regardless of the location of the veterinarian, includes veterinary surgery, obstetrics, dentistry, and all other branches or specialties of veterinary medicine."); Idaho Code Ann. §§ 54-2103(41)(a), 54-2114; 225 Ill. Comp. Stat. § 115/5 ("It shall be unlawful for any person who is not licensed in [Illinois] to provide veterinary medical services from any state to a client or patient in this state through telephonic, electronic, or other means, except where a *bona fide* veterinarian-client-patient relationship exists."); Miss Code Ann. § 73-39-59(3) ("A veterinarian-client-patient relationship cannot be established solely by telephonic or other electronic means."). *See also* Utah Code Ann. § 58-28-604(2) (same); 59 Okla. Stat. Ann. § 698.2.18 (veterinary telemedicine means "the transmission of diagnostic images such as, but not limited to, radiographs, ultrasound, cytology, endoscopy, photographs and case information over ordinary or cellular phone lines to a licensed veterinarian or board-certified medical specialist for the purpose of consulting regarding case management with the primary care licensed veterinarian who transmits the cases"); 63 Pa. Stat. § 485.3(10)(ix) (practicing of veterinary medicine includes rendering advice or recommendation by electronic transmission of data); Tex. Code Ann. § 801.351(c) ("A veterinarian-client-patient relationship may not be established solely by telephone or electronic means."). *See generally* Gregory M. Dennis, *Veterinary Telemedicine: Law & Jurisdiction*, Northeast Veterinary Conference (Providence, R.I., Aug. 9, 2004); Gregory M. Dennis, *How Should Legislatures Respond to Telemedicine?*, 18(5) Trends (Oct.–Nov. 2002); Gregory M. Dennis, *General Practitioners' Responsibilities in the Telemedicine World*, 18(4) Trends (Aug.–Sept. 2002); Gregory M. Dennis, *Legal Implications of Veterinary Telemedicine & E-Health*, American College of Veterinary Radiology (Chicago, Ill., Nov. 30, 2000) & American Veterinary Medical Association convention (Salt Lake City, Utah, July 25, 2000); and Gregory M. Dennis, *Legal Implications of Veterinary Telemedicine & Telecare*, World Veterinary Cong. (Lyon, France, Sept. 24, 1999).
169. *See, e.g.*, Stoll v. Cornell Univ. Coll. of Veterinary Med., 94 N.Y.2d 162, 701 N.Y.S.2d 316, 723 N.E.2d 65 (1999) (Cornell University College of Veterinary Medicine is a *private*, rather than a state university, and therefore

was *not* subject to the requirements of the New York Freedom of Information Act).

170. *E.g.*, Gilreath v. Ohio State Univ. Veterinary Hosp., 2002 Ohio 5408 (Ct. Cl. 2002); Austin v. State, 54 Ill. Ct. Cl. 375 (2002); Block v. State, 53 Ill. Ct. Cl. 128 (2000); Carter v. State, 20 Ill. Ct. Cl. 213 (1951).
171. *See, e.g.*, Loman v. Freeman, 375 Ill. App. 3d 445, 874 N.E.2d 542 (4th Dist. 2006), *aff'd*, 229 Ill. 2d 104, 890 N.E.2d 446, 459 (2008) (Illinois Court of Claims did not have exclusive jurisdiction over a malpractice claim that a veterinarian employed at the University of Illinois Veterinary Teaching Hospital had breached a duty of care applicable to *all* veterinarians from the common law and independent of employment with the state).
172. 790 P.2d 836 (Colo. 1990) (*en banc*).
173. Hartsough v. State, 762 P.2d 758 (Colo. App. 1988).
174. *E.g.*, Ga. Code Ann. § 43-50-80 (*Relief from liability for rendering emergency care*); Kan. Stat. Ann. § 47-841 (*Veterinarian not liable for good faith volunteer actions*); Mo. Rev. Stat. § 340.287 (*Veterinary emergency care, no civil liability, exceptions (Good Samaritan law)*); N.J. Stat. Ann. § 45:16-9.11 (*Nonliability for civil damages for rendering emergency care*); 42 Pa. Cons. Stat. Ann. § 8331.1 (*Veterinary Good Samaritan civil immunity*).
175. *E.g.*, Kan. Stat. Ann. § 47-841: *Veterinarian not liable for good faith volunteer actions.*

> (b) Any licensed veterinarian who in good faith renders or attempts to render emergency care at the scene of an accident or emergency to the *human* victim or victims thereof shall not be liable for any civil damages as a result of any act or omission by such persons rendering or attempting to render the emergency care.

(emphasis added).

176. Hoffa v. Bimes, 2008 Pa. Super. 181, ¶ 13, fn. 2, 954 A.2d 1241, 1247, fn. 2 (2008) (stating "The interpretation and application of the Veterinary Immunity Act is a question of law to be resolved in the first instance by the trial court and not the jury.").
177. 2008 Pa. Super. 181, 954 A.2d 1241 (2008).
178. In *Hoffa v. Bimes*, as the veterinary practice's anesthetist was absent, the horse had to be transported to the University of Pennsylvania for surgery. 2008 Pa. Super. 181, ¶ 9, fn. 1, 954 A.2d at 1246, fn. 1.
179. *Id.* ¶ 8.
180. *Id.* ¶ 9.
181. *See generally* Cheryl M. Bailey, Annotation, *Veterinarian's Liability for Malpractice*, 71 A.L.R.4th 811, § 29: *Failure to Warn or to Obtain Informed Consent* (1989).
182. *E.g.*, Lawrence v. Big Creek Veterinary Hosp., L.LC., 2007 Ohio 4627, ¶ 31 (App. 11th Dist. 2007).

183. *See, e.g.*, Zimmerman v. Robertson, 254 Mont. 105, 854 P.2d 338, 342 (1993) (veterinary "malpractice claim premised on a theory of lack of informed consent is a separate cause of action rather than an 'element' in an otherwise professional negligence" action); Emes Stable v. Univ. of Pa., 1988 U.S. Dist. LEXIS 2972, 1988 WL 33893 (E.D. Pa. 1988); Ladnier v. Norwood, 616 F. Supp. 940 (E.D. La. 1985), *aff'd*, 781 F.2d 490, 494 (5th Cir. 1986) (veterinarian had not breached a duty to warn a racehorse trainer about the possibility of a fatal reaction to administration of vitamin E to a horse to treat anhydrosis, in view of testimony unequivocally establishing that equine specialists did not consider the risk of a fatal reaction (estimated as one in every 25,000 dosages) substantial enough to warrant a warning and that nearly all drugs used in equine medicine had a similar remote chance of a fatal reaction); Hull v. Tate, 45 Okla. Bar Assn. J. 2455 (1971) (same, probability of adverse reaction was one out of 10,000 injections). *But see* Ullmann v. Duffus, 2005 Ohio 6060, ¶¶ 27–28 (10th Dist. App. 2005), *appeal denied*, 109 Ohio St. 3d 1406, 845 N.E.2d 523, *reh'g denied*, 109 Ohio St. 3d 1498, 848 N.E.2d 859 (2006) (stating "Our research has revealed no case in which an Ohio court has recognized a tort claim for lack of informed consent against a veterinarian. Even if Ohio courts recognized a claim for lack of informed consent against a veterinarian, expert testimony would be required 'to establish what the claimed undisclosed risks and dangers . . . are, and if disputed, whether those particular undisclosed risks did in fact materialize and cause the patient's injuries. These issues are beyond the knowledge of the lay person and require expert testimony.'").
184. While alternative, complementary, and/or holistic veterinary medicine can be practiced by a veterinarian, state statutes or regulations may have an intended or unintended consequence with regard to potential liability of such veterinary practitioners. By way of example, CONN. GEN. STAT. ANN. § 22-351a: *Liability for intentionally killing or injuring companion animal*, precludes the assessment of punitive damages and attorneys' fees in a judgment against a veterinarian "while following accepted standards of the practice of the [veterinary] profession." CONN. GEN. STAT. ANN. § 22-351a(d). Consequently, could an alternative, complementary, or holistic veterinarian be vulnerable to the assessment of punitive damages and attorneys' fees because he or she was not following accepted standards of the practice of veterinary medicine? A similar provision may be found in CONN. GEN. STAT. ANN. § 53-247: *Cruelty to animals*, pertaining to the assessment of fines up to $5,000.00 and/or imprisonment up to five years. CONN. GEN. STAT. ANN. § 53-247(b).

    Another example is 20 MO. CODE REGS. § 2270-6.011(5) declaring that Missouri veterinarians "at all times shall conform their practice to the *currently accepted standards for the profession of veterinary medicine* as these standards are set forth [in the Missouri Veterinary Practice Act] or by any rule lawfully promulgated by the board or as otherwise found to be accepted within the profession as gauged by reasonable conduct of other professionals engaged in the practice of veterinary medicine" (emphasis added).

Finally, the *A.V.M.A. Guidelines for Alternative and Complementary Veterinary Medicine, Recommendations for patient care,* recommends that "owner consent should be obtained prior to initiating any treatment, including CAVM." *Available at* http://www.avma.org/issues/policy/comp_alt_medicine.asp. *See also* Gregory M. Dennis, *Legal Issues Concerning Alternative & Complementary Veterinary Medicine* (Fort Collins, Colo.: Colo. State Univ., Coll. of Veterinary Med. & Biomedical Scis., Medical Acupuncture for Veterinarians, May 1, 2008); Gregory M. Dennis, *The Law and Complementary & Alternative Veterinary Medicine* (Kan. City, Mo.: Am. Holistic Veterinary Med. Ass'n, Sept. 13, 2004).

185. 2007 Ohio 4627 (11th Dist. App. 2007).
186. *See generally* Dana G. Allen, John K. Pringle & Dale Smith, *Xylazine, in* Handbook of Veterinary Drugs 493–94 (J. B. Lippincott Co. 1993).
187. *See, e.g., Acepromazine, id.* at 453 ("Priapism can occur in the horse, more commonly in stallions or recently castrated geldings, or in combination with etorphine. Thus, its use in stallions should be avoided.").
188. *See generally Butophanol [Torbugesic], id.* at 79–80.
189. "Priapism: persistent abnormal erection of the penis, accompanied by pain and tenderness. It is seen in disease and injuries of the spinal cord, and may be caused by vesical calculus and certain injuries to the penis." Saunders Comprehensive Veterinary Dictionary, *supra* note 2, at 1454.
190. "Phallectomy: amputation of the penis." Saunders Comprehensive Veterinary Dictionary, *supra* note 2, at 1369.
191. *Lawrence,* 2007 Ohio 4627, ¶¶ 30–31.
192. *Id.* at ¶ 46.
193. *See generally* Duane Fleming & John F. Scott, *The Informed Consent Doctrine: What Veterinarians Should Tell Their Clients,* 224(9) J.A.V.M.A. 1436 (May 1, 2004).
194. *Board Enhances AVMA Visibility*: "Informed consent" versus "owner consent," J.A.V.M.A. News (Dec. 15, 2007), *available at* http://www.avma.org/onlnews/javma/dec07/071215d.asp.
195. *See* Pruitt v. Box, 984 S.W.2d 709, 711 (Tex. App. El Paso 1999) (stating "the more appropriate standard [for veterinary malpractice] may be, as in other professional malpractice cases *where money* or personal property *is at stake,* a general negligence standard utilizing a standard of care applicable to a professional of ordinary skill and care in similar communities" (emphasis added).).
196. *See* James F. Wilson, Legal Consents for Veterinary Practices with Spanish Translation: Understanding the Legal Consent Doctrine

AND HOW TO ACHIEVE IT: DIFFERENTIATING CONSENT TERMINOLOGY, pp. 2–3 (Priority Press Ltd., 4th ed. 2006).

197. *E.g.*, Hoffa v. Bimes, 2008 Pa. Super. 181, ¶ 13, 954 A.2d 1241, 1247 (2008) (during an emergency situation, the law "dispenses with the need to secure the informed consent of the horse's owner prior to administering 'emergency care'").

198. "Zoonosis pl. zoonoses: disease of animals transmitted to humans. . . . direct [zoonosis:] one transmitted by contact or via an inanimate vehicle and which requires only one reservoir vertebrate (passing directly from animal to humans without the involvement of a vector or intermediate host) to maintain a cycle of infection, *e.g.* rabies. *See also* Cyclozoonosis, Metazoonosis, Saprozoonosis." SAUNDERS COMPREHENSIVE VETERINARY DICTIONARY, *supra* note 2, at 1957.

199. More than 250 zoonotic diseases have been identified. *See* Jessica Ryen Doyle, *Deadly Diseases You Can Catch from Your Pet*, FOXNEWS.COM (June 18, 2008).

200. *See generally* McNew v. Decatur Veterinary Hosp., 85 Ga. App. 54, 68 S.E.2d 221 (1951) (*un*successful claim that a veterinarian had failed to warn the plaintiff of the dangerous condition of its pup after being told by the owner of the pup's condition. The puppy had been brought to veterinary clinic after being bitten by a rabid dog and it was later released back to the owner); Placko v. Fawver, 55 Ill. App. 3d 759, 13 Ill. Dec. 492, 371 N.E.2d 187 (1977) (veterinarian who failed to take steps to assure that the body of a suspected rabid cat was not disposed of, was found liable where, because no test could be performed to determine whether in fact the cat was rabid, the child had to undergo series of painful rabies injections); Life for God's Stray Animals, Inc. v. New N. Rockdale County Homeowners Ass'n, 253 Ga. 551, 322 S.E.2d 239 (1984) (animal shelter was found to be a public nuisance, in part because of the spread of various zoonotic agents via the release of large amounts of animal waste giving rise to the possibility of transmission of zoonotic diseases to humans through well water); City of Fort Scott v. Brown, 133 Kan. 401, 300 P. 1093 (1931) (veterinary clinic declared a public nuisance because of unsanitary conditions that included, among other things, the veterinarian permitting diseased tissue from sick animals to remain on the premises); Leverett v. Town of Limon, 567 F. Supp. 471 (D. Colo. 1983) (large-animal veterinarian on outskirts of town operated a practice that at times had 200 or more head of cattle present. Inconsistency existed between municipality's zoning ordinances and maps whether the location of the veterinarian's practice was zoned residential or business-industrial. Municipality issued citation against veterinarian and found him to be in violation of zoning ordinances and that he had to shut down his practice at that location. The veterinarian brought a 42 U.S.C. § 1983 civil rights action. The federal district court denied the veterinarian's substantive due process

claim when it found that there was "a reasonable relationship between the number of cattle kept in a restricted area within a municipality and the risk of various diseases, including zoonotic diseases, *i.e.*, those transmissible from the cattle to humans." 567 F. Supp. at 474. However, the court found for the veterinarian on the basis of denial of *procedural* due process because of a biased official participating in the zoning proceedings against the veterinarian. 567 F. Supp. at 474–75.); Baylis v. Wilmington Med. Ctr., Inc., 477 A.2d 1051 (Del. Super. 1984), *aff'd*, 567 A.2d 418 (Del. 1989) (medical malpractice action for improper treatment of a patient who was suspected of having *toxicariasis*); Steele v. United States, 463 F. Supp. 321 (D. Alaska 1978) (optometrist was found negligent in failing to timely refer a 4-year-old child to an ophthalmologist. The court found that the child lost his eye because of *toxocara canis* and that if the optometrist had promptly referred the child to an ophthalmologist, the child might not have lost his eye).

201. Jessica Ryen Doyle, *Deadly Diseases You Can Catch from Your Pet*, FOXNEWS .COM (June 18, 2008) ("A Corpus Christi, Texas, man and his daughter spent weeks in the hospital because of a diseased cockatiel bought from a PetSmart, according to a lawsuit filed Tuesday by the man's family."); Josh Katz, *"Parrot Fever" Death Results in Lawsuit*, FINDINGDULCINEA.COM (July 1, 2008) ("After a [Corpus Christi, Texas] man died and his daughter fell into a coma, their family is suing PetSmart for selling them the cockatiel that allegedly caused the illness." "A man who bought a hamster from a Rhode Island PetSmart reportedly contracted the lymphocytic choriomeningitis virus (LCMV) from the animal, and then donated his liver to [another man], who died from the transplant."); Latham v. Wal-Mart Stores, Inc., 818 S.W.2d 673, 676 (Mo. App. E.D. 1991) (store was not strictly liable under products liability law for injuries to purchaser's husband caused by contracting psittacosis from a bird purchased at the store); Malicki v. Koci, 121 Ohio App. 3d 723, 727, 700 N.E.2d 913, 915 (8th Dist. 1997) (plaintiffs who received a parakeet as a gift and thereafter contracted psittacosis were allowed to maintain a negligence action against the pet store.).

202. *See generally* Jennifer G. Wright et al., *Infection Control Practices and Zoonotic Disease Risks Among Veterinarians in the United States*, 232(12), J.A.V.M.A. 1863 (June 15, 2008); Kate Hurley, *Zoonotic Disease: The Enemy in Our Midst*, ANIMAL SHELTERING (July–Aug. 2004); J. A. Allert, *Reducing Risk of Zoonotic Parasitic Diseases—A Shared Responsibility*, 207(4) J.A.V.M.A. 403 (Aug. 15, 1995); James F. Wilson et al., *New Directions Regarding Liability and Treatments for Zoonotic Parasitic Diseases*, VETERINARY FORUM (Nov., 1995). *See also* SMITHKLINE BEECHAM ANIMAL HEALTH, WHEN YOUR DOG HAS INTERNAL PARASITES (1990).

203. KATIE STENERODEN, D.V.M., M.P.H., STATIONARY VETERINARY CLINIC BIOLOGICAL RISK MANAGEMENT 17 (Iowa State Univ., Ctr. for Food Sec. & Pub. Health, Mar. 2005).

204. *Id.* at 18.
205. "Bartonella: a genus of gram-negative, coccoid or rod-shaped bacteria in the family Bartonella-ceae. *B. bacilliformis* is the cause of Oroya fever or Carrión's disease in humans and occasionally dogs, in South America. *B. henselae* causes cat-scratch disease, bacillary anigomatosis, and endocarditis in humans." SAUNDERS COMPREHENSIVE VETERINARY DICTIONARY, *supra* note 2, at 183.
206. STENERODEN, *supra* note 203, at 18.
207. 719 P.2d 474 (Okla. Civ. App. 1985).
208. "Brucellosis: infection by *Brucella* spp. It causes different syndromes in each animal species. (1) Bovine brucellosis, caused by *B. abortus*, is characterized by abortion in late pregnancy and subsequent infertility. (2) Ovine brucellosis, caused by *B. ovis*, is characterized by epididymitis in rams and resulting infertility. (3) Brucellosis in pigs, caused by *B. suis*, is a chronic disease manifested by infertility and abortion in sows, orchitis in boars and heavy piglet mortality. (4) Caprine brucellosis, caused by *B. melitensis*, is manifested principally by abortion although other signs including loss of weight, mastitis, lameness and orchities are also reported. (5) There is no specific brucella organism in horses but *B. abortus* occurs not infrequently as bursitis in fistulous withers and poll evil. (6) In dogs, *B. canis* causes late abortions in bitches, and infertility and scrotal dermatitis in males." SAUNDERS COMPREHENSIVE VETERINARY DICTIONARY, *supra* note 2, at 256. *See also* the definition for *Brucella*.
209. *Sloan*, 719 P.2d at 475.
210. STENERODEN, *supra* note 203, at 6.
211. "Toxoplasmosis: a contagious disease of all species caused by the sporozoan parasite *Toxoplasma gondi*. The principal manifestation in animals is as abortion in ewes. It is also a cause of sporadic cases of pneumonia, central nervous system disease, and less often retinochoroidis, and hepatitis in dogs and cats. Clinical signs include fever, malaise, lymphadenitis, abortion, fetal malformation. Major importance as a zoonosis from bradyzoities in meat." SAUNDERS COMPREHENSIVE VETERINARY DICTIONARY, *supra* note 2, at 1814.
212. "Psittacosis: a disease of psittacine birds caused by *Chlamydophila psittaci* and also the zoonotic disease caused by infection with this species; first seen in parrots and later found in other birds and domestic fowl, in which it is called Ornithosis. It is transmissible to humans. In birds psittacosis causes a systemic infection and signs including diarrhea and ocular and nasal discharge." *Id.* at 1483.
213. STENERODEN, *supra* note 203, at 7.
214. *Id. See also* HOW TO PREVENT TRANSMISSION OF INTESTINAL ROUNDWORMS FROM PETS TO PEOPLE: RECOMMENDATIONS TO VETERINARIANS (Div. of Parasitic Diseases, Ctrs. for Disease Control and Prevention & Am. Ass'n of Veterinary Parasitologists, Mar. 1995).

215. 825 F.2d 908, *reh'g denied*, 834 F.2d 425 (5th Cir. 1987), *cert. denied*, 485 U.S. 1099 (1988).
216. *Id.* at 913–14 (emphasis in original).
217. *Id.* at 914, n.7. *See* Bartlett v. MacRae, 54 Or. App. 516, 635 P.2d 666 (1981) (wrongful death action against a veterinarian for dispensing poisonous cattle dye in an improperly labeled container that was accidentally drunk by the plaintiff's decedent. The veterinarian was found 30 percent at fault, the decedent 70 percent at fault.).
218. 943 F. Supp. 1023 (D. Minn. 1996).
219. *See* Brandt v. Marshall Animal Clinic, 540 N.W.2d 870 (Minn. App. 1995) (malpractice action against a veterinarian and a state law product liability claim against an animal vaccine manufacturer arising from injuries to dairy cattle. State law claims against the vaccine manufacturer were preempted by APHIS regulations.).
220. *See generally* Brooks v. Goettl, 2006 WL 3691000 (W.D. Tex. 2006) (Wisconsin plaintiff who had picked up two miniature horses in Texas, for which a Texas veterinarian issued a health certificate allegedly based upon having seen the horses two days before for probably a minute and without checking the horses' temperature, pulse, or respiration or checking their medical history, sued the veterinarian for veterinary malpractice, negligence *per se*, breach of express warranty, fraud, negligent misrepresentation, strict products liability, promissory estoppel, intentional infliction of emotional distress, and breach of contract, because of an outbreak of equine strangles in the Wisconsin plaintiff's herd after the Texas horses arrived; summary judgment for veterinarian denied. *Id.* at *2.); Moreland v. Lowdermilk, 709 F. Supp. 722 (W.D. La. 1989) (presence of infection of parasites in a racehorse and its owner having not timely and properly maintained a de-worming program was the cause of the horse's death and not any actions or inactions by the veterinarians); Streeter v. Vaughan, 39 Wash. 2d 225, 233–34, 235 P.2d 193, 198–99 (1951) (unsuccessful fraud action by a cattle buyer against a veterinarian who had stated cattle were disease-free).
221. 76 F.3d 1261 (2nd Cir. 1996).
222. "Bovine viral leukosis: a highly fatal, systemic, malignant neoplasm of the reticulendothelial system of cattle. It is characterized by tumors composed of aggregations of neoplastic lymphocytes in almost any organ with a great variety of clinical syndromes resulting. The causative retrovirus is transmitted in a number of ways, including insect vectors, but only to cattle over about 1.5 years of age." SAUNDERS COMPREHENSIVE VETERINARY DICTIONARY, *supra* note 2, at 238.
223. *E.g.*, Ossining Union Free Sch. Dist. v. Anderson LaRocca Anderson, 73 N.Y.2d 417, 541 N.Y.S.2d 335 (1989).
224. In *Dorking*, the lawsuit was allowed to proceed against the *private* veterinarian, but the USDA was dismissed on the basis of governmental immunity under the Federal Tort Claims Act.

225. 67 F.3d 1340 (7th Cir. 1995).
226. *Id.* at 1347 (citations omitted).
227. *Id.*
228. 163 N.W.2d 904 (Iowa 1969).
229. "Anaplasmosis: a disease caused by *Anaplasma* spp. In cattle it is chronic, often remitting disease characterized by fever, jaundice, emaciation and anemia, but never hemoglobinuria. It is transmitted by a number of insect vectors, especially ticks. In sheep and goats the disease is subclinical. *See also* Babesiosis." SAUNDERS COMPREHENSIVE VETERINARY DICTIONARY, *supra* note 2, at 84.
230. Two justices of the Iowa Supreme Court dissented in *Hubbard*, declaring the state should be subject to suit because the cattle owner's action was "simply a malpractice claim against a veterinarian employed by the state, who was negligent in the performance of his professional duties." 163 N.W.2d at 913.
231. 550 N.E.2d 334 (Ind. 1990).
232. *Id.* at 338.
233. 502 So. 2d 573 (La. 1987).
234. *Id. See also* Neary v. Regents of Univ. of Cal., 185 Cal. App. 3d 1136, 230 Cal. Rptr. 281 (1st Dist. 1986); William C. Mitchell, Ltd. v. Brown, 576 N.W.2d 342 (Iowa 1998). *See generally* Gregory M. Dennis, *Personal Privacy and Confidentiality*, *in* BLACKWELL'S FIVE-MINUTE VETERINARY PRACTICE MANAGEMENT CONSULT 400–01 (Ames, Iowa: Blackwell Publ'g 2007).
235. 20 Ill. Ct. Cl. 213 (1951).
236. "Malignant edema: an acute infection of wounds by *Clostridum septicum*, *C. chauvoei*, *C. perfringens*, *C. sordellii* or *C. novyi*. The inflammation causes severe swelling and discoloration of skin and exposed tissues. There may be local subcutaneous emphysema and a frothy exudate, depending on the identity of the invading organism. There is a high fever and a profound toxemia; death follows within a few hours if treatment is not provided." SAUNDERS COMPREHENSIVE VETERINARY DICTIONARY, *supra* note 2, at 1095.
237. *See* Huie v. Wipperfurth, 632 So. 2d 1109, 1112 (Fla. App. 5th Dist. 1994) (stating "We, therefore, reluctantly conclude that the independent contract defense recognized in *Wendland* is no longer viable in an action brought against a dog owner under [FLA. STAT. ANN. §] 767.04 [dog owner liability statute]."). *See generally* Wendland v. Akers, 356 So. 2d 368, 371 (Fla. App. 4th Dist. 1978), *cert. denied*, 378 So. 2d 342 (Fla. 1979) (stating "In capsulized form we hold: the owner of a dog is not liable to a third party for damages from being bitten or otherwise injured by such document *subsequent to the delivery of possession and control of the dog to a qualified veterinarian for care or treatment and the acceptance of such employment and possession by the veterinarian*, in the absence of a showing of active

negligence by the owner which contributes directly to and becomes the proximate cause of said injury" (emphasis added).).

238. A. Hotlgrieve, *Shielding Clients from Injury Protects against Malpractice Claims*, 201 J.A.V.M.A. 1681 (Dec. 1, 1992). *See also* James F. Wilson, *Standards of Care for Animal Restraint: Reasonable and Prudent Daily Practice*, VETERINARY FORUM 21 (Nov. 1993).
239. Joseph H. King, Jr., *The Standard of Care for Veterinarians in Medical Malpractice Claims*, 58 TENN. L. REV. 1, 33–34 (1990).
240. *Id.* at 34–35.
241. *E.g.*, Smith v. Hugo, 714 So. 2d 467, 468 (Fla. App. 4th Dist. 1998).
242. *Id.* at 468 (stating "Under the [trial] court's instruction, the jury had the proper basis to resolve the issue of negligence and *comparative negligence*" (emphasis added).).
243. 320 N.C. 621, 359 S.E.2d 780 (1987), *rev'g* Branks v. Kern, 83 N.C. App. 348 S.E.2d 815 (1986).
244. *Id.* at 624, 359 S.E.2d at 783, 68 A.L.R.4th at 821.
245. *See, e.g.*, Melnychuk v. Ronaghan, 1999 CA. AB. CA. 170 (Alberta App. 1999) (a veterinarian had no duty to warn when the client was already aware of the risk of injury the scalpel posed).
246. *See generally* Cheryl M. Bailey, Annotation, *Liability for Injuries Caused by Cat*, 68 A.L.R.4TH 823 (1989).
247. *E.g.*, Smith v. Roans, 605 So. 2d 10 (La. App. 2nd Cir. 1992) (court not only recognized that dog bites were an occupational hazard of the veterinary profession but even went further to suggest the dog's conduct during the examination was not unreasonable and, in fact, was a part of his right of *self-defense*); Nelson v. Hall, 165 Cal. App. 3d 709, 715, 211 Cal. Rptr. 668, 673 (3rd Dist.); Scozzafava v. Lieb, 190 Cal. App. 3d 1575, 236 Cal. Rptr. 129, 130, fn. 3 (1st Dist. 1987); Molinari v. Tuskegee Univ., 339 F. Supp. 2d 1293, 1299 (M.D. Ala. 2004). *See generally* Tyra v. Delta Veterinary Clinic, Inc., 687 S.W.2d 931 (Mo. App. S.D. 1985) (veterinary assistant who was directed by the clinic's veterinarian to go to the veterinarian's farm and unload feed and sustained a back injury while doing so was covered by the workers' compensation act and *not* exempt from the act by reason of being engaged in an agricultural pursuit); Katie Burns, *Study Links Occupational Exposure With Risk of Miscarriage: Anesthetic Gates, Radiation, Pesticides Are Areas of Concern for Pregnant Workers*, J.A.V.M.A. (May 15, 2008), *available at* http://www.avma.org/onlnews/javma/May08/080515n.asp.
248. 339 F. Supp. 2d 1293 (M.D. Ala. 2004). *See also* PROSSER AND KEETON ON THE LAW OF TORTS § 68, at 495–96 (5th ed. 1984) ("*Effect of Comparative Negligence on Assumption of Risk*. The rise of comparative negligence has forced the courts and commentators to consider afresh the proper role for the assumption of risk defense. Indeed, several comparative negligence statutes by their terms abolish assumption of risk, in addition to

contributory negligence, as defenses that will bar liability altogether. Most of the statutes, however, are silent on assumption of risk, and so the matter has been thrown over to the courts.").

249. *Id.* at 1299.
250. *Id.* at 1300–01.
251. *See, e.g.*, Salko Farm & Stable, L.L.C. v. Baus, 2007 WL 1976241, at *5 (Conn. Super. 2007) (the administration of a drug "by a veterinarian for the purpose of providing treatment, and that it was obtained and maintained to enable a veterinarian to do so when needed, is a part of the practice of veterinary medicine"). *See also* Phillips v. Baus, 2007 WL 1976219, at *5 (Conn. Super. 2007) (same); Block v. State, 53 Ill. Ct. Cl. 128 (2000); Ladnier v. Norwood, 616 F. Supp. 940 (E.D. La. 1985), *aff'd*, 781 F.2d 490 (5th Cir. 1986).
252. *E.g.*, Lawrence v. Big Creek Veterinary Hosp., L.L.C., 2007 Ohio 4627 (App. 11th Dist. 2007) (acepromazine administered to a male horse allegedly resulting in a permanent erection).
253. *See, e.g.*, Ullmann v. Duffus, 2005 Ohio 6060 (App. 10th Dist. 2005), *appeal denied*, 109 Ohio St. 3d 1406, 845 N.E.2d 523, *reh'g denied*, 109 Ohio St. 3d 1498, 848 N.E.2d 859 (2006).
254. *E.g.*, Animal Medicinal Drug Use Clarification Act of 1994 (AMDUCA), 21 U.S.C. § 360b. In 1994 Congress passed AMDUCA, which basically codified an existing Food and Drug Administration, Center for Veterinary Medicine, Compliance Policy Guide 7126.06 on extralabel drug use by veterinarians and F.D.A. Compliance Policy Guide 7125.35 on human-labeled drugs distributed and used in animal medicine. *See, e.g.*, Phillips v. Baus, 2007 WL 1976219 (Conn. Super. 2007) (alleging violation of AMDUCA and the Connecticut Unfair Trade Practices Act by a veterinarian administering a compound drug (betamethasone) to a show horse). *See also* Salko Farm & Stable, L.L.C. v. Baus, 2007 WL 1976241 (Conn. Super. 2007). *See generally* B. Buttitta, *Has Landmark Legislation Lost its Luster?*, 10(11) Veterinary Product News 1 (Nov. 1998).
255. *See generally* Downing v. Dixon, 313 S.W.2d 644, 650 (Mo. 1958) (stating "It has been settled many times that the violation of a statute or ordinance is negligence *per se* . . . but it is also well settled that the violation must be shown to have been the proximate cause of the injury.").
256. 313 Pa. Super. 75, 459 A.2d 417 (1983), *aff'd*, 376 Pa. Super. 557, 546 A. 2d 665 (1988), *appeal denied*, 524 Pa. 608, 569 A.2d 1367 (1989).
257. *Id.* at 80–81, 459 A.2d at 419–20.
258. 206 N.W.2d 713 (Iowa 1973).
259. 1986 WL 6670 (Ohio App. 9th Dist. 1986).
260. *Id.* at *1, citing Swoboda v. Brown (1935) Ohio State 513, syllabus four, 2 Ohio Op. 516, 196 N.E. 274 (1935).
261. 85 Idaho 64, 375 P.2d 704 (1962).

262. "You are instructed that the violation of a statute or regulation made by a State Agency under authority of statute, intended for the protection of a person and others like situated, which results in his injury and is the proximate cause of it, is negligence *per se*." 85 Idaho at 73–74, 375 P.2d at 709.
263. 85 Idaho at 76, 375 P.2d at 711.
264. 54 Or. App. 516, 635 P.2d 666 (1981).
265. 54 Or. App. at 519–20, 636 P.2d at 667–68.
266. *See generally* Jay M. Zitter, Annotation, *Measure, Elements, and Amount of Damages for Killing or Injuring Cat*, 8 A.L.R.4TH 1287 (1981); J. A. Connelly, Annotation, *Measure and Elements of Damages for Killing or Injuring Dog*, 1 A.L.R.3D 997 (1965).
267. *See generally* Bruce A. Wagman & Jayne M. DeYoung, *Actions Involving Injuries to Animals*, 90 AM. JUR. PROOF OF FACTS 1, §§ 20–32 (2006); Sam A. Mackie, *Veterinary Malpractice*, 32 AM. JUR. PROOF OF FACTS 3d 351, § 10: Elements of damages; Checklist at 377–78 (1995).
268. Phillips v. Baus, 2007 WL 1976219, at *4 (Conn. Super. 2007). *See also* Salko Farm & Stable, L.L.C. v. Baus, 2007 WL 1976241, at *4 (Conn. Super. 2007) (same).
269. *See, e.g.*, Wright v. Edison, 619 S.W.2d 797, 801–02 (Mo. App. E.D. 1981) (the measure of damages of injury to an animal is the difference between the fair market value of the animal immediately before and immediately after the purported injury); Ruden v. Hansen, 206 N.W.2d 713 (Iowa 1973) (the measure of damages for loss of livestock (hogs) is the difference between the reasonable market value of the animals immediately before and after the veterinarian's negligent act. Also, the farmer could recover the expense of feeding gilts from the date of purchase until farrowing but could not recover the cost of extra pig feed allegedly made necessary to raise unhealthy pigs. Nor could the farmer recover for loss of anticipated future profits.); Frost v. Taylor, 649 S.W.2d 264 (Mo. App. S.D. 1983) ($1,500 damage award for death of a 14-month old female Walker dog; no specification or breakdown as how amount was determined); Ponder v. Angel Animal Hosp., Inc., 762 S.W.2d 846 (Mo. App. S.D. 1988) (plaintiff-client was not entitled to an award of damages in her action against a veterinarian for alleged negligent castration of her dog where there was no evidence of reduction in value due to the castration or any evidence showing monetary loss to the plaintiff); Collins v. Ubanoski, 1989 WL 131120 (Tex. App. Houston 1989) (jury awarded plaintiff $31,450 for the loss of steer due to veterinary malpractice. However, the only evidence of the animal's market value that was presented to the jury was that the animal was worth $2,256 immediately before the negligent act and $500 after the wrongful act. Consequently, as there was no evidence presented to the jury that would have supported a verdict of $31,450, the verdict

had to be set aside and a new trial ordered. The Texas Court of Appeals noted that market value meant "the amount that would be paid in cash by a willing buyer who desires to buy, but is not required to buy, to a willing seller who desires to sell, but is under no necessity of selling." Further, in determining market value "the highest and best use to which the animal may have been used" is to be considered.); Julian v. DeVincent, 155 W. Va. 320, 184 S.E.2d 535 (1971) (plaintiff, whose dog was killed by defendant's dog, could not recover damages in the absence of evidence showing the value of its dog); Cantling v. Han. & St. Joe. R.R. Co., 54 Mo. 385, 391 (1873) (no recovery for the loss of two dogs, other than fair market value).

See generally Rebecca J. Huss, *Valuation in Veterinary Malpractice*, 35 Loy. U. Chi. L. J. 479 (Winter 2004); Margit Livingston, *The Calculus of Animal Valuation: Crafting a Viable Remedy*, 82 Neb. L. Rev. 873 (2004).

270. *E.g.*, Petco Animal Supplies, Inc. v. Schuster, 144 S.W.3d 554 (Tex. App. 3rd Dist. 2004) (while mental anguish, intrinsic value for loss of companionship, lost wages, and punitive damages were not recoverable, the dog owner was entitled to recover replacement value and to be reimbursed for costs to train a new dog).
271. *E.g.*, Burgess v. Shampooch Pet Indus., Inc., 35 Kan. App. 2d 485, 131 P.3d 1248 (2006) (recognized that where an animal that had been injured had no "fair market value," so as to determine the amount of the owner's damages, then "the measure of damages may include, but is not limited to, the reasonable and customary cost of necessary veterinary care and treatment").
272. *See, e.g.*, Bueckner v. Hamel, 886 S.W.2d 368, 371 (Tex. App. Houston 1994) (while the owner could be entitled to the value of an animal wrongfully killed and for the breeding value of such animal, the owner was *not* entitled to a damage award for the loss of future progeny from the animal).
273. Levine v. Knowles, 218 So. 2d 217 (Fla. App. 3rd Dist. 1969) (verdict of $1,000 against a veterinarian for negligent disposal of the body of a dead dog was excessive where the only evidence before the jury was that the dog, when alive, was worth $100. For the first appeal *see* Levine v. Knowles, 197 So. 2d 329 (Fla. App. 3rd Dist. 1967).).
274. *E.g.*, Safford Animal Hosp. v. Blain, 119 Ariz. 296, 580 P.2d 757 (App. 1978) (a cow that escaped from a veterinary hospital ran into and injured the veterinarian's neighbor who was trying to help the veterinarian to capture the cow).
275. *See, e.g.*, Mazella v. Fairfield Equine Assocs., P.C., 2005 WL 2452908 (S.D.N.Y. 2005).
276. *See* Bartlett v. MacRae, 54 Or. App. 516, 635 P.2d 666 (1981) (wrongful death action against a veterinarian for dispensing a poisonous cattle dye in an improperly labeled container that was accidentally drunk by the plaintiff's decedent. The jury attributed 30 percent fault to the veterinar-

ian and the remaining 70 percent to the decedent.). *See generally* Sherman v. Kissinger, 146 Wash. App. 855, 860, ¶ 1, 195 P.3d 539, 542, ¶ 1 (2008) (unlike for humans, there is no cause of action for wrongful death of an animal).

277. *See generally* William A. Reppy, Jr., *Punitive Damage Awards in Pet-Death Cases: How do the Ratio Rules of State Farm v. Campbell Apply?*, 1 J. ANIMAL LAW & ETHICS 19 (2006) (discussing State Farm Mut. Auto. Ins. Co. v. Campbell, 538 U.S. 408 (2003)).

278. While there has been much discussion about whether or not an animal owner should be allowed to recover emotional pain and suffering, mental distress, and/or loss of companionship damages for the death of or injury to an animal, most states still do not allow such a recovery for ordinary negligence or malpractice. *See generally* Victor E. Schwartz and Emily J. Laird, *Non-Economic Damages in Pet Litigation: The Serious Need to Preserve a Rational Rule*, 33 PEPP. L. REV. 227 (2006); Jay M. Zitter, Annotation, *Recovery of Damages for Emotional Distress Due to Treatment of Pets and Animals*, 91 A.L.R.5TH 545 (2001).

Two states that were considered to allow emotional pain and suffering or distress damages for loss of an animal subsequently changed their position to not allowing such damages to be recoverable. For instance, in Campbell v. Animal Quarantine Station, 63 Haw. 557, 632 P.2d 1066 (1981), mental distress was deemed a proper item of damage recovery for death of a family pet caused by defendant's negligent conduct. However, in 1986 the Hawaii legislature statutorily negated emotional loss damages arising "solely out of damage to property or material objects." HAW. STAT. ANN. § 663-8.9(a). *See, e.g.*, City of Tyler v. Likes, 41 Tex. Sup. Ct. J. 174, 962 S.W.2d 489, 500 (1997) (the Hawaii "state legislature in 1986 reversed that policy, enacting a statute barring liability for negligent infliction of emotional distress based solely on damage to property, HAW. REV. STAT. ANN. § 663-8.9 (Michie 1995)"). Hawaii Senate Bill 1301 (2007), carried over to the 2008 session, might restore such an action but not against a veterinarian unless he or she had been grossly negligent or engaged in a wanton act or omission.

Byas v. Kennedy, 867 So. 2d 1195 (Fla. App. 1st Dist. 2004), a veterinary malpractice action, ruled that an earlier Florida decision—Knowles Animal Hosp., Inc. v. Willis, 360 So. 2d 37 (Fla. App. 3rd Dist. 1978), *cert. denied*, 368 So. 2d 1369 (Fla. 1979)—that had allowed emotional pain and suffering damages for loss of an animal had been effectively negated by a 1995 decision of the Florida Supreme Court adopting the "impact rule" that requires some physical impact upon the plaintiff before the recovery of damages for emotional distress can be recovered. *E.g.*, Zell v. Meek, 665 So. 2d 1048 (Fla. 1995). The *Byas* court found another earlier decision—LaPorte v. Associated Indeps., Inc., 163 So. 2d 267, 269 (Fla. 1964)—to be distinguishable as *LaPorte* involved malicious conduct toward a cat (throwing a garbage can at it) compared to simple negligent behavior by a veterinarian who was trying to provide treatment.

See also Kondaurov v. Kerdasha, 271 Va. 646, 657, 629 S.E.2d 181, 186–87 (2006) (stating "We conclude that permitting such an award [for emotional grief for loss of a pet] would amount to a sweeping change in the law of damages, a subject properly left to legislative consideration."); Carbasho v. Musulin, 217 W. Va. 359, 362, 618 S.E.2d 368, 371 (2005) ("Our statutory law, as well as this Court's decision in *Julian* [*v. DeVincent*, 155 W. Va. 320, 184 S.E.2d 535, 536 (1971)], clearly establish that damages for sentimental value, mental suffering, and emotional distress are not recoverable for the death of a pet dog. Not only is that the law of this State, but it is also the general rule in a majority of jurisdictions. *See, e.g.*, Oberschlake v. Veterinary Assocs. Animal Hosp., 151 Ohio App. 3d 741, 785 N.E.2d 811 (2003); Koester v. VCA Animal Hosp., 244 Mich. App. 173, 624 N.W.2d 209 (2000); Harabes v. Barkery, Inc., 348 N.J. Super. 366, 791 A.2d 1142 (2001); Zeid v. Pearce, 953 S.W.2d 368 (Tex. App. 1997); Jason v. Parks, 224 A.D.2d 494, 638 N.Y.S.2d 170 (1996); Nichols v. Sukaro Kennels, 555 N.W.2d 689 (Iowa 1996). *But see* Campbell v. Animal Quarantine Station, 63 Haw. 557, 632 P.2d 1066 (1981); Knowles Animal Hosp., Inc. v. Wills, 360 So. 2d 37 (Fla. Dist. Ct. App. 1978)."); Julian v. DeVincent, 155 W. Va. 320, 184 S.E.2d 535, 536 (1971) (plaintiff could not recover damages for the sentimental value of its dog); Petco Animal Supplies, Inc. v. Schuster, 144 S.W.3d 554 (Tex. App. 3rd Dist. 2004) (mental anguish, intrinsic value for loss of companionship, lost wages and punitive damages are not recoverable); Myers v. City of Hartford, 84 Conn. App. 395, 853 A.2d 621, *cert. denied*, 271 Conn. 927, 859 A.2d 582 (2004) (not allowing infliction of emotional distress claim for premature and improper euthanasia of a stray dog); Liotta v. Segur, 36 Conn. L. Rep. 621 (2004) (dog owner could not assert a negligent infliction of emotional distress claim and recover mental anguish damages arising from an injury to its dog that ultimately resulted in it having to be euthanized); Oberschlake v. Veterinary Assocs. Animal Hosp., 151 Ohio App. 3d 741, 785 N.E.2d 811 (2nd Dist. 2003) (veterinary malpractice action, rejecting dog owners' emotional pain and suffering claims and dog's pain and suffering claim brought by his owners as "pet guardians"); Ullmann v. Duffus, 2005 Ohio 6060 ¶ 30 (10th Dist. App. 2005), *appeal denied*, 109 Ohio St. 3d 1406, 845 N.E.2d 523, *reh'g denied*, 109 Ohio St. 3d 1498, 848 N.E.2d 859 (2006); Pacher v. Invisible Fence of Dayton, 154 Ohio App. 3d 744, 798 N.E.2d 1121 (2nd Dist. 2003); Krasnecky v. Meffen, 56 Mass. App. 418, 422–23, 777 N.E.2d 1286, 1289 (2002), *appeal denied*, 438 Mass. 1106, 782 N.E.2d 516 (2003) (denying sheep owners' claims for emotional distress and loss of companionship damages); Fackler v. Genetzky, 257 Neb. 130, 595 N.W.2d 884 (1999), *appeal after remand*, 263 Neb. 68, 638 N.W.2d 521 (2002) (rejecting claim for emotional pain and suffering for the negligent death of two horses brought against a veterinarian. However, the Nebraska Supreme Court appeared to leave open for another day the question if such damages could be allowed for an *intentional* injuring or killing of an animal. *Citing* Richardson v. Fairbanks N. Star Borough, 705 P.2d 454 (Alaska 1985) and Gill v. Brown, 107 Idaho 1137, 695 P.2d 1276 (App. 1985).); Zeid v. Pearce, 953 S.W.2d 368 (Tex. App. El Paso 1997) (refused to allow a pet owner to recover emotional pain and suffering damages from a veterinarian whom the owner accused was negligent for having vaccinated a dog. The court noted that since at least 1891 (*e.g.*, Heiligmann v. Rose, 81 Tex. 222, 16 S.W. 931 [1891]), Texas had adhered to the rule that the only recovery possible for loss of a dog was the animal's market value, if any, or some special or pecuniary value to the owner that could be ascertained by reference to the dog's usefulness or services. 953 S.W.2d at 369.); City of Canadian v. Guthrie, 87 S.W.2d 316, 318 (Tex. Civ. App. Amarillo 1932) (horse owner could *not* recover sentimental value damages for loss of horse); Nichols v. Sukaro Kennels, 555 N.W.2d 689 (Iowa 1996) (declining to recognize a claim by pet owners for emotional pain and suffering when their toy poodle was attacked and killed by another dog at a kennel); Jason v. Parks, 224 App. Div. 2d 494, 638 N.Y.S.2d 170 (1996) (declined to recognize a claim against a veterinarian for a client's emotional pain and suffering for death or injury to a pet); McDonald v. Ohio State Univ. Veterinary, 67 Ohio Misc. 2d 40, 644 N.E.2d 750 (1994) (while sentimental value is not recoverable for injury to an animal, the owner was entitled to recover expenses incurred in trying to rehabilitate a pedigree show dog after a negligently performed surgery); Carroll v. Rock, 220 Ga. App. 260, 469 S.E.2d 391, 394 (1996) (trial court allowed evidence of the pet owner's mental condition following escape of her cat and its disappearance from a veterinary clinic. The admission of such evidence was reversible error as the pet owner had made no claim for either negligent or intentional infliction of emotional distress.); Janovski v. Presser Animal Hosp., Ltd., 157 Ill. App. 3d 818, 821, 510 N.E.2d 1084, 1087 (1987) (dog owner could *not* recover for loss of companionship resulting from veterinarian's negligently caused death of dog); Miller v. Parana, 426 Pa. Super. 189, 626 A.2d 637 (1993) (in an action for intentional infliction of emotional distress arising from the defendant-veterinarian's alleged beating to death of the plaintiff's dog, the veterinarian's conduct did *not* rise to the level of outrageousness necessary to support an award of damages.); Daughen v. Fox, 372 Pa. Super. 405, 539 A.2d 858, *appeal denied*, 520 Pa. 605, 553 A.2d 967 (1988) (under no circumstances may there be recovery of damages for the loss of companionship of a pet); Peloquin v. Calcasieu Parish Policy Jury, 367 So. 2d 1246 (La. App. 3rd Cir.), *appeal after remand*, 378 So. 2d 560 (La. App. 3rd Cir. 1979) (plaintiffs stated a sufficient cause of action for loss of their cat, which had been destroyed by a local animal shelter. At the trial following the remand from the Louisiana Court of Appeal, the jury returned a verdict that the cat that had been destroyed by the local animal shelter was *not* the plaintiffs' cat. Therefore, the plaintiffs recovered nothing. *E.g.*, Peloquin v. Calcasieu Parish Police Jury, 378 So. 2d 560, 561 (La. App. 3rd Cir. 1979).); Wilcox v. Butt's Drug Stores, 38 N.M. 502, 35 P.2d 978, 979 (1934) (action for wrongful death of a dog where druggist had sold strychnine tablets to a dog owner to be used as a laxative and dog promptly died. While the owner had a cause of action against the druggist, owner could not recover for the sentimental value of the dog.). *But see* Burgess v. Shampooch Pet Indus., Inc., 35 Kan. App. 2d 485, 131 P.3d 1248 (2006) (recognized that where an animal that had been injured had no "fair market value," so as to determine the amount of the owner's damages, then "the measure of damages may include, but is not limited to, the reasonable and customary cost of necessary veterinary care and treatment"); Am. Legal Def. Fund, Inc. v. Glickman, 332 U.S. App. D.C. 104, 154 F.3d 426 (1998), *cert. denied*, 526 U.S. 1064 (1999) (zoo visitor could maintain an action under the Endangered Species Act for aesthetic injury for having allegedly seen nonhuman primates in non-humane conditions at a zoo); Am. Soc. for the Prevention of Cruelty to Animals v. Ringling Bros., 354 U.S. App. D.C. 432, 317 F.3d 334 (2003) (former circus employee could maintain an action under the Endangered Species Act for aesthetic and emotional injury from allegedly having seen elephants mistreated); Wright v. Edison, 619 S.W.2d 797, 801–02 (Mo. App. E.D. 1981) (in an action for damages to a house and personal possessions therein caused by buyers during remodeling before the closing date on the sale of the house, sellers were not entitled to future damages because of the alleged nervousness of their cat who had been left in the house. *Nervousness* of the cat could be considered a factor in arriving at opinion as to the cat's *current* monetary value, but jury should *not* be allowed to speculate on *future* behavior of the cat.). *See generally* Lewis v. DiDonna, 294 App. Div. 2d 799, 743 N.Y.S.2d 186 (2004) (negligence action against a pharmacy for mislabeling a prescription for a dog); Hey v. Moran & Maxi Drug, Inc., 2002-569-A, PC 01-3682 (R.I. 2003) (action alleging a pharmacist had improperly filled a prescription resulting in a dog having to be euthanized); Klein v. St. Louis Transit Co., 117 Mo. App. 619, 93 S.W. 281, 282–83 (St. L. 1906) (pet owner may *not* recover damages for its mental suffering resulting from the loss of its pet).

279. *E.g.*, Langford v. Emergency Pet Clinic, 96 Ohio App. 3d 174, 178, 644 N.E.2d 1035, 1037 (8th Dist.), *appeal denied*, 71 Ohio St. 3d 1045, 641 N.E.2d 203 (1944) (affirmed the dismissal of a dog owner's action for intentional or negligent infliction of emotional distress for allegedly improper burial of its dog in a mass grave); Annunziata v. Millar, 241 N.J. Super. 275, 287, 574 A.2d 1021, 1027 (1990) (involved animal remains buried in a pet cemetery behind a veterinary clinic, which was to be closed. "Here we are not dealing with human remains. If deference is to be given to human

remains—and there is a consensus in society for that—the same cannot be said to apply to animals—no matter how much affection they have engendered in the hearts of their owners. If the owner wishes something of a permanent nature for his or her pet's remains, the owner may contract for and pay for that. There are commercial pet cemeteries available. The plaintiff owners here chose not to do so."). *Contra*, Corso v. Crawford Dog & Cat Hosp., Inc., 97 Misc. 2d 530, 531, 415 N.Y.S.2d 182, 183 (1979) (wrongfully withholding or destroying a pet's body by an organization that was supposed to have arranged for the pet's funeral gave rise to an actionable tort lawsuit. "As in the case where a human body is withheld [citations omitted], the wrongful withholding or, as here, destruction of the dog's body, gives rise to an actionable tort.").

280. Superseded, in part, by Wagman & DeYoung, 90 Am. Jur. Proof of Facts 3d, *Actions Involving Injuries to Animals* (2006).

CHAPTER 5

Animal-Related Contract and Sales Disputes

JULIE I. FERSHTMAN

I. Introduction

Animals are complex subjects of contracts. Unlike contracts involving basic goods and services, contracts involving animals can require numerous details that take into account the animal's continuing needs. Statutes in many states can be applied to animal-related disputes, such as the Uniform Commercial Code and deceptive trade practice laws. It often makes good sense for counsel to invoke these laws when they could add the potential to recover legal fees.

II. Common-Law Issues

A. Bailments

Animal ownership requires boarding the animal on occasion. The boarding relationship can potentially create bailment and agistment arrangements.

Black's Law Dictionary (7th ed.) defines a "bailment" as "[a] delivery of personal property by one person (the bailor) to another (the bailee) who holds the property for a certain purpose under an express or implied-in-fact contract. Unlike a sale or gift of personal property, a bailment involves a change in possession but not in title."[1] Traditionally, where the subject of the bailment is damaged, lost, or destroyed, courts have imposed a presumption of negligence on the bailee. Under that approach, the bailor must first come forth and prove that a bailment arrangement existed and the extent of damage to the goods. Thereafter, the bailee must then come forth with evidence that the loss or damage was not due to the bailee's negligence.[2]

Courts do not automatically impose this presumption against bailees. Courts have declined to do so, for example, where the bailee did not have exclusive control and access to the item at issue or where the bailee was in no better position than the bailor to prevent, know, or ascertain the cause of the loss.[3] And not all courts are convinced that animals, which are alive and mobile, deserve to be the subjects of a bailment and, consequently, receive the same treatment in the eyes of the law as inanimate objects that can be kept in controlled and secure conditions.[4]

"Agistment" has been defined as "a species of bailment whereby one agrees to keep and care for another's animals."[5]

Ultimately, litigation involving bailments frequently involves the legal standard of negligence. That is, the inquiry focuses on whether the one given possession and custody of an animal belonging to another for care and keeping has given the animal "reasonable care." In addition, states may have unique legal provisions pertaining to bailment arrangements. In Washington, for example, a court held that professional bailees cannot legally disclaim liability for their own acts of negligence.[6] Kentucky passed legislation, specific to boarding of horses, that provides an exception to the general rule that damages to bailed property that was delivered in good condition creates a rebuttable presumption of negligence on the part of the bailee.[7]

Disputes have existed over the years involving injuries to animals that include

- A stable that provided its boarded horses with hay that had blister beetles, causing several of the horses to die.
- The death of a dog at a boarding kennel, allegedly due to an improper administration of medication.
- The death of horses at a stable due to a barn fire of undetermined origin.

Res ipsa loquitur has been raised in bailment cases, with little success. In one case from Kentucky, for example, racehorses perished in a barn fire, and the owner of a few of them brought suit. The court rejected the application of *res ipsa loquitur* based on the facts and recognized that "[t]he fact that some mystery accompanies an accident does not justify the application of the doctrine of res ipsa loquitur."[8]

B. Fraud or Misrepresentation

From the standpoint of the buyer's counsel, claims of fraud present challenges as to pleading and proof. In the pleading stages, Federal Rule of Civil Procedure 9(b) and comparable state rules of procedure require that parties alleging fraud or mistake in their pleadings "must state with particularity the circumstances constituting fraud or mistake. Malice, intent, knowledge, and other conditions of a person's mind may be alleged generally."

Fraud can occur through active misrepresentation or by concealment when the party had some form of duty to make a disclosure.

Generally, a prima facie case of fraud or misrepresentation includes these elements:

1. A misrepresentation
2. Of a material fact or opinion to another
3. Made for the purpose of inducing reliance by the other party
4. Which induces reliance by the other party
5. To his or her detriment.[9]

It is widely accepted that a fraudulent statement must relate to a present or preexisting fact. In animal sales transactions, for example, a claim of fraud could potentially be predicated on statements regarding a horse's current physical capabilities to compete in jumping events. By comparison, a fraud claim would likely fail if based on the seller's opinion that a particular horse offered for sale should win blue ribbons in the future.

In an attempt to overcome the difficulties of proving that the defendant intended to defraud, counsel for plaintiffs could consider a few options.

First, counsel might evaluate whether the jurisdiction recognizes claims of innocent misrepresentation, as these claims require lesser degrees of proof. Innocent misrepresentation "may be actionable if the declarant has the means of knowing, ought to know, or has the duty of knowing the truth" of a representation that turns out to be false.[10]

Second, counsel can consider the possibility of making a claim of negligent misrepresentation. A claim of negligent misrepresentation "merely requires proof that the defendant failed to exercise reasonable care or competence to obtain or communicate true information."[11] In some states, a claim for negligent misrepresentation requires that the parties have a special relationship of trust and confidence.[12]

Third, counsel might want to evaluate whether the applicable facts and law warrant a claim under the Uniform Commercial Code, such as a claim for breach of implied warranties. Claims of this type do not require proof of the seller's intent to deceive.

A common defense in sales fraud litigation is that the buyer accepted the animal "as is" and cannot thereafter be heard to complain. This position has succeeded in some cases,[13] but has been rejected by some courts. In *Richie and Pat Bonvie Stables, Inc. v. Irving*,[14] for example, the plaintiffs purchased a horse at an auction that was represented as never having been injected and being "100 percent," when the horse had actually been through surgery. Although the sales catalog included an "as is" clause, the court refused to accept it and found that such clauses could not shield defendants from its fraudulent misrepresentation and concealment.

Defenses to a fraud claim include lack of misrepresentation, the plaintiff's lack of reliance on the defendant, plaintiff's failure to mitigate, and the plaintiff's ratification of the complained-of transaction by failure to respond within a prompt period of time. In *Vanier v. Ponsoldt*,[15] for example, the plaintiff bought an Arabian stallion at an auction but sensed that the auction was conducted in a fraudulent manner, yet the plaintiff continued making installment payments on the horse afterward. The court held that the plaintiff's actions constituted ratification of the sale because he failed to repudiate it in a timely manner.

C. Breach of Fiduciary Duties

A fiduciary relationship exists where the parties are under a duty to act for or get advice for the benefit of another upon matters within the scope of trust relations, and where special confidence is reposed in another who in equity and good conscience is bound to act in good faith and with due regard to interests of one reposing confidence.[16] The relationship is sometimes described as a "confidential relationship" in that a special confidence is reposed between the parties.[17]

Agency relationships commonly give rise to fiduciary duties. As the *Restatement of Agency (Second)* § 1 indicates, agency results from the manifestation of consent, as well as from actual consent, by one person to another that the other shall act on his or her behalf and be subject to his or her control. Fiduciary duties imposed on agents include the duty of full disclosure, duty of loyalty, and duty of faithfulness to the principal.[18] Sales agents for buyers of horses can qualify as fiduciaries.[19]

Courts have held that one seeking to establish the existence of a fiduciary relationship should do so by a preponderance of the evidence.[20] An excellent resource for counsel evaluating cases involving claims of a fiduciary relationship and fiduciary duties is the *Restatement of Agency*

(Second), which addresses the creation of the fiduciary relationship and types of fiduciary duties.

D. Replevin

An action for replevin requires a party to show that he or she has title to an item, such as a horse, and that he or she is entitled to immediate possession.[21] In *Rapuano v. Rapuano*,[22] the plaintiff sued to recover possession of a horse that had been stabled with her daughter. The court noted that statute prevented the commingling of a cause of action for replevin with any other cause of action except conversion. Also, in *Livengood v. Markusson*,[23] the court held that the owner of a pet cat has a property right, and is therefore entitled to recover the possession of the cat by replevin proceedings.

III. *Statutory Issues*

A. Uniform Commercial Code and Breach of Warranties

State Uniform Commercial Codes have been applied to animal sales. However, counsel should carefully research the applicable state UCC before asserting such claims, because a few state UCCs include specific provisions making them inapplicable to certain types of animals. For example, Missouri has eliminated implied warranties for livestock sales.[24] Kentucky law provides no implied warranties that animals are free of disease or sickness.[25] Other states, such as Florida, have exempted certain animals, such as cattle and hogs, from implied warranties.[26]

In determining whether a state Uniform Commercial Code applies to a particular transaction, counsel can make three inquiries: (1) the seller must qualify as a "merchant" under the law; (2) the transaction must qualify as a "sale of goods"; and (3) the warranty must not have been excluded or modified in a legally sufficient manner.

Certain types of animals, typically livestock, have qualified as "goods" for purposes of applying the UCC to sales.[27] Also, a seller was liable for breach of warranty by selling chicks that were infected with a disease.[28] Commercial sellers of animals have qualified, but one case held that cattle ranchers are not "merchants" as to sales of cattle for purposes with which they were not familiar.[29]

Counsel representing buyers have every incentive to include a theory of breach of implied warranty or breach of express warranty because the particular standards of proof are much more lenient than that of claims of common-law fraud and misrepresentation. In the equine sale case of *Randazzo v. McCarthy*,[30] for example, the court dismissed the fraud claims but allowed the plaintiff to pursue its claims of breach of implied warranty.

1. *Breach of Implied Warranty of Merchantability*[31]

Section 2-314 of the Uniform Commercial Code provides that unless excluded or modified, a warranty that the goods shall be merchantable is implied in a contract for their sale if the seller is a merchant with respect to goods of that kind. This provision also states, in Section 2-314(2), that goods to be merchantable "must be at least such as (a) pass without objection in the trade under the contract description; and . . . (c) are fit for the ordinary purposes for which such goods are used." Section 2-314(3) provides that unless excluded or modified, implied warranties may arise from course of dealings or usage of the trade.

2. *Breach of Implied Warranty of Fitness for a Particular Purpose*

Section 2-315 of the Uniform Commercial Code states that an implied warranty of fitness for a particular purpose may exist "[w]here the seller, at the time of contracting, has reason to know any particular purpose for which the goods are required and that buyer is relying on the seller's skill or judgment to select and furnish suitable goods . . ."

One court held that merely because a stallion is sold does not necessarily mean that the horse is fit for use as a breeding stallion,[32] or that a Thoroughbred mare is fit for breeding purposes and to be used as a broodmare.[33] One court held that an implied warranty was not created regarding a young bull's future breeding capacity because the information was impossible to predict at the time of the sale.[34]

In another case, where the buyer purchased a male dog for breeding purposes, but the dog had an undescended testicle that might be a hereditary condition that would decrease the dog's value as a stud, the seller was found to have breached his implied warranty of merchantability.[35]

3. *Breach of Express Warranty*

Counsel need to carefully evaluate whether the statements on which a plaintiff relies as "representations" or "warranties" truly qualify as a matter of law as express warranties. Under the UCC, an express warranty is made to a buyer that relates to "goods" and must become "part of the basis of the bargain." Express warranties need not be made in writing and they need not be part of a written contract. Statements in advertisements and catalogs can constitute express warranties if they become part of the basis of the bargain.[36]

Representations regarding a horse's condition and abilities might qualify as express warranties.[37] Representations regarding a horse's age could also qualify.[38] Representations regarding the abilities of milk cows to produce milk could qualify as an express warranty that the cattle were suitable for their intended use, thereby allowing the buyer to recover damages.[39]

General statements of "soundness" might not qualify. For example, in *Sessa v. Riegle*,[40] the court held that "words to the effect that 'the horse is sound'" spoken during a telephone conversation between the parties to a horse sale did not constitute an express warranty.[41]

In defense of an express warranty case, the seller can argue that the buyer, before entering into the contract, examined the goods as fully as he desired, or refused to examine the goods, which prevented the buyer from creating an implied warranty as to defects that an examination ought to have revealed.[42]

Further, the element of reliance on statements of the seller deserves intensive investigation. Courts have dismissed equine sale cases where buyers had independent information sources prior to the sale, such as a veterinarian who performed a prepurchase veterinary examination,[43] or a horse trainer who offered his opinion on the suitability and qualities of the horse being sold.

Where defects are patent and the seller demanded that the buyer inspect the horse to discover the defect, the breach of warranty claim may not apply.[44]

4. *Monetary Damages in Breach of Warranty Claims*

Breach of warranty claims can involve several possible damages, including the following:

- *Difference in value.* Some states provide that the buyer can recover the difference in value between the value as warranted and the lesser actual value.[45]
- *Lost profits.* States may provide that lost profits can be recovered in a breach of warranty action.[46]
- *Expense of maintaining the horse.* Courts in some states have allowed the buyer to recover reasonable expenses associated with the care and keeping of the horse.[47]
- *Expense of shipping the animal.* Shipping charges related to the buyer's purchase and subsequent return to the seller could potentially be recovered.[48]
- *Interest.* Interest could potentially be recoverable from the time of the demand.

- *Attorney fees.* Under the laws of some states, attorney fees could be recoverable in breach of warranty claims in addition to other damages.[49]
- *Inconvenience and "mental stress."* Damages of this type are unlikely in breach of warranty cases.[50] In one case, however, the court found that the defendant breached warranties by selling the plaintiff a quarter horse suffering from founder and ordered the defendant seller to pay the plaintiff, in addition to other damages, $500 for inconvenience and mental stress.[51]
- *Injuries to people.* If the buyer suffered injuries from a horse that was alleged to be misrepresented, recovery of personal injuries is possible.[52]

5. *Rescission*[53]

Rescission can be pursued as a remedy for breach of warranty under the Uniform Commercial Code. Section 2-601 provides that before the sale concludes, the buyer can reject goods that fail to conform to specifications of the contract. Section 2-608 allows the buyer to revoke acceptance of the goods if the buyer later discovers that they fail to conform to the terms of the agreement.

Rescission should be sought within a reasonable period of time. A horse buyer's delay of 21 months before seeking rescission was not deemed to be unreasonable, especially based on continued assurances from the seller.[54] In another case, a horse buyer's three-year delay before seeking rescission was deemed untimely.[55]

In addition, the buyer's exercise of a considerable degree of dominion and control over the animal at issue, such as breeding the horse even though the buyer has challenged the animal's quality and fitness, could potentially prevent rescission,[56] but not always.[57]

6. *Defenses to Warranty Claims*[58]

Defenses in breach of warranty claims can include the following, where applicable and where supported by the facts:

- *Warranties were disclaimed.* Warranties can be disclaimed under the UCC, and written disclaimers in contracts have effectively barred litigation involving sales of animals.[59] Section 2-316 addresses disclaimers of implied warranties. This rule provides that an implied warranty of merchantability can be disclaimed or waived if the document provides that the goods are sold "as is" or "with all faults" or similar language. In addition, Section 2-316(2) provides that the "language must mention 'merchantability' and must be conspicuous." But "as-is" disclaimers are not always enforced.[60]

- *No warranties were made.* If the alleged statements were mere "puffing" and sales talk, they may not, as such, qualify as warranties.[61]
- *No "merchant" status of the seller.* The seller's "merchant" status could trigger application of the UCC Section 2-314, which provides that the seller must be a "merchant with respect to the goods of that kind."
- *Merchantability.* The goods at issue were "merchantable." Plaintiff bears the burden of proof that the goods were "unmerchantable" within the meaning of Section 2-314(2).
- *No reliance.* Reliance on part of the buyer can be a fact issue for the jury.[62]
- *No examination of the goods to discover defect.* Under the UCC, when a buyer refuses to examine the goods before use under circumstances where an examination would reveal the defect at issue, the implied warranty of fitness for a particular purpose can be waived.[63]
- *Untimely notice.* Section 2-607 requires notice of a breach of warranty within a "reasonable time" or else the buyer's remedy could be barred. A defense can be asserted that the plaintiff failed to give timely notice and therefore cannot maintain an action for breach of warranty.[64]
- *Usage of trade.* Under Section 2-316(3)(c), "an implied warranty can also be excluded or modified by course of dealing or course of performance or usage of trade." Section 1-205 defines "usage of trade" as "any practice or method of dealing having such regularity of observance in a place, vocation or trade as to justify an expectation that it will be observed with respect to the transaction in question."

B. Consumer Protection and Deceptive Trade Practice Statutes

State deceptive trade practice laws have been applied to animal-related sale disputes. For example, horse breeders and sellers have been found liable under state consumer protection act and deceptive trade practice laws.[65] Deceptive trade practice laws have also been applied to horse training services.[66] But not all disputes may trigger a violation of these laws because courts might, instead, deem them to be mere breach of contract cases.[67] And other courts have held that the state deceptive trade practice statute cannot apply to the factual setting of a horse purchase because the act complained of did not have a sufficient impact on the public interest.[68]

Counsel representing plaintiffs in sales litigation have every incentive to evaluate whether a deceptive trade practice law applies, as these laws often provide for recovery of attorney fees. Some even include provisions for recovery of treble damages. Given the reality that significant amounts of money are not always at stake in animal-related litigation, the potential for recovery of these damages can make the cases worthwhile for counsel to pursue.

C. Special Pet Purchase Protection Statutes

Approximately 17 states (as of March 2008) have enacted some form of law protecting consumers who buy dogs or cats.[69] One of these statutes, the New Jersey Pet Purchase Protection Act,[70] has already generated litigation. In one case,[71] the plaintiff purchased a dog from a breeder, but the animal died five days later due to a congenital condition. The court upheld an award for the buyer based on this law.

IV. Other Defenses

A. No Reliance

Since the buyer's reliance on the seller is a critical element of a sales fraud case, the defense can seek evidence that the buyer did not rely on the seller or that certain events and actions around the time of the sale "broke the chain of reliance." This defense has been applied, for example, where the buyer brings in third parties to inspect the animal before the sale.[72]

B. Statements of "Puffing" Are Not Actionable

Some cases have held that buyers do not justifiably rely, for purposes of a case of sales fraud or misrepresentation, on mere statements of "puffing" by the seller.[73]

C. Statute of Frauds

Even seasoned business people frequently deal on a handshake in buying and selling animals. With the prevalence of verbal contracts, this can raise issues regarding application of the statute of frauds. In two somewhat recent cases, a state statute of frauds barred animal-related litigation. An oral agreement regarding care, training, and racing of a horse was found to be void based on the statute of frauds in *Hutchins v. Patoine*.[74] And in

Valentino v. Davis,[75] the court would not enforce a contract involving the breeding and care of horses based on the statute of frauds. By comparison, other courts have declined to bar litigation on the basis of the statute of frauds.[76]

D. Animal Was Sound Prior to Sale

In the equine sales case of *Simpson v. Widger*,[77] where the horse was found to have soundness problems, the court noted that the seller did not breach an express warranty by making representations before the sale that the horse was sound, because the horse was "serviceably sound" and capable of doing his job with minor unsoundness. The court stated that "[n]ot many horses can be certified as 100 percent sound . . . [and] the practical horseman seeks serviceable soundness. He regards mere minor troubles—those that do not incapacitate a horse for his job but only mar his looks—more as blemishes than as true unsoundnesses."[78] The point of *Simpson* was that the term "sound" in the context of horse dealing should mean "serviceably sound." Consequently, representations that a horse was sound, even if the horse harbored certain minor blemishes, were true and could not form the basis of a cause of action for breach of express warranty.

V. Litigation Strategies

A. Counterclaims

The jurisdiction's rules of procedure, such as Federal Rule of Civil Procedure 13(a), might require that a compulsory counterclaim be asserted with the responsive pleading. Defendants in disputes involving possession and ownership of animals can consider asserting counterclaims. A counterclaim might seek, for example, costs of care and keeping of the animal; reimbursement of veterinary care and other expenses incurred on the animal for which payment has not been made; and reimbursement of boarding expenses for the animal.

B. Interrogatories and Document Requests

1. By Buyer's Counsel to the Defendant Seller

In a sale dispute, counsel should undertake discovery to determine facts such as the following:

- Purchase information and documentation on the animal when the defendant acquired it and before resale to the plaintiff.

- Veterinarians that attended to the animal.
- Veterinary service and billing records applicable to the animal.
- Identities of farriers that attended to the animal (if a horse).
- Farrier service and billing records on the animal (if a horse).
- Identities of all prior owners of the animal.
- Identities of all trainers of the animal.
- Identities of all lessees of the animal.
- The animal's complete show, race, or produce record.
- All facilities where the animal was kept.
- Witnesses to the complained-of sale and to statements made.
- All policies of insurance applicable to the animal.
- All applications for insurance on the animal.
- All insurance claims on the animal.
- All advertisements regarding the animal.

2. *By Seller's Counsel to the Plaintiff Buyer*

Counsel for the seller in a sales dispute should undertake discovery to determine details from the buyer such as:

- Facilities or places where the animal was kept after purchase.
- Trainers whom plaintiff retained to handle, show, or work with the animal after this purchase by plaintiff.
- Veterinarians who examined, treated, or attended the animal after the plaintiff's purchase.
- Shows or competitions in which the animal was entered after purchase by plaintiff.

C. Depositions

Although budgetary constraints might make depositions undesirable, they are worth the effort and expense in most cases. Depositions are especially useful to gather spontaneous answers from parties or key witnesses as compared to interrogatory answers (which counsel usually draft). In cases where the credibility of parties and witnesses is an especially important factor, depositions can allow counsel to examine the witness's demeanor and manner of testifying. Also, the deposition transcript can help counsel prepare for trial and can be used for impeachment of witnesses during trial.

In litigation where the parties have expert witnesses, the deposition can be particularly important for probing the expert for his or her qualifications beyond what appears in his or her curriculum vitae. This information can be especially useful for trial preparation and for review by your own expert witness.

D. Trial[79]

At the voir dire stages, prospective jurors should be asked about their ownership and experiences with the type of animal at issue, and whether they have litigation experience of their own. They should also be asked whether they can keep an open mind where the transaction involves the sale of an animal or an animal-related service.

If the case involves injuries to an animal or the animal's health, keep in mind that most jurors will be unfamiliar with animal conformation. Charts and models could be very useful to help the jury understand the animal's anatomy.

Chances are unlikely that the jurisdiction will have applicable standard civil jury instructions for animal-related sales or contract litigation. In that event, counsel can consider drafting their own jury instructions and presenting them to the court and opposing counsel at the proper time citing references to authorities on which the instruction is based.

APPENDIX A

Sample Demand Letter in an Equine Sale Dispute

[Date]

Via Certified Mail and Regular Mail

Sam and Sue Seller

2222 Right Road

Anytown, Texas

Re: Sale of "Lemon," 2005 American Quarter Horse Gelding

Dear Mr. and Mrs. Seller:

We write as attorneys for Betty and Bob Buyer, who purchased a 2005 American Quarter Horse gelding registered as "LEMON" from you on December 30, 2009, for $45,000.00 (this horse will hereafter be referred to as "the horse").

As you are aware, the Buyers and their agent, Alex Agent, specifically advised you before the sale that they wanted to purchase a horse with the expressed intended purpose of being an all-around Youth Activity horse to be shown frequently and in numerous AQHA events at the highest level of competition by their 14-year-old daughter, Daphine. In making the decision to purchase the horse, the Buyers relied on your repeated representations that the horse was fit and suitable as an all-around Youth Activity performance horse, and, in particular: (1) the horse was sound and had no lameness problems of a permanent nature; and (2) although the horse had previously tested "N/H" (positive) for the Hyperkalemic Periodic Paralysis (HYPP) syndrome, the only symptoms he ever exhibited were merely minor muscle twitches.

However, on December 30, 2009, the date when the Buyers brought their daughter and agent over to your facility to finalize the purchase and haul the horse, Mr. Seller personally watched as the horse exhibited signs of lameness. The horse repeatedly refused to take the right lead while being longed or during brief rides at your facility by the Buyers' daughter, Daphine, and their agent, Mr. Agent. The horse also appeared short-strided in his right hind foot. As you are aware, none of these problems existed in late November 2009, when the Buyers' agent had the horse thoroughly examined by a veterinarian in Oklahoma. On December 30, 2009, the horse's problems were called to Mr. Seller's attention, but he personally assured the Buyers and their agent that the horse was sound but was simply out of shape since it had not been ridden since November 2009. Since Mr. Seller is a highly experienced farrier and professed to be familiar with the horse's condition, the Buyers relied on these assurances in submitting the final payment and hauling the horse away that day.

Contrary to the representations made by Mr. Seller, however, the horse showed no signs of improvement. The horse remained lame from the day he arrived at his new home in Texas on December 31, 2009.

As you may recall, the Buyers' agent personally notified you of the horse's serious lameness condition in early February 2010, but you improperly refused to either accept a return of the horse or refund all or part of the Buyers' money. That call had been preceded by numerous examinations and tests conducted by several veterinarians as well as a hospitalization at the Texas State University Large Animal Clinic. On February 5, after extensive testing, Texas State University issued its diagnosis of chronic laminitis on the right rear hoof. To determine the extent of the problem, as chronic or acute, that veterinary clinic ordered the horse to be returned for further testing in mid-February. You were also advised that examination confirmed the following diagnosis: chronic laminitis of the right hind foot. The attending veterinarians at Texas State believe that this foot had demonstrated signs of trauma weeks before December 30, 2009, when the Buyers purchased the horse.

Undoubtedly, had the Buyers known of these problems, no sale would ever have occurred. Therefore, it is our strong belief that the horse was totally unmerchantable as a Youth Activity show horse on December 30, 2009, when the sale took place. It is also our belief that you knew or should have known of the horse's serious lameness problems before the sale was finalized.

Despite the highest quality of care and attention that the Buyers have continually given the horse, several nationally prominent veterinarians with equine lameness specialties have all reached the same conclusion that no amount of care will ever make him capable of competing as a Youth Activity performance horse. These veterinarians include Diane Doctor, D.V.M. (it is our understanding that she personally conveyed to you her diagnosis), Victor Vetty, D.V.M., and Michael Medicine, D.V.M.

It is our clients' strong belief that your sale of the horse to the Buyers has violated the law; in particular, breach of implied and express warranties, breach of contract, breach of fiduciary duty, negligent and/or fraudulent misrepresentation, and breach of the state Consumer Protection Act, among others. Accordingly, if the Buyers are forced to litigate this matter in a court of law, they will seek full rescission of the sale, together with other compensatory damages including, but not limited to, board fees, veterinary bills, medications, and farrier bills, all of which may potentially be trebled pursuant to the Consumer Protection Act. The Buyers will also not hesitate to seek recovery of their attorney fees.

Unfortunately, no amount of money damages will ever compensate the Buyers and their 14-year-old daughter, Daphine, for the agonizing pain and disappointment she has suffered as her dreams and hopes for the horse to be her prize Youth Activity show horse during the show season, and many seasons afterward, will never be realized.

Therefore, solely in the interests of promptly resolving this matter, without the burden and expense of litigation, our clients, Mr. and Mrs. Buyer, hereby demand that you immediately do the following: (1) refund the entire $45,000.00 purchase price to Mr. and Mrs. Buyer; (2) irrevocably return the horse to your facility; and (3) evidence the transfer of ownership to you by signing a form required by the American Quarter Horse Association.

Unless satisfactory arrangements are made with our office to fully accomplish all of the above three measures by July 1, 2010, Mr. and Mrs. Buyer will have no alternative but to promptly pursue their legal remedies.

Sincerely,
Lawrence Lawyer
Counsel for Betty and Bob Buyer

APPENDIX B

Sample Response to Demand Letter in an Equine Sale Dispute

[Date]
Re: Peter Purchaser v. High Road Farm

Dear Mr. Demanding:

This firm has been retained to represent the interests of High Road Farm.

We have specifically been asked to respond to your letter of May 1, 2010, to High Road Farm. In that letter, you purport to assert a written demand on behalf of Peter Purchaser for relief against High Road Farm. Under State Statute ________. However, your letter does not comply with the requirements of that statute and, accordingly, we cannot and will not accept it as making any claim under State Statute ________. Your letter does not comply with that statute because, among other reasons, it does not comply with the provisions of State Statute ________ requiring a letter "reasonably describing the unfair or deceptive act or practice relied upon and the injury suffered." In addition, State Statute ________ is not applicable to the instant situation or to what "facts" are set forth in your letter.

Although your letter states that High Road Farm engaged in an unfair and deceptive business practice, your letter contains only a conclusory allegation that High Road Farm misrepresented "UNSTOPPABLE'S" jumping history, suitability for Mr. Purchaser, and alleged tendency to stop when approaching a jump. Your letter, however, sets forth no facts or grounds upon which this assertion is based. You make no statement whatsoever as to what, if anything, was said by our client and in what way any such statement was a misrepresentation.

A fair and impartial review of the facts of this matter demonstrates that High Road Farm has not violated State Statute ________ in any manner. High Road Farm categorically denies that it made any misrepresentation of any sort, but especially as to "UNSTOPPABLE'S" jumping history, suitability for Peter Purchaser, or any purported tendency to stop when approaching a jump.

While High Road Farm certainly offered "UNSTOPPABLE" for sale, it did not seek out your client as a potential buyer. Rather, your client, through his trainer, approached representatives of High Road Farm stating that they had observed "UNSTOPPABLE'S" performance during the previous year and wanted to buy the horse. Indeed, Terry Trainer went so far as to say that your clients "had to have it," referring to "UNSTOPPABLE." When Terry Trainer was informed what the horse's jumping record was, he responded to the effect of "I know, I know," indicating that he had watched the horse from April to December of the previous year on at least a half dozen occasions at shows during which the rider was Chris Competitor. Mr. Purchaser likewise said words to the effect of "You don't have to tell me. I've followed his career." Additionally, Mr. Purchaser stated that the reason he was buying the horse was that he had seen how successful Chris Competitor was in riding the horse.

In addition to the above facts, Terry Trainer rode the horse prior to purchase and tried him over a series of jumps to determine whether or not they desired to go forward with the purchase. Mr. Trainer jumped the horse through a course of jumps that measured 3' to 3'3." Terry Trainer said at the time that Peter Purchaser was only going to do mini-medals, or a course no higher than 2'6", for one year. Subsequent to the sale, it came to our client's knowledge that the classes that Mr. Purchaser rode in were higher than what was represented to us.

The presale test rides with "UNSTOPPABLE" took approximately 40–45 minutes. Terry Trainer rode the horse through a whole course on several occasions for a total of 25–30 jumps. Additionally, a complete physical, x-rays, and blood work was done to your clients' complete satisfaction. According to reports by your client (see the enclosed letter), the "vetting looks fine." Lastly in this regard, the bill of sale notes that the sale of "UNSTOPPABLE" was "as is," subject to the veterinary examination that was performed.

In the year and a half following the sale, High Road Farm had two communications in writing from Mr. Purchaser, copies of which are attached. On May 28, 2007, Mr. Purchaser indicated that he "is really enjoying 'UNSTOPPABLE.'"

On June 1, 2008, Mr. Purchaser once again wrote High Road Farm. For the first time, he raises the concept that he would like to sell "UNSTOPPABLE." Mr. Purchaser went on to say that before he would consider other options, he wanted to offer to High Road Farm the chance to buy "UNSTOPPABLE" back because of Chris Competitor's "close affection for him." Nowhere does he say that there was any misrepresentation, but specifically there is no mention of any misrepresentation (or any discussion for that matter) concerning the horse's show jump history, suitability, or any alleged tendency to stop prior to completing a jump.

In May of 2008, Wanda Witness of High Road Farm saw Terry Trainer beating "UNSTOPPABLE" in a wash rack because he would not sit still and observed Mr. Purchaser "ground tying" him. Lastly, in this regard, Olivia Observer also saw the horse in the fall of 2008 at the Medal Finals. She observed Terry Trainer beating "UNSTOPPABLE" with a dressage whip, which was an extra long whip with a stinger. She was appalled at this treatment at the hands of Mr. Trainer and at that time it was apparent that the horse would not jump over a crossrail or even a pole lying on the ground.

As Mr. Purchaser is aware, combining a horse with a particular rider is an inexact science at best, and it is often difficult to predict a successful relationship between rider and horse. By analogy, one could buy the latest, most improved model of golf clubs, but that would not necessarily guarantee a champion golfer. It is unfortunate that "UNSTOPPABLE" has not worked out the way your client hoped, but we suggest that the responsibility for the same lies elsewhere.

Your client Mr. Purchaser bought "UNSTOPPABLE" on the basis of what he and his trainer saw at many shows, after thorough testing and upon the advice of a professional trainer, not on any representation made by our client and not on any recitation of a jump history per se. Accordingly, High Road Farm rejects your demand to refund the purchase price. What High Road Farm will do, however, is what it has offered to do in the past. In return for payment of basic boarding expenses, estimated to be approximately $750.00 per month, High Road Farm would be willing to board "UNSTOPPABLE" for at least one month and evaluate his salability as a jumping horse at the present time. Alternatively, if your client agrees to pay the boarding expenses, High Road Farm would offer to help sell the horse, although it cannot guarantee a sale nor a sale within a particular time frame.

As you are undoubtedly aware, our client enjoys an excellent reputation in its field. It takes your allegations, which border on slander, very seriously. Inasmuch as it has no insurance that would pay for legal expenses in the event of a lawsuit, please be advised that High Road Farm will take full avail of its rights under State Statute ________ to assert a counterclaim for a frivolous lawsuit. The facts of this case go well beyond the doctrine of caveat emptor, or buyer beware. Terry Trainer was a professional trainer who was engaged on behalf of Mr. Purchaser to ensure that Mr. Purchaser was purchasing a horse of a quality commensurate with the purchase price. If you have any additional information or further substantiation of your claim, either by way of factual documentation or legal precedent, High Road Farm will be more than happy to reconsider its position.

Naturally, the foregoing in no way constitutes, nor should it be considered, a waiver or relinquishment by High Road Farm of any and all defenses and rights available to it under applicable laws and statutes. Additionally, the foregoing in no way restricts or limits High Road Farm from relying upon and asserting other facts and grounds that are, or may become available to it.

Very truly yours,
Sally Serious
Counsel for High Road Farm

APPENDIX C

Sample Complaint in a Sales Fraud Case

STATE OF MICHIGAN
IN THE CIRCUIT COURT FOR THE COUNTY OF EQUINE

BOB and BETTY BUYER,
Plaintiffs,

Civil Action No.: 45678
The Honorable Jim Dandy

vs.

SAM SELLER,
Defendant.

Complaint

Plaintiffs, BOB and BETTY BUYER, for their Complaint against Defendant SAM SELLER, state as follows:

Jurisdictional Allegations

1. Plaintiffs are residents of the City of Appaloosa, County of Equine, State of Michigan.
2. Upon information and belief, Defendant Sam Seller is a resident of the City of Andalusia, State of Shetland.

3. Jurisdiction of the Circuit Court is appropriate pursuant to ________________ because Plaintiffs seek equitable relief.
4. Venue in this Court is appropriate since the horse at issue, for which equitable relief is sought, is located within this County.

General Allegations

5. Plaintiffs adopt by reference the allegations contained in paragraphs 1 through 4 of the Complaint as if fully set forth herein.
6. In and before June 2009, Plaintiffs were actively looking to purchase a horse for their 11-year-old daughter to show in Pinto Horse Association, American Paint Horse Association, and open show competition that was well-trained, compliant, easy to handle, and competitive.
7. Prior to June 17, 2009, and at all times relevant hereto, defendants owned a 2002 American Paint Horse gelding registered as "PERFECT SHOW HORSE." (This horse will hereafter be referred to throughout this Complaint as "the Horse.")
8. Defendant consigned the Horse to be sold at the Perfect Horse Quarter & Paint Horse Sale in Quartertown, Michigan, that took place on June 16, 17, and 18, 2009.
9. In the catalog for the auction sale, Defendant represented and warranted the Horse to be "a nice 16.1 all-around gelding. He has APHA [American Paint Horse Association] points in Halter, Hunter Under Saddle, and Western Pleasure. He is a very nice mover, slow legged, and pretty. Ready to go to the show pen today. Sound, no bad habits. . . ."
10. The Horse went through the auction on or about June 17, 2009. However, no sale occurred as a result.
11. While the Horse was still on the auction grounds, Plaintiffs learned from their niece, who was attending the auction, that the Horse was being offered for sale privately.
12. Thereafter, Plaintiffs' niece spoke with Defendant on the grounds of the auction regarding the Horse. During these discussions, Plaintiffs' niece specifically and repeatedly advised Defendant that the Horse, if purchased by Plaintiffs, was intended to be ridden and shown right away by Plaintiff BETTY BUYER's 11-year-old daughter, a novice rider, in Pinto Horse Association, American Paint Horse Association, and open show competition for youth riders.

13. In response, Defendant made several representations and warranties to Plaintiffs' niece regarding the Horse that include, but are not limited to, the following:

    a. the Horse would be safe and quiet enough for an 11-year-old novice rider to handle, ride, and show at the caliber of horse shows described;
    b. an 11-year-old novice rider could competitively show the horse in English and Western riding events "right away" in these shows;
    c. the Horse was a "really good-minded gelding";
    d. the Horse had never been lame and never "had any issues" with his feet;
    e. the Horse was "ready to go to the show pen today";
    f. the Horse was "sound [with] no bad habits"; and
    g. the Horse would suit the needs of Plaintiffs and their 11-year-old daughter.

14. In reliance on the representations Defendant made to Plaintiffs' niece, Plaintiff BETTY BUYER came to see the Horse in person, discuss the Horse with Defendant, and ride him.
15. Defendant made several representations and warranties to Plaintiff BETTY BUYER regarding the Horse that included, but were not limited to, the following:

    a. the Horse would be safe and quiet enough for an 11-year-old novice rider to handle, ride, and show at the caliber of horse shows described;
    b. an 11-year-old novice rider could competitively show the horse in English and Western riding events "right away" in these shows;
    c. the Horse was a "really good-minded gelding";
    d. the Horse had never been lame and never "had any issues" with his feet;
    e. the Horse was "ready to go to the show pen today";
    f. the Horse was "sound [with] no bad habits"; and
    g. the Horse would suit the needs of Plaintiffs and their 11-year-old daughter.

16. While presented at the auction grounds, the Horse displayed a calm and compliant demeanor for Plaintiff BETTY BUYER, her daughter, and her niece, all of whom saw the Horse.

17. At the time the Horse was being presented to Plaintiff BETTY BUYER and her niece, as indicated previously, he demonstrated no signs of lameness or erratic behavior.
18. In reliance on the many representations and warranties that Defendant, individually and collectively, made as set forth previously, and in reliance on the Horse's demeanor and condition displayed on the auction grounds, Plaintiffs entered into an agreement to purchase the Horse from Defendant for Seven Thousand and Five Hundred ($7,500) Dollars.
19. On June 17, 2009, Plaintiffs then transported the Horse to their facility in the City of Appaloosa, County of Equine, State of Michigan.
20. Within about two (2) days after the sale to Plaintiffs, the Horse's behavior began to show drastic and dangerous changes. For example, the Horse would suddenly, and without any prompting or warning, buck and rear while being ridden. The Horse also displayed a "flighty" and dangerous disposition when being handled.
21. Consequently, the Horse was dangerous to be handled and/or ridden by anybody, much less by the Plaintiffs' 11-year-old daughter.
22. In the days that followed Plaintiffs' purchase of the Horse, his dangerous behavioral problems consistently repeated themselves.
23. On August 3, 2009, Dr. Lameness Specialist, an equine specialist veterinarian, evaluated the Horse. His professional assessment, a copy of which is attached hereto, states, *inter alia:*

    a. the Horse was particularly dangerous to be around, even for a professional;
    b. it would be totally inappropriate and foolish to allow anyone but the most experienced horsemen around the Horse; and
    c. the Horse was lame in the right and left front feet and right front fetlock joint and showed radiographic changes of a chronic nature in the navicular bones and right front fetlock joints.

24. Within a reasonable time after Plaintiffs purchased the Horse, they contacted Defendant and demanded that Defendant rescind the sale and take the Horse back in exchange for Plaintiffs' purchase money, but Defendant failed or refused to comply.
25. Defendant did offer, in response to Plaintiffs' demands, to accept the return of the Horse in exchange for Plaintiffs' receipt of a

different horse that was in Defendant's possession, a registered American Paint Horse mare. Defendant represented that this mare would be more suitable for Plaintiffs' needs and assured Plaintiffs that they would make the trade in a few weeks, after they gave the mare some additional training.

26. Based on Defendant's assurances that he would replace the Horse with a different horse that was represented to be more suitable, Plaintiffs refrained from taking any further action to rescind the sale and from making any further demands on Defendant.
27. After several weeks followed, however, Defendant refused to make the trade as promised.
28. In a further attempt to resolve the dispute and to seek rescission of the sale of the Horse, Plaintiff BOB BUYER met defendant SAM SELLER, personally, on the grounds of the auction in November 2009. Defendant again refused.
29. Plaintiffs made a final demand that Defendant rescind the sale of the Horse. Defendant failed or refused to respond.
30. Plaintiffs are now left with a horse that is unsound, is not what Defendant represented and warranted, is dangerous to ride, is dangerous to handle, is dangerous to be around, and is wholly unsuitable as a show horse for the Plaintiffs' 11-year-old daughter.

Count I: Rescission—Fraudulent Misrepresentation

31. Plaintiffs adopt by reference the allegations contained in paragraphs 1 through 30 of the Complaint as if fully set forth herein.
32. Defendant, in order to induce the Plaintiffs to purchase the Horse, intentionally made several written and oral representations to them regarding the Horse that included, but were not limited to, the following:

    a. the Horse would be safe and quiet enough for an 11-year-old novice rider to handle, ride, and show at the caliber of horse shows Plaintiffs described;
    b. an 11-year-old novice rider could competitively show the horse in English and Western riding events "right away" in these shows;
    c. the Horse was a "really good-minded gelding";
    d. the Horse had never been lame and never "had any issues" with his feet;
    e. the Horse was "ready to go to the show pen today";

f. the Horse was "sound [with] no bad habits"; and
g. the Horse would suit the needs of Plaintiffs and their 11-year-old daughter.

33. Defendant's statements were false when stated.
34. Defendant misrepresented those facts regarding the Horse in the manner set forth above under circumstances where Defendant knew or should have known them to be false, or Defendant acted with reckless disregard as to their truth or falsity.
35. In purchasing the Horse, Plaintiffs relied on the written and oral representations and warranties from Defendant regarding the condition, suitability, temperament, training, soundness, and qualities of the Horse.
36. All of the misrepresentations made by Defendant regarding the Horse were material to the Plaintiffs' decision to purchase him.
37. Defendant had actual knowledge that the condition, temperament, training, soundness, and abilities of the Horse were important to the Plaintiffs and that the Plaintiffs specifically wanted to buy a horse that was suitable for competing in Pinto Horse Association, American Paint Horse Association, and open horse shows by Plaintiffs' 11-year-old daughter immediately after the sale. Further, Defendant knew that Plaintiffs would likely not have purchased the Horse if they had known the truth about the Horse's condition, temperament, training, abilities, and unsoundness.
38. Defendant had a duty to verify the statements before inducing reliance upon them by Plaintiffs to consummate the sale of the Horse.
39. Plaintiffs' daughter was unable to show the Horse in any events under saddle during the 2009 horse show season in the manner contemplated by the purchase, which caused Plaintiffs and their daughter great disappointment, frustration, humiliation, anguish, and emotional suffering.
40. The Horse has no value whatsoever as a show horse for Plaintiffs and their daughter and limited value far below the sale price that Plaintiffs paid to Defendant. Further, Plaintiffs have expended substantial sums in the ongoing maintenance expenses applicable to the Horse.
41. As a direct and proximate result of the Defendant's misrepresentations, upon which Plaintiffs relied to their detriment, Plaintiffs have suffered substantial damages that include the cost of the Horse as well as substantial ongoing expenses in maintaining the

horse that include, but are not limited to, medications, supplements, veterinary expenses, farrier expenses, costs, attorney fees, and litigation expenses.

WHEREFORE, for the foregoing reasons, Plaintiffs respectfully request that this Honorable Court do the following:

A. Rescind the sale of the Horse;
B. Order Defendant to immediately return Plaintiffs' purchase price of Seven Thousand and Five Hundred ($7,500) Dollars;
C. Order Defendant to pay Plaintiffs the amount of moneys that Plaintiffs have expended in the care, keeping, and training of the Horse from the date of purchase to the date of judgment;
D. Order Defendant to pay Plaintiffs consequential damages and damages for mental anguish and emotional distress in an amount in excess of $25,000;
E. Order Defendant to pay interest and Plaintiffs' court costs, and attorney fees and other damages as authorized pursuant to the Michigan Consumer Protection Act, Michigan Compiled Laws §§ 445.901, *et seq.*, and the Michigan Uniform Commercial Code, Michigan Compiled Laws §§ 440.2101, *et seq.*; and/or
F. Order such further and other relief as the Court may deem just and proper.

Count II: Rescission—Mutual Mistake/Failure of Consideration

42. Plaintiffs adopt by reference the allegations contained in paragraphs 1 through 41 of the Complaint as if fully set forth herein.
43. In the alternative, all parties labored under the false impression that the Horse was a show horse that was capable of being handled, ridden, and shown competitively and immediately by the Plaintiffs' 11-year-old daughter and that only in that condition was the Horse worth the sales price that Plaintiffs paid to the Defendant.
44. Plaintiffs would not have agreed to purchase the Horse at the agreed-upon price or at any price if Defendant had not made the misrepresentations.
45. In view of the foregoing, only if the Horse was in the condition and had the abilities believed by Plaintiffs would he have been worth the sales price that Plaintiffs paid to Defendant.
46. Therefore, there has been a mutual mistake of fact and a total failure of consideration.

47. As a direct and proximate result of the Defendant's misrepresentations, upon which Plaintiffs relied to their detriment, Plaintiffs have suffered substantial damages that include the cost of the Horse as well as substantial ongoing expenses in maintaining the Horse that include, but are not limited to, medications, supplements, veterinary expenses, farrier expenses, costs, attorney fees, and litigation expenses.

WHEREFORE, for the foregoing reasons, Plaintiffs respectfully request that this Honorable Court do the following:

A. Rescind the sale of the Horse;
B. Order Defendant to immediately return Plaintiffs' purchase price of Seven Thousand and Five Hundred ($7,500) Dollars;
C. Order Defendant to pay Plaintiffs the amount of moneys that Plaintiffs have expended in the care, keeping, and training of the Horse from the date of purchase to the date of judgment;
D. Order Defendant to pay Plaintiffs consequential damages and damages for mental anguish and emotional distress in an amount in excess of $25,000;
E. Order Defendant to pay interest and Plaintiffs' court costs, and attorney fees and other damages as authorized pursuant to the Michigan Consumer Protection Act, Michigan Compiled Laws §§ 445.901, *et seq.*, and the Michigan Uniform Commercial Code, Michigan Compiled Laws §§ 440.2101, *et seq.*; and/or
F. Order such further and other relief as the Court may deem just and proper.

Count III: Innocent or Negligent Misrepresentation

48. Plaintiffs adopt by reference the allegations contained in paragraphs 1 through 47 of the Complaint as if fully set forth herein.
49. In the alternative, the representations and warranties of Defendant with respect to the condition, suitability, temperament, training, soundness, and abilities of the Horse were made innocently and without malice but nevertheless were false, misleading, or omitted material facts and had the effect of deceiving the Plaintiffs. The damages suffered by Plaintiffs were every bit as great as they would have been if the representations were made by Defendant in bad faith and with an intent to mislead the Plaintiffs.

50. Plaintiffs relied on the written and oral representations of Defendant in making the decision to purchase the Horse, and, in the exercise of due care and diligence in their part, could not have known of the false, misleading, or omitted material facts.
51. As a direct and proximate result of the Defendant's improper and unlawful misrepresentations and conduct, upon which Plaintiffs relied to their detriment, Plaintiffs have suffered substantial damages that include the cost of the Horse as well as substantial ongoing expenses in maintaining the Horse that include, but are not limited to, medications, supplements, veterinary expenses, farrier expenses, costs, attorney fees, and litigation expenses.
52. The losses incurred by Plaintiffs have inured to the benefit of the Defendant.

WHEREFORE, for the foregoing reasons, Plaintiffs respectfully request that this Honorable Court do the following:

A. Rescind the sale of the Horse;
B. Order Defendant to immediately return Plaintiffs' purchase price of Seven Thousand and Five Hundred ($7,500) Dollars;
C. Order Defendant to pay Plaintiffs the amount of moneys that Plaintiffs have expended in the care, keeping, and training of the Horse from the date of purchase to the date of judgment;
D. Order Defendant to pay Plaintiffs consequential damages and damages for mental anguish and emotional distress in an amount in excess of $25,000;
E. Order Defendant to pay interest and Plaintiffs' court costs, and attorney fees and other damages as authorized pursuant to the Michigan Consumer Protection Act, Michigan Compiled Laws §§ 445.901, *et seq.*, and the Michigan Uniform Commercial Code, Michigan Compiled Laws §§ 440.2101, *et seq.*; and/or
F. Order such further and other relief as the Court may deem just and proper.

Count IV: Breach of Express and Implied Warranties under the Michigan Uniform Commercial Code, Michigan Compiled Laws §§ 440.2104, *et seq.*

53. Plaintiffs adopt by reference the allegations contained in paragraphs 1 through 52 of the Complaint as if fully set forth herein.

54. Defendant is a "merchant" as that term is defined in § 104 of the Michigan Uniform Commercial Code, Michigan Compiled Laws § 440.2104 with respect to the sale of horses.
55. Plaintiffs and Defendant entered into a contract whereby Defendant sold the Horse to Plaintiffs for Seven Thousand and Five Hundred ($7,500) Dollars.
56. The Horse was subject to implied warranties of merchantability under the Michigan Uniform Commercial Code, Michigan Compiled Laws § 440.2314.
57. Defendant held himself out as being knowledgeable, if not an expert, in regard to horses and show horses.
58. Plaintiff BETTY BUYER and her niece told Defendant the particular purpose for which they were interested in buying the Horse.
59. When they purchased the Horse to be ridden, handled, and shown by the Plaintiffs' 11-year-old novice daughter, Plaintiffs relied on the Defendant's skill and expertise.
60. The Horse was subject to implied warranties of fitness for a particular purpose under Michigan Compiled Laws § 440.2315.
61. The Horse was also subject to implied warranties of merchantability under Michigan Compiled Laws § 440.2313.
62. To induce Plaintiffs to purchase the Horse, Defendant also made certain express warranties and representations to Plaintiffs regarding the Horse. These express warranties were made through the auction catalog description of the Horse, through Defendant's words on the grounds, and through Defendant's conduct, that included, but are not limited to, the following:

    a. the Horse would be safe and quiet enough for an 11-year-old novice rider to handle, ride, and show at the caliber of horse shows Plaintiffs described;
    b. an 11-year-old novice rider could competitively show the horse in English and Western riding events "right away" in these shows;
    c. the Horse was a "really good-minded gelding";
    d. the Horse had never been lame and never "had any issues" with his feet;
    e. the Horse was "ready to go to the show pen today";
    f. the Horse was "sound [with] no bad habits"; and
    g. the Horse would suit the needs of Plaintiffs and their 11-year-old daughter.

63. Defendant's representations and warranties, individually and collectively, formed a part of the basis of the bargain between Plaintiffs and Defendant.
64. The Horse did not perform as warranted and represented by Defendant in that he was not sound and was completely unsuitable and dangerous to be handled, ridden, or shown by Plaintiffs' daughter or others.
65. At the time of sale from Defendant to Plaintiffs, the Horse was also lame in both front feet, and the right front fetlock joint and showed radiographic changes of a chronic nature in the navicular bones and right front fetlock joints.
66. Plaintiffs relied on Defendant's skill and expertise when they agreed to purchase the Horse.
67. The Horse's poor condition, temperament, training, soundness, and abilities, as described in the foregoing paragraphs, render him unfit for the ordinary purpose for which horses, in general, and show horses, in particular, are used.
68. The Horse was not of average quality in the horse industry, in general, and the show horse industry, in particular, at the time Defendant sold him to the Plaintiffs.
69. As a direct and proximate of the Horse's poor condition, temperament, training, soundness, and abilities when sold to Plaintiffs, the Plaintiffs and their 11-year-old daughter cannot utilize him for the ordinary purposes of sound, safe, reliable performance as a show horse for their 11-year-old daughter, or for anyone, to ride and handle.
70. As a direct and proximate result of the Defendant's improper conduct, the Defendant has violated the Michigan Uniform Commercial Code.
71. As a direct and proximate result of the Defendant's breaches of express and implied warranties, Plaintiffs have suffered damages that include the cost of the Horse as well as substantial ongoing expenses in maintaining the Horse that include, but are not limited to, medications, supplements, veterinary expenses, farrier expenses, costs, attorney fees, and litigation expenses. Damages also include the cost and inconvenience of obtaining another show horse for Plaintiffs' daughter and costs and attorney fees in attempting to obtain relief from Defendant's wrongful and unlawful conduct.

WHEREFORE, for the foregoing reasons, Plaintiffs respectfully request that this Honorable Court do the following:

A. Rescind the sale of the Horse;
B. Order Defendant to immediately return Plaintiffs' purchase price of Seven Thousand and Five Hundred ($7,500) Dollars;
C. Order Defendant to pay Plaintiffs the amount of moneys that Plaintiffs have expended in the care, keeping, and training of the Horse from the date of purchase to the date of judgment;
D. Order Defendant to pay Plaintiffs consequential damages and damages for mental anguish and emotional distress in an amount in excess of $25,000;
E. Order Defendant to pay interest and Plaintiffs' court costs, and attorney fees and other damages as authorized pursuant to the Michigan Consumer Protection Act, Michigan Compiled Laws §§ 445.901, *et seq.*, and the Michigan Uniform Commercial Code, Michigan Compiled Laws 440.2101, *et. seq.*; and/or
F. Order such further and other relief as the Court may deem just and proper.

Count V: Breach of Contract

72. Plaintiffs adopt by reference the allegations contained in paragraphs 1 through 71 of the Complaint as if fully set forth herein.
73. Plaintiffs and Defendant entered into a valid contract that required Defendant to provide Plaintiffs with a horse that was sound, well-trained, of good temperament, safe, reliable, and suitable for riding, handling, and showing in Pinto Horse Association, American Paint Horse Association, and open show competition by an 11-year-old novice rider.
74. Plaintiffs performed all acts required of them under the contract, including payment of the full purchase price to Defendant.
75. Defendant failed to do what the contract required of him. The Horse they provided was unsound, of bad temperament, dangerous to handle, ride, or be around and unquestionably was unfit to be handled or shown by an 11-year-old.
76. As a direct and proximate result of the Defendant's breaches of contract, Plaintiffs have suffered damages that include the cost of the Horse as well as substantial ongoing expenses in maintaining the Horse that include, but are not limited to, medications, supplements, veterinary expenses, farrier expenses, costs, attorney fees, and litigation expenses. Damages also include the cost and inconvenience of obtaining another show horse for Plaintiffs' daughter and costs and attorney fees in attempting to obtain relief from Defendant's wrongful and unlawful conduct.

77. As a result of Defendant's breach of their contract with Plaintiffs, Plaintiffs are also entitled to recover exemplary damages from Defendant.

WHEREFORE, for the foregoing reasons, Plaintiffs respectfully request that this Honorable Court do the following:

A. Rescind the sale of the Horse;
B. Order Defendant to immediately return Plaintiffs' purchase price of Seven Thousand and Five Hundred ($7,500) Dollars;
C. Order Defendant to pay Plaintiffs the amount of moneys that Plaintiffs have expended in the care, keeping, and training of the Horse from the date of purchase to the date of judgment;
D. Order Defendant to pay Plaintiffs consequential damages and damages for mental anguish and emotional distress in an amount in excess of $25,000;
E. Order Defendant to pay interest and Plaintiffs' court costs, and attorney fees and other damages as authorized pursuant to the Michigan Consumer Protection Act, Michigan Compiled Laws §§ 445.901, *et seq.*, and the Michigan Uniform Commercial Code, Michigan Compiled Laws 440.2101, *et. seq.*; and/or
F. Order such further and other relief as the Court may deem just and proper.

Count VI: Michigan Consumer Protection Act, Michigan Compiled Laws §§ 445.901, *et seq.*

78. Plaintiffs adopt by reference the allegations contained in paragraphs 1 through 77 of the Complaint as if fully set forth herein.
79. Plaintiffs are "persons" within the meaning of the Michigan Consumer Protection Act, Michigan Compiled Laws § 445.902(c).
80. Defendant was engaged in "trade or commerce" as defined in Michigan Compiled Laws § 445.902(d).
81. Defendant's conduct, as set forth previously, constituted unfair, unconscionable, or deceptive methods, acts, or practices in the conduct of trade and commerce within the meaning of the Michigan Consumer Protection Act, Michigan Compiled Laws §§ 445.901, *et seq.*, and, in particular, by the following acts or omissions:

   a. Representing that goods or services have . . . characteristics, uses, [or] benefits . . . which they do not have. . . . [Michigan Compiled Laws § 445.903 (c)];

b. Representing that goods or services are of a particular standard, quality, or grade, . . . if they are of another [Michigan Compiled Laws § 445.903 (e)];
c. Failing to reveal a material fact, the omission of which tends to mislead or deceive the consumer, and which fact could not reasonably be known by the consumer [Michigan Compiled Laws § 445.903 (s)];
d. Charging the consumer a price that is grossly in excess of the price at which similar property or services are sold [Michigan Compiled Laws § 445.903 (z)];
e. Making a representation of fact or statement of fact material to the transaction such that a person reasonably believes the represented or suggested state of affairs to be other than it actually is [Michigan Compiled Laws § 445.903 (bb)]; and/or
f. Failing to reveal facts that are material to the transaction in light of representations of fact made in a positive manner [Michigan Compiled Laws § 445.903 (cc)].

82. As a direct and proximate result of Defendant's improper conduct, Defendant has violated the Michigan Consumer Protection Act, Michigan Compiled Laws §§ 445.901, *et seq.*
83. As a direct and proximate result of the Defendant's improper conduct, described previously, the Plaintiffs have been materially damaged.

WHEREFORE, for the foregoing reasons, Plaintiffs respectfully request that this Honorable Court do the following:

A. Rescind the sale of the Horse;
B. Order Defendant to immediately return Plaintiffs' purchase price of Seven Thousand and Five Hundred ($7,500) Dollars;
C. Order Defendant to pay Plaintiffs the amount of moneys that Plaintiffs have expended in the care, keeping, and training of the Horse from the date of purchase to the date of judgment;
D. Order Defendant to pay Plaintiffs' consequential damages and damages for mental anguish and emotional distress in an amount in excess of $25,000;
E. Order Defendant to pay interest and Plaintiffs' court costs, and attorney fees and other damages as authorized pursuant to the Michigan Consumer Protection Act, Michigan Compiled Laws §§ 445.901, *et seq.*, and the Michigan Uniform Commercial Code, Michigan Compiled Laws §§ 440.2101, *et seq.*; and/or

F. Order such further and other relief as the Court may deem just and proper.

[COUNSEL FIRM/NAME/SIGNATURE BLOCK]

Demand for Trial by Jury

Plaintiffs demand a trial by jury of all issues so triable herein.

[COUNSEL FIRM/NAME/SIGNATURE BLOCK]

APPENDIX D

Sample Affirmative Defenses in a Sales Fraud Case

A. Plaintiff's Complaint fails to state a claim upon which relief can be granted.
B. Plaintiff's Complaint is barred, in whole or in part, since any damages alleged were proximately caused by the culpable acts of others over whom Defendant has no control and for whom Defendant cannot be held accountable.
C. Plaintiff's Complaint is barred, in whole or in part, since the proximate cause of any alleged damages was Plaintiff, based on the quality of care and attention she gave to the horse after the sale took place.
D. Plaintiff's Complaint is barred, in whole or in part, since Plaintiff failed to give proper and timely notice of any breached warranties as required under the Michigan Uniform Commercial Code.
E. Plaintiff's Complaint is barred, in whole or in part, since none of the complained-of statements qualified as "express warranties" and, alternatively, no breach of warranties took place.
F. Plaintiff's Complaint is barred, in whole or in part, since even assuming that any "express warranties" were made, they were not "part of the basis of the bargain."

G. Plaintiff's Complaint is barred, in whole or in part, since any statements made by Defendant were merely statements of opinion and not "express warranties."
H. Plaintiff's Complaint is barred, in whole or in part, since there was no reliance on Defendant by Plaintiff and any purported reliance was not reasonable.
I. Plaintiff's Complaint is barred, in whole or in part, since Defendant is not a "merchant" for purposes of invoking the Michigan Uniform Commercial Code.
J. Plaintiff's Complaint is barred, in whole or in part, since the horse at issue was merchantable at the time of sale and was fit for its ordinary purposes.
K. Plaintiff's Complaint is barred, in whole or in part, since no fraud or misrepresentation existed as Defendant was unaware that the horse at issue had any lameness or unsoundness problems, contrary to the allegations in the Complaint.
L. Plaintiff's Complaint is barred, in whole or in part, since Defendant made no false or misleading statements whatsoever.
M. Plaintiff's Complaint is barred, in whole or in part, since Defendant made no statements whatsoever about the horse's future performance and even if such statements were made they do not qualify as fraudulent representations.
N. Plaintiff's Complaint is barred, in whole or in part, since the horse at issue was merchantable at the time of sale and was fit for its ordinary purposes.
O. Plaintiff's Complaint is barred, in whole or in part, since the horse at issue conformed to any contract at the time of sale.
P. Plaintiff's Complaint is barred, in whole or in part, since the horse did not have any "defects," infirmities, or "nonconformities" that would, in general or in particular, entitle Plaintiff to seek or receive revocation of acceptance.
Q. Plaintiff's Complaint is barred, in whole or in part, since Plaintiff has failed to plead fraud with particularity as required under Federal Rule of Civil Procedure 9(b).
R. Plaintiff's Complaint is barred, in whole or in part, because Plaintiff has not sought revocation of acceptance within an appropriate or reasonable time.
S. Plaintiff's Complaint is barred, in whole or in part, because Plaintiff has failed to mitigate her damages.
T. Plaintiff's Complaint is barred, in whole or in part, since Plaintiff has failed to plead fulfillment of conditions precedent on Plaintiff's part.

U. Defendant reserves the right to amend his answer to plead further and other affirmative defenses after a reasonable opportunity for discovery.

[COUNSEL FIRM/NAME/SIGNATURE BLOCK]

APPENDIX E

Sample Complaint in a Breach of Fiduciary Duty Case

PLEASANT CIRCUIT COURT
CIVIL BRANCH

POLLY PLAINTIFF Plaintiff,	Hon. ______________ Case No. ____________

vs.

DANIEL DEFENDANT and
DIANE DEFENDANT,
Defendants.

Complaint

NOW COMES Plaintiff, POLLY PLAINTIFF, by counsel, and for her cause of action states as follows:

Count I

1. That the Defendants, DANIEL AND DIANE DEFENDANT, reside at Riverview Farm, River Run Road, Horse Country, Kentucky 45678.
2. That the Defendants owe to the Plaintiff the liquidated sum of $25,000.00, being Plaintiff's one-third of the sales proceeds from the sale of the Saddlebred filly CALIFORNIA SUN in February

2010, which Defendants have collected but refuse to pay Plaintiff despite demand made.

3. That the Defendants owe to the Plaintiff a complete accounting of all transactions involving any and all horses purchased or sold by the Defendants in which the Defendants acted as agent for the seller or buyer.

Count II

4. That the Plaintiff realleges and reiterates all allegations set forth above in Count I.
5. That the Defendants, DANIEL AND DIANE DEFENDANT, while acting as agents for the Plaintiff, advised the Plaintiff to purchase the American Saddlebred mare GEORGIA PEACH.
6. That the Defendants, DANIEL AND DIANE DEFENDANT, further advised the Plaintiff that the mare was being sold by the Pleasant County Bank which had repossessed the mare and was selling her to satisfy a debt.
7. That the Defendants, DANIEL AND DIANE DEFENDANT, advised the Plaintiff that they would not receive a commission on this transaction.
8. That on November 11, 2008, the Plaintiff purchased the mare for $80,000.00, which was the price recommended by the Defendants.
9. That recently the Plaintiff discovered that the mare had been sold to Bob Buyer on that same date.
10. That the Defendants either owned an interest in the mare when it was sold to Plaintiff or received a commission on the sale, in breach of their fiduciary duties to the Plaintiff.
11. That Defendants owe to the Plaintiff the sum received as commission or profit.

WHEREFORE the Plaintiff demands as follows:

A. That the Plaintiff have Judgment against the Defendants for an amount of damages to be determined by the Court for repayment of the amounts owed by the Defendants to the Plaintiff as set forth in Count II, which amount and damages are in excess of any minimum dollar amount to establish the jurisdiction of the Court.

B. That the Plaintiff have Judgment against the Defendants for damages to be determined for breach of Defendants' fiduciary duty, which damages are in excess of any minimum dollar amount to establish the jurisdiction of this Court.

C. That the Plaintiff be awarded prejudgment interest on all sums owed, plus interest on the Judgment at the legal rate of twelve percent (12%) from the date of Judgment until paid in full, plus her costs expended.
D. That the Defendants be ordered to provide a full accounting of all transactions involving any horses purchased or sold by the Plaintiff in which the Defendants acted as Plaintiff's agent.
E. Any and all relief to which Plaintiff may appear entitled.

Respectfully submitted,
By:__________________________

APPENDIX F

Sample Answer and Counterclaim in a Breach of Fiduciary Duty Case

REDRESS MUNICIPAL COURT

ALICE AGGRIEVED, Plaintiff,	Hon. ________________ Case No. _____________

vs.

PETER, PAUL, AND MARY EQUINE,
Defendants.

Answer

Come the Defendants, PETER, PAUL, AND MARY EQUINE, by counsel, and for their answer to the Plaintiff's Complaint states as follows:

First Defense

Plaintiff's Complaint fails to state a claim upon which relief can be granted.

Second Defense

Plaintiff is guilty of laches, has waived, or is otherwise estopped from asserting the claims in her Complaint.

Third Defense

1. Defendants admit the allegations contained in Paragraph 1 of Plaintiff's Complaint.
2. Defendants admit with respect to Paragraphs 5, 6, 7, 8, 9, and 10 of Plaintiff's Complaint that said sums are owed to Plaintiff, but affirmatively states that Defendants have tendered or offered payment of said amounts, which tenders and offers have been refused by Plaintiff, and Defendants therefore deny the remaining allegations of said paragraphs.
3. Defendants deny the allegations of Paragraph 2. With respect to the allegations of Paragraph 3 of Plaintiff's Complaint, Defendants admit possession of said photographs, but affirmatively state that said photographs were a gift from Plaintiff to Defendants and Plaintiff is therefore not entitled to return thereof.
4. With respect to the allegations contained in Paragraph 5 of Plaintiff's Complaint, Defendants state that they agreed to provide to Plaintiff a replacement switch of equal value for a lost switch and did provide said replacement, which replacement switch remains in the possession of the Defendants and has been tendered for delivery to Plaintiff, but that Plaintiff refuses to accept delivery thereof. Defendants deny the remaining allegations of said paragraph.
5. With respect to the allegations contained in Paragraph 6 of Plaintiff's Complaint, Defendants state that one-half of the charges for refinishing said buggy were paid by Defendants, the balance thereof being paid by Plaintiff in return for the Defendants' having permitted the Plaintiff to use said buggy from March, 2009, until July, 2010, and Defendants therefore deny the allegations of said paragraph.
6. Defendants admit so much of the allegations of Paragraphs 17 and 18 as state that Plaintiff purchased said mare at public auction for $40,000.00 and that the Defendants owned an interest in said mare at the time of the sale, but Defendants specifically deny the remaining allegations of said paragraphs.
7. Defendants are without sufficient knowledge or belief as to the truth of the allegations contained in Paragraph 19 of Plaintiff's Complaint, and the same are therefore denied.

8. Defendants specifically deny the allegations contained in Paragraphs 11, 12, 13, 14, 15, 16 of Plaintiff's Complaint.
9. Defendants deny each and every other allegation not specifically admitted herein.

Counterclaim

For their Counterclaim against the Plaintiff herein, Defendants state as follows:

Count I

1. During the period from March, 2009 until July, 2010, Defendants acted as advisors and trainers for Plaintiff with respect to her activities in the American Morgan Horse industry.
2. At the outset of Defendants and Plaintiff's business relationship, Plaintiff was aware of the universal custom in the Morgan Horse industry that advisors and trainers such as the Defendants are paid a commission of ten percent of the gross sales price of a horse purchased upon his or her recommendation at the time of purchase and an additional commission of ten percent upon the subsequent sale of any such horse.
3. As a special accommodation to Plaintiff, Defendants agreed with Plaintiff not to be paid a commission at the time of purchase of any horses by Plaintiff, but that Defendants would receive, and Plaintiff agreed Defendants would receive, a commission of ten percent of the gross sales price of any horse so purchased by Plaintiff upon its subsequent sale.
4. That the Morgan horses set forth on Exhibit "A" hereto were pur chased by Plaintiff upon Defendants' recommendation and subsequently resold by the Plaintiff. The gross sales price for Plaintiff's interest therein is set forth on Exhibit "A," and Defendants are entitled to a commission thereon in the amount of $50,000.00, representing ten percent of the total gross sale proceeds to Plaintiff from the sale thereof.
5. That in addition to the horses set forth on Exhibit "A," Plaintiff purchased upon Defendants' recommendation, the Morgan horses set forth on Exhibit "B" hereto, which horses are still owned by Plaintiff and which Plaintiff refuses to sell in order to deny Defendants a commission thereon. Defendants state they are entitled to judgment awarding them a commission equal to ten percent of the gross sales price thereof upon sale by the Plaintiff, or in the alternative, are entitled to a judgment awarding

them a ten percent commission on the gross value thereof in the event Plaintiff refuses to sell said horses at the time of judgment.

Count II

1. Defendants reallege and reaffirm each and every allegation set forth in Count I of their Counterclaim herein.
2. Defendants have, for a period of many years, enjoyed a good reputation in the American Morgan Horse industry, which is of fundamental importance to the success of Defendants' business and occupation as a trainer of American Morgan horses.
3. That during the period from July, 2010, and continuing until the present date, Plaintiff has communicated statements to third parties in the American Morgan Horse industry, and others, which statements are false and slanderous and have directly impugned the reputation of Defendants in their trade or business.
4. That said statements include statements by the Plaintiff that the Defendants are dishonest and that Defendants are not competent in the trade or business of training American Morgan horses.
5. That said statements were made by Plaintiff intentionally and maliciously and for the specific purpose of adversely affecting Defendants' reputation in the American Morgan Horse industry, with a resultant loss of business opportunities and profits to the Defendants.
6. That as a direct and proximate result of the Plaintiff's slanderous statements, Defendants have been damaged in a precise amount unknown to the Defendants, but which amount exceeds the jurisdictional minimum of this Court, $25,000.

WHEREFORE, Defendants demand that the Plaintiff's Complaint be dismissed and held for naught; demand judgment against the Plaintiff under Count I of their Counterclaim herein in the amount of $100,000 plus an additional amount for commissions still owed by the Plaintiff; demand judgment under Count II of their Counterclaim herein in an amount that is unknown to the Defendants, but that exceeds the jurisdictional minimum of this Court, $2,500.00; demand their costs herein expended including a reasonable attorney's fee; trial by jury; and all other relief to which they are entitled.

Respectfully submitted,
By:______________________________

APPENDIX G

Sample Complaint in a Breach of Bailment Case

STATE OF MICHIGAN
IN THE CIRCUIT COURT FOR THE COUNTY OF CONCHO

PRESTON PLAINTIFF, Plaintiff,	The Honorable ________ Civil Action No. ________

vs.

BREEDING STABLES, LLC;
BETTY BREEDER; ATLAS ANIMAL CLINIC;
and VETERINARIAN JOHN DOE,
Defendants.

Complaint

NOW COMES the Plaintiff, Preston Plaintiff, by and through his attorneys, and for his cause of action against the above-named Defendants, shows unto this Honorable Court as follows:

1. Plaintiff resides in the City of Racetown, County of Concho, State of Michigan.
2. Defendant Breeding Stables, LLC ("Stables"), upon information and belief, is a Michigan Limited Liability Company engaged in the business of breeding horses for profit and is located and doing business in the County of Concho, State of Michigan.
3. Defendant Betty Breeder ("Breeder"), upon information and belief, is an employee and/or principal and/or owner of Defendant Breeding Stables, LLC, and resides in the County of Concho, State of Michigan.
4. Defendant Atlas Animal Clinic ("Clinic"), upon information and belief, is engaged in the practice of veterinary medicine and is located in the County of Concho, State of Michigan.

5. Defendant Veterinarian John Doe ("Doe"), whose identity is yet unknown, upon information and belief, is engaged in the practice of veterinary medicine and is an employee and/or principal and/or owner of Defendant Atlas Animal Clinic and resides in the County of Concho, State of Michigan.
6. All of the acts and omissions of which Plaintiff Complains occurred in the County of Concho, State of Michigan, and the amount in controversy exceeds $25,000 exclusive of costs, interest, and attorneys fees.

Facts

7. Plaintiff incorporates by reference the allegations in paragraphs 1 through 6.
8. Plaintiff was the owner of a Thoroughbred racing mare named FLASH, which horse was the winner of a number of races, had foaled valuable offspring, and had value substantially in excess of $25,000.
9. On or about May 21, 2009, Plaintiff delivered FLASH to, and she was accepted into the care and custody of, Defendants Breeding Stables, LLC, and Betty Breeder for purposes of being bred to a stud horse owned by Stables and/or Breeder.
10. At the time FLASH was so delivered, she was in excellent health and physical condition.
11. On or about May 22, 2009, Defendant Doe, acting for himself and on behalf of Defendant Clinic and at the hire and request of Defendants Stables and Breeder, performed a physical examination of FLASH that involved insertion of Doe's arm into the rectum of FLASH.
12. In the course of the examination, Doe detected the presence of blood on his examination glove, an indication that a tear in the rectum had occurred.
13. Neither Doe nor Breeder contacted Plaintiff to advise of the problem or to request instructions on treatment, but instead elected to feed the horse and turned her out to pasture overnight.
14. On or about May 23, 2009, Breeder contacted Plaintiff, advised that FLASH might have sustained a Grade 2 torn rectum, and requested permission to transport the horse to the Veterinary Medical College at Michigan State University for "a second opinion." Permission was granted, and Breeder transported the horse.

15. That same day, doctors at the College called Plaintiff and advised that FLASH was gravely ill with a Grade 4 rectal tear and peritonitis and would not survive, and requested permission to perform euthanasia. Permission was granted, and FLASH died that day.
16. A necropsy was performed that confirmed a rectal tear with associated severe acute septic peritonitis.

Count I: Negligence of Defendants Breeding Stables, LLC, and Betty Breeder

17. Plaintiff incorporates by reference the allegations in paragraphs 7 through 16.
18. At all times pertinent hereto, Defendants Stables and Breeder held themselves out to the public, and to Plaintiff in particular, as skilled and experienced in the business and practice of breeding horses like FLASH.
19. At all times pertinent hereto, Defendants Stables and Breeder owed to Plaintiff various duties, among them being the duty to:

    a. Take proper care of FLASH while she was in their care and custody and to deliver FLASH back to Plaintiff in like condition as she was received;
    b. Take all necessary precautions to prevent harm from coming to FLASH;
    c. Engage the services of veterinarians that were competent to perform necessary physical examinations prior to breeding;
    d. Engage the services of veterinarians who would render or obtain proper medical treatment in the event of a mishap;
    e. Communicate promptly and fully with Plaintiff regarding the condition of his horse and, in the event of a mishap, promptly seek Plaintiff's informed consent for treatment; and
    f. Perform all acts appropriate and customary in the business of breeding other people's horses for profit.

20. Defendants Stables and Breeder negligently breached some or all of said duties.
21. As a direct and proximate result of the breach by Defendants Clinic and Doe, Plaintiff sustained damages in the form of loss of the value of FLASH, loss of future profits from racing and breeding FLASH, out of pocket expense for medical care, treatment, transportation for FLASH's last illness, and disposal of her remains, and other damages not yet known.

WHEREFORE, Plaintiff, Preston Plaintiff, prays for judgment against the Defendants in whatever amount above Twenty-Five Thousand ($25,000.00) dollars to which Plaintiff is found to be entitled by the trier of fact, plus court costs, interest, and attorney fees so wrongfully sustained.

Count II: Breach of Contract/Bailment

22. Plaintiff incorporates by reference the allegations in paragraphs 17 through 21.
23. Plaintiff's delivery of FLASH to, and acceptance into their care and custody by, Defendants Breeding Stables, LLC and Betty Breeder for purposes of being bred to a stud horse owned by Stables and/or Breeder, together with discussions between Plaintiff and Defendants prior to delivery, created a contract between Plaintiff and Defendants.
24. Alternatively, Plaintiff's delivery of FLASH, and acceptance into their care and custody by, Defendants Breeding Stables, LLC and Betty Breeder for purposes of being bred to a stud horse owned by Stables and/or Breeder, together with discussions between Plaintiff and Defendants prior to delivery, created a bailment between Plaintiff and Defendants.
25. As express and/or implied conditions of said contract, Defendants Stables and Breeder agreed to:

    a. Take proper care of FLASH while she was in their care and custody and to deliver FLASH back to Plaintiff in like condition as she was received;
    b. Take all necessary precautions to prevent harm from coming to FLASH;
    c. Engage the services of veterinarians that were competent to perform necessary physical examinations prior to breeding;
    d. Engage the services of veterinarians who would render or obtain proper medical treatment in the event of a mishap;
    e. Communicate promptly and fully with Plaintiff regarding the condition of his horse and, in the event of a mishap, promptly seek Plaintiff's informed consent for treatment; and
    f. Perform all acts appropriate and customary in the business of breeding other people's horses for profit.

26. Defendants Stables and Breeder breached some of all of the terms of said contract and/or bailment, causing loss to Plaintiff as stated previously.

WHEREFORE, Plaintiff, Preston Plaintiff, prays for judgment against the Defendants in whatever amount above Twenty-Five Thousand ($25,000.00) dollars to which Plaintiff is found to be entitled by the trier of fact, plus court costs, interest, and attorney fees so wrongfully sustained.

Count III: Negligence of Atlas Animal Clinic and Veterinarian John Doe

27. Plaintiff incorporates by reference the allegations in paragraphs 21 through 26.
28. At all times pertinent hereto, Defendants Clinic and Doe held themselves out to the public as skilled and experienced in the practice of large animal veterinary medicine.
29. At all times pertinent hereto, Defendants Clinic and Doe owed to Plaintiff various duties, among them being the duty to:

    a. Take proper care of FLASH while she was in their care and custody and to deliver FLASH back to Plaintiff in like condition as when she was received;
    b. Take all necessary precautions to prevent harm from coming to FLASH;
    c. Engage the services of veterinarians who were competent to perform necessary physical examinations prior to breeding;
    d. Properly perform necessary physical examinations;
    e. Engage the services of veterinarians who would render or obtain proper medical treatment in the event of a mishap;
    f. Properly render or obtain proper medical treatment in the event of a mishap;
    g. Communicate promptly and fully with Plaintiff regarding the condition of his horse and, in the event of a mishap, promptly seek Plaintiff's informed consent for treatment; and
    h. Perform all acts appropriate to the standard of care and customary in the practice of large animal veterinary medicine.

30. Defendants Clinic and Doe negligently breached some or all of said duties.
31. As a direct and proximate result of the breaches by Defendants Clinic and Doe, Plaintiff sustained damages in the form of loss of the value of FLASH, loss of future profits from racing and breeding FLASH, out of pocket expense for medical care, treatment, transportation for FLASH's last illness, and disposal of her remains, and other damages not yet known.

WHEREFORE, Plaintiff, Preston Plaintiff, prays for judgment against the Defendants in whatever amount above Twenty-Five Thousand ($25,000.00) Dollars to which Plaintiff is found to be entitled by the trier of fact, plus court costs, interest, attorney fees so wrongfully sustained.

Demand for Trial by Jury

NOW COMES the Plaintiff, Preston Plaintiff, by and through his attorneys, and hereby demands a trial by jury relative to the above cause of action.

[Attorney Signature]

APPENDIX H

Sample Answer and Affirmative Defenses in a Breach of Bailment Case

STATE OF MICHIGAN
IN THE CIRCUIT COURT FOR THE COUNTY OF CONCHO

PRESTON PLAINTIFF, Plaintiff,	The Honorable _______________ Civil Action No. _______________

vs.

BREEDING STABLES, LLC;
BETTY BREEDER; ATLAS ANIMAL CLINIC;
and VETERINARIAN JOHN DOE,
Defendants.

Answer to Complaint

Defendants BREEDING STABLES, LLC, and BETTY BREEDER only, (hereafter, "the Breeder Defendants"), by their attorney, for their Answer to the Plaintiff's Complaint, state as follows:

Parties, Jurisdiction, and Venue

1. The Breeder Defendants neither admit nor deny the allegations contained in paragraph 1 as they are without sufficient knowledge and information to form a belief as to the truth thereof.
2. Admitted.
3. The Breeder Defendants admit only that Betty Breeder is Manager and an owner of Breeding Stables, LLC. However, the Breeder Defendants deny that any allegations are properly asserted against her for the reason that all actions she took in connection with Plaintiff and his horse were conducted in her capacity as a representative of Breeding Stables, LLC. Consequently, Plaintiff has improperly joined her as a party Defendant in this case and the Breeder Defendants hereby demand that she be stricken from this case.
4. The Breeder Defendants neither admit nor deny the allegations as they have no application to it.
5. The Breeder Defendants neither admit nor deny the allegations as they have no application to it.
6. The Breeder Defendants admit only that the facility that boarded Plaintiff's horse is located in Concho County, Michigan, and that the veterinary services of Atlas Animal Clinic were provided in Concho County, Michigan. The Breeder Defendants deny the allegation that the amount in controversy exceeds $25,000 as it is untrue. The Breeder Defendants deny the allegations as they are false to the extent that they suggest or infer that these Defendants, individually or collectively, are liable to Plaintiff for any amount whatsoever.

Facts

7. The Breeder Defendants adopt by reference their answers to paragraphs 1 through 6 of the Complaint as if fully set forth herein.
8. The Breeder Defendants neither admit nor deny the allegations as they are presently without sufficient knowledge and information to form a belief as to the truth thereof but leave Plaintiff to his proofs.
9. The Breeder Defendants admit that Plaintiff brought the horse "FLASH" to the facility owned by Breeding Stables, LLC for purposes of bring stabled and bred to a stallion. Defendants deny that Plaintiff brought the horse to Betty Breeder in her individual capacity, unrelated to the stable business, as such allegations are false.

10. The Breeder Defendants neither admit nor deny the allegations as they are presently without sufficient knowledge and information to form a belief as to the truth thereof but leave Plaintiff to his proofs.
11. The Breeder Defendants admit only that a prebreeding examination was performed on or about May 22, 2009, and Plaintiff specifically knew about this examination before it was done and consented to it. The Breeder Defendants further admit that BREEDING STABLES, LLC, retained this veterinary facility, as it successfully and professionally handled prebreeding examinations there for years.
12. The Breeder Defendants admit only that a veterinarian from Atlas Animal Clinic, Dr. John Doe, did notice some blood after he attempted the examination that day, but these Defendants deny that the veterinarian suspected a tear on that date.
13. The Breeder Defendants deny the allegations as they are false. Further, the allegations are false to the extent that they suggest or infer that there was found to be a "problem" with the mare; in fact, Dr. John Doe did not suspect a rectal tear at the time and so advised these Defendants.
14. The Breeder Defendants admit that on or about May 23, 2009, Betty Breeder contacted Plaintiff numerous times to advise that Dr. John Doe suspected a rectal tear and that he recommended that the mare be transported to the Veterinary Medical College at Michigan State University for further examination and possible treatment. Further, these Defendants admit that after they made a few calls to the Plaintiff and waited patiently for his answer, permission was finally given to transport the mare.
15. Upon information and belief, the Breeder Defendants deny the allegations as they are false. These Defendants admit, however, that Plaintiff instructed the MSU Veterinary Clinic to euthanize the mare.
16. The Breeder Defendants neither admit nor deny the allegations as they are presently without sufficient knowledge and information to form a belief as to the truth thereof but leave Plaintiff to his proofs.

Count I: Negligence (Asserted against Breeding Stables, LLC, and Betty Breeder)

17. The Breeder Defendants adopt by reference their answers to paragraphs 1 through 16 of the Complaint as if fully set forth herein.

18. The Breeder Defendants admit only that BREEDING STABLES, LLC, is an equine business that, among other things, breeds horses. These Defendants neither admit nor deny the allegations regarding how it allegedly "held themselves out to the public and to the Plaintiff in particular" as they are merely characterizations set forth by the Plaintiff and/or mental impressions allegedly held by the Plaintiff and are not presented as allegations of fact.
19. The Breeder Defendants neither admit nor deny the allegations that they owed Plaintiffs "various duties," including, but not limited to, those specified in subparts (a) through (f) as they state conclusions of law for which no answer is required. The Breeder Defendants submit that they breached no legal duties to Plaintiff.
20. The Breeder Defendants deny the allegations as they are false.
21. The Breeder Defendants deny the allegations as they are false.

WHEREFORE, Defendants BREEDING STABLES, LLC, and BETTY BREEDER respectfully request that this Honorable Court dismiss the Plaintiff's Complaint with prejudice and award these Defendants their court costs, including attorney fees.

Count II: Breach of Contract/Bailment

22. The Breeder Defendants adopt by reference their answers to paragraphs 1 through 21 of the Complaint as if fully set forth herein.
23. The Breeder Defendants neither admit nor deny the allegations in regard to the creation of a contract between the parties as they state conclusions of law for which no answer is required. These Defendants admit only that in May 2009 Plaintiff delivered the broodmare "FLASH" to the facility owned by BREEDING STABLES, LLC, for breeding and boarding.
24. The Breeder Defendants neither admit nor deny the allegations in regard to the creation of a bailment between the parties as they state conclusions of law for which no answer is required. These Defendants admit only that in May 2009 Plaintiff delivered the broodmare "FLASH" to the facility owned by BREEDING STABLES, LLC, for breeding and boarding. The Breeder Defendants submit that they took appropriate action and discharged all legal duties appropriately at all times.

25. The Breeder Defendants neither admit nor deny the allegations contained in paragraph 25 of the Complaint, including subparts (a) through (f), as they state conclusions of law, not allegations of fact, and therefore require no answer. The Breeder Defendants submit that they took appropriate action and discharged all legal duties appropriately at all times.
26. The Breeder Defendants deny the allegations as they are false.

WHEREFORE, Defendants BREEDING STABLES, LLC, and BETTY BREEDER respectfully request that this Honorable Court dismiss the Plaintiff's Complaint with prejudice and award these Defendants their court costs, including attorney fees.

Count III: Negligence of Atlas Animal Clinic and Veterinarian John Doe

27. The Breeder Defendants adopt by reference their answers to paragraphs 1 through 26 of the Complaint as if fully set forth herein.
28. The Breeder Defendants neither admit nor deny the allegations as they have no application to them.
29. The Breeder Defendants neither admit nor deny the allegations in paragraph 29, including subparts (a) through (h), as they have no application to them.
30. The Breeder Defendants neither admit nor deny the allegations as they have no application to them.
31. The Breeder Defendants neither admit nor deny the allegations as they have no application to them.

WHEREFORE, Defendants BREEDING STABLES, LLC, and BETTY BREEDER respectfully request that this Honorable Court dismiss the Plaintiff's Complaint with prejudice and award these Defendants their court costs, including attorney fees.

Affirmative Defenses

In further answer and by way of affirmative defense, Defendants BREEDING STABLES, LLC, and BETTY BREEDER, state that they will or may rely on the following defenses if applicable and if supported by facts to be determined through discovery:

A. Plaintiff's Complaint fails to state a claim upon which relief can be granted.
B. Plaintiff's Complaint is barred, in whole or in part, since any alleged damages were proximately caused by the culpable acts of another party (Atlas Animal Clinic and its staff) over whom the Breeder Defendants have no control and for whom the Breeder Defendants cannot be held accountable.
C. Plaintiff's Complaint is barred, in whole or in part, since any complained-of acts of the Breeder Defendants, or either of them individually, were not the proximate cause of the Plaintiff's alleged damages.
D. Plaintiff's Complaint is barred, in whole or in part, since Plaintiff has improperly joined as a party defendant Betty Breeder in her individual capacity, even though all business dealings with Plaintiff that are the subject of this litigation were in fact conducted through the duly established Michigan Limited Liability Company BREEDING STABLES, LLC.
E. Plaintiff's Complaint is barred, in whole or in part, due to the sole, comparative, or contributory negligence of the Plaintiff himself.
F. Plaintiff's Complaint is barred, in whole or in part, due to the statute of frauds.
G. Plaintiff's Complaint is barred, in whole or in part, because Plaintiff has failed to mitigate his damages failed to plead the existence of a tort separate and independent of a contract.
I. Plaintiff's Complaint is barred, in whole or in part, since the corporate Defendant BREEDING STABLES, LLC, and all persons associated with that entity, took all reasonable measures and exercised the legally required degree of care.
J. The Breeder Defendants reserve the right to amend their answer to plead further and other affirmative defenses after a reasonable opportunity for discovery.

Reliance on Jury Demand

The Breeder Defendants rely on the jury demand previously sought by Plaintiff as applicable to all claims and defenses in this action.

[Attorney Signature]

APPENDIX I

Sample Interrogatories from Plaintiffs to Defendant in an Equine Sale Case

STATE OF MICHIGAN
IN THE CIRCUIT COURT FOR THE COUNTY OF EQUINE

BOB and BETTY BUYER,
Plaintiffs,

Civil Action No.: 45678
The Honorable Jim Dandy

vs.

SAM SELLER,
Defendant.

Plaintiffs' First Set of Interrogatories

Instructions and Definitions

For purposes of these Interrogatories and Requests for Production of Documents served by Plaintiffs to Defendant, the following definitions and instructions shall apply:

A. All information is to be divulged that is in the possession of Defendant as well as his attorneys, consultants, investigators, agents, or their other representatives (except for information governed by applicable privileges).
B. These Interrogatories are to be regarded as continuing and Defendant is instructed to provide, by way of supplementary answers, additional information as may later be obtained by him or on his behalf that will augment or otherwise modify any answers not given to these Interrogatories.
C. "Complaint" refers to the Plaintiffs' Complaint in this case.
D. "The Horse" refers to a 2002 American Paint Horse gelding registered with the American Paint Horse Association as "PERFECT

SHOW HORSE" that Defendant sold to Plaintiffs that is the subject of the Complaint and this litigation.

E. "Document" shall have its customary broad meaning and shall include, without limitation, the following items, whether printed, recorded or reproduced by any other mechanical process, or written or produced by hand, including but not limited to: letters, writings, correspondence, photographs, e-mails, downloads, memoranda, drawings, notes, transcripts, contracts, agreements, telegrams, books, magazines, advertisements, statements, notices, reports, diaries, logs, calendars, videos, movies, audiotapes, CDs, diskettes, or materials similar to any of the foregoing.

Interrogatories

INTERROGATORY NO. 1: Identify (by full name, home address, business address, home telephone number, and business telephone number) each person that you believe has information relevant to the issues raised in Defendant's Answer to Complaint and Affirmative Defenses concerning the sale discussions, sale negotiations, and sale transaction for the purchase and sale of the Horse.

INTERROGATORY NO. 2: With respect to each person identified in your previous answer, please describe with reasonable particularity the information you believe he or she possesses.

INTERROGATORY NO. 3: Identify all persons that you believe overheard any discussions between yourself (i.e., any or all of the Defendants) and the Plaintiffs (either separately, together, or with others) concerning the quality of the Horse, the worth or value of the Horse and/or that horse's suitability as a show horse for the Plaintiffs (or either of the Plaintiffs individually) before Defendants (or either of them) received payment for the purchase of the Horse.

INTERROGATORY NO. 4: For each person identified in response to Interrogatory No. 3:

a. please identify (by full name, home address, business address, home telephone number, and business telephone number) him or her; and
b. describe the substance of what you claim each such person overheard.

INTERROGATORY NO. 5: State what you paid (or what items you traded or services rendered in exchange for money) when you bought or acquired the Horse before this horse was sold to the Plaintiffs.

INTERROGATORY NO. 6: With respect to the monetary *value* of the Horse at the time when you bought or acquired him:

a. state what you believed this amount *actually was* at the time when you bought or acquired the Horse; and
b. state how you arrived at that determination of value.

INTERROGATORY NO. 7: With respect to the monetary value of the Horse at the time when you sold the Horse to the Plaintiffs:

a. state what you believed this amount actually was at the time the sale was completed; and
b. state how you arrived at that determination of value.

INTERROGATORY NO. 8: With respect to all veterinarians, equine chiropractors, myotherapists, and/or equine massage therapists who examined, treated, or attended the Horse before the Horse was sold to Plaintiffs (or either of them) and while Defendants owned or maintained the Horse, please state:

a. full name(s), business name(s), business address(es), and telephone number(s);
b. the date(s) when the Horse was under the care of each such person.

INTERROGATORY NO. 9: With respect to all farriers, blacksmiths, and/or horseshoers who have examined, treated, or attended the Horse before the Horse was sold to Plaintiffs (or either of them) and while Defendant owned or maintained the Horse, please state:

a. full name(s), business name(s), business address(es), and telephone number(s);
b. the date(s) when the Horse was under the care of each such person.

INTERROGATORY NO. 10: With respect to all horse shows or schooling shows in which the Horse was entered after before the Horse was sold to

Plaintiffs (or either of them) and while Defendant owned or maintained the Horse, please state:

a. the location(s) and date(s) where each such show took place;
b. all events or class(es) in which the Horse was entered;
c. name(s) of all exhibitors and/or handlers;
d. the Horse's placing(s), if any, in each such horse show, clinic, schooling show, and/or equine event identified in answer to Interrogatory No. 10(a); and
e. attach to your answers to these Interrogatories copies of all documents in regard to the Horse's involvement in each horse show, clinic, schooling show, and/or equine event identified in answer to Interrogatory No. 10(a).

INTERROGATORY NO. 11: With respect to each person you will or may call as a witness at the trial of this action, either in person or by deposition, please state:

a. name, address, and telephone number;
b. a synopsis of the expected testimony of each witness identified in Interrogatory No. 11(a); and
c. attach to your answers to these Interrogatories copies of all documents given to or received by you from any person(s) referenced in response to Interrogatory No. 11(a) regarding this lawsuit.

INTERROGATORY NO. 12: Please state the name, address, and telephone number of each person who is expected to be called as an expert witness on behalf of the Defendant at the trial of this case together with the subject matter on which the expert is expected to testify.

INTERROGATORY NO. 13: With respect to Affirmative Defense E, which asserts that "[*repeat Defendant's specific affirmative defense here*]," please state:

a. all facts upon which you will rely in support of this defense;
b. all documents of any kind upon which you will rely in support of this Affirmative Defense; and
c. attach to your answers to these Interrogatories copies of all documents referenced in answer to Interrogatory Nos. 13(a) through 13(b).

[COUNSEL FIRM/NAME/SIGNATURE BLOCK]

Plaintiffs' Request for Production of Documents

Pursuant to Local Court Rule ____________, Plaintiffs request that the following documents and things be produced for inspection and copying within twenty-eight (28) days from the time this request is served. These items may be produced by mailing or hand-delivering them within the time permitted by court rule to: Lawrence Lawyer, 12345 Easy Street, Morgantown, MI 45678. Clear and complete copies of documents may be served in place of originals.

1. All documents identified in answer to Interrogatory No. 10(e).
2. All documents identified in answer to Interrogatory No. 11(c).
3. All documents identified in answer to Interrogatory No. 13(d).
4. All written sales documentation between Defendant and the person(s) or entity/ies from whom Defendant purchased the Horse before the sale to the Plaintiffs.
5. All photographs of the Horse.
6. All videotapes of the Horse.
7. All communications, whether by letter or e-mail, with anyone in regard to the Horse applicable to the time period before he was purchased by the Defendant.
8. All communications, whether by letter or e-mail, with anyone in regard to the Horse applicable to the time period before he was purchased by Plaintiffs from the Defendant.
9. All documents from Defendant's veterinarian regarding the Horse.
10. All Coggin's Tests regarding the Horse.
11. All written prepurchase examinations regarding the Horse.
12. All canceled checks reflecting the purchase or acquisition of the Horse by Defendant before this Horse was sold to the Plaintiffs.
13. All farrier records, documents, bills, or receipts for services provided to the Horse while at the Defendant's facility and/or while Defendant owned the Horse.
14. All veterinary records, documents, bills, or receipts for services provided to the Horse while at the Defendant's facility and/or while Defendant owned the Horse.
15. The show and/or performance record of the Horse applicable to the time period before this horse was sold to the Plaintiffs.
16. All advertisements in regard to the Horse in any print publication, posting, or Web site.
17. All auction consignment records in regard to the Horse.
18. All documents of any kind in regard to the Horse (other than documents that are specifically governed by an applicable privilege).

19. All documents that Defendant will or may introduce into evidence at the trial of this case.

[COUNSEL FIRM/NAME/SIGNATURE BLOCK]

APPENDIX J

Sample Defendant's Interrogatories to Plaintiff in an Equine Sale Case

[NOTE: Interrogatories like these were utilized by the Defendant in an equine sale case in which the Plaintiff alleged that the horse had been represented as "sound" but was lame at the time of sale. When the Plaintiff answered these interrogatories, it was determined that Plaintiff represented repeatedly to his equine mortality insurance company that the horse was sound, contrary to the allegations in the Complaint. The lawsuit was dropped soon after.]

STATE OF ILLINOIS
IN THE CIRCUIT COURT FOR THE COUNTY OF HORSE

BELINDA BUYER, Plaintiff,	Civil Action No.: 12345 The Honorable Jane Bright
vs.	
SALLY SELLER, Defendant.	

Defendant's First Set of Interrogatories

General Instructions and Definitions

For purposes of these Interrogatories, the following definitions and instructions shall apply:

A. These Interrogatories and document requests shall be continuing in nature so as to require supplemental answers, in writing and under oath, if Plaintiff and/or her attorneys obtain further or different information from the time the original answers are served through the time of trial.
B. The answers should include all information obtained by Plaintiff or by others on her behalf, such as her attorneys, consultants, investigators, agents, or other representatives of the Plaintiff and her attorneys.
C. "Plaintiff" refers to BELINDA BUYER and her attorneys, consultants, investigators, agents, or other representatives or persons who may have obtained information for or on behalf of the Plaintiff.
D. "The Horse" refers to a 2006 Thoroughbred stallion registered with the Jockey Club as No. 98765 as "MAN O' PEACE" that Defendant sold to Plaintiff that is the subject of the Complaint and this litigation.
E. "Complaint" refers to the Plaintiff's Complaint in this case.
F. "Document" shall have its customary broad meaning and shall include, without limitation, the following items, whether printed, recorded, or reproduced by any other mechanical process, or written or produced by hand, including but not limited to: letters, writings, correspondence, photographs, e-mails, diskettes, memoranda, drawings, notes, transcripts, contracts, agreements, telegrams, books, magazines, advertisements, statements, notices, reports, diaries, logs, calendars, videos, movies, audiotapes, CDs, or materials similar to any of the foregoing.

Interrogatories

INTERROGATORY NO. 1: With respect to all stables, barns, or facilities where the Horse was kept from January 1, 2006, to the present, please state the name(s), street address(es), and telephone number(s), as well as the name of the owner(s) of each facility and the barn manager(s) at each facility. Please also provide the date(s) in which the Horse was stabled at each facility.

INTERROGATORY NO. 2: With respect to all horse trainers whom Plaintiff or her agents or representatives retained to handle, show, or work with the Horse after this horse was sold to Plaintiff, please state the name(s), address(es), and telephone number(s), as well as the name of the owner(s) of each facility and barn manager(s) at each facility. Please also provide the date(s) in which the Plaintiff retained each horse trainer.

INTERROGATORY NO. 3: With respect to all equine transportation individuals and/or business entities who handled and/or transported the Horse in a horse trailer after this horse was sold to Plaintiff, please state the name(s), address(es), and telephone number(s). Please also provide the date(s) in which the Horse was handled and/or transported by each such person or entity.

INTERROGATORY NO. 4: With respect to all veterinarians, equine chiropractors, myotherapists, and/or equine massage therapists who have examined, treated, or attended the Horse after the horse was sold to Plaintiff, please state the name(s), business name(s), address(es), telephone number(s), and the date(s) when the Horse was under the care of each such person.

INTERROGATORY NO. 5: With respect to all farriers, blacksmiths, and/or horseshoers who have examined, treated, or attended the Horse after the horse was sold to Plaintiff, please state the name(s), business name(s), address(es), telephone number(s), and the year(s) when the Horse was under the care of each such person.

INTERROGATORY NO. 6: With respect to all horse shows in which the Horse was entered after the Horse was sold to Plaintiff, please state:

a. the location(s) and date(s) where each such horse show took place; and
b. the Horse's placing(s), if any, in each such horse show, clinic, schooling show, and/or equine event identified in answer to Interrogatory No. 6(a).

INTERROGATORY NO. 7: Please state the insurer, broker, and/or agency to whom application(s) was/were submitted involving the Horse and all date(s) of application for the following types of insurance, as well as the date(s) in which such policy/ies was/were issued:

a. equine mortality insurance;
b. equine major medical insurance;
c. Accident, Sickness, or Disease Insurance (or Accident, Sickness, and Disease Insurance); and
d. equine loss of use insurance.

INTERROGATORY NO. 8: For each type of insurance specified in response to Interrogatory 6, please state when the Plaintiff, or her agents or designees, submitted a claim for benefits; the insurance company or companies to whom the claim(s) was/were submitted; and the amount requested in the claim.

INTERROGATORY NO. 9: With respect to each person Plaintiff will or may call as a witness at the trial of this action, either in person or by deposition, please state the name(s), address(es), telephone number(s), and a synopsis of the expected testimony of each person identified.

INTERROGATORY NO. 10: Please state the name, address, and telephone number of each person who is expected to be called as an expert witness on behalf of the Plaintiff at trial together with the subject matter on which the expert is expected to testify.

First Set of Requests for Production of Documents

Definition

"Document" refers to all writings and other materials described in Federal Rule of Civil Procedure 34(a) that are, or were, in the possession, custody, or control of Plaintiff, her agents, or any person acting on her behalf, including, without limitation, the following items, whether printed, recorded, or reproduced by any other mechanical process, or written or produced by hand, including but not limited to: letters, writings, correspondence, photographs, e-mails, diskettes, memoranda, drawings, notes, transcripts, contracts, agreements, telegrams, books, magazines, advertisements, statements, notices, reports, diaries, logs, calendars, videos, movies, audiotapes, CDs, or materials similar to any of the foregoing.

Documents for Production

1. Copies of all invoices ever given to or received by Plaintiff or her agents or representatives from equine veterinarians, equine chiropractors, myotherapists, and/or equine massage therapists involving the Horse.
2. Copies of all invoices ever given to or received by Plaintiff or her agents or representatives from any equine-related magazine, newsletter, or Web site involving the Horse.
3. All documents ever given to or received by Plaintiff or her agents or representatives from veterinarians, equine chiropractors, myotherapists, and/or equine massage therapists involving the Horse.

4. Copies of all equine mortality insurance applications that Plaintiff or her agents or representatives submitted at any time involving the Horse.
5. Copies of all major medical insurance applications that Plaintiff or her agents or representatives submitted at any time involving the Horse.
6. Copies of all equine loss of use insurance applications that Plaintiff or her agents or representatives submitted at any time involving the Horse.
7. Copies of all Accident, Sickness, or Disease Insurance (or Accident, Sickness, and Disease Insurance) applications that Plaintiff or her agents or representatives submitted at any time involving the Horse.
8. Copies of all Veterinary Certificates of Examination (or similar documentation) that Plaintiff or her agents or representatives ever submitted to any insurance broker, agency, or company involving the Horse.
9. Copies of all equine insurance claims that Plaintiff or her agents or representatives submitted at any time involving the Horse, as well as copies of documents received from the insurer(s) in response to the claim(s).
10. Copies of all documents that Plaintiff or her agents or representatives received at any time from any equine insurance company, insurance broker, and/or insurance agent involving the Horse.
11. Copies of all documents Plaintiff or her agents or representatives received from any veterinarian, farrier, myotherapist, equine chiropractor, and/or equine massage therapist at any time involving the Horse.
12. Copies of all documents that Plaintiff or her agents or representatives received at any time from any horse boarding facility, horse trainer, and/or stallion station involving the Horse.
13. Copies of all documents that Plaintiff or her agents or representatives received at any time from any equine transportation persons or entities involving the Horse.
14. All documents that Plaintiff will or may introduce into evidence at the trial of this case.
15. Copies of all advertisements placed by Plaintiff or her agents or representatives at any time involving the Horse, whether or not the advertisements were actually placed in magazines, Web sites, or other publications.

[COUNSEL FIRM/NAME/SIGNATURE BLOCK]

Notes

1. Black's Law Dictionary 136–37 (7th ed. 1999).
2. Cornia v. Wilcox, 898 P.2d 1379, 1383 (Utah 1995). In these situations, the bailee can show that reasonable care was given and that the loss could occur even in the exercise of reasonable care. *See also*, Annotation, *Cause of Action for Loss of or Injury to Animal by an Animal*, 38 Causes of Action 2d 281 (2008).
3. Staheli v. Farmer's Coop of S. Utah, 655 P.2d 680, 684 (Utah 1982).
4. Cornia v. Wilcox, 898 P.2d 1379, 1385 (Utah 1995) (declining to strictly apply the standard bailment principles because of factors differentiating cattle that grazed on public lands from inanimate objects "stored under lock and key in a confined area").
5. Baker v. Hansen, 666 P.2d 315, 320 (Utah 1983), *quoted in* Cornia v. Wilcox, 898 P.2d 1379, 1383 (Utah 1995).
6. Adam Karp, *Professional Bailees May Not Disclaim Liability*, ABA-TIPS Animal Law Comm. Newsl. 7 (Spring 2006).
7. Ky. Rev. Stat. § 422.280.
8. Barruter Farm v. Upson Downs Farm, 2006 WL 259608 (Ky. Ct. App. 2/10/2006).
9. See Restatement (Second) of Torts §§ 525, 552, 552C (1977).
10. 37 Am. Jur. 2d *Fraud and Deceit* § 119, at 153 (2001).
11. 37 Am. Jur. 2d *Fraud and Deceit* § 120, at 154 (2001).
12. 37 Am. Jur. 2d *Fraud and Deceit* § 129, at 160 (2001).
13. See the next section, for example, regarding disclaimers in sale transactions governed by the Uniform Commercial Code.
14. 796 A.2d 899 (N.J. Ct. App. 2002).
15. 833 P.2d 949 (Kan. 1992).
16. *See* Black's Law Dictionary 564 (5th ed. 1979).
17. *See* Steelvest, Inc. v. Scansteel Serv. Ctr., Inc., 807 S.W.2d 476 (Ky. 1991).
18. Nonanimal cases addressing these duties include Fed. Pants, Inc. v. Stocking, 762 F.2d 561 (7th Cir. 1985); Wilcox v. St. Croix Labor Union Mut. Homes, Inc., 567 F. Supp. 924 (D.V.I. 1983) (examining an agent's duty to act in good faith).
19. *See, e.g.*, Bradshaw v. Thompson, 454 F.2d 75 (6th Cir. 1972).
20. *See, e.g.*, Farrell v. Lincoln Nat'l Bank, 320 N.E.2d 208 (Ill. 1974); Baskin v. Dan, 239 A.2d 549 (Conn. 1967).
21. *See, e.g.*, Rapuano v. Rapuano, 2001 WL 1332431 (Conn. Super. 10/12/2001).
22. *Id.*
23. 164 N.E. 61 (Ohio 1928).
24. Mo. Rev. Stat. § 400.2-326(5).
25. Ky. Rev. Stat. § 355.2-316(3)(s).
26. Fla. Stat. Ann. § 672.316(3)(d).

27. *See, e.g.*, Sessa v. Riegle, 427 F. Supp. 760, 764 (E.D. Pa. 1977); Keck v. Wacker, 413 F. Supp. 1377 (E.D. Ky. 1976); Alpert v. Thomas, 643 F. Supp. 1406 (D. Vt. 1986).
28. Vlases v. Montgomery Ward & Co., 377 F.2d 846 (3d Cir. 1967).
29. Fear Ranches, Inc. v. Berry, 470 F.2d 905 (10th Cir. 1972).
30. 2005 WL 2361588 (Conn. Super. Ct. 2005).
31. For more information, see Annotation, *Implied Warranty of Fitness on Sale of Livestock*, 53 A.L.R.2d 884 (1957); Annotation, *Elements and Measure of Damages for Breach of Warranty in Sale of Horse*, 91 A.L.R.3d 419 (1979).
32. Wood v. Ross, 26 S.W. 148 (Tex. Ct. App. 1894).
33. Burnett v. Hensley, 92 N.W. 678 (Iowa 1902).
34. Frederickson v. Hackney, 198 N.W. 806 (Minn. 1924).
35. Dempsey v. Rosenthal, 468 N.Y.S.2d 441 (N.Y. Ct. App. 1983).
36. Appleby v. Hendrix, 673 S.W.2d 295 (Tex. Ct. App. 1984) (holding that advertisement for Arabian stallion qualified as an express warranty); Torstenson v. Melcher, 241 N.W.2d 103 (Neb. 1976) (holding that a catalog advertisement for a bull qualified as an express warranty).
37. *See, e.g.*, Norton v. Lindsay, 350 F.2d 46 (10th Cir. 1965) (examining statements regarding soundness); Yuzwak v. Dygert, 534 N.Y.S.2d 35 (N.Y. Ct. App. 1988) (addressing representations by seller that a horse was quiet and easy to handle); Arine v. McAmis, 603 P.2d 1130 (Okla. 1979).
38. Morningstar v. Hallett, 858 A.2d 125 (Pa. Super. 2004).
39. Mitchell v. Rudasill, 332 S.W.2d 91 (Mo. Ct. App. 1960).
40. 427 F. Supp. 760 (E.D. Pa. 1977).
41. In Sessa v. Riegle, 427 F. Supp. 760, 766 (E.D. Pa. 1977), *aff'd*, 568 F.2d 770 (3d Cir. 1978), the court noted that "because horses are fragile creatures, susceptible to a myriad of maladies, detectable and undetectable, only where there is an 'understanding' that an ignorant buyer is relying totally on a knowledgeable seller not 'to make a mean deal,' are statements as to soundness taken to be anything more than the seller's opinion or commendation."
42. *See* U.C.C. § 2-316, cmt. 8.
43. In Simpson v. Widger, 709 A.2d 1366, 1373 (N.J. Ct. App. 1998), a breach of warranty case, the plaintiff sued alleging that the seller represented the horse to be "sound" but the seller allegedly knew that the horse at the time of the sale had ring bone disease that could adversely affect the horse's ability to compete. The court dismissed the case, in part, on the basis that the buyer did not rely on the seller. Before the purchase, the buyer had an independent examination of the horse by an equine veterinarian.
44. *See, e.g.*, Calloway v. Manion, 572 F.2d 1033 (5th Cir. 1978).
45. *See, e.g.*, Rowland v. Scarborough Farms, L.L.C., 2007 WL 1704393 (Ga. Ct. App. 6/14/07); O'Brien v. Wade, 540 S.W.2d 603 (Mo. Ct. App. 1976); Loisseau v. Gates, 140 N.W. 258 (S.D. 1913); Stewart v. Riley & Johnson, 66 So. 488 (Ala. 1914); Schleicher v. Gentry, 554 S.W.2d 884 (Ky. Ct. App. 1977).

46. *See, e.g.*, Glann v. White, 148 N.W. 210 (Mich. 1914) (allowing jury to decide whether buyer of team of horses could recover consequential damages when horses were ill and unable to work).
47. *See, e.g.*, Balch v. Newberry, 253 P.2d 153 (Okla. 1953) (holding that buyer in breach of warranty claim allowed to recover purchase price and expenses in caring for the dog); Cooper v. Ragsdale, 153 P. 516 (Kan. 1915); Springer v. Puckett, 139 P. 1115 (Colo. Ct. App. 1914); Berkey v. Lefebure & Sons, 99 N.W. 710 (Iowa 1904) (holding that expenses of keeping stallion were recoverable).
48. Jones v. Healy, 261 N.Y.S. 464 (N.Y. Ct. App. 1932) (awarding as damages freight charges on stallion); Hostetler v. Bartholomew, 147 P. 1134 (Kan. 1915) (awarding expenses of shipping horse).
49. Manula v. Wheat, 2007 WL 3232081 (E.D. Ark. 10/31/07); Arine v. McAmis, 603 P.2d 1130 (Okla. 1979).
50. Stewart v. Shanahan, 277 F.2d 233 (8th Cir. 1960) (recognizing that remand was appropriate because plaintiff in a warranty case was not entitled to recover damages for "grievous mental anguish and distress of body and mind").
51. Smith v. Andrepont, 378 So. 2d 479 (La. Ct. App. 1979).
52. *See, e.g.*, Hall v. Klien, 1999 WL 682584 (Ohio Ct. App. 9/3/99) (ruling for seller on personal injury claim asserting allegations of breached warranties because seller made no warranty of gentleness and horse had no prior propensity to buck); Bruce v. Fiss, Doerr & Carroll Horse Co., 62 N.Y.S. 96 (N.Y. Ct. App. 1900) (allowing buyer who was kicked by horse to recover damages for his personal injuries). *But cf.* Mullerleile v. Brandt, 116 P. 868 (Wash. 1911) (denying recovery to plaintiff).
53. For more information, see Annotation, *Measure and Elements of Recovery of Buyer Rescinding Sale of Domestic Animal for Seller's Breach of Warranty*, 35 A.L.R.2d 1273 (1954).
54. Hayes v. Equine Equities, Inc., 480 N.W.2d 178 (Neb. 1992).
55. Chernick v. Casares, 759 S.W.2d 832 (Ky. Ct. App. 1988).
56. Calloway v. Manion, 872 F.2d 1033, 1039 (5th Cir. 1978).
57. *See* White Devon Farm v. Stahl, 389 N.Y.S.2d 724 (N.Y. Super. 1976) (finding that the buyer's breeding of subfertile stallion while seeking rescission was not unreasonable and profits could offset the damages on rescission).
58. For more information, see Annotation, *Elements and Measure of Damages for Breach of Warranty in Sale of Horse*, 91 A.L.R.3d 419 (1979).
59. Brennan v. Shapiro, 785 N.Y.S.2d 100 (N.Y. Ct. App. 2004) (enforcing "as is" disclaimer in bill of sale and holding that claims not set forth in the document were barred); Cohen v. N. Ridge Farms, 712 F. Supp. 1265 (E.D. Ky. 1989) (enforcing auction terms and conditions with disclaimer enforced); Ray L. Atchison Constr. Co. v. Sossaman, 717 P.2d 988 (Colo. Ct. App. 1985) (upholding disclaimer of warranties in sale contract for breeding cattle).

60. *See, e.g.*, Chick v. Brimm, 2002 WL 31999427 (Del. Comm. Pleas 9/30/2002) (finding seller's failure to disclose broken bone in racehorse was a breach of warranty that was not overridden by "as-is" language in the terms of auction); Alpert v. Thomas, 643 F. Supp. 1406 (D. Vt. 1986) (addressing issues in sale of stallion); Slyman v. Pickwick Farms, 472 N.E.2d 380 (Ohio Ct. App. 1984).
61. In Yuzwak v. Dygert, 534 N.Y.S.2d 35 (N.Y. Ct. App. 1988), the defendant asserted that no warranties were made that the horse was "good for children" as these such statements were mere "puffing," and not representations; the court held that this was an issue for the jury to decide.
62. Yuzwak v. Dygert, 534 N.Y.S.2d 35 (N.Y. Ct. App. 1988).
63. Ladner v. Jordan, 2002 WL 31656663 (Miss. Ct. App. 11/26/2002); Forbis v. Reilly, 684 F. Supp. 1317 (W.D. Pa. 1988) (dismissing breach of warranty case brought by buyer who was deemed experienced with several "professional trainers and veterinarians at her disposal" who failed to consult with any of them after being made aware of a defect in the horse).
64. Miron v. Yonkers Raceway, Inc., 400 F.2d 112 (2d Cir. 1968) (finding untimely the rejection of a purchase of a racehorse with broken leg when plaintiff tried the day after purchase to reverse the sale since x-rays did not identify the date when the fracture occurred).
65. Beck Bay Farm, LLC v. Collucio, 230 F. Supp. 2d 176 (D. Mass. 2002) (applying Massachusetts statute); Cronin v. Bacon, 837 S.W.2d 265 (Tex. Ct. App. 1992) (applying Texas statute); Fancher v. Benson, 580 A.2d 51 (Vt. Super. 1990) (applying Vermont statute); Travis v. Wash. Horse Breeders, 769 P.2d 418 (Wash. 1988) (applying Washington statute); Archibald v. Act III Arabians, 741 S.W.2d 957, 958 (Tex. Ct. App. 1987), *rev'd and remanded*, 755 S.W.2d 84 (Tex. 1988).
66. Archibald v. Act III Arabians, 741 S.W.2d 957, 958 (Tex. Ct. App. 1987), *rev'd and remanded*, 755 S.W.2d 84 (Tex. 1988).
67. *See, e.g.*, Perry v. Green, 437 S.E.2d 150 (S.C. Ct. App. 1993).
68. *Id.*
69. *See, e.g.*, ARIZ. REV. STAT. § 44-1799–1799.09 (Arizona pet dealers statute); ARK. CODE ANN. §§ 4-97-101–109 (Arkansas Pet Store Retail Protection Act).
70. N.J. STAT. ANN. §§ 56:8-92–97.
71. Maguire v. Mohrmann, 935 A.2d 1259 (N.J. Super. 2007).
72. For example, in Sessa v. Riegle, 427 F. Supp. 760 (E.D. Penn. 1977), no reliance was found where the buyer sent an agent to inspect the horse. In Hall v. Klien, 1999 WL 682584 (Ohio Ct. App. 6 Dist. 1999), no reliance was found because the buyer brought two persons with her to examine the horse.
73. Sheffield v. Darby, 535 S.E.2d 776 (Ga. Ct. App. 2000) (holding that reliance cannot be predicated on mere statements of opinion or puffing, such as the statement that a horse would make a good show horse); Leal v. Holtvogt, 702 N.E.2d 1246 (Ohio Ct. App. 1998); Forbis v. Reilly, 684 F. Supp. 1317

(W.D. Pa. 1988) (finding buyer may not blindly rely on the representations of the seller but must exercise common diligence and ordinary prudence); Slyman v. Pickwick Farms, 472 N.E.2d 380 (Ohio Ct. App. 1984).
74. 2003 WL 21911138 (Me. Super. 6/25/03).
75. 2000 WL 261133 (N.Y. Ct. App. 3/9/2000).
76. Hitzke v. Easterday, 701 N.W.2d 654 (Wisc. Ct. App. 2005) (involving statute of frauds issues in sale of a pony).
77. 709 A.2d 1366 (N.J. Ct. App. 1998).
78. *Id.*
79. For more information, see Annotation, *Fraud in the Sale of a Show Horse*, 39 AM. JUR. TRIALS 540; Annotation, *Misrepresentation in Sale of Animal*, 35 PROOF OF FACTS 2d 607.

CHAPTER 6

The Disabled, Service Animals, and the Law

GARY C. NORMAN

I. Introduction

While companion animals furnish their human counterparts with certain documented positive benefits, particularized benefits inure to qualified individuals with disabilities who find themselves partnered with animals. In contexts that range from travel to housing, a special status arises for animals that receive training to furnish assistance to people with disabilities.

A. Historical Perspectives

Peer-reviewed research reflects that animals can positively affect human health and behavior, including a sustained increase in health-engendering behaviors such as increased amounts of exercise. Companion animals positively influence the systolic and diastolic blood pressure measurements of humans.[1] For instance, studies document that animals cause a reduction of blood pressure measurements among spouses and aid in the management of the significant health risk factor and chronic condition of hypertension.[2] Additional effects of animals include improvement of the physical and emotional well-being of their human counterparts, especially of children in medical facilities, older adults, and those otherwise residing within institutional settings.[3] A study of the effects of companion animals on Medicare beneficiaries conducted by the University of California at Los Angeles found that among such beneficiaries, those who owned pets experienced fewer medical care visits.[4] In further degree, the human counterparts of animals, inclusive of the handlers of service animals, "suffer deep emotional distress when coping with the loss of their . . . animal whether by separation or death."[5]

Animals have positively influenced their human counterparts throughout history. The Greeks furnished horseback rides to raise the spirits of incurably ill people.[6] The founder of modern nursing, Florence Nightingale, testified to the benefits of pet animals for the sick.[7] Dogs were initially partnered with the vision impaired in Germany as a response to the aftermath of World War I in which thousands of soldiers returned with damaged sight.[8] The use of dogs to assist other kinds of people with disabilities, such as the hearing impaired and mobility impaired, dates from the mid to late 20th century.[9]

With their documented benefits on the human condition, it is no wonder that animals would be called into service by and for people with disabilities. Consequently, several statutes were enacted to extend legal protections to people with disabilities partnered with these special animals.

B. Legal Scope

Service animals clearly constitute something more than just mere pets, and as such, their specialized training triggers critical access rights and obligations.[10] The following laws provide the handlers of service animals certain rights of reasonable accommodations:

1. Public services, programs, and activities are covered by Title II of the Americans with Disabilities Act of 1990 (ADA) and Section 504 of the Rehabilitation Act of 1973, as amended.
2. Places of public accommodation are covered by Title III of the ADA and various state laws.
3. Housing is covered by the Federal and State Fair Housing Acts.
4. Private and public transportation is covered by Titles II and III of the ADA.
5. Air travel is covered by the Air Carriers Access Act of 1986.
6. Emergency preparedness is addressed in the Pets Evacuation and Transportation Standards Act of 2006.

For each, the general principle is that of reasonable accommodations of access for service animals. The counterbalance is that individuals, entities, or places of public accommodations covered under the law need not permit access to a service animal or alleged service animal if such access would constitute a fundamental alteration or pose an undue burden. This chapter defines service animals, the rights and obligations of the public and the handlers of such specialized animals under federal law, and the defenses that may counterbalance handlers' rights.

II. Considerations on the Definition of the Service Animal

A. Statutory Definition of Service Animal

The definition of service animals is broad. In the view of the established service animal civil rights movement, expanding the range of animals considered as service animals may be well intended, but of concern. Two recent issuances, a final rule published to update the implementing regulations for Part 382 of the Air Carriers Access Act of 1986 and a Notice of Proposed Rulemaking (NPRM) for the implementing regulations to the ADA, address the dispute about what should or should not constitute service animals.

The statutory language of Title III of the ADA and the implementing regulation found at 28 C.F.R. § 36.104 defines a service animal as "any guide dog, signal dog, or other animal individually trained to do work or perform tasks for the benefit of an individual with a disability."[11] The other significant statutory and regulatory panoply that guarantee the reasonable accommodation of access generally follow the language of this definition.[12]

The definition evidences that no prohibition restrains what kind of animal a person with a disability may use for assistance work. For an animal to achieve the status of a service animal under this foregoing definition, rather, the three criteria are

1. The animal is individually trained.
2. The animal is trained to perform specific work or tasks.
3. The work or tasks that the animal is trained to perform must relate directly to the specific disability of the person.

In addition, it is critical to note that the ADA does not specify a concrete list of tasks that an animal must perform in order to achieve the status of a service animal.[13] As a guide for what kinds of tasks a service animal performs for people with disabilities, the Title III Technical Assistance Manual illustratively describes that they do the following:

1. Guide people with impaired vision,
2. Alert individuals with impaired hearing to the presence of intruders or sounds,
3. Provide minimal protection or rescue work, or
4. Pull a wheelchair or retrieve dropped items.[14]

Expressing that an animal must receive training beyond that of the average pet to validate it as a service animal, the court in *Access Now, Inc. v. Town of Jasper* indicated that the ADA does not establish the type or amount of training for service animals.[15]

Guidance that the Department of Transportation issued in May 2003, in order to clarify the rights and obligations of passengers with disabilities who travel with service animals, can be interpreted as expanding the gambit of the definition of service animals under Part 382 regulations for the Air Carriers Access Act of 1986 (ACAA) to include "emotional support animals."[16]

Under the broad definition of "service animal" found in the ADA and the 2003 expanded definition under the ACAA, a potential for conflict or, more likely, confusion, exists. Some courts and commentators argue that emotional support animals should not be included in the definition of the service animal. In the viewpoint of one court, categorizing so-called emotional support animals as service animals would cause public confusion and would unfortunately dilute existing access protections, as there is a porous demarcation line between an emotional support animal and a pet.

Rebecca F. Wisch at the Animal Legal and Historical Center of the Michigan State University College of Law indicates that state legislators reflect reluctance to enact a broad definition for service animals.[17] Indicating the concern of some state legislators that, if the definition for service animal in their code expanded to include emotional support animals, far too many individuals with perceived disabilities would seek admittance to places of public accommodation with animals whose purpose is whimsical companionship rather than measurable assistance, she provides copies of the Florida and North Dakota statutory provisions on service animals as examples of narrow definitions of service animals.[18]

Florida provides:

> (d) "Service animal," means an animal that is trained to perform tasks for an individual with a disability. The tasks may include, but are not limited to, guiding a person who is visually impaired or blind, alerting a person who is deaf or hard of hearing, pulling a wheelchair, assisting with mobility or balance, alerting and protecting a person who is having a seizure, retrieving objects, or performing other special tasks. A service animal is not a pet.[19]

North Dakota states:

> "Assistance dog" includes a dog that has been specially trained to assist an individual with a disability. The term includes guide dogs that guide individuals who are legally blind, hearing dogs that alert individuals who are hard of hearing to specific sounds, and service dogs for individuals with disabilities other than blindness or deafness. The term does not include a dog that is not trained to mitigate an individual's disability, but the presence of which is to provide for the comfort, protection, or personal defense of an individual.[20]

The current ADA definition, and even the definition proposed by the Coalition of Assistance Dog Organizations, does not encompass service animals in training.[21] Myriad state codes, however, define service animals to include service animals in training, or otherwise extend the coverage of protections for the handlers of service animals to the trainers of service animals in training.[22]

A limit exists as to the definition of a service animal in other respects. In *Burnham v. Department of Social and Health Services*, a court in Washington State held that service animals cannot be considered to constitute Durable Medical Equipment (DME) or a prosthetic device eligible for reimbursement under welfare and health insurance benefits.[23] In this interesting case, an individual with mental health or psychiatric disabilities who received substantial kinds of public benefits, including Supplemental Security Income and food stamps, filed with the social services department for financial assistance in paying for costs she incurred in caring for her service animal.[24] The social services department denied the application, and on administrative appeal, an administrative judge upheld such determination, concluding that service animals do not constitute DME or a prosthetic device.[25] Relying on what can be fairly interpreted as a technical construction of Washington legislation, the court indicated that the definition of prosthetic device is geared to remedy a physical malady or deformity, and as the appellant had mental health disabilities, a service animal did not meet the definition.[26]

In *Assenberg v. Anacortes Housing Authority*, the court found that snakes did not constitute service animals, where a tenant failed to produce sufficient follow-up evidence of how they benefited said tenant's claimed disability.[27]

Worth noting is the extent to which terminology for guide dogs touches on trademark law. The able-bodied public residing in the metro area where a specific school is located may call a guide dog in reference to the name of a particular school in whose proximity it is associated.[28] For example, in Michigan, there is a training school for guide dogs named Leader Dogs for the Blind. In Michigan, an average citizen on the street might consequently exclaim, "See that blind guy and his leader dog?"

In addition, just as the kinds of service animals have changed and are changing over time, so is the terminology utilized to define them. For instance, "guide dog" and "dog guide" are used interchangeably in this chapter, as it is popular for the handlers of guide dogs to refer to them as dog guides.

B. Agencies Address Definition of Service Animal

Federal departments have recently sought to address the definition of the service animal in such issuances as the NPRM to the ADA and the Final Rule to the ACAA. The NPRM to the ADA indicates that issues have arisen with respect to the definition of the service animal since its original promulgation at Part 36 in 1990.[29]

Indicating that a broad array of animals can furnish measurable assistance to people with disabilities, the NPRM strikes a balance between the advocacy of the established service animal civil rights movement, on the one hand, who argue against emotional support animals being included in its brand, and the advocates of people with mental health disabilities on the other, who contend that animals that furnish mental support are service animals. The NPRM indicates that the definition will be revised to exclude emotional support animals and will otherwise be revised to include animals who furnish assistance to people with learning and mental health disabilities.[30]

The Final Rule to the ACAA, published in June 2008, retains a more inclusive definition for the service animal, encompassing emotional support animals.[31] Acknowledging that able-bodied passengers may claim that their pets constitute service animals, the Final Rule consequently allows carriers to request documentation that an emotional support animal is a trained service animal and to impose advance notification requirements on handlers when determining the difference between a pet and an emotional support animal.[32]

Interestingly, the Final Rule recognizes that, for purposes of an airport, access of emotional support animals might be different depending on the circumstances; for example, an eating establishment could probably deny an emotional support animal, whereas an emotional support animal might enjoy access on an aircraft under the ACAA.[33] Carriers never need allow access to such animals as snakes, who pose a health and safety issue.[34] Carriers should determine the access of other kinds of alleged service animals, such as miniature horses, on a case-by-case basis and in accordance with such suggested criteria as weight and size.[35]

III. Training Standards and Certification

Because more and more people with disabilities seek to employ a variety of animals as service animals, briefly exploring the extent to which service animals must be certified and to what extent states provide for such certification is warranted.

Various statutory and regulatory panoply, including the ADA, do not specify what type of individuals (e.g., licensed instructors) should train animals in order that they can achieve the status of service animals.[36] Training and placing some service animals, such as dog guides, however, constitutes, or is perceived as constituting, a professional vocation. Correspondence conveyed by the International Association of Assistance Dog Partners (IAADP) in 2007 to the New York General Assembly expresses that training should not be restricted to professional trainers.[37] According to IAADP, as long as an animal can ultimately meet the scope of the proposed revised definition for service animals that the association has advocated, the training of such service animals does not matter, whether it is received through an organization, as is the typical circumstance with dog guides, or through private or self-directed sources.[38] Significant waiting lists plague those who can benefit from the assistance of signal dogs and other service animals.[39] Protecting the rights of individuals to train their own service animals is of consequence and is critical for this foregoing fact.[40]

Guidance issued by the Department of Transportation on the question of the access of service animals in air travel acknowledges not all service animals receive training through a formal program and may alternately receive training from their disabled handler.[41] At the same time, IAADP, a cross-disability education and advocacy nonprofit that is a leading voice on service animal policy, is concerned that any animal might be employed as a service animal and that such animal might not possess the kind of training and behavioral attributes to validate it as a legitimate, well-trained, and socially acceptable service animal.[42] Therefore IAADP has developed a set of criteria for training and public behavior of service animals.[43] This criteria may be useful when seeking to prove or defend against whether a particular animal constitutes a service animal.

California, solely with respect to dog guides, establishes a detailed statutory and regulatory scheme respecting the trainers, training, and placement of dog guides. According to the decision in *Lentini v. Cal. Ctr. for the Performing Arts*, which is discussed later when addressing defenses under the ADA, handlers of service animals need not possess certification in order to receive access.[44]

In West Virginia, however, a state court of appeals held that it is the burden of a tenant who requests the access of a service animal as a reasonable accommodation pursuant to the Fair Housing Act[45] and the West Virginia Fair Housing Act[46] to demonstrate that such animal is or has been individually trained and performs assistance for the benefit of such tenant.[47] The court also wrote that it is reasonable for a landlord or person similarly situated to demand that a tenant who requests the reasonable accommodation of the access of an alleged service animal furnish:

1. An assurance that the claimed service animal is properly trained,

2. A writing to the effect from its trainer that it is so trained, and
3. A statement from a licensed physician specializing in the field of disability that certifies that the alleged service animal is necessary to ameliorate the effects of a disability.[48]

North Carolina requires an extensive certification, implemented under the auspices of the Department of Health and Human Services, to certify a service animal.[49]

In Maryland, General Assembly Delegate Christopher Shank introduced a bill to establish an accreditation function under the auspices of the Maryland Department of Disabilities.[50] Delegate Shank withdrew the bill because of substantial opposition waged by the national and Maryland service animal advocacy communities against its illegal provisions.[51]

An author and disability policy advocate, Susan L. Duncan, R.N., argues that the intent of the ADA is not to evaluate the legitimacy of a service animal but rather to ensure that people with disabilities receive access to public goods and services to the fullest extent possible.[52] She contends that the panoply of the ADA does not require certification of service animals, the proof of disability, or of the training of a service animal.[53] In her opinion, certification, even if required, would not be a guarantor of quality, but would rather just equal the perceptions of the individual performing the evaluation.[54] The NPRM to the ADA appears to agree with Duncan in that its text expresses that the DOJ has opted not to impose certification requirements as a measure of what should constitute a service animal.[55]

IV. Overview: Accommodating Service Animals under Federal Law

A federal statutory antecedent to the ADA is the Rehabilitation Act of 1973, as amended. This landmark statute prohibits discrimination against an otherwise qualified individual with a disability, solely based on the disability, in any program or activity that receives federal financial assistance.[56] Sections 501 (employment) and 504 (public accommodations) cover federal executive agencies, including the United States Postal Service.[57]

According to *McWright v. Alexander*, Section 501 of the Rehabilitation Act imposes affirmative obligations on federal agencies to ensure equal opportunity to the disabled by conducting fair and open employment practices. The regulations that implement this part of the Rehabilitation

Act provide that the federal government "shall become a model employer of individuals with handicaps."[58] Federal agencies must provide reasonable accommodations of the known physical or mental limitations of a qualified employee with a disability, unless the agency demonstrates that the accommodation would impose an "undue hardship" on the operation of its program.[59] In either the employment or the general public accommodations context, entrance of a service animal would constitute a reasonable accommodation.

In November 2005, the General Services Administration issued a Final Rule regarding federal property management that prohibits animals on federal grounds, except for official business.[60] People with disabilities, however, may bring dog guides or animals being trained to serve as dog guides onto federal grounds.[61] Additional regulatory panoply protects the access rights of service animals in the context of the grounds of various departments and agencies of the federal government.[62]

In a decision of the state court of appeals in *Whittier Terrace Association v. Hampshire* that was rendered before the enactment of the provisions of the ADA regarding the accommodation of service animals, a privilege to a reasonable accommodation for a tenant with a mental health disability to an assistance cat was found to exist under Section 504 of the Rehabilitation Act, 29 U.S.C. § 794.[63] A landlord brought action to evict a tenant based on violation of a no-pets policy.[64] After stating that the individual could be deemed disabled, a medical witness gave sufficient testimony to demonstrate a link between the disability and the assistance provided by the cat. The court wrote:

> Under the federal law (and regulations) a handicapped individual is qualified if, through reasonable adjustments to accommodate his handicap, he can meet the essential eligibility requirements for participation in the Federally assisted program or activity. Such accommodations are deemed reasonable (and are mandated) where they will not result in an undue financial or operational hardship on the program or agency.[65]

No reasons supported the eviction of the tenant except for the simple presence of the cat in violation of a rule of the landlord.[66] The court cited to *Majors v. Housing Authority of DeKalb*, where a showing of psychological dependence by a mentally ill patient on a dog was held to require an exception to a no-pets clause in a residential lease.[67] Sections 501 and 504 of the Rehabilitation Act, as opposed to the ADA (discussed later), require a receipt of financial assistance before its provisions apply.

Congress amended the Rehabilitation Act to provide that the standards of the ADA apply in circumstances that seek to determine whether the provisions of the Rehabilitation Act have been violated.[68] The Rehabilitation Act incorporates the ADA's definition of "reasonable accommodation," and decisions applying the ADA are useful guidance. Conversely, Rehabilitation Act precedent is useful and can be relied on in interpreting the ADA.[69]

V. Service Animals at Your Feet on Board: Air Carriers Access Act

A. Introduction

In response to a decision of the U.S. Supreme Court holding that unsubsidized carriers did not constitute recipients of federal assistance, thus falling outside of the scope of the Rehabilitation Act of 1973, as amended, Congress enacted and President Reagan signed into law the Air Carrier Access Act of 1986 (hereinafter the Act).[70]

The Act prohibits discrimination on the basis of disability by all domestic carriers, authorizing the Department of Transportation to issue regulations that ensure nondiscrimination while maintaining the safe carriage of all passengers.[71] The panoply of the Act precedes the ADA. As such, the ADA does not include air carriers within its purview.[72]

Under the Act, "any individual or private entity that directly or indirectly, by lease or other arrangement, engages in air transportation" possesses the following kinds of obligations that will be addressed in turn further:[73]

1. Operate in a nondiscriminatory manner,
2. Provide accessible and usable facilities,
3. Provide access features in certain new and renovated aircraft, and
4. Provide access to communications and information.[74]

B. Prohibition against Unlawful Discrimination

The implementing regulations to the nondiscrimination provisions of the Act, which are found at 14 C.F.R. §§ 382.7 and 382.57, prohibit

1. Discrimination against any otherwise qualified individual with a disability, by reason of such disability, in the provision of air transportation.

2. Requiring a person with a disability to accept special services (including, but not limited to, pre-boarding) not requested by the passenger.
3. Excluding a qualified individual with a disability from or denying the person the benefit of any air transportation or related services that are available to other persons, even if there are separate or different services available for persons with a disability. . . .
4. Taking any action adverse to an individual because of an assertion, on his or her own behalf, or on behalf of others, of rights protected by the Act, and
5. Imposing charges for providing facilities, equipment, or services.[75]

Language contained in the implementing regulations also states, "Carriers shall, in addition to meeting the other requirements of this part, modify policies, practices, or facilities as needed to ensure nondiscrimination, consistent with the standards of section 504 of the Rehabilitation Act, as amended."[76]

In May 2003, the Department of Transportation issued a document to update guidance issued in 1996 regarding service animals.[77] This guidance seemingly expanded access to emotional support animals. The guidance provides some useful information about rights and responsibilities of both carriers and the handlers of service animals. The guidance states that in accordance with Part 382, carriers must

1. Permit service animals to accompany qualified individuals with a disability on a flight;
2. Accept as evidence that an animal is a service animal identifiers such as identification cards or other written documentation, or other means of proof, such as harnesses, tags or credible verbal assurances;
3. Permit a service animal to accompany a qualified individual with a disability in any seat in which the person sits, unless the animal obstructs an aisle or other area that must remain unobstructed in order to facilitate an emergency evacuation or to comply with FAA regulations. If a service animal cannot be accommodated at the seat location of the qualified individual with a disability whom the animal is accompanying, the carrier shall offer the passenger the opportunity to move with the animal to a seat location in

the same class of service, if present on the aircraft, where the animal can be accommodated, as an alternative to requiring that the animal travel in the cargo hold;
4. Refrain from the imposition of charges for providing facilities, equipment or services; and
5. Provide a Complaints Resolution Official to resolve disagreements that may arise between the carrier and qualified individuals with disabilities.[78]

1. *Boarding*

Part 382 of the regulations mandates that people with disabilities, certainly including those partnered with a service animal, be subject to the same security screening procedure as able-bodied individuals.[79] Subsection (a) of that regulation states:

> Qualified individuals with a disability shall undergo security screening in the same manner, and be subject to the same security requirements, as other passengers. Possession by a qualified individual with a disability of an aid used for independent travel shall not subject the person or the aid to special screening procedures if the person using the aid clears the security system without activating it. Provided, that this paragraph shall not prohibit security personnel from examining a mobility aid or assistive device which, in their judgment, may conceal a weapon or other prohibited item. Security searches of qualified individuals . . . whose aids activate the security system shall be conducted in the same manner as for other passengers. Private security screenings shall not be required . . . to a greater extent, or for any different reason, than for other passengers.[80]

In implementing the foregoing regulatory provision, the Transportation Security Administration developed the following policy regarding the screening of service animals and their handlers:

1. It is recommended that persons using an animal for assistance carry appropriate identification. Identification may include: cards or documentation, presence of a harness or markings on the harness, or other credible assurance of the passenger using the animal for their disability.
2. At no time during the screening process will the disabled person be required to be separated from his or her service animal.

3. Security Officers have been trained not to communicate, distract, interact [with], play [with], feed, or pet service animals. The Security Officer should ask permission before touching a service animal or its belongings.
4. Passengers with disabilities must assist with the inspection process by controlling their service animal while the Security Officer conducts the inspection. In addition, control of the animal must be maintained in a manner that ensures the animal cannot harm the Security Officer.
5. Passengers and their service animals who must depart the secure boarding area to relieve their animal, as many airports do not possess relieving areas, must undergo the full screening process again. The officer is to upgrade the returning service animal team to the front of the screening line to expedite the screening process.
6. Passengers are to advise Security Officers of the best manner in which the screening process through the metal detector can be achieved, i.e., whether the passenger and service animal should walk through together or separately.
7. Where the metal detector alarms in the situation where a disabled passenger and the service animal have walked together, both members of the team must undergo additional screening, and
8. Where the metal detector alarms in the situation where a disabled passenger and the service animal have walked through separately, additional screening must be conducted on whoever set off the alarm. If the dog set off the alarm, the security officer will then perform a physical inspection of the dog and its belongings (collar, harness, leash, backpack, vest, etc.).[81]

When on an aircraft, handlers of service animals typically find the floor space in certain areas of the cabin to be more suitable and hence comfortable. For example, the bulkhead on most aircraft provides an enhanced amount of room on the floor for a service animal. In addition, the regulation at Section 382.38(a)(3), which regards seating accommodations, indicates that carriers shall provide, on request, a bulkhead seat.[82] Furthermore, Subsection (b) concerns advance requests for seating accommodations, providing that carriers will

1. Block an adequate number of seats as to accommodate the disabled.
2. Designate a certain number of seats as "priority seats" and not assign these seats to able-bodied passengers, until 24 hours before

the scheduled departure of the flight. At any time up until 24 hours before the scheduled departure of the flight, the carrier shall assign a seat to an individual who requests it. If an individual with a disability does not make a request at least 24 hours before the scheduled departure of the flight, the carrier shall meet the individual's request to the extent practicable, but is not required to reassign a seat assigned to another passenger.

3. Provide notice that all passengers assigned priority seats are subject to being reassigned to another seat if necessary to provide a seating accommodation to a disabled passenger. The carrier may provide this notice through its computer reservation system, verbal information provided by reservation personnel, ticket notices, gate announcements, counter signs, seat cards or notices, frequent-flier literature, or other appropriate means. If the individual with a disability does not check in at least an hour before the scheduled departure of the flight, the carrier shall meet the individual's request to the extent practicable, but is not required to reassign a seat assigned to another passenger.[83]

The regulation at 14 C.F.R. § 382.33 allows carriers or airports to impose advance notice requirements on qualified individuals with disabilities.[84] In addition, the regulation at § 382.33(a)(7) regarding the ability of a qualified individual with a disability to receive services or accommodations as part of a group may be of concern to service animal teams who are traveling as a group, such as travel to annual national conventions of advocacy nonprofits, such as the American Council of the Blind or the National Federation of the Blind.[85] The provision states that advance notice may be required in order to provide accommodations to people with disabilities who are traveling as a group of ten or more persons when their travel had been arranged in a group setting.[86]

The 2003 guidance states, with regard to service animals in training, that

> Airlines are not required otherwise to carry animals of any kind (except for service animals) either in the cabin or in the cargo hold. Airlines are free to adopt any policy they choose regarding the carriage of pets and other animals provided that they comply with other applicable requirements, e.g., the Animal Welfare Act. Service animals in training . . . are not pets. However, "in training" status indicates that they do not yet meet the legal definition of service animal.

However, like pet policies, airline policies regarding service animals in training vary. Some airlines permit qualified trainers to bring service animals in training aboard an aircraft. Trainers of service animals should consult with airlines, and become familiar with their policies.[87]

2. Access to Facilities and Information

Part 382 of the regulations requires ready and usable access to the following services while in the airport:

1. Accessible parking near the terminal
2. Signs indicating accessible parking and the easiest access from those spaces to the terminal
3. Accessible medical aid facilities and travelers aid stations
4. Accessible restrooms
5. Accessible drinking fountains
6. Accessible ticketing systems at primary fare collection areas
7. Amplified telephones and text telephones (TTYs) for use by persons with hearing and speech impairments
8. Accessible baggage check-in and retrieval areas
9. Jet ways and mobile lounges
10. Level entry boarding ramps, lifts, or other means of assisting an individual with a disability on and off an aircraft and assistance within the airport
11. Information systems, and
12. Signs indicating the location of specific facilities and services.[88]

In addition, Part 382 indicates that with respect to physical access, a carrier or airport is deemed to be in compliance if it meets requirements applying to places of public accommodation under Department of Justice Title III implementing regulations, including the ADA Accessibility Guidelines.[89] Carriers must ensure access to the following information concerning facilities and services:

1. The location of seats, if any, with movable armrests and any seats which the carrier . . . does not make available to qualified individuals with a disability.
2. Any limitations on the ability of the aircraft to accommodate qualified individuals with disabilities, including limitations on the availability of boarding assistance to the aircraft, with respect to the departure and destination points and any intermediate stops. The carrier shall

provide this information to any passenger who states that he or she uses a wheelchair for boarding, even if the passenger does not explicitly request the information.

3. Any limitations on the availability of storage facilities, in the cabin or in the cargo bay, for mobility aids or other equipment commonly used by persons with a disability.
4. Whether the aircraft has an accessible lavatory.
5. Safety briefings and information the carrier provides to other passengers in the terminal or on the aircraft in an accessible manner, including, but not limited to, information concerning ticketing, flight delays, schedule changes, connections, gate assignments and the checking and claiming of luggage. . . .
6. In the event that special information concerning the transportation of animals outside the continental United States is either required to be or is provided by the carrier, the information shall be provided to all passengers traveling with animals outside the continental United States with the carrier, including those traveling with service animals.[90]

3. *Decision Interpreting Coverage of Southwest's Web Site as Place of Public Accommodation*

Access to Web sites of carriers is a critical issue that affects the ability of people with disabilities, especially those with vision disabilities, to enjoy the increasing range of goods and services furnished by means of the Internet. A federal district court in Florida dismissed a lawsuit that sought to require Southwest Airlines to ensure accessibility to its Web site for people who require screen-readers to access its wealth of information.[91] In *Access Now, Inc., v. Southwest Airlines Co.*, the court granted the airline's motion to dismiss, indicating that Southwest's Web site does not constitute a place of public accommodation covered by Title III of the Americans with Disabilities Act.[92] On appeal, the Court of Appeals for the Eleventh Circuit affirmed the lower court, writing that since the plaintiffs had filed under the Act, and as such, presented a new theory on appeal, that the Web site of Southwest Airlines, as a whole, constituted a travel service covered by Title III of the ADA, it could not reach the merits of the appeal.[93]

Another ruling on a pretrial motion did find a nexus between the challenged service, Target.com, and the full enjoyment of the services of the public accommodation, the brick and mortar store of Target, and, as such, discrimination was actionable under Title III.[94]

However, the final rule at Nondiscrimination on the Basis of Disability in Air Travel,[95] which updated the Act, refrains from announcing a position on whether carriers are obligated to ensure accessibility to Web sites. That stated, carriers cannot charge disabled passengers for providing via telephone the same information or services that would have been furnished through the Web site.

C. Foreign Travel

As the Air Carriers Access Act of 1986 initially did not cover foreign carriers, the Aviation Investment and Reform Act for the 21st Century (AIR 21) amended the Act to cover foreign carriers.[96]

An issue that arose in the context of foreign travel of service animals is the extent to which carriers transporting to foreign destinations, such as the United Kingdom, have to comply with domestic access requirements of the United States.

On February 28, 2000, the United Kingdom instituted the Pet Travel Scheme, which enables dog guides from certain countries and territories to enter its country without undergoing a six-month quarantine and related requirements, including having to transport as manifest cargo in sealed containers in the cargo hold of the carrier.[97] The British Department for Environment Food and Rural Affairs required carriers in the United States to execute a contract with their agency in order for dog guides to fly in the cabin to the United Kingdom.[98] In summer 2004, the National Federation of the Blind passed Resolution 2004–13 to allow dog guides to fly in the cabin to the United Kingdom.[99]

On February 26, 2007, the Department of Transportation (DOT) published guidance in the *Federal Register* requiring domestic and foreign carriers to generally comply with the Act.[100] The *Federal Register* notice indicates that the failure of a carrier to acquire necessary permission from applicable licensing authorities in the United Kingdom would constitute a violation.[101] In addition, the airline may not limit the duration of a flight for which a service animal may repose in the cabin of the carrier.[102] The DOT also decided that domestic carriers may not mandate that service animals wear a special harness that can be attached to a seat belt on take-off and landing—a practice on which the United Kingdom airlines presently insist.[103] Finally, foreign carriers that require an absorbent mat to be placed under the service animal may continue this practice, but carriers must provide and not charge for the mat.[104]

Notably, the United Kingdom does not adhere to all of the policy and legislative pronouncements of the European Union; as such, the procedure for handlers of service animals to prepare for a trip to the Continent is different. This is a fact this author learned when preparing for a foreign policy fellowship in which he engaged in October 2008. For travel to many member states of the European Union within the continent, an international health certificate completed by a licensed veterinarian is required. Service animals are not required to travel in the cargo hold or to undergo a quarantine. In addition, the European Union recently enacted its own statute and set of implementing regulations to increase the access of people with disabilities, including those partnered with service animals, to air travel to, within, and from its borders.[105] Consequently, the opportunities for traveling abroad appear ever more clear and accessible for the handlers of service animals.

D. Defenses

Part 382 of the Act also furnishes a defense against reasonable accommodations where such accommodations "would constitute an undue burden or would fundamentally alter. . .[the] program."[106] Specifically, the regulation at Section 382.31, regarding the refusal of transportation, states:

> Carrier personnel . . . may refuse to provide transportation to any passenger on the basis of safety, and may refuse to provide transportation to any passenger whose carriage would violate the Federal Aviation Regulations. In exercising this authority, carrier personnel shall not discriminate against any qualified individual with a disability on the basis of disability and their actions shall not be inconsistent with the provisions of this Part. In the event that such action is inconsistent with the provisions of this Part, the carrier shall be subject to remedies provided under § 382.65 . . .[107]

The regulation also provides:

> When a carrier refuses to provide transportation to any person on a basis relating to the individual's disability, the carrier shall specify in writing to the person the basis for the refusal, including, where applicable, the reasonable and specific basis for the carrier's opinion that transporting the person would or might be inimical to the safety of the flight. This written explanation shall be provided within 10 calendar days of the refusal of transportation.[108]

For purposes of the Act, examples of undue burdens include

1. Asking another passenger to give up the space in front of his or her seat to accommodate a service animal,
2. Denying transportation to any individual on a flight in order to provide an accommodation to a passenger with a service animal,
3. Furnishing more than one seat per ticket, and
4. Providing a seat in a class of service other than the one the passenger has purchased.[109]

Furthermore, according to the 2003 guidance, which with respect to exotic animals is followed in the 2008 final rule, discussed previously, certain species, such as snakes and spiders, pose safety or health concerns that are not capable of mitigation.[110] Those species do not enjoy access to the cabin of aircraft.[111] The access of other animals, such as the miniature horse, should be evaluated on a case-by-case basis.[112] Factors to be evaluated include

1. Weight,
2. State and foreign country restrictions, and
3. Whether or not the animal would pose a direct threat to the health or safety of others, or cause a fundamental alteration.[113]

E. Remedies: Lots of Greenbacks for Discrimination?

Provided that a service animal can be interpreted to fall within the phrase "assistive device," one of the more interesting regulatory provisions is at Section 382.43 that regards the treatment of mobility aides and assistive devices.[114] Under Section 382.43(b) of the regulations, the criteria for calculating the compensation for replacement of a damaged, lost, or destroyed assistive device is its original purchase price.[115] People with disabilities cannot be forced to sign a waiver of liability for the damage or loss of an assistive device.[116]

The Eleventh Circuit Court of Appeals in *Love v. Delta Airlines* concluded that no private right of action can be inferred from the Act.[117] People with disabilities, certainly including those partnered with service animals, can only seek redress to alleged violations by filing a complaint with the DOT.[118]

In that regard, a position paper of the National Council on Disability (NCD), which contends the Air Carriers Access Act of 1986 should receive dutiful amendment to allow for a private right of action, states:

> Despite improved enforcement of the . . . Act by the Department . . . since the 2000 . . . amendments, people with disabilities continue to experience widespread discrimination . . . While earlier court decisions recognized an implied private right of action . . . since the Supreme Court's decision in Sandoval, which changed the test for determining whether a private right of action exists, two circuit courts have ruled that the ACAA does not allow private suits. Under Sandoval, Congress must expressly provide for a private right of action in the statute. Thus, only by expressly allowing for a private right of action under the ACAA will victims of discrimination . . . be able to seek redress for their . . . disability-based discrimination by . . . carriers. NCD . . . calls on Congress to amend the ACAA to establish a private right of action for the recovery of compensatory and punitive damages for violations of the ACAA and for the recovery of attorneys' fees.[119]

1. *A Case Regarding JNOV and Medical Damages against Northwest Airlines*

In a suit against Northwest Airlines in which a dog guide handler claimed she sustained injuries because of the cramped space afforded to her dog on the floor, a court determined that the Airline Deregulation Act[120] did not preempt the claims of the handler.[121] The court also found that there was sufficient evidence to sustain the verdict of the jury, but that there was no legally sufficient basis for the jury to refuse to award medical expenses to the handler.[122] The jury awarded her general damages in the amount of $5,000, but awarded no damages to account for her medical expenses.[123] In ruling on plaintiff's judgment notwithstanding the verdict (JNOV), the court wrote, "Section 1305 . . . [does] not apply to preempt state tort claims arising from injury caused by aircraft operation and maintenance."[124] The court found that the instant case involves operations as opposed to services that would be preempted by federal law, reasoning:

> Service animals are very similar to carry-on baggage which must be properly accommodated to avoid injury. Northwest has advanced no reason to treat animate baggage, such as a seeing-eye dog, differently from inanimate baggage, such as bottles of rum. In the instant case, the plaintiff's claims concern the way that the airline handled the dog, not the passenger, and allege that the airline violated its own rules and regulations by not moving the dog when it was apparent that it could not be accom-

> modated at the seat with its master. This claim plainly relates to the handling of a passenger's baggage. Whether Northwest employees complied with their own regulations regarding treatment of service animals . . . clearly relates to the operation of a flight as interpreted by the court in Hodges.[125]

The court's reasoning indicated that an airline could breach a duty to the handler of a service animal by not following its own flight operational plans respecting passengers with service animals.[126] The court also found that there was sufficient evidence before the jury to infer that the damages to the plaintiff were sustained as result of the flight.[127] The court then considered the issue of damages. The plaintiff claimed the jury improperly considered medical reimbursement of Medicare and Medicaid in assessing the award. The court wrote that under the collateral source rule, a tort recovery cannot be diminished because of external third-party reimbursement, such as Medicare.[128]

2. *Compliance Reviews: As Good as Greenbacks?*

The Enforcement Office of the DOT engages in such collaborative policymaking efforts as forums, in which carriers and the advocacy communities are brought together to monitor and address problems. Staff at the Enforcement Office also conduct informal compliance reviews. In August 2002, the DOT established a toll-free telephone hotline for disability-related air travel service problems.[129]

On April 20, 2005, the DOT published a request in the *Federal Register* for public comment on a draft of a technical assistance manual it had created in accordance with AIR 21.[130] The DOT issued a final version of the technical assistance manual on July 19, 2005.[131]

F. Future Issues

Myriad protections under the Act entitle the handlers of service animals to access the goods and services afforded by carriers. In the circumstance of dog guides, the various stages of training discussed earlier are an important conduit through which that particular dog morphs from plain pet into a highly trained service animal. Access rights are not provided to the handlers or trainers of service animals in training aboard carriers as is the circumstance for handlers of service animals. That is clearly an avenue for rulemaking that should be explored—at least in the context of dog guides in training and other animals that are receiving training to become legitimate service animals.

Remedies under the Act are administrative in nature. Disability advocates contend that remedies need to be enhanced to include a private right of action. The decision involving the dog guide handler who sustained injuries in transit in the cabin of Northwest is important not only because of the issue of space, which can be challenging when traveling with a dog guide, but also because as more and more animals who are claimed to be service animals enter the cabin of carriers, there is a chance that a dog guide or other legitimate service animal could receive injuries from the occasional pet that makes it aboard.

In sum, the Act, an important predecessor to the Americans with Disabilities Act of 1990, represents a stride forward in improving the access of people with disabilities, including those partnered with service animals. Educating carriers and airport security and other staff about the Act is a significant issue.

VI. Service Animals in Your Apartment: Some Say Yes, I Say No?

Opportunities for fair, just, and accessible housing constitute a core component for independent living of people with disabilities.[132] With respect to housing accommodations, people with disabilities who are partnered with service animals experience a range of encounters from the positive—"What a great dog guide!"—to the negative—"What do you mean, you want to have a dog guide on the premises?"

Three years after the enactment of one of the critical pieces of civil rights–era legislation, the Voting Rights Act, Congress enacted, and President Johnson signed, the Fair Housing Act.[133] Though it did not initially include people with disabilities within its panoply, the Fair Housing Act received dutiful amendment in the late 1980s to ensure that people with disabilities could equally enjoy housing services through the provision of reasonable accommodations.[134] President Reagan signed the amended version of the Fair Housing Act, known as the Fair Housing Amendments Act (FHAA), into law on September 13, 1988.[135] The House Report accompanying the FHAA indicates that its enactment is intended as a "clear pronouncement of a national commitment to end the unnecessary exclusion of persons with [disabilities] from the American mainstream."[136]

A. Reasonable Accommodations

The thrust of the FHAA is reasonable accommodations. Under the FHAA, reasonable accommodations categorize into two generalized areas—structural modifications or changes to ensure that a person with a disability can equally enjoy the premises, and changes in policies or procedures to enable a person with a disability to equally enjoy such housing.[137] Decisions under the Rehabilitation Act provide useful guidance in interpreting the protections of the FHAA.[138]

The FHAA reads as follows:

> It shall be unlawful . . .
>
> (f)(1) To discriminate in the sale or rental, or otherwise to make unavailable or deny, a dwelling to any buyer or renter because of a handicap of—
>
> (A) That buyer or renter . . .
>
> [or] (2) To discriminate against any person in the terms, conditions, or privileges of sale or rental of a dwelling, or in the provision of services or facilities in connection with such dwelling, because of a handicap of—
>
> (A) That person . . .
>
> (3) Discrimination includes a refusal to make reasonable accommodations in rules, policies, practices, or services, when such accommodations may be necessary to afford such person equal opportunity to use and enjoy a dwelling . . .[139]

In a joint statement of explanatory guidance issued by the Office of Fair Housing and Equal Opportunity of the Department of Housing and Urban Development and the Civil Rights Division of the Department of Justice, a reasonable accommodation is "a change, exception, or adjustment to a rule, policy, practice, or service that may be necessary for a person with a disability to have an equal opportunity to . . . enjoy dwelling, including public and common use spaces."[140] The guidance further states, "Since rules, policies, practices, and services may have a different effect on persons with disabilities than on other persons, treating persons with disabilities exactly the same as others will sometimes deny them an equal opportunity to use and enjoy dwelling."[141] An example of a reasonable accommodation set forth in this guidance is the modification of a "no-pets policy" to allow the access of a service animal on the premises of a property.[142]

In addition, the implementing regulation to the FHAA affirms this guidance with a similar example:

> A blind applicant for rental housing wants to live in a dwelling unit with a seeing eye dog. The building has a no pets policy. It is a violation . . . for the owner or manager of the apartment complex to refuse to permit the applicant to live in the apartment with a seeing eye dog because, without the seeing eye dog, the blind person will not have an equal opportunity to use and enjoy a dwelling.[143]

B. The Ugly Face of Discrimination: An Overview of Its Nature and Burdens of Proof

As one court expressed, discrimination under the FHAA can be actual or constructive, but in any event, "Until an accommodation request is denied, there is no discrimination under 42 U.S.C. § 3604(f)(3)(B)," and, as such, no cause of action.[144] Discrimination can take a variety of forms, including as part of the application and screening process in the context of renting. This usually occurs in the following contexts:

1. Inquiries concerning disability status,
2. Refusal to rent to an applicant specifically based on disability, and
3. Refusal to rent to a person with a disability on the same terms that are provided to the able-bodied.[145]

Thus, the frameworks for instigating or defending against an action under the FHAA have been described by one set of commentators as

1. Direct evidence of intentional discrimination,
2. Shifting analysis of burdens of proof and production, as is set forth in the context of fair employment law, commonly referred to as the McDonnell Douglas Prima Facie Case,
3. Disparate impact, and/or
4. Failure to provide reasonable accommodations.[146]

An important consideration in either instigating or defending against an action is the burden of proof and/or production. In *Assenberg v. Anacortes Housing Authority*, the court provided an important framework for either proving or defending against a service animal claim. The court stated:

A plaintiff has the burden of proving four elements . . .

1. He is [disabled] within the meaning of § 3602(h) and defendant knew or should have known of that fact.
2. An accommodation was necessary to afford the . . . person an . . . equal opportunity to use and enjoy the dwelling. . . .
3. The accommodation was reasonable. . . . [and]
4. Defendant refused to make the requested accommodation.[147]

It is worth emphasizing, as one court did, that reasonable accommodations constitute a fact-specific inquiry that must be conducted on a case-by-case basis; therefore, actions instigated under the FHAA "will infrequently be proper for resolution on summary judgment."[148]

C. Case Examples of Discrimination

In *Zatopa v. Lowe*, a tenant who had AIDS and long-term clinical depression sought a reasonable accommodation of allowing him to have an emotional support animal, which was a pit bull mix, in his apartment.[149] The court noted, "An accommodation need not satisfy the particular preference of the disabled person in order to be held reasonable." The court concluded that the defendant's offer of a "safe and gentle" dog breed was a reasonable accommodation.

In *Dubois v. Ass'n of Apartment Owners of 2987 Kalakaua*, the Court of Appeals for the Ninth Circuit held that a condominium association did not deny a request for accommodation of a service animal by requesting additional medical information from a treating physician regarding what tasks the said service animal furnished; and, in the interim, pending this information, the association granted residents a temporary exemption from its no-pets rule.[150]

In *Croley v. Hunting Creek Club Condominium Ass'n*, the court indicated that, for purposes of winning on a claim of unlawful discrimination pursuant to the FHAA, a moving plaintiff bears the burden to furnish proof that the defendant had denied the use of said service animal.[151] In that case, the plaintiff claimed that he had to relinquish the use of his alleged service animals because of a refusal of a condo association to modify its policy of allowing only service animals weighing under 40 pounds.

Finally, in *Proffer v. Columbia Tower*, a court stated that a violation of the FHAA did not occur where a plaintiff received the accommodation of having a service animal, but where a defendant denied her the additional accommodation to have extraneous animals she claimed she was training for the future needs of people with disabilities.[152]

Of course, the foregoing is not an exhaustive manifest of decisions interpreting the provisions of the FHAA. Instead, these cases evince examples of what the shape and form of reasonable accommodations constitute and do not constitute under the FHAA.

D. My Emotional Support Animal and I Demand Accommodations Here—Does My Apartment Complex Have a Legal Obligation?

Protections clearly exist under the FHAA to ensure that the handlers of service animals, such as dog guides, can enjoy equal housing opportunities. If not, with its scope, the handlers benefit from a statutory scheme through which such handlers can seek redress. Emotional support animals pose an interesting question in the context of the coverage of the FHAA and accommodations requested pursuant to its provisions.

While the established service animal community would probably dispute that an emotional support animal should receive the same accommodation of a modification of a no-pets policy, several courts and several administrative rulings have found, particularly in the circumstance of state panoply broader than the FHAA, that emotional support animals and their handlers are entitled to the same level of protection.[153] An interesting article published in the *Vermont Bar Journal* contends that if the thrust of the Americans with Disabilities Act of 1990 and related panoply, such as the FHAA, is to ensure that people with disabilities enjoy the broadest feasible access to goods and services, then people with mental health disabilities should not be forced to endure a heightened level of scrutiny with their emotional support animals when tendering requests for reasonable accommodations.[154] The article also provided what appears to be required of handlers of emotional support animals in the context of rental housing, stating:

> In the rental housing situation, disabled persons will have to show, again through medical testimony, that in order to have full use and enjoyment of their homes, they must have the emotional support animal living with them. In essence, then, the service animal is performing the critical task of providing the disabled person with independence and inclusion he or she would not otherwise enjoy. . . . And, is that not the point."[155]

Clearly, the issue of the coverage of emotional support animals under the FHAA will be and continue to be in flux and change.

E. Defenses

Three exceptions to the general principle of reasonable accommodations in the context of housing are

1. The FHAA does not cover a person who owns no more than three homes and sells or rents a home without discriminatory advertising;
2. The FHAA does not cover buildings of four or fewer units where the owner occupies one of the units; and
3. The FHAA does not cover private clubs or religious organizations that restrict occupancy in housing units to its members.[156]

The FHAA allows for defenses of fundamental alteration and undue burden. In *Judy B. v. Borough of Tioga*, the court concluded that the test for determining whether an accommodation is reasonable is whether it either imposes undue financial and administrative burdens or requires a fundamental alteration in the nature of a program.[157] In *Smith & Lee Associates, Inc. v. City of Taylor*, the court indicated that an accommodation is reasonable if it does not require a fundamental alteration in the nature of a program, impose undue financial and administrative burdens, or undermine the basic purpose that the requirement seeks to achieve.[158]

The FHAA also allows for a defense against allowing the access of a service animal where such an animal would pose a direct threat. For instance, in *Rakuz v. Spunt*, the court found that adverse actions undertaken by a landlord against a tenant for his failure to pick up the waste of his service animal did not violate the FHAA.[159]

F. Remedies

The FHAA allows for either administrative remedies, pursued through the Department of Housing and Urban Development, or a private right of action.[160] Administrative remedies include civil monetary penalties and other capped damages.[161] In private actions, the FHAA provides for damages, including damages for the loss of civil rights, injunctions, and attorney fees at the discretion of the court.[162]

The FHAA provides important protections to people with disabilities partnered with service animals. The ability of a service animal to reside with its disabled handler can constitute a critical aspect of independent living for such handler in the community. As more and more individuals age in the community, there may be a concomitant increase in the kinds of animals that are present in the public who are called on for specialized assistance. As such, housing providers must learn of their obligations under the FHAA. On the other hand, the handlers of service animals possess their own responsibilities, such as being a good tenant. The hope is that the foregoing provides a good starting point for considering the best ways in which to either file litigation or to defend a client against actions. Most of all, it is hoped that this will provide valuable information for housing providers and handlers to resolve their disputes so that they need not resort to the courts.

VII. Americans with Disabilities Act of 1990

A. General Comments

The ADA passed in the Senate on September 7, 1989, and after five different committees conducted hearings, in the House on May 20, 1990.[163] On July 26, 1990, President George H. W. Bush signed the ADA into law.[164] In the process of enacting the ADA, Congress reviewed prior pieces of legislation as a model. The ADA contains a specific provision stating that except as otherwise provided in the Act, nothing in the Act shall be construed to apply a lesser standard than the standards applied under Title V of the Rehabilitation Act, including Section 504 and regulations issued therewith.[165]

In enacting the ADA, Congress intended to provide a mandate for the eradication of exclusion and discrimination of people with disabilities.[166] Many recognize the ADA as "a milestone on the path to a more decent, tolerant, progressive society."[167] Senator Paul Simon provided remarks on access of service animals that evinced a strong commitment for their increased and unfettered access. The Senator stated:

> One form of discrimination faced by thousands of people with disabilities in public accommodation is prohibiting entry by an assistive animal. Part of the problem lies in ignorance . . . Regretfully, many people still don't understand that these animals are well-trained and certified, and don't create public disturbances nor pose any public health risk whatsoever. Generally speaking . . . it is safe for a trained assistive animal to go, including restaurants and other public accommodations [to any place of public accommodation]. . . . It should be further understood that a person with a disability using a guide, signal or service

> dog should not be separated from the dog. . . . A person with a disability and his or her assistive animal function as a unit and should never be involuntarily separated. Nor is there any need for this separation. To require it would be discriminatory under the Americans with Disabilities Act.[168]

The ADA provides several titles that include protections from work to the courthouse and from the local grocer to communications. The Titles of the ADA that apply most directly to service animals are

> Title I—employment, set forth at 42 U.S.C. §§ 12111–12117
>
> Title II—public services that public entities furnish, for example, state governments, set forth at 42 U.S.C. §§ 12131–12165
>
> Title III—goods or services that places of public accommodation furnish, set forth at 42 U.S.C. §§ 12181–12189.

B. Title II

1. *Overview*

Access to the goods and services of public entities is critical to all citizens, inclusive of people with disabilities. Protections for people with disabilities in the context of public entities fall under Title II. The ADA defines public entities to include any state or local government, any department, agency, special purpose district, or other instrumentality of a state or local government, the National Railroad Passenger Corporation, and any commuter authority. Title II of the ADA requires public entities to ensure that their programs and services are accessible so that people with disabilities can equally engage in the life of the community.[169]

Like Title III, for which extensive explanation is furnished later, the implementing regulation at 28 C.F.R. § 35.130(b)(7) requires public entities to modify their policies, procedures, programs, and services to ensure that they are accessible to persons with disabilities, including those partnered with service animals.[170]

2. *Examples of Access Protections, If Any, for Service Animal Handlers*

A. Local Government

Access issues often arise in the context of the request of a handler, or the family member of a handler, for an exception to a local ordinance to allow the access of a service animal. In *Access Now v. Town of Jasper*, plaintiffs sought declaratory judgment and injunctive relief against defendant pursuant to Title II of the ADA, 42 U.S.C.S. § 12131, for its claimed failure to provide reasonable accommodations of an exception to a town ordinance in order that a minor daughter could have a miniature horse as a service animal.[171] Granting judgment in favor of the defendant, the court found that the daughter did not constitute a qualified individual with a disability for purposes of 42 U.S.C. § 12131(2), the miniature horse did not equal a service animal, and as such, no accommodations to its policies on animals were required.[172] As the minor daughter's purported medical conditions did not "substantially limit her in a major life activity," such as walking, the court focused on the fact that the daughter's own treating physician had never prescribed the miniature horse for the mitigation of the alleged disability.[173] The court stated that the plaintiff furnished no evidence demonstrating that the miniature horse constituted an individual trained service animal, rather than just a pet.[174]

The court provides information on what is required to prove discrimination based on disability, stating:

> 1. [Offering] evidence that the disability was actually considered by the public entity in making its decision . . . or
> 2. [Showing] that the public entity could have . . . accommodated the disability but refused to do so.[175]

B. Quarantine Restrictions

One of the pressing issues under Title II is that of quarantine restrictions. In 1979, the American Council of the Blind initially expressed its opposition to certain quarantine regulations and policies enforced by the state of Hawaii through Resolution 79-07 stating that such restrictions "deny the . . . constitutionally guaranteed right of free and unrestricted travel between and among the states, commonwealths, and territorial possessions." Amazingly, more than two decades would pass before a court would hand down a decision critically affecting the access rights of service animals with respect to the restrictions imposed on their travel by quarantine regulations and policies.[176]

In *Crowder v. Kitagawa*, a class of visually impaired persons partnered with dog guides sought exemption from Hawaii's imposition of a 120-day quarantine on carnivorous animals entering the state.[177] Hawaii law permitted disabled persons seeking to bring a dog guide into the state to stay free of charge in an apartment or cottage at the quarantine station for the duration of the 120-day quarantine period.[178] Hawaii also permitted the quarantined dog guide, after an initial ten-day observation period, to train with its owner on the quarantine station grounds, and to train off the station grounds for up to four hours a day, three days per week, if accompanied by a department inspector and subject to the restriction that the dog not have any contact with other animals or humans.[179]

The Ninth Circuit rejected the defendants' argument that it did not violate the ADA as the quarantine constituted a public health measure, observing, "Congress intended to prohibit outright discrimination, as well as those forms of discrimination which deny disabled persons public services disproportionately due to their disability."[180] The court stated, "Although Hawaii's quarantine requirement applies equally to all persons entering the state with a dog, its enforcement burdens visually impaired persons in a manner different and greater than it burdens others. Because of the unique dependence upon guide dogs among many of the visually impaired, Hawaii's quarantine effectively denies these persons—the plaintiffs in this case—meaningful access to state services, programs, and activities while such services, programs, and activities remain open and easily accessible by others."[181] The court held that "what constitutes reasonable modification is highly fact-specific, requiring case-by-case inquiry," and remanded the action to the district court "for determination of the factual dispute whether the plaintiffs' proposed modifications to Hawaii's quarantine [were] reasonable under the ADA."[182]

c. Access to Public Transportation

Included within the panoply of the regulations is the obligation to accommodate a service animal in order that such service animal and its handler can enjoy equal access to public transportation.[183]

d. What to Do? Law Enforcement Faces Off with Assistance Dogs

As is true with any other citizen, people with disabilities partnered with service animals find both benefits and challenges when seeking to utilize or interact with law enforcement. Historically, government has possessed the authority and the responsibility to protect the public through what are called its police powers. One of the core components of this police power is law enforcement. State and local government agencies or departments in executing their police power consequently fall within the purview of Title II of the ADA.

In many states, an access denial can result in civil liability and criminal penalties.[184] For instance, Washington State provides for sanctions of misdemeanors, gross misdemeanors, felonies, or gross felonies for interference with a service animal.[185] In Maryland, penalties include a $500 fine for access denial or interference with a service animal handler, and a

$25 fine for access denials or interference of or with the trainers of service animals in training.[186]

In addition, some states also sanction the theft of a service animal. For instance, Tennessee provides, "A person who intentionally or knowingly unlawfully kills the animal of another, with the intent to deprive the owner of the right to the animal's life and without the owner's effective consent, commits theft of that animal."[187]

Isolated reports indicate that more and more police professionals and prosecutors are learning, or have learned, that their individual state sanctions access denials under a "White Cane Law," and are or have undertaken official actions consistent with that newfound knowledge.[188] Indeed, a blind prosecutor in New York reflected on how her dog guide served a vital role as a prosecutorial tool or facilitator: in one instance by providing the comfort needed to enable a molested girl to discuss a criminal offense perpetrated against her, and in myriad other circumstances by consoling the families of murder victims.[189] On the other hand, people who enjoy partnership with dog guides continue to report negative experiences with law enforcement.[190] Therefore, a need for dialogue among the handlers of service animals and law enforcement professionals still remains, as handlers of service animals may call on the police to enforce their civil rights. A technical assistance guide provides valuable information for law enforcement:

1. Law enforcement officers "may not refuse to assist" someone who uses a dog guide, which is an extension of the handler, or "insist that the [handler] put the guide away as a prerequisite to receiving service."
2. Police officers must take whatever special measures are needed to ensure that the handler's safety is not jeopardized should a handler need to be separated from a dog guide.
3. ". . . Knowledge of ADA requirements is therefore critical."
4. "Proof of disability," or "identification or certification of a guide or other legitimate service animal," may not be requested.[191]

The technical assistance guide delineates the additional following advice for law enforcement:

1. Verbally identify oneself to a person partnered with a dog guide,
2. Never pet service animals without permission, and
3. During an interview with a service animal handler, such animal may perceive any latent stress and/or anxiety of its handler. Allow-

> ing the dog to sniff a hand held with palm facing upward can serve to reduce the anxiety of all parties.[192]

Of the utmost importance is the recommendation that law enforcement agencies and departments appoint a special-needs liaison to educate about and resolve any perceived or actual questions or issues that may arise with respect to the ADA generally and service animal access specifically.[193]

C. Title III

1. General Principles

The statutory and regulatory panoply for Title III of the ADA establishes the general rule that "no individual shall be discriminated against on the basis of disability in the full and equal enjoyment of the goods, services, facilities, privileges, advantages, or accommodations of any place of public accommodation by any person who owns, leases (or leases to), or operates a place of public accommodation."[194] Discrimination is defined as including "a failure to make reasonable modifications in policies, practices, or procedures, when such modifications are necessary to afford such goods, services, facilities, privileges, advantages, or accommodations to individuals with disabilities, unless the entity can demonstrate that making such modifications would fundamentally alter the nature of such goods, services, facilities, privileges, advantages, or accommodations."[195]

The legislative history of the ADA, especially, with reference to Title III, contains statements concerning the access of service animals. The Education and Labor Committee indicated that

> A public accommodation which does not allow dogs must modify that rule for a blind person with a seeing-eye dog, a deaf person with a hearing-ear dog, or a person with some other disability who uses a service dog. Refusal to admit the dog in these circumstances is tantamount to refusing to admit the person who is in need of the dog. Moreover, a public accommodation may not require the person with the disability to be separated from the service, guide, or seeing-eye dog once inside the facility.[196]

The Judiciary Committee specifically stated that refusing to modify a "no-pets policy" violates the ADA. This important committee stated, "It is discriminatory to fail to make reasonable modifications in policies and practices when such modifications are necessary to provide goods or services, unless it can be demonstrated that the modifications would fundamentally alter the nature of the goods or services provided. For example, it is discriminatory to refuse to alter a no-pets rule for a person with a disability who uses a guide or service dog."[197]

The statute directs the Department of Justice to promulgate regulations implementing Title III of the ADA.[198] The implementing regulation states, "Generally, a public accommodation shall modify policies, practices, or procedures to permit the use of a service animal by an individual with a disability."[199] In its interpretive commentary, contained in Appendix B to the implementing regulations, the DOJ states:

> Section 36.302(c)(1) of the final rule now provides that generally, a public accommodation shall modify policies, practices, and procedures to permit the use of a service animal by an individual with a disability. This formulation reflects the general intent of Congress that public accommodations take the necessary steps to accommodate service animals and to ensure that individuals with disabilities are not separated from their service animals. It is intended that the broadest feasible access be provided to service animals in all places of public accommodation, including movie theaters, restaurants, hotels, retail stores, hospitals, and nursing homes . . .[200]

As the DOJ is the department charged with implementing Title III, its views deserve deference.[201] Therefore, the statute, the implementing regulation, and the interpretative guidance pronouncements of the DOJ reflect the general rule that the handlers of service animals enjoy rights of accommodations when working in places of public accommodation.

2. *Access to Differing Places of Public Accommodations*

Resolving access denials or even defending against them can involve different avenues. Litigation may be brought against alleged misfeasors under the ADA. In other instances, alleged access denials will involve the filing of a complaint, or defending against a complaint, in an administrative state agency and/or the DOJ. In many instances, the DOJ will seek to resolve access denials of service to service animal handlers out of court through consent decrees and/or settlements. In yet other instances, the DOJ may refer parties to resolve their ADA-related cases through the mediation program operated under the auspices of one of its contractors, the Key Bridge Foundation.[202]

Important educational outreach occurs through such out-of-court resolutions. As such, the differing kinds of establishment-specific cases will be discussed both through the context of court-rendered decisions or rulings and by out-of-court settlements.

A. Snoopy "Chilling" on the Sun Deck: Is He Allowed to Take a Cruise?

The implementing regulation and its appendix to Title III indicate that a cruise ship is a place of public accommodation, and as such falls under the purview of Title III.[203] Cruise ships typically contain one or more of the kinds of places of public accommodations enumerated in the ADA.[204] The Department of Transportation cogently observed, "[C]ruise ships are self-contained floating communities."[205] "In addition to transporting passengers, cruise ships house, feed, and entertain passengers and thus take on aspects of public accommodations."[206]

Two federal courts have held that a cruise ship is a place of public accommodation, subject to the requirements of Title III of the ADA.[207] In *Stevens v. Premier Cruise Lines*, the Eleventh Circuit wrote:

> Because Congress has provided such a comprehensive definition of "public accommodation," we think that the intent of Congress [to apply Title III to cruise ships] is clear enough. . . . Cruise ships, in fact, often contain places of lodging, restaurants, bars, theaters, auditoriums, retail stores, gift shops, gymnasiums, and health spas. And a public accommodation aboard a cruise ship seems no less a public accommodation just because it is located on a ship instead of upon dry land. In other words, a restaurant aboard a ship is still a restaurant. Very important, Congress made no distinctions—in defining "public accommodation"—based on the physical location of the public accommodation. We conclude, therefore, that those parts of a cruise ship which fall within the statutory enumeration of public accommodations are themselves public accommodations for the purposes of Title III.[208]

In sum, cruise ships are generally subject to Title III. Therefore, cruise ships, if flagged as domestic vessels, must comply with Title III of the ADA.[209] Cruise ships must allow service animals to accompany their handlers aboard. This means that Snoopy can indeed enjoy his chance to "soak in the rays," but only if he is a service animal. On the other hand, should Snoopy, the service animal, desire to disembark and visit St. Lucia, a different issue arises as access to foreign nations triggers more complicated questions.

B. Service Animals under the Table at a Bistro

On October 15, 1992, in correspondence to Senator George J. Mitchell, the DOJ clarified that the protections guaranteed under Title III cover eating establishments.[210] The ADA Title III Technical Assistance Manual specifically includes a restaurant as a place of public accommodation in exemplifying obligations to modify policies and procedures to allow the access of a service animal. The manual states, "An individual who is blind wishes to be accompanied in a restaurant by her guide dog. The restaurant must permit the guide dog to accompany its owner in all areas of the restaurant open to other patrons and may not insist that the dog be separated from her."[211] As with places of lodging discussed subsequently, out-of-court settlements and other forms of negotiated solutions to access denials are typical.

The United States District Court for the Southern District of Indiana issued a consent order in *U.S.A. v. Top China Buffet, Inc.* The order recounts that a disabled woman and her service animal, along with her husband and daughter, sought entrance to eat at the eating establishment; but, as is the unfortunate response of handlers from time to time, they heard "no dogs allowed here."[212] The order adjudged and decreed that

> 1. The [eating establishment] shall not discriminate against any individual on the basis of disability in the full and equal enjoyment of the goods, services, facilities, privileges, advantages or accommodations . . . by excluding or providing unequal treatment to persons with disabilities who use service animals.
> 2. The eating establishment will adopt a policy and procedure regarding the access of service animals.
> 3. The eating establishment will issue a communication to its employees, both in English and in other languages, notifying of the said policy, and will also provide training on such policy.
> 4. The eating establishment will provide training on the policy to all new employees within twenty hours of their entrance on duty.
> 5. The policy on the access of service animals will be posted in a conspicuous area at all times where employees can see its contents.
> 6. The eating establishment will, within sixty days of the entrance of the order, develop a poster and/or sign that is no less than 2′ × 2′, that provides the following language and is in accordance with the corresponding:

a. "Individuals with disabilities accompanied by their service animals are welcome at the Top China Buffet Restaurant."

b. The sign shall comply with the requirements of § 4.30 of the ADA Accessibility Guidelines for Buildings and Facilities (hereinafter referred to as the "ADAAG") as contained in Appendix A to 28 C.F.R. Part 36, including the requirement that the message be stated in Braille. Within 120 days of the entry of this Consent Order, pursuant to . . . § 4.30 of the ADAAG, the Defendant shall install the sign on the wall or window adjacent to the latch side of the entry door of the restaurant at a height of 60 inches from the finished floor to the centerline of the sign and provide proof of this sign to the United States Attorney for the Southern District of Indiana.

7. The eating establishment must pay the service animal handler $5,000, and must pay a civil money penalty in the amount of $2,400 to the federal government.[213]

c. Service Animals under the Bed: Places of Lodging

Reports in the media reflect that the travel industry, including places of lodging, increasingly allow customers to bring their dogs with them.[214] Despite the burgeoning market for "dog friendly" hotels, it is clear that places of public accommodation, including inns, hotels, and motels, that are not owner-occupied establishments renting five or fewer rooms, fall, and have historically fallen, under the purview of Title III.[215] As the American Foundation for the Blind (AFB) points out in its technical assistance guide, places of lodging are required to allow the access of a service animal, unless such access would constitute a fundamental alteration in the nature of the goods and services provided or jeopardize the safe operation of such place of public accommodation.[216] Examples of areas where service animals and their handlers should be similarly allowed as any able-bodied guest include poolside, lobbies, laundries, and business centers.[217]

An important point that the AFB technical assistance guide states is that places of lodging are not required to provide a relief area for a dog guide per se.[218] Public accommodations, including places of lodging, however, must modify policies and practices to permit the access of a service animal.[219] No decisions or other forms of legal analysis specifically address the issue of relief areas as a reasonable accommodation in the context of lodging. In any event, the AFB technical assistance guide does indicate that places of lodging and the handlers of service animals should work collaboratively to address relief areas.[220]

An informative guide developed for the hotel and tourism industry in California states, "Hotel operators are not required to provide special services like food, water, doggy bags, leashes, etc. Staff is not required to clean a service animal's mess, but if staff cleans the rooms generally and put guest items away, they should do the same with the animal's accoutrements."[221]

Recent DOJ settlements or compliance reviews have resulted in some of the following required measures to be undertaken on the part of inns, hotels, and motels to address alleged access denials or prospective access denials. Those measures include

1. An acknowledgement that persons with disabilities may be accompanied by service animals when utilizing the facilities of an inn, hotel, or motel.
2. An acknowledgement that persons with disabilities partnered with service animals are not required to furnish evidence of identification or certification of their service animals or of their individual disability to be permitted access. In that regard, no signage, harness, or other indicia is required to identify an animal as a service animal.
3. The creation of and training on a policy and procedure to govern the access of service animals.
4. Some amount of compensation to the complainant to be paid by the inn, hotel, or motel.
5. The adoption of a notice, in 24-point print or larger, in a conspicuous place in the lobby that reads: "Individuals with disabilities are welcome . . . No pet fee or other special fee, surcharge, or deposit is required due to the use of a service animal."[222]

D. Shopping at a Boutique for That Pampered Pup

In *Stan v. Wal-Mart Stores, Inc.*, a legally blind individual partnered with a dog guide was told once by a Wal-Mart employee and on a separate occasion by a Sam's Club employee that she could not bring her dog guide into the stores.[223] Managers at the stores, which are places of public accommodation for purposes of Title III of the ADA, apologized to the handler, told her that she was permitted to bring her dog into the stores, and assured her that they would train their employees to ensure that the same mistake would not occur again.[224] The court stated that to establish liability under Title III, the plaintiff must demonstrate:

1. A disability,
2. Defendants are owners or operators of a place of public accommodation, and
3. Defendants discriminated against Plaintiff by denying her a full and equal opportunity to participate in Defendants' stores on the basis of her disability.[225]

The court wrote that for purposes of an action for injunctive relief, which the plaintiff sought in this case, standing and irreparable harm must be demonstrated.[226] The court stated that rude treatment without an actual restriction on the ability to enter a place of public accommodation would not likely arise to an injury under the ADA.[227] The court also wrote that to have standing for injunctive relief, a likelihood of future discrimination must be demonstrated.[228]

The defendant stores had official policies allowing the access of service animals on which all employees received at least a modicum of training.[229] The district court had granted summary judgment in favor of defendant stores because there was "no indication in the record" that the plaintiff would likely suffer discrimination on account of her disability at the defendants' stores in the future and the plaintiff thus lacked standing to obtain injunctive relief.[230] The court found that, assuming the plaintiff did have standing and that the conduct of the stores constitutes a violation of the ADA, irreparable harm entitling plaintiff to relief was not demonstrated, because the evidence in the record reflected that she and her service animal were allowed access on several occasions and that the stores provided remedial training to its employees subsequent to the alleged access denial on the part of staff.[231] Thus, this decision indicates that "summary judgment is warranted where all the evidence . . . demonstrates that the defendants have taken all necessary steps to ensure that no individual with a disability is excluded, denied services, segregated or otherwise treated differently than other individuals."[232]

Therefore, the general principle is that of access for the handler of a service animal. As discussed further later, with an inability to win punitive damages, an important form of relief sought under Title III is injunctive in nature. The *Stan* decision provides interesting information on the framework for Title III actions and an analysis of injunctive relief.

E. Sphygmomanometers and Stethoscopes: But Look, a Dog

According to DOJ technical assistance furnished in 1993, unless a medical facility constitutes a religious entity or a subdivision under the control of a religious entity, such a medical facility falls under the definition of a place of public accommodation, and as such, is subject to Title III of the ADA, including requirements for the reasonable accommodation of a service animal.[233]

However, the technical assistance acknowledges that medical facilities may exclude service animals if such access would either cause a fundamental alteration or constitute a legitimate and significant health and safety risk.[234] In providing for the exception to the general principle for broadest feasible access, the technical assistance provides that appropriate medical personnel of a facility must make an individualized assessment before excluding a service animal and narrowly tailor any such exclusion to specific areas of the facility, such as an operating room.[235]

In *Branson v. West*, the court found that the Veterans Administration violated Section 501 of the Rehabilitation Act by refusing to allow a physician partnered with a mobility assist dog to use her dog at the workplace.[236] Because the Veterans Administration failed to produce evidence indicating that a service animal would not provide the benefits described or that such service animal would require financial expenditure and/or cause fundamental changes to operational policies, the court wrote that no reasonable trier of fact could conclude that the service animal was not a reasonable accommodation.[237] The court wrote, "Whether the admission of a service dog is reasonable and required by the employer under the Rehabilitation Act is a fact intensive inquiry requiring consideration of the costs, efficacy, and benefits of each particular situation."[238] Without consideration of each set of facts, the court was not willing to broadly hold that a service animal is or should be permitted in every federal facility.[239]

For purposes of Section 501 of the Rehabilitation Act, but certainly applicable to Section 504, the court stated that three elements govern the analysis of a claim:

1. There must be a qualified individual with a disability,
2. The medical facility must render reasonable accommodations for the known disabilities of the qualified individual with such disability, and
3. A reasonable accommodation need not be made by the medical facility if it would impose an undue hardship.[240]

In *Day v. Sumner Regional Health Systems, Inc.*, in 2006, a woman with multiple disabilities sought entrance to a medical facility with her service animal, and was rebuffed by medical staff after trying to bring her dog with her into the emergency room.[241] The defendant medical facility moved to dismiss, arguing that the regulation at 28 C.F.R. Pt. 36 provides general guidelines respecting service animal access "and does not expressly create an absolute universal right of access for all service animals."[242] The court wrote that "[i]n determining the existence of a 'direct threat,' a place of public accommodation must not base its calculus on stereotypes or generalizations about the effects of a disability but rather must make 'an individualized assessment, based on reasonable judgment that relies on current medical knowledge. . . .'"[243] The court dismissed the motion, indicating that the plaintiff alleged ongoing or future harm; allegations that, based on the record, could not be overcome by an argument of direct threat.[244]

In *Pool v. Riverside Health Services, Inc.*, a Kansas district court held that a hospital did not violate the ADA when it refused to allow a service animal to accompany its handler in the hospital.[245] The hospital subsequently adopted a written policy permitting the presence of service animals in public areas, but excluding such service animals from nonpublic areas, such as the emergency room. The court found this policy reasonable, based on the hospital's testimony that explained the purpose of the exclusion was to institute safeguards against infection.[246]

The *Pool* court also observed that:

> Service animals provide to thousands of Americans a critical means of access to the world. Federal policy as reflected in the ADA is designed to support this access. This policy, however, is not unlimited; it does not compel hospitals to jeopardize the health and safety of their patients.

In *Smith v. Moorman*, the Sixth Circuit Court of Appeals held that the Veterans Administration Medical Center did not violate the ADA by refusing the request of a patient to keep his dog with him during the course of his hospitalization. The Sixth Circuit found that the record reflected the patient fairly received medical treatment and that the exclusion of the service animal was based on appropriate medical reasons.[247]

The best and the most recent guidance of the access of service animals at medical facilities is set forth in an Office of Civil Rights, Department of Health and Human Services, 2006 fact sheet. For standard service animals, that is, domestic animals such as dogs used for guide and signal work, the fact sheet reflects a general principle that service animals are guaranteed the broadest feasible access to medical facilities, including inpatient rooms, applicable intensive care units, emergency rooms, and general public areas.[248] The 2006 guidance also indicates that staff should consider and incorporate the use of service animals during rehabilitation and discharge planning.[249]

In addition, the claim that a service animal cannot be accommodated based on the risk of infection is specious, as well-behaved, well-trained, and vaccinated service animals pose no more significant risk of transmitting infection than people.[250] In light of this, if immunocompromised patients can receive visitors without wearing protective gear or resorting to protective measures, such as specialized gowns, then service animals should also receive access to such patients as well.[251] According to the guidance, standard cleaning and infection control measures are sufficient to avoid any issues with the presence of service animals.[252] A narrowly tailored individualized exclusion may be appropriate in medical facilities in some circumstances where a service animal poses a risk to health and safety. For example, exclusion of service animals may be proper where equipment for advance life support is present and the access of the able-bodied is restricted. According to the 2006 guidance, however, service animals cannot be excluded by staff just because such staff deems they can provide similar services of a particular service animal.[253] In excluding service animals, medical facilities must engage in an individualized assessment that is rendered by qualified personnel.[254]

3. *Defenses*

A place of public accommodation may request that a service animal be removed when such removal is necessary for its safe operation.[255] For instance, a place of public accommodation would be within its legal purview to request, based on concrete, as opposed to speculative, evidence, the removal of a service animal who posed a direct threat to the health and/or safety of others by acting in a vicious or consistently disruptive manner.[256] The decision provided below recognizes that in the context of removing service animals based on disruptive behavior, such removals cannot be based on an isolated or unobtrusive disruption. In the Ninth Circuit decision *Lentini v. California Center for the Arts*, the court affirmed the decision and order of the district court that a nonprofit performance arts center modify its policies and procedures, its activities and services, as to allow the broadest feasible access to a woman and her service animal.[257] The court found that modifications comported with the meaning of 42 U.S.C. § 12182(b)(2)(A)(ii) and that such modification to allow the entrance of the service animal would not constitute a fundamental alteration.[258] The court described the appellee as a quadriplegic who is mobility impaired and who utilizes a small, black Shih Tzu/poodle mix as her service animal as he provides tasks such as retrieving dropped items.[259] The court recounted that the center possessed a policy that no animals were allowed in its premises, except for certified service animals.[260] Additionally, an unwritten policy provided that recognizable service animals were to be granted admission without any questions.[261]

During 1997 and 1998, ticket agents of the center told the appellee that she could not bring her dog into the premises.[262] After receiving assurance that the dog equaled a service animal, they permitted the appellee to enter with her dog.[263] At two performances in 1998, the dog barked, but ceased upon request.[264] On an occasion in 1999, however, the dog was denied entrance.[265] Flouting the denial, the woman entered with her service animal.[266] Security staff told her that she could not attend the performance with the dog, but could attend if she left the dog in her automobile.[267] When she did not vacate the premises, the local police were called, and when their efforts failed to mediate the situation, she was threatened with a citizen's arrest.[268]

The district court conducted a bench trial on the appellee's complaint that included, among others, claims for declaratory and injunctive relief under Title III of the ADA.[269] On August 13, 2001, the district court filed its findings of fact and conclusions of law, finding in favor of the appellee on all counts except for her claims of retaliation and negligence.[270] The district court delivered findings of fact that related specifically to the discriminatory treatment suffered at the performance arts center, including that appellants stated the only dogs allowed are Seeing Eye dogs, that they refused to listen to the explanation that the appellee's dog was a service dog, and that no mention was ever recorded about the dog being a disturbance at previous performances.[271]

Determining that the dog's barking was intended to alert its handler to a potentially dangerous situation, the Ninth Circuit found that the center possessed an unwritten and exclusive policy regarding service animals who had barked at prior performances regardless of the barking's sound level and reason.[272] The court also found that the center did not possess a similar policy for the exclusion of a human who had uttered noises or had caused disruption at a prior performance.[273] Finding and concluding that, except in certain circumstances, barking would be an appropriate service for a qualified individual with a disability, the court affirmed the findings of the district court and ordered the center to modify its policies to grant the broadest feasible access pursuant to Title III of the ADA.[274]

The court also stated that in the rare circumstances where a disruption might rise to the level as to permit the exclusion of a service animal, this determination is to be based on a comparative analysis of similar disruptions of human counterparts.[275] The court cited to *Crowder v. Kitagawa* in stating: "'The determination of what constitutes reasonable modification is highly fact-specific, requiring case-by-case inquiry.'"[276] The court wrote that the order of the district court struck a proper balance that allows access to service animals but permits their exclusion in limited circumstances.[277]

Insofar as in both instances where the service animal barked, patrons did not complain, the court wrote that a comparative analysis of dog and human disruptions is not an unreasonable gauge as to whether a particular bark outburst is inappropriate.[278]

Note that the place of public accommodation must still provide the goods or services to the handler that it would have furnished to any other patron.[279] For instance, the place of public accommodation might have to provide a sighted guide to a vision-impaired person or have to comply with other access requirements, such as Braille signage.

In the context of housing, if a service animal engages in extreme disruptions, or its handler fails to properly and consistently manage its needs, a landlord would be justified in denying a request for an accommodation to permit the continued access of the said service animal.[280] Thus, it is critical that the handlers of service animals endeavor to the best of their abilities to control, care for, and maintain the highest standards of training and partnership possible.

A. Fundamental Alteration

A key defense to providing a reasonable accommodation is that of fundamental alteration. In the context of service animal access, this defense appears as part of myriad different factual milieu.

i. Allergies and Religious Tenets Fundamental alteration is often couched in the context of a defense called direct threat. The regulation at 28 C.F.R. § 36.208 provides a defense for denying access to a service animal, and reads, "This part does not require a public accommodation to permit an individual to participate in or benefit from the goods, services, facilities, privileges, advantages and accommodations of that public accommodation when that individual poses a direct threat to the health or safety of others." The interaction in which the handler of a dog guide or other service animal encounters an exclusion based on an allergy or a religious belief therefore triggers the issue of who is correct.

Under the ADA, allergies and religious beliefs are not valid reasons for excluding or banning a dog guide or other legitimate service animal.[281] Certainly instances arise where an allergy can rise to the level of a disability that may require, on request, a reasonable accommodation.[282] Instructive guidance on this issue is set forth in a legal opinion for the City of Cincinnati, Ohio.[283]

In May 1999, a resident of Cincinnati, Ohio, sought entrance to a taxicab with her dog guide but was denied such access.[284] After refusing to transport the dog guide team, the driver claimed he possessed an allergy and that his religion prohibited him from being in the presence of the dog.[285]

The legal counsel found that the dog guide handler experienced discrimination and unequal treatment despite the fact that the next cab in line drove her to her destination.[286] In some circumstances, allergies may arise to the level of a disability, thus triggering the panoply of the ADA; in addition, the belief that dogs are ritually unclean is protected under the First Amendment to the United States Constitution.That stated, acting on a specious claim of an allergy or exercising a personal religious belief in a way that denies transportation violates the ADA.[287]

Moreover, an informative guide for the transit industry states:

> Allergies generally should not be problematic for fixed route drivers who have little direct contact with service animals. The issue may be more critical for paratransit drivers who come into closer contact with service animals and passengers onboard their vehicles. Paratransit drivers who are allergic to animals should not be assigned to transport passengers traveling with service animals.[288]

A decision of the Ninth Circuit in *Lockett v. Catalina Channel Express, Inc.* provides instructive analysis of the issue of service animals posing a direct threat, based on the dander or other allergens they might leave. The court affirmed an order granting summary judgment in favor of a ferry operator who discriminated against a passenger partnered with a dog guide.[289] Initiated by a request from a regular passenger who possessed allergies to dander, a ferry operator excluded animals from a lounge aboard its ferry that is equivalent to a first-class cabin on an airplane.[290] The ferry operator refused to sell a blind passenger a ticket in the lounge, based on the presence of her dog guide.[291]

The district court held that the ferry's refusal to admit the dog guide to the lounge comported with the provisions found at 28 C.F.R. §§ 36.208, 36.301(a) and 36.302(c), based on health and safety concerns.[292] The Ninth Circuit stated, "in light of the purposes of the ADA," the ferry operator's "refusal to sell the [handler] a ticket to the . . . lounge cannot be justified as a separate arrangement under 42 U.S.C. § 12182(b)(1)(A)(iii)."[293] In some limited circumstances, however, providing a separate but equal accommodation does not violate the statute, according to the court. To apply, there must be

1. A separate arrangement or facility, which
2. Was necessary for the disabled person, and
3. Was "as effective as" that for which it was a substitution.[294]

The court stated that the ferry operator did not offer the handler a separate arrangement or facility, but relegated her to the general passenger area.[295] Thus, this provision does not apply.[296] The court also wrote that even if the provision were applicable, the general passenger area was not "as effective as" the lounge.[297] The court stated, "Construing the subsection to allow the relegation of an individual with a disability to tourist class, or to the back of the airplane, on the rationalization that the individual was allowed to travel on the same plane, would distort the letter and intent of the subsection."[298]

However, the court also stated that 28 C.F.R. § 36.208 permits the ferry operator to ask the dog guide team to travel in the general passenger area, or coach, while it investigated the matter. The court held that the ferry operator's one-time request that the dog guide team accept passage in the general passenger area was a reasonable judgment under 28 C.F.R. § 36.208.[299]

Furthermore, according to the court, the entity asserting a direct threat as a basis for excluding a service animal handler also bears the burden of demonstrating that the individual handler poses a significant risk to the health and safety of others.[300]

As this discussion demonstrates, a party bears the burden to demonstrate that allergies or religious beliefs pose such a problem as to permissibly allow the exclusion of a service animal under the rubric of direct threat. Of course, places of public accommodation may find themselves called on to balance the rights of accommodations guaranteed to legitimate service animal teams under the ADA and the health or religious concerns of other individuals. While this poses a challenge, the clear answer is that such counterbalancing concerns cannot lay as a pretext to engage in unlawful discrimination.

ii. Educational Settings The editor of the *Braille Monitor*, a blindness lifestyle and policy magazine published by the National Federation of the Blind (NFB), stated, "People are sometimes puzzled at the . . . frustration expressed by many in the blindness community when we talk about our struggle to receive service from . . . rehabilitation or education establishments."[301] In light of this statement, an interesting case that touches on the concept of fundamental alteration under the ADA arises in the context of a young woman, Stephanie Dohmen, partnered with a dog guide. She sought training at a rehabilitation facility influenced and/or operated by the NFB, but was told that she could not utilize her dog guide while on its premises at such training.[302]

NFB philosophy holds that while in rehabilitation training, whether or not partnered with a dog guide, a blind person must master the techniques of blindness, which, in the organization's view, means the long white cane and not partnership with a dog guide.[303] In line with this philosophy, a requirement of many NFB-operated or -influenced rehabilitation facilities is that students with dog guides must not only train with a white cane but also leave their dog guide in their room or dorm when in training.[304]

Dohmen attended a blindness adjustment course at the facility in 2001 but had to leave early for health reasons.[305] In 2002 she sought readmittance to the facility to complete the course.[306] When she requested to bring her dog guide she was told the dog was not allowed based on the policy of the Iowa Department for the Blind, which states that dog guides cannot accompany their handlers while at rehabilitation facilities.[307]

On November 26, 2002, Guide Dog Users, Inc. (GDUI) and four dog guide schools filed a formal complaint with the DOJ on behalf of Dohmen against the Iowa Department for the Blind.[308] A press release issued by these organizations quotes the response of a director of one of the dog guide schools that dog guides do not constitute effective mobility aides for the blind.[309]

The formal complaint describes the position of the rehabilitation facility: "The Iowa Department for the Blind [the rehabilitation facility] holds that participants in their orientation and adjustment to blindness program *must learn to be self-reliant and independent* and that *the presence of . . . dogs would frustrate* the purpose and *fundamentally alter the nature of the program. . . .*"[310] The formal complaint requests that the DOJ enforce the ADA by forcing the State of Iowa Department for the blind to immediately bring its policies into compliance with the civil rights of all blind persons, including the handlers of service animals.

Clearly, as expressed in the formal complaint provided on behalf of Dohmen, GDUI opposes and condemns the position of the rehabilitation facility. GDUI additionally announced its policy stance on the issue of dog guides and rehabilitation facilities in a 2003 position paper, *Use of Guide Dogs in Public Rehabilitation Programs*.[311] Referring to the general mandates and protections of the Rehabilitation Act, the position paper states:

> One of the . . . challenges for blind individuals during initial rehabilitation training involves learning to navigate the environment with limited or no vision. All United States guide dog training programs require proof of proficiency in orientation and mobility prior to training with the dog. Once a person has become proficient enough at orientation and mobility to successfully complete training at a guide dog program, he or she may then choose the mobility aid, white cane or guide dog that best suits his or her needs during all phases of travel. This choice must be

> respected and honored by all public agencies but especially those whose purpose is to promote the well-being and independence of persons who are blind if those agencies are to be compliant with the Rehabilitation Act and its principles of informed choice, self determination and personal responsibility. . . .[312]

In contrast, the NFB passed a resolution at its 2003 summer national convention to reaffirm its commitment to informed choice of consumers to attend cane training programs, but "insist that this right not be endangered by misinterpretation for the purpose of furthering a political agenda." The resolution provided that a few misguided persons, in odds with the body of proven methodology for adjusting persons to blindness, seek to distort informed choice by altering the nature of programs to enable the access of dog guides at rehabilitation facilities.[313]

The resolution stated,

> WHEREAS, in enacting the informed choice right as part of the Rehabilitation Act, Congress intended that individuals would be able to select among programs and not that they would be granted legal standing to alter programs to suit individual demands, any more than higher education students have the right to control the curriculum at a public or private university.[314]

Notably, a 1996 letter from the Department of Justice to Senator Dianne Feinstein stated that a college could, depending on the circumstances, constitute either a place of public accommodation or a public entity.[315]

In 2003 Dohmen filed a complaint against the Iowa Department for the Blind in Iowa State Court under federal and state disability laws.[316] In 2006 the state court granted summary judgment to the Department for the Blind for lack of jurisdiction for Dohmen's failure to exhaust administrative remedies.[317] In June 2008 the appellate court reversed and remanded, finding that the Department for the Blind waived the defense for lack of jurisdiction.[318]

The important point worth mentioning is that if the blind cannot properly treat dog guide handlers, how is the well-intended, but misinformed, sighted public supposed to comply with the ADA?

iii. What Happens When Allowing Access Seemingly Violates the Health Code In *Johnson v. Gambrinus Co./Spoetzl Brewery*, appellant brewery challenged the judgment of the United States District Court for the Southern District of Texas that found a violation of the ADA and Section 121.003(c) of the Texas Human Resources Code (1997) when appellant refused to permit appellee tourist, who was blind, to tour the brewery with his dog guide.[319] The dog guide handler sought to purchase a ticket to attend a tour of a microbrewery but was rebuffed by the ticket agent and again upon further inquiry by the brewmaster, who based his decision upon his interpretation of applicable federal, state, and local health codes.[320] The ticket agent told the dog handler he could not attend the tour with his dog but could attend with a human guide.[321] Declining to enjoy the tour without his dog guide, he waited for his friends outside.[322]

On appeal, the microbrewery asserted:

1. "Broadest feasible access" constitutes a goal and not a legal standard by which to adjudge alleged violations under the ADA, and
2. It cannot be held liable for a state law violation when a federal statute, the Food, Drug and Cosmetic Act, 21 U.S.C. §§ 301–395, mandates its actions.[323]

After finding that no reason existed to distinguish the burdens of proof under Titles II and III, the court delineated the following burdens of proof:

1. The plaintiff has the burden of proving that a modification was requested and that the requested modification is reasonable, which is met by introducing evidence that the requested modification is reasonable in the general sense, that is, reasonable in the run of cases.
2. While the defendant may introduce evidence indicating that the plaintiff's requested modification is not reasonable in the run of cases, the plaintiff bears the ultimate burden of proof.
3. If the plaintiff meets this burden, the defendant must render the requested modification or accommodation, unless it is demonstrated that such modification would constitute a fundamental alteration. The kind of evidence that demonstrates this burden must be based on the circumstances of the parties and not on that of the requested modification.[324]

The court then stated that a modification of a no-pets policy to allow the access of a service animal in a place of public accommodation is reasonable in the "run of cases."[325] The interpretation of the DOJ, that service animals are to receive the broadest feasible access, is not arbitrary and capricious.[326]

The court affirmed the judgment of the district court, finding that appellee met his burden of proving that the requested modification was reasonable but that appellant failed to meet its burden of proving that the modification would fundamentally alter the nature of the brewery, or would jeopardize its safe operation.[327] The court held that 21 U.S.C. § 342 of the Food, Drug, and Cosmetic Act did not compel appellant's "no animals" policy because dogs could go on parts of the brewery tour without violating the regulation.[328]

B. Mistake Is Not a Defense

In *Brown v. Lopez*, a blind patron partnered with a dog guide attempted to purchase a meal at a Mexican restaurant only to be rebuffed, first by the waitress and then, after furnishing identification, by the manager.[329] Holding that 42 U.S.C.S. § 12182 of the ADA encompasses not only intentional discrimination, but also the discriminatory effects of benign neglect, apathy, and indifference, the appellate court reversed and remanded the decision of the trial court and indicated that mistake or misunderstanding does not comprise a defense under the ADA.[330]

C. Religious and Other Organizations

Religious entities enjoy an exemption under Title III.[331] This equally applies when an organization is controlled by a religious entity. For instance, a hall utilized for Knights of Columbus meetings would not be covered by Title III when it is used for that specific purpose, but such a hall would be covered when rented to the public. Title III also does not apply to private clubs or establishments exempted from coverage under Title II of the Civil Rights Act of 1964.[332]

D. Remedies

Private rights of action are available under the ADA. The enforcement remedies of Section 504 of the Rehabilitation Act of 1973, 29 U.S.C. § 794a, are incorporated by reference into the ADA. These remedies are similar to those of Title VI of the Civil Rights Act of 1964, and include damages and injunctive relief. Note, however, in *Barnes v. Gorman*, the U.S. Supreme Court held, in a unanimous decision, that punitive damages may not be awarded under Section 202 of the ADA and Section 504 of the Rehabilitation Act of 1973, as amended.[333] If a suit is brought by the Department of Justice, the possible remedies include injunctive relief, damages to individuals, and civil penalties.[334]

E. Closing Thoughts on Title III

The ADA furnishes broad protections for the handlers of service animals with broadest feasible access. Of course, no rights are absolute. The ADA allows for several defenses, although the moving party possesses the burden of proof. One of the key defenses constitutes fundamental alteration. Of all the sub-issues discussed in the context of fundamental alteration, the discrimination that Dohman alleged probably constitutes the important pending resolution as it reflects how even the blind are not immune from misinformation about the rights of handlers. There are remedies available under the ADA, including damages, injunctive relief, and civil penalties; however, the Supreme Court has concluded that the ADA does not allow for the recovery of punitive damages.

VIII. Emergency Preparedness

The events of September 11, 2001, and the hurricanes of 2005 galvanized both Americans and federal, state, and local governments into planning for the prevention, mitigation, and recovery from a disaster or emergency. Tales and experiences emanating during and after the hurricanes of 2005 not only depicted profound human suffering and tragedy, but also evidenced the degree to which the human-animal bond can bear a particular brunt of disasters. In some circumstances, people ordered to evacuate by first responders refused to do so when they could not bring their pets. Service handlers encountered access denials at emergency shelters.[335]

Congress enacted, and President George W. Bush signed into law, the Pets Evacuation and Transportation Standards (PETS) Act of 2006.[336] The PETS Act amends Sections 613, 611, and 403(a)(3) of the Robert T. Stafford Disaster Relief and Emergency Assistance Act to ensure that state and local emergency-preparedness operational plans address the needs of individuals with household pets and service animals following a disaster and/or emergency. The PETS Act provides:

> **Standards for State and Local Emergency Preparedness Operational Plans—**
>
> In approving standards for State and local emergency preparedness operational plans . . . the Director shall ensure that such plans take into account the needs of individuals with household pets and service animals prior to, during, and following a major disaster or emergency.
>
> **Emergency Preparedness Measures of the Director—**
>
> The Director may make financial contributions, based on programs or projects approved by the Director, to the States and local

> authorities for animal emergency . . . preparedness purposes, including the procurement, construction, leasing, or renovating of emergency shelter facilities and materials that will accommodate people with pets and service animals. Thus, as part of this, the Federal Emergency Management Agency is directed to include expenses related to companion and service animals under their cost-sharing programs with states and local communities during major disasters.
>
> **Providing Essential Assistance to Individuals with Household Pets and Service Animals Following Disaster—**
>
> First responders will engage in the provision of rescue, care, shelter and essential needs to individuals with household pets and/or service animals as well as to the pets and service animals themselves.[337]

The provisions of the PETS Act are obviously broad. Thus, it is worth noting some implications of the PETS Act as states and local governments seek to implement its provisions. Society historically views the word "pets" as encompassing obvious animals, such as dogs and cats. More and more, society is recognizing animals historically viewed as livestock, such as horses, as companion animals and even service animals. Thus, an issue could conceivably arise as to what constitutes a pet for purposes of compliance with the PETS Act.[338]

Since first responders already possess arguable obligations under Titles II and III of the ADA, it would seem that the requirement that service animals be accommodated at emergency shelters is duplicative.[339]

IX. Identifying If Lassie Is a Dog Guide or Just a Great Thespian

Identifying service animals can prove a challenge, consequently causing confusion if and to what extent inquiries of whether an animal constitutes a service animal are appropriate.

A. ADA Provisions

Service animals may or may not wear special harnesses or collars and possess identifying papers.[340] The ADA does not mandate that service animals be specifically identified with certification papers, a harness, special collar, or any other form of identification.[341] If a place of public accommodation or public entity is not certain whether an animal constitutes a service animal, then such place of public accommodation or public entity may tender an inquiry to the handler.[342]

In *Grill v. Costco Wholesale Corp.*, the court upheld a private membership shopping club's policy that required its employees to first look for visible identification that the animal comprised a service animal and, if no such identification existed, to tender task-based inquiries to determine if the animal constituted a service animal.[343] In the second Costco case of *Dilorenzo v. Costco Wholesale Corp.*, the court concluded that a store did not exceed the bounds of the ADA by inquiring about the training of a purported service animal of a patron and providing such patron with a copy of its policy on service animals.[344] The court wrote that the claim ultimately stood on whether the store exceeded the bounds of a legitimate inquiry into whether the dog was a service animal.[345] The court wrote:

> Whether a given policy sets forth standards of conduct within statutory bounds is a question of facial validity, which in the case of Costco's service dog policy, was upheld in *Grill v. Costco Wholesale Corp.* The existence of a legal policy notwithstanding, a public accommodation can still act in a manner that violates the ADA. . . . Either way, Costco does not violate the ADA simply by violating its . . . own policy.[346]

Regarding the ability of a store to tender an inquiry into whether a dog constitutes a service animal, the *Dilorenzo* court wrote:

> That Costco had a right to make an inquiry in the first place cannot seriously be questioned. This follows from DOJ interpretations regarding "legitimate inquiry," the *Grill* case, as well as common sense. In operating its business, Costco has the authority to exclude ordinary pets from its facilities, and yet must also comply with federal anti-discrimination law, which under most circumstances includes permitting service animals into its warehouses. Given these two co-existing conditions, an occasion for some kind of inquiry is bound to arise.[347]

The court also stated, "Clearly an inquiry would cease to be legitimate if it was used to harass or discourage people with disabilities from availing themselves of public accommodation. In this way, unduly repetitive questioning, after an adequate answer has been given, could suggest a pretext for discrimination, constituting an illegitimate inquiry."[348]

In *Thompson v. Dover Downs, Inc.*, the Delaware Supreme Court wrote that a place of public accommodation, a business, could exclude a service animal if the handler refused to answer questions about its training.[349] Although brought under Delaware state law, the court stated that the state law and the ADA's provisions regarding service animals were essentially the same. The court relied on the fact that the place of public accommodation had contacted the DOJ information line confirming that while the individual could not be asked about his disability, such place of public accommodation was permitted to inquire into the dog's training.

Therefore, the nature of a permissible inquiry on the part of a third party may include one or more of the suggested points below:

1. Do you have a disability? (Note, however, the inquiry cannot proceed beyond this level of detail.)
2. Is this animal a service animal?
3. Has this animal been individually trained to assist you with your disability?
4. How does this animal assist you with your disability?

Rebecca F. Wisch at the Animal Legal and Historical Center of the Michigan State University College of Law writes instructive language regarding identification of prohibitions on places of public accommodations relative to service animals that states:

> The impetus behind a requirement of proof of training is to eliminate an abuse of the system by owners of "ordinary pets." One thing remains clear in all these situations: the ADA does not require a disabled person to disclose the nature of his or her disability to a business owner. A permissible inquiry starts and ends with the dog's qualifications. The goal of such laws is to make equal access to public places a reality for all individuals.[350]

B. State Analysis in Attorney General Opinion

Nevada possesses one of the most specific statutory provisions regarding identification.[351] To address circumstances when it is difficult to determine if a service animal is indeed a service animal, Nevada tracks the federal law and specifically sets forth the kinds of questions a place of public accommodation can ask:

1. If the animal is a service animal or service animal in training, and
2. What tasks the animal is trained to perform or is being trained to perform.[352]

While Montana grants the same rights guaranteed to people with disabilities to the trainers of service animals, its statutory language evidences a concern about identifying what are and are not legitimate service animals in training. As such, its provision on identification provides:

> (4) For the purposes of this section, a service animal in training that is a dog shall wear a leash, collar, cape, harness, or backpack that identifies in writing that the dog is a service animal in training. Other service animals in training must also be identifiable by written identification as a service animal in training. The written identification for service animals in training must be visible and legible from a distance of at least 20 feet.[353]

However, guidance on identification for service animals is set forth in a 2001 opinion of the Maryland Attorney General. The opinion concluded that "A service animal need not be specially licensed or identified to accompany its owner in a place of public accommodation."[354]

X. *State Protections Briefly Explored*

All 50 states have laws requiring access to public accommodations and housing for persons with disabilities using service animals.[355] State-based protections for service animals can be classified into the following areas:

1. Accommodation laws,
2. Laws that sanction theft, intentional interference, and/or harm by uncontrolled pets and/or their owners to a service animal,
3. Licensing laws for service animals, and
4. Wrongful impersonation.[356]

As the ADA does not apply to service animals in training, protections for the trainers of service animals in training are provided in many states. For instance, Montana states that the same rights of access guaranteed to service animals are also equally afforded to the trainers of service animals in training.[357]

Of all the issues that could be discussed in the context of state-based protections, the recent effort to enact what are known as anti-attack laws in the several states is one of the most important. These laws seek to sanction and ultimately prevent the circumstance of an uncontrolled pet and/or its handler intentionally or recklessly attacking and harming a service animal.[358]

Nevada has one of the more strict laws that sanction willfully or maliciously injuring, obstructing, intimidating, or willfully or maliciously killing a service animal or service animal in training.[359] Nevada provides for gross misdemeanors and felonies and for restitution for the replacement cost of the service animal or service animal in training.[360]

In addition, statutes that provide sanctions for the injury or death of a service animal are critical, even from the rare unfortunate, nefarious acts of an individual with a disability. As reported in *Philadelphia Weekly*, a blind person, who had also allegedly beaten his wife and children, killed his dog guide by multiple blunt force traumas.[361] The police arrived at the man's garage finding him endeavoring to revive his dead dog guide.[362] After providing a litany of false responses, the man admitted to killing the dog guide.[363] The police charged the man and a judge delivered a sentence under the animal cruelty statute of a criminal misdemeanor.[364] The offender received

1. A sentence of four to 23 months in the county correctional facility,
2. Court-prescribed counseling, and
3. A fine of $1,000 that is to serve as restitution to his guide dog school, Leader Dogs for the Blind, and for the cost of the dog guide, which ranges more than $40,000.[365]

If the judge had known about Pennsylvania's existing anti-attack statute, an additional set of sanctions would have been available with which to sentence this terrible crime. Further, this conviction calls attention to a critical issue that has ultimate consequences for the handlers of service animals insomuch as rights of access and accommodations depend on positive public perception. That is, service animals constitute sentient beings requiring commitment, dedication, and proper care and management. Thus, it is worthwhile for the established service animal advocacy community and attorneys who represent them not only to ensure the passage of anti-attack statutes in the remainder of the several states, but also to contemplate whether every possibly qualified individual with a disability should be allowed to acquire a service animal. Protections for service animals against their handlers may also be necessary.

Some states sanction the theft of a service animal. For instance, Washington recognizes the act of unlawfully purloining a service animal as a theft in the first degree.[366] All of the foregoing provide important protections, and in some instances, exceed those of the ADA.

XI. Scooby, Snoopy, and Lassie All Say Bye—Concluding the Chapter

From the grocer to that important flight out to the coast, the handlers of service animals possess the right to have a reasonable accommodation be rendered to permit the access of their service animal. Protections furnished under federal law do not generally cover service animals in training. Many states, however, furnish similar protections to the trainers of service animals in training. No right is absolute. Thus, rights and responsibilities straddle both communities—those who are not partnered and those who are partnered with service animals. Therefore, defenses and remedies exist to sanction or vindicate an alleged access denial.

Notes

1. Erica Friedman & S. A. Thomas, *Pet Ownership, Social Support and One Year Survival among Post-Myocardial Infarction Patients in the Cardiac Arrhythmia Suppression Trial*, 76 AM. J. CARDIOLOGY 1213–17 (1995); Erica Friedman et al., *Social Interaction and Blood Pressure: Influence of Companion Animals*, 171(8) J. NERVOUS & MENTAL DISORDERS 461–65 (1983).
2. Karen Allen, Ph.D., *Pets and Human Cardiovascular Health*, http://nursing.msu.edu/habi/Allen_talk.doc (last visited Feb. 19, 2008).
3. Sandra B. Barker, *Therapeutic Aspects of the Human-Companion Animal Interaction*, 16(2) PSYCHIATRIC TIMES (Feb. 1999), http://www.psychiatrictimes.com/p990243.html (last visited Feb. 3, 2008); *What a Difference a Dog Makes*, 49 (19) DIABETES FORECAST (1996); Susan L. Duncan, R.N., *Loneliness: A Health Hazard of Modern Times*, 13(1) INTERACTIONS 5–9 (1995).
4. Nancy Templeman, *Pet Ownership Can Bring Better Health According to the Latest Research*, VA. COOP. EXTENSION (Apr. 28, 1997), http://www.ext.vt.edu/news/releases/042897/pet&health.html (last visited Feb. 19, 2008).
5. Elizabeth Paek, *Fido Seeks Full Membership in the Family: Dismantling the Property Classification of Companion Animals by Statute*, 25 U. HAW. L. REV. 481, 493 (Summer 2003).
6. Kelly Henderson, M.Ed., *No Dogs Allowed?: Federal Policies on Access for Service Animals*, 7(2) ANIMAL WELFARE INFO. CTR. NEWSL. (Summer 1996) (citing L. M. Hines & L. K. Bustad, *Historical Perspectives on Human-Animal Interactions*, 66(1) NAT'L. FORUM 4–6 (1986)).
7. *See* FLORENCE NIGHTINGALE, NOTES ON NURSING: WHAT IT IS AND WHAT IT IS NOT (Dover 1969).

8. Int'l Guide Dog Fed'n, History, http://www.ifgdsb.org.uk/page.asp?code=00010018 (last visited Feb. 29, 2008).
9. *See* Henderson, *supra* note 6.
10. Elizabeth Blandon, *Reasonable Accommodation or Nuisance? Service Animals for the Disabled*, 75 FLA. B. J. 12 (2001).
11. 28 C.F.R. § 36.104 (2008), *see* 42 U.S.C. §§ 12181–112189 (2008).
12. Fair Housing Act, 42 U.S.C. § 3604(f) (2008); 14 C.F.R. pt. 382 (2008).
13. Access Now, Inc. v. Town of Jasper, 268 F. Supp. 2d 973 (E.D. Tenn. 2003) (citing Green v. Hous. Auth. of Clackamas County, 994 F. Supp. 1253 (D. Or. 1998)).
14. U.S. DEP'T OF JUSTICE, AMERICANS WITH DISABILITIES ACT TITLE III TECHNICAL ASSISTANCE MANUAL III-4.2300 (1994 & Supp.).
15. *See Access Now*, 268 F. Supp. 2d at 980 (citing Green v. Hous. Auth. of Clackamas County, 994 F. Supp. 1253, 1256 (D. Or. 1998)).
16. Office of the Sec'y, Dep't of Trans., Notice of Policy Guidance concerning Service Animals in Air Transportation, 68 Fed. Reg. 24,874 (May 9, 2003).
17. Rebecca F. Wisch, *Detailed Discussion of Assistance Animal Laws*, ANIMAL L. & HISTORICAL CTR. (Mich. State Univ. Coll. of L., 2007), http://www.animallaw.info/articles/ddusassistanceanimal.htm (last visited Feb. 29, 2008).
18. *Id.*
19. *Id.* (citing FLA. STAT. § 413.08(d) (2007)).
20. *Id.*
21. Guide Dog Users, Inc. & Int'l Assoc. of Assistance Dog Partners, Position Paper: Proposed Changes to the Definition of "Service Animal" (Jan. 11, 2002), http://www.gdui.org/cadopaper.html (last visited June 24, 2008) (To address the proliferation of animals employed into assistance work, the established service animal civil rights movement (e.g., dog guides) formed an umbrella advocacy organization to provide one voice on what kinds of animals should meet the definition of service animals. This umbrella organization is called the Coalition of Assistance Dog Organizations, and has advocated that the definition at Part 36 be changed such that a more narrow scope of specifically defined animals be considered service animals.).
22. ARIZ. REV. STAT. ANN. § 11-1024(E) (West 2008) (Arizona extends the same protections afforded to handlers of service animals to the trainers of service animals); CAL. PENAL CODE § 365.5(g)(2), (i) (West 2008) (California extends the protections afforded to handlers of dog guides, assistance dogs, and service animals to trainers); CONN. GEN. STAT. ANN. § 46a-64(a)(5) (West 2008) (Connecticut extends the same protections to handlers of service animals to trainers of service animals, particularly dog guides, as long as such trainer possesses membership in a dog guide school training organization and has and can produce evidence of their authority of the

service animal training institution to train the animal.); FLA. STAT. ANN. 413.08 (West 2008) (Florida extends the protections granted to people with disabilities to the trainers of service animals. Additionally, FLA. STAT. 1496, Fla. 110th Reg. Sess. [Mar. 13, 2008], is before the Florida legislature to include the protections afforded to the disabled to volunteer puppy raisers, volunteers who help to acclimate dog guides to social settings, as long as the animals they are training to be future service animals are on leash, the volunteers possess credentials of their training institution, and the animal is wearing indicia of the school through which it is being trained.); 720 ILL. COMP. STAT. ANN. 630/1 (West 2008) (Illinois extends the protections afforded to service animals, specifically dog guides and seizure alert dogs to the trainers of such animals); IND. CODE ANN. § 016-23-2(d) (West 2008) (stating "[a] guide dog trainer, while engaged in the training process of a guide dog, is entitled to access to any public accommodation."

23. 63 P.3d 816 (Wash. App. 2003), *review denied by* Burnham v. Dep't of Soc. & Health Servs., 79 P.3d 445 (Wash. App. 2003).
24. *Burnham*, 63. P.3d at 817.
25. *Id*. at 818.
26. *Id*. at 820–21.
27. No. C05-1836RSL, 2006 WL 1515603 (W.D. Wash. May 25, 2006), *aff'd*, 268 Fed. Appx. 643 (9th Cir. Wash. Mar. 5, 2008), *cert. denied*, 129 S. Ct. 104 (2008).
28. *Id*.
29. Nondiscrimination on the Basis of Disability by Public Accommodations and in Commercial Facilities, 73 Fed. Reg. 34,508, 34,520 (June 17, 2008).
30. *Id*.
31. Nondiscrimination on the Basis of Disability in Air Travel, 73 Fed. Reg. 27,614, 635 (May 13, 2008).
32. *Id*. at 27,635–37.
33. *Id*.
34. *Id*.
35. *Id*.
36. Gary Norman, *Service Animals and the Law*, 40 MD. B.J. 56 (Sept.–Oct. 2007).
37. Letter from the Int'l Assoc. of Assistance Dog Partners to Senator George Winner, Chair of the Investigations & Gov't Operations Comm. (2007), http://www.iaadp.org/nystatelegislature2007.html.
38. *Id*.
39. *Id*.
40. *Id*.
41. Office of the Sec'y, Dep't of Trans., Notice of Policy Guidance concerning Service Animals in Air Transportation, 68 Fed. Reg. 24,874 (May 9, 2003).

42. Int'l Assoc. of Assistance Dog Partners, Service Animal Regulations under ADA , http://www.iaadp.org/CADO2005.html (last visited June 24, 2008).
43. Int'l Assoc. of Assistance Dog Partners, IAADP Minimum Training Standards for Public Access, http://www.iaadp.org/iaadp-minimum-training-standards-for-public-access.html (last visited June 24, 2008).
44. 370 F.3d 837 (9th Cir. May 27, 2004).
45. 42 U.S.C. §§ 3601–3631 (1988).
46. W. Va. Code §§ 5-11A-1 to 11A-20 (2008).
47. 210 W. Va. 380, 557 S.E.2d 787, 2001 W. Va. LEXIS 178, at *2–3 (Dec. 10, 2001).
48. *Id.*
49. N.C. Gen. Stat. §§ 168-4.2, 168-4.3 (2008).
50. Norman, *supra* note 36 (citing Md. Service Animal Reform Act of 2006, Md. H. 1457, 420th Gen. Assembly, 2006 Reg. Sess. (2006)).
51. *Id.*
52. Susan L. Duncan, RN, *APIC State-of-the-Art Report: The Implications of Service Animals in Health Care Settings*, 28(2) Am. J. Infection Control 170 (2000), http://www.deltasociety.org/download/APIC.pdf (last visited Jan. 15, 2008).
53. *Id.* at 173.
54. *Id.*
55. Nondiscrimination on the Basis of Disability by Public Accommodations and in Commercial Facilities, 73 Fed. Reg. 34,508, 34,520 (June 17, 2008).
56. 29 U.S.C. § 794 (2008).
57. *Id.*
58. 29 C.F.R. § 1614.203(b) (2008).
59. Office of Pers. Mgmt., Federal Employment of People with Disabilities, http://www.opm.gov/DISABILITY/appempl.asp (last visited Apr. 13, 2008).
60. Fed. Mgmt. Regulation, Real Property Policies Update, 70 Fed. Reg. 67,786 (Nov. 8, 2005).
61. *Id.* at 67,786, 807.
62. *See* Dogs and Other Animals, 46 C.F.R. § 386.19 (2007); Dogs and Other Animals, 4 C.F.R. § 25.12 (2007) (stating that no dogs or animals may be brought into the office of the Government Accountability Office, except dog guides); Pets, 36 C.F.R. § 2.15 (2007) (prohibiting the possession of pets in public buildings or in modes of conveyance, except for guide dogs for the vision impaired and signal dogs for the hearing impaired).
63. 532 N.E.2d 712 (Mass. App. Ct. 1989).
64. *Id.*
65. *Id.*
66. *Id.*

67. 652 F.2d 454 (5th Cir. 1981) (establishing that a service animal is necessary to use and enjoy the benefits and advantages of housing).
68. 29 U.S.C. § 791(g) (2008).
69. 56 Fed. Reg. 35,544, 35,545 (1991).
70. Air Carrier Access Act of 1986, Pub. L. No. 99-435, 100 Stat. 1080, 49 U.S.C. § 1374 (1986).
71. DOT v. PVA, 477 U.S. 597 (1986).
72. 28 C.F.R. § 36.104 (2008).
73. Air Carrier Access Act of 1986, *supra* note 70.
74. 14 C.F.R. §§ 382.7, 382.23, 382.39, 382.43, 382.45, 382.47 (2008).
75. *Id.* §§ 382.7(a), 382.57 (2008).
76. *Id.* § 382.7.
77. 14 C.F.R. pt. 382 (1996); 61 Fed. Reg. 56,409, 56,420 (Nov. 1, 1996).
78. Office of the Sec'y, Dep't of Trans., Notice of Policy Guidance concerning Service Animals in Air Transportation, 68 Fed. Reg. 24,874, 24,877 (May 9, 2003), 14 C.F.R. §§ 382.7, 382.55(a) (2008).
79. *Id.* § 382.49(a)–(c).
80. *Id.* § 382.49(a).
81. Transp. Sec. Admin., Service Animals, http://www.tsa.gov/travelers/airtravel/specialneeds/editorial_1056.shtm (last visited Feb. 11, 2008).
82. 14 C.F.R. § 382.38(a)(3) (2008).
83. *Id.* § 382.38(b)(1), (2).
84. 14 C.F.R. § 382.33 (2008).
85. 14 C.F.R. § 382.33(a)(7) (2008).
86. *Id.*
87. Office of the Sec'y, Dep't of Trans., Notice of Policy Guidance concerning Service Animals in Air Transportation, 68 Fed. Reg. 24,874, 24,876 (May 9, 2003).
88. Accessible Journeys, Inc., Details of the Air Carriers Access Act (2004), http://www.disabilitytravel.com/airlines/air_carrier_act_details.htm (last visited Feb. 7, 2008); 14 C.F.R. §§ 382.23, 382.39, 382.40 (2008).
89. *Id.*
90. 14 C.F.R. §§ 382.45(a)(1)–(4), (b)–(c); 382.55 (2008).
91. Access Now, Inc., v. Sw. Airlines Co., 227 F. Supp. 2d 946 (S.D. Fla. 2002), *appeal dismissed*, 385 F.3d 1324 (11th Cir. 2004).
92. *Id.*
93. *Id.*
94. Nat'l. Fed'n of the Blind v. Target Corp., 452 F. Supp. 2d 946 (N.D. Cal. 2006).
95. 73 Fed. Reg. 27,614 (May 13, 2008).
96. Pub. L. No. 106-181, 49 U.S.C. § 41705(a) (2000) (In a May 18, 2000, notice, the DOT stated, "The Department rule implementing . . . Part 382 . . . does not by its terms address foreign . . . carriers but the Office of Aviation Enforcement and Proceedings . . . gives notice that it intends to use

the provisions of that regulation as guidance in investigating any complaints it receives of non-compliance by foreign carriers. . . .").

97. Peter Donahue, *Guide Dog Users Await In-Cabin Air Routes to U.K.*, Harness Up (Fall 2004), http://www.nfb-nagdu.org/harnessup/fall04-a.html (last visited Feb. 28, 2008).
98. *Id.*
99. *Id.*
100. Office of the Sec'y, Dep't of Trans., *Carriage of Service Animals in Air Transportation into the United Kingdom and Foreign Health Documentation Requirements for Service Animals in Air Transportation Notice*, Fed. Reg. Notice (July 17, 2007), http://airconsumer.ost.dot.gov/rules/UKServiceAnimalJulyNotice.doc (last visited Apr. 5, 2008).
101. *Id.*
102. Joan Froling, *New Guidance on Air Travel with an Assistance Dog to the U.K.*, IAADP, http://www.iaadp.org/new-guidance-air-travel-uk.html (last visited Apr. 15, 2008).
103. *Id.*
104. *Id.*
105. *Id.*
106. 14 C.F.R. § 382.7 (2008).
107. *Id.* § 382.31(d), (e).
108. *Id.*
109. Office of the Sec'y, Dep't of Trans., Notice of Policy Guidance concerning Service Animals in Air Transportation, 68 Fed. Reg. 24,874, 24,877 (May 9, 2003).
110. *Id.*
111. *Id.*
112. *Id.*
113. *Id.*
114. 14 C.F.R. § 382.43 (2008).
115. *Id.* § 382.43(b).
116. *Id.*
117. 310 F.3d 1347, 1359–60 (11th Cir. 2002).
118. 14 C.F.R. pt. 382 (2008).
119. Lex Frieden, Chairperson, Nat'l Council on Disability, Position Paper on Amending the Air Carrier Access Act to Allow for Private Right of Action (July 8, 2004), http://www.ncd.gov/newsroom/publications/2004/aircarrier.htm (last visited Apr. 16, 2008).
120. 49 U.S.C. § 1305 (1995).
121. Christoph v. Nw. Airlines, Inc., 1995 U.S. Dist. LEXIS 10266 (E.D. La. July 17, 1995).
122. *Id.*
123. *Id.*
124. *Id.* at *4 (citing Hodges v. Delta Airlines, 44 F.3d 334 (5th Cir. 1995)).

125. *Id.* at *5–6.
126. *Id.* at *7.
127. *Id.* at *8.
128. *Id.* at *9 (citing Williamson v. St. Francis Med. Ctr., 559 So.2d 929 (La. App. 2 Cir. 1990)).
129. Office of the Sec'y, Office of the Gen. Counsel, Dep't of Trans., Implementing the Air Carrier Access Act: A Status Report From the Department of Transportation (Jan. 2004), http://airconsumer.ost.dot.gov/legislation/acaa/200401-implementing.doc (last visited Feb. 13, 2008).
130. Nondiscrimination on the Basis of Disability in Air Travel, Request for Comments, 70 Fed. Reg. 20,640 (Apr. 20, 2005).
131. Nondiscrimination on the Basis of Disability, 70 Fed. Reg. 41,482 (July 19, 2005); *see also* Key Bridge Foundation Center for Mediation, http://www.keybridge.org.
132. Bronk v. Ineichen, 54 F.3d 425, 428 (7th Cir. 1995).
133. *See* Adaptive Env'ts, Inc., Historical Context of the Americans with Disabilities Act, http://www.dbtac.vcu.edu/whatsada-history.aspx (last visited Apr. 16, 2008).
134. *Id.*
135. PARALYZED VETERANS ASS'N., UNDERSTANDING THE FAIR HOUSING AMENDMENTS ACT, http://www.unitedspinal.org/pdf/fair_housing_amendment.pdf (last visited Apr. 16, 2008).
136. H.R. REP. NO. 100-711, at 18 (1988), *reprinted in* 1988 U.S.C.C.A.N. 2173, 2179.
137. PARALYZED VETERANS ASS'N, UNDERSTANDING THE FAIR HOUSING AMENDMENTS ACT, *supra* note 135.
138. Bryant Woods Inn, Inc., v. Howard Planning Bd., 124 F.3d 597, 603 (4th Cir. 1997); Shapiro v. Cadman Towers, Inc., 51 F.3d 328, 334 (2d Cir. 1995); United States v. Cal. Mobile Home Park Mgmt. Co., 29 F.3d 1413, 1416–17 (9th Cir. 1994); Smith & Lee Assoc., Inc. v. City of Taylor, 13 F.3d 920, 930 (6th Cir. 1993).
139. 42 U.S.C. § 3604 (2008).
140. Joint Statement of the Dep't of Hous. & Urban Dev. and the Civ. Rights Div. of the Dep't of Justice (May 17, 2004), http://www.fairhousing.com/include/media/pdf/finaljointstatement051704.pdf (last visited Feb. 24, 2008).
141. *Id.*
142. *Id.*
143. 24 C.F.R. § 100.204, ex. 1 (2008).
144. Prindable v. Ass'n. of Apt. Owners of 2987 Kalakaua, 304 F. Supp. 2d 1245 (D. Haw. 2003).
145. NAT'L HOUS. LAW PROJECT, FAIR HOUSING INFORMATION SHEET # 1: EARLY TERMINATION OF A LEASE, http://www.nhlp.org/hjn2006/hjn2006/Workshop%206b%20Materials.pdf (last visited Apr. 16, 2008).

146. Diane E. Citrino, Edward G. Kramer, & David G. Oakley, *Cause of Action for Handicap Discrimination in Housing in Violation of the Federal Housing Act [42 U.S.C.A. §§ 3601 et seq.] and Related Federal Statutes*, *in* 1 CAUSES OF ACTION 2D §§ 8–14 (2007).
147. Assenberg v. Anacortes Hous. Auth., No. C05-1836RSL, 2006 WL 1515603 (W.D. Wash. May 25, 2006), *aff'd*, 268 Fed. Appx. 643 (9th Cir. Wash. Mar. 5, 2008), *cert. denied*, 129 S.Ct. 104 (2008) (court found in favor of the defendant, a public housing authority, where an individual who claimed he was disabled failed to request a reasonable accommodation for the modification of a no-pets policy to allow the access of his snake, and where such individual was illegally using narcotics).
148. Janush v. Charities Hous. Dev. Corp., 169 F. Supp. 2d 1133, 1136 (N.D. Cal. 2000).
149. No. C 02-02543, 2, 10 (N.D. Cal. Aug. 7, 2002).
150. 453 F.3d 175 (9th Cir. 2006).
151. No. 105CV1326CMHBRP, 2005 WL 5269272 (E.D. Va., Dec. 13, 2005), *aff'd*, 201 Fed. Appx. 953 (4th Cir. 2006).
152. No. 98-CV-1404-K (AJB), 1999 WL 33798637 (S.D. Cal. Mar. 4, 1999).
153. *Debate over Companion Animals Continues to Rage*, 11 ADA COMPLIANCE GUIDE NEWSL. (Nov. 2007).
154. Beth A. Danon, Esq., *Emotional Support Animal or Service Animal for ADA and Vermont's Public Accommodations Law Purposes: Does It Make a Difference?*, 32 VT. B. J. 21 (Summer 2007).
155. *Id.*
156. BAZELON CTR. FOR MENTAL HEALTH LAW, WHAT "FAIR HOUSING" MEANS FOR PEOPLE WITH DISABILITIES, http://www.bazelon.org/issues/housing/publications/wfhm.pdf (last visited Apr. 20, 2008).
157. 889 F. Supp. 792 (N.D. Pa. 1995).
158. 13 F.3d 920 (6th Cir. 1993), *remand to* 872 F. Supp. 423 (E.D. Mich. 1995), *aff'd in part, rev'd in part*, 102 F.3d 781 (6th Cir. 1996).
159. 654 N.E.2d (Mass. App. Ct. 1995).
160. Rebecca J. Huss, *No Pets Allowed: Housing Issues and Companion Animals*, 11 ANIMAL L. REV. 69 (2005); Diane E. Citrino, Edward G. Kramer, & David G. Oakley, *Cause of Action for Handicap Discrimination in Housing in Violation of the Federal Housing Act [42 U.S.C.A. §§ 3601 et seq.] and Related Federal Statutes*, *in* 1 CAUSES OF ACTION 2D §§ 33–34 (2007).
161. *Id.*
162. *Id.*
163. Adaptive Env'ts, Inc., Historical Context of the Americans with Disabilities Act, http://www.dbtac.vcu.edu/whatsada-history.aspx (last visited Apr. 20, 2008).
164. *Id.*
165. *Id.*
166. S. REP. NO. 101-116, at 20 (1989); H.R. REP. NO. 101-485, pt. 2, at 50 (1990).

167. PGA Tour, Inc. v. Martin, 532 U.S. 661 (2001) (citing Bd. of Trs. of Univ. of Ala. v. Garrett, 531 U.S. 356, 375 (2001) (Kennedy, J., concurring)).
168. 135 CONG. REC. S10,800 (1989).
169. Disability Rights Sec., Civ. Rights Div., Dep't of Justice, The ADA and City Governments: Common Problems (May 9, 2000), http://www.usdoj.gov/crt/ada/comprob.htm (last visited Mar. 26, 2008).
170. 28 C.F.R. § 35.130(b)(7) (2008).
171. 268 F. Supp. 2d 973 (E.D. Tenn. 2003).
172. *Id.* at *12.
173. *Id.*
174. *Id.* at *6.
175. *Id.* at HN 11.
176. Am. Council of the Blind, 1979 Resolutions, http://www.acb.org/resolutions/res79.html (last visited Feb. 22, 2008).
177. 81 F.3d 1480 (9th Cir. 1996).
178. *Id.* at 1482.
179. *Id.*
180. *Id.* at 1483.
181. *Id.*
182. *Id.* at 1486.
183. 49 C.F.R. § 37.167(d) (2008).
184. Indep. Living Research Utilization, Questions & Answers about Service Animals and the Law: Which Animals Do the ADA & State Law Recognize; Outstanding or Unanswered Questions, ILRU Program (Apr. 14, 2004), http://www.ilru.org/html/training/webcasts/handouts/2004/04-29-Conway/questions.html (last visited Apr. 2, 2008).
185. WASH. REV. CODE ANN. § 409.91.170(6) (2008).
186. MD. CODE ANN. HUMAN SERVS. § 7-705(e)(1)(ii)–(2)(ii) (2008).
187. TENN. ST. § 39-14-208 (2008).
188. Amy A. Breyer, Update on Illinois Guide Dog Trial, Animal Law Blog, http://animallawonline.blogspot.com (Mar. 5, 2008) (last visited Apr. 2, 2008).
189. Wendy Lin, *A Prosecutor's Best Friend: Retired Guide Dog Tips Scales of Blind Justice Toward Victims*, NEWSDAY (Nov. 12, 1989), *available at* http://vachss.com/dogs/av_dogs/sheba.html (last visited Apr. 2, 2008).
190. Kathy Podgers, Police Policy Fails to Protect Guide Dog from Bike on Crowded Sidewalk, From the Port, http://fromtheport.blogspot.com/2005/09/police-policy-fails-to-protect-guide.html (last visited May 2008).
191. Denise M. Decker, Ph.D., GDUI Fact Sheet (Dec. 2007), http://www.gdui.org/tip-sheet-for-law-enforcement.doc (last visited Apr. 2, 2008).
192. *Id.*
193. *Id.*
194. 42 U.S.C. § 12182(a) (2008); 28 C.F.R. § 36.302 (2008).
195. 42 U.S.C. § 12182(b)(2)(A)(ii).

196. H.R. Rep. No. 101-485, at 106 (1990), *reprinted in* 1990 U.S.C.C.A.N. 303, 389.
197. *Id.*
198. 42 U.S.C. § 12186(b).
199. 28 C.F.R. § 36.302(c)(1).
200. *Id.* at App. B.
201. Bragdon v. Abbott, 524 U.S. 624 (1998).
202. *See* Key Bridge Found., http://www.keybridge.org/2008_training.html (last visited Apr. 22, 2008).
203. 28 C.F.R. pt. 36, App. B at 587 (finding "places of public accommodation operated in mobile facilities, such as cruise ships . . . [to be] covered under this part, and . . . included in the definition of 'facility.'"); Title III Technical Assistance Manual III-1.2000(D) (1994 & Supp.).
204. 42 U.S.C. § 12181(7) (2008).
205. 56 Fed. Reg. 45,584, 600 (1991).
206. *Id.*
207. *See* Stevens v. Premier Cruise Lines, 215 F.3d 1237, 1241 (11th Cir. 2000); Deck v. Am. Haw. Cruises, Inc., 51 F. Supp. 2d 1057, 1061 (D. Haw. 1999).
208. *Stevens*, 215 F.3d at 1241.
209. Walter Johnson, *Supreme Court Holds Title III Applies to Foreign-Flagged Cruise Ships*, Emp. L. Alert (June 12, 2005), http://www.nixonpeabody.com/linked_media/publications/ELA_06132005.pdf (last visited Apr. 2, 2008).
210. Letter from Dep't of Justice to Hon. George J. Mitchell (Oct. 15, 1992), http://justice.gov/crt/foia/tal197.txt (last visited Apr. 1, 2008).
211. ADA Technical Assistance Manual III-4-2000 (2000), http://www.dbtac.vcu.edu/adaportal/Private_Business/Browse_TAM_III/Chapter_4/III-4-2000.html (last visited Apr. 1, 2008).
212. U.S.A. v. Top China Buffet, Inc., No. IP 02-1038 C Y/F (S.D. Ind. Oct. 24, 2003), http://www.ada.gov/topchina.htm.
213. *Id.*
214. See Claude Solnik, *Long Island Hospitality Industry: Room for Rover*, Long Island Bus. News, May 23, 2008; Michael Martinez, *Upscale Lodgings Join Trend of Catering to Pets*, Buffalo News, Feb. 17, 2008, at G2.
215. Scott Marshall, Assoc. Exec. Dir. for Gov't. Relations, Am. Found. for the Blind, Self-Evaluation Checklist for Hotels and Motels to Ensure Access to Services and Facilities by Customers Who Are Blind, Deaf-Blind, or Visually Impaired, http://www.empowermentzone.com/adahotel.txt (last visited Mar. 31, 2008).
216. *Id.*
217. Martin H. Orlick, *Adopting Pet and Service Animal Policies to Avoid Lawsuits from Disabled Hotel Guests*, Global Hospitality Advisor (Sept. 2004), http://www.hotel-online.com/News/PR2004_3rd/Sept04_PetPolicy.html (last visited Apr. 4, 2008).

218. Marshall, *supra* note 215. However, this would seem to contradict the general requirement that places of public accommodation grant the broadest feasible access.
219. 28 C.F.R. § 36.302 (2008).
220. *Id.*
221. Orlick, *supra* note 217.
222. Settlement Agreement with Charles W. & Vivian Gabrielson, Owners of the Terrace Motel, DJ No. 202-13-181 (2005), http://www.ada.gov/terracemotel.htm (last visited Mar. 31, 2008); Settlement Agreement with the Travel Inn, DJ No. 202-11e-82 (2006), http://www.ada.gov/travelinn.htm (last visited Mar. 31, 2008); Voluntary Compliance Agreement with Calvary Baptist Church and Hotel Salisbury, Inc. (May 16, 2007), http://www.ada.gov/salisbury.htm (last visited Mar. 31, 2008).
223. 111 F. Supp. 2d 119 (N.D. N.Y. 2000).
224. *Id.*
225. *Id.* at 123 (citing Calvarese v. City of Oswego, No. 96-CV-602, 1998 WL 315091 (N.D. N.Y. June 10, 1998)).
226. *Id.*
227. *Id.*
228. *Id.* at 25 (citing Levy v. Mote, F. Supp. 2d 538 (D. Md. 2000).
229. *Id.*
230. *Id.*
231. *Id.* at 125–26.
232. Camarillo v. Carrols Corp., 518 F.3d 153 (2d Cir. 2008).
233. Letter from the Disability Rights Sec., Civ. Div., Dep't of Justice, to Hon. Senator John C. Danforth (May 10, 1993), http://www.usdoj.gov/crt/foia/tal302.txt (last visited Mar. 23, 2008).
234. *Id.*
235. *Id.*
236. No. 97 C 3538, 1999 WL 311717 (N.D. Ill. May 11, 1999).
237. *Id.* at *1.
238. *Id.* at *10 (citing Vande Zande v. State of Wisc. Dep't of Admin., 44 F.3d 538, 544–45 (7th Cir. 1995)).
239. *Id.* at *27.
240. *Id.*
241. No. 3:07-0595, WL 4570810 (M.D. Tenn. Dec. 26, 2007).
242. *Id.* at *3 (citing Docket Entry No. 9 at 3).
243. *Id.*
244. *Id.* at *4–5.
245. No. 94-1430 PFK, 1995 WL 519129 (D. Kan. Aug. 25, 1995).
246. *Id.* at *4–5.
247. 47 Fed. Appx. (6th Cir. 2002).
248. Office of Civ. Rights, Dep't of Health & Human Servs., Animals in Health-Care Facilities, Fact Sheet (Dec. 22, 2006).

249. *Id.*
250. *Id.*
251. *Id.*
252. *Id.*
253. *Id.*
254. *Id.*
255. Disability Rights Sec., Civ. Rights Div., Dep't of Justice, Commonly Asked Questions about Service Animals in Places of Business (1996 and 2002 Supp.), http://www.ada.gov/qasrvc.htm (last visited Apr. 1, 2008).
256. *Id.*
257. 370 F.3d 837 (9th Cir. 2004).
258. *Id.*
259. *Id.* at 837–38.
260. *Id.* at 841.
261. *Id.*
262. *Id.*
263. *Id.*
264. *Id.*
265. *Id.*
266. *Id.* at 841–42.
267. *Id.*
268. *Id.*
269. *Id.*
270. *Id.*
271. *Id.* at 842–43.
272. *Id.*
273. *Id.*
274. *Id.*
275. *Id.*
276. *Id.* at 844–45 (quoting Crowder v. Kitagawa, 81 F.3d 1480, 1486 (9th Cir. 1996)).
277. *Id.*
278. *Id.*
279. Commonly Asked Questions about Service Animals in Places of Business, *supra* note 255.
280. Woodside Village-Stratford Ass'n v. Hertzmark, 647 A.2d 759 (Conn. App. Ct. 1994).
281. Joan Froling, *The Dog Phobia Case*, 2(3) PARTNERS FORUM, *available at* http://www.iaadp.org/work_access3.html (last visited Mar. 29, 2008).
282. *Id.*
283. Letter from James L. Johnson, Assistant City Solicitor, to Kent Ryan, Dir. of Public Safety (May 4, 1999), http://www.dimenet.com/disnews/archive.php?mode=P&id=1087.
284. *Id.*

285. *Id.*
286. *Id.*
287. *Id.*
288. Rosemary G. Mathias, Assisting Passengers Traveling with Service Animals, Final Rpt. (Jan. 1997), http://ntl.bts.gov/DOCS/96-0138-7.html.
289. 496 F.3d 1061, 1064 (9th Cir. 2007).
290. *Id.* at 1063.
291. *Id.*
292. *Id.* at 1064.
293. *Id.* at HN4.
294. *Id.*
295. *Id.*
296. *Id.*
297. *Id.* at 1065.
298. *Id.*
299. *Id.*
300. *Id.* (citing Bragdon v. Abbott, 524 U.S. 624, 649–50 (1998)).
301. Robert Leblond, *The True Meaning of Regulations: A Vocabulary Lesson from the School of Hard Knocks*, BRAILLE MONITOR (Jul. 1993), http://www.etext.org/Politics/Braille.Monitor/monitor-9307 (last visited Mar. 2, 2008).
302. Guide Dog Users, Inc., Iowa Case, http://www.gdui.org/iowa.html (last visited Mar. 2, 2008).
303. EDWIN C. VAUGHAN & JAMES H. OMVIG, EDUCATION AND REHABILITATION FOR EMPOWERMENT (Info. Age Publ'g Inc. 2005).
304. *Id.*
305. Letter from Guide Dog Users, Inc., to Disability Rights Sec., Civil Rights Div., Dep't of Justice (Nov. 19, 2002), http://www.gdui.org/complaint.html.
306. *Id.*
307. *Id.*
308. Press Release, Guide Dog Users, Inc., Training Schools File Formal Complaint Against Iowa Dep't of the Blind (Nov. 26, 2002), http://www.gdui.org/iowa.html#press (last visited Mar. 2, 2008).
309. *Id.*
310. Letter from Guide Dog Users, Inc., to Disability Rights Sec., Civ. Rights Div., Dep't of Justice (Nov. 19, 2002) (emphasis added), http://www.gdui.org/complaint.html.
311. GDUI Advocacy & Legis. Comms., Position Paper: Use of Guide Dogs in Public Rehabilitation Programs (2003), http://www.gdui.org/iowapos.html (last visited Mar. 2, 2008).
312. *Id.*
313. Nat'l Fed. of the Blind, Informed Choice, Resolution 2003-101 (July 4, 2003), http://nfb.org/legacy/bm/bm03/bm0309/bm030910.htm (last visited Mar. 2, 2008).

314. *Id.*
315. Letter from Disability Rights Sec., Civ. Div., Dep't of Justice, to Hon. Senator Dianne Feinstein (Apr. 23, 1996), http://www.usdoj.gov/crt/foia/tal685.txt.
316. Dohmen v. Iowa Dep't. for the Blind, 755 N.W. 2d 144 (Iowa App. 2008).
317. *Id.* at *1.
318. *Id.* at *3–4.
319. 116 F.3d 1052 (5th Cir. 1997).
320. *Id.* at 1056.
321. *Id.*
322. *Id.*
323. 116 F.3d 1052.
324. *Id.* at 1059–60.
325. *Id.*
326. *Id.*
327. *Id.* at 1052.
328. *Id.*
329. No. 04-02-00664-CV, 2003 WL 21918587 (Tex. App. Aug. 13, 2003).
330. *Id.*
331. 42 U.S.C. § 12187 (2008).
332. 42 U.S.C. §§ 2000a-3(a) (2008); 42 U.S.C. § 12187.
333. 536 U.S. 181 (2002).
334. Letter from John L. Wodatch, Chief, Disability Rights Sec., Civ. Div., Dep't of Justice, to Suzanne Lacampagne, Esq. (Feb. 25, 1993), http://www.usdoj.gov/crt/foia/cltr052.txt.
335. William Wan, *A Lesson from Katrina: Pets Matter*, Wash. Post, Jan. 2, 2006, at B1; Anita Kelso Edson, *Hurricane Katrina—Guide Dog Rescued*, ASPCA.org, *reprinted in* 12(1) Partners Forum (Int'l Ass'n of Assistance Dog Partners, Oct. 2005), http://www.iaadp.org/newsletters/iaadp-partnersforum-v12-n1-web.doc (last visited Mar. 16, 2008).
336. Pub. L. No. 109-308, 120 Stat. 1725 (Oct. 6, 2006).
337. *Id.*
338. Hillary A. Leonard & Debra L. Scammon, *No Pet Left Behind: Accommodating Pets in Emergency Planning*, 26(1) J. Pub. Policy & Mkt. 49 (Spring 2007), http://www.business.utah.edu/humis/docs/person_1229_1194036940.pdf (last visited Mar. 16, 2008).
339. Gary Norman, *Giving Pets and Service Animals Shelter from the Storm*, Md. B. Bulletin (Sept. 2007).
340. Commonly Asked Questions about Service Animals in Places of Business, *supra* note 255.
341. *Id.*
342. *Id.*
343. 312 F. Supp. 2d 1349 (W.D. Wash. 2004).
344. No. 2007 LEXIS 73536 (W.D. Wash. Oct. 2, 2007).

345. *Id.* at *13.
346. *Id.* at *11–12 (citing *Grill*, 312 F. Supp. 2d 1349 (W.D. Wash. 2004)).
347. *Id.* at *13–14.
348. *Id.*
349. 887 A.2d 458 (Del. 2005).
350. Wisch, *supra* note 17.
351. NEV. REV. STAT. § 651.075(1)(f) (2008).
352. *Id.* § 651.075(2)(a).
353. MONT. CODE ANN. § 49-4-214(4) (2008).
354. J. Joseph Curran, Jr., 86 Op. Att'y. Gen. 120 (June 13, 2001).
355. Joan Black, CCLV CHRONICLE , May 4, 2002, www.ccbnet.org/chron02.htm (last visited Jan. 7, 2009).
356. Wisch, *supra* note 17.
357. MONT. CODE ANN. § 49-4-214(1), (3) (2008).
358. Guide Dog Users, Inc., Legislative Handbook (2001), http://www.gdui.org/handbook.html (last visited Apr. 23, 2008).
359. NEV. REV. STAT. § 426.790(1) (a)–(c) (2008).
360. *Id.* § 426.790(2)(a)–(c).
361. Brian Hickey, *Justice Is Blind*, PHILA. WEEKLY (May 14, 2003), http://www.philadelphiaweekly.com/articles/5583/archives (last visited Mar. 2, 2008).
362. *Id.*
363. *Id.*
364. *Id.*
365. *Id.*
366. WASH. REV. CODE ANN. § 9.91.170(6) (2008).

CHAPTER 7

Animal Insurance Litigation

JULIE I. FERSHTMAN

I. Introduction

This chapter focuses on disputes between policyholders and insurance companies when the subject of the insurance is an animal. Animal insurance policies, typically insuring horses and livestock, have existed for several decades. In recent years, specialized policies have emerged that offer coverage for veterinary expenses of house pets, show dogs, and dogs used for breeding.[1] Some insurers offer policies of mortality insurance on police dogs. As of March 2008, no known cases exist involving disputes related to dog and pet insurance policies. Because considerable case law exists involving livestock insurance coverage disputes, however, counsel handling disputes under pet health care policies or other forms of animal-related insurance are encouraged to review existing cases for possible similarities.

This chapter discusses insurance litigation involving insurance policies that are issued on the lives of animals. These types of policies include animal mortality insurance (sometimes combined with endorsements such as loss of use, major medical expense, surgical expense, herd policy, limited mortality, specified perils, and agreed value), stallion and mare infertility insurance, and prospective foal insurance. This chapter does not address liability insurance policies such as commercial general liability insurance policies, homeowner's insurance disputes, professional liability policies, and association policies.

When disputes arise involving policies insuring animals, several courts have recognized their unique nature and have shown a willingness to depart from legal standards that would apply to other types of insurance policies.

The most common insurance coverage disputes in animal insurance policies, particularly equine and livestock mortality policies, are addressed in the next section. Counsel are also strongly cautioned to read the applicable insurance policy very carefully. Policy terms can differ greatly among insurers, even for the same type of coverage.[2]

II. Coverage Issues Involving Animal Insurance Policies

A. General Condition of Animal at Policy's Inception

Livestock mortality insurance policies usually include the general condition that "at the commencement of this insurance each animal hereby insured is in sound health and free from any illness, disease, lameness, injury or physical disability whatsoever."[3] This general condition has generated litigation.

In one case involving the "sound health" condition, the issue was whether the determination that the insured horse was in "sound health" upon application is based on an objective standard or a subjective standard from the standpoint of the insured party. In *Lasma Corp. v. Monarch Insurance Co. of Ohio*,[4] an Arabian mare had existing, but nondisclosed, health conditions at the policy's inception. Later, upon the presentation of a claim, the insurer denied liability based on the "sound health exclusion." At trial, the court instructed the jury that the policy's "sound health" condition would be satisfied if the *insured parties* subjectively and "reasonably believed" that the mare was in sound health when the policy was applied for (as opposed to applying an objective standard of whether the mare actually was in "sound health"). The court's ruling suggested that the insured's subjective belief of "sound health" controlled and the insurer was found liable.

In *Lucini-Parish Insurance, Inc. v. Buck*,[5] the insured horse died soon after the application was submitted but before the policy was issued. At issue was whether the horse would have satisfied the policy's general condition that "at the commencement of this insurance each animal hereby insured is in sound health and free from any illness, disease, lameness, injury or physical disability whatsoever." The insured horse owner prevailed.

Whether an insurer could effectively waive this policy condition of "sound health at inception" in an equine mortality policy was an issue raised in another case in which the horse was not sound at commencement.[6] The court held that the condition was not waived under the circumstances presented in that case.

B. Condition of Timely Notice to Insurer

Livestock mortality policies typically require that the insured party timely notify the company (or its designated contact person) if the insured horse becomes injured or ill. Although notice requirements vary among insurers, one livestock mortality policy sets forth the notice requirement this way:

> Insured's responsibility
>
> 1. *Immediately notify US or YOUR agent* by telephone or telegraph;
> 2. Employ a licensed veterinarian, at YOUR expense, to treat the animal;
> 3. Secure proper care and, if required, allow the animal to be removed for treatment at YOUR expense.
>
> * * *
>
> *We reserve the right to deny a claim if YOU do not comply with these conditions.*

Provisions of this type in livestock mortality policies have generated considerable litigation when the insured party submits notice to the insurer that is deemed to be too late. The litigation typically centers on the question of whether (1) the insured party violated the policy's "notice" requirement; (2) whether the insurer is required to prove that it was actually prejudiced by the late notice;[7] and (3) whether the issue results in a loss of coverage. With great frequency, courts have sided with insurers on issues of late notice, although the outcome of these cases can vary with the circumstances of the late notice and the language of the policy.[8]

Some courts have held that the specialized and unique nature of equine insurance makes coverage forfeited when the insured violates the notice requirement—regardless of the issue of prejudice. In *Arigato Stables v. American Live Stock Insurance Co.*,[9] the plaintiff, who owned and insured a Thoroughbred, gave the insurer late notice under a mortality policy. The issue was whether to extend the state's proof of prejudice requirement, which existed with other (nonanimal) types of insurance, to the equine mortality policy. Taking into account the specialized nature of equine insurance, the court stated:

> We are satisfied that this policy . . . is specifically tailored to the peculiar circumstances of the Thoroughbred breeding business and that the court should not rewrite the terms of the contract for the parties. We are not dealing with a contract that will affect the rights of third policies who have liability claims. . . . *It is clear that the conditions set forth in the policy serve a necessary purpose with respect to the risk assumed by the insurer.*[10]

C. Euthanasia and Humane Destruction Disputes

Differentiating animal mortality insurance policies from life insurance policies applicable to humans is the potential that the insured party could cause the insured animal to be destroyed and then collect proceeds of the policy. Legal disputes have arisen over the years as to *when* and *whether* to euthanize an insured animal while maintaining the right to bring a claim for mortality insurance benefits.

In any insurance dispute involving humane destruction issues of equines, counsel should refer to the humane destruction guidelines established by the American Association of Equine Practitioners (AAEP). The AAEP's "Guidelines for Recommending Euthanasia" state:

> The AAEP recommends that the following criteria be considered in evaluating the necessity for intentional euthanasia of a horse. It should be pointed out that each case should be addressed on

its individual merits and that the following are guidelines only. Not all criteria must be met in each case.

> 1. Is the condition chronic, incurable, and the cause of inhumane pain and suffering?
> 2. Does the immediate condition present a hopeless prognosis for life?
> 3. Is the horse a hazard to itself or its handlers?
> 4. Will the horse require continuous medication for the relief of pain for the remainder of its life?[11]

The publication also states:

> **EUTHANASIA JUSTIFICATION**—Justification for euthanasia of a horse for humane reasons should be based on medical, not economic considerations; and further, the same criteria should be applied to all horses regardless of age, sex or potential value.[12]

Disputes have arisen when animal owners either euthanize the insured animal without insurer approval or procure a veterinary opinion supporting euthanasia that the insurer disputes. In *Bunch v. Underwriters at Lloyd's London*,[13] for example, the court ruled that the plaintiff violated an "intentional slaughter" exclusion by euthanizing his horse and as a result was not entitled to recover benefits under an equine mortality policy. The plaintiff in *Bunch* had veterinary support for the euthanasia decision. After his veterinarian euthanized the horse, the plaintiff submitted the claim. The problem was, he never sought *advance approval* from the insurer. The court held that the plaintiff had violated the policy's "intentional slaughter" exclusion because he failed to show—even with the veterinary support—that the animal was "suffering" from a disease that was "incurable and so excessive that immediate destruction is necessary for humane reasons."[14]

Similarly, in *Abraham v. Insurance Co. of North America*,[15] the plaintiff/insured had an equine mortality policy on his horse but failed to fulfill a condition within the policy that required the plaintiff to produce a certificate by a qualified veterinarian that "destruction was necessary in order to immediately relieve incurable suffering." By all indications, the plaintiff intentionally destroyed his own horse. The insurer denied the claim. Siding with the insurer, the court held that the plaintiff's failure to fulfill the policy's veterinary certification requirement prevented him from recovering policy benefits.[16]

Finally, an old but interesting case stands for the proposition that an insured *cannot* "hasten the death of the horse" and then seek payment under an equine mortality policy. In *Tripp v. Northwestern Live-Stock Insurance Co.*,[17] the plaintiff owned a horse that was insured under an equine mortality insurance policy, but he euthanized it two hours before the policy was scheduled to lapse. The defendant insurer denied his claim, invoking provisions in the mortality policy that excluded intentional slaughter. The plaintiff later sued. Ruling in favor of the insurer, the court stated:

> The entire contract of insurance shows that *it was not intended that defendant should be liable for any willful act which tended to hasten the death of the horse insured, but that it should be relieved from liability by such act.*
>
> * * *
>
> The burden was on the plaintiff to show that the disease from which the horse suffered was the cause of, and not merely a pretext for, his death during the life of the policy and that he has wholly failed to show. We conclude that the district court rightly directed a verdict for the defendant and its judgment is affirmed.[18]

D. Postmortem Requirements

Equine mortality insurance policies typically include a condition requiring postmortem veterinary examinations upon the death of a horse. While it is possible that some insurers may be inclined to waive this requirement, depending on the nature of a particular claim, counsel should be cautious that a violation could forfeit coverage.

The following is a sample of a policy's postmortem requirement:

> It is a condition precedent to any liability of the Company hereunder that:
>
> * * *
>
> (c) in the event of the death of an insured animal the Insured shall immediately at his own expense arrange for a post-mortem and autopsy examination to be made by a qualified Veterinary Surgeon,

* * *

> *And any failure by the Insured to do so shall render the Insured's claim null and void and release the Company from all liability in connection therewith*, whether the Insured has personal knowledge of such events or such knowledge is confined to the representatives of the Insured or other persons who have care, custody or control of the animal(s).

In *Jahn v. Great American Assurance Company*,[19] the insurer denied a claim on a $125,000 equine mortality policy, in part because the insured horse owner failed to comply with the policy's postmortem requirement upon the horse's demise. Rather than procure the postmortem, the insured had the horse buried. The court found that the plaintiff's failure to procure a postmortem report, combined with several other violations of the policy, justified the insurer in denying the equine mortality claim.

III. Damages

In addition to seeking the amount of coverage at issue, or a legal defense, and prejudgment interest as allowed by applicable law, policyholders might have claims to seek additional damages against insurers, which are explored next.

A. Attorneys' Fees

Counsel representing insureds with claims against insurers have every incentive to seek an award of attorneys' fees. Typically, attorneys' fees are not recoverable in litigation against an insurer involving a policy of insurance,[20] unless a state statute allows their recovery[21] or the court finds that the nonprevailing insurer acted in bad faith.[22] States differ considerably in their willingness to award attorneys' fees, and counsel should research current case law in the applicable jurisdiction.

Insurers can sometimes defeat requests for these and other damages if they can successfully prove that the claim at issue was "fairly debatable."[23] Some states even require the insured party to show the absence of a reasonable basis for denying benefits.[24]

B. Penalty Interest

For claims that are not properly or timely paid, statutes in several states allow insured parties to recover penalties against insurers, typically in the form of an interest rate. Under some state laws, these statutory penalties can be as high as 25 percent.[25]

C. Unfair Trade Practices Act or Insurance Practices Act

State trade practices acts or unfair insurance practices acts address wrongful acts by insurers. Not all of these statutes, however, allow policyholders a private right of action for their violation. With this in mind, counsel should review these statutes' case law carefully.

D. Punitive Damages

Several jurisdictions allow a court to consider awarding punitive damages against an insurance company that is found to have wrongly failed or refused to pay policy benefits or otherwise breached its general covenant of good faith and fair dealing.[26] One equine insurance case involved a considerable punitive damage award against an insurer.[27]

IV. Litigation Considerations for Counsel

A. Timing for Instituting Litigation

If the dispute involves coverage for an animal, such as equine mortality insurance, the question for counsel for both the policyholder and the insurance company is, when is the right time to initiate suit? Sometimes disputes are prone to early resolution or action for a few reasons:

First, in policies of equine insurance, for example, provisions may exist to resolve valuation disputes in actual cash value policies by securing an "umpire" appraiser.

Second, insurance policies often have a statute of limitations that can severely limit the time in which disputes can be brought. That period, according to several policies, is one year. Many states make these limitations periods enforceable.[28]

Third, these disputes are often subject to early settlement, especially if an insurer can be convinced that the state has an applicable bad-faith statute and that the circumstances at issue in the claim, based on the facts, could warrant imposition of this statute.

B. State Insurance Bureau Complaints

State bureaus of insurance have departments specifically designed to investigate complaints against insurers, brokers, agents, and/or adjusters. Most state governmental Web sites offer online complaint forms.

Counsel should consider whether these processes are appropriate for a particular dispute instead of, or in addition to, litigation.

C. Burden of Proof

Counsel representing policyholders should be mindful that they bear the burden of proof in the litigation. They will need to prove that

- The insured is entitled to coverage under the policy terms.
- The loss is encompassed within the policy period.
- Conditions precedent under the policy that were required to be performed by the policyholder were satisfied.

Depending on the case, counsel for the insurer will need to prove that:

- The claimant has failed to comply with material terms or conditions of the policy, such as the condition of notice or the general condition that the animal be in sound health at the policy's inception.
- The policy was procured through misrepresentation.
- The policy has lapsed or the claimant is otherwise untimely in his or her request for coverage.
- An applicable exclusion in the policy bars coverage.

D. Venue

Counsel will need to select a forum for the litigation that is most advantageous to their clients. A review of the applicable case law in the state could yield useful insights into whether the state courts or the federal courts are more favorable.

Typically, insurers prefer federal courts for coverage disputes. Federal courts are widely believed to be more capable of handling and managing complex litigation, and some insurers find these courts to be more conservative than state courts. On the other hand, plaintiff's counsel might prefer federal courts because they frequently schedule short deadlines and impose facilitation and case review conferences, which can promote prompt resolution of the case. Counsel seeking federal jurisdiction are encouraged to review the Federal Declaratory Judgments Act.[29]

E. Arbitration

Many insurance policies include language obligating the parties to arbitrate their disputes. From the standpoint of the insured, arbitration might be undesirable because it removes the matter from a jury and can involve submission of the dispute to a specialized forum that might be perceived as being pro-insurer. Counsel seeking to avoid arbitration should examine the policy as well as applicable case law to determine whether the dispute at issue is truly arbitrable. If a matter has been arbitrated, counsel seeking to challenge the award should examine the Federal Arbitration Act[30] and applicable local statutory and case law to determine whether the award can be vacated.

F. Discovery

In litigation involving alleged denials of policy benefits, counsel representing policyholders often seek a copy of the claim file and underwriting file applicable to the client. This information is particularly useful in litigating bad-faith claims against the insurer, but it offers little help when the inquiry is merely whether coverage exists under the policy.

Upon receiving discovery requests for the claims and/or underwriting files, counsel for insurers will need to consider whether all documents are discoverable or, instead, subject to qualified privileges or exclusions such as Federal Rule of Civil Procedure 26(B)(3) involving documents prepared in anticipation of litigation or preparation for trial. Courts have disagreed considerably on these issues, and the discoverability should be carefully evaluated based on the applicable law.

Discovery disputes have also arisen regarding attorney-client privilege. Whether or not the insurer can justifiably raise this argument depends on applicable state law. In some states, where the insurer takes the position that it relied on counsel in formulating its coverage position, attorney-client communications would be discoverable.

Disputes have also arisen when the policyholder's counsel seeks discovery of other claim files. Courts nationwide have differed on whether other claim files can, and should, be discoverable.

G. Motions

Coverage litigation typically involves the filing of motions for summary judgment or partial summary judgment. Counsel for insurers can bring motions for partial summary judgment in an attempt to narrow the claims. For example, if the complaint contains claims against the insurer for bad faith denial of benefits, but the jurisdiction does not recognize such a cause of action, counsel for the insurer can consider an early motion to strike or for summary judgment in an attempt to dismiss such claims.

Doing so can potentially limit the scope of discovery and focus any settlement discussions on recognized causes of action.

For matters that are headed for trial, motions in limine can be very effective to narrow and eliminate evidence that could otherwise be introduced at trial. Counsel for the policyholder might consider motions seeking to eliminate prior claim history of the particular animal or claimant. Counsel for the insurer might consider pretrial motions seeking to eliminate any references at trial to the insurer's financial condition, the insurer's profitability, loss ratios, other litigation or complaints brought against the particular insurer, and how the insurer has handled other claims in the past.

Notes

1. These policies are known to be held by less than 4 percent of pet owners. *See Pet Healthcare Insurance*, ABA-TIPS ANIMAL LAW COMM. NEWSL. (Spring 2008), p. 13.
2. For more information, see Annotation, *Livestock or Animal Insurance: Risks and Losses*, 47 A.L.R.4TH 772 (1986); Annotation, *Personal Injuries Inflicted by Animals as Within Homeowner's or Personal Liability Policy*, 96 A.L.R.3d 891 (1979).
3. However, at the insurer's discretion, if the application materials or information in the company's possession reveal a health condition, the insurer could either refuse to issue the policy or could accept the risk but impose an exclusion that makes the animal insurable subject to the condition. For example, equine insurance policies have been issued with "lameness exclusions" or "colic exclusions" where the horse has a documented history of such conditions. As issued, the policy would include an appropriate exclusion endorsement.
4. 764 P.2d 1118 (Ariz. 1988).
5. 836 P.2d 627 (Neb. 1992).
6. Tate v. Charles Aguillard Ins. & Real Estate, Inc., 508 So. 2d 1371 (La. 1987).
7. In many states when a violation of the notice requirement is at issue, the insurer will be required to prove that it was prejudiced by the delayed notice. Wolfson v. Ins. Co. of Fla., 451 So. 2d 1005 (Fla. App. 1984) (finding genuine issues of material fact on the issue of whether the insurer was prejudiced by the insured's late notice of a horse's demise); Hood v. Fireman's Fund Ins. Co., 412 F. Supp. 846 (S.D. Miss. 1976) (discussing late notice given after cattle destroyed in a flood). *But cf.* Ins. Co. of N. Am. v. Hopper, 69 S.W.2d 728 (Ky. 1934) (holding where horse was properly treated by a veterinarian, the failure to immediately notify the insurer did not adversely affect coverage).

8. Cases enforcing the policy's notice condition and denying coverage due to untimely notice include Jahn v. Great Am. Assurance Co., 2004 WL 765240 (N.D. Ill. Apr. 6, 2004); Hiscox Dedicated Corp. Member, Ltd. v. Wilson, 246 F. Supp. 2d 684, 693–94 (E.D. Ky. 2003); Arigato Stables v. Am. Live Stock Ins. Co., 493 A.2d 584 (N.J. App. 1985); Patti v. Monarch Ins. Co. of Ohio, 401 N.Y.S.2d 682 (N.Y. Super. 1977); Circle 4 Stables, Inc. v. Nat'l Sur. Corp., 451 S.W.2d 564. 567 (Tex. App. 1970); Underwriters at Lloyd's, London v. Harkins, 427 S.W.2d 659, 664 (Tex. Civ. App. 1968); Menard v. Citizens Ins. Co. of N.J., 134 So. 2d 85, 87 (La. App. 1966); Hartford Live Stock Ins. Co. v. Henning, 266 S.W. 912 (1924); Hough v. Kaskaskia Live Stock Ins. Co., 230 Ill. App. 341 (1923).
9. Arigato Stables v. Am. Live Stock Ins. Co., 493 A.2d 584 (N.J. App. 1985).
10. *Id.* at 585 (emphasis added).
11. Am. Assoc. Equine Prac. *Guidelines for Recommending Euthanasia, in* The Veterinary Role in Equine Insurance (4th ed. March 2006).
12. *Id.*
13. Bunch v. Underwriters at Lloyd's London, 343 So. 2d 994 (La. 1977).
14. *Id.* at 995.
15. Abraham v. Ins. Co. of N. Am., 84 A.2d 670 (Vt. 1951).
16. *Id.* at 674.
17. Tripp v. Nw. Live-Stock Ins. Co., 59 N.W. 1 (1884).
18. *Id.* at 2 (emphasis added).
19. Jahn v. Great Am. Assurance Co., 2004 WL 765240 (N.D. Ill. Apr. 6, 2004).
20. *See* Advance Watch Co. v. Kemper Nat'l Ins. Co., 878 F. Supp. 1034, 1043 (E.D. Mich. 1995), *rev'd on other grounds*, 99 F.3d 795 (6th Cir. 1996) (finding no entitlement to attorneys' fees upon successful suit against insurer); Previews, Inc. v. Cal. Union Ins. Co., 640 F.2d 1026, 1029–30 (9th Cir. 1981) (California law).
21. Numerous states have enacted statutes that obligate insurers to pay the plaintiff's attorneys' fees when the insurer has been found to have wrongfully refused to pay. *See* Cal. Ins. Code § 1619 (2005) (finding failure to pay claim for 30 days, if failure deemed vexatious and without reasonable cause); Fla. Stat. Ann. § 627.428(1) (1982); Mo. Ann. Stat. § 375.296 (2002); Ga. Code Ann. § 13-6-11 (1984); Del. Code Ann. tit. 18, § 4102 (1968) (discussing property insurance policies).
22. *See* Alyeska Pipeline Serv. Co. v. Wilderness Soc'y, 421 U.S. 240, 258–59 (1975); Christian v. Am. Home Assurance Co., 577 P.2d 899, 906 (Okla. 1977).
23. *See* Bibeault v. Hanover Ins. Co., 417 A.2d 313 (R.I. 1980).
24. *See* Anderson v. Cont'l Ins. Co., 271 N.W.2d 361 (Wisc. 1978).
25. *See* La. Rev. Stat. § 22:658 (2008) (setting a 25 percent penalty in fire and theft policies, and 12 percent for certain other policies); Me. Rev. Stat. tit. 24-A, § 2436 (1973) (awarding interest at the rate of 1½ percent per

month); MICH. COMP LAWS § 500.2006(4) (2004) (allowing 12 percent interest).

26. *See, e.g.*, Chodos v. Ins. Co. of N. Am., 178 Cal. Rptr. 831, 839–41 (awarding punitive damages awarded under policy where insurer obligated to pay auto repair costs); Olson v. Rugloski, 277 N.W.2d 385 (Minn. 1979) (stating insurer could be subject to award of punitive damages if its refusal to pay a claim rendered the insurer guilty of "fraud, oppression, or malice"). *But cf.* Kewin v. Mass. Mut. Life Ins. Co., 409 Mich. 401 (Mich. 1980); Smith v. Harleysville Ins. Co., 418 A.2d 705 (Pa. Super. 1980) (finding no liability for punitive damages).
27. Am. Bankers Ins. Co. v. Caruth, 786 S.W.2d 427 (Tex. App. 1990) (discussing equine mortality policy).
28. In Tom Thomas Org., Inc. v. Reliance Ins. Co., 242 N.W.2d 396 (Mich. 1976), for example, the inland marine policy contained a 12-month limitation on lawsuits, but plaintiff's institution of litigation after that time resulted in dismissal.
29. 28 U.S.C. § 2201 (1948).
30. 9 U.S.C. § 10 (2002) (examining how a federal court can vacate an arbitration award).

CHAPTER 8

Legal Issues Involving Animal Associations and Individuals Helping Animals

ZANDRA ANDERSON

I. Introduction

Animal law in some aspects is new. There are old laws about animals being chattel or about dog bites, but there are few laws regarding liability issues for the individual animal rescuer and rescue organization. However, this is an area of the law that is growing and taking form as animal laws are enacted and case law defines our common law.

This area of the law in all likelihood will continue to grow, particularly as pets are treated more and more as family members. Almost half of American households are comprised of unmarried people and over one-quarter of households are comprised of people living alone, demographics which have steadily increased over the past 30 years.[1] Consequently, pets have in many cases become the focus of single people without children. The pet industry is a multibillion-dollar business and continues to grow with no signs of decline.[2]

This chapter discusses existing animal law and the potential for liability with regard to animal rescue and those who rescue animals. Since this area of the law is not well established in some aspects, there is not an abundance of case law or statutory law. Thus this chapter focuses on recurring issues with rescue that potentially create liability concerns.

II. Establishing an Animal, Rescue, or Humane Organization

There are issues to be considered when dealing with the rescue of animals in need. Often, individuals rescue animals and dutifully find them suitable homes. The true issues arise when a group of people decide to band together for the purpose of rescuing animals.

A. Benefits and Drawbacks of Establishing an Association or Organization

An attorney who is involved with or asked to represent such a group should be prepared to advise on the advantages and drawbacks of establishing a formal organization. The obvious benefit of forming an association of like people is that there is power in numbers. The work of rescue can be divided. The group will have greater access to potential fosters and homes for abandoned animals. It is easier to persuade the community to donate to a group rather than to an individual rescuer.

The benefits of establishing some sort of association of people to help animals include

- Division of work regarding the care of the animals;
- Greater ability to attract donations of both money and supplies;
- Larger network of people to find potential adopters and fosters;
- Enhanced capability to help a larger number of animals; and
- Backup system for members to take some time off.

The challenges of establishing some sort of association of people to help animals include

- Internal politics;
- Agreeing on group goals;
- Establishing group-approved procedures for caring for and placing the animals;
- Peacefully establishing who will be the leaders; and
- Resolving disputes in the group.

B. Benefits and Drawbacks of Establishing a 501(c)(3) Charitable Corporation

Typically, rescue groups are composed of lay people who like to help animals. Some forge ahead without any considerations of legalities, but eventually as they grow or are faced with a situation of potential liability, they may seek legal advice as to how they can best protect themselves as volunteers and continue their mission of saving animals.

A 501 corporation is a charitable corporation that is exempt from tax as per the Internal Revenue Code, 26 U.S.C. 501(c)(3), which covers the following types of organizations:

> Corporations, and any community chest, fund, or foundation, organized and operated exclusively for religious, charitable, scientific, testing for public safety, literacy, or educational purposes, or to foster national or international amateur sports competition (but only if no part of its activities involve the provision of athletic facilities or equipment), or *for the prevention of cruelty to children or animals,* no part of the net earnings of which inures to the benefit of any private shareholder or individual, so substantial part of the activities of which is carrying on propaganda, or otherwise attempting, to influence legislation (except as otherwise provided in subsection (h)), and which does not participate in, or intervene in (including the publishing or distributing or statements), any political campaign on behalf of (or in opposition to) any candidate for public office.[3]

As readily ascertainable from the code, animal rescues are covered. The question then becomes whether or not it is a good idea to incorporate. There are some very good reasons to incorporate, but similarly there are reasons not to do it. The benefits of establishing a charitable corporation include the following:

- Limitation on liability;
- People who donate may take their donations as a tax benefit;
- Donations are more easily encouraged if there is a tax benefit;

- Credibility and perception of the group are enhanced by the establishment as a corporation;
- Corporate donors are much easier to attract; and
- Public relations are aided by the appearance of an established charity.

There are also drawbacks to establishing a charitable corporation:

- Tax filings are necessary;
- An accountant or someone knowledgeable about accounting must be utilized to make sure that the charitable status is not violated and that IRS filings are prepared correctly;
- Liability is limited but not extinguished;
- Officers and directors must be established;
- Corporate books and a bank account must be maintained; and
- Generally, a charity cannot contribute funds for political issues.

III. Protections of 501(c)(3) Status

The protections afforded 501(c)(3) charitable corporations concern liability and recoverable damages. However, these protections are not absolute, and they vary by state. The question is whether the party sued will have some immunity from liability based on either being a charity or being a volunteer for a charity. If so, then the charity or the volunteer may have defenses to allegations in a lawsuit or may enjoy a cap on the amount of damages that can be awarded against them.

It is important to investigate what your state statutes provide regarding charitable immunity. Be knowledgeable about what your state law provides, but keep in mind that the courts will go out of their way to protect people, particularly children, who have been injured or killed by animals.

In Texas, liability for charitable organizations is addressed in the Remedies Code,[4] which is analyzed in the following sections. As an example of how liability is commonly analyzed, the following key issues of concern provide a framework for researching the law regardless of the state involved.

A. Immunity from Liability for Volunteers

In determining the liability of a charitable organization, check your state's statutes to ascertain the situations in which such an organization is exempt from liability. Typically, volunteers have some degree of protection.

Regarding the liability of volunteers, the Texas Civil Practice and Remedies Code provides as follows:

> VOLUNTEER LIABILITY. (a) Except as provided by Subsection (d) and Section 84.007, a volunteer of a charitable organization is immune from civil liability for any act or omission resulting in death, damage, or injury if the volunteer was acting in the course and scope of the volunteer's duties or functions, including as an officer, director, or trustee within the organization.[5]

This provision grants volunteers immunity from "civil liability" from their acts or omissions. Although not expressly stated in the provision above, volunteers are not liable for their negligent acts or omissions.

B. Limitations on Liability for the Charitable Organization

Typically, the organization itself will enjoy immunity from liability to one degree or another. Your state's statutes will provide to what degree the charitable organization will or will not be liable.

The following is an example of the limitation on liability that states extend to their charitable corporations. Regarding the liability of the charitable organization, the Texas Civil Practice and Remedies Code provides as follows:

> ORGANIZATION LIABILITY. Except as provided in Section 84.007 of this Act, in any civil action brought against a nonhospital charitable organization for damages based on an act or omission by the organization or its employees or volunteers, the liability of the organization is limited to money damages in a maximum amount of $500,000 for each person and $1,000,000 for each single occurrence of bodily injury or death and $100,000 for each single occurrence for injury to or destruction of property.[6]

This provision allows the charitable organization (nonhospital kind) to be sued for negligence but limits the amount of liability. That means that dog-rescue groups established under these tax-exempt provisions of a 501(c)(3) corporation may indeed be sued and found liable for damages for its acts and omissions. Importantly, the organization may be sued for the acts and omissions of both its employees and volunteers. This means the organization itself can be sued for negligence.

However, this provision limits the amount of liability that can be recovered against a charitable organization. In Texas, as stated in the provision above, the cap on the amount of damages is $1,000,000 per single occurrence of injury or death, with a limit of $500,000 that can be received by an individual litigant. As illustration, four successful plaintiffs in the same suit might recover $500,000, $200,000, $175,000, and $125,000, for a total of $1,000,000. The total equals the limit of the exposure regardless of the number of plaintiffs and the extent of their injuries.[7] Similarly, a Texas charitable organization may be liable for property damage, but only up to $100,000 for each single occurrence regardless of the number of litigants and the extent of the property damage.[8]

C. Limitations on Employee Liability

Often the employees of charitable organizations do not have personal liability for the negligent acts, but the organization does. This is another area of concern for the practitioner, so it is important to research how your state determines employee liability.

Regarding the liability of employees of a charitable organization in Texas, the Civil Practices and Remedies Code provides as follows:

> EMPLOYEE LIABILITY. Except as provided in Section 84.007 of this Act, in any civil action brought against an employee of a nonhospital charitable organization for damages based on an act or omission by the person in the course and scope of the person's employment, the liability of the employee is limited to money damages in a maximum amount of $500,000 for each person and $1,000,000 for each single occurrence of bodily injury or death and $100,000 for each single occurrence for injury to or destruction of property.[9]

The code is clear that an employee may be sued, but the limits on employee liability are the same as those for the charitable organization. As indicated in the previous section, the Texas charitable organization is liable for the negligent acts of its employees and volunteers.[10] Therefore, this limitation is a protection to both the employee and the charitable organization.

D. Exceptions to Immunity

Be on the lookout for any exceptions to immunity that your state may have. The exceptions can be key to determining whether or not it is in the best interests of the organization you represent to incorporate.

1. *Volunteers Negligently Operating a Motor Vehicle*

In Texas, volunteers are liable for their own negligence when they are driving a car to the extent that they would be personally liable were they not driving in a volunteer capacity.

Regarding the liability of a volunteer for driving a motor vehicle, the Civil Practices and Remedies Code provides:

> VOLUNTEER LIABILITY. (d) A volunteer of a charitable organization is liable to a person for death, damage, or injury to the person or his property proximately caused by any act or omission arising from the operation or use of any motor-driven equipment, including an airplane, to the extent insurance coverage is required by Chapter 601, Transportation Code, and to the extent of any existing insurance coverage applicable to the act or omission. (e) The provisions of this section apply only to the liability of volunteers and do not apply to the liability of the organization for acts or omissions of volunteers.[11]

This means that volunteers performing a volunteer act, such as delivering a dog for a rescue, are not immune for their negligent acts while driving a car. They are liable for the minimum limits required in the Transportation Code, or if they have bought an insurance policy with greater limits, then they can be liable up to those limits. The minimum amounts of liability insurance required by Sec. 601 of the Texas Transportation Code are as follows:

> MINIMUM COVERAGE AMOUNTS. (a) The minimum amounts of motor vehicle liability insurance coverage required to establish financial responsibility under this chapter are:
>
> (1) $25,000 for bodily injury to or death of one person in one accident;
> (2) $50,000 for bodily injury to or death of two or more persons in one accident, subject to the amount provided by Subdivision (1) for bodily injury to or death of one of the persons; and
> (3) $25,000 for damage to or destruction of property of others in one accident.[12]

The volunteer is at least liable for the lowest limits required by the state. Since these limits are lower than the limitations on charitable organization liability, the charitable organization is not completely shielded from liability arising from the acts of one of its volunteers when driving. The volunteer can be liable to the extent of his or her insurance and the organization can be liable for anything over that amount.

2. *Willful or Gross Negligence*

As discussed previously, a charitable rescue may be liable for negligent acts, but there is a limit to the liability. However, if a charitable rescue is found by a jury to be willfully negligent, then there is no limit to its liability. If a jury finds for gross negligence, then the rescue could be liable for that even if they are insured for their negligent acts. Most insurance policies do not cover grossly negligent acts, so that puts even the insured rescue at risk.

In Texas, the applicable provision is as follows:

> APPLICABILITY. (a) This chapter does not apply to an act or omission that is intentional, willfully negligent, or done with conscious indifference or reckless disregard for the safety of others.[13]

This means that Texas law does not shield the charitable organization, including its employees or volunteers, from acts that go beyond negligence. If an act is intentional there is no protection from liability, nor is there any limit on liability. The same is true for acts that are found to be willfully negligent or done with a conscious indifference or reckless disregard for the safety of others. All of these acts described go beyond ordinary negligence, and the organization is not shielded from liability or the amount of damages that may be recovered.

E. Summary: Establishing an Animal Organization

- Clarify goals of the individuals and group—what purpose are they trying to serve by establishing a rescue organization?
- Identify the state laws regarding benefits enjoyed by charitable corporations.
- Clarify whether or not the group wants to keep up with the corporate filings and tax filings for a charitable corporation.
- Identify the state laws, if any, that cap the liability of a charitable organization and its volunteers.
- Determine if establishing a 501(c)(3) charitable organization is cost effective for the group.
- Consider the risk of liability versus the benefit to the community and animals being saved in light of the many ways to diminish exposure of the rescue.

IV. *Liability of the Animal, Rescue, or Humane Organization*

Most humane organizations or animal rescues focus primarily on placing dogs and cats. Certainly, other animals can be the subject of cruelty seizures and may find their way into these shelters, but most adoptions are of cats and dogs. It is uncommon for a rescue group to run into legal problems over cats, although one animal shelter was sued over a cat attacking a child while the animal was being shown for adoption.[14] There are some serious concerns for rescue groups regarding the placement of dogs. The following sections address liability issues concerning the placement of dogs.

A. Can a Rescue Group or Individual Rescuer Be Sued for Negligence in Placing a Dog?

Negligence means failure to use ordinary care; that is, failing to do that which a person of ordinary prudence would have done under the same or similar circumstances or doing that which a person of ordinary prudence would not have done under the same or similar circumstances. This is essentially the definition given to civil juries all over the country that are charged with determining whether someone is negligent.

A Texas case, *Koepke v. Martinez*, directly deals with the issue of negligence in disclosing information about the propensity of a dog.[15] Koepke sold a shar-pei to Teresa Canales. Canales was unable to pick the dog up from Koepke personally, so her employee, Maria Martinez, paid Koepke and took the dog to her house. The next day the dog attacked her husband, Andres Martinez, while he was trying to feed it.

Andres Martinez sued Koepke for his injuries, claiming negligence, misrepresentation, strict liability, and gross negligence, alleging that Koepke was negligent in not disclosing that the dog had aggressive tendencies. The jury indeed found that Koepke was negligent.

However, in another Texas negligence case involving a dog, "liability is premised usually on the negligence of the owner or keeper in the keeping or handling of the animal."[16] Since Koepke was not the owner of the dog at the time of the attack, the appellate court reversed the judgment against him. Judge Dorsey, joined by two other judges, dissented and chastised the appellate court, stating that it "seriously erred" in its holding.[17] In his dissent, the judge does not just refer to the dog simply as a shar-pei, but rather a "Chinese fighting dog."[18] He reasoned that "[s]urely there is a duty to disclose dangerous propensities of an animal to one who takes custody of him who has no reason to believe the dog will attack."[19]

Additionally, Judge Dorsey stated, "It is undisputed that the seller did not tell Martinez or Canales that the *breed* of dog was known as a *Chinese attack dog*, or its propensity for aggressive behavior."[20] Importantly,

Koepke testified that he never knew of the dog having aggressive tendencies. Regardless, this opinion argues that there should be negligence for not disclosing information about the *breed*.

Although this opinion was the dissent (in an en banc hearing), which is not controlling, it was joined by two other judges. This dissent may well foreshadow the law to come as legislatures and courts all over the country are voicing a concern over certain breeds that allegedly attack or bite.

An important point about this case is that Martinez did not lose on Koepke's failure to disclose the propensities of the breed of the dog, but rather because Koepke was not the owner at the time of the attack. Also, Martinez alleged misrepresentation concerning the aggressive tendencies of the dog, but the jury rendered its verdict on the negligence action. So, can a rescue or rescuer be sued for the negligent placement of a dog? Absolutely. *Koepke* hinged on what was disclosed about the propensities not only of the actual dog, but of the breed. This is of importance to placing any kind of dog, whether it is a Chihuahua or a German shepherd.

Because a rescue organization can be sued for its role in placing a dog, it is very important to fairly assess the dog and fully disclose any known propensities of the animal.[21] This applies to all animals, but the greatest potential for liability is in the placement of dogs, regardless of their size, because all dogs have the potential to bite.

B. Ethical and Legal Considerations of Full Disclosure in Adopting Animals

When representing a rescue organization, it is important to counsel the rescuer and rescue group to disclose everything they know about the specific dog they are trying to place and about its breed. A rescuer who fudges a little bit in an effort to get the dog a home can put the rescue at risk for misrepresentation and negligence. Adopters rely on the information given them in deciding whether to adopt a dog. If they are relying on false information, partial truths, or omissions, they might adopt a dog they would otherwise pass on. It is crucial that the information they get be correct and with full disclosure.

The rescue must correctly state the dog's breed. If a dog is a mix, for example between a German shepherd and a Labrador retriever, the dominant breed, if any, must be stated first: If the dog is more characteristic of a Lab, then it would be a Lab/shepherd mix. If the more dominant breed is German shepherd, then the dog would be identified as a shepherd/Lab mix. The rescue needs to make sure that the breed is stated correctly, and if there is doubt, to ask an expert in the particular breed.

Certainly, some dogs are so mixed they are just mixed. There is nothing wrong with stating a dog is a "mix" if the rescue cannot identify the breed. By contrast, there is something wrong with stating a dog is a mix if the rescue knows full well that the dog is, for example, a pit bull or a pit bull mix. This is clearly an important distinction.

All too often, pit bulls are not properly identified. They have been erroneously called mixes, boxers, mini-boxers, bulldogs, bull terriers, American bulldogs, ridgebacks, shar-peis, and even Boston terriers. They have also been called AmStaffs, Staffie Bulls, or American Staffordshire Terriers, though the dog on the street that ends up in rescue is likely to be an American Pit Bull Terrier and not its cousin, the American Staffordshire Terrier, an American Kennel Club–registered dog.

Whether the rescue is making a mistake or is trying to "help" the dog have a better chance of getting a home, misstating the breed is a disservice to the dog and a good way to get your rescue sued. An owner who does not know the full truth about the dog he or she is adopting will not know how to take care of the dog properly. That is setting the dog up for failure and will only serve to further tarnish the breed's reputation.

Proper placement includes a consideration of the dog or dogs already living in the potential adopter's home. For example, some dogs should not be placed with small dogs; taking a chance on such placement can set the organization up for a lawsuit, particularly if someone gets hurt breaking up an altercation. Some hounds, particularly retired racing greyhounds, may not be a good match to be adopted with cats or small dogs due to their prey drive.

Every breed has its own characteristics that should be disclosed to the potential adopter.[22] The following are some factors to consider in counseling the rescue organization on placement of dogs that will help diminish their liability:

- Whether the dog is good with other dogs, cats, kids, all adults;
- Whether the potential adopter has other pets, and if they will peacefully reside with the adopted dog;
- The age, size, and breed of all other dogs;
- Whether the dog is predisposed to dog aggression;
- Whether the dog will be kept inside.

Adopting dogs is not a perfect science, but the more the rescue knows and discloses about the breed and the particular dog, the less likely it is that things will go awry with the adoption and it will reduce the number of dogs that are returned. Last, but certainly not least, full disclosure reduces the risk of the rescue being sued for anything untoward that goes on with an adopted dog.

C. Proper Screening of the Adopter or New Owner

A corollary to fully disclosing information about the breed of the dog and the particular animal is that the new owner or adopter should be properly screened. The chance of a responsible placement that shields the rescue group from potential liability is enhanced by screening the potential adopter.

Placing an animal in an untenable situation leaves open the possibility for liability or unintended legal consequences to the rescue group. Failure to screen the new owner can potentially put the rescue group at risk.

1. Determine What Other Animals the New Owner Has

Before a placement is made, the organization should inquire about the ownership of other animals, their size and gender, and whether they are intact. This information will help determine if the new animal will have a good chance to peacefully coexist with the rest of the animals.

If a new owner has a small dog, there are certain large dogs that should not be placed with small dogs. If this is not heeded and the larger dog attacks the smaller dog, the owner could be injured in trying to break up the fray. Worse yet, a child could be injured in trying to separate fighting dogs. If the rescue organization failed to take this into consideration before the placement, that leaves them vulnerable for a potential lawsuit for negligent placement and possible misrepresentation.

If a child was the one trying to extricate the small dog from the larger dog, and if the child is injured in the process, the risk of liability is increased.

2. Determine the Age of Everyone in the Family

Similarly, the age of everyone living in the family should be considered in an effort to effect the best placement of a dog and lessen the risks of liability. There are certain dogs that are unsuitable for small children. Small dogs are particularly vulnerable to children, whose play can precipitate biting. Some dogs, because of what they have endured on the streets, need a quiet environment. In adopting to older people or people with children, it is wise to consider whether an overly exuberant dog could knock the adopter down. If a child is injured because of a poor placement by a rescue organization, it is reasonable to consider that the parents might be looking for any potentially liable parties to pay for the injuries to their child.

V. Liability of a Rescue Organization for Placement of Original Owner's Animal with a New Owner: Who Owns the Dog?

Most animals that come into shelters are not feral. In other words, they at some time had an owner. Generally, no questions arise when an animal is placed in a new home. However, it does happen, and then the organization is faced with a dilemma: What do you do when the original owners present themselves after the waiting period for reclaiming their pet and the animal has already been adopted?

A. The Stray or At-Large Animal

A stray animal is one that is loose on the streets and has either been abandoned by its owner or has gotten away somehow. These animals are also referred to as being at-large. Many cities and counties have at-large laws providing that pets cannot run loose, like dogs and sometimes cats, even ferrets. Some cities and counties do not have such laws, particularly in rural areas.

1. Impoundment

In the case of at-large animals, typically there are laws, usually ordinances or regulations, that provide how long a city or a county must hold the dog or cat if it is brought in to an established shelter or a municipal or county pound. This is called impoundment.

The period of impoundment is usually several days (three to six days is common) that the shelter must wait to give the owner time to reclaim the animal. These laws usually provide that the shelter can adopt them or euthanize them after the impoundment period. Some laws provide that animals can be sold. Therefore, the shelter or pound would have to maintain the animal for at least 72 hours (three days) before putting the dog up for adoption or euthanizing it. An owner who comes to claim the animal typically has to pay an impoundment fee and show proof of rabies vaccinations. Sometimes there are fines for the animal being at-large, and there are usually fines if the animal is not wearing its tag or the owner does not have a license or does not have proof of the rabies vaccination.

2. Owner Claims the Animal After It Has Been Adopted

Most cities and counties have an abundance of stray animals, many of which die because no one claims them. That is the norm. However, it frequently happens that the original owner comes to claim the animal after the waiting period elapsed and the animal was placed in a new home.

The shelter is faced with the problem of what should be done now that there are two alleged owners—the original owner and the new adopter.

In all jurisdictions, animals are considered property. An action for property can be brought based on the applicable statute of limitations. If a rescue organization or an individual rescuer has adopted out someone's pet, the organization or individual potentially faces a lawsuit over the animal. It is important to determine if your jurisdiction answers the ownership issue in its ordinances, regulations, or statutes.

If an original owner presents to claim an animal that has already been adopted, a conflict of law may arise. On the one hand there are typically local laws that address when a rescue organization may place an animal for adoption. On the other hand, since animals are property, the owner's rights to his or her animal have not been extinguished because the pet got loose. The question then becomes which of them has the superior right to the animal. This conflict is created if the local animal laws do not address the issue. This is a common ambiguity in animal law.

In one case,[23] a lost dog was placed by a local rescue organization, Underdog Rescue, after being received from the local animal control. Local law required that a notice be placed in three locations indicating that the pound had the dog, which was not done in this case. The court ordered the return of the dog to the owner because the city failed to post the notices and so animal control services "never acquired title to the dog and that the transfer to McKenzie/Underdog was illegal."[24]

The adopter argued for an award of money based on her paying the fee for the dog and having kept it for a period of time. The court ruled that she was entitled to be reimbursed, but that the cost should be divided among the adopter, the city, and the animal rescue.[25] The court reasoned that the adopter failed to return the dog to animal control, that animal control failed to post the notices, and that the rescue failed to verify whether animal control posted notices.[26] While this case is unreported (like so many animal cases), it is important because it shows how these conflicts play out in the courts.

By contrast, a minority view is stated in a Vermont case, *Morgan v. Kroupa*, involving a dog that broke loose from its collar and ran away.[27] The dog's owner alerted the local humane society and posted signs in an effort to locate his dog. A woman found the dog and rescued him from running loose next to a highway. She contacted the local humane society and was told to keep the dog until the owner could be found, but she never heard back from it. She, too, posted signs and even placed two announcements on a radio station regarding the dog. After a year, the original owner found out that the woman had the dog. He asked for the dog back and she refused, but the dog jumped in his truck and he drove away with it. The woman sued and the court refused to treat the dog per the state's lost property statute. The court awarded her the dog since she had cared for it for a year and made efforts to return the dog.[28] This states the minority position, which allowed for the original owner's rights in his property to be disregarded.

The *Morgan* case was expanded in a later Vermont case, *Lamare v. North Country Animal League*.[29] In this case, an owner lost an AKC-registered German shepherd. It ended up in the local animal control. The owner called family, friends, and neighbors in search of the dog to no avail. Animal control posted notices in three places that the dog was found, as is required by city ordinance. After the requisite waiting period, animal control gave the dog to the Animal League. The owner contacted the Animal League, and was told to fill out an application, but the Animal League denied the application in favor of other adopters. The owner sued. The court applied *Morgan* and determined that the owner's rights were extinguished when the owner did not retrieve the dog from animal control and said that the owner failed to "conscientiously" search for the dog.[30]

The minority view as stated in these Vermont cases has come under fire because the owner's rights were disregarded and because these holdings can prompt dogs to be stolen. In the *Lamare* case, only a month had passed when the owner tried to get the dog back from the rescue organization but was denied. Many people are not aware of how to find a lost dog, so this case is very tough on people who lose their pets.

By contrast, the problem created by an adoption that is challenged by the original owner was played out in *Woods v. KittyKind*.[31] Though unreported, the case is important because it illustrates just how these conflicts arise and how the law in this instance is determined in favor of the owner.

Woods returned from a weekend trip to find that her cat was missing on September 27, 2004. She posted signs and contacted local shelters. She found out in early October that her cat had been taken in by KittyKind, Inc., a rescue organization for cats. Her cat had been adopted and KittyKind refused to give her the name of the adopter so that she could get her cat back.

Woods alleged that KittyKind failed to take proper steps to locate the owner including waiting five days (the local waiting period for impounded animals). She sought to enjoin KittyKind from placing pets before waiting five days and checking local registries for owners looking for their lost pets. KittyKind countered by stating that after the wait period, local law allows for organizations like KittyKind to place animals for adoption.

The court dealt with the heart of the matter in all rescue cases and astutely pointed out that KittyKind did not present any statute or local law that "once a party has been properly given custody of a cat or dog which was believed to be abandoned, the original owner loses his or her custody rights to the animal."[32] The court furthered reasoned:

> There is a distinction between allowing a shelter to make a lost animal available for adoption and extinguishing the original owner's rights to the animal. One does not necessarily follow from the other.[33]

This case illustrates the conflict that exists within the law that can put rescue organizations and original owners at odds. In this case, the court ordered that KittyKind divulge the name, address, and phone number of the adopter so that the original owner could get her cat back.[34]

As in this case, most local laws do not extinguish the property rights of the original owners. They do, however, allow shelters to place animals for adoption after the local waiting period has expired. The practitioner representing rescue organizations should be prepared for this sort of issue. While most adoptions will not be challenged, eventually most rescue groups will be faced with an ownership issue.

Some important points of the *KittyKind* case are as follows:

- Most statutes and local laws provide for a waiting period before adopting an animal but do not extinguish the property rights of the owner.
- The owner of an animal can assert his or her rights after an animal has been placed if the owner's property rights have not been clearly extinguished by statute or local laws.
- The courts will consider the efforts of the owner to find the lost animal to give support to the return of the animal or to divulge the adopter's identity.
- The courts will consider the lack of efforts of the rescue organization to give support to the return of the animal or to divulge the adopter's identity.
- The rescue organization may be well served by making an effort to locate the owner of the animal before placing it for adoption unless it came from a local animal control that has already waited the requisite number of days.
- Most courts will not dispossess owners of their pets lightly.

When rescue organizations put out effort to care for and place an animal, they sometimes lose sight of the owner's rights and desire to have his or her pet returned. Counseling the rescue organization client from the beginning on handling these situations will soften the blow when an original owner wants their animal back. As their attorney, you will find it much easier to take a proactive approach than to try to reason with people in an emotionally charged situation when the issue actually occurs. Representation can become difficult particularly when the group considers the animal their "own" and because they may have vested time and money into the animal.

3. *How to Handle Ownership Questions and Avoid a Potential Lawsuit*

Where there are no state or local laws that address this ownership dilemma, some organizations will contact the new adopter, explain the situation, and ask if they will voluntarily release the animal back to the owner. Since Texas does not have any statutes addressing this matter, various established rescue organizations were surveyed informally in jurisdictions where the local laws do not address this ownership matter.[35]

None of the shelters surveyed would divulge the adopter's identity to the original owner without a court order, but would make contact with the adopter if the owner presented shortly after the lapse of the waiting period. The ones surveyed reported success in getting the pets back to the original owner and none have been sued over the issue. The behavior and attitude of the original owner toward the rescue organization greatly affected its willingness to cooperate.

4. *How to Handle Ownership Issues Contractually*

The rescue organization can put a clause in its contract to cover itself in the event an original owner returns to claim a dog or cat, providing a grace period during which the adopter agrees to relinquish the animal back to the rescue organization. A long grace period could have a chilling effect on adoptions, so the length of the grace period will have to be weighed by the organization.

5. *If Local Laws Do Not Address All Rescue Organizations, How Are Strays or At-Large Animals Affected?*

Check your local laws to determine which rescue organizations are addressed. There are rescue groups popping up all over the country. There are breed rescues for particular breeds of dogs. There are all-breed rescues that take all breeds of dogs including mutts. There are cat rescues, and there are rescues that take cats and dogs. However, local laws pertaining to impoundment and holding periods do not necessarily address all rescue organizations. Some address only animal control and shelters run by cities and counties, which are commonly called pounds. Some local laws may include other humane organizations that actually house the animals, like the Societies for the Prevention of Cruelty to Animals or the Humane Societies (each are locally autonomous and independent from the national organizations).

If your local laws do not address all rescue organizations, then what laws apply regarding the holding period for a stray animal or an at-large animal? This is another area of concern that is commonly a loophole in the law. Often the small rescue groups, many of which utilize fosters and have no facility, are not addressed in local laws. In representing them, it is always best to err on the side of safety and counsel them to wait the local holding period before adopting out an animal. It is also wise that they make an effort to locate the original owner. Regardless, they can still be sued by the original owner if a dispute as to ownership arises.

6. *Local Laws Rarely Affect the Individual Rescuer*

Local laws usually do not address the individual rescuer of an animal, the Good Samaritan who picks up a stray. In fact, some state and local laws specifically exempt this person from applicable laws. However, it is not uncommon for individual "do-gooders" to be involved in the rescue and placement of animals on a regular basis. They will post dogs on the Internet and try to get them adopted. In fact, there is a steep network of such rescuers all over the country. They constantly find dogs and cats (mostly dogs) and tell their tales to get them adopted. These individuals sometimes find themselves in the midst of a lawsuit if they adopt out someone's pet.

In representing and counseling individuals who are involved in such rescue efforts, it is wise that they abide by local laws for holding an animal before they place it and that they make attempts to find the original owner. This is not going to prevent someone from suing them, but it will show that there was a good-faith attempt on the part of the rescuer to return the dog and will thwart any possible theft allegations. As a practical matter, the individual rescuer is an easier target for a lawsuit than an established shelter.

7. *Try to Determine Ownership during the Waiting Period*

How to determine ownership is a common issue that arises in animal rescue, particularly with dogs and cats. It is also an issue that is typically not addressed by local laws. When a rescue takes in an animal, there should be some attempt to determine its owner. There also needs to be a way that anyone claiming the animal can prove it is theirs.

As the popularity of microchipping rises, it is wise to encourage rescue organizations to scan the animals they take in that are strays. Many veterinary clinics have scanners and if the group is large enough, a scanner should be purchased. If an owner goes to the trouble of microchipping their pet, they obviously want their pet returned if it gets loose. Placing or euthanizing a pet that is chipped runs the risk of a lawsuit by a pet owner who is obviously motivated to keep the pet.

It is advisable to require proof of identity of the person claiming the animal, too. It is reasonable that the rescue organization request proof of ownership by the production of vet records, pictures, registration papers, pet licenses, and microchipping.

If any dispute arises later regarding ownership, then the rescue group can demonstrate its efforts to determine the true owner. Having a protocol for determining ownership also deters people who go to shelters to claim an animal for untoward purposes.

B. The Owner Turn-In or Owner Surrender

An owner turn-in, commonly referred to as an OTI in the rescue world, is someone who relinquishes or surrenders a pet to a pound, shelter, animal control facility, or rescue organization. They are turning over a pet they no longer want.

The rescue organization should be carefully counseled on two key points of such a turn-in. First, the group needs to have a well-drafted contract for an owner turn-in. The contract should clearly state that this is a voluntary turn-in and that the owner clearly understands and acknowledges that all rights in the animal are forever relinquished. The owner's signature should be witnessed. Upon signing this contract, all ownership and property rights are extinguished.

Second, the rescue organization needs to determine that the person turning in the animal is indeed the owner. All too often rescue groups are faced with an annoyed neighbor or a vindictive spouse who is turning in a pet in an act of spite or vengeance. Thus it is advisable to get proof of identification of the individual turning in the animal. This will not only cut down on the risk of getting sued over the placement or euthanasia of such an animal, it will also help eliminate the unscrupulous person who is turning in a pet belonging to another.

If you are representing what is commonly called a kill shelter, one that euthanizes animals if the population gets too large, then verifying that the person turning in an animal is the legal owner is even more important. Because these shelters are typically overcrowded, the dogs or cats that have been turned in by their owners are the first slated for euthanasia.

Legally, shelters have to wait for the hold period to expire prior to putting down the strays whose owners are not determined, so in times of overcrowding, the owner turn-ins are the first to go. This is often true regardless of pedigree or adoptability.

The last thing a rescue organization wants is to deal with an upset individual because a spouse or a neighbor turned in their animal and it was adopted or worse, killed. This puts the organization at risk of being sued and is a public relations nightmare.

In *Animal Hospital of Elmont, Inc. v. Gianfrancisco*,[36] Gianfrancisco was unable to pay his vet bill; the vet clinic warned him if the bill was not paid and the dog picked up within 11 days, it would rely on statutes for abandoned animals. After the waiting period lapsed, a vet employee turned the puppy over to the local Society for the Prevention of Cruelty to Animals, claiming that the dog was hers. As an OTI, the dog was killed in less than 48 hours. The suit was brought by the vet for the fees and boarding; the owner countered for the cost of the dog. The court awarded both of them damages against each other.[37] The shelter was not sued, but it certainly could have been for failing to verify ownership of the dog.

C. Animals Seized by Local Authorities

1. Awarded to Shelters

Depending on state statutes, rescue organizations may be awarded animals that have been legally seized in cruelty cases. In these cases, the property rights of the original owner are extinguished by court order and the animal becomes the property of the receiving agency.

In some jurisdictions, the owner may appeal such an award. Once the appeals, if available, are extinguished, the owner has forever lost ownership and property rights in the animal. It is imperative to determine under your state and local laws if an appeal of the cruelty seizure is allowed so that you can advise your shelter client when they can offer the animal for adoption or dispose of it.

If you represent the dog owner in one of these cases, you must ensure that the shelter does not mistakenly kill the animal during the pendency of your appeal. One way to do this is to establish a rapport with the shelter personnel. Call them frequently to remind them that the animal is not to be killed.

2. Animals Seized as Evidence in Possession of the Shelter

Animal control will be in possession of animals seized as evidence that have to be maintained until the disposition of the case. In some jurisdictions, the local Society for the Prevention of Cruelty to Animals or Humane

Society takes responsibility for animals during cruelty seizures or seizures for dogfighting and maintains them while the case is pending, which may eventuate (not often) in the animals being returned to the owner.

In *Snead v. SPCA of Pennsylvania*,[38] Snead's dogs had been seized because she was charged with dogfighting, but the charges were dropped without her knowledge. Failing to tell Snead that she could pick up her 12 dogs (11 pit bull terriers and one French shepherd), the shelter waited the required two days and euthanized the dogs. The court awarded Snead damages of $154,926.73, including $100,000 in punitive damages.[39] On appeal, the award of punitive damages was reversed, but her actual damages and legal fees were allowed.[40]

Some important points of this case:

- Dogs are property, which gives the owner rights.
- Owners' rights in their property are not extinguished because their animals were seized by authorities.
- Shelters can incur liability by failing to properly care for the property of others.
- Careful screening for the true owner and legal status of the dogs would have revealed that the charges were dropped and saved these dogs from being unnecessarily euthanized.
- Careful screening for the true owner and legal status of animals in the care of the shelter reduces and/or eliminates the risk of the shelter being sued and importantly of causing undue grief to owners, while avoiding public relations problems with the community.

D. Animals at Large or Seized Due to Disasters

There is no better teacher about handling animals during and after a disaster than Hurricane Katrina. Many people who evacuated from New Orleans and the Gulf Coast thought they would return to their homes shortly and so did not make long-term provisions for their pets. Rescue efforts were hastily put together for the animals in need, but the rescuers faced perplexing problems of what to do with the animals, since many owners were unable to return to their homes. Though the state enacted emergency laws to extinguish ownership rights if the owner failed to reclaim animals within a certain time frame, the courts have consistently ignored the legislature's enactments in favor of owners.

Arguello v. Behmke[41] illustrates the conflict created between the original owner and a new owner who adopted a Katrina dog, as well as the problems endured by rescue organizations in the wake of a disaster like Hurricane Katrina. A week after evacuating from her Louisiana home, Arguello returned for her three dogs, two beagles and a Great Dane, and took them to the Lamar Dixon Shelter, which was set up to provide temporary housing for animals whose owners were victims of the hurricane. Arguello had signed a bailment with Lamar Dixon for them to keep her dogs and had been in telephone contact with the shelter, but when she attempted to retrieve her dogs she learned that her Great Dane, Chopper, had been transferred to another rescue and then placed with Behmke. Behmke refused to return the dog, and Arguello sued Behmke on an action for replevin.

The court reasoned that it was clear that Arguello never intended to abandon Chopper or give up her ownership rights; that Arguello would have had to abandon her ownership rights in the property or make a claim after the six-year statute of limitations, neither of which happened in this case; and that pursuant to the original contract between Arguello and Lamar Dixon, the shelter should have contacted her before moving Chopper and she should have been apprised of the contract that was entered into by the second shelter.[42] The court concluded that Chopper should be returned to Arguello.[43] It further stated that even if all the contracts were valid, a court of equity should not serve injustice or hardship.[44]

Some important points from this case:

- The courts are not inclined to extinguish the property rights of owners.
- The courts are particularly disposed to returning pets to their original owners in the wake of disasters.
- Contractual agreements of third parties (like between the two rescue organizations regarding ownership) do not extinguish the property rights of owners.
- The statute of limitations is applied to property cases involving animals.
- A bailment situation can be created when dogs are found that does not eliminate the owner's property rights.
- There is always some risk when rescue organizations take in animals and adopt them to new owners.
- While there is some risk, on balance these challenges do not often occur.

E. Establishing Disputed-Ownership Policies

An organization that chooses to act as intermediary in ownership disputes between the alleged original owner and the adopter should first establish policies and procedures to handle these issues appropriately and consistently.

It is best to have one person designated to handle custody matters. The designee should interact calmly with the alleged original owner, get proof of ownership (vet records, licenses, pictures, registration, lost dog signs, and so on), and explain that while no promises can be made about the return of the animal, the adopter will be contacted and the owner will be called at a later date. Once all the information is obtained from the alleged original owner, the organization must determine whether the original owner's animal and the adopted animal appear to be the same. There is absolutely no need to disturb an adoption if the information does not match up. In one instance of mistaken identity, a rescue accepted a dog that had very long hair and was in dire need of grooming. Pictures were taken of the dog both before and after grooming. Someone saw the "after" pictures on a Web site and thought the dog was hers. However, her dog had been shaved, and its hair could not possibly have grown so long in the period of time that it was missing. This is a practical example of how some ownership queries can be handled.

In situations in which it does appear that the adopted dog belonged to the claimant owner, the rescue group should contact the adopter, explain the situation, and allow the adopter time to decide whether to return the dog (if there is not a contract provision stating that the adopter must do so). An adopter who relinquishes the animal should be offered the option of another dog or return of the adoption fee. Reimbursement of veterinarian and other costs can be sought from the reclaiming owner.

Alternatively, the rescue organization can take the position that the adoption is final and that it cannot be disturbed regardless of an alleged owner coming forward. This hard-line approach may dissuade many original owners from suing the group, but others will fight tooth and nail to get their pet back.

VI. The Importance of Contractual Agreements in Protecting the Rescue Organization and Ensuring Responsible Placement of Animals

No animal should be adopted to a new owner without an adoption contract. Not even a friendly adoption between friends or neighbors should be done without the benefit of a contract. A contract prevents misunderstandings and is a recorded representation of what is required and what the new owner represented that he or she would do. It is important legally, but also psychologically as a formal commitment to an animal. The adoption contract is the cornerstone for responsibly placing animals.

In addition to the adoption contract, an application will help weed out potential problems with adopters. It is a very good way to obtain useful information from the adopter that will lead to the responsible placement of animals, particularly dogs and cats. Rescue organizations should utilize both an application and a contract.

A. The Adoption Application: Soliciting Information to Ensure a Responsible Adoption and Protect the Rescue Organization

The application is an important tool in properly placing animals and tends to eliminate people who are not interested in providing a good home. Some rescuers fear that having to fill out an application and a contract might seem too onerous and will scare away potential adopters, but this concern is generally unfounded. Anyone who is interested in making a commitment to an animal will not have a problem filling out an application and signing a contract.

However, an application process will thwart unscrupulous people who do not want to divulge personal information, such as those seeking fighting dogs ("power breeds" such as American Pit Bull Terrier, German shepherd, shar-pei, Akita, Doberman pinscher, and Rottweiler). The application process will also deter people known as "bunchers," who pose as legitimate adopters but are seeking dogs and cats for untoward purposes such as bait for fighting dogs or to be sold for science.

1. *Elements of a Good Application*

A good application will cover at least the following information:

a. Full Identification of the Potential Adopter

The full name, address, zip code, all phone numbers, date of birth, and a copy of the current driver's license with picture (front and back if information is on the back) should be obtained. The rescue organization may wish to run a background check on the individual, particularly if a power breed is requested. Some organizations who adopt out those breeds of dogs do not adopt to individuals with a criminal record, particularly if the record is drug-related. It is relatively easy and inexpensive to get a criminal background check done on the Internet. Also, some jurisdictions have that information online. For example, the Jury Information Management System in Harris County, Texas, retrieves any civil or criminal actions filed in that county. A countywide search is a good start, particularly if the potential adopter has lived in the county for an extended period of time.

The potential adopter must provide an actual residence address, not just a mailing address, because some municipalities restrict the total number of pets a person may have and some restrict the number of dogs a person may own. The rescue organization should follow the law of the jurisdiction where the adopter resides in determining whether he or she can have another animal. It does not make sense to adopt to someone who may have animal control seize the animals for exceeding the legal limit.

B. Home Ownership and Homeowners' Associations

A homeowners' association may have pet-ownership rules that are more restrictive than the prevailing local law. These rules may restrict the number of dogs, their size, and even the breed of dogs owned. There can also be provisions about fencing, fencing height, prohibitions on chaining or tethering, and other provisions. Some homeowners' associations do not allow fencing at all, a large factor in owning a dog. These considerations are equally applicable to condo associations or townhouse associations since some of them do not allow even small dogs.

C. Leasing or Renting

An adopter who rents should provide the name and contact information of the complex, landlord, or management company. The landlord or the management company will commonly have pet restrictions. They may even have rules banning certain breeds. This is a serious consideration because some leasing contracts provide that if pets are there in contravention of the rules, the property manager can confiscate them. The last thing the rescue organization wants is for an adopted animal to end up back in the pound.

Some leasing managers have been known to enter a person's apartment or house while the lessee was not home so that animal control can take the pets. Once that happens, there are no guarantees that the pet owner or the rescue from which the pets came will ever get them back. Seizures like this raise Fourth Amendment issues, but as a practical matter you cannot count on winning on these arguments since the courts that handle seizures are the lower courts and the pet owner usually is required to appear in court within a short period of time. Many never even have time to hire an attorney.

D. Number, Kind, and Sex of Other Pets

To safeguard against injury or return, it is important to ascertain what other pets are in the household. Some dogs—for example, American Pit

Bull Terriers, Rottweilers, Akitas, and Chow Chows—are less aggressive with the opposite sex, and such placement reduces the chance for fighting. Most dogs are like that to some degree. For the same reasons, these dogs should also be placed with dogs of similar size.

In placing dogs with other animals, it is important to consider what they were bred for. Hunting dogs (also referred to as the sporting breeds) and terriers were bred to be prey-driven, and thus might not be good with cats or small dogs. Because they hunt, when these kinds of dogs see something dart across their line of vision, they instinctively go into action. That's nature, but it can be at the expense of another smaller animal, like a cat, ferret, or a toy-sized dog.

E. Age of Everyone in the Home

Some dogs are better suited for people of a certain age. For example, a large, rambunctious puppy could knock over small children. On the other end of the continuum, a tiny dog might not be the best option for a family with small children for the safety of the dog. Likewise, it is important to consider what type of dog to place with an elderly person who is not surefooted. Taking these factors into consideration helps ensure a responsible adoption that does not result in the animal being returned or a liability issue for the rescue.

F. Work Schedule of the Adopter(s)

Adopters who work long hours need to consider the daily and long-term needs of a dog or a puppy. Who will walk the dog or let it outside when nature calls? Who will socialize the dog, train it, and give it enough stimulation to make it a good pet? If an adopter will not have enough free time to care for a dog, perhaps an independent cat would make a more appropriate pet.

G. Where the Animal Will Stay and How It Will Be Cared For

It is beneficial to have the potential adopter answer questions about where the animal will live, how it will be cared for, and where will it be kept when the owners go out of town or on vacation. Rescue organizations often have rules about how they want their animals placed, so this question is an effective screening tool. If, for example, a person would like to adopt a cat and indicates the cat will be an inside and outside cat, this might offend rescue organizations that believe cats should be inside-only pets.

Similarly, if a person is looking for a guard dog to be loose on a business property at night, many rescues will reject the application. Many smaller organizations require that their dogs be inside dogs. However, some of the bigger, better-known humane organizations allow dogs to be outside dogs and do not even screen on this issue.

Certain dogs cannot be tossed safely into a backyard and left without supervision. Some dogs climb, jump, or dig under fences. This is especially true of dogs that are stressed to begin with or have separation anxiety.

The rescue organization can predict how the animal will be treated from the potential adopters' answers to this section. This helps to make sure that the placement will be a good one for the animal.

2. *How an Application Benefits a Rescue Organization*

The application is an invaluable tool in proper placement of animals. If there are problems with the adoption later on, untruthful answers on the application can serve to support the rescue organization's position that the animal should be returned to them. The application should have a provision for the adopter to sign that his or her responses are true and correct. If it is later found out that some or all of the information provided is untrue, then the application can be used in an effort to reclaim the animal.

The application can also be utilized to limit potential liability of the rescue organization. By proper screening, adoptions can be made that minimize the risk of getting sued. For example, if a group places a large male Akita in a family with another large male Akita, those two dogs have a greater chance of fighting because they are the same gender. If a fight breaks out and a child tries to intervene and gets injured, there is potential liability based on that adoption, particularly if the rescue group failed to ask what other dogs the family owns or failed to heed what had been divulged on the application.

Stated positively, if the application contains key information and it is heeded, then the rescue organization has minimized potential exposure to suits. To continue the previous example, placing an appropriate female Akita has a higher likelihood of success and reduces the possibility of a fight amongst the dogs. The application can be used to point out potential red flags about the feasibility of a good adoption. (See Appendix A: Application for Adoption.)

B. The Adoption Contract: Binding the Adopter, Protecting the Rescue

The adoption contract should succinctly set out what is expected of the adopter. This will give the adopter notice of what the requirements are and how they will be reinforced. The contract should also protect the animal by contractually committing the adopter to follow through on his or her promises. There is also a huge psychological commitment gained by having an adoption contract. While minors cannot be bound to a contract, it is a good idea to have them sign so that they are a part of the adoption and feel responsible for the animal, too.

1. *Key Elements of a Rescue Organization's Adoption Contract*

The adoption agreement should include those things the organization expects of the adopters and a way to enforce them. While not all contract requirements may be enforceable by courts, the provisions addressing the humane treatment of animals and proper care most likely will be.

a. Proper Identification of the Adopters and the Animal to Be Adopted

The adopter should be identified thoroughly, including a copy of his or her driver's license as an attachment to the agreement. If something goes awry with the placement, the rescue organization wants to be able to locate the adopter.

Similarly, the animal needs to be identified and, if possible, photographed. If the animal is microchipped, the identifying information should be included on the contract. If there are ever any issues with the adopter properly caring for the animal, it is important to be able to correctly identify it if the organization attempts to reclaim it.

b. Organization's Expectations of the Adopter

The rescue organization must decide what they expect of an adopter and clearly state it in the contract. The minimum standards of proper care and veterinary attention should be included, but there may be other requirements sought by the organization. For example, many organizations require that the pet be an inside-only animal. Some organizations do not want a dog's ears or tail to be surgically altered or a cat to be declawed. Some even dictate the animal's feeding regimen. As a practical matter, if the contract is too onerous, potential adopters may be dissuaded by the expectations.

Even though the courts may not enforce all aspects of animal adoption contracts, they can be an effective way to weed out people who are not willing to abide by the requisites set by the organization. There is no way to be certain what a court will enforce. Regardless, commemorating the expectations in a written form will help attract responsible owners.

c. Disclaimer and Hold-Harmless Provision

The adoption contract should contain a disclaimer about the animals since often there is no information about their history and no way to predict their future behavior. After they relax and settle into their new home, their true personality will be revealed.

It is wise to have a hold-harmless provision in the rescue contract to protect the organization if, for example, an adopted dog bites someone. The rescue can contractually protect itself for the untoward actions of an adopted dog by including this clause.

D. Return of Animal to the Rescue Organization If the Adopter Can No Longer Keep It

Custody questions, not liability issues, are the most frequent sources of dispute between a rescue organization and its adopters. Adoption contracts usually have a provision about returning the dog or cat to the rescue organization if the adopter cannot keep the animal. The best, reputable rescue organizations will always accept an animal back into their program if something happens with the adoption. This is something that should be clearly explained.

The transfer of the animal is an area of common dispute in adoptions. For example, if an adopter decides she cannot afford to properly care for the animal adopted, she may alert the rescue, but before the animal is relinquished, a friend may offer to take it. Many rescues want the animal back or at the very least want the new owner to submit an application and contract of his own. Often the new owner does not understand why he should comply with the rescue's request and refuses. Similarly, it is hard for the adopter to understand why she cannot freely give away her pet to another family.

E. Return of Animal to the Rescue Organization in the Event of Death of the Adopter

Most reputable organizations will accept an animal back into their program for any reason, because the emphasis is on the well-being of the rescued animal. Sometimes the provisions of the contract go so far as to require the return of the animal in the event of the death of the adopter. This puts the beneficiaries at odds with the rescue, since animals are property.

If there is a will or trust provision for the pet, then there is a conflict between that document and the adoption contract if it provides for the return of the animal in the event of death. If the owner dies intestate, then the rescue organization has a stronger argument to contend that the property reverts back to the rescue organization. One argument in favor of the rescue getting the animal back is that the adopter entered into a contract regarding property that inures to the benefit of the rescue organization against his successors. The counterargument is that the adopter cannot bind his beneficiaries contractually. It will be interesting to see if these provisions of adoption contracts are actually held enforceable by the courts. My suspicion is that they will not be enforceable unless the animal is being treated cruelly.

F. Return of Animal to the Rescue Organization Due to Breach of the Adoption Contract

If an adopter breaches the adoption contract, the rescue organization can decide if it wants to pursue the return of the animal. Getting the animal returned depends on what part of the contract the adopter breached. If the animal is being cruelly treated, courts are more likely to enforce the contract.

However, there are some contract provisions that might not be enforceable. For example, some groups require that dogs be fed only a raw diet. If the adopter decides to feed the dog kibble instead, it is likely that provision will not be enforceable. In fact, some judges are likely to award sanctions for what they perceive to be a frivolous claim.

Yes, there may be a contract provision violated, but that does not necessarily mean that the rescue will win in court. Lay rescuers have a hard time understanding this. Rescuers often question, "What's the point of having a contract if it's not enforceable?" As an attorney, it is easy to see a number of good reasons to have a contract and even include provisions that might not be enforced. The commitment to an animal is memorialized, which underscores the importance of good care regardless of whether or not all the provisions of the contract would pass judicial scrutiny.

It is important to counsel your rescue clients to pick their battles, as these sorts of "feel good" contract provisions are probably not enforceable anyway. That is not to advise against including them in your contracts. By all means do include them, because many adopters will not want to violate their agreements. Some provisions are really seeking a psychological commitment rather than a legal one anyway.

G. Ownership Disputes

The adoption contract is an excellent way to handle ownership disputes before they ever happen. In the event that the rescue has convincing evidence that an original owner has claim to an adopted dog, the contract can provide that the adopter has to return the dog to the rescue. However, rescue groups typically do not want to put such language in their contracts for fear of daunting the adoption process. There should be some language that holds the rescue harmless for adopting an animal in good faith.

H. Spaying and Neutering Provisions

Many rescue organizations release dogs on spay/neuter contracts, requiring that the adopter have the animal fixed within the time allotted by law. The attorney for these groups needs to check with state and local laws for any provisions that might affect these agreements. Some states allow for animals to be adopted on spay/neuter contracts and even provide the key elements in the statute. The enforceability of these provisions is enhanced by state requirements for the altering of pets that leave shelters. However, these statutes may not affect all rescue groups.

Absent any state or local provisions for the enforcement of contractual spay/neuter agreement, any suit over a breach of that part of the contract will be determined on a case-by-case basis. (See Section IX, Responsibility of Animal Associations and Individual Rescuers for Spaying and Neutering, *infra*.)

2. How to Draft the Contract to Protect the Organization from a Lawsuit

The key parts of an adoption contract that afford protection to the rescue from litigation are contained in the disclaimers. The contract containing solid disclaimers about the animal, its origins, health, and temperament, will best protect the organization from any liability lawsuits. Of course, make sure the disclaimers contain the truth. For example, if the adoption contract has appropriate disclaimers about the temperament of a dog, but the rescue group fails to disclose that the dog nipped one of its volunteers, the disclaimer is worthless. A dog's known aggression toward cats must be disclosed: If the dog goes after the adopter's cat and a child intervenes, the rescue has significant exposure for failing to disclose important information about the particular dog. A breed's known propensities should also be disclosed; for example, that hounds are prey-driven and so may not be suitable in a home with cats. The rescue would be at risk if it failed to disclose the characteristics of the breed as well as the characteristics of the individual animal.

Adoption contracts should be used even if the adopter is someone known to the rescue group or the individual rescuer. Even if the adopter is a friend or relative, a contract should be utilized. Perhaps the application can be waived, but a contract, even a simple one, should be executed. (See Appendix B: Adoption Contract; Appendix C: Additional Contract Terms for Certain Breeds; and Appendix D: Short Adoption Contract Form.)

C. The Owner Turn-In Contract: Key Elements

The owner turn-in contract is used when the owner of an animal wants to relinquish his or her property rights in the animal to the rescue organization. It is essential to determine if the animal being turned in is indeed the property of the purported owner.

1. *Identify the Person Alleging to Be the Owner*

It is important to properly identify the person claiming to own the animal. It is advisable to photocopy the person's driver's license and obtain addresses (home and business), phone numbers, date of birth, and place of employment. If the person is married, ascertain whether the spouse is aware that the animal is being turned in. This is a chief source of problems for rescue groups because a vindictive spouse can turn in an animal to spite the other spouse or may be turning in property that does not belong to him or her.

The contract must have a place for the alleged owner to sign that he or she is the sole owner of the animal or that the other spouse agrees to the turn-in. It is a good practice to check with the other spouse before disposing of the animal. This can be discreetly done as a verification process and will save the organization from finding itself at odds with a spouse who may actually be the real owner.

2. *Specify That Property Rights Are Extinguished in the Transfer*

The owner turn-in contract must make exceedingly clear that the ownership rights in property are being transferred to the rescue organization. It is advisable to put that language in capital or bold letters. This is extremely important because many rescue organizations that are high-kill may euthanize the animal or put it up for adoption the same day it arrives. This can become a source of problems for the rescue when a former owner has a change of heart and comes back the next day to reclaim a dog or cat. (See Appendix E: Owner Relinquishment Agreement.)

VII. Liability of Rescuers and Rescue Groups for Defamation

Libelous e-mails and Internet postings can easily become the subject of defamation suits. If the charitable rescue group you represent is the subject of a barrage of e-mails disparaging the group, the damage can be devastating to donations. Donations are the lifeblood of charities, so defamatory comments can affect the flow of money into the organization. The chilling effect on donations is easily tracked by a decline in donations shortly after the remarks and for a period after.

A. Talk Is Not Cheap If It Is Slander

The liability for defamation applies equally to rescuers and dog owners. Defamation is actually broken down into two parts, slander and libel.

Slander refers to the spoken word and libel refers to the written word. Defamation is the spreading of false statements that disparage the person about whom the statements were said. Truth is always a defense in a defamation case.

In the case *Stearns v. McManis,* Stearns and McManis co-owned a Saint Bernard.[45] Their relationship became strained when McManis brought some more Saint Bernards to Houston to sell. Stearns accused McManis of being a "puppy miller." The court pointed out:

> The term is considered disparaging by dog fanciers. It describes one whose primary interest is in selling puppies for profit with little concern for their health or for improving the breed.[46]

The jury found that such statements were made with malice and were not true. Apparently, Stearns had made these statements to other Saint Bernard owner's when McManis tried to join the Saint Bernard club and was rejected. The fact that he was rejected proved that people had actually relied on the statements of Stearns, so the jury returned a verdict in favor of McManis. He was awarded $200 in damages and $1,000 in punitive damages. Although that sum is not very much, it demonstrates that juries will award damages for that type of disparagement even for the fancy of a dog.

B. The Humane Society of Dallas Bites Back: The Rescue Organization as the Defamed Plaintiff

A newspaper reporter wrote an article about a family who saw their (presumably lost) pet at an adoption being held by the Humane Society.[47] The Humane Society contended defamation and business disparagement based on the article. The newspaper contended successfully that the article was fair comment and was protected speech. The Humane Society did not win that one, but it does go to show that rescue organizations also do not take lightly what they perceive as disparaging comments made about their efforts. Keep in mind that donations are the key to their success, so they do not want to jeopardize receiving them by a poor public perception.

C. Alleged Defamation over Cruelty Determination: The Individual as the Defamed Plaintiff against a Rescue Organization

In the case *Barnett v. Tarrant County Humane Society,* a kennel owner had 176 Weimaraners.[48] Of that number, 112 were in such terrible condition they had to be destroyed. As reported in the *Fort Worth Star-Telegram,* the

Humane Society alleged that many of the plaintiff's dogs had distemper and mange, that her kennels had not been cleaned for months, that the dogs had received no care for a period spanning several months, and that some of the dogs had almost no hair. The kennel owner contended that such statements were false and constituted libel and slander. Although the plaintiff lost because the court found that these allegations were indeed true, this certainly points out how these suits can evolve. It also shows how hoarders are often in a total state of denial about problems with their animals.

In a similar case, *Tabaj v. Fayette SPCA*, Tabaj sued a rescue organization for defamation for alleging that he was cruel to animals on their property.[49] The allegations were contained in citations that were later dropped. The rescue organization attempted to argue that it was immune from liability because it is legally recognized as the animal care and control society for the township. The court did not grant the summary judgment based on immunity, but did on the basis that the statements in the citations were privileged.

Importantly, the *Tabaj* case did not discuss the compensation received by the society for acting as the animal control agency in the township. Other cases have been decided in favor of immunity based on the city's delegation of animal control functions to humane organizations, with compensation.

D. Posting Alleged Defamatory Remarks on an Internet Bulletin Board

In November 2001, a local television station aired a "Whistle Blower 2" episode investigating the Atlanta Humane Society. The series severely criticized the organization's management of Fulton County animal control, particularly its euthanasia policies, its failure to place animals for adoption, and its failure to assist in investigating animal cruelty cases. The director of the organization was Bill Garrett.

Subsequent to the airing of this program, Kathie Mills posted some comments about the Atlanta Humane Society and Garrett on her Web site, Kitty Village.[50] This case illustrates how rescuers get worked up and the sort of things they will say about each other. The case states:

> Mills operated an internet animal rescue website known as Kitty Village. After the television series aired, Mills participated in an internet message board discussion of the programs. During that discussion, she made inflammatory statements about AHS and Garrett, including referring to Garrett as "Mr. Kill," stating that

> he "was not worthy to lick the dog or cat poop off our shoes" and that he was "evil." She relied upon the program's accusations to speculate that AHS policy with regard to euthanasia, adoption, and cruelty investigations was calculated to "maximize profits," and stated that she was withdrawing support for another humane organization led by Garrett "until they get a leader who does not delight in slaughtering pets for fun and profit."[51]

As in many places, the humane society had for many years taken over the responsibility of most of Fulton County's animal control responsibilities, for which they received public tax money. As such, the Atlanta Humane Society was treated as a governmental entity, which could not be the subject of defamation. Accordingly, the organization could not maintain a suit for defamation.

This case shows that rescue organizations and individuals should carefully consider what they say, write, or post to the Internet. Counsel for rescue organizations should advise their clients that as a rule of thumb, they should not say, write, e-mail, or post anything they would not want a jury to read. The same applies to anything they might forward in an e-mail.

E. Alleged Defamation Could Curtail Donations to Charitable Rescue Organization

In *Murphy v. Daytona Beach Humane Society*,[52] Murphy, who operated a group called the Taxpayers Dogwatch Committee, alleged mismanagement and improper use of tax funds by the humane society. The humane society alleged that Murphy's actions were an attempt to hamper the operation of the organization and would have an adverse affect on donations for the new facility they wanted to build. Therefore, the organization sought an injunction to cause Murphy to cease making these comments and accusations, but fell short of actually alleging libel.

The court determined that a charitable corporation does not have a property interest in the solicitation of funds from the public similar to that which a for-profit corporation has in protecting its business. In fact, the court stated:

> Private corporations which claim the confidence of the public and seek the possession of public funds are among the subjects that may be criticized in accordance with the rules of fair comment, and it has even been said that bona fide criticism of such

> corporations should be encouraged as a means of public security, rather than suppressed.[53]

An injunction had been granted but was overturned by the appellate court on the basis that an injunction for libel must be accompanied by some property interest, which was not met by the charitable corporation. Note, however, that this case addresses the availability for injunctive relief, which is sparingly granted.

F. The DNA: They Sent What on E-mail?

In the rescue world, DNA means Do Not Adopt, and it refers to a person or a group whom the writer does not believe should ever get an animal. This is a popular subject of rescue e-mails, and in fact many people and groups maintain lists of DNAs for future reference in placing animals. Some lists are valid and include people who have been convicted of animal cruelty. Sending those via e-mail is probably not problematic if worded to reflect on the facts and state the truth.

However, as rescue people can have rather lofty expectations for adopters, occasionally the person who is the subject of a DNA has merely refused to agree to an onerous requirement of the rescuer or rescue organization. These DNAs sent out via e-mail often contain the individual's personal information including driver's license number and even Social Security numbers. Obviously this makes rescue groups vulnerable to defamation charges, and groups must be reminded in no uncertain terms that personal information obtained in the adoption process by rescue organizations should never be made public.

G. Sending E-mail from an Employer's Account

Some of the most inflammatory e-mails are sent from corporate accounts of employers. In fact, the plaintiff attorney in a defamation case should check to see whether the sender has e-mailed from his or her employer's account. This can be a great source of leverage, as senders confronted with the possibility of notification to their employers are usually willing to make amends. The employee will usually not want to jeopardize his or her job and will hastily make a retraction, and if not, the employer will probably not want to be involved in some fray about animal rescue.

Since defamation cases are not easy to make, extracting retractions and apologies is a viable way to handle these matters and is made all the easier if the remarks were generated on an employer's account. This can be an easy and inexpensive way to shut down the defamatory buzz.

Animal rescue clients should be counseled not to send anything that could be remotely considered defamatory from their employer's corporate account. The best advice is that rescue e-mail should be sent from personal accounts and not from work. This avoids any problems with an employer getting ensnared in a defamation suit. Additionally, e-mail received and sent by the employee is private if sent on a personal account. The employer can read whatever passes through its corporate e-mail account.

In a local example, some rescuers were sending e-mail from their place of employment, a large law firm. Some members of the firm read the e-mails that were alleged to be defamatory and untrue about some shelters. It was revealed that one of the shelters was a client of the law firm. You can imagine that some fur was flying around the office when these e-mails were discovered.

While corporate employers will have a good defense that such statements were not authorized by them, there is nothing stopping the clever attorney from including what might be a deep pocket into a defamation suit. It could be claimed that the employer has a duty to monitor the e-mails being sent by its employees on the company's corporate account.

VIII. Liability of Animal Shelters Run by Government Entities

A. Liability for Torts

The liability of government-run animal shelters for torts is contingent on to what degree the state allows its governmental entities to be sued. Governmental entities enjoy sovereign immunity, but may be sued for tort actions to the degree that state law provides for exceptions.

It is imperative to determine the state law for governmental liability for a tort action. Certain actions on the part of governmental entities and their employees can be exempt from liability, so this needs to be determined to ascertain if a cause of action is viable against a government-run animal shelter. Similarly, this determination will also provide defenses to liability based on governmental immunity.

B. Liability for Damages Arising from Torts

Similarly, if a cause of action may be pursued for governmental liability for a tort, the damages that are recoverable are typically limited by state statutes. There is a cap on damages that a plaintiff can receive if he or she prevails against a governmental entity on a tort claim.

State law must be reviewed to determine if there is an applicable limit on the damages that can be recovered. Caps on damages tend to vary according to whether the facility is run by the state, a county, or a municipality.

State statutes must be likewise reviewed to determine if attorneys' fees, interest, court costs, and exemplary damages are recoverable.

C. Notice Provisions

An important consideration for the practitioner is to determine what, if any, notice provisions are contained in state laws when suing governmental entities. The failure to give proper notice to the governmental entity of a potential claim can be a complete bar to filing suit if not followed properly.

D. Liability for the Placement of Animals: Sovereign Immunity

Shelters are concerned about liability for the negligent placement of animals with adopters. The same contract provisions that can help insulate a nongovernment shelter from liability are applicable to government-run shelters.

Additionally, the government-run shelters likely enjoy immunity from liability for tortuous acts to some degree and perhaps even totally, so that must be determined according to state law to fully assess any potential liability for the placement of animals.

Government-run shelters are wise to utilize breed-specific rescues in the placement of animals because the rescues will have particular expertise in the personality and behavior traits particular to the breed. The breed rescue will thus be in a better position to properly assess the animal and more fully screen adopters. This is particularly true in the placement of breeds that need special consideration.

The breed rescues also usually have more time to work with an animal before it is adopted, and their screening process for adopters tends to be far more in depth and may include home visits to determine suitability of the breed for the potential adopter's lifestyle. This level of scrutiny both of the animal and the adopter decreases potential for untoward occurrences.

In addition to potentially insulating the shelter from liability by utilizing breed rescues, the shelter can enjoy greater placement of animals, thereby reducing their euthanasia numbers and increasing their placement numbers.

IX. Responsibility of Animal Associations and Individual Rescuers for Spaying and Neutering

A. Legal Responsibility of the Rescue Organization for Spaying and Neutering

When representing rescue organizations, it is imperative to check your state and local laws to determine what responsibility, if any, your client has for spaying and neutering the animals it places. These laws address the placement of cats and dogs as a rule.

If spaying and neutering is required by state or local laws, the onus is often put on the rescue organization to make sure this is done. Often, the organization has a choice. It can spay or neuter the pets itself, or have the adopter sign a spay/neuter contract agreeing to get the animal fixed within the time allotted by law. This puts the burden on the rescue organization to follow up with the new owners to make sure the animal was fixed per the contract.

The spay/neuter contract is sometimes preferable to altering puppies and kittens at a very early age. If the animals are very young, there is a risk of severing or damaging their ureters, which can make the animal incontinent, and of affecting their hormonal development. A spay/neuter contract that allows for the animal to be altered when it is older can be used to avoid these potential problems, and is often provided for in the statute or ordinances.

In Texas, for example, state law provides that rescue groups must spay or neuter the animals or have the adopter sign a contract agreeing to do so. The statutes found in the Texas Health and Safety Code provide:

> REQUIREMENTS FOR ADOPTION. Except as provided by Section 828.013, a releasing agency may not release a dog or cat for adoption unless the animal has been sterilized or the release is made to a new owner who signs an agreement to have the animal sterilized.[54]

The requisites of the spay/neuter agreement are set out in the statute:

> STERILIZATION AGREEMENT.
>
> (a) The sterilization agreement used by a releasing agency must contain:
>
> (1) the date of the agreement;

(2) the names, addresses, and signatures of the releasing agency and the new owner;
(3) a description of the animal to be adopted;
(4) the sterilization completion date; and
(5) a statement, printed in conspicuous, bold print, that sterilization of the animal is required under Chapter 828, Health and Safety Code, and that a violation of this chapter is a criminal offense punishable as a Class C misdemeanor.

(b) The sterilization completion date contained in the sterilization agreement must be:

(1) the 30th day after the date of adoption in the case of an adult animal;
(2) the 30th day after a specified date estimated to be the date an adopted infant female animal becomes six months old or an adopted infant male animal becomes eight months old; or
(3) if the releasing agency has a written policy recommending sterilization of certain infant animals at an earlier date, the 30th day after the date contained in the written policy.[55]

This provision allows for puppies and kittens to be adopted at a young age but not have to be surgically altered until later. This gives the rescue organizations an opportunity to work with very young animals safely.

In some jurisdictions there can even be criminal sanctions for failing to spay and neuter an adopted animal per the contract signed. Of course, enforcement is always an issue, but it shows to what lengths some states and localities go to ensure that adopted animals are not adding to pet overpopulation.

As indicated in the Texas sterilization statute, any violation is a criminal offense and is punished as a Class C misdemeanor. In Texas, this is the most minor type of criminal offense, carrying a fine and no jail time. Nevertheless, the sterilization completion date and the fact that a violation is a criminal offense should be in bold print in the contract to emphasize the importance of the agreement.

B. Individual Rescuer's Responsibility for Spaying and Neutering

Typically, the individual who has done a good deed and saved an animal from likely death is exempt from state and local spaying/neutering laws. However, read the laws closely because it might be a different result if the individual is rescuing animals on an ongoing basis.

In the Texas sterilization statute, the responsibility rests on the "releasing agency." Releasing agency is defined as

> a public or private animal pound, shelter, or humane organization. The term does not include an individual who occasionally renders humane assistance or shelter in the individual's home to a dog or cat.[56]

This definition clearly covers rescue organizations of all kinds, including those with or without shelters, but it does not cover individuals who "occasionally" rescue dogs or cats. There is no definition for "occasionally," so an argument could be made that this requirement covers individuals who rescue cats and dogs on an ongoing basis.

X. Liability of the Individual for Helping and Rescuing Animals

A. Feral Cat Colonies

Many individuals maintain feral cat colonies. However, in some jurisdictions, a person who feeds an animal even for a brief time is deemed to own it. Additionally, some jurisdictions do not allow cats to be at large. Therefore, there is a conflict if the person feeding the feral cats is now deemed the owner and is in violation of at-large laws for cats.

1. Consideration of Local At-Large Laws

Some local laws prohibit cats from being loose while others specifically exempt them from at-large laws. It is important to consider the existing at-large laws to first ascertain if cats may be at large. Even in cities that do not allow cats to be at large, the wording of the ordinances tend to indicate that it applies to owned cats or possessed cats.

a. Cities Allowing Cats to Be at Large by Specifically Exempting Them

Los Angeles is an example of a city that specifically exempts cats from at-large laws:

> ANIMALS AT LARGE.
>
> No person owning or having possession, charge, custody or control of any animal, except cats which are not in heat or season, shall cause, permit or allow the animal to stray, run, or in any

> manner to be at large in or upon any public street, sidewalk or park, except as otherwise expressly provided in section 63.44 of this Code, or in the bed of the Los Angeles River or upon any unenclosed lot or land.[57]

Cats are specifically excepted unless they are in heat. These types of ordinances take into consideration the perceived differences between cats and dogs. Traditionally, cats have been perceived as more capable of taking care of themselves and as hunters in the wild. They have also been thought of as useful for controlling rodents. Therefore, it is not uncommon to have at-large laws that do not apply to cats.

B. Cities Allowing Cats to Be at Large by Omission

Many city at-large laws exclude cats by simply not mentioning them. These laws address dogs without ever mentioning cats. Houston is an example of a city that prevents dogs from being at large and is silent regarding cats:

> Running at large prohibited.
>
> (a) It shall be unlawful for any person owning or having in his possession any dog to allow such dog to be at large without the owner or person in charge thereof having direct physical control over such dog. An owner or person having in his possession a dog may allow the dog to be at large on property that does not provide the animal with access to a sidewalk or street.
>
> (b) It shall be unlawful for any person owning or having in his possession a dangerous dog, as defined in section 6-151 of this Code, to allow that dog to be at large. A person who violates this subsection shall, upon conviction, be assessed a fine of not less than $500 nor more than $2,000. Each day that any violation of this subsection continues shall constitute and be punishable as a separate offense.[58]

Cats are never mentioned. It is lawful for cats in Houston to be at large similar to Los Angeles, but expressed by an omission.

C. Cities That Prohibit Cats from Being at Large

By contrast there are cities that have at-large ordinances that apply equally to dogs and cats. However, the laws applying to cats are often not enforced. This small city in Houston, Texas, Hilshire Village (incorporated municipality in the larger city), has such a law:

> RUNNING AT LARGE PROHIBITED; NUMBER OF ANIMALS PERMITTED; SPECIAL RESTRAINT REQUIRED; AUTHORITY TO IMPOUND
>
> (a) It shall be unlawful for any dog, cat, or other animal possessed, kept, or harbored to run at large.
>
> (b) No owner shall possess, harbor, or keep:
>
> > (1) More than a total of four (4) animals over the age of six (6) months; and/or
> > (2) The offspring of such animals [as are permitted in (b)(1)] under the age of six (6) months; provided, the combined total of such animals and their offspring does not exceed twelve (12);
> > (3) Animals for breeding for the generation of profit. Livestock are excepted from the provisions of this article and shall be subject to the limitations of Article 2.1000 of this article.
>
> (c) The animal control officer is authorized to impound animals running at large.[59]

Any animal owned may not be at large and this ordinance specifically mentions that cats are included.

2. Local Laws That Prohibit Maintaining Feral Cat Colonies

Some local laws consider anyone who feeds an animal to be the owner. If that city or county forbids cats to be at large, then the person feeding the animal could be in violation of at-large laws and subject to fines and penalties.

An example of this is Harris County, Texas. In this county, feeding an animal will make the person the "custodian" of it:

> *Custodian:* A person or agency which feeds, shelters, harbors, has possession or control, or has the responsibility to control an animal, including, but not limited to, the owner of the animal.[60]

Their laws also provide that cats may not be at large. Interestingly, any cat or dog that is not restrained (on a leash) is considered a stray:

> *Stray:* Any animal not under restraint as defined by these Regulations. The display of a vaccination tag or license tag does not change the fact that the dog or cat is a stray for the purposes of these Regulations.[61]

The laws clearly do not allow for cats to be at large and specifically include them in the impoundment regulations:

> All dogs and cats must be kept under restraint while in the unincorporated areas of Harris County, Texas. The custodian of a dog or cat is not authorized to have, harbor or keep any unlicensed dog or cat, or to allow any dog or cat to become a stray.[62]

Considering local laws as a whole, it can be deduced that liability can arise from an individual maintaining a feral cat colony or even from feeding one stray cat. Since animal control all over the country is typically at the bottom of funding priority for cities and counties, these laws are often overlooked. However, if your client for some reason is detected or reported, he or she may face consequences including criminal sanctions (usually fines).

3. *Trap and Kill Jurisdictions*

The local jurisdictions that do not allow for the maintenance of feral colonies may employ the trap and kill method of managing free-roaming cats. The laws allow for feral cats to be trapped. They are then transferred to whatever local agency impounds animals, and if the cats are not claimed after the waiting period, they are euthanized. Some ordinances do not have a waiting period for a feral cat, but that puts the burden on the collecting agency to determine with certainty that the cat is feral.

In *Christman-Resch v. City of Akron*, the plaintiff challenged a city ordinance prohibiting at-large cats and allowing them to be impounded just like a dog.[63] Christman-Resch argued that the ordinance is unconstitutional, violating due process, equal protection, and unreasonable search and seizure, and that trapping and euthanizing cats is not a governmental function. The city pointed out that it traps cats only in response to a citizen complaint and does not drive around looking for cats to impound. The city also listed numerous problems allegedly caused by free-roaming or feral cats, including scratching cars, defecating in gardens, spraying on windows, carrying disease, using a child's sandbox as a litter box, and exacerbating asthma. The court ruled that there were no violations of any constitutional rights and that this was a proprietary function of the city and therefore allowed.[64]

4. *Catch and Kill Jurisdictions*

While some cities do not expressly provide for trapping, if at-large cats are prohibited, animal control is allowed to catch the loose animals. If no one claims them, they are euthanized or put up for adoption. Feral cats are not suitable for adoption as inside pets, so they are euthanized.

Some cities will conduct a "sweep" to find and catch loose dogs and cats. These sweeps are typically in response to a volume of calls from concerned citizens in a particular area of a city. It is common for word of an upcoming sweep to spread around the Internet with warnings from rescuers. Some animal control facilities make the sweep known to the public in an effort to educate the public on the importance of keeping their animals indoors. Additionally, there are some jurisdictions that do not even hold feral cats the requisite number of days to see if they will be claimed.[65]

An example of a local county that has at-large cat laws is Harris County, Texas, though it does not actively trap cats. Cats that are caught by animal control are treated in the same manner as dogs:

> Animal Control shall keep all healthy unclaimed dogs and cats for a period of three (3) working days. At the expiration of that time if a dog or cat has not been claimed or redeemed by the owner, it may be put up for adoption, sold, or humanely killed. All actions taken under this section shall be conducted as required under the Animal Welfare Act (7 U.S.C. Section 2131 *et. seq.*).[66]

5. *Catch and Relocate Jurisdictions*

Some jurisdictions, while there may not be ordinances to this effect, employ a practice of catching feral cats and relocating them to be barn cats.[67] This is done with the barn owner's agreement, and while it may not solve all feral cat issues, it is worth mentioning as a partial solution to dealing with feral cats in jurisdictions that do not have laws providing for cat colonies.

6. *Local Laws Allowing Feral Cat Colonies*

Some local laws make provisions for maintaining feral cat colonies. These laws allow for the cats to be trapped, neutered, and then released (TNR) to roam as feral cats again. Some jurisdictions refer to these laws as trap, neuter and "return" instead of "release." Both have the same meaning.

If there are such laws, then the person who is feeding the colony cannot be guilty of violating at-large laws. It is common in these jurisdictions that local spay/neuter facilities offer incentives and even free altering of feral cats.

The Spay Neuter Assistance Program (SNAP) in Texas has a feral cat day once per month. Feral cats that have been trapped may be brought in on one Sunday of the month and they are altered for free. The trapper is given care instructions and after the cat has been monitored for the requisite number of days, it may be released back into the area from which it came. Interestingly, these special days at the clinics are held despite the fact that most cities where they conduct the surgeries ban at-large cats. As mentioned, at-large cat laws are not enforced as stringently as at-large dog laws.

However, feral-cat laws vary widely from city to city. As indicated previously, some laws do not address feral cats directly, so the legal status must be deduced from taking into consideration all the laws regarding cats. By contrast, a growing number of local governments subscribe to the belief that cat populations can be controlled with maintained feral cat colonies, which offer a humane alternative to merely catching and killing cats.

An example of a city ordinance that allows for feral cat colonies to be legally maintained is found in Speedway, Indiana. People who maintain feral cat colonies are not considered the owners of these cats. However, owned cats may not be at large. This ordinance clearly distinguishes between an owned cat and a feral cat in terms of its legally being at large. (See Appendix F: Sample Feral Cat Colony Ordinance (Speedway, Indiana).)

The caretakers of the colony provide food, water, shelter, and/or veterinary care to the cats. The city can pick up loose cats and have them neutered; the cat's ear is slightly notched at the tip to indicate that it has been altered. Recognized groups can be designated by the city to trap, neuter, and return cats. They become the designee of the city.

7. Classifying Feral Cats as Pests

There is a distinction between feral cats and free-roaming cats. A free-roaming cat is any cat that roams free, but may include domestic cats whose owner allows them to be an inside/outside cat or totally an outside cat. Feral cats are wild and do not include domestic cats. A domesticated cat may become feral.

Some states do not define cats as feral or free-roaming. Wisconsin recently attracted attention when an advisory board to its Natural Resources Board recommended that free-roaming cats without collars be labeled an "unprotected species." While this did not pass, it drew the ire of cat fanciers because these cats could have been killed as a pest animal. Proponents of this measure argue that free-roaming cats destroy the habitat of some songbirds, while the cat fanciers said it was cruel to kill the cats.

8. Summary: Legal Considerations of Feral Cat Colonies

The attorney handling feral cat matters should consider the following issues:

- Are there local laws that allow for the maintenance of feral cat colonies?
- Are there local laws that prohibit the feeding of stray animals or animals at large?
- Are there local laws that prevent cats being at large?
- Are there local trap and kill laws?
- If there are trap and kill laws, is there a waiting period before the cats can be disposed of?
- Are there local laws allowing cats to be impounded like dogs?
- If impoundment laws apply, what is the waiting period before the cats can be disposed of?
- Are there local laws providing that a person who feeds an animal for a period of time is deemed the owner?
- Are there local laws that sanction the feeding of stray animals?

B. The Classic Clash of Birds and Cats: *State of Texas v. Stevenson*

There is no appellate case law in Texas dealing with feral cats. However, there was a recent case in Galveston, Texas, that underscores the clash of bird enthusiasts and people who care for feral cats. *State of Texas v. Stevenson* involved feral cats, an ornithologist who shot and killed one of them, and the toll booth operator who fed the cats. It embodies the classic tension between birders and cat fanciers. The case is an example of how individuals can become liable for their actions in the furtherance of attempting to help both birds and cats.

As reported in the *New York Times Magazine*:

> On the evening of Tuesday, Nov. 7, 2006, [Jim] Stevenson took a break from watching the election returns to look at some birds at San Luis Pass, a ripply channel connecting Galveston Bay to the gulf. Stevenson parked his white Dodge van with "Galveston Ornithological Society" bannered on its side, near the end of the San Luis Pass bridge, a tollway that connects Galveston Island to

> Follets Island. He found a spot in the low grass-speckled dunes and waited. Soon enough, he saw a handful of piping plovers, a federally listed endangered species. Then he saw something else: a scraggly cat stalking the plovers. A colony of about a dozen feral cats had been sleeping under the bridge. The cats liked to wander into the dunes for the same reason Stevenson did: the birds.
>
> "Piping plovers are tame, abiding little creatures," Stevenson told me. "They roost in the dunes and can't see or hear a cat creep up on them."
>
> Stevenson said he tried to protect the birds by capturing the cat. He failed and returned home frustrated. Late that night, he worried [about] the problem. "The American taxpayers spend millions of dollars to protect birds like piping plovers," he said, "and yet here are these cats killing the birds, and nobody's doing anything to stop it."
>
> The next morning, Stevenson decided to act. He loaded his .22 rifle in the van and took off for San Luis Pass. He spotted the same cat under the bridge. Stevenson put the animal in his sights and pulled the trigger.
>
> "The cat dropped like a rock," he said.
>
> Up on the bridge, a tollbooth attendant named John Newland heard the shot. Newland, a quiet man in his 60s, often fed the cats under the bridge. He called them his babies. Newland bolted out of his tollbooth and saw Stevenson's van. "I got you!" Newland screamed. "You quit shooting my cats!"
>
> Stevenson fled, but the cops caught up to him near his house. A Galveston police officer cuffed him, read him his rights and threw him in jail.[68]

Thus, the classic case of a bird fancier and a cat fancier at odds was born. A hailstorm of controversy ensued. Birders were in support of Stevenson while cat fanciers were appalled. The case played out with both sides presenting their conflicting views regarding whether or not feral cats indeed pose a threat to birds. Stevenson even alleged that he had received death threats regarding the case.

Stevenson, an ornithologist who teaches life science at College of the Mainland and Galveston College, was charged with animal cruelty. Part of the defense of the case was that feral cats were not covered in the Texas Penal Code because the law provided that a person commits the offense of cruelty if, without legal authority, he killed an animal "belonging to another." The toll booth operator, John Newland, contended that the cats were his. The case was premised on Newland owning the cats and that they were not feral.

The trial lasted a week and on November 16, 2007, the jurors stated that they were hopelessly deadlocked. They, too, obviously were just as divided as people are in general over this issue. The judge dismissed the case because the jury could not deliver a verdict.

The Texas Legislature in its 2007 session closed the loopholes for feral cats and stray dogs. They now enjoy the same protection under the code as animals fortunate enough to have owners. The statute now defines "animal" as follows:

> (2) "Animal" means a domesticated living creature, including any stray or feral cat or dog, and a wild living creature previously captured. The term does not include an uncaptured wild living creature or a livestock animal.[69]

Further, the legislature did away with the language "belonging to another," so there is no need for the animal to be owned for someone to be guilty of cruelty.

Interestingly, subsequent to the trial of Stevenson, John Newland, the toll booth operator who fed the cats, was charged with a Class C Misdemeanor for keeping too many animals. The charge was dropped because the applicable city ordinance defined cats as "domesticated members of the feline species," but the cats in question were not domesticated. The city asked Newland to agree to quit feeding the cats, but he declined. As it stands, he was not breaking a law.

C. Individual Animal Rescuer Liability

Many state and local laws regarding the rescue and placement of animals address humane societies and established animal shelters. However, growing numbers of individuals are becoming involved in the rescue and placement of abandoned animals.

1. Is the Individual Rescuer Subject to the Same Regulations as an Animal Shelter for Care of Rescued Animals?

Yes and no. Often state and local laws make exceptions for the person who is acting as a Good Samaritan and takes in a stray animal. These laws typically refer directly to established organizations, so it leaves open many questions the individual rescuer faces.

A. How Long Must an Individual Rescuer Keep an Animal Before Placing It?

It is wise for the individual rescuer to keep a stray animal at least as long as the local prevailing laws provide for the owner to reclaim the animal. The individual rescuer should make an effort to locate the original owner by networking with local shelters, posting signs, and watching for ads for lost animals.

B. Lawsuits Regarding Ownership

The individual rescuer is much more vulnerable to a lawsuit if the original owner seeks to reclaim the pet. Prevailing property laws set the statute of limitations on property cases, so the rescuer's exposure can extend for a number of years. Practically speaking, these suits do not occur very often, but it is certainly something to consider when counseling the individual rescuer or a small rescue organization.

2. *Consideration of State and Local Laws Addressing the Individual Animal Rescuer*

A. Spaying and Neutering

It is important to check state or local laws to determine if the individual rescuer has any responsibility for spaying and neutering animals before adopting them to new owners, or for securing an agreement that the pet will be altered by the new owner. Often the individual rescuer is exempt from these requirements, or omitted from the law altogether.

B. Number of Animals Allowed

Most local laws restricting the number of pets do not address the issue of ownership, but instead specify how many animals can be kept on the homeowner's premises. An individual rescuer is not exempt from these laws. This is very hard for rescuers to understand and even harder for them to heed. It is very common for the individual rescuer to be in violation of local laws limiting the number of animals that may be on the person's property.

However, some local laws allow multiple-pet licenses with an annual permitting fee and an inspection by local animal control. Sometimes these permits are allowed based on the size of the property and the distance of the animals to the next landowner. Kennel licenses also allow for additional animals to be kept on the premises, but they usually have restrictions on how and where such an operation can be run (generally, not in residential areas).

c. Vaccinations

Most laws regarding the requirement for a rabies vaccination do not distinguish between the owner or possessor of an animal. Therefore, the individual rescuer should follow local rabies laws.

3. Is the Individual Rescuer Subject to the Same Liability as the Rescue Organization?

The individual rescuer can potentially be sued for the negligent placement of an animal or the withholding of information just as an organization can. As a practical matter, the rescue organization is more vulnerable to this type of suit because of the perception that they should know more about the animal placed than a single individual. The individual rescuer is certainly subject to any claim of defamation.

XI. Probate Litigation Involving Animal Organizations

This section is not intended to be an exhaustive treatment of probate matters as they relate to rescue organizations. It is for the purpose of making counsel aware that this is an area of concern for any animal group that is named in someone's will.

Rescue organizations are sued more often over probate matters than liability issues. Why? A disgruntled family member may not understand why Fluffy and Fido got an inheritance and he got nothing. While there is probably a very good reason, this is why rescue organizations blessed with being beneficiaries under wills are also cursed with lawsuits challenging them. In representing rescue organizations, it is important to be aware of the possibility of these challenges.

A. Problems That May Arise When an Animal Organization Is the Beneficiary in a Will

An organization that is a named beneficiary in a will may find itself in a legal battle over the estate of the decedent. The rescue may find itself as a defendant in a probate issue. On the other hand, the organization will need to be prepared to defend its inheritance and what was rightfully willed to it.

1. Pretermitted Spouse Challenges Will Benefiting Rescue Organization

In a case addressing the issue of a pretermitted spouse, Tomsche challenged his late wife's will, which was executed one year prior to their marriage.[70] He sought to inherit under a statute benefiting a spouse left out of a will that was drawn prior to marriage. By doing so, he would gain that part of her devise to the society. In this case, the society defended its inheritance and while it did not get the original one-half, it was able to keep one-third.[71]

2. Capacity Challenged Regarding New Will in Favor of Rescue Organizations

In the case *Miami Rescue, Inc. v. Roberts*, Manucy was being taken care of by a longtime friend, Roberts, and had named Roberts as her sole beneficiary.[72] At a point, Manucy began to suffer a delusion that Roberts let her dog die, stole money from her, and abandoned her. While delusional, she changed her will to leave her estate to four charities, two of which were animal rescue groups. Roberts contested the will and the court found that Manucy was indeed suffering from an insane delusion that negated the later will.

3. Capacity Challenged Regarding New Will Excluding Rescue Organization

Capacity to execute a new will was challenged by the beneficiaries in a previous will, which included the Orlando Humane Society.[73] In *Hack v. Janes*, the Orlando Humane Society along with the other beneficiaries under the original will challenged the new will on the basis that a new beneficiary, Janes, had exercised undue influence over the decedent to change her will.[74] The court determined that Janes did not unduly influence the testator.[75] However, the important point is that rescue organizations may find themselves in a position to support a will or to challenge it in order to protect and guard the interests of the group.

4. Will Benefiting Rescue Organization Challenged Based on Improper Execution

An unreported case clearly shows how relatives, even ones that are not close to the decedent, will challenge a will particularly if the beneficiary is an animal organization.[76] In this case, Peterson left his estate to Lake of the Woods Humane Society in Minnesota. Because Peterson was ill and did not want to be seen, he had the will brought to his house and he signed there. His personal representative then took the will to the bank where a friend who worked at the bank compared the signature to the one on file with the bank. The friend, who was also a notary, notarized

Peterson's signature, got two witnesses to sign, and notarized their signatures, too. When Wolf, a distant relative, learned how the will was executed, she challenged it. In this case, the court allowed the will to stand because there was a self-proving affidavit and it was determined that the will expressed the wishes of the decedent.[77] Regardless, this case demonstrates that even a relative who was not close to the decedent will challenge a will benefiting an animal organization.

5. Relative Challenges Will Benefiting Rescue Organization Based on Construction of Will

In *Waldecker v. Pfefferle*, Lovett gave her entire estate to the Erie County Humane Society with the provision that they take care of her Siamese cat, Sinbad.[78] She was very clear in her will and stated:

> All my life I have been an animal lover and specifically have had cats as friends and companions, and therefore, all my property, whether real, personal or mixed, of whatsoever character and wheresoever situated, which I may now own or hereafter acquire, or have the right to dispose of at the time of my decease, I give, devise and bequeath to the Erie County Humane Society, 220 W. Perkins Avenue, Sandusky, Ohio 44870. I direct that the Erie County Humane Society shall out of the proceeds of my estate, pay for the proper care and veterinary service of my Siamese cat, SINBAD, for the remainder of its natural life.[79]

One might think this was clear and unequivocal, but not when money is involved and the recipient of it is an animal organization and a cat. Lovett died in 1996, and Sinbad died in 1997. The decedent's relatives argued that the will failed because the will was actually a trust for the cat. Clearly this was not the case, but that did not prevent this suit and a later one (barred by *res judicata*) from being filed to try to retrieve the money from the Humane Society. While this is an unreported case, it is important because it illustrates to what degree relatives will go to bust a will in favor of an animal rescue organization.

6. Rescue Organizations Challenge Distribution under a Will

Beneficiaries under a will often challenge the amount of distribution they receive. Rescue organizations are no different. In *Rodman v. Rodman*, two different humane societies were beneficiaries under a will.[80] Twenty-five percent of the estate was left to six beneficiaries, which included the two humane societies. No provisions were made for the remaining 75 percent of the estate. This suit ensued because the six argued to be viewed as four groups each getting 25 percent of the estate. While their suit failed, it does illustrate the point that rescue organizations armed with able counsel will challenge wills just like any other beneficiary.

B. How an Animal Organization Can Preserve Its Rights as a Beneficiary in a Will

The aforementioned cases illustrate the following points:

- Relatives have a tendency to challenge wills that favor animal organizations, particularly if the estate is substantial.
- Rescue groups that are beneficiaries of wills need to be prepared for legal challenges to their taking under wills.
- Rescue organizations have rights as beneficiaries that should be guarded for the benefit of the organization.
- Officers of charitable rescue organizations have a fiduciary duty to the corporation to protect its interests, including those derived from being a beneficiary of will.

The best way to protect a rescue organization from being embroiled in a probate dispute is to be proactive as much as possible. If the rescue organization is aware of the desired bequest prior to the execution of the will, then it is possible to work with the benefactor in the drafting of language that will ensure that his or her wishes are carried out. (Of course, the attorney for the rescue group should not draft the will, but suggestions may be made to protect the benefactor's intent.) If possible, the rescue group or its attorney should keep a copy of the will.

The more an organization can prepare for bequest issues, the better. In a famous case of animal as beneficiary, Leona Helmsley's bequest of $12 million for the care of her beloved dog Trouble, a Maltese, has been the subject of media frenzy particularly since the dog got more money than her brother or her grandchildren, two of whom were explicitly left out of the will.[81] Helmsley had created a trust for Trouble, but a New York judge ruled that Helmsley was "mentally unfit" when she made out her will, cut Trouble's inheritance to $2 million, gave the two disinherited grandchildren $3 million each, and placed the remainder in a charitable trust.[82] While the bequest does not benefit a rescue organization, this is another example of how leaving a large sum of money to benefit an animal can really stir some people and may end in litigation.

APPENDIX A

Application for Adoption

Fido & Fluffy Rescue Organization Application

Please understand that not all families and dogs are compatible. Every effort is made to match traits exhibited by a dog with the characteristics you desire in a dog. Our goal is to ensure the welfare of the dog by placements in the best possible home.

To be considered as an adopter, you must:

- Be 21 years of age or older and have identification showing present address.
- Be willing and able to invest the time and money required to provide proper care for the dog. The estimated annual cost to care for a dog is over $600.00.
- Be prepared to pay an application fee of $ __________ and an adoption fee of $ __________.
- Application and adoption fees are nonrefundable.
- Consent to reference checks and home visits.
- Complete application and sign required contracts.
- If for any reason contractual obligations are not met, the dog will become property of the Rescue. If for any reason the dog has to be "given up," it is to be returned to Fido & Fluffy Rescue.

I agree to the considerations above:

Signature ____

Date ____

THANK YOU FOR VISITING OUR SHELTER TODAY. How did you hear about the adoption program? ______________________________

Have you previously applied to adopt from Fido & Fluffy Rescue? _____

Name ____________________________ Driver's Lic. ________________

Home Phone _________ Work Phone _________ Cell Phone _________

Address ___________________ City/State ____________ Zip _________

Number of adults in household ______________________________

Number of children _________ Ages of children ___________________

Does anyone have allergies?________________________________
Explain: ____

Do you ☐ Own ☐ Live with relative ☐ Rent—Landlord's name and telephone number ____________________________________
If renting, do you have your Landlord's permission to have a pet? ☐ Yes ☐ No Is a deposit required? ☐ Yes ☐ No
Amount of deposit required ____________
Has the deposit been paid? ☐ Yes ☐ No
Do you live in a ☐ House ☐ Condo ☐ Apartment ☐ Mobile Home ☐ Townhouse What restrictions on size and/or number of pets apply in your subdivision or apartment complex? ______________________
Is there a breed restriction? ☐ Yes ☐ No
Do you operate a business in your home? ☐ Yes ☐ No Type _________

Animal Care Information

Why do you want to get a dog?______________________________
How long have you considered this decision? ____________ Do all the adults agree to this adoption? ☐ Yes ☐ No
Who will be responsible for the care of this dog? _________________

Where will the dog be kept during the day?_______ Night?_________
Where will the dog be kept when you go on vacation? __________ How many hours per day will the dog be left with no one home? ____ Where will it be kept when unattended? ____________________________
Will this dog spend most of its time ☐ Inside ☐ Outside
If outside, how may hours per day? ___________________________

What type of food will you feed this dog? ___________ Can you invest the time and effort to allow this dog to adjust to its new home? ☐ Yes ☐ No How long seems reasonable for this? ______________________
Explain: ____
____
____

If you have to give up the dog, what will you do with it?____________
If the dog were lost, what would you do? ________________________
____
____
____
____

If this dog requires surgery or special care, what would you do? _______
____
____

How much would you spend on your dog in an emergency situation? __
____
____

How many pets do you have? _________ List the pets you now have in your household:

Cat, Dog, etc.	Neu-tered	Sex	Age	Vac-cines Current	Kept Where	Breed	Weight

List the previous three pets you have owned:

Cat, Dog, etc.	Neutered	Kept Where	Time Owned	What happened to this pet?

What veterinarian will you use? ______________________________
Date of last visit: _____________

Dog Compatibility

Please explain why you picked the dog you are applying to adopt: _____
____
____

Do you want a dog for a: (mark all that apply) ☐ House Pet ☐ Watch Dog ☐ Children's Pet ☐ Company for Another Pet ☐ Hunting Dog ☐ Fighting Dog ☐ Companion ☐ Outside Dog ☐ Gift for: ________________
☐ If Watch Dog, explain: ______________________________
☐ Other: ____

What do you consider valid reasons for giving up a dog: (mark all that apply) ☐ Moving ☐ Fleas ☐ Vet bills ☐ Destructive ☐ Biting ☐ Grew too big ☐ Digging ☐ Chewing ☐ Unable to train ☐ Having a baby ☐ Barking too much/too little ☐ Too rough with children ☐ Other:______________

What will you do if the dog demonstrates the following behaviors?
Digging: ____
Chewing: ____
Not getting along with other pets:_________________________
Difficulty adjusting to household:_________________________

What preferences and personality traits are you wanting in a dog? ______
____
____

What breed of dog are you looking for? _________ Size/Weight________
Sex __________ Color ____________ Hair Length ________________
Activity level? ☐ Low ☐ Medium ☐ High ☐ Playful ☐ Lap Dog ☐ Laidback ☐ Outgoing
☐ House-trained ☐ Good with children ☐ Quiet ☐ Past puppy stage ☐ Gets along with cats ☐ Other: ___________________________
What traits do you consider undesirable? ______________________
____
____

Daily Care of This Dog

Where will this dog be kept: ☐ At home ☐ At work ☐ Both ☐ Other: ___
____

How will you keep this dog confined? (mark all that apply) ☐ House ☐ Kennel ☐ Fence ☐ Chain ☐ Patio ☐ Garage ☐ Leash ☐ Crate ☐ Other:
____

If crated or kenneled, how many hours a day? __________ Type and size of crate: __________________________

Do you have a yard? ☐ Yes ☐ No If yes: ☐ Partially fenced ☐ Open ☐ Completely fenced

If fenced: Type _____________ Height ____________ Condition ________

Where will this dog be allowed to relieve itself?____________________

You will probably have to house-train a new puppy. Please explain your method of house-training: ____

____

With any new dog, there may be "accidents" during the adjustment period. How will you handle the adjustment process? _______________

____

How often will you exercise this dog? ______________________________

Where and how will you exercise this dog?__________________________

How will you transport this dog? ___________ Do you plan to take this dog to training classes, and if yes, what kind? _______________________

How would you prevent heartworms? ______________________ Are the dog(s) you have at home now (or was the dog you last owned) on a heartworm preventative? ☐ No ☐ Yes—what type? _________________

Dogs often live in excess of ten years. Are you prepared to assume responsibility for that long? ☐ Yes ☐ No

Are you familiar with: ☐ Parvovirus ☐ Distemper ☐ Bordetella ☐ Rabies ☐ Parasites

Is there anything else that you think is important or that you would like to add? ____

I certify that the above information is true and correct. I understand that false information may result in nullifying this adoption. Fido & Fluffy Rescue reserves the right to approve or deny adoption to anyone for any reason. Fido & Fluffy Rescue's main interest is in the well-being and proper placement of the dog.

**DO NOT FORGET DRIVER'S LICENSE AND SIGNATURE ON BACK OF PICTURE COPY.

Signature of Applicant ______________________________ Date _________

Driver's License Number ____
Social Security Number____

**Note: You will be asked to show your driver's license and a copy will be made. For mail-in applications, please send a copy of the driver's license of all adults in the household.

Mail-in applicants, please copy a picture from the Web site of the dog you are adopting and sign the back of copied picture.

FOR COUNSELOR USE ONLY: ☐ APPROVED ☐ DENIED
DOG'S NAME ____________________ TAG NUMBER ________________
SHELTER NUMBER __________ BREED ________ SEX ____ AGE_____
MICROCHIP NO. (if any)____
COMMENTS: ____

APPENDIX B

Adoption Contract

Fido & Fluffy Adoption Contract

This Adoption Contract is entered into between Fido & Fluffy Rescue (hereinafter Rescue) and ____________________ (hereinafter Adopter) on this ___ day of ______, 20__, regarding the adoption of:

Name of dog: ____
Gender: ____________ Spayed or Neutered: _____ Date Altered:______
Breed:______________ Approximate Age: _______
Rabies Tag No.:______ Veterinarian: ____________
Microchip No. (if any): ____
Rescue No.: ____

Adopter has provided the following identifying information:

Full name (includes any names ever used): ______________________
Home Address: ____
Business Address: ____
All Telephone & Cell Numbers: ________________________________
Fax Number: ____________ E-mail Address: ___________________
Driver's License Number: ___________________ (attach a copy of the front and back of license which is made a part of this Agreement)
Date of Birth: ____
Place of Birth: ____

Adopter agrees as follows:

1. That _________ (name of dog) will be an inside dog and will not be kept in a yard or dog run, but will live inside the home with Adopter;
2. That provisions will be made for the dog to relieve itself on a regular basis;
3. That when the dog is in any yard it will be attended and not alone in the yard without access to get back into the house;
4. That all fences will be a minimum of six (6) feet in height if the dog is to be allowed off lead in the yard;
5. That the dog will be given daily exercise which is in addition to being let out in the yard to relieve itself;
6. That Adopter will provide quality food, water, and veterinary care for ________ (name of dog) for its entire life including heartworm and flea prevention;
7. That Adopter will comply with all state and local laws regarding vaccinating and licensing of the dog;
8. That Adopter will not cosmetically alter the dog by cropping its ears or docking its tail;
9. That the dog is not to be used for resale or profit;
10. That the dog is not be used for any illegal purpose including but not limited to any combative use including dogfighting, sparring, and rolling;
11. That the dog will not be used as a guard dog and will not be trained as an attack or protection dog;
12. That the dog will not be tethered or chained regardless of any local laws that may allow such;

13. That if for any reason that Adopter is unable to keep ______ (name of dog), Adopter agrees to return the dog to Rescue and such return of the dog will be at Adopter's expense;
14. Not to give the dog away if Adopter cannot or does not want to keep the dog;
15. That should Adopter want to give the dog away to a third party, Rescue may at its election allow the transfer of the dog if the third party is approved by Rescue;
16. That the dog will wear a collar with current rabies tag and an identification tag in addition to any microchipping or tattooing;
17. That when the dog is outside of the house or an enclosed structure it will be on a leash of not more than six (6) feet long and that a Flexi-Lead (retractable lead) will never be used;
18. That the dog will never be transported loose in the open bed of a truck;
19. That the dog will not ever be left unattended in a vehicle;
20. That Adopter will treat the dog with respect and dignity, will regularly groom it, and will devote time each day to it;
21. That Adopter will always supervise the dog with children;
22. ________ (name of dog) has been evaluated by a veterinarian, ________________________________ (medical records attached), and the following is known about the dog's medical status: ________________________;
23. Adopter acknowledges that he/she fully understands that while ________ (name of dog) has been evaluated by a veterinarian, the full medical history of the dog is not known because it is a rescue dog. Adopter agrees that any and all veterinary bills are the sole responsibility of Adopter from the date of this contract through the entire lifetime of the dog. Adopter holds harmless Rescue for any medical condition that ________ (name of dog) may have including any disclosed and all unknown to Rescue; ________ (name of dog)'s temperament has been evaluated by Rescue and the following is known: ________________________;
24. Adopter acknowledges that there is no way that Rescue can fully evaluate _______ (name of dog)'s temperament in a rescue situation and that the dog's full personality will not be known until it has settled down in Adopter's home. Adopter assumes all responsibility for the actions of the dog from the date of this contract

throughout the entire time Adopter owns the dog. Adopter agrees to hold harmless and indemnify Rescue for any and all actions of the dog from the date of this contract forward;

25. Should Adopter fail to comply with any of these provisions, this shall be deemed a breach of contract and Rescue has the right to regain possession of the dog. Adopter agrees that should Rescue make demand for the return of the dog, that the dog will be returned in no more than one (1) day (24 hours) from the date of the demand whether written or oral. Should Adopter fail to return the dog and Rescue has to seek return from a court of competent jurisdiction, Adopter agrees to pay liquidated damages of $1000.00 in addition to attorney's fees, cost of court, case expenses, and any other expense to which Rescue may show themselves to be entitled. Adopter agrees that the adoption fee is forfeited if any of the terms of this contract are breached;
26. This contract is to be governed by the laws of the State of ______ and any disputes will be handled and resolved in ______________ County, ________;
27. Adopter agrees and acknowledges that no guarantees have been made by Rescue regarding the health and or temperament of _________ (name of dog). Adopter agrees to accept the dog based on these terms and that if for any reason the dog is returned that the adoption fee is forfeited;
28. Adopter agrees and acknowledges that there will be at least two home visits, one scheduled before the dog is placed and one unscheduled (without notice) after the dog is placed, and that Adopter will make his or her home available for inspection including the yard and any other area to which the dog has access;
29. Adopter acknowledges that all information contained herein is true and correct, and if any information is found to be false, that the adoption will not be accepted and that if the dog is already placed, that the dog will be immediately returned to Rescue upon demand;
30. Adopter acknowledges that this is the full agreement of the parties and that there are no other representations or promises made other than the ones stated herein;
31. Adopter acknowledges that this Agreement is binding on the entire family of Adopter, his or her heirs, next of kin, executors, assigns, and administrators; and

32. This contract reflects the entirety of the Agreement between Adopter and Rescue. If any part of it fails, that will not affect the other provisions from being in full force and effect.

For and in consideration of $ _____ as an adoption fee paid to ________ (rescue organization), the rescue organization hereby transfers ownership of ________ (name of dog) to Adopter.

AGREED:

ADOPTER
Printed Name: ____
Date: ____

ACCEPTED:

FIDO & FLUFFY RESCUE
BY: (Printed Name of Fido & Fluffy Rescue Representative) __________
Title: ____
Date: ____

Adopter's Initials _____ Page 5 of 5

APPENDIX C

Additional Contract Terms for Certain Breeds

Additional Terms to Fido & Fluffy Agreement When Adopting Certain Breeds

(E.g., American Pit Bull Terrier, Staffordshire Bull Terrier, American Staffordshire Terrier, Akita, German shepherd, Doberman pinscher, Chow Chow)

33. Adopter acknowledges that there are special considerations in adopting a *(insert breed)* and that while there may be exceptions, Adopter agrees to abide by extra terms to ensure the best possibility for success of the adoption.
34. Adopter agrees that he/she will not adopt, buy, or accept another dog smaller than ________ (name of dog adopted), the *(insert breed),* for the safety of the smaller dog.
35. Adopter agrees that he/she will not adopt, buy, or accept another dog that is the same gender as ______________________ (name of dog adopted).
36. Adopter agrees that any dog that he/she adopts, buys, or accepts will be of the same size or larger than ______________________ (name of dog adopted) and will be opposite of ______________'s gender.
37. Adopter agrees that he/she will contact Rescue prior to adopting, buying, or accepting another dog so that the addition of any new dog can be discussed with Adopter.
38. Adopter agrees that if Rescue counsels against Adopter accepting any new dog, that Adopter will abide by suggestion of Rescue. Rescue agrees to fairly assess the situation so that there will not be potential safety problems for Adopter or _____________ (name of dog adopted).
39. Adopter agrees that he/she will have the new dog evaluated by Rescue or someone suggested by Rescue at the expense of Adopter if deemed necessary by Rescue.
40. Adopter agrees that if any new dog is accepted by Rescue, then Adopter agrees that ___________________ (name of dog adopted) and the new dog will be crated separately whenever Adopter is away from the home, and they will not be left unattended together in any fenced yard.
41. Adopter agrees that if he/she accepts a new dog and if the situation proves untenable with ____________________ (name of dog adopted) and the new dog, Adopter will find other accommodations for the new dog, not ________ (name of dog adopted).
42. Adopter agrees to feed ________ (name of dog adopted) and any new dog separately in places where each dog cannot see the other dog, and to pick up bowls after feeding.
43. Adopter agrees to supervise ________ (name of dog adopted) and the new dog while playing with toys and not to leave toys out.
44. Adopter agrees to have _________________ (name of dog adopted) trained in obedience and to commence training within thirty (30) days of adoption. Adopter agrees that if he/she gets

another dog, that dog will likewise be obedience trained within thirty (30) days of adoption.

45. Adopter agrees that if he/she adopts, buys, or accepts another dog, the new dog will be spayed or neutered.
46. Adopter agrees that __________________ (name of dog adopted) will never be allowed off lead in a dog park, or off lead unless in a fenced, secure enclosure, with the exception of any sanctioned dog events that ________ (name of dog adopted) trained for and is properly entered (e.g., agility, tracking, or search and rescue).
47. Adopter agrees that __________________ (name of dog adopted) will not be allowed off lead around dogs not owned by Adopter and that __________________ will be kept at least six (6) feet from such dogs.

APPENDIX D

Short Adoption Contract Form (Limited Use)

Fido & Fluffy Short Form (Limited Use for Known Adopter Only)

Name of Dog: __________________ Breed: ________________________
Age: ______ Spayed/Neutered: ________ Microchip: ______________
This Agreement is between ______________________ of Fido & Fluffy Rescue, who is placing the above described dog, __________________ (name of dog), and (Adopters).

Adopters agree as follow:

1. To have ________ (name of dog) evaluated by a competent veterinarian, to give it all vaccinations indicated, and to have it tested for heartworms and parasites on an annual basis or as needed by its condition;
2. If ________ (name of dog) is heartworm positive, to put it on Heartgard to treat for any heartworms;

3. To have ________ (name of dog) spayed within thirty (30) days after this adoption, but if it is heartworm positive to have it spayed/neutered as indicated by the veterinarian;
4. To keep ________ (name of dog) groomed and its nails clipped;
5. To administer heartworm and flea preventive on a regular basis as prescribed by the veterinarian;
6. That ________ (name of dog) will be an inside dog and will have access to the outside to relieve itself;
7. To love, pet, nurture, properly care for, and always treat ________ (name of dog) with the kindness and dignity it deserves;
8. That if for any reason Adopters cannot care for or keep ________ (name of dog), it will be returned to Fido & Fluffy Rescue;
9. That if any of the provisions of this Agreement are violated and/or not met, ________ (name of dog) will be returned to Fido & Fluffy Rescue immediately upon demand;
10. That if there are any costs associated with the return of ________ (name of dog) to Fido & Fluffy Rescue, such costs will be paid by the Adopters;
11. That Adopters will ensure that the Minor Children will abide by this agreement;
12. The following is known about ______________ (name of dog): ____________;
13. The consideration for this Agreement concerning ________ (name of dog) is an adoption fee of ________________, which has been paid by the Adopters.

Signed this __________________ day of ____________, 20__.

For and in consideration of $ _____ as an adoption fee paid to _________ (rescue organization), the rescue organization hereby transfers ownership of ___________ (name of dog) to Adopters.

AGREED BY ADOPTERS:

ADOPTER ____

MINOR ____
MINOR ____

ACCEPTED: ____
FIDO & FLUFFY RESCUE
By: Printed Name: ____

APPENDIX E

Owner Relinquishment Agreement

Owner Relinquishment Agreement

1. Name of Owner: ______________________________
2. Address of Owner: ______________________________
3. Telephone Nos. of Owner: ______________________________
4. Driver's License No.: (attach copy of license to agreement) _____ ______________________________
5. Animal relinquished: ☐ Dog ☐ Cat ☐ Bird ☐ Ferret ☐ Other: ______ Microchip: ______
6. Age of Animal: ____ Gender: ____ Altered: _____ Weight: ______
7. Reason for Relinquishment: ______________________________
8. Name of Animal: ________________ Breed: ______________
9. Was animal obtained from a breeder? ________ If so, breeder's name and number: ______________________________ ______________________________.
10. Was the animal obtained from a rescue organization? _______ If so, name and number of organization: ________________ ______________________________.
11. Is the animal up-to-date on vaccinations? _____ Heartworm preventative? ____
12. Name and number of veterinarian: ______________________________ ______________________________
13. Are there any temperament issues with the animal and if so describe: ______________________________ ______________________________ ______________________________.
14. Is there anyone who co-owns the animal with you? ______ If so, please provide the name, address, and telephone numbers for the co-owner (includes spouse, boyfriend, girlfriend, or life partner): ______________________________.

I, ______________________________, owner of the above described __________________ (dog, cat, bird, ferret, other), hereby relinquish any and all interests and rights in the animal and transfer them to _______ __________________________ (name of rescue organization). I certify that I am the owner of the animal free and clear of any other interests. I certify that this animal is free of any dangerous or vicious propensities and that I have not failed to disclose any such information. The information given is correct and complete. I fully understand that this contract fully extinguishes all ownership rights I have in this animal and conveys them to ______________________________ (rescue organization). I fully understand that ______________________________ (rescue organization) becomes the owner of the animal immediately upon my execution of this agreement and ________________ (rescue organization) may place the animal for adoption or may do whatever they see fit and appropriate for the animal. I fully acknowledge there are no guarantees that the animal will be adopted. I agree to release, hold harmless, indemnify, and defend ______________________________ (rescue organization) including their board of directors, officers, volunteers, agents, and members from any and all claims of any kind whatsoever that may be made as a result of the relinquishment and ultimate disposition of the ______________ (dog, cat, bird, ferret, other) as afore described.

Signed this ________________ day of ____________ , 20__.
Owner of ____
Witness on Behalf of ______________________________________
(rescue organization)

APPENDIX F

Sample Feral Cat Colony Ordinance (Speedway, Indiana)

Ordinance No. 1060

An Ordinance to Amend Chapter 7.05 of the Speedway Municipal Code Regarding Animals

WHEREAS, the presence and proliferation of free-roaming cats in the Town of Speedway, Indiana (the "Town") poses a burden and nuisance to its citizens and the general public as well as a potential threat to the health and safety of individuals, household pets and other animals in the Town; and

WHEREAS, the Town Council of the Town of Speedway, Indiana (the "Town Council"), being the governing body of the Town, has determined that a process to allow for the registration, caretaking, feeding, vaccination and trapping, neutering and return of free-roaming cats through a managed program is in the public interest of the Town; and

WHEREAS, the Town Council now desires to amend Section 7.05 of the Speedway Municipal Code to provide for such managed program.

NOW THEREFORE, BE IT ORDAINED by the Town Council of the Town of Speedway, Indiana that Chapter 7.05 of the Speedway Municipal Code is amended to read as follows:

1. **Section** 7.05.010 of the Speedway Municipal Code is hereby deleted in its entirety and replaced with the following:

> **7.05.010 Definitions.** For the purposes of this Chapter, the following terms shall have the following meanings:
>
> **"Animal"** means any living, nonhuman vertebrate creature.
>
> **"Authorized employee"** means any employee of the Speedway Police Department or the Speedway Street Department.
>
> **"Colony"** means one or more free-roaming cats, whether unmanaged or managed.
>
> **"Colony caretaker"** means a person who provides food, water, and/or shelter for free-roaming cats in a managed colony. Colony caretakers shall not be deemed to be owners or keepers of such animals.
>
> **"Designee"** means an organization recognized by the Speedway Police Department/Animal Control that uses the trap-neuter-return method for stabilizing and reducing the free-roaming cat population.

"Ear tip" means a surgical procedure removing approximately four-tenths of one inch (0.4") from the tip (pinna) of the left ear of an unowned, free-roaming cat at the time of spay/neuter and vaccination to identify that cat as having been spayed or neutered and vaccinated as part of the trap-neuter-return method to stabilize and reduce the free-roaming cat population.

"Free-roaming cat" means any homeless, stray, feral or undomesticated cat.

"Managed colony" means a colony of free-roaming cats that is registered with the Speedway Police Department/Animal Control or its designee and is maintained by a colony caretaker using the trap, neuter, return method to stabilize and reduce the free-roaming cat population.

"Town" means the Town of Speedway, Indiana.

"Town Council" means the Town Council of the Town of Speedway, Indiana.

"Veterinarian" means a person licensed to practice veterinary medicine in the State of Indiana.

"Wild Animal" means an animal whose species usually lives in the wild or is not domesticated and includes the following:

(a) Red and gray foxes;
(b) Coyotes;
(c) Wolves (all species); and
(d) Bears

2. **Section** 7.05.030 of the Speedway Municipal Code is hereby deleted in its entirety and replaced with the following:

7.05.030 Confinement of cats and dogs.

It shall be unlawful for the owner or any other person having the possession, care, custody or control thereof, to permit any dog or cat to run at large upon public streets or walks or parks or upon private property of the Town, other than the dog or cat owner's property, unless such dog be attached to a leash of not more than twelve feet in length, of sufficient strength to restrain such dog and each dog or cat shall be kept under the control of the person accompanying it.

(1) Duty of the Police Chief of the Speedway Police Department. It shall be the duty of the Police Chief or an authorized employee, to apprehend all dogs and cats running loose and place them in a kennel designated by the Town Council. It shall also be the duty of the Police Chief or an authorized employee, to notify the owners of all licensed dogs and cats having an identification tag attached to them when apprehended that the dog or cat is being held in the kennel. The Police Chief or authorized employee, may, at his/her discretion, release any apprehended cat found to be bearing identification in the form of an ear tip.

(2) Dogs and cats to be held five days. All dogs and cats apprehended for running loose shall be kept in the kennel until claimed or for a period of five days, whichever occurs first. If the dog or cat is not claimed within five days, the animal shall be turned over to the Marion County animal control's office, or destroyed.

Cats in the kennel found to be bearing identification in the form of ear tip, may, at the discretion of the Police Chief or authorized employee, be released to its managed colony, or the Town's designee.

(3) Owner claiming licensed dog or cat. The owner of a licensed dog or cat apprehended for running loose may obtain the cat or dog by paying to the Clerk-Treasurer of the Town a boarding fee of Two Dollars ($2.00) for each day or fraction of a day thereof the cat or dog is in the kennel plus a fine of Thirty Dollars ($30.00). A "day" as used in this section shall be defined as twenty-four hours from the time the dog or cat is actually placed in the kennel.

(4) Owner claiming unlicensed dog or cat. The owner of any unlicensed dog or cat apprehended for running loose may obtain the unlicensed dog or cat by paying to the Clerk-Treasurer of the Town a boarding fee of Two Dollars ($2.00) for each day or fraction thereof the dog or cat is in the kennel plus a fine of Forty

Dollars ($40.00). A "day" as used in this section shall be defined as twenty-four hours from the time the dog is actually placed in the kennel.

3. Section 7.05.070 of the Speedway Municipal Code is hereby deleted in its entirety and replaced with the following:

7.05.070 Vaccination required.

(a) Each owned dog and cat over the age of three months which is kept in the Town shall have been vaccinated against rabies by a veterinarian within the preceding three hundred sixty-five days. It shall be unlawful for a person to own a dog or cat not in compliance with this section.

(b) Upon the vaccination of an animal a certificate of rabies vaccination shall be issued at least in triplicate with one copy given to the animal owner. Such certificate shall be presented upon request by any police officer of the Town. A metal vaccination tag shall be worn by the animal at all times.

4. Section 7.05.071 of the Speedway Municipal Code is hereby added to include the following:

7.05.071 Unauthorized Caretaking Prohibited.

(a) It shall be unlawful to provide food, water or shelter to a colony of free-roaming cats (1) that is not registered with the Speedway Police Department/Animal Control or its designee, and (2) without implementing the trap, neuter, return method as set forth in this Chapter.

(b) A person who violates any provision of this section shall be punished as provided in section 7.05.190 of this Chapter; provided, however, a fine imposed for the first such violation shall not be less than Thirty-Five Dollars ($35.00); subsequent or continued violations may also result in the animals' impoundment by the enforcement authority.

5. Section 7.05.072 of the Speedway Municipal Code is hereby added to include the following:

7.05.072 Managed Free-Roaming Cats.

(a) The Speedway Police Department/Animal Control or its designee, in order to encourage the stabilization and reduction of the free-roaming cat population in the Town, may:

(1) Trap any free-roaming cat in a humane manner;

(2) Have the cat surgically sterilized, ear-tipped, and vaccinated against rabies by a licensed veterinarian;

(3) Release the cat for adoption or other disposition in accordance with law or to a colony caretaker who will maintain the cat as part of a managed colony of free-roaming cats.

(b) The enforcement authority may impound free-roaming cats in violation of this Chapter and dispose of the cats in accordance with applicable law. Any free-roaming cat impounded by the enforcement authority that bears an appropriate ear-tipping indicating it belongs to a managed colony may, at the discretion of the Speedway Police Department/Animal Control or its designee, be returned to its managed colony unless illness or injury present an imminent danger to public health or safety. Seriously ill or injured cats with no reasonable prognosis for humane rehabilitation for survival outdoors may be humanely euthanized.

6. Section 7.05.073 of the Speedway Municipal Code is hereby added to include the following:

7.05.073 Colony Caretaker Responsibilities.

(a) Colony caretakers shall abide by colony management guidelines devised by the Speedway Police Department/Animal Control or its designee regarding the provision of food, water, shelter and veterinary care for cats within the managed colony.

(b) A person who violates this section shall be punished as provided in Section 7.05.190 of this Chapter; provided, however, a fine imposed for the first such violation shall not be less than Thirty-Five Dollars ($35.00); subsequent or continued violations may result in the caretaker's removal from management of the managed colony.

PASSED AND ADOPTED on the 22nd day of May, 2006.

Notes

1. United States Census Bureau, May 2006.
2. American Pet Products Manufacturer, Industry Statistics and Trends (2007–2008).
3. 26 U.S.C. 501(c)(3) (1986, as amended) (emphasis added).
4. Charitable Immunity and Liability, TEX. CIV. PRAC. & REM. CODE ANN. ch. 84 (2007).
5. *Id.* at § 84.004(a).
6. *Id.* at § 84.006 (added by Acts 1987, 70th Leg., ch. 370, § 1, effective Sept. 1, 1987).
7. *Id.*
8. *Id.*
9. *Id.* at § 84.005 (added by Acts 1987, 70th Leg., ch. 370, § 1, effective Sept. 1, 1987).
10. *Id.* at § 84.006.
11. *Id.* at § 84.004(d), (e).
12. TEX. TRANSP. CODE ANN. § 601.072 (2008).
13. TEX. CIV. PRAC. & REM. CODE ANN. § 84.007(a).
14. Lieberman v. Powers, 70 Mass. App. Ct. 238, 873 N.E.2d 803 (Sept. 26, 2007) (Parent brought an action against the director of the Animal Rescue League of Boston because a cat jumped down on the head of his child, injuring the child. The cats were being shown in a small room and were free. Summary judgment in favor of shelter was overturned because court determined there was a fact issue about the advisability of showing cats in this manner.).
15. Koepke v. Martinez, 84 S.W.3d 393 (Tex. App.-Corpus Christi 2002), *petition denied*.
16. Dunnings v. Castro, 881 S.W.2d 559, 562 (Tex. App.-Houston [1st] 1994), *writ denied, as cited by* Koepke v. Martinez, 84 S.W. 3d 393, 396.
17. Koepke v. Martinez, 84 S.W.3d 393 (Tex. App.-Corpus Christi 2002), *reh'g overruled*, 133 S.W. 3d 633, Dissenting Opinion on Motion for Rehearing en Banc.
18. *Koepke* at 633.
19. *Id.* at 634.
20. *Id.* (emphasis added).
21. *See, e.g.*, Earl v. Piowaty, 42 A.D.3d 865, 839 N.Y.S.2d 861 (N.Y. App. Div. 2007) (A young boy was bitten by a dog when he reached down to pet it. The boy alleged he was talking softly to the dog, but another account

indicated the boy was excited about winning a game and shouted at the dog when he grabbed it while it was asleep, which startled the animal. The mother of the boy that was attacked sued both the owner of the dog and the rescue organization that placed the dog on a theory that they had knowledge of a known propensity of this dog for biting, as apparently a child had been slightly nipped previously by the dog in a game of Frisbee.); Claps v. Animal Haven, Inc., 34 A.D.3d 715, 825 N.Y.S.2d 125 (N.Y. App. Div. 2006) (Suit involving a person who was bitten by a dog that was being shown for adoption by a rescue while in a pet supply store. Held that the rescue organization had no knowledge of vicious propensity.); Galgano v. Town of N. Hempstead, 840 N.Y.S.2d 794, 41 A.D.3d 536, 2007 WL 1704612, 2007 N.Y. Slip Op. 05223 (N.Y. App. Div., June 12, 2007) (No. 2006-00735, 5679/04) (Shelter was sued for placing a dog that subsequently bit someone. Summary judgment granted because shelter did know of dog's propensities and the fact that the dog was turned in was not tantamount to knowledge.); D.C. v. Petco Animal Supplies Stores, Inc., 16 Misc. 3d 1114(A), 2007 WL 2116499, 2007 N.Y. Slip Op. 51413(U) (N.Y. Sup. Ct., July 16, 2007) (No. 1670/06) (Petco was sued for a dog bite that occurred on a store's sidewalk while a rescue organization was conducting adoptions. The rescue did not know of any dangerous propensity of the dog, so that was imputed to Petco, and the complaint was dismissed.); Chase v. City of Memphis, 971 S.W.2d 380 (Tenn. July 21, 1998) (No. 02S01-9703-CV-00019) (City held liable based on release of dogs that had bitten contingent on owner enrolling them in obedience school. City failed to check that owner had followed conditions of release of dogs. Dogs had been involved in numerous incidents and later killed a neighbor. City liability for damages was capped.).

22. It is incumbent on the rescue to understand the breeds that they are placing in order to adopt them safely and responsibly. Each breed of dog has its own characteristics based in part on the purpose for which they were bred. Greyhounds are bred for speed and hunting. Therefore, these dogs will be prey-driven, and while they are great pets, they might not be a candidate for placement with cats or particularly rabbits. The new owner also needs to be aware that if they ever get loose, they dart like wild and are hard to catch. Labrador retrievers are bred to retrieve game. Therefore, these dogs will have a tendency to retrieve and usually like water. An adopter who has a swimming pool should thus be cautioned that there can be a risk of the dog drowning if it does not know how to find the steps of the pool in order to get out. German shepherds have been bred to be guard dogs and can be fiercely loyal to a fault. They also are herding dogs, and their tendency to nip at the heels of other dogs and even people can get the dogs in trouble. Terriers were historically bred to hunt small prey, so the potential owner needs to understand that this might not be the dog to let loose at the dog park. Chihuahuas are a toy breed bred as a companion dog, but ounce for ounce, they can be one

of the most aggressive dogs. They cannot be underestimated because of their size. Special care should be taken in placing them with small children both for the sake of the child and these tiny dogs.

23. Thomas v. City of Minneapolis & Sharon Keller/Underdog Rescue, 2007 WL 1121465 (Minn. Ct. App.).
24. *Id.*
25. *Id.*
26. *Id.*
27. Morgan v. Kroupa, 167 Vt. 99, 702 A.2d 630 (1994).
28. *Id.* at 101.
29. Lamare v. N. Country Animal League, 170 Vt. 115, 743 A.2d 598 (1997).
30. *Id.* at 602.
31. Woods v. KittyKind, Inc., 2005 WL 1404712, 2005 N.Y. Slip Op. 50911(U) (N.Y. Sup. Ct.); *see, e.g.*, Feger v. Warwick Animal Shelter, 29 A.D. 3d 515, 814 N.Y.S. 700 (allegation that shelter knowingly placed a stolen champion cat for adoption).
32. *Id.* at 1.
33. *Id.*
34. *Id.*
35. The author contacted three of the major animal shelters in Houston, Texas. There are no ordinances that purport to divest ownership of animals after a particular time, and Texas does not have lost property statutes.
36. Animal Hosp. of Elmont, Inc. v. Gianfrancisco, 100 Misc. 2d 406, 418 N.Y.S.2d 992 (N.Y. Dist. Ct. July 20, 1979). *See, e.g.*, Moskoff v. City of Akron, 1994 WL 162282 (Ohio Ct. App. 9th 1994) (Dogs were seized by Humane Society but another shelter, Buckeye Animal Shelter & Services, claimed the dogs. Because Humane Society euthanized some of the dogs, Buckeye argued that the society was not trying to protect dogs from harm.).
37. *Id.* at 418.
38. Snead v. Soc'y for the Prevention of Cruelty to Animals of Pa., 929 A.2d 1169, 2007 WL 1990510 (Pa. Super.), 2007 PA Super 204. *But see, e.g.*, Churchwell v. City of Big Spring, 2004 WL 905951 (Tex. App.-Eastland 2004) (City sued for failing to euthanize dog that was returned to his owner after it had bitten someone. Summary judgment granted based on sovereign immunity and failure to properly state a claim pursuant to the Texas Tort Claims Act.); Hegarty v. Addison County Humane Soc'y, 176 Vt. 405, 848 A.2d 1139 (Apr. 2, 2004) (Horses were seized by Humane Society without a warrant and owner sued for conversion. Court held society had statutory authority to seize horses without warrant.).
39. *Snead*, 2007 WL 1990510 at 1175.
40. *Id.*
41. Arguello v. Behmke, No. HNT-C-14002-06, 2006 WL 205097 (N.J. Super. Ct. Ch. Div. Jan. 26, 2006).
42. 2006 WL 205097 at *4.
43. *Id.* at 4.

44. *Id.* at 7.
45. Stearns v. McManis, 543 S.W. 2d 649 (Tex. Civ. App.-Houston [1st] 1976).
46. *Id.*
47. Humane Soc'y of Dallas v. Dallas Morning News, 180 S.W. 3d 921 (Tex. App.-Dallas 2005), no writ.
48. Barnett v. Tarrant County Humane Soc'y, 608 S.W. 2d 823 (Tex. Civ. App.-Tarrant 1980), no writ; *See also* Harris v. Bucks County S.P.C.A., 7 Pa. D. & C.3d 489 (Pa. Com. Pl. 1977) (SPCA employee denounced a proposed reenactment of a 112-mile cattle drive done in 1778 by George Washington as "callous exploitation." Court ruled SPCA was stating its side and no defamation.).
49. Tabaj v. Fayette Soc'y for the Prevention of Cruelty to Animals, 53 Pa. D. & C.4th, (Pa. Com. Pl. July 23, 2001) (No. 00361 Sept. Term 2000).
50. Atlanta Humane Soc'y v. Mills, 274 Ga. App. 159, 618 S.E. 2d 18, 5 Fulton County Daily Rep. 2150 (June 3, 2005) (No. A03A2480, A03A2481), *reconsideration denied* (July 6, 2005), *cert. denied* (Oct. 24, 2005).
51. *Id.*
52. Murphy v. Daytona Beach Humane Soc'y, 176 So. 2d 922, (Fla. App. 1st June 29, 1965) (No. G-256).
53. *Id.* at 926.
54. TEX. HEALTH & SAFETY CODE ANN. § 828.002 (added by Acts 1991, 72nd Leg., ch. 373, § 1, effective Jan. 1, 1992).
55. *Id.* § 828.003 (added by Acts 1991, 72nd Leg., ch. 373, § 1, effective Jan. 1, 1992).
56. TEX. HEALTH & SAFETY CODE, ch. 828 Dog & Cat Sterilization, § 828.001(2) (2007).
57. L.A. MUN. CODE, ch. V, Public & Safety Protection, art. 3, § 53.06 (amended by Ord. No. 160,401, effective Nov. 1, 1985).
58. Code 1968, § 6-56; Ord. No. 69-985, § 2, 7-2-69; Ord. No. 70-2, § 2, 1-6-70; Ord. No. 71-942, § 1, 5-25-71; Ord. No. 85-2217, § 2, 12-12-85; Ord. No. 92-1449, § 6, 11-4-92; Ord. No. 07-148, § 8, 1-31-07. CITY OF HOUSTON ORDS., art. 4 Dogs & Cats, div. 3, § 6-101.
59. Ordinance 323 (adopted Dec. 17, 1987), § 3. CODE OF ORDS., Hilshire Vill., Tex., ch. 2, Animal Control, art. 2.300 (1987).
60. HARRIS COUNTY ANIMAL REGS., Rabies Vaccinations.
61. HARRIS COUNTY ANIMAL REGS., Leash Law.
62. HARRIS COUNTY ANIMAL REGS. § 4, Restraint & Impoundment.
63. Christman-Resch v. City of Akron, 159 Ohio App. 3d 673; 825 N.E. 2d 189, 2005 Ohio 715 (Ohio Ct. App.-9th Feb. 23, 2005) (No. 22140).
64. *Id.* at 676.
65. Justice for Animals, Inc. v. Lenoir County S.P.C.A., Inc., 360 N.C. 48, 619 S.E.2d 494 (N.C. Ct. App. Feb. 1, 2005) (No. COA04-69) (cats were determined to be feral by a poke method and then euthanized before the 72-hour waiting period elapsed). *But see* Havlik v. Multnomah County, 164 Or. App. 522, 992 P.2d 942 (Dec. 22, 1999) (No. CA A105086) (employee

at animal control filed worker's compensation claim based on depression caused in part by overcrowding due to the change in policy of holding feral cats).

66. Harris County Animal Regs. § 4, Restraint & Impoundment.
67. *See, e.g.*, Beck v. Cornell Univ., 42 A.D.3d 609, 839 N.Y.S.2d 5752007 N.Y. Slip Op. 05800 (N.Y. App. Div.-3d July 5, 2007) (No. 501364) (A feral cat colony was being maintained on campus, but then the university decided to trap and relocate cats. Employees were instructed not to feed cats, but plaintiff did and posted signs on his cat food that it was private property. He was fired and filed suit alleging in part that it was cruelty to not feed cats. Court found otherwise.).
68. Bruce Barcott, *Kill the Cat That Kills the Bird?*, N.Y. Times Mag., Dec. 2, 2007, *available at* http://www.nytimes.com/2007/12/02/magazine/02cats-v--birds-t.html.
69. Tex. Penal Code, § 42.092 Cruelty to Non-Livestock Animals (a)(2).
70. Estate of Mason v. Fort, 616 So. 2d 322 (Miss. Apr. 1, 1993) (No. 90-CA-1070).
71. *Id.* at 325.
72. Miami Rescue, Inc. v. Roberts, 943 So. 2d 274, 31 Fla. L. Weekly D2979 (Fla. App.-3d Nov. 29, 2006) (No. 3D06-1037). *See also In re* Estate of Vanoni, 798 A.2d 203, 2002 PA Super 98 (Pa. Super. Apr. 5, 2002) (No. 501 EDA 2001), *reargument denied* (June 6, 2002) (Decedent's will leaving entire estate to the local humane society challenged by his two children on the basis of capacity. Held against humane society.).
73. Hack v. Janes, 878 So. 2d 440, 27 Fla. L. Weekly D676 (Fla. App. 5th Mar. 22, 2002) (No. 5D00-2394).
74. *Id.*
75. *Id.* at 444.
76. *In re* Estate of Peterson, 2006 WL 1529520 (Minn. App.). *See also In re* Estate of Hoffmann, 1998 WL 612911 (Minn. App.) (cancer society challenged later will benefiting humane society and unsuccessfully alleged fraud).
77. *Peterson*, 2006 WL 1529520 at 2.
78. Waldecker v. Pfefferle, 2002 WL 31521467 (Ohio App. 6th).
79. *Id.* at 4.
80. Rodman v. Rodman, 21 N.C. App. 397, 204 S.E.2d 695 (May 1, 1974) (No. 742SC64).
81. Sewell Chan, *Leona Helmsley's Unusual Last Will*, N.Y. Times (Aug. 29, 2007), http://cityroom.blogs.nytimes.com/2007/08/29/leona-helmsleys-unusual-last-will.
82. Jane Wells, *Trouble for Leona Helmsley's Trouble*, CNBC (June 16, 2008), http://www.cnbc.com/id/25197630/site/14081545.

CHAPTER 9

Remedies in Animal-Related Litigation

JOAN E. SCHAFFNER

I. Introduction

Animals are classified as personal property under the law. This classification dictates the remedies available for harm to or loss of an owned animal or pet. Traditionally courts have been reluctant to recognize value of a pet beyond the fair market value of the individual animal. Increasingly, however, as humans' relationships with their pets have changed and their pets have become more like family members, courts are recognizing that their value to their owners may include noneconomic damage. This is a dynamic area of the law as it relates to pets and thus it is important to follow the recent scholarly writings on the subject, newly enacted statutes, and new cases in your jurisdiction and others addressing the availability of noneconomic damages in an animal law case.

The availability of remedies to owners of pets is of great import to lawyers and clients alike. Although clients may wish to file suit against someone who has wrongfully injured or killed their pet as a matter of principle, and/or to publicize the issue, for example in the case of a grossly negligent veterinarian, most clients do not have the resources to bring suit if the available monetary remedy will not at the very least exceed the cost of the suit. The lack of a truly compensable remedy for the loss of one's pet has prevented many people from filing suit. Unless the animal is an economically valuable race horse or show dog, for example, the fair market value of the animal is negligible compared to the costs of suit and thus few suits are filed. As courts recognize that the true value of the animal includes companionship to the owner, and that many owners are as attached to their pets as they are to other human family members, thus warranting emotional distress damages and consequential damages for lost wages and other expenses for caring for an injured pet, more suits will be brought and owners will be more accurately compensated for their losses.

In the most egregious cases, punitive damages may be available and this will provide increased incentive to file suit and hold the wrongdoer accountable. Moreover, specific remedies, such as injunctive relief, may also be available in certain situations, providing another incentive to file suit.

This chapter explores the various remedies potentially available in a suit involving an animal. As the other chapters of this book make clear, there are a variety of animal-related cases. Cases arising in property, tort, contract, wills and trusts, and others will each invoke a particular remedy. The remedy available is dependent upon the substantive claim brought. Each of the substantive chapters address what type of remedy may be available. This chapter addresses the remedy in more detail and focuses on the valuation and specific issues that arise in seeking the remedy once liability has been established.

This chapter is organized around the function and form of the remedy rather than the substantive basis for relief. Remedies fall into two primary categories: substitutionary and specific relief. Substitutionary relief is monetary relief based upon the factfinder's valuation of the owner's loss. The owner neither gets what she started with nor what she was promised. Thus the money is substitutionary in two ways: (1) the money substitutes for the owner's original entitlement and (2) the factfinder's valuation substitutes for the owner's valuation of her loss. Substitutionary remedies perform one of the following functions: compensation, punishment, or restitution. Specific relief seeks to either avoid harm, undo the harm, or repair the harm in kind. Such remedies include injunctions, specific performance or cancellation under a contract, and return of property. Their functions are either preventive, coercive, declaratory, or ancillary (an aid to enforce the primary remedy). The more common relief is substitutionary, as in the case of an owner seeking monetary compensation for the loss of or injury to her animal. However, specific relief is available in cases of contracts to purchase animals, return of an animal stolen or lost and recovered by another, or judicial orders to prevent the killing of or harm to animals, often in "public" cases such as the enforcement of the Endangered Species Act. Since this book is a resource for the attorney engaged in "private" animal law cases of the type that the typical practitioner will encounter, remedies involving "public" cases to enforce federal statutes or treaties will not be addressed. Finally, although the context of a given animal law case varies, this chapter will focus primarily on relief to the owner of an animal for the harm to or loss of the animal and utilize this terminology. When other contexts arise they will be addressed as appropriate.

II. Damages

A. Compensatory

Compensatory damages are designed to place owners in their "rightful position," the position they would have been in had the wrong not occurred, by "compensating" them as closely as possible for the harm to their animal. The key to achieving an accurate "rightful position" is to provide compensation for all losses proximately caused by the wrong and to value each loss based upon relevant market and/or the reasonable owner's valuation. The following subsections will address each potential loss involved in the harm to one's animal and discuss the likelihood of recovery and the means for valuing the loss if recoverable.

1. Loss to the Animal

The animal does not have separate standing under the law to seek damages, thus no court has allowed recovery for the animal's pain and suffering. For example, in *Oberschlake v. Veterinary Assoc. Animal Hospital,*[1] Poopi was taken to the vet to have its teeth cleaned; however, while the dog was under anesthesia, the vet tried to spay it although it had already been spayed as a puppy. Poopi's owners sought recovery for Poopi's own emotional distress of being wrongfully "spayed" twice. The court stated succinctly: "Although Poopi was obviously directly involved in the incident, a dog cannot recover for emotional distress—or indeed for any other direct claims of which we are aware. We recognize that animals can and do suffer pain or distress, but the evidentiary problems with such issues are obvious. As a result, the claims on Poopi's behalf were . . . not viable."[2]

2. Loss to the Owner

A. Economic Property Loss

The owner may recover the property loss of an animal, which traditionally is the fair market value, if any, and "some special or pecuniary [economic] value to the owner, that may be ascertained by reference to the usefulness and services of the dog."[3] If the animal is injured, the recovery is the difference between the fair market value before and after the harm[4] or the costs to repair, for example, veterinary costs. Generally, the recovery for injury to the pet is the costs of veterinary treatment with some courts limiting the amount of such recovery to the animal's fair market value.[5] Courts have recognized that limiting recovery to fair market value generally provides minimal compensation because most pets have little or no market value. In such cases, some courts allow owners to receive full compensation of their out-of-pocket economic losses.

For example, in *Hyland v. Borras,*[6] Borras's bulldog trespassed onto Hyland's property and attacked her ten-year-old shih tzu, causing serious injuries. The veterinarian costs and other related out-of-pocket expenses were $2,500, but the "replacement cost" for the shih tzu was $500. Although the normal rule for loss of personal property where the "repair costs outweigh the replacement costs" is either "the diminution in the value of the property, or its replacement costs,"[7] the court stated the rule must be flexible to properly compensate plaintiff under the circumstances. The court noted that "animals kept for companionship have no calculable market value beyond the subjective value of the animal to owner, and that value arises purely as a result of their relationship and the length and strength of the owner's attachment to the animal."[8] The court here found that Hyland had raised, loved, and devoted time to her dog since it was a puppy and thus Borras must be held liable for her recovery expenses in order to properly compensate her. Moreover, the court said, awarding the economic losses that defendant caused will deter owners from negligently allowing their dogs to run loose.[9] This court clearly understood the difference between normal personal property with value to the owner that generally diminishes with time as it becomes used and a pet, whose value to the owner increases with time as their relationship develops. Thus while a ten-year-old Ford car may be worth much less than the current market value for the current model, a ten-year-old shih tzu is worth much more than the current market value of a "new" shih tzu.

There are, of course, cases where the animal is economically valuable. For example, if the animal is pedigreed and/or used to breed, or the animal provides special services to a disabled owner,[10] the economic loss is considerable and recoverable if properly supported with evidence of the economic loss. Often in the case of pedigreed animals, there is a market for the specific animal, and thus the fair market value for loss of the animal is fairly easily established by introducing evidence of the price paid for the animal, offers made by others to purchase the animal, and the price of similar animals. Secondary evidence includes proof of the animal's registration papers, physical characteristics, and prior breeding, as well as awards won by the animal in shows or races.[11]

Further, a consequential loss may include the lost income likely to have been received by the owner from the animal.[12] It is more difficult to establish potential future earnings from the animal; however, evidence of past income received and demonstration of the likelihood of continued income may suffice. In the case of animals used for breeding, courts generally refuse to compensate for the loss of future progeny as too speculative but may include the animal's breeding potential in the valuation of the lost animal.[13] Other losses that may be recoverable include reimbursement for money spent on the animal for training, microchipping, or other similar expenses.[14]

For example, in *Bueckner v. Hamel*, the defendant shot a Dalmatian and Australian shepherd owned by the Hamels.[15] Both dogs were relatively young, two and three years old respectively, purebred, and registered with reputable clubs. The Hamels introduced evidence that they had purchased the dogs with the intent to breed them, that they had already picked out a male for the Australian shepherd, and that the dogs could be expected to breed once per year and produce six to eight puppies; they also introduced as evidence the market price for the puppies. In this case the dogs had not yet been bred. The court allowed the introduction of the evidence to assess the value of the two dogs themselves but disallowed recovery for prospective progeny. The court upheld the trial court's damage award of $1,825 as legally and factually sufficient.[16]

In another case, *Petco v. Schuster*, Licorice, a 14-month-old miniature schnauzer, slipped its leash and ran away from a Petco employee who had taken the dog out for a bathroom break during its grooming, and was ultimately killed in traffic. The owner recovered the replacement value (fair market value) of Licorice ($500), her expenses to send Licorice to training school ($892), and her expenses for microchip implantation ($52.40).[17]

B. Noneconomic Property Loss

Generally courts refuse to include noneconomic damage as a component of the animal's "special or intrinsic value." However, scholars and some courts are beginning to recognize the loss of companionship as a noneconomic element of damage from the loss of a pet.[18] Traditionally, courts have recognized the "intrinsic" value of certain types of property, such as heirlooms or trees, generally when the property otherwise has no market value. For example, one's family heirlooms, or family films, while having no real market value, have a special value to the owner and courts may award a reasonable amount for the "intrinsic" value of the item lost.[19] Moreover, the intrinsic value of a tree includes an aesthetic value based on the appearance of the tree and a utilitarian value based on the shade the tree provides.[20] Thus the intrinsic value of the animal to the owner is the value of their companionship and may be recoverable.

Additionally, under traditional rules, the owner can often recover lost utility from the property. Thus, the key is to demonstrate to the court the utility the property served to the owner and to compensate the owner for a reasonable valuation of that lost utility.[21] In the case of a typical family pet, the primary utility of the pet is to provide the owner "companionship." Thus, the owner under traditional property law should be able to recover the loss of companionship resulting from the loss of the pet. However, few courts have awarded loss of companionship, either because they refuse to recognize companionship as the utility of the pet or because they find that the pet has a market value and thus intrinsic value is not recoverable.[22]

One reason offered for the reluctance to award noneconomic damages is the difficulty in setting an appropriate amount reflective of the actual value lost. However, there are many instances of courts awarding noneconomic damages where valuation is difficult, such as for emotional pain and suffering. Types of evidence that could be used to both support the award of loss of companionship and determine a reasonable value for such loss include

- Statistics from studies of the human/animal bond and social and emotional interactions that have shown that some 80 percent of animal owners treat their pets as members of family, 50 percent keep photos of their pet in their wallet or on their desk at work and/or share their bed with their pets, and 25 percent celebrate their pets' birthdays;
- During the Katrina disaster many people risked their life rather than leave their animals behind;
- The benefits of the bond between pets and their owners that include alleviating boredom, preventing loneliness and isolation, helping patients recuperate, and reducing depression, anxiety, and stress in many individuals; and
- Evidence of the money the owner has spent on the pet for food, medical care, entertainment, socializing, and sheltering.[23]

c. Economic Consequential Loss

In addition to the direct loss of the animal and the lost income from the animal, the owner may incur additional consequential losses caused by the defendant's wrong. For example, in *Petco* the owner sought reimbursement for lost wages incurred from her time taken off from work searching for Licorice before the dog was found dead.[24] In general, consequential damages are limited when too remote, speculative, or avoidable. The Texas court in *Petco* held these damages unrecoverable since the lost property, Licorice, was unrelated to the owner's job.[25] The court distinguished claims for lost property from claims for personal injury where lost wages are recoverable in order to make the plaintiff whole. Moreover, under a breach of contract theory, based on the grooming contract with Petco, the court held the lost wages too remote and thus unforeseeable. Such damages were not contemplated by the parties under the contract and were thus not recoverable.[26] However, had the owner demonstrated that a reasonable person would search for his or her dog and introduced evidence of the reasonable costs incurred from such a search, she may have been able to recover something for that expense.

An owner may incur costs related to the care of an injured animal. No cases have addressed this type of recovery. One interesting theory advanced by animal law litigator Adam Karp is that such a loss may be analogized to a repair cost since the owner would otherwise have to hire a vet tech, for example, to care for the injured animal. In the human context courts generally allow the cost of nursing services to care for an injured or sick child or spouse, and a minority of courts allow the recovery of lost wages if the parent or other spouse remains home from work to care for the injured person.[27] However, normally the veterinary costs would be considered the "repair costs" recoverable in an animal case.[28]

D. Noneconomic Personal Loss to Owner

Some states may allow owners to recover for their own emotional injury caused by the loss of their pet under a theory of intentional or negligent infliction of emotional distress. The basic elements of such a claim are (1) defendant's outrageous behavior; (2) intent to cause emotional distress to owner; (3) owner's severe emotional suffering; (4) the owner in proximity to witness the outrageous conduct; and (5) in the case of negligent infliction, physical harm to the owner.[29] Most cases fail because either the defendant's conduct is not deemed outrageous enough, the owner's emotional distress was not severe enough, the owner did not witness the conduct, and/or the defendant did not know the owner of the animal killed. However, in the most outrageous case where, for example, a person intentionally and with premeditation shoots a neighbor's dog merely because the dog is on the person's property, and the owner is present, recovery may be available.[30]

Interestingly, a 1981 case from Hawaii, *Campbell v. Animal Quarantine Station*,[31] allowed recovery for the emotional distress of an entire family that resulted from the improper and negligent handling and transport of their pet dog resulting in the dog's death from heat prostration. Although the family did not witness the death nor even the dead body and were not themselves physically injured, the court held that Hawaii recognizes a claim for the emotional distress resulting from the negligent destruction of property, citing *Rodrigues v. State*.[32] In *Rodrigues*, the state highway department was found negligent for failing to protect an owner's home from severe water damage caused by the failure of the highway culvert to drain surface waters after it became blocked with beach sand and was forced to compensate the homeowners for their resulting emotional distress. Interestingly, the dissent in *Rodrigues* faulted the majority for allowing such recovery, arguing that "the policy behind recognizing the value of an attachment to material possessions [is flawed]. This attachment should neither be encouraged by society nor made a basis for recovery in a court of law in an age when man has surrounded himself with a veritable plethora of material possessions approaching the limits of what even an affluent society needs or can afford."[33] The Hawaii legislature abolished the claim for emotional injury from loss of property unless it also results in "physical injury to or mental illness of" the person.[34] While most courts still refuse to allow such recovery, the loss of one's pet is distinguishable from the loss of "material possessions" and may persuade some courts, today, to allow such recovery for "sentient" property.

There may also be a basis for recovery of emotional distress damage "arising from the breach of duties incident to . . . contracts dealing with intensely emotional noncommercial subjects such as preparing a corpse for burial."[35] In *Petco*, the court refused recovery for emotional distress for breach of the grooming contract stating that such a contract does not fall into the narrow class of contracts dealing with intensely emotional noncommercial subjects. "These 'special relationship' cases generally have three common elements: (1) a contractual relationship between the parties; (2) a particular susceptibility to emotional distress on the part of the plaintiff; and (3) the defendant's knowledge of the plaintiff's particular susceptibility to the emotional distress based on the circumstances."[36] Arguably, a contract to provide care for one's sick or injured animal might fall within that narrow class, although no cases to date have so held.

Nevertheless, if the owner does have a basis for recovering emotional distress, the valuation is similar to other claims that result in emotional injury to a person. For example, to value the emotional loss from witnessing the killing of a pet, the lawyer should introduce evidence of the owner's loss of appetite, insomnia, depression, anger, withdrawal, inability to concentrate, nightmares, and visits to a counselor or therapist proximately caused by the event. The owner should demonstrate that there was a reasonable need for such counseling. Generally, the more horrific the defendant's conduct, for example the manner of killing the pet, the more value is assigned to the emotional injury. This is appropriate since the level of emotional injury does relate to the nature of the wrong. However, if there is also a claim for punitive damages, the lawyer should be careful to distinguish the valuation of the emotional injury designed to *compensate* the owner from the punitive damage designed to *punish* the defendant, discussed later.

Moreover, it is important to distinguish the direct *emotional injury to the owner* caused by the defendant's actions and the *loss of companionship* to the owner from the loss of their pet. The first loss arises from the claim that the defendant directly harmed the owner in causing the owner's emotional injury, the second loss arises from the defendant destroying the owner's property, their pet, and from the owner's utility loss of that property, the companionship, discussed previously.

E. State Statutes Allowing Recovery

Since 2000, a few states (e.g., Connecticut, Tennessee, and Illinois) have enacted statutes that expressly allow for damages for the loss of a pet, including noneconomic damages. The basic elements of these statutes are definition of "pet" or "companion animal"; conduct establishing liability; the damages allowed; and exemptions from liability.

i. **Definition of "Pet"** The statutes generally define what animal qualifies as a "pet" for purposes of recovery. The primary purpose is to limit recovery of damages to certain species and to those who own the animals for purposes of companionship rather than farming, research, or other commercial purpose. Thus, for example, Connecticut defines "companion animal" as "a domesticated dog or cat that is normally kept in or near the household of its owner or keeper and is dependent on a person for food, shelter, and veterinary care, but does not include a dog or cat kept for farming or biomedical research practices."[37] Interestingly, Illinois allows recovery for any "animal" to which a person has a right of ownership, neither limiting the owner's utility of the animal to that of companionship nor the species to dog or cat.[38]

ii. **Conduct Establishing Liability** States may hold a person liable for intentional or negligent conduct that harms an animal. Connecticut limits liability to "any person who intentionally kills or injures a companion animal."[39] Similarly, Illinois limits liability to a person who engages in "an act of aggravated cruelty" as defined under the criminal code or killed by a person acting in bad faith.[40] Under Tennessee's statute, a person may recover when a "pet . . . is killed or sustains injuries that result in death caused by the unlawful and intentional, or negligent, act of another or the animal of another."[41] However, in the case of negligence, the animal must have suffered the death or injury while on the property of its owner or under the control and supervision of its owner.

iii. **Damages Allowed** Each of these states allows economic and non-economic or punitive damages within certain limits. Economic damages allowed include "expenses for veterinary care, the fair monetary value of the companion animal, . . . burial expenses"[42] and "other expenses incurred by the owner in rectifying the effects of the cruelty, pain and suffering of the animal."[43] Noneconomic damages include "emotional distress suffered by the owner."[44]

Tennessee limits noneconomic damages to compensate "for the loss of the reasonably expected society, companionship, love and affection of the pet" to $5,000.[45] Punitive damages (discussed more fully in the next section) are expressly provided under statute in Connecticut and Illinois with proscribed limits. For example, Illinois limits such damages to "not less than $500 but not more than $25,000 for each act of abuse or neglect to which the animal was subjected."[46] These states also allow recovery for reasonable attorneys' fees.[47]

iv. Exemptions The state may also exempt certain actors from specific types of damages. Negligent veterinarians are exempt from liability for noneconomic damages in Tennessee. Veterinarians in Connecticut are exempt from punitive damages and attorneys' fees "while following accepted standards of practice of the profession."[48] Moreover, state actors and animal-related nonprofits are similarly exempt from liability for punitive damages and attorneys' fees.[49]

B. Punitive or Exemplary Damages

Punitive damages are designed to punish the wrongdoer. They do not really "remedy" anything but are sometimes necessary to make it economically feasible for private plaintiffs to enforce important rights. Given the problems with obtaining adequate compensatory damages for the loss of one's animal because of the reasons stated previously, the ability to recover punitive damages in the egregious cases make it more economically feasible for owners to file suit.

Punitive damages generally are recoverable for the death of an animal under a tort theory if the owner can prove, by clear and convincing evidence, fraud or malice on the part of the defendant.[50] Punitive damages are not recoverable for breach of contract.

Punitive damage awards are highly sensitive to the specific facts of the case. The more egregious the conduct and malicious the intent, the greater opportunity for a large award. The factors considered in the determination of a punitive damage award include degree of reprehensibility, defendant's wealth, reasonable ratio to compensatory damages, profitability, analogous civil or criminal fines, and the potential for multiple liability.[51] One problem owners may encounter is with the "reasonable ratio to compensatory damages" factor, given the recent Supreme Court cases that have held that a ratio of punitive damages to compensatory damages that exceeds single digits may be unconstitutional under the Due Process Clause.[52] The Court does allow a larger ratio when compensatory damages are quite low.[53] This is the situation in most animal cases.[54] Thus it is unlikely the Court would find that a ratio in excess of nine in a case where a pet was maliciously killed would be unconstitutional since the fair market value, and hence typical compensatory damages awarded, is generally minimal.[55]

Further, some states impose treble damages on owners whose dogs cause injury after they had been ordered retrained. Thus, for example, in

Massachusetts: "If a dog which the selectmen of a town, chief of police of a city or the county commissioners, or, upon review, a district court, shall have ordered to be restrained shall wound any person, or shall worry, wound or kill any live stock or fowls, the owner or keeper of such dog shall be liable in tort to the person injured thereby in treble the amount of damages sustained by him."[56]

III. Restitution

In the "pure" sense, restitutionary relief is designed to restore to the plaintiff all that the defendant wrongfully gained at the plaintiff's expense. In many cases, the amount of damages to compensate for the plaintiff's loss is equal to the restitutionary relief if the value of the loss to the plaintiff equals the value of the gain to the defendant. However, in certain cases the value of the property to the plaintiff and defendant may differ or the defendant may use the property to realize profits. In these cases restitutionary damages may exceed compensatory damages.

In a criminal case, courts often order the defendant to pay restitution to the owner or third party even though they are not parties to the criminal case. The restitution here is generally for the purpose of compensating the owner or third party but may also be deemed punitive in nature. For example, when a person kills another's pet and is criminally charged for animal cruelty, the court may order the defendant to pay the owner restitution. Thus, in the *Bueckner* case discussed previously, Bueckner, the defendant who killed the Hamels' Dalmatian and Australian shepherd, had been prosecuted criminally and ordered to pay the Hamels $375 in restitution. Bueckner asserted the defense of accord and satisfaction in the civil case, arguing that the restitution he paid to the Hamels discharged any obligation he might owe them.[57] The court disagreed but did offset the amount of compensatory damages awarded by the amount of restitution. There is no indication how the criminal court arrived at the $375 for restitution.

Similarly, restitution is also common in criminal cases where an owner's dog injures or kills another's pet, the court finds that the dog is "dangerous," and orders the owner of the dog to pay restitution to the other pet's owner. In these cases the dog is generally impounded by animal control and the court further orders the owner to pay restitution to animal control for the expenses incurred while the dog was impounded.[58] The restitution here is clearly designed to compensate animal control.

Restitution is also used to reflect specific relief to remedy in-kind. Thus when a person has wrongful possession of an animal, the owner may sue the person for replevin and seek return of the animal in restitution.[59] If the owner of the animal uses the animal for breeding, racing, or showing, for example, the owner can recover for the lost income he would have realized during the time he was not in possession of the animal under compensatory damages as described previously. Furthermore, the owner may have a claim for disgorgement of profits against the defendant, if the defendant, while in wrongful possession of the animal, gained a profit from the use of the animal.

IV. Other Specific Relief

A. Injunctions

Injunctive relief is an equitable specific remedy designed to avoid future harm. The majority of animal law cases in which injunctive relief is sought arise in the "public" law context under federal statutes or treaties, for example, the Endangered Species Act.[60] Similarly, injunctive or declaratory relief is a common remedy sought under the Administrative Procedure Act to seek compliance or enforcement of the Animal Welfare Act.[61] Such cases are beyond the scope of this text.[62]

Injunctive relief is equitable and thus requires a showing that the legal remedy is inadequate. For injunctions involving property, the issue is whether the property is "unique." Thus, in injunctive relief cases involving animals, the primary issue will be whether the court deems the animal "unique."

Parties may frequently seek preliminary injunctive relief to maintain the status quo and avoid irreparable harm during the pendency of the lawsuit. The equitable criteria for granting preliminary relief to a plaintiff are (1) strong likelihood of success on merits; (2) possibility of irreparable injury to plaintiff if the relief is not granted; (3) balance of hardships favoring plaintiff; and (4) advancement of public interest.[63] Some courts consider the criteria more as a sliding scale or balancing test weighing the probable success on the merits and the balance of hardships to the parties.[64] Thus, if the plaintiff can show either a very strong case on the merits or severe irreparable harm, the court is more likely to award the preliminary relief. Irreparable harm involves more than mere substantial harm. Irreparable harm is harm that cannot be adequately compensated with monetary damages either because of the nature of the harm or because of the difficulty in calculating the damage accurately to compensate for the harm.

Typical cases involve Thoroughbred horses or purebred dogs for their return or to prevent their sale by another. In *Kinderhill Select Bloodstock, Inc. v. United States*,[65] the Internal Revenue Service seized Thoroughbred horses from the owner as a levy for back taxes owed. The IRS had scheduled the sale of the horses and the owner sought a preliminary injunction preventing their sale until ownership of the horses had been determined. The owner successfully argued that the horses were unique because of the difficulty in assessing their fair market value and that, in fact, these specific horses were the horses he wanted and other horses would not adequately compensate him. The court agreed and held that the horses were indeed unique and thus the harm to the owner would be irreparable if they were sold. The court relied on cases where certain property such as works of art and historical artifacts were deemed unique.[66] The court nevertheless denied the preliminary injunction due to the owner's failure to demonstrate likelihood of success on the merits.[67]

Similarly, in *Saunders v. Regeer*,[68] the court found that Misty, a pedigreed, registered, female Irish setter was unique and issued a preliminary injunction against the sale or removal of Misty pending trial. In a rather eloquent description of the value of dogs, the court stated:

> There is no need to dwell upon the value of dogs to mankind, the seeing-eye dog to the blind, the dogs used in warfare, to carry food and messages under fire and through most hazardous conditions, those canines used to detect criminals, lost persons and to protect our property and, most importantly, the companionship they afford human beings, whether sick or well, young or old. Lord Byron in his "Inscription on the Monument of a Newfoundland Dog" attests to the undisputed value of a dog when he says,
>
> > "The poor dog, in life the firmest friend,
> > The first to welcome, foremost to defend."[69]

In contrast, the court in *Wortz v. Patterson*[70] concluded that the controversy over the sale of Muffin, a trotting horse, was essentially financial. The court was persuaded by the facts here. Muffin's owner could have resolved the controversy by paying defendant some $5,000 to avoid the horse's sale by the defendant. The court held that plaintiff was not entitled to an injunction here where she could regain title to Muffin "by settling her financial problems with the defendant."[71]

An interesting case involving wolf dog owners' request for a preliminary injunction is *Michigan Wolfdog Assoc., Inc. v. St. Clair County*.[72] The owners of wolf dogs challenged the constitutionality of the Michigan Wolf-Dog Cross Act that defined all wolf dogs as dangerous; imposed limitations on ownership of wolf dogs, including sterilization, microchipping, prohibition of transfer, and special enclosures for the dogs; and allowed officers to enter private property without a search warrant to seize such dogs, and kill them if the dog potentially exposed a human or other animal to rabies or injured a human or other animal.[73] The owners challenged the Act on the following grounds: void for vagueness and depriving plaintiff of adequate notice and opportunity for hearing in violation of due process, unreasonable search and seizure in violation of the Fourth Amendment, and discriminating against them in violation of equal protection under the law.[74] The issue of irreparable harm here did not turn on the uniqueness of the animal but rather on whether the owners or their dogs would suffer irreparable harm if the preliminary injunction enjoining enforcement of the Act was not issued. The owners here argued irreparable harm to their dogs arising from (1) forced sexual sterilization of the dog, (2) microchipping, and (3) harm from their economic inability to construct adequate facilities or transfer their dog to one who can. The court admitted that sterilization would cause irreparable harm to the dogs but that this harm was not outweighed by the threat of harm to the public from enjoining the statute along with the court's finding that the plaintiffs were unlikely to win on the merits.[75]

Nuisance cases are the other classic cases for injunctive relief involving animals. Owners that allow their dogs to bark incessantly and at odd hours of the night, or fail to maintain their premises adequately, thus causing injury to their neighbors' well-being, may be found liable of creating a private nuisance.[76] The court will issue an injunction in such cases where the nuisance and resulting injury is proven. However, "equity will not interfere where the apprehended nuisance or injury is doubtful, contingent, conjectural, or merely problematic."[77]

B. Specific Performance

Many animal cases involve contracts that address, for example, the purchase and sale, breeding, care, training, or burial of an animal. Basic contract principles apply. Specific performance is an equitable remedy and requires a showing that the legal remedy is inadequate; in other words, when the contract involves property deemed "unique chattel." As in the cases for injunctive relief, the primary issue in specific performance cases involving animals is whether the court deems the animal to be "unique chattel."

In *Harris v. Barcroft*,[78] defendant purchased Dobra, a Doberman pinscher, and "agreed that plaintiff would have the first pick and one half of the puppies from the first two litters and the right to select the stud for these breedings."[79] After problems arose with the breeding efforts, plaintiff brought suit for specific performance and defendant countered requesting rescission of the contract. The appellate court disagreed with the trial court's finding that Dobra, of championship caliber, was not unique.[80] However, the court found that plaintiff came to equity with unclean hands after attempting to take Dobra illegally from defendant, and denied specific performance.

Similarly, the court in *Morris v. Sparrow*[81] held that a certain horse, Keno, was unique. Sparrow filed suit for specific performance under a contract in which Morris had agreed to deliver Keno to Sparrow in consideration for Sparrow's work at Morris's cattle ranch. While Sparrow worked at the ranch, he broke and trained Keno in his spare time. The court found that "when one has made a roping horse out of a green, unbroken pony, such a horse would have a peculiar and unique value."[82]

An interesting case involving a contract to train a race horse is *Finnegan v. Foraker.*[83] Finnegan owned a farm where he trained standard-bred racehorses. Foraker contracted with Finnegan to have full control over the horse for six months to train the horse; they would split the costs and prize winnings realized; and if the horse improved the agreement could be extended another year. Handsome Count, a trotter, was in poor shape when Finnegan took it. Finnegan cared for and trained Handsome Count, which won its third and sixth starts under Finnegan's guidance. Eventually, Finnegan turned the horse out for several weeks to rest and when it returned to racing it did not do well. Foraker demanded the horse's return and Finnegan refused. Foraker's wife then took Handsome Count in the predawn hours from Finnegan, and the Forakers gave the horse to another trainer. Finnegan filed suit for the return of the horse and an injunction forbidding anyone else to train it for at least one year pursuant to the contract.[84]

The court first noted that the proper theory of the case was for specific performance under the contract together with incidental injunctive relief necessary for enforcement.[85] Foraker argued that equitable relief was improper as Finnegan had an adequate remedy at law, replevin, if he established legal right to his possession and that specific performance was inappropriate because the contract was for Finnegan's personal services. The court determined that "Finnegan bargained for a chance to realize his gain based upon the purse winnings of the horse[ ] under his control. . . . If the horse has been wrongfully taken from his control, then he is either deprived of the opportunity to establish the potential value of his services or, at best, his share of the winnings will be made to depend upon the abilities of another trainer. In neither event can the true value of his services be ascertained."[86] Quoting *Elliott v. Jones*, the court stated:

"[A] particular horse with unique or peculiar traits and qualities different from horses in general, and which has promises of development by training so as to become valuable for speed in racing contests, has a prospective but now unascertainable value, and, therefore, a contract respecting it is properly a subject for a decree for specific performance, because of the inadequacy of the legal remedies."[87] The court further stated that replevin was inadequate because the right to possession during the action requires the posting of a bond equivalent to the value of the property and "since a bond for the value of Handsome Count would have no relation to his potential purse-winnings, and . . . his potential monetary realization from the horse cannot be accurately determined while the animal is out of his possession,"[88] it is inadequate.

To summarize, an animal will be deemed unique property under many circumstances but it does depend upon the type of animal, its characteristics, and the owner's use of the animal. Generally, when the specific relief involves Thoroughbred horses or pedigreed dogs to be used for racing or breeding, the court will find the animal is unique. Moreover, if the person has a unique relationship with the animal, as for example Sparrow's relationship to Keno, or Finnegan's agreement relating to Handsome Count, the court will find the animal is unique and award specific equitable relief if otherwise warranted.

V. Attorneys' Fees and Ancillary Remedies

A. Attorneys' Fees

The American Rule is that each party bears the costs of their attorneys' fees. However, many state and federal statutes allow the prevailing party recovery of attorneys' fees and/or costs under certain circumstances, and certain contracts also allow for recovery of fees. Cases involving animals brought pursuant to these statutes are no different. Thus the availability of attorneys' fees is a function of the basis for the claim. For example, a prevailing dog owner's claim against a society for the prevention of cruelty to animals for wrongfully killing her dog filed under the civil rights statutes may recover attorneys' fees,[89] the prevailing dog owner in *Petco* whose dog escaped from the groomer and was found dead could recover reasonable attorneys' fees under breach of contract,[90] and a condominium owner's personal injury action against a dog owner whose dog injured her would have been entitled to the recovery of attorneys' fees in action to enforce governing documents of common interest development had she prevailed.[91]

The recovery is limited to reasonable attorneys' fees.[92] The courts consider several factors to determine the reasonableness of the fees requested: (1) number of hours; (2) result obtained, (3) importance of the case, (4) amount involved, (5) intricacies of the facts or law, (6) expertise of counsel, (7) the contingent nature of the fee, and (8) the typical rate for similar counsel in the legal area and geographical region.[93] A typical case involving one's pet will likely not warrant a large attorneys' fee award as the importance of the case will be relatively slight, the amount at issue will be relatively small, as discussed previously, and the law and facts will be relatively simple.

However, there are cases where the fees awarded are quite substantial. For example, in *Petco*, the court found 45 hours at $150 per hour a reasonable attorneys' fee even though the case was decided by default judgment. The attorney did have to draft pleadings, file motions, and conduct factual investigation and legal research into the availability of damages for the wrongful killing of a dog.[94] In *Vanier v. Ponsoldt*,[95] the court determined that $88,814 was a reasonable amount for attorneys' fees and expenses for the vendor of an Arabian horse who sued the vendee for failure to make payments as agreed in the amount of $155,555. The court found that the litigation was complicated, the witnesses and evidence were scattered throughout the country, and the record was voluminous. Similarly, in *Albritton v. McDonald*,[96] the court awarded $2,000 in attorneys' fees against a seller who knowingly sold the purchaser a horse infected with equine infectious anemia ("swamp fever"), which then infected two other horses owned by the purchaser. The court awarded $1,985 in compensatory damages but noted that there were six hearings, a trial that lasted two days, and numerous pleadings and briefs filed on appeal.

B. Ancillary Remedies

Ancillary remedies are remedies designed to enforce the primary remedy granted by the court. Thus, a contempt sanction is ancillary relief to enforce an injunction and garnishment or attachment of property is ancillary relief to enforce a damages award. There are no special considerations involved in animal cases. Of course since animals are property, an animal may be the target of attachment or levy to satisfy the owner's liability for damages. Thus in *Kinderhill Select Bloodstock, Inc.*,[97] discussed previously, the IRS seized the owner's Thoroughbred horses as levy on back taxes. In some situations, the animal may be considered exempt property pursuant to the state statute.

APPENDIX A

Selected Secondary Sources on Remedies in Animal Law Cases

Damages in General

Bruce Wagman & Jayne DeYoung, *Actions Involving Injuries to Animals*, 90 Am. Jur. Proof of Facts 3d 1, ch. II.B (Damages and Other Remedies).

Robin Miller, *Damages for Killing or Injuring Dog*, 61 A.L.R.5th 635.

Jay Zitter, *Measure, Elements and Amount of Damages for Killing or Injuring Cat*, 8 A.L.R.4th 1287.

Jay Zitter, *Recovery for Damages for Emotional Distress Due to Treatment of Pets and Animals*, 91 A.L.R.5th 545.

Susan Hankin, *Not a Living Room Sofa: Changing the Legal Status of Companion Animals*, Rutgers J.L. & Pub. Pol'y 314, pt. III (Changes in Damage Awards) (Winter 2007).

Margit Livingston, *The Calculus of Animal Valuation: Crafting a Viable Remedy*, 82 Neb. L. Rev. 783 (2004).

Debra Squires-Lee, *In Defense of Floyd: Appropriately Valuing Companion Animals in Tort*, 70 N.Y.U.L. Rev. 1059 (1995).

Noneconomic Damages for Loss of Animal

Adam Karp, *Interference with Human-Companion Animal Relationship: Where "Use" = "Companionship" and "Loss of Use" = "Loss of Companionship,"* ABA-TIPS Animal Law Comm. Newsl. 1 (Fall 2006).

Victor Schwartz & Emily Laird, *Non-Economic Damages in Pet Litigation: The Serious Need to Preserve a Rational Rule*, 33 Pepp. L. Rev. 227 (Jan. 2006).

Elaine Byszewski, *Valuing Companion Animals in Wrongful Death Cases: A Survey of Current Court and Legislative Action and a Suggestion for Valuing Pecuniary Loss of Companionship*, 9 Animal L. 215 (2003).

William C. Root, *Man's Best Friend: Property or Family Member? An Examination of the Legal Classification of Companion Animals and Its Impact on Damages Recoverable for Their Wrongful Death or Injury*, 47 Vill. L. Rev. 423 (2002).

Geordie Duckler, *The Economic Value of Companion Animals: A Legal and Anthropological Argument for Special Valuation*, 8 ANIMAL L. 199 (2002).

Sonia Waisman & Barbara Newell, *Recovery of "Non-Economic" Damages for Wrongful Killing of Injury of Companion Animals: A Judicial and Legislative Trend*, 7 ANIMAL L. 45 (2001).

Steven Wise, *Recovery of Common Law Damages for Emotional Distress, Loss of Society, and Loss of Companionship for the Wrongful Death of a Companion Animal*, 4 ANIMAL L. 33 (1998).

Veterinary Malpractice

Rebecca Huss, *Valuation in Veterinary Malpractice*, 35 LOY. U. CHI. L.J. 479 (Winter 2004).

Punitive Damages

William Reppy, *Punitive Damage Awards in Pet-Death Cases: How do the Ratio Rules of State Farm v. Campbell Apply?*, 1 J. ANIMAL L & ETHICS 19 (May 2006).

APPENDIX B

List of Available Remedial Forms

Motions for Preliminary Injunction, 4A WEST'S FED. FORMS, DIST. COURTS–CIVIL § 5284, § 5285 (3d ed.).

Affidavit in Support of Order to Show Cause (Containing Temporary Restraining Order) for Preliminary Injunction in Relation to Unique Chattel, 4 WEST'S MCKINNEY'S FORMS CIVIL PRACTICE LAW AND RULES § 10:326 (N.Y.C.P.L.R. 7109).

Complaint to Enjoin Destruction of Unique Property, 21B AM. JUR. PL. & PR. FORMS REPLEVIN § 18.

Complaint for Prejudgment Seizure & Restraining Order for Property in Immediate Danger of Destruction, 21B AM. JUR. PL. & PR. FORMS REPLEVIN § 242.

Counterclaim for Injunctive Relief for Return of Pedigreed Dog, 7A ILL. CIV. PRAC. FORMS § 172:22.

Judgment Granting Specific Performance of Contract to Sell Personalty, 22B Am. Jur. Pl. & Pr. Forms Specific Performance § 109.

Complaint under Americans with Disabilities Act Seeking Injunction to Admit Service Animal, 8 Ill. Civ. Prac. Forms § 189:4.

Notes

1. 151 Ohio App. 3d 741 (Oh. Ct. App. 2003).
2. *Id.* at 745, para. 18; *see also* Gluckman v. Am. Airlines, Inc. 844 F. Supp. 151 (S.D.N.Y. 1994).
3. Bueckner v. Hamel, 886 S.W.2d 368, 375 (Tex. App. 1994).
4. Nichols v. Sukaro Kennels, 555 N.W.2d 689, 692 (Iowa 1996).
5. Robin Miller, *Damages for Killing or Injuring Dog*, 61 A.L.R.5th 635 para. 11[a], [b] (citing cases including Nichols v. Sukaro Kennels, 555 N.W.2d 689 (Iowa 1996); Zager v. Dimilia, 524 N.Y.S.2d 968 (Village Ct. 1988); Burgess v. Shampooch Pet Indust., Inc. 131 P.3d 1248 (Kan. Ct. App. 2006)).
6. 719 A.2d 662 (N.J. Sup. Ct 1998).
7. *Id.* at 663.
8. *Id.* at 664.
9. *Id.*
10. Carbasho v. Musulin, 217 W. Va. 359, 361 n.3 (W. Va. 2005).
11. *See* Miller, *supra* note 5, ch. III.
12. *See, e.g.*, Quave v. Bardwell, 449 So. 2d 81, 84 (La. App. 1st Cir. 1984).
13. *See Bueckner*, 886 S.W.2d at 370–71.
14. *See* Petco Animal Supplies, Inc. v. Schuster, 144 S.W.3d 554, 568 (Tex. App. 2004).
15. *Bueckner*, 886 S.W.2d at 370.
16. *Id.* at 372, *see also* Mitchell v. Heinrichs, 27 P.3d 309 (Alaska 2001).
17. *Petco*, 144 S.W.3d at 558–59.
18. *See, e.g.*, LaPorte v. Assoc. Indep., Inc. 163 So. 2d 267 (Fla. 1964); Jankoski v. Preiser Animal Hosp., Ltd., 157 Ill. App. 3d 818 (1st Dist.), *appeal denied*, 117 Ill. 2d 544 (1987); Brousseau v. Rosenthal, 443 N.Y.S.2d 285 (NYC Civ. Ct. 1980); Stephens v. Target Corp., 482 F. Supp. 2d 1234, 1236 (W.D. Wash. 2007).
19. *See, e.g.*, Mieske v. Bartell Drug Co., 92 Wash. 2d 40 (Wash. 1979); Brown v. Frontier Theaters, 369 S.W.2d 299 (Tex. 1963).
20. *See Petco*, 144 S.W.3d at 563.
21. *See* Adam Karp, *Interference with Human-Companion Animal Relationship: Where "Use" = "Companionship" and "Loss of Use" = "Loss of Companionship,"* ABA-TIPS Animal Law Comm. Newsl. 1 (Fall 2006).
22. *See, e.g.*, Stettner v. Graubard, 368 N.Y.S.2d 683 (Town Ct. 1975); Pickford v. Masion, 98 P.3d 1232 (Wash. Ct. App. Div. 2 2004); Carbasho v. Musulin, 618 S.E.2d 368 (W. Va. 2005).
23. *See generally* Debra Squires-Lee, *In Defense of Floyd: Appropriately Valuing Companion Animals in Tort*, 70 N.Y.U.L. Rev. 1059 (1995).

24. *Petco*, 144 S.W.3d at 565–66.
25. *Id.* at 566.
26. *Id.*
27. *See* Depouw v. Bichette, 833 N.E.2d 744, 747–48 (Ohio App. 2d Dist. 2005) (citing Kerns v. Lewis, 249 Mich. 27, 227 N.W. 727 (1929); Keeth v. State, 618 So. 2d 1154 (La. App. 1993)).
28. *See, e.g.*, Kaiser v. US, 761 F. Supp. 150, 156 (D.D.C. 1991).
29. *See* Restatement (Second) of Torts § 46(1).
30. Burgess v. Taylor, 44 S.W.3d 806 (Ky. Ct. App. 2001); Richardson v. Fairbanks N. Star Borough, 705 P.2d 454 (Ala. 1985); Knowles Animal Hosp. v. Wills, 360 So. 2d 267 (Fla. App. 3d Dist. 1978); La Porte v. Assoc. Indep. Inc, 163 So. 2d 267 (Fla. 1964); *see also* William Reppy, *Punitive Damage Awards in Pet-Death Cases: How Do the Ratio Rules of* State Farm v. Campbell *Apply?*, 1 J. Animal L & Ethics 19, pt. II (May 2006); Elaine Byszewski, *Valuing Companion Animals in Wrongful Death Cases: A Survey of Current Court and Legislative Action and a Suggestion for Valuing Pecuniary Loss of Companionship*, 9 Animal L. 215 (2003).
31. 63 Haw. 557 (1981).
32. Rodrigues v. State, 472 P.2d 509 (1970).
33. *Id.* at 523 (dissent).
34. Haw. Rev. Stat. § 663–8.9 (1986).
35. *Petco*, 144 S.W.3d at 562; Corso v. Crawford Dog and Cat Hosp., Inc. 415 N.Y.S.2d 182 (NYC Civ. Ct. 1979). *But see* Langford v. Emergency Pet Clinic, 96 Ohio App. 3d 174 (8th Dist. Cuyahoga County), *dismissed, appeal not allowed*, 71 Ohio St. 3d 1405 (Ohio 1994).
36. *See* Gilmore v. SCI Tex. Funeral Servs. Inc., 234 S.W.3d 251, 256–57 (Tex. 2007) (citing *Freeman*, 183 S.W.3d at 890).
37. Conn. Gen. Stat. § 22-351a(a); *see also* Tenn. Code Ann. 44-17-403(b).
38. 510 Ill. Comp. Stat. § 70/16.3.
39. Conn. Gen. Stat. § 22-351a(b).
40. 510 Ill. Comp. Stat. § 70/16.3.
41. Tenn. Code Ann. § 44-17-403(a)(1).
42. Conn. Gen. Stat. § 22-351a(b).
43. 510 Ill. Comp. Stat. § 70/16.3.
44. *Id.*
45. Tenn. Code Ann. § 44-17-403(a)(1), (d).
46. 510 Ill. Comp. Stat. § 70/16.3.
47. Conn. Gen. Stat. § 22-351a(c); 510 Ill. Comp. Stat. § 70/16.3.
48. Conn. Gen. Stat. § 22-351a(d).
49. Conn. Gen. Stat. § 22-351a(d); Tenn. Code Ann. § 44-17-403(e).
50. *Petco*, 144 S.W.3d at 566, *LaPorte*, 163 So. 2d at 267.
51. Grimshaw v. Ford Motor Co., 174 Cal. Rptr. 348 (Cal. App. 4th Dist. 1981).
52. BMW v. Gore, 517 U.S. 559 (1996); State Farm v. Campbell, 538 U.S. 408 (2003).

53. *State Farm*, 538 U.S. at 425.
54. Geordie Duckler, *The Economic Value of Companion Animals: A Legal and Anthropological Argument for Special Valuation*, 8 ANIMAL L. 199, 213 (2002).
55. *See generally* Reppy, *supra* note 30, at 47–48.
56. MASS. GEN. LAWS ANN. ch. 140, § 159.
57. *Bueckner*, 886 S.W.2d at 372–73.
58. *See* Chapter 10, Criminal Law.
59. *See, e.g.*, Long v. Noah's Lost Ark, Inc., 158 Ohio App. 3d 206 (Ohio App. 7th Dist. 2004); Buczkowicz v. Lubin, 80 Ill. App. 3d 200 (Ill. App. 3d Dist., 1980).
60. *See, e.g.*, Natural Res. Def. Council v. Winter, 502 F.3d 859 (9th Cir.), *stay vacated by* 508 F.3d 885 (9th Cir. 2007). The Supreme Court ultimately reversed in Winter v. Natural Res. Def. Council, 128 S. Ct. 365 (2008).
61. *See, e.g.*, Animal League Def. Fund v. Veneman, 496 F.3d 826 (9th Cir. 2006) (seeking declaration that the U.S. Department of Agriculture's decision not to adopt a policy providing guidance to entities regulated under the Animal Welfare Act in how to ensure the psychological well-being of primates under their care was arbitrary and capricious).
62. These cases also raise difficult standing issues, also beyond the scope of this text.
63. Judge Posner describes the test as follows: Issue a preliminary injunction when $P \times Hp > [(1-P) \times Hd]$ (+/–) Hpi where: P = probability of success, Hp = irreparable injury to P if injunction denied, Hd = irreparable injury to D if injunction granted, and Hpi = injury to public or third parties. *See* Barbara Ann White, *Risk-Utility Analysis and the Learned Hand Formula: A Hand That Helps or a Hand That Hides?*, 32 ARIZ. L. REV. 77, 121 n.236 (1990) (citing Am. Hosp. Supply Corp. v. Hosp. Products Ltd., 780 F.2d 589, 593 (7th Cir. 1986)).
64. *See generally* Charles Wright, Arthur Miller, & Mary Kay Kane, *Grounds for Granting or Denying a Preliminary Injunction*, 11A FED. PRAC. & PROC. CIV. 2D § 2948.
65. 835 F. Supp. 699 (N.D.N.Y. 1993).
66. *Id.* at 700.
67. *Id.* at 701.
68. 271 N.Y.S. 2d 788 (N.Y. 1st Dist. 1966).
69. *Id.* at 791.
70. 1981 WL 15139 (Del. Ch. 1981).
71. *Id.* at *1.
72. 122 F. Supp. 2d 794 (E.D. Mich. 2000).
73. MICH. COMP. LAWS § 287.1001–.1023 (2000).
74. *Michigan Wolfdog*, 122 F. Supp. 2d at 797–98.
75. *Id.* at 808–09. *See also* Walsh v. St. Mary's Church, 670 N.Y.S.2d 220 (Sup. Ct. App. Div. 3rd Dept. 1998) (the threat of removal of the remains of family pets constitutes irreparable harm).

76. *See generally* Phillip White, Jr., *Keeping of Domestic Animal As Constituting Public or Private Nuisance*, 90 A.L.R.5th 619.
77. *See* Ann Melley, 58 Am. Jur. 2d *Nuisances* § 342 (citing Missouri v. Illinois, 180 U.S. 208 (1901)).
78. 543 P.2d 656 (Or. 1975) (*en banc*).
79. *Id*. at 656.
80. *Id*. at 657.
81. 287 S.W.2d 583 (Ark. 1956).
82. *Id*. at 585.
83. 1977 WL 5178 (Del. Ch. 1977).
84. *Id*. at *3.
85. *Id*.
86. *Id*. at *4.
87. *Id*. (quoting Elliott v. Jones, 101 A. 872, 873 (1917)).
88. *Id*.
89. Snead v. Soc'y for Prevention of Cruelty to Animals of Pa., 929 A.2d 1169 (Pa. Super. 2007).
90. *Petco*, 144 S.W.3d at 567.
91. Chee v. Amanda Goldt Prop. Mgmt., 50 Cal. Rptr. 3d 40, 50–56 (Cal. App. 1st Dist. 2006) (pursuant to Cal. Civ. Code § 1354(f)(2003)).
92. *See generally* Jane Draper, *Excessiveness or Inadequacy of Attorney's Fees in Matters Involving Commercial and General Business Activities*, 23 A.L.R.5th 241 (originally published in 1994).
93. *Id*. 2[b]; *see also Petco*, 144 S.W.3d at 567.
94. *Petco*, 144 S.W.3d at 567.
95. 251 Kan. 88 (Kan. 1992) (applying Kentucky law).
96. 363 So. 2d 925 (La. App. 2d Cir. 1978).
97. 835 F. Supp. 699 (N.D.N.Y. 1993).

CHAPTER 10

Criminal Law

DANA M. CAMPBELL
PAMELA D. FRASCH

I. Introduction

This chapter is intended to help attorneys and others become effective advocates for animals while working with their local prosecutors' offices to ensure that animal abuse cases are carefully reviewed and vigorously prosecuted once the investigation is complete. It is not intended to serve as an investigations guide. In addition, prosecutors who don't often handle animal abuse cases may find benefit from the information contained herein.

Please note that defendants are referred to herein as "he," both for convenience and because the majority of defendants in animal abuse cases are male.[1]

Except where specifically noted, the general term "abuse" is used here to encompass acts of cruelty, neglect, abandonment, sexual assault, and fighting of animals. The term "prosecutor" means district attorney, state's attorney, city or county prosecutor, and any other person responsible for bringing animal abuse cases into court on the government's behalf.

II. Common Types of Animal Cruelty Cases

From the definition of "animal" to determining what type of activity is considered to be criminal "neglect," "abuse," or "cruelty," each state has developed unique animal cruelty laws.[2] Every state has basic misdemeanor prohibitions against cruelty and neglect. Forty-five states have at least one felony-level animal cruelty law, typically applied to the most heinous forms of cruelty or for multiple convictions.[3] Most states include prohibitions against abandoning an animal without making appropriate provision for its continuing care, and most states have a prohibition against the sexual assault of an animal. The following is a discussion of the typical criminal charges filed under these statutes, as well as possible defenses to them.

A. Neglect

"Neglect" is one of the vaguest terms within the animal cruelty laws, but it can be summed up generally as the failure to provide one or all of the following: food, shelter, water, and veterinarian care.[4] Problems arise when the language lacks specificity. For example, does "adequate shelter" mean that the area needs to be clear of feces? Is melted snow sufficient to meet the requirement for "water"? Vague terms, coupled with the fact that the different species protected under the animal cruelty laws have very different needs, can result in confusion and difficulty in investigating and prosecuting animal abuse cases.

Some states have worked to provide more direction by passing laws with much more detail as to what are considered "minimum standards" for generic animal care.[5]

Of course, as in most abuse cases, you may still need a veterinarian or other expert witness to explain any examination, diagnosis, or condition and the causal connection with neglect of the animal's basic needs. Asking your expert, "How much . . . ?" and "How long until . . . ?" questions will help the jury or judge better understand the prolonged and painful suffering involved in a neglect case. For example: How long does it take for fly larvae to develop in body cavities or wounds? How long did it take this animal body to decompose? What percentage of body weight did this animal lose while in defendant's custody? How long would it take for an animal like this to lose this much weight? Were there any food remnants found in its digestive system? How long would an animal have to go without food for there to be nothing left in the digestive system? Is cannibalism among dogs a normal behavior? How long could a dog go without food before resorting to cannibalism?

Another problem commonly encountered in neglect cases is determining how many counts to file in cases involving large numbers of animals, such as in a hoarder, breeder, or "rescuer-gone-bad" case.[6]

Determining the proper owner or caretaker of animals and who was responsible for the neglect (if it occurred over a long duration) can also complicate a case.[7]

B. Abuse

Animal abuse[8] cases are much like domestic violence cases in which the victim has gone into hiding before trial or is otherwise unavailable—you need to build your case on evidence other than the victim's testimony. Because of this challenge, the more evidence seized, the easier the case is to prove, making the investigation stage critical. Unfortunately, many inexperienced or uncaring investigators treat animal abuse cases like a stolen property case: They show up, take a report, and that's it. More appropriate is to treat an animal abuse case like an assault or murder case: Scrupulously document the scene with photos and/or video; seize the body and preserve it for lab testing (no freezing, as it destroys the cells for testing); if the animal is alive, place it in a safe environment; seize the weapon and anything containing the animal's tissue, blood, or hair; question those at the crime scene and canvass the neighbors to learn what they may have seen or heard in the days and hours leading up to the crime; seize veterinary records and any other records indicating ownership of, or otherwise relating to, the animal; and, as with any crime, document the chain of custody for anything seized. Engage a veterinarian or veterinary school to examine the animal or carcass to determine the extent of injuries or cause of death and to rule out other unrelated possibilities.

Just as important as proving the physical act of abuse is proving the mental state of the defendant at the time of the abuse. Rarely will there be direct evidence of this—announcements or letters by the defendant stating, "I hate the dog and I am going to shoot it dead," are unusual—so you will have to make the argument based on what is available. At the Animal Legal Defense Fund (ALDF), we have seen every kind of abuse imaginable, and even some we could never have imagined: beating, stabbing, poking, shooting with guns or arrows, slicing with machetes, dragging behind cars, setting afire, microwaving, throwing, stomping, strangling, allowing other animals to attack, and more. The point is that these very deliberate acts do not just occur accidentally or negligently. Often, by virtue of the nature of the abuse itself, you can fairly easily argue that the necessary mental state was present; just remember to argue the point.

Most states include crimes of omission as well as commission as part of their abuse laws—for example, neglect. Crimes of omission arguably require a different mens rea. Failure to feed a dog or provide it shelter should not require the same mental state as beating a dog to death. Even if your state laws do not specify different mental states, be prepared to argue the obvious intent of the statute and refer to any general annotation or legislative comment that supports this assumption.

Typical abuse defenses include:

1. "I wasn't there," or "I was there, but it wasn't me."
2. "The animal was attacking me/my child/my pets."
3. "I was training or disciplining the animal."
4. "I was temporarily insane—the animal urinated on the carpet/chewed up a piece of furniture/etc."

Defense 1 will be borne out (or not) based on the quality of your evidence.

Defense 2 is more problematic. Most people will be sympathetic to a defense-of-self-or-others type of argument, and some state laws specifically allow it.[9] Whether the abuse occurred on the animal's own property or someone else's, the type of animal involved (pit bulls are given less latitude than, say, Chihuahuas), and witness statements of the circumstances leading up to the abuse, are all factors that may affect the case. It may be helpful to file a motion in limine raising the issue of whether the prosecutor can introduce character evidence by neighbors or others familiar with the abused animal showing its peaceful nature and harmless past, to counter this defense.

Defense 3 will be easier to prove in places that don't have an outright exemption in their animal cruelty laws for training methods. In those places, if the training involved caused pain or injuries to the animal as defined by the cruelty law, your burden is met and the defense fails. However, in states like Oregon that do have a training exemption,[10] you may need to go further and find an expert, or several, to show that the training method used by the defendant is beyond the boundaries of what is generally accepted in the field in that part of the state.

Defense 4 should be handled just like a temporary insanity defense in any other type of criminal case. Once a defendant files his notice of intent to use this defense, it becomes a battle of the mental health experts to examine the defendant and testify about the defendant's condition and the credibility of the defense posited in that particular case. However, the quality of the initial investigation (e.g., the detailed observation and precise description of the defendant's demeanor and statements) is key to a reliable forensic psychological evaluation of an offender's state of mind at the time of the offense, as these evaluations often occur months after the initial arrest, after the defense has provided notice of intent to assert an insanity defense.

C. Abandonment

Unless someone is caught in the act of leaving an animal on the side of the road, or moves from the property leaving unattended animals behind, you will not see many arrests for abandonment.[11] Nevertheless, sometimes the above circumstances do occur (particularly in rental units for the latter circumstance) or an animal is identifiable and can be traced back to its abandoning owner. The tricky part of this type of case is proving who was the responsible owner or caretaker of the animal[12] and finding a way to counter a possible defense argument that the animal escaped and was not abandoned.

The other issue to check is whether your state is one in which either the definition of abandonment, or the crime itself, states that it is not a defense to the crime of abandonment that an animal was left near an animal shelter if no arrangements were made with the shelter to house the animal.[13]

D. Sex Offenses

Sexual assault of an animal is specifically outlawed in many states as an offense separate from general animal abuse. Before these provisions were enacted, prosecutors found it difficult to determine what charges to file when an animal was sexually assaulted but no provable injuries resulted from the sex act itself. A charge of animal sexual assault is different from other animal abuse charges in that the sexual act itself is the crime, without requiring any proof of pain or injury being caused to the animal as a result of the abuse to the animal. Usually the mens rea is stated as acting with the purpose of "arousing or gratifying the sexual desire" of the perpetrator.[14]

E. Hoarders and Breeders

The term "collector" is used interchangeably with "hoarder" to describe people who keep large numbers of animals in their house or property in squalid conditions. However, animal welfare workers prefer the term hoarder[15] as it more closely describes a pathological behavior that is an unhealthy preoccupation for keeping things, as opposed to the more benign "collector" who may be engaged in a perfectly acceptable hobby (e.g., collecting dolls or stamps).

Animal breeders who allow indiscriminate breeding can find themselves with far too many animals to care for. "Puppy mill" is a term used for a dog breeder who maximizes profits by spending little to nothing on caring for his dogs, forcing females to have litter after litter with no time to recover in between. All of these scenarios result in large-scale neglect cases that overtax the resources of the various agencies charged with bringing hoarders to justice.

In one of the first-ever studies done on the hoarding phenomenon, Dr. Gary Patronek of Tufts University Cummings School of Veterinary Medicine identified numerous common characteristics of hoarders in the 54 cases submitted for the study from ten animal welfare agencies.[16]

Results showed most hoarders are:

- Female (76 percent)
- Older than 40 (83 percent), with 46.3 percent being older than 60 years of age
- Unmarried (75 percent)
- Living in single-person households (more than 50 percent)
- Unemployed, retired, or on disability

•

- Cat owners (65 percent), and dog owners (60 percent), with farmed animals involved in 11 percent of cases and birds in 11 percent of cases
- Hoarding a median of 39 animals per case, with four cases involving more than 100 animals
- Unable or unwilling to care for their animals: 80 percent of the cases had animals who were found dead or in poor condition (severely malnourished, poor skin and coat, with obvious disease or injury)
- Living in filth: 77.6 percent of the residences were described as heavily cluttered and unsanitary, with 69.4 percent of the cases having accumulations of animal feces and urine in the human living areas; 32.7 percent of the homes did not have a working bathroom
- In denial: 58 percent refused to acknowledge to the investigating officer that a problem existed

Hoarders give a variety of reasons to explain the large numbers of animals present,[17] including a love for the animals, animals as surrogate children, feelings that no one else would care for the animals, and fear the animals would be euthanized if taken to a shelter.[18]

The information in Dr. Patronek's study correlates to the information ALDF has in its National Animal Cruelty Database, except that in recent years we have seen an increasing number of cases involving well over 200 animals on a hoarder's property. Our experience, as well as a new study on hoarding, shows that hoarders have a high risk of recidivism following a conviction, and often move to new locales in other states where they are unknown to the media and law enforcement.[19] For this reason, it is important for prosecutors to ensure that hoarders are not only directed in court to obtain expert psychiatric help and routed to local senior service or other aid agencies, but also have a conviction on their record that will alert authorities to this harmful tendency, wherever they eventually turn up.

Much evidence needs to be collected, organized, and preserved on the scene of a hoarding case. Thus, it is important for investigators to work with their prosecutor well before the day of the planned seizure. The prosecutor can ensure that the search warrant is in order (it is unlikely hoarders would give investigators consent to enter, because hoarders are usually sensitive to having anyone visit their property due to its poor condition). The prosecutor can also work with investigators to determine how best to catalog and record the numerous veterinary reports, photos, and animals taken at the scene, critical to preparing the eventual complaint and trial. For example, it is customary for each animal to be labeled with a numbered collar and a similarly numbered piece of paper, visible in a photo, and again with its kennel or living area, for use in compiling individual charges based on each animal's identifying characteristics and condition. Each animal should have a brief on-site initial exam and report done by the on-scene veterinarians (if possible) or as soon as possible after they arrive at a safe environment. This precludes defense claims that the animals' poor health conditions developed after the seizure.

You will also need to arrange safe lodging for all of the animals to be seized in a way that won't tip off the hoarder. If there are not enough shelter openings, you may need to consider discreetly finding sanctuaries and shelters outside the immediate area, foster homes, or even county fairgrounds to house large animals. Other tips, articles, and checklists for large-scale hoarding investigations are included in a very helpful manual entitled *How to Investigate Animal Cruelty in New York State: A Manual of Procedures*, by the New York State Humane Association, Inc., which can be found at http://nyshumane.org/manual.htm.

After animal neglect charges are filed, it is time to seek two more protections for the animals and their caregivers: a cost of care bond or forfeiture hearing if your state allows it[20] and a motion for prime setting (or whatever the procedure is called in your jurisdiction) to have the case receive a priority swift setting on the court's docket so that the animals are kept "in custody" only a minimum amount of time before the case is finally resolved.

F. Animal Fighting

Hog dog contests are just the latest example of the many ways animal exploiters use animals to make money. Thus the term "animal fighting" has broadened to encompass much more criminal activity now than it did just a few years ago, including more animals than the typical dogs and gamecocks, and in some places making spectators, promoters, fight premises owners, and profiteers criminally liable as well.[21]

For dogfighting and cockfighting cases, the Humane Society of the United States (HSUS) has perhaps the best training videos available for law enforcement and prosecutors. The videos explain how fighting rings operate, the training tools and animal injuries to recognize as being unique to the "sport," and more. HSUS also has some of the country's foremost expert witnesses to testify on the above for fighting cases. If you know or suspect there are dogfight or cockfight enterprises going on in your county, contact HSUS for support at http://www.hsus.org/ace/18708.

G. Farmed Animal Cases

The primary problem in prosecuting cruelty against farmed animals is that some or all of them may be excluded from protection because of an outright exemption for specific species or agricultural practices, or as a result of a narrow definition of "animal" within the animal cruelty codes. Therefore, along with exemptions from the animal cruelty laws for hunting, veterinary, and laboratory practices, you will often see exemptions using such terms as "good animal husbandry,"[22] "generally accepted agricultural practices,"[23] "livestock,"[24] "poultry,"[25] "production animals,"[26] and so on. In other places, the definition of "animal" may include "nonhuman vertebrate" but not "livestock,"[27] or a "live, nonhuman vertebrate creature" while excluding "animals kept or owned for agricultural purposes."[28] One saving grace may be that if the animals were treated outside the normal animal husbandry or training practices for the area, they may not be exempt from protection under the animal cruelty laws. This would likely require a local expert to testify as to the local standards and then compare these standards with how the animals were actually treated in your case. Clearly then, it is essential to check a state's definitions of "animal" in the animal cruelty code and any exemptions before assuming a case may go forward.

A secondary problem is finding experts in the area who are capable of examining and assessing large animals to determine whether and how they have been mistreated, and who can testify on the local animal husbandry standards for a region or type of practice.[29]

Finally, the seizure and safekeeping of abused farmed animals until trial can be difficult if shelter facilities are scarce or not set up for large animals. In advance of the anticipated seizure, alternative arrangements may need to be made with foster ranches or farms, or even at a county's fair barns and grounds.

Farm Sanctuary, which can be found at http://www.farmsanctuary.org/, is a good resource to start with if you have a farmed animal case, as it does accept some farmed animals on a space-available basis. Also, the organization has accrued valuable experience in investigating and promoting the prosecution of farmed animal cruelty cases.

III. Common Motions in Animal Cruelty Cases

A. Motion to Suppress Evidence

A motion to suppress evidence is filed by defendants as a matter of course in nearly every type of criminal case. Usually they seek to suppress evidence obtained as a result of a search or confession that the defendant alleges was done improperly. A hearing is then scheduled to establish the facts surrounding the search (was there an applicable warrant exception or valid warrant?) or the voluntary nature of the confession. These motions generally should be challenged by using the same constitutional provisions and case law that are commonly used in any nonanimal cruelty criminal case.

In the rare instance in which such a motion is granted, thus excluding some or all of the evidence seized in the case, the prosecutor must then decide if there is enough admissible evidence remaining with which to prove the case beyond a reasonable doubt.

Because animals are property under the law, animal control agents or police officers are often reluctant to seize animals without a warrant (even if the animal is in immediate danger) because they believe they would not be acting within their authority. Too often this hesitation results in the abused animal dying or being removed by the defendant before a warrant is obtained, especially if it is a weekend or after hours when a judge is harder to reach. Enforcement officers must be made aware that, as in any other crime, if there is evidence of a crime, the evidence of the crime—in this case the animal—may be seized.

Plain view or exigent circumstances may also support taking an animal into custody, thus treating the animal the same way that an officer would treat contraband if observed on private property.

Different states and courts may rule differently on these evidentiary subjects, but the most important thing to instill in enforcement officers is that the care of the animal is paramount. As long as charges are filed for animal cruelty and the officer is acting in good faith and on probable cause, the worst-case scenario is that the evidence will be suppressed, because the remedy for a bad seizure is to suppress the evidence from the trial. However, in the meantime, the animal will have been removed from the dangerous environment and may be used as part of an agreement to dismiss the case as long as the defendant agrees to forfeit the animal. Protecting the animal should be the first priority.

B. Motion to Examine the Carcass or Other Evidence

Occasionally you will see a motion to examine the carcass filed by defendants who want access to the animal's body to do their own independent testing and analysis of cause of death or injuries. As with any other evidence, the prosecutor should arrange to be present whenever the defense is present or has designated someone or a lab to handle your case's evidence, at a time and place convenient to both parties.

Sometimes, by the time this motion is filed, the animal's dead body may have already been destroyed following the necropsy. Is the destruction fatal to your case? The answer is generally "no," unless the defendant can show the destruction was done or directed to be done in bad faith by the state and the defendant can prove he would be prejudiced without the examination. In a rare reported animal cruelty case on this point, the court noted that the defendants had ample opportunity to examine the animals and related documents on their condition at the time of seizure.[30] The court relied on standards established in other types of criminal cases, in which evidence was destroyed, to find for the state.[31]

C. Motion for Particular Bail or Release Conditions

Courts have significant discretion in bail matters, so take the opportunity to have the prosecutor ask for what she can at the bail hearing to protect the animals, such as a "no contact with animals" order as a condition of release. Sometimes this means that the defendant will have to relinquish other animals still in his custody that were not seized. Convince the court that arrangements can and should be made to get these animals out of harm's way until final disposition or a forfeiture hearing can take place. It is important to specify and emphasize "no contact" as opposed to "no possession" to prevent the defendant from transferring his animals to others in his home, relatives, or friends with whom he has frequent contacts.

Defendant could also be ordered at this time to post a bond to cover the costs of care of seized animals in states or municipalities that allow for such a measure.

Finally, if there are surviving animals who may be going to foster homes, shelters, back to innocent owners, or other appropriate places, you may want to ask the court to limit or prohibit defendant's contact with these care providers, or for law enforcement-supervised visits with the animals, to prevent the defendant from harassing the animal care providers.

IV. Special Procedural and Other Unique Issues in Animal Cruelty Cases

A. Forfeiture or Foster Care until Trial, Costs of Care in the Interim

The time between seizure of abused animals and conclusion of the criminal trial can be months or even years. Thus, the expenses of caring for an animal seized by police or humane agents in an abuse case can easily cost thousands of dollars. In hoarding cases involving many animals, costs can quickly rise into the five- and even six-digit range, enough to bankrupt the best-financed animal shelters or municipality. Shelters without the resources to house large numbers of animals may consider adapting ALDF's Sample Foster Care Forms for Animal Shelters, available at http://www.aldf.org, as part of a foster care program to establish temporary foster homes for the animals. If the animals are lucky and media coverage of the seizure is good, there will be enough foster home providers in the area who come forward to care for them. But this option is less than ideal, as foster providers must typically agree to bear the entire cost of rehabilitating and caring for the animal with no guarantee that they will ultimately be able to permanently adopt the animal. Foster providers may also be required to seek specific permission from the court every time they need veterinary intervention for the animal. This can be costly, both in terms of money and time.

Petitioning the court to require the defendant to post a "cost of care" bond from which the animal care facility can draw to cover the animals' ongoing expenses is now possible in a growing number of states that have passed such legislation.[32] Failure to post the bond can often result in the animals being immediately released to the shelter for permanent placement, without waiting for final disposition of the case.

Another possible route is to seek pretrial forfeiture of the animals so that they can be placed in permanent homes before trial.[33] Because forfeiting animals amounts to a taking of "property" without compensation, constitutional due process requirements of notice and a hearing must be met. This usually means there must be a court hearing to decide if there is probable cause to believe the defendant will be convicted of abuse at trial (the standard may differ slightly depending on the wording of each state's forfeiture laws or case history). If the prosecutor is reluctant to move for such a hearing due to inexperience with the law or a perception that it is a civil matter rather than a criminal one, ALDF can work with you to assist the prosecutor, or to seek the appointment of a special prosecutor for the forfeiture hearing.

It is also important to remember that abusers will sometimes, though rarely, voluntarily waive their rights of ownership in the animal if simply asked by animal control or other officials to sign a release.

B. The Link between Animal Abuse and Human Violence

The connection between violence against humans and violence against animals is a phenomenon that has been extensively studied and documented by law enforcement and mental health professionals. If the law enforcement community in your jurisdiction does not take animal abuse in and of itself seriously, it can be very compelling to show that animal abusers are highly likely to engage in other forms of violent and antisocial criminal behavior.

The Massachusetts SPCA, together with Northeastern University, reviewed the criminal records of 153 people charged with intentional cruelty to animals for the ten-year period both prior to and following the animal abuse. They compared this information with a control group of "neighbors" who had not been engaged in animal abuse at any time. According to the study, 70 percent of the animal abusers also committed violent, property, drug, or disorderly crimes, compared to only 22 percent of the control group. *The animal abusers were also shown to be five times more likely than their nonabusive neighbors to commit violent crimes against people.* More than a quarter of the abusers were under age 18, with 50 percent falling under age 30; 97 percent of the abusers were male.[34]

One of the first studies of the connection between animal cruelty and violent crimes involved 84 prison inmates charged with violent crimes. Of those, 75 percent had early records of animal abuse.[35]

In a significant study of 152 federally imprisoned inmates, 25 percent of the aggressive inmates had committed five or more acts of animal abuse as children compared to only 6 percent of nonaggressive inmates. (The inmates' aggressiveness levels were assigned based on their behavior *after* entering prison.) At least one act of animal abuse in childhood was reported by 60 percent of the criminals.[36]

In a study of 53 New Jersey families referred to youth and family services for child abuse, 88 percent of the families had at least one member of the household who physically abused animals (sometimes the abuser was the child acting out his or her own abuse).[37]

Among women seeking shelter from domestic violence in Utah, 71 percent who shared their homes with companion animals reported that their male partners had threatened to or had harmed or killed their companion animals. Of the women with children, 32 percent reported that one of their children also had committed acts of animal cruelty.[38]

In addition to reviewing the literature on the role of companion animals in the development of the social lives of children, the authors of this next report conducted their own study of adult prisoners and institutionalized juveniles. Of 81 violent offenders in Minnesota, 86 percent had owned a companion animal sometime in their life that they considered special to them. More than 60 percent of the offender and the control groups lost their special companion animals through death or theft, but more companion animals died of gunshots in the offender group. Of 238 teenagers living in psychiatric or juvenile institutions, 91 percent said they had owned a special companion animal. The companion animals of the institutionalized group suffered more abuse, but the abuser was usually someone other than the child.[39]

News accounts throughout the years have also revealed a disturbing similarity among serial killers like Ted Bundy, Jeffrey Dahmer, and Albert De Salvo (a.k.a. "The Boston Strangler"): They all committed or witnessed brutal acts of animal abuse before growing up to commit serial murders of humans. The same is true of many teenage "school shooters," such as Mississippi's Luke Woodham and Oregon's Kip Kinkel, who abused animals and later killed their parents and classmates.

The Humane Society of the United States created the First Strike campaign in 1997, aimed at creating awareness of the link between animal cruelty and violent crimes. Among a number of resources, the program provides expert testimony and information on this link to prosecutors and law enforcement working on high-profile animal cruelty cases. Its resources can be found at http://www.hsus.org/hsus_field/first_strike_the_connection_between_animal_cruelty_and_human_violence/.

C. Proving Ownership or Custody

Animal ownership can be difficult to establish; yet it is often essential to prove a neglect case (that is, showing who is responsible, under the statute, for caring for the animal). Most people simply do not think they need to keep proof of ownership of an animal for any reason. Nevertheless, here is a checklist that may be helpful to help establish animal ownership:

- In a neglect case, charge all parties on the premises for whom there is probable cause and try them together. Let them point their fingers blaming each other in court (they must not be allowed to have separate trials or this won't work), but in the end the argument is that neglect is a failure to act, and if they all had access to both the premises and the animals and they all failed to act, they all should be held responsible.
- Check with animal control or other local licensing authorities to see who licensed the animals (if they are licensed).
- If the animal was adopted or purchased, find a bill of sale or adoption receipt with the buyer's name, or request it as part of discovery.
- Check with the purported owner's veterinarian, if any, to see who was primarily responsible for bringing the animal in for treatment or for paying the bills.
- Check with neighbors, the suspect's family members, or store clerks to see who was visibly exercising control or care over the

animal, walking, buying food, and so on. Especially in more rural areas, feed stores know all of their clients. This can help establish either that the person never came in to buy the starving animal food, or that the buyer/owner did come in, and can be identified.

- Ensure that any search warrant includes a provision to seize papers, receipts, financial records, and veterinary and other documents (in both electronic and paper form) that might indicate ownership.

D. Proving Pain or Cause of Death

Proving that the animal suffered pain or that the cause of death was due to criminal abuse is an essential element of cruelty cases.[40] However, the following checklist may also be helpful:

- Typically it is wise to decline a defendant's offer to stipulate to the qualifications of your veterinarian or other expert. Rather, the better practice is to insist on laying this foundation as part of your direct examination of the witness to ensure that the jury has an appreciation for the quality of your expert's training and education, thus bolstering your veterinarian's credibility as an expert.
- Once you have established the veterinarian's qualifications, ask if she has had a chance to review the reports and/or evidence in the case.
- Ask what she found as a result of the exam—as she's testifying, follow along with the veterinarian's report and ask follow-up questions.
- For any type of cruelty case, it is important for the jury to understand the length and extent of suffering that occurred. You can establish this by asking questions such as: How many cuts were present from the (machete/knife/scissors)? How long would it take to bleed to death in that manner? Do animals have nerve endings that experience pain much like humans? How long does it take for fly larvae to develop in body cavities or gaping wounds? How long would it take for an animal like this to lose this much weight? Were there any food remnants found in the digestive system? How long would an animal have to starve for there to be nothing in the digestive system? Is cannibalism among dogs a normal behavior? How long would a dog have to go without food before resorting to cannibalism?

- Often the time (or the time range) of death is a key element (e.g., in alibi cases), so when relevant, have the veterinarian render an opinion on this issue.
- Don't forget to ask your expert to state, unequivocally, her final opinion on the cause of death or emaciated condition, and whether the animal suffered pain, for every animal in the case.
- Depending on the veterinarian's answer to that question, ask: Is there any other possible condition that could explain your findings? A preexisting condition you found, an old injury, or other explanation? (Be sure you know the answer to this before asking!)
- Always take every opportunity to use pictures or other visual aids. Show them to the veterinarian and ask her if this is how she recalls the injury appearing. Ask the police if this is the condition they found the animal in when they arrived on the scene. The old saying "A picture is worth a thousand words" is especially true when prosecuting cruelty cases. Don't hesitate to use this valuable tool.[41]

E. Jury Issues

1. *Voir Dire*

As in any trial, selecting your jurors may be the most important step toward winning the case. A good article on the subject of selecting a jury for an animal cruelty case is *Effective Voir Dire in Animal Cases*, by Lawrence Weiss.[42] The article does a good job of describing the characteristics for prosecutors to seek in potential jurors and why these characteristics are important. Also, a list of sample voir dire questions for you to consider is attached as Appendix D at the conclusion of this chapter.

2. *Jury Instructions*

Sample Jury Instructions for an animal cruelty case are included as Appendix E at the conclusion of this chapter.

V. Considerations for Plea Bargains and Sentencing in Animal Cruelty Cases

A. Creating a Criminal Record for the Defendant

Often, prosecutors will give a "diversion" type of plea deal to a first-time abuser, and that can be a mistake. (Diversion agreements involve delaying entry of a plea until certain conditions, like counseling, are met. If there are no new crimes committed during the diversionary period, usually a year, the charges are dismissed—creating no criminal record for the defendant.) Many abusers, and particularly hoarders, move from state to state, which means no one in the justice system would have any way to know of diversion agreements for prior offenses in other states. What may appear to be a first-time offense for this prosecutor may be a fourth abuse offense for the defendant.

Familiarize yourself with the law of diversionary programs in your state. These programs generally require the consent of the prosecutor and define the types of crimes that can be considered. Usually, violent crimes do not qualify, although animal cruelty is often not treated as a violent crime. Know the law on this issue, and find out whether there is a separate prosecutor in the office who handles diversions, as it may not be the same prosecutor who will be handling the case. It is important to reach that prosecutor immediately to make sure that the defendant does not get diverted or accepted to such a program. Be prepared to argue that animal cruelty is a violent crime that should not be eligible for such a program.

Also, based on what we know about the link between animal cruelty and violent crime,[43] the ability to track a person's history of violence through convictions can be an important tool for a judge in determining whether to grant a restraining order to the abuser's wife or family, or in deciding who should have custody of their children.[44]

B. Jail Time and Suspended Sentences

There is no better way to send a message to the abuser and the greater community that animal cruelty will not be tolerated than by sentencing a defendant to a meaningful jail term with some time suspended as a strong incentive to stay out of trouble during the remainder of his probationary period.[45]

C. Community Service

Community service sentences are always a good idea, as they give the defendant time to think about what he has done to get there, while benefiting his community. However, some judges may think they are being creative by requiring the community service to be performed in an animal shelter, as it will teach him respect for animals. This can be a recipe for disaster. Most shelters do not want the offenders there, and do not have the necessary staff to provide constant oversight of the offender to ensure that he does not harm the resident, and quite vulnerable, animals. It is highly recommended, therefore, that community service be completed only in locations where the offender does not have any access to animals.

D. Restitution

Restitution represents a belief in the fundamental fairness of financially restoring injured parties to the place they were before defendant's actions caused the harm. It is a rare case in which there is no restitution due; even in cases where the defendant has harmed his own animal, veterinary bills and the county's costs of caring for the animal until its permanent placement need to be paid by someone. These bills properly rest on the defendant's shoulders.

Restitution should always be requested by the prosecutor, whether as part of a plea bargain or after trial. Local shelters, in particular, face extraordinary veterinary and other expenses when they agree to accept abused animals.[46] Without restitution, these shelters suffer tremendous economic hardship, and may opt to refuse to accept animals seized in future cruelty cases.

In cases in which large numbers of animals are involved and the costs of care over time are quite high, or there are other complicating factors (e.g., determining the value of someone's beloved companion animal), a separate restitution hearing may be ordered. In that case, the prosecutor will present evidence supporting the amount sought, and the defendant will present evidence disputing the amount sought. For this reason, it is important that all medical costs and care expenses between the time of seizure and the restitution hearing or sentencing be meticulously documented with receipts and tracking reports. ALDF has sample spreadsheets that have been presented in court to document the costs of care in cases involving multiple animals. Usually, the shelter will be able to recover a daily cost of care per animal, figured at a prevailing rate for that area, and including overhead expenses such as staffing, lighting, water, food, and the like. This rate is then multiplied by the number of days each animal spends in the shelter and the number of animals being held, and is in addition to specific expenses like veterinary fees or trailer rentals for transport to the shelter.

E. Counseling

As noted previously, some states now have laws that require counseling for defendants convicted of animal abuse.[47] Although counseling can be very helpful, the field as it relates to animal abusers is still developing. So, before insisting on counseling as part of a sentence, you should review the available programs in your area and whether they have any definite measures for success, such as rates of recidivism of program participants. For more information, you may want to review the AniCare Model of Treatment for Animal Abuse, developed by Society & Animals Forum (formerly Psychologists for the Ethical Treatment for Animals), which can be accessed at http://www.psyeta.org/AniCare.html.

F. No-Contact Orders

See supra Section III.C., Motion for Particular Bail or Release Conditions.

VI. Identifying Cases in Your State

A. Media

Many of the cases pursued by ALDF come from newspaper, Internet, or other media reports forwarded to us by concerned citizens. Many times, media reports lack critical information or provide misinformation about a case; however, they can still provide enough information for you to determine whether case assistance would be useful. Inaction (such as a failure to file charges or an unreasonable delay in moving forward) or those cases where there is too little action (such as filing an insufficient type or number of charges) are examples of the type of information commonly included in media reports relating to cases in which your legal assistance may be warranted and where your involvement can make a difference in the outcome.

B. Animal Shelters and Other Advocacy Groups

Becoming active with local shelters or rescue groups as a volunteer or board member will put you in contact with your local animal community and no doubt lead to learning about cases in which animals have been, or should be, seized for their own protection as a prelude to a criminal abuse case. Keep your ears open, and make sure that people know you are willing to provide legal assistance for such cases.

Pet-abuse.com also maintains a cruelty database that tracks animal abuse cases throughout the country. The cases, which can be searched by state, included alleged and open animal abuse cases as well as convictions.[48]

The Michigan State University College of Law's Animal Legal & Historical Web Center offers more than 800 cases and 1,000 U.S. statutes, as well as FAQs for attorneys about animal law issues.[49]

C. Law Enforcement

Developing positive relationships with local police officers, county sheriffs, prosecutors, or animal control or humane agents can often lead to direct contacts for advice or other legal assistance on cruelty cases. Look for opportunities to develop these relationships and discuss your willingness to be a resource to help with the legal aspects of cruelty investigations and prosecutions. Do not assume that law enforcement agents are familiar with animal cruelty laws, as they often rely on animal control agencies rather than handling these cases themselves. If you are active in a local animal law committee of the bar association or other lawyers group, consider using that forum to create and provide law enforcement agents with easily portable "pocket books" that outline the cruelty laws in your state and provide the names and numbers of emergency or 24-hour veterinarians and wildlife rehabilitators listed by county or region.

D. Identifying and Contacting the Appropriate Prosecutor

It can be very useful to contact the prosecutor early on in the case to determine the procedural posture of the case and offer assistance and suggestions as outlined in this chapter. Thus, identifying the prosecutor assigned to the case is essential.

If you are lucky, the name of the prosecutor assigned to the case will be evident in the news story or referral source that brought the case to your attention. In all other cases, you will need to do some sleuthing. Before calling the prosecutor's office, make sure you have as much information about the case as possible. The defendant's name, approximate date of the offense, victim's name, or the case number (if known) will help the prosecutor's office quickly determine which prosecuting attorney has been assigned to the case.

If you call and are told there is no prosecutor yet assigned, ask when the assignment will be made or if there is a date set for a first appearance in court. Note the information so that you can make a timely follow-up call. You may also want to ask whether there is someone typically assigned to handle all of the office's animal abuse cases and, if there is, ask to speak to that person. If there is no one, this may be a good time to start talking to the chief prosecutor or first deputy about the importance of having the expertise and consistency that a prosecutor dedicated to handling animal abuse cases would provide the office. Consider sending a letter of introduction and one of ALDF's "Resources for Prosecutors" brochures as a follow-up to your call. You may even want to direct them to the Los Angeles City Attorney Office's Animal Protection Unit, which can be found at http://www.lacity.org/atty/Advocating/attyaniprunit.htm, so they can speak with one of their prosecutors as to how and why such a unit was created.[50]

VII. Prosecutorial Discretion and Considerations

In virtually every jurisdiction, the prosecutor's office has complete discretion regarding whether to bring charges, and which ones to file. You can provide invaluable assistance by ensuring that your prosecutor's office takes into account the following considerations.

A. Felony or Misdemeanor Abuse

Every state has at least one misdemeanor law prohibiting cruelty and neglect; all but five states have at least one felony-level animal cruelty law.[51] Usually, animal cruelty laws (whether they be misdemeanor or felony level) are further broken down into degrees of severity. Thus, preliminary questions that must be answered before deciding on the precise charges to be brought include: what level of severity was the cruelty, and does the conduct or prior criminal record of the defendant allow or require a felony charge? If a felony case can be established, encourage the prosecutor to file the higher charges or, at a minimum, to file both felony and misdemeanor charges. A felony conviction becomes part of the defendant's history identifying him as a violent offender and a potential future danger. It also makes a greater range of penalties possible and sends a message to the community that animal abuse is taken seriously by law enforcement and the community.[52]

B. Multiple Counts

In cases involving more than one animal victim, the better practice is to file one count for each animal victimized because it can give the prosecutor more options in a plea bargain and because it more accurately reflects the nature of the case—you wouldn't file one count of homicide when three people died, and animal cases are no different in that regard.

Although bringing multiple charges for multiple animals means more work for the prosecutor at the time of drafting the charges, the effort pays off later in preparing for trial and in keeping animals not included in the counts from being returned to their abuser.

C. Related Counts

Prosecutors should also consider appropriate charges outside the traditional animal cruelty statutes. Indeed, it is often the case that the only way in which a prosecutor can charge a felony-level offense is to look at alternative charges, such as arson. Because animals are considered property under the law, a number of property-related charges can be considered—for example, criminal property damage, theft, or arson. Many states have made the theft of a companion animal a felony offense. In addition, consider charges such as child endangerment, domestic violence, criminal mischief, disorderly conduct, or trespass. Also consider using your local health and zoning codes if the premises in which the animals were kept are dangerous or unsanitary.

If a weapon was used in the abuse, consider weapons charges, which often carry additional sentencing consequences, especially when a firearm was used. Moreover, when a case does involve the use of a firearm, remind the prosecutor to consider presenting the case to the United States Attorney's Office for review as well, as the federal sentences for cases involving the use of a firearm are substantial. Dogfighting enterprises can also have federal penalties available depending on the circumstances; Racketeer Influenced Corrupt Organizations (RICO) laws may be another state or federal avenue for pursuing charges.

Sometimes, animal cruelty acts are committed by defendants who are also domestic violence offenders. If a defendant has a history of domestic violence or is subject to a restraining order, an animal cruelty crime may also be deemed a violation of the restraining order or a form of harassment or violent threat against the (human) victim.

Finally, if the case involves felony crimes within a jurisdiction bound by state sentencing guidelines, be sure to encourage the prosecutor to charge all applicable *Blakely*[53] sentencing enhancement factors to support an upward departure sentence.

D. Juveniles

It can be useful to think of criminal courts for juveniles as a parallel universe to the adult courts—they have most of the same basic rights and responsibilities as adults, but the procedures and possible sentences are entirely different. In many states, juvenile court proceedings are closed to the public and media, and the records are sealed and confidential, making it difficult to learn whether a juvenile has been charged, let alone his name or the case status. (Note, however, that depending on the victims' rights laws of each state, the person victimized by the juvenile defendant may still be allowed to be present in juvenile court and speak at sentencing. The victim is also typically notified of court dates and plea negotiations.) Juvenile cases don't go to trial; rather, they are "adjudicated." Perhaps more than with any other type of defendant, juveniles are seen by some judges and others in the system as having the greatest potential for reform, especially if they are in court on a first offense.

Interestingly, in September of 2001, the United States Department of Justice's Office of Juvenile Justice and Delinquency Prevention issued a 15-page bulletin, *Animal Abuse and Youth Violence*, that reported on the research linking animal abuse to juvenile-perpetrated violence, analyzed the motives of child and adolescent animal abusers, and discussed the importance of including information about animal abuse in assessments of youth at risk for committing interpersonal violence. The report can be found at http://www.ncjrs.gov/pdffiles1/ojjdp/188677.pdf.

With juvenile cases treated by courts as cases under seal with the utmost confidentiality, and no nationwide government tracking system available that includes crimes against animals, it is difficult for the prosecutor and court to get a clear picture of a juvenile abuser's prior history with animal abuse or other violent crimes, especially if the juvenile moves from state to state. However, it is always wise to remind the prosecutor to check with her local juvenile department to confirm the offender's local history, and to check for any references to an interstate compact transfer involving the youth, as those records may help provide some background on a juvenile offender's out-of-state history.

E. Resources Available to the Prosecutor

Providing the prosecutor with all of the information that she needs to handle the case will result in more effective prosecutions. Prosecutors' offices are often overburdened and underfunded. When faced with competing priorities, animal cruelty cases sometimes receive the least amount of attention and resources. However, if the case is made easy to handle with little work, it is likely to be processed more appropriately. As with law enforcement officers, it is important that you do not assume the prosecutor is completely familiar with animal cruelty laws. Any information you can provide on potential charges or additional evidence, if presented in the right way, may help keep the case alive.

1. *Follow-Up Investigations*

A prosecutor's case in court is only as good as its underlying investigation, which is why it is especially important to ensure all has been done that can be done up front. Waiting to file charges while at the same time asking the original investigators (or the prosecutor's in-house investigators) to do more work on a case is not at all uncommon for all types of cases and should be done whenever there appear to be gaps in the investigation or a possibility of building an even stronger case for trial. In some instances, the case initially presented to the prosecutor will not be sufficient for charges to be filed unless and until the follow-up work is done. The prosecutor should not have qualms about making such a request of her office's investigators, or with the original investigating officers.

Follow-up can be as easy as asking investigators to question the suspect for purposes of encouraging a confession, or canvassing the suspect's neighbors to see if they heard or saw any animal cruelty before or during the incident in question. Other requests may be more difficult, such as obtaining a warrant to return to the crime scene and retrieve a forgotten weapon—or even the dead animal body—or submitting evidence to forensic labs for further analysis. Due to the inexperience that many traditional investigators have with handling animal abuse cases, it is especially important to consider that more work may need to be done in order to move the case toward trial or plea instead of dismissal.

That said, it is important to attempt to get things right from the beginning to ensure that a case is not prematurely dismissed. Full names of witnesses and contact phone numbers are essential to ensure that the case can be prosecuted and further investigated if needed. Complaints or indictments must be correct and precise. For example, in states where the incident date is a material element of the charged offense, cases have been lost or dismissed due to an incorrect date for the offense, when a simple amendment to the complaint upon the first court appearance could have solved the problem, or the complaint could have stated that the crime occurred within a short range of time instead of on a specific date. It is important not to guess the date on which the cruelty occurred. It is much better to write a complaint that states "sometime between the dates November 4 and November 8." Otherwise, the prosecutor is burdened with the unnecessary task of proving that the act happened on a precise date. If she is unable to do so, a dismissal or an acquittal may result.

2. *Laboratories and Other Scientific Tools*

Be sure your contacts in law enforcement and the prosecutor's office are aware of resources in their region that can help bolster their case by providing better quality evidence. For example, many states have one or more veterinary schools that offer diagnostic, forensic, and necropsy services to investigators for little or no charge. Other types of specialty labs or veterinarian specialists may also be available, and should be included in any list of resources you provide.

Sometimes it is necessary to remind investigators that animal abuse cases can benefit from the same tools and procedures as those used in human abuse cases; for example, fingerprint or blood or hair analysis, lab testing of possibly poisoned bait, detailed professional analysis of crime scene evidence, and so on. In cases where an animal has died, as with humans, it is important to remind your contacts that the animal body should be preserved in a refrigerated environment, not a freezer, as a freezer will destroy the animal's tissue, thus making later analysis useless.

3. *Veterinarians and Other Expert Witnesses*

Most animal abuse cases will require an expert to help analyze the evidence or testify at court, or both. Usually that expert will be a veterinarian, who can establish an animal's cause of death, describe its injuries, and provide other important forensic information to the judge or jury, such as what a healthy animal should weigh in a starvation case, or the fact that a dog was shot at close range from the back based on the stippling pattern and the trajectory of the bullet.[54] As soon as abuse or neglect is suspected, a veterinarian should be brought in by law enforcement to examine the animal (either at the scene or as soon as possible after seizure) and make a written report of his or her findings. This also will foreclose the suspect's ability to claim that the animal's condition developed after the animal was seized, not before. Even in cases where the cause of death seems apparent, such as gunshot wounds, a definitive cause of death should be obtained to rule out any other possible theories or preexisting conditions that could cause death. You would not want to be the prosecutor who learns in court for the first time that an animal who suffered obvious wounds was also being seen by the owner's veterinarian for late-stage cancer, which could plant a seed of reasonable doubt in the minds of the jury as to whether it was the cancer or the abuse that caused death.

Many different types of experts for animal cruelty cases, such as animal behaviorists, wildlife rehabilitators, farriers, species experts such as elephant or turtle specialists, zoo veterinarians, and others can help both the prosecutor and the jury understand any number of different points, such as

- What do certain species of animals need to survive?
- Did an animal suffer pain as a result of various injuries? (For example, will a bull hook thrust into an elephant's thick skin hurt the elephant?)
- How long would an animal have to be neglected to have such long hooves, low body weight, and poor teeth?

Because animals cannot testify themselves (sign-language-proficient primates notwithstanding), it is the evidence and the experts that are left to tell the animals' stories to the jury.[55]

4. Visual Aids for Trial

Visual aids are incredibly useful tools in any lawyer's case, and that is especially true in an animal abuse case where the victim will never enter the courtroom. Jurors (and judges, too) appreciate lawyers who can make their time in court more interesting by using appropriate visual aids to accompany the testimony and arguments. This can be done by bringing out all evidence that appeals to the senses, and is a concept that should be kept in mind by investigators collecting evidence at the scene. You can talk about a dog who was burned by a sadist, or you can reach into the evidence bag and show the jury a clump of singed hair and a burned dog bed recovered by the investigator while he is testifying so the jurors can see it, and smell it, for themselves. Police can verbally describe how overpowering the stench was upon entering a cat hoarder's house, but how much more effective would it be to have a 12-inch-by-12-inch sample of the crusted fecal matter and other debris that was covering the floor for the jury to see and smell during the officer's testimony? It makes a powerful, lasting impression—so do bloody baseball bats, clothes, and towels used during the criminal act or to clean up afterward.

Make sure that any photos to be used in court are enlarged so they may be easily seen by the jury. All photographs should be dated and initialed by the photographer so that they can be authenticated in court. Photos are often the most effective means of convincing the jury of the crime. In photographing abused animals on scene or shortly after their seizure, be sure to take clear photographs of the entire animal as well as specific injuries in both close and long range, while completely filling the frame.

While photos and videos of the crime and the scene are of course part of the case, don't forget other types of helpful visual evidence: the weapon used (you would be surprised how often this is overlooked when police respond to an animal abuse case—often it can still be recovered after a follow-up request); blood-spattered clothing, rugs, or other items; a comparison photo of the now-healed neglected horse to hold up next to your photo of the neglected horse when she was 500 pounds underweight; the food bowl holding caked dirt or mold; the water bowl with green sludge; x-rays of broken bones; poster-board copies of compelling veterinarian or police reports, and so on.

Obviously, it is important that the prosecutor specifically evaluate the case for visual aids available or still needed early on in the case. For photos, this is especially important as the animals' physical appearance is steadily changing for the better. In the event follow-up is needed, the prosecutor still will have time to properly prepare or create the aids before trial.

VIII. Communication with the Prosecutor and Judge

A. Prosecutors

Building relationships with your local prosecutors is something that should be happening well before you actually need to call on them for a specific case. Here are some ideas on how to develop and maintain a productive and cooperative relationship, colloquially known as the "Three Be's":

1. Be Squeaky

As in the saying, "The squeaky wheel gets the oil":

- Ask to meet with the prosecutor designated to handle the case(s).
- Emphasize how important it is for you, your supporters, and taxpayers to see tough enforcement of animal laws and tough positions on sentencing abusers.
- Bring copies of relevant statutes with you.
- Write and/or call the prosecutor anytime a case arises that you would like to see prosecuted and ask others to do the same.
- Pack the courtroom on hearing days.

2. Be a Resource

Offer to assist whenever necessary to:

- Recommend a veterinarian in your area who might make a good expert witness.
- In neglect cases, educate the prosecutor on proper standards of care.
- If you can, offer to provide or find facilities for holding seized animals.
- Work on sponsoring or testifying in support of laws affecting and improving the welfare of animals.
- Be available to volunteer for rescues on large cases and make sure local law enforcement agencies and your prosecutor know you are available.

3. Be Prepared

When the prosecutor does call on you for help:

- Be available to assist with legal research, writing, or other tasks as requested.
- Have your referral veterinarian list handy.

- Have copies of (and be familiar with) animal protection laws. Be prepared to discuss the technical aspects of the laws.
- If you work with a shelter or other facility, ensure that staff is trained and ready for large-scale rescues.

B. Judges

Your state ethical rules should be your guide as to when and how to communicate with a judge on a pending case. Ex parte contacts with a judge are prohibited universally, but some states have a broader view of who is considered a "party" or "interested party" in a case, making it difficult to advise on this topic. You would probably be safe in submitting any letters, briefs, or memos to the judge as long as you send the same to the prosecutor and defense attorney on the case and note that you have done so on the original sent to the judge. Once the case has gone to trial, and therefore no longer is pending, you generally are allowed to send a letter or otherwise communicate with the judge regarding suggestions for an appropriate sentence if there was a conviction. However, before any communication, thoroughly review your local rules and any relevant laws.

IX. Available Resources

ALDF has a long history of assisting prosecutors and law enforcement agencies on all types of cruelty cases. The following are some examples of the type of support ALDF can provide.

A. Expert Witness Database

Understanding animal physiology and all of the possible maladies and injuries that can arise in abuse cases nearly always requires the use of at least one expert in each case, and ALDF has the resources to help make the search easier. Whether the need is for a farrier to testify on hoof neglect, a wildlife rehabilitator, or a veterinarian amenable to being called to court as a witness, ALDF keeps a database of contact information for these animal experts.

B. Research

In addition to its staff attorneys, ALDF has developed a network of several hundred volunteer lawyers all around the country, anxious to be called upon to do research work for briefs, motions, and memos, litigate cases as special prosecutors, or provide any other legal help needed.

C. Telephone Advice and Ideas from Prosecutors

Animal cases often involve new and sometimes difficult issues; being able to discuss these issues with someone who has handled them before can provide the insight and confidence needed to go forward. Throughout the years, ALDF has been fortunate to be able to provide assistance to prosecutors from our former prosecutors on staff who provide support and assistance.

D. Other

See Appendix G for further reading suggestions and other resources.

X. *Conclusion*

Animal abuse and neglect are serious crimes that require a serious response. It is our hope that the information contained within this chapter will assist those attorneys interested in using their legal skills to address this problem. ALDF is dedicated to protecting the lives and advancing the interests of animals using the legal system. We encourage you to contact us if we can provide more information or support for your efforts.

APPENDIX A

Sample Indictment

In the United States District Court for the Eastern District of Virginia
Richmond Division

UNITED STATES OF AMERICA,
Plaintiff,

vs.

PURNELL A. PEACE,
a/k/a "P-Funk" and "Funk,"

QUANIS L. PHILLIPS,
a/k/a "Q,"
TONY TAYLOR,
a/k/a "T,"
MICHAEL VICK,
a/k/a "Ookie,"
Defendants.

Indictment

JULY 2007 TERM - At Richmond, Virginia

Count One

(Conspiracy to Travel in Interstate Commerce in Aid of Unlawful Activities and to Sponsor a Dog in an Animal Fighting Venture)

THE GRAND JURY CHARGES THAT:

1. Beginning in or about early 2001 and continuing through on or about April 25, 2007, in the Eastern District of Virginia and elsewhere, defendants, PURNELL A. PEACE, also known as "P-Funk" and "Funk," QUANIS L . PHILLIPS, also known as "Q," TONY TAYLOR, also known as "T," and MICHAEL VICK, also known as "Ookie," did knowingly and willfully combine, conspire, confederate and agree with each other, and with persons known and unknown to the Grand Jury, to commit the following offenses against the United States, to wit:

   a. traveling in interstate commerce and using the mail or any facility in interstate commerce with intent to commit any crime of violence to further any unlawful activity and to promote, manage, establish, carry on, and facilitate the promotion, management, establishment, and carrying on of an unlawful activity, to wit: a business enterprise involving gambling in violation of Virginia Code Annotated Sections 3.1-796.124(A)(2), 18.2-326, and 18.2-328, and thereafter performing and attempting to perform acts to commit any crime of violence to further any unlawful activity and to promote, manage, establish, and carry on, and to facilitate the promotion, management, establishment, and carrying on of the unlawful activity, in violation of Title 18, United States Code, Section 1952;

b. knowingly sponsoring and exhibiting an animal in an animal fighting venture, if any animal in the venture has moved in interstate commerce, in violation of Title 7, United States Code, Section 2156(a)(1); and
c. knowingly buying, transporting, delivering, and receiving for purposes of transportation, in interstate commerce, any dog for purposes of having the dog participate in an animal fighting venture, in violation of Title 7, United States Code, Section 2156(b).

Manner and Means of the Conspiracy

2. It was part of the conspiracy that the defendants and their co-conspirators would and did:

    a. purchase and develop a parcel of property to serve as the main staging area for housing and training pit bulls involved in the animal fighting venture and for hosting dog fights;
    b. establish a kennel name to represent the animal fighting venture in dog fighting competitions;
    c. purchase pit bulls for use in dog fighting competitions;
    d. train and breed pit bulls for participation in dog fighting competitions;
    e. travel to other locations in interstate commerce to participate in dog fighting competitions;
    f. sponsor and exhibit dogs in animal fighting competitions in interstate commerce involving dogs that have moved across state lines;
    g. provide funding for the expenses associated with the ongoing animal fighting venture, including improvements on the property, dog food, medicine, travel expenses, and purse fees for dog fighting competitions; and
    h. develop the animal fighting venture's pool of pit bulls by testing the fighting prowess of dogs within the venture, providing veterinary treatment for injured dogs slated to stay with the kennel, and destroying or otherwise disposing of dogs not selected to stay with the ongoing animal fighting venture.

Overt Acts

3. In furtherance of the conspiracy and to effect the objects thereof, at least one of the following overt acts, among others, was com-

mitted by the defendants and other conspirators in the Eastern District of Virginia and elsewhere:

2001–2002: Establishment of "Bad Newz Kennels" at 1915 Moonlight Road, Smithfield, Virginia:

4. At some point in or about early 2001, QUANIS L. PHILLIPS, also known as "Q," TONY TAYLOR, also known as "T," and MICHAEL VICK, also known as "Ookie," decided to start a venture aimed at sponsoring American Pit Bull Terriers in dog fighting competitions.
5. In or about May 2001, TAYLOR identified the property at 1915 Moonlight Road, Smithfield, Virginia, as being a suitable location for housing and training pit bulls for fighting.
6. On or about June 29, 2001, VICK paid approximately $34,000 for the purchase of property located at 1915 Moonlight Road, Smithfield, Virginia. From this point forward, the defendants, aided and assisted by others known and unknown to the Grand Jury, used this property as the main staging area for housing and training the pit bulls involved in the dog fighting venture and hosting dog fights.
7. In or about 2001, the exact dates being unknown to the Grand Jury, PURNELL A. PEACE, also known as "P-Funk" and "Funk," PHILLIPS, TAYLOR, and VICK started acquiring pit bulls for the fighting operation from various locations inside and outside of Virginia, including purchasing approximately 4 dogs from an individual in North Carolina, approximately 1 dog from an individual in New York, approximately 6 dogs and 6 puppies from an individual in Richmond, Virginia, and a female pit bull named "Jane" from an individual in Williamsburg, Virginia.
8. In or about early September 2001, PHILLIPS, TAYLOR, and VICK purchased approximately 4 pit bull puppies for approximately $1,000 from an individual known to the Grand Jury in Williamsburg, Virginia. One of these puppies was a male pit bull named "Magic."
9. In or about early 2002, VICK, accompanied by PEACE, purchased approximately 4 pit bulls from Cooperating Witness Number 1 (C.W.#1) in Virginia. C.W.#1 had previously purchased one of the pit bulls from an individual in North Carolina.
10. In or about early 2002, PEACE, PHILLIPS, TAYLOR, and VICK established a dog fighting business enterprise known as "Bad Newz Kennels." At one point, the defendants obtained shirts

and headbands representing and promoting their affiliation with "Bad Newz Kennels."

11. Beginning in 2002 and continuing through at least 2005, the exact dates being unknown to the Grand Jury, "Bad Newz Kennels" members, aided and assisted by others known and unknown to the Grand Jury, continued to develop the 1915 Moonlight Road property for the ongoing dog fighting venture, including building: a fence to shield the rear portion of the compound from public view; multiple sheds used at various times to house training equipment, injured dogs, and organized fights; a house to be occupied by the defendants and others associated with maintaining the property; and kennels and buried car axles with chains for the pit bulls. The buried car axles allow the dog chains to pivot, allowing the pit bulls to avoid getting tangled in the chains.

2002: Execution of "Bad Newz Kennels" Pit Bulls that Performed Poorly in "Testing" Sessions:

12. In or about February 2002, PEACE and VICK "rolled" or "tested" some of their fighting dogs against other dogs owned by C.W.#1 and others in Virginia Beach, Virginia. "Rolling" or "testing" a fighting dog means placing the dog in a short fighting match to determine how well the animal fights. One of the pit bulls sponsored by PEACE and VICK in this "testing" session did not fight very well.
13. In or about February 2002, PEACE executed the pit bull that did not perform well in the "testing" session by shooting it with a .22 caliber pistol.
14. In or about the summer of 2002 at various times, the exact dates being unknown to the Grand Jury, PEACE, PHILLIPS, TAYLOR, and VICK "rolled" or "tested" additional "Bad Newz Kennels" dogs by putting the dogs through fighting sessions at 1915 Moonlight Road to determine which animals were good fighters.
15. In or about the summer of 2002, PEACE executed at least one dog that did not perform well in a "testing" session at 1915 Moonlight Road by shooting the animal.
16. In or about the summer of 2002, PHILLIPS executed at least one dog that did not perform well in a "testing" session at 1915 Moonlight Road by shooting the animal.
17. In or about the summer of 2002, TAYLOR executed at least two dogs that did not perform well in "testing" sessions at 1915 Moonlight Road by shooting one dog and electrocuting the other.

2002: Fights Involving "Maniac," a Male Pit Bull Owned by an Individual from North Carolina, Versus Dogs Owned by "Bad Newz Kennels":

18. In or about the spring of 2002, PEACE, PHILLIPS, and TAYLOR traveled from Virginia to North Carolina with a male pit bull named "Seal" to participate in a dog fight against a male pit bull named "Maniac," owned by an individual from North Carolina. The purse for the dog fight was established at approximately $500 per side, for a total of approximately $1,000.
19. In or about the spring of 2002, PEACE, PHILLIPS, and TAYLOR sponsored "Seal" in a dog fight against "Maniac."
20. In or about the spring of 2002, "Bad Newz Kennels," represented by PEACE, PHILLIPS, and TAYLOR, lost the purse when "Maniac" prevailed over "Seal."
21. In or about late 2002, an individual traveled from North Carolina to Virginia with a male pit bull named "Maniac" to participate in a dog fight against a pit bull named "Zebro," owned by a person unknown to the Grand Jury. "Bad Newz Kennels" hosted the dog fight at 1915 Moonlight Road and established the purse at approximately $1,000 per side, for a total of approximately $2,000.
22. In or about late 2002, a person unknown to the Grand Jury, aided and assisted by TAYLOR and VICK, sponsored "Zebro" in the fight against "Maniac."
23. In or about late 2002, a person unknown to the Grand Jury, aided and assisted by TAYLOR and VICK, lost the purse when "Maniac" prevailed over "Zebro."

Late 2002: A Fight Involving "Chico," a Male Pit Bull Owned by "Bad Newz Kennels," Versus a Pit Bull from Alabama:

24. In or about late 2002, individuals unknown to the Grand Jury traveled from Alabama to Virginia with a male pit bull to participate in a dog fight against a male pit bull named "Chico" owned by "Bad Newz Kennels." "Bad Newz Kennels" hosted the dog fight at 1915 Moonlight Road and established the purse at approximately $1,000 per side, for a total of approximately $2,000.
25. In or about late 2002, PHILLIPS and TAYLOR, sponsored "Chico" in a dog fight against the male pit bull from Alabama.
26. In or about late 2002, "Bad Newz Kennels," represented by PHILLIPS and TAYLOR, won the purse when "Chico" prevailed over the male pit bull from Alabama.

Late 2002: "Bad Newz Kennels" Hosting Other Kennels' Dog Fights at 1915 Moonlight Road:

27. In or about late 2002, "Bad Newz Kennels," represented by PEACE, PHILLIPS, and TAYLOR, hosted one regular fight and a "Grand Champion Fight" (meaning that each dog was fighting for his fifth consecutive win) at 1915 Moonlight Road between male pit bulls from North Carolina and Maryland.
28. In or about late 2002, "Bad Newz Kennels," represented by PEACE, PHILLIPS, and TAYLOR, hosted a fight at 1915 Moonlight Road between a male pit bull sponsored by the "Junior Mafia" of North Carolina versus a male pit bull sponsored by a person known to the Grand Jury from Williamsburg, Virginia.

2002–2003: Fights Involving "Jane," a Female Pit Bull Owned by "Bad Newz Kennels," Versus Pit Bulls From New York and North Carolina and a Fight in New Jersey:

29. In or about late 2002, PEACE, PHILLIPS, TAYLOR, and another individual known to the Grand Jury traveled from Virginia to Maryland with a female pit bull named "Jane" to participate in a dog fight against a female pit bull owned by "Show Biz Kennels" of New York. The purse for the dog fight was established at approximately $1,000 per side, for a total of approximately $2,000.
30. In or about late 2002, PEACE, PHILLIPS, and TAYLOR sponsored "Jane" in a dog fight against the female pit bull owned by "Show Biz Kennels."
31. In or about late 2002, "Bad Newz Kennels," represented by PEACE, PHILLIPS, and TAYLOR, won the purse when "Jane" prevailed over the female pit bull owned by "Show Biz Kennels."
32. In or about the spring of 2003, PEACE, PHILLIPS, TAYLOR, VICK, and two other individuals known to the Grand Jury, traveled from Virginia to North Carolina with a female pit bull named "Jane" to participate in a dog fight against a female pit bull owned by individuals from North Carolina unknown to the Grand Jury. The purse for the dog fight was established at approximately $1,500 per side, for a total of approximately $3,000.
33. In or about the spring of 2003, PEACE, PHILLIPS, TAYLOR, and VICK sponsored "Jane" in a dog fight against the female pit bull from North Carolina.
34. In or about the spring of 2003, "Bad Newz Kennels," represented by PEACE, PHILLIPS, TAYLOR, and VICK, won the purse when "Jane" prevailed over the female pit bull from North Carolina.

35. In or about late 2003, PEACE, PHILLIPS, TAYLOR, and another individual known to the Grand Jury traveled from Virginia to New Jersey with a female pit bull named "Jane" to participate in a dog fight against a female pit bull owned by individuals unknown to the Grand Jury. The purse for the dog fight was established at approximately $5,000 per side, for a total of approximately $10,000.
36. In or about late 2003, PEACE, PHILLIPS, and TAYLOR sponsored "Jane" in a dog fight against the female pit bull owned by the individuals unknown to the Grand Jury.
37. In or about late 2003, "Bad News Kennels," represented by PEACE, PHILLIPS, and TAYLOR, won the purse when "Jane" prevailed over the female pit bull owned by the individuals unknown to the Grand Jury.

2003–2004: Fights Involving "Big Boy," a Male Pit Bull Owned by "Bad Newz Kennels," Versus Pit Bulls From South Carolina and New Jersey:

38. In or about the spring of 2003, an individual unknown to the Grand Jury traveled from South Carolina to Virginia with a male pit bull to participate in a dog fight against a male pit bull named "Big Boy," owned by "Bad Newz Kennels." "Bad Newz Kennels" hosted the dog fight at 1915 Moonlight Road and established the purse at approximately $1,000 per side, for a total of approximately $2,000.
39. In or about the spring of 2003, PEACE, PHILLIPS, TAYLOR, and VICK sponsored "Big Boy" in a dog fight against the male pit bull from South Carolina.
40. In or about the spring of 2003, "Bad Newz Kennels," represented by PEACE, PHILLIPS, TAYLOR, and VICK, won the purse when "Big Boy" prevailed over the male pit bull from South Carolina.
41. In or about late 2003, PEACE, PHILLIPS, TAYLOR, and VICK traveled from Atlanta, Georgia to South Carolina with a male pit bull named "Big Boy" to participate in a dog fight against a male pit bull owned by an individual from South Carolina unknown to the Grand Jury. The purse for the dog fight was established at approximately $3,600 per side, for a total of approximately $7,200.
42. In or about late 2003, PEACE, PHILLIPS, TAYLOR, and VICK sponsored "Big Boy" in a dog fight against the male pit bull from South Carolina.
43. In or about late 2003, "Bad Newz Kennels," represented by PEACE, PHILLIPS, TAYLOR, and VICK, won the purse when "Big Boy" prevailed over the male pit bull from South Carolina.

44. In or about the spring of 2004, individuals unknown to the Grand Jury traveled from New Jersey to Virginia with a male pit bull to participate in a dog fight against a male pit bull named "Big Boy," owned by "Bad Newz Kennels." "Bad Newz Kennels" hosted the dog fight at 1915 Moonlight Road and established the purse at approximately $1,500 per side, for a total of approximately $3,000.
45. In or about the spring of 2004, PEACE, PHILLIPS, TAYLOR, and VICK sponsored "Big Boy" in a dog fight against the male pit bull from New Jersey.
46. In or about the spring of 2004, "Bad Newz Kennels," represented by PEACE, PHILLIPS, TAYLOR, and VICK, won the purse when "Big Boy" prevailed over the male pit bull from New Jersey.

March 2003: Fights Involving Two Pit Bulls Owned by an Individual from North Carolina Versus Pit Bulls Owned by "Bad Newz Kennels":

47. In or about June 2002, Cooperating Witness Number 2 (C.W.#2) observed PEACE, VICK, and others unknown to the Grand Jury representing "Bad Newz Kennels" and "Hard Core Kennels" participate in two separate dog fights against "D.C. Kennels" at a location around Blackstone, Virginia. C.W.#2 approached an individual unknown to the Grand Jury after the fight to offer "Bad Newz Kennels" a future fight with two of his pit bulls, a 35-pound female pit bull and a 47-pound male pit bull.
48. In or about the late summer of 2002, an individual unknown to the Grand Jury from "Bad Newz Kennels" agreed to fight C.W.#2's pit bulls in or around March 2003.
49. In or about March of 2003, C.W.#2 traveled from North Carolina to a location near Blackstone, Virginia with his 35-pound female pit bull and a 47-pound male pit bull to participate in the dog fight matches against members of "Bad Newz Kennels."
50. In or about March of 2003, PEACE, VICK, and other individuals unknown to the Grand Jury sponsored a female pit bull in a dog fight against the 35-pound female pit bull owned by C.W.#2. The purse for the dog fight was established at approximately $13,000 per side, for a total of approximately $26,000.
51. In or about March of 2003, PEACE, VICK, and other individuals unknown to the Grand Jury sponsored a female pit bull in a fight against the 35-pound female pit bull owned by C.W.#2.
52. In or about March of 2003, "Bad Newz Kennels," represented by PEACE, VICK, and others unknown to the Grand Jury, lost the purse when the 35-pound female pit bull owned by C.W.#2 prevailed over the "Bad Newz Kennels" pit bull.

53. In or about March of 2003, PEACE, after consulting with VICK about the losing female pit bull's condition, executed the losing dog by wetting the dog down with water and electrocuting the animal.
54. In or about March of 2003, PEACE, VICK, and other individuals unknown to the Grand Jury sponsored a male pit bull in a dog fight against the 47-pound male pit bull owned by C.W.#2. The purse for the dog fight was established at approximately $10,000 per side, for a total of approximately $20,000.
55. In or about March of 2003, PEACE, VICK, and other individuals unknown to the Grand Jury sponsored a male pit bull in a fight against the 47-pound male pit bull owned by C.W.#2.
56. In or about March of 2003, "Bad Newz Kennels," represented by PEACE, VICK, and others unknown to the Grand Jury, lost the purse when the 47-pound male pit bull owned by C.W.#2 prevailed over the "Bad Newz Kennels" pit bull.
57. In or about March of 2003, VICK retrieved a book bag from a vehicle containing approximately $23,000 in cash. The cash was provided to C.W.#2 as payment for winning both dog fight matches.

March 2003: A Fight Involving "Cleo," a Female Pit Bull From New York, Versus a Pit Bull Owned by "Bad Newz Kennels":

58. In or about March of 2003, PEACE, VICK, and other individuals unknown to the Grand Jury sponsored a female pit bull in a dog fight against a female pit bull named "Cleo," owned by an individual unknown to the Grand Jury from New York and handled during the fight by C.W.#1. The purse for the dog fight which took place in Surry County, Virginia, was established at approximately $3,000 per side, for a total of approximately $6,000.
59. In or about March of 2003, PEACE met C.W.#1 and led him to the fight location in Surry County. Virginia.
60. In or about March of 2003, PEACE, VICK, and other individuals unknown to the Grand Jury sponsored a female pit bull in a fight against the female pit bull named "Cleo."
61. In or about March of 2003, "Bad Newz Kennels," represented by PEACE, VICK, and others unknown to the Grand Jury, lost the purse. The "Bad Newz Kennels" female pit bull jumped out of the ring and "scratched" the fight. Following an agreement to allow a rematch between the dogs, "Cleo" beat the "Bad Newz Kennels" female pit bull.
62. In or about March of 2003, PEACE executed the losing dog by shooting it with a pistol.

Fall 2003: A Fight Involving "Magic," a Male Pit Bull Owned by "Bad Newz Kennels," Versus a Male Pit Bull in South Carolina:

63. In or about the fall of 2003, PEACE, PHILLIPS, TAYLOR, and VICK traveled from Atlanta, Georgia to South Carolina with a male pit bull named "Magic" to participate in a dog fight against a male pit bull owned by individuals from South Carolina unknown to the Grand Jury. The purse for the dog fight was established at approximately $1,500 per side, for a total of approximately $3,000.
64. In or about the fall of 2003, PEACE, PHILLIPS, TAYLOR, and VICK sponsored "Magic" in a dog fight against the male pit bull from South Carolina.
65. In or about the fall of 2003, "Bad Newz Kennels," represented by PEACE, PHILLIPS, TAYLOR, and VICK, won the purse when "Magic" prevailed over the male pit bull from South Carolina.

Fall 2003: A Fight Involving a Male Pit Bull From North Carolina Versus a Male Pit Bull Owned by "Bad Newz Kennels":

66. In or about the fall of 2003, Cooperating Witness Number 3 (C.W.#3) traveled to Surry County, Virginia, with a male pit bull from North Carolina to participate in a dog fight against a male pit bull named "Tiny," owned by "Bad Newz Kennels." "Bad Newz Kennels" hosted the dog fight at 1915 Moonlight Road and established the purse at approximately $3,500 per side, for a total of approximately $7,000.
67. In or about the fall of 2003, an individual unknown to the Grand Jury met C.W.#3 and led him and others accompanying C.W.#3 to 1915 Moonlight Road, Smithfield, Virginia.
68. In or about the fall of 2003, PEACE, PHILLIPS, TAYLOR, and VICK sponsored "Tiny" in a fight against the male pit bull sponsored by C.W.#3. During the fight, C.W.#3 was criticized by a person unknown to the Grand Jury from "Bad Newz Kennels" for C.W.#3's having yelled out VICK's name in front of the crowd during the dog fight.
69. In or about the fall of 2003, "Bad Newz Kennels," represented by PEACE, PHIILIPS, TAYLOR, and VICK, won the purse when "Tiny" prevailed over the male pit bull owned by C.W.#3.
70. In or about the fall of 2003, PEACE told C.W.#3 that he would give him a rematch in the future.

Late 2003: A Fight Involving "Trouble," a Female Pit Bull Owned by an Individual from North Carolina, Versus a Pit Bull Owned by "Bad Newz Kennels":

71. In or about late 2003, Cooperating Witness Number 4 (C.W.#4) traveled to Surry County, Virginia, with a female pit bull named "Trouble," a dog that originally came from Florida, to participate in a dog fight against a female pit bull owned by "Bad Newz Kennels." "Bad Newz Kennels" hosted the dog fight at 1915 Moonlight Road and established the purse at approximately $7,000 per side, for a total of approximately $14,000.
72. In or about late 2003, an individual unknown to the Grand Jury met C.W.#4 and led him and others accompanying C.W.#4 to 1915 Moonlight Road, Smithfield, Virginia.
73. In or about late 2003, PEACE placed a side-bet with C.W.#4 of approximately $4,000 on the "Bad Newz Kennel" dog to win the fight.
74. In or about late 2003, PEACE, VICK, and other individuals unknown to the Grand Jury sponsored a female pit bull in a fight against the female pit bull named "Trouble."
75. In or about late 2003, "Bad Newz Kennels," represented by PEACE, VICK, and others unknown to the Grand Jury, lost the purse when "Trouble" prevailed over the "Bad Newz Kennels" pit bull.
76. In or about late 2003, VICK paid C.W.#4 the purse money of approximately $7,000 and approximately $4,000 for the side-bet entered by PEACE.

Early 2004: A Fight Involving "Too Short," a Male Pit Bull Owned by "Bad Newz Kennels," Versus a Pit Bull from Maryland:

77. In or about early 2004, individuals unknown to the Grand Jury traveled from Maryland to Virginia with a male pit bull to participate in a dog fight against a male pit bull named "Too Short" owned by "Bad Newz Kennels." "Bad Newz Kennels" hosted the dog fight at 1915 Moonlight Road and established the purse was at approximately $3,000 per side, for a total of approximately $6,000.
78. In or about early 2004, PEACE, PHILLIPS, TAYLOR, and VICK sponsored "Too Short" in a dog fight against the male pit bull from Maryland.
79. In or about early 2004, "Bad Newz Kennels," represented by PEACE, PHILLIPS, TAYLOR, and VICK, won the purse when "Too Short" prevailed over the male pit bull from Maryland.

2004–2005: "Bad Newz Kennels" Continues Hosting Dog Fights at 1915 Moonlight Road, Smithfield, Virginia:

80. From in or about late 2004 through 2005 at various times, the exact dates being unknown to the Grand Jury, PEACE, PHILLIPS, VICK, and others known and unknown to the Grand Jury continued operation of the animal fighting venture at 1915 Moonlight Road and hosted approximately 10 dog fights on the property. Many of these fights were held on the second floor of a shed on the property. Participants in these fights came from various places, including New York, Texas, and North Carolina.

Early 2007: "Bad Newz Kennels" Dog Fighting Operation Continues at 1915 Moonlight Road, Smithfield, Virginia:

81. In or about early 2007, the exact dates being unknown to the Grand Jury, PEACE, PHILLIPS, VICK, and others known and unknown to the Grand Jury continued operation of the animal fighting venture at 1915 Moonlight Road.
82. In or about April 2007, PEACE, PHILLIPS, VICK, and two others known and unknown to the Grand Jury "rolled" or "tested" additional "Bad Newz Kennels" dogs by putting the dogs through fighting sessions at 1915 Moonlight Road to determine which animals were good fighters.
83. In or about April 2007, PEACE, PHILLIPS, and VICK executed approximately 8 dogs that did not perform well in "testing" sessions at 1915 Moonlight Road by various methods, including hanging, drowning, and slamming at least one dog's body to the ground.
84. On or about April 25, 2007, PEACE, PHILLIPS, and VICK possessed various items associated with the continued operation of the dog fighting operation at 1915 Moonlight Road, including the sheds and kennels associated with housing the fighting dogs and hosting dog fights; approximately 54 American Pit Bull Terriers, some of which had scars and injuries appearing to be related to dog fighting; a "rape stand," a device in which a female dog who is too aggressive to submit to males for breeding is strapped down with her head held in place by a restraint; a "break" or "parting" stick used to pry open fighting dogs' mouths during fights; treadmills and "slat mills" used to condition fighting dogs; and other items.

(In violation of Title 18, United States Code, Section 371).

Forfeiture Allegation

Pursuant to Rule 32.2(a) Fed. R. Crim. P., the defendants are hereby notified that, if convicted of the offense charged in Count One, the defendants shall forfeit to the United States their interest in any property constituting, or derived from, proceeds obtained directly or indirectly as the result of such violation, including any assets which may be directly forfeitable as proceeds or subject to forfeiture as a substitute asset.

(In accordance with Title 18, United States Code, Section 981(a)(1)(C), as incorporated by 28 U.S.C. § 2461(c).)

A TRUE BILL

____
FOREPERSON
CHUCK ROSENBERG
UNITED STATES ATTORNEY
By: Michael R. Gill
Assistant United States Attorney

APPENDIX B

Sample Subpoena Duces Tecum

Subpoena
DUCES TECUM

(Benton County Grand Jury)

In re the **GRAND JURY INVESTIGATION**
Of ______________________________ DA No. ________________

IN THE NAME OF THE STATE OF OREGON, TO:
Custodian of Records for JOHN DOE SMITH, DVM

YOU ARE HEREBY COMMANDED TO APPEAR before the BENTON COUNTY GRAND JURY in the Benton County Courthouse, at 120

NW 4th Street, Corvallis, Oregon, as a witness for the State of Oregon on __________ at 9:00 a.m. and you are directed to bring the following records with you:

All reports, photos, x-rays, chart notes and records regarding the care and treatment of [______________] including all dental records, if any, for the purposes of: (a) determining the cause of death and (b) attempting to identify the burned animal remains discovered in the investigation of the above captioned criminal investigation.

In lieu of your personal appearance on the above-specified date and time, you may produce the above-described documents to Detective [*insert name*] (or his designee) who is assisting the grand jury with its investigation of this case.

APPENDIX C

Sample Forfeiture Petition

IN THE CIRCUIT COURT OF THE STATE OF OREGON
FOR THE COUNTY OF CLACKAMAS

STATE OF OREGON, Plaintiff, vs. SHELLIE A. ANDERSON, Defendant. OREGON HUMANE SOCIETY, a non-profit corporation, Petitioner, vs. SHELLIE A. ANDERSON, Respondent.	PETITION FOR FORFEITURE OF SEIZED ANIMALS PURSUANT TO ORS 167.347 (HEARING REQUESTED within 14 days of filing date, per ORS 167.347(2)) Circuit Court Case No. CR07-10803

COMES NOW the Oregon Humane Society, a non-profit organization incorporated under the laws of the State of Oregon, by and through its attorney, Scott A. Heiser of the Animal Legal Defense Fund, and respectfully petitions this Court for an order of immediate forfeiture of two horses seized by authorities during a search of Shellie Anderson's property located at 22143 South Evergreen Drive, Beavercreek, Clackamas County, Oregon, on or about February 22, 2007. To that end, Petitioner alleges as follows:

1. That on or about February 22, 2007, while executing a duly authorized search warrant issued on February 20, 2007, two horses were impounded by the Clackamas County Sheriff's Office pursuant to ORS 167.345(2) and placed into the custody of the Petitioner. Both of these animals are being held and supervised by the Petitioner pending the outcome of a related criminal action under this same case number charging the Respondent/Defendant with multiple violations of ORS 167.325. See the Clackamas County District Attorney's Information, which is a part of this court's case file (note that as the filing of this petition, the defendant has avoided execution and service of a duly authorized arrest warrant).
2. There is probable cause to believe that the animals mentioned in this Petition were subjected to neglect by the Respondent/Defendant in violation of ORS 167.325. See Exhibit 1, the February 20, 2007, Affidavit of Oregon Humane Society Special Agent Austin Wallace, filed in support of application for the above-referenced search warrant, which is attached and incorporated into this petition as Exhibit 1; and Exhibit 2, the February 22, 2007, Incident Report of Austin Wallace documenting the facts of this case (Oregon Humane Society Case No. 2744), which is attached and incorporated into this petition as Exhibit 2, both of said documents are summarized as follows:

    a. On January 24, 2007, Petitioner received a voice mail from Deborah Alto of 22231 South Evergreen Drive, Beavercreek, reporting neglected horses located at 22143 South Evergreen Drive, Beavercreek, Clackamas County, Oregon. Mrs. Alto described the horses as very thin and stated that they were not receiving food. Mrs. Alto had previously contacted the Clackamas County Sheriff's Office regarding this issue. In January 2006, Respondent/Defendant was investigated by Petitioner for a similar complaint.

b. On February 4, 2007, Agent Wallace visited Respondent/Defendant's home and observed two horses, an older mare, "Lady," and a younger colt, "Duran." Based on Agent Wallace's training and experience, both horses appeared to be considerably underweight. After taking pictures of both horses, Agent Wallace posted a notice on Respondent/Defendant's gate advising her to have the horses seen by a licensed veterinarian within 48 hours or if they were being seen by a veterinarian, to provide proof by contacting Petitioner.
c. On February 6, 2007, Respondent/Defendant contacted Agent Wallace stating that her horses had not received water during the freezing temperatures and "that would cause them to look sucked up." Respondent/Defendant could not commit to a period of time her horses were without water. Additionally, Respondent/Defendant could not describe a feeding regimen for her horses and further, when asked about her finances, stated "I don't have an income."
d. On February 7, 2007, Deputy Morgan Guthner of the Clackamas County Sheriff's Office contacted Agent Wallace and informed him that he spoke with Respondent/Defendant's neighbor Luke Smith of 17484 S. Steiner Road. Luke Smith told Deputy Morgan Guthner that he had helped Respondent/Defendant feed her horses many times because she had financial problems and furthermore that he had previously helped to worm the horses.
e. On February 12, 2007, Agent Wallace, Deputy Morgan Guthner and Deputy Jones of the Clackamas County Sheriff's Office visited 22143 South Evergreen Drive to speak with Respondent/Defendant. Respondent/Defendant was not home, but the parties noted that there was no hay, both horses were chewing on grass less than a quarter inch tall, visible chew marks on the fences possibly indicated inadequate food, and the water trough was unclean.
f. On February 13, 2007, Agent Wallace spoke with Respondent/Defendant's neighbor Luke Smith of 17484 S. Steiner Road. Mr. Smith said that Respondent/Defendant had twice made comments that she feels bad that she cannot feed her horses more.
g. On February 13, 2007 Agent Wallace received a faxed statement from Mrs. Alto documenting her observations of Respondent/Defendant's horses since 2003. The statement cites incidents of neglect. See Exhibit 2.

h. On February 14, 2007, Agent Wallace spoke to Respondent/Defendant and was informed that Respondent/Defendant's veterinarian Dr. Sunholm was examining the horses. Agent Wallace spoke to Dr. Sunholm subsequent to his visit. Dr. Sunholm stated that in his opinion "Lady" was 200 lbs. underweight and "Duran" was 150 lbs. underweight. Dr. Sunholm made additional findings as to the horses' health and conditions. See Exhibit 2. Finally, the last time Dr. Sunholm examined Respondent/Defendant's horses was three years prior to his current visit. This examination was at the request of Deputy Robin Iverson of the Clackamas County Sheriff's Office. The horses were underweight and undernourished at that time.

i. On February 22, 2007, subsequent to the execution of the duly authorized search warrant issued on February 20, 2007, Respondent/Defendant's horses were impounded by the Clackamas County Sheriff's Office pursuant to ORS 167.345(2) and placed into the custody of the Petitioner. Petitioner's Staff Veterinarian, Dr. Kris Otteman, examined the horses using the Henneke body condition scoring system. Per Henneke regulations, both horses returned an unacceptable body score. See Exhibit 2. Additionally, "Duran's" hooves indicated a lack of regular care.

3. In the event that Respondent/Defendant elects to post a security deposit or bond with the Court Clerk, pursuant to ORS 167.347(3), said sum should be in an amount sufficient to repay all reasonable costs incurred, and anticipated to be incurred, by the Petitioner in caring for the animals from the date of initial impoundment on or about February 22, 2007, through to the date of trial for the criminal charges referenced here. The sum to be paid should be not less than the combined sum of $1,056.74 (the total costs incurred between February 22, 2007, and April 25, 2007), and $8.28 (the anticipated cost per day), for each day between April 26, 2007, and the date an Order is entered granting this Petition. See Exhibit 3, two Costs of Care spreadsheets prepared by Agent Wallace, attached and incorporated by reference herein.

WHEREFORE, Petitioner prays for judgment against Respondent/Defendant as follows:

1. For the immediate forfeiture of the two horses mentioned herein and for such other relief as may be just and equitable; or
2. In the alternative, requiring Respondent/Defendant to post a security deposit or bond, within 72 hours of the hearing of this matter, in an amount determined by the court to be sufficient to repay all reasonable costs incurred, and anticipated to be incurred, by Petitioner in caring for the animals from February 22, 2007, to the date of the criminal trial, as is set forth at ORS 167.347(3).

Respectfully submitted on June 20, 2007.

____

APPENDIX D

Sample Jury Voir Dire

General Questions

I. Background

1. What is your name and address?
2. Tell me about your occupation.
    a. What do you do?
    b. How long have you been there?
    c. What jobs did you hold before this one?
    d. Have you ever held a job in:

        Animal processing?
            Meat processing/butcher shop/slaughterhouse?
            Leather shop/tannery?
        Ranching, farming, or raising animals for food?
        Raising (puppy mills) or training animals for consumers, racing?
        Any field dependent on animals? (e.g., feedstock business, animal supplies)
        Pharmaceuticals?

Rodeo, circus?
Veterinary medicine?
Pet shop/store?
Animal shelter?
If yes to any of the above, could you tell me more?

e. Have you ever worked for an employer that was targeted by animal rights demonstrations?
If so, could you tell me about this?
How did it affect you?
f. Do you have any special experience, training, knowledge, or education in ____, or that may contribute to your understanding of this case (depends on case)?

3. Tell me about your educational background.

a. What is your college alma mater?
b. What was your college major?
c. What types of activities were you involved in?

II. Familiarity with Parties and the Case

4. Are you personally related to or do you have family or close friends who are personally related to any of the parties, attorneys, witnesses, or the judge in this case?

a. If so, could you tell me more about this? Employment, dealings, etc.?
b. Have you ever owned stock in ____ (if a large company is at issue)?

5. Have you heard anything about any of the parties in this case that has affected your opinions of the parties in this case?

a. Do you have any other preconceived opinions about any of the parties involved in this case?
b. If so, could you tell me more about these opinions?

6. What have you seen or heard about this case, if anything?

a. What types of opinions have you expressed about this case, if any?
b. Do you feel that you could dismiss what you've heard about this case if you are selected as a juror, thus reaching a verdict based solely on what is presented by the parties to the case?

III. Previous Experience with and Attitude about the Judicial System

7. Have you ever served as a juror? If so, could you tell me about your prior jury experience?
8. Have you ever been sued or sued another party?
   If so, could you tell me about this?
9. Have you ever been the victim of a crime? Has a family member or close friend?
   If so, could you tell me more about this?
10. Have you ever been a complainant or witness in a criminal investigation, grand jury proceeding, or trial?
    Have you ever testified before a grand jury?
11. Have you ever been a defendant in a criminal case?
    Have you ever been charged with or convicted with animal abuse, neglect, or abandonment?
12. Is there anything about your prior experience or involvement in a trial or case that would hinder your ability to act as an impartial juror for this case?

IV. Law Enforcement

13. Have you ever served in the military or the guard? Has a family member or close friend?

    a. Any in active duty?
    b. Ever involved in law enforcement during active duty?

14. Have you ever worked for or had any association with any municipal, state, federal police force, FBI, CIA, Justice Department law enforcement agency, prosecutor's office, or government agency, including animal control agencies? Has a family member or close friend?
    If so, could you tell me more about this association?
    What type of work?
15. What type of interaction have you generally had with law enforcement?
16. Have you had any previous brushes or run-ins with the law?
    If so, could you tell me more about them?
17. How do you feel about the trustworthiness of law enforcement officials?
18. Will it be difficult for you to be impartial because the credibility of law enforcement officials will likely be in conflict with laypersons?

V. Attitude toward the Criminal Justice System

19. Do you have any friends or family members who are attorneys?
20. How do you feel about the role that attorneys play in our criminal justice system?
21. How do you feel about the role that government plays in our criminal justice system?
22. How do you feel about the role that the jury plays in our system?

VI. Understanding of Law

23. As you know, the burden of proof in a criminal trial is "beyond a reasonable doubt." This differs from the civil standard of "preponderance of the evidence." Will you be able to deliberate with the other jurors keeping in mind this higher burden of proof that the state is required to prove?
24. Do you understand that the court will instruct you that a person who is accused of a crime is presumed innocent until such time as the prosecution overcomes this presumption of innocence and proves him or her guilty beyond a reasonable doubt?
25. The rules of law will be stated for the jury before deliberation. Will you have any hesitation or unwillingness to accept these statements as rules of law that you will be required to follow?
26. Do you have any doubts that you would be able to apply the law as explained, even if you personally disagree with it?

VII. Personal Tastes, Preferences, Activities, Beliefs

27. Tell me about the organizations you belong to—community, social, work, or recreational.

    a. What types of volunteer activities do you or have you participated in?
    b. Have you ever belonged to an organization such as the NRA, Safari International, Ducks Unlimited?

28. Do you give to charities? If so, which ones?
29. How do you generally spend your free time?

    a. What types of hobbies do you have?
    b. How do you spend your time with family and friends?

30. What types of TV programs do you watch?
31. Do you read newspapers or magazines? If so, which ones do you regularly read?

32. What is the last book you read?
33. Do you have a special dietary regimen?
34. Have you ever participated in civil rights demonstrations or protests of any kind?
    If so, could you tell me more about these?
35. What is your opinion about the ownership of weapons?
    a. Do you own any weapons?
    b. Have you ever shot or killed an animal?
       If so, could you tell me about the surrounding circumstances?
36. Do you own any animals?
    a. From where did you get him/her/them?
    b. Is/are your animal(s) spayed or neutered?
    c. Do you get along with your animals?
    d. What are your thoughts about how people should treat animals that are in their care?
    e. Have you ever had to give away or sell your animals?
       If so, under what circumstances and to whom?
    f. Do you know what a companion animal is?
37. What is your knowledge and understanding of animal exploitation? Animal testing?
    a. What are your thoughts, if any, about the ability of animals to suffer and experience pain?
    b. What are your thoughts about euthanizing animals?
       Note: this may bring pro-animal responses as well.
38. Do you have any religious or ethical beliefs that would prevent you from passing judgment on another person?
39. Do you have any ideas or beliefs that would hinder your ability to follow the instructions that will be given by the judge?
40. Do you have any preconceived notions about the credibility of certain types of people?

VIII. Attitude during Trial

41. If the time should arise that one of the attorneys makes an objection, do you understand that the objection will be based on rules of evidence, such that the attorney will be objecting to what he or she believes is an unfair or improper method for offering evidence? Will you hold it against an attorney for making objections based on these rules of evidence that the attorney is aiming to uphold?

42. Will you be able to hear all the witnesses with an open mind, and then make a decision with the other jurors when it is time for deliberations?
43. Do you believe the amount of time a person has to observe a subject would bear on the strength of identification?

IX. General Ability to Serve as a Juror

44. Do you have any medical conditions that would interfere with your ability to serve as a juror?
45. Do you have any difficulty understanding English?
46. Do you have any difficulty hearing, seeing, understanding, or sitting for what may be long periods of time?
47. Do you believe you may not be able to sit, listen, and pay careful attention to the opening statements, or to the evidence, over the course of the trial?

X. General Responsibility as a Juror

48. Do you understand that your primary responsibility as a juror rests in determining the innocence or guilt of the accused?
49. Do you understand that while it may appear that the attorneys for both sides are engaged in a duel, as a juror, you must remember your main job is to reach a verdict based on the facts and the evidence presented to you? When evidence is presented that you haven't clearly heard, will you speak up and ask to hear the evidence again?
50. How do you feel about a juror providing assistance to the prosecution, helping to solve the case or providing missing evidence?
51. Do you understand that you cannot resort to guesswork in reaching a verdict?
52. If you are unclear about the law during deliberation, will you ask the bailiff to have the judge repeat the instructions of law again?
53. Do you understand that it is our duty as citizens to follow the law, even though our ideas of what the law ought to be may differ from what the law actually is?
54. Will you follow the law as instructed, despite any feeling of sympathy you might feel for either of the parties in this case? Will you prevent any feeling of sympathy from interfering with your returning a verdict based solely and wholly on the law and evidence of the case?

XI. Impartial Juror

55. Do you know of any reason that I have not asked you about, why you could not be a fair and impartial juror for both sides in this case?
56. Both parties are seeking fair and impartial jurors; do you feel that you can be one of those?
57. Is there any reason why you would prefer not to sit on this jury?

Horse-Abuse Specific

1. Have you ever owned a horse? (Use as part of question 36)
   If so, have you ever had to sell one of your horses?
   If so, under what circumstances and to whom?
   If not, what type of interaction have you had with horses?
2. Have you ever worked processing animal products, including in a (Use as part of question 2d):
   Saddle shop?
   Farm supply business?
3. Have you ever gone to, watched, or bet on horse races? (Use as part of question 29)

Dog-Neglect Specific

1. Have you ever owned, or had any experience with, a dog? (Use as part of question 36)
   If so, could you tell me more?
2. Do you ever go to dog races or dog shows? (Use as part of question 29)

Aggravated Animal Abuse

Violent Tendencies

1. Have you ever threatened to hurt a person or animal in anger?
2. Have you ever hit or injured a person or animal in anger?

Acceptance of Violent Tendencies in Others

1. Have you ever witnessed another person threaten to hurt a person or animal?
2. Have you ever witnessed another person hurt or injure a person or animal?

3. If yes (to either of the above), how did you respond, what was your reaction?

Animals as Property/Things

1. How do you feel about a person's power over his or her property?
2. How do you feel about ownership of animals as property?

Animals' Inability to Feel Pain

1. Do you believe people can feel pain when hurt or injured?
2. How do you feel about whether or not animals can feel pain when hurt or injured?

Animal Abuse—Sexual Assault

Tendency to Dabble in Lewd and Deviant Sexual Behavior

1. As we're all aware, adults are legally permitted to view certain types of pornography. Have you ever exercised your right to do so?
2. What are your feelings about categorizing certain types of pornography as illegal?

Belief in Domination over Animals

1. What are your feelings about the dominion of people over animals?
2. What are your feelings about animals serving the needs of people?
3. Do you believe there are limits? If so, please tell me more about these limits.

Abandonment

Irresponsible

1. How do you feel about leaving animals, such as house cats and dogs, for example, home alone?
2. If you have animals, what do you do with them when you go away?
3. If you have animals, what would you do with them if you were to move?

Inability to Understand the Duties of Animal Caretakers/Owners/Guardians

1. How do you feel about allowing domesticated animals to fend for themselves?
2. When a person no longer wishes to keep an animal, how do you feel that a person should proceed?

Animal Fighting

Tendency to Like Violent Sports

1. Could you tell me about the types of sporting events you enjoy watching? (wrestling, hockey)

Belief That Animal Fighting's Illegality Is Unimportant, Doesn't Have to Follow the Law

1. As you likely already realize, animal fighting has been made illegal by our state legislature. How do you feel about the use of government personnel, such as police officers and animal control officials, to enforce against animal fighting?
2. What more or less, do you believe, should be done about animal fighting? Why?

Lack of Compassion

1. Have you ever been in the presence of an animal that was sick, injured, or hurt?
2. If so, could you tell me more about the surrounding circumstances?
3. How did you react to the incident?

Part of Upbringing or Personal Taste

1. Could you tell me about how you know about animal fighting? How did you first, if ever, hear about it?
2. Have you or someone you know, friend, family member, or someone close to you, ever attended an animal fight in the past?
3. Have you ever seen video recordings of animal fights, or do you know of a friend, family member, or someone close to you, who has seen them?

APPENDIX E

Sample Jury Instructions

IN THE CIRCUIT COURT OF THE STATE OF OREGON
FOR THE COUNTY OF BENTON

STATE OF OREGON
Plaintiff,
________________________,

STATE'S REQUESTED JURY INSTRUCTIONS

vs.

________________________________,
Defendant.

Court No. ______________
DA No. _________

Comes now, Scott Heiser, District Attorney for Benton County, Oregon, and respectfully requests the Court give the following jury instructions:

No.	UCrJI No.	Title
1	1001	Introduction
2	1003	Precautionary Instructions
3	1004	Functions of the Court and Jury
4	1005	Evaluating Witness Testimony
5	1006	Inferences
6	1007	Innocence of Defendant—Proof Beyond a Reasonable Doubt
7	1023	Direct and Circumstantial Evidence
8	1028	Witness False in Part
9	1031	Criminal Charge
10	1034	Intentionally
11	1035	Knowingly
12	1036	Recklessly
13	3000	Definitions (*Animal; Physical Injury*)

14	3001	Animal Abuse in the Second Degree (Count 2)
15	3007	Sexual Assault of an Animal or Animal Carcass (Count 1)

Respectfully submitted on ____ November 20___ , by:

____

APPENDIX F

Sample Verdict

IN THE CIRCUIT COURT OF THE STATE OF OREGON
FOR THE COUNTY OF BENTON

STATE OF OREGON
Plaintiff, **VERDICT**

______________________ ,

vs. Court No. ______________

______________________ ,
Defendant.

We the jury, being first duly impaneled and sworn in the above-entitled Court and cause, do find the defendant on charge of:

Count 1: SEXUAL ABUSE OF AN ANIMAL OR ANIMAL CARCASS
______ Guilty of Child Neglect in the Second Degree
______ Not Guilty of Child Neglect in the Second Degree

Count 2: ANIMAL ABUSE IN THE SECOND DEGREE
______ Guilty of Harassment
______ Not Guilty of Harassment

Date: ______________________________
Presiding Juror: ______________________________

APPENDIX G

Suggested Readings and Other Resources

Articles

Lydia S. Antoncic, *A New Era in Humane Education: How Troubling Youth Trends and a Call for Character Education Are Breathing New Life into Efforts to Educate Our Youth About the Value of All Life*, 9 ANIMAL L. 183 (2003).

Frank R. Ascione, *Animal Abuse and Youth Violence*, JUV. JUST. BULL. (U.S. Department of Justice, Office of Juvenile Justice and Delinquency Prevention), Sept. 2001.

Angela Campbell, *The Admissibility of Evidence of Animal Abuse in Criminal Trials for Child and Domestic Abuse*, 43 B.C.L. REV. 463 (March 2002).

Randall Lockwood & Ann Church, *Deadly Serious: An FBI Perspective on Animal Cruelty*, HSUS NEWS, Fall 1996.

Janet Mickish & Kathleen Schoen, *Protection Orders and Animal Abuse in Family Violence*. 35 COLO. LAW. 105 (Sept. 2006).

Stephan Otto, Model Animal Protection Laws Collection, Animal Legal Def. Fund, http://www.aldf.org (2006).

Gary J. Patronek, *Hoarding of Animals: An Under-Recognized Public Health Problem in a Difficult-to-Study Population*, 114 PUB. HEALTH REP. 81 (Jan/Feb. 1999).

Allie Phillips, *The Dynamics Between Animal Abuse, Domestic Violence and Child Abuse: How Pets Can Help Abused Children*, 38 PROSECUTOR 22 (Sept./Oct. 2004).

Joseph G. Sauder, *Enacting and Enforcing Felony Animal Cruelty Laws to Prevent Violence Against Humans*, 6 ANIMAL L. 1 (2000).

Lawrence Weiss, *Effective Voir Dire in Animal Cases*, 2 ANIMAL L. 187 (Spring 1996).

Books

AM. HUMANE ASS'N, RECOGNIZING & REPORTING ANIMAL ABUSE: A VETERINARIAN'S GUIDE (1998).

FRANK R. ASCIONE, CHILDREN AND ANIMALS: EXPLORING THE ROOTS OF KINDNESS AND CRUELTY (Purdue Univ. Press, 2005).

FRANK R. ASCIONE, SAFE HAVENS FOR PETS: GUIDELINES FOR PROGRAMS SHELTERING PETS FOR WOMEN WHO ARE BATTERED (2000).

FRANK R. ASCIONE & PHIL ARKOW, CHILD ABUSE, DOMESTIC VIOLENCE, AND ANIMAL ABUSE: LINKING THE CIRCLES OF COMPASSION FOR PREVENTION AND INTERVENTION (Purdue Univ. Press, 1999).

RANDALL LOCKWOOD & FRANK R. ASCIONE, EDS., CRUELTY TO ANIMALS AND INTERPERSONAL VIOLENCE: READINGS IN RESEARCH AND APPLICATION (Purdue Univ. Press, 1998).

NEW YORK STATE HUMANE ASS'N, HOW TO INVESTIGATE ANIMAL CRUELTY IN NEW YORK STATE: A MANUAL OF PROCEDURES (updated June 2004), http://nyshumane.org/manual.htm.

SONIA S. WAISMAN, PAMELA D. FRASCH, & BRUCE A. WAGMAN, ANIMAL LAW: CASES AND MATERIALS 3D (Carolina Academic Press, 2006).

Animal Advocacy Groups

American Horse Defense Fund http://www.ahdf.org	The American Horse Defense Fund's mission is to facilitate the protection, conservation, and humane treatment of members of all equine species. AHDF works to address inhumane treatment of horses, ponies, donkeys, mules, and burros, both wild and domesticated, through education, advocacy, and litigation in the state, federal, and international arenas.
American Humane Association http://www.americanhumane.org 303-792-9900	The AHA is a network of individuals and organizations working to prevent cruelty, abuse, neglect, and exploitation of children and animals and to assure that their interests and well-being are humanely guaranteed by an aware and caring society.
Animal Protection Institute http://www.api4animals.org 916-447-3085	API advocates for the protection of animals from exploitation. Campaigns address animals used in entertainment, captive exotic animals, companion animals, compassionate consumerism, farmed animals, and wildlife protection.
Association of Veterinarians for Animal Rights http://www.avar.org 530-759-8106	VAR works toward the acquisition of rights for all nonhuman animals by educating the public and primarily the veterinary profession about a variety of issues concerning nonhuman animal use.
Doris Day Animal League http://www.ddal.org 202-546-1761	The Doris Day Animal League's mission is to reduce the pain and suffering of nonhuman animals through legislative initiatives, education, and programs to enforce existing statutes and regulations protecting animals.

Farm Sanctuary http://www.farmsanctuary.org 607-583-2225	Farm Sanctuary was founded in 1986 to combat the abuses of industrialized farming and to encourage a new awareness and understanding about "farm animals." Farm Sanctuary also reaches out to legislators and businesses and works to bring about institutional reforms.
Fund for Animals http://www.fundforanimals.org 888-405-FUND	The Fund operates five direct animal care operations that provide medical treatment for animals: the Cleveland Amory Black Beauty Ranch, a large sanctuary in east Texas; the Wildlife Center in Southern California for injured wildlife; the rabbit sanctuary in South Carolina; the Cape Wildlife Center in Massachusetts; and the Rural Area Veterinary Services (RAVS) program, which provides medical services to remote communities worldwide.
Humane Society of the United States http://www.hsus.org 202-452-1100	The HSUS works to protect animals through education programs and anticruelty campaigns, legislation, advocacy, emergency rescue services, and litigation. HSUS also offers experts and training on handling the crime of animal fighting and on shelter management.
Performing Animal Welfare Society http://www.pawsweb.org 209-745-2606	Dedicated to the rescue of performing and exotic animals from cruel confinement and performances that cause pain, PAWS is a place where abandoned or abused performing animals and victims of the exotic animal trade can live in peace and contentment.
Society & Animals Forum http://www.psyeta.org/AniCare.html 301-963-4751	Society & Animals Forum (formerly Psychologists for the Ethical Treatment of Animals) works with social scientists, mental health providers, and other animal protection organizations to reduce the suffering and exploitation of both human and nonhuman animals. It also offers the "first-ever" psychological intervention program for treatment of animal abuse, the AniCare Model, with a companion program for children.
United Animal Nations http://www.uan.org 916-429-2457	Founded in 1987, United Animal Nations (UAN) is North America's leading provider of emergency animal sheltering and disaster relief services and an advocate for the critical needs of animals. UAN assists animals by helping to prevent, mitigate, and resolve crises.
United Poultry Concerns http://www.upc-online.org 757-678-7875	Dedicated to the respectful and compassionate treatment of domestic fowl.

World Animal Net Directory http://www.worldanimal.net 617-524-3670	Established in 1997 by veterans of the international animal protection movement to improve communication and coordination between the world's animal protection groups on target campaigns, WAN offers a database of animal protection societies.

Additional Legal Resources

Animal Legal Defense Fund http://www.aldf.org National Headquarters 707-795-2533 Criminal Justice Program 503-231-1602	Since 1979, the Animal Legal Defense Fund has been leading the fight to protect the lives and advance the interests of animals through the legal system. ALDF's Criminal Justice Program works with prosecuting attorneys, police officers, and humane investigators to ensure the vigorous enforcement of all animal protection laws and provides guidance in developing animal protection legislation and animal law classes at law schools.
Animal Legal & Historical Web Center http://www.animallaw.info	As of publication of this chapter, there are over 700 full text cases (U.S., historical, and U.K.) and 975 U.S. statutes available on this site, with Michigan and California being particularly comprehensive, along with over 38 topics that give directions and comprehensive explanations on some of the more interesting issues of animal law.
Animal Legal Reports Services http://www.AnimalLegalReports.com	ALRS covers legal cases, jury verdicts, and settlements pertaining to animal welfare in a bimonthly reference source for veterinarians, lawyers, clubs, associations, government, welfare, and law enforcement officials.
Animal and Plant Health Inspection Service of USDA http://www.aphis.usda.gov/animal_welfare/index.shtml	APHIS is the federal agency charged with enforcement of the Animal Welfare Act and other laws related to animals used in commerce.
Center for Animal Law Studies http://law.lclark.edu/org/cals/	Founded in 2008, the Center for Animal Law Studies at Lewis & Clark is the home for the animal law programs and activities of Lewis & Clark Law School. The Center collaborates with the national nonprofit Animal Legal Defense Fund to educate and support law students and legal professionals in the rapidly developing field of animal law through classes, conferences, scholarship, and clinical opportunities.

Cornell Law School Legal Information Institute http://www.law.cornell.edu/	Online law library for researching state and federal laws and cases.
LawyerExpress http://www.lawyerexpress.com	Designed for lawyers, this site includes links to traditional legal research sources as well as to legal news, periodicals, company information, news, and more.
North Carolina Wesleyan College's Criminal Justice Mega-Sites http://faculty.ncwc.edu/mstevens/415/linklist.htm	A comprehensive collection of links to many criminal justice-related Web sites.
National Institute for Animal Advocacy http://www.nifaa.org	Trains advocates to win strong state and local animal protection laws through political action.

Notes

1. For example, ALDF's National Animal Cruelty Database shows that more than 75 percent of the defendants in the thousands of cases reported to ALDF are male. The Pet-Abuse.com national database shows that of nearly 8,500 animal abusers, more than 75 percent were male.
2. Stephan Otto, Director of Legislative Affairs for ALDF, created a compendium of every state's animal cruelty laws and placed them into top, middle, or bottom tiers based on the laws' strengths and comprehensiveness. Each state statute cited in this chapter will also indicate the state's ranking.
3. The states that do not have some form of felony animal cruelty law are Arkansas, Idaho, Mississippi, North Dakota, and South Dakota.
4. For definitions of neglect, *see, e.g.*, Ga. Code Ann. § 16-12-4(a)(3) (2007) (middle tier): "'Willful neglect' means the intentional withholding of food and water required by an animal to prevent starvation or dehydration"; Ariz. Rev. Stat. § 13-2910(H)(3) (2007) (middle tier): "'Cruel neglect' means failure to provide an animal with necessary food, water or shelter"; Colo. Rev. Stat. § 18-9-201(4) (2007) (top tier): "'Neglect' means failure to provide food, water, protection from the elements, or other care generally considered to be normal, usual, and accepted for an animal's health and well-being consistent with the species, breed, and type of animal."
5. *See, e.g.*, Or. Rev. Stat. § 167.310(5) (2007) (top tier); Animal Legal Def. Fund, "Model Animal Protection Laws Collection," *available at* http://www.aldf.org.
6. *See infra* Sections VII.B., Multiple Counts, and II.E., Hoarders and Breeders.
7. *See infra* Section IV.C., Proving Ownership or Custody.

8. Definitions of "abuse" include the following: "[E]very act, omission, or neglect whereby unnecessary or unjustifiable physical pain or suffering is caused or permitted," CAL. PENAL CODE § 11199(d)(2) (2007) (top tier); animal abuse in the first degree is when a person "intentionally, knowingly or recklessly: (a) Causes serious physical injury to an animal or; (b) Cruelly causes the death of an animal," OR. REV. STAT. § 167.320(1)(a)–(b) (2007) (top tier).
9. *See, e.g.*, KY. REV. STAT. ANN. § 525.130(2)(g) (2007) (bottom tier).
10. OR. REV. STAT. § 167.335(11) (2007) (top tier).
11. Definitions of "abandonment" include the following: When a person "intentionally, knowingly, recklessly or with criminal negligence leaves a domestic animal at a location without providing for the animal's continued care," OR. REV. STAT. § 167.340(1) (2007) (top tier); "completely forsaking or deserting an animal originally under one's custody without making reasonable arrangements for custody of that animal to be assumed by another person," DEL. CODE ANN. tit. 11, § 1325(a)(6) (2007) (top tier); to "forsake an animal entirely or to neglect or refuse to provide or perform the legal obligations for care and support of an animal by its owner," FLA. STAT. ANN. § 828.13(1)(a) (2007) (top tier).
12. *See infra* Section IV.C., Proving Ownership or Custody.
13. *See, e.g.*, OR. REV. STAT. § 167.340(2) (2007) (top tier).
14. *See, e.g.*, OR. REV. STAT. § 167.333(1)(b) (2007) (top tier).
15. *See, e.g.*, 510 ILL. COMP. STAT. 70/2.10 (2007) (top tier): "'Companion animal hoarder' means a person who (i) possesses a large number of companion animals; (ii) fails to or is unable to provide what he or she is required to provide under [this statute]; (iii) keeps the companion animals in a severely overcrowded environment; and (iv) displays an inability to recognize or understand the nature of or has a reckless disregard for the conditions under which the companion animals are living and the deleterious impact they have on the companion animals' and owner's health and well-being."
16. *See* Gary J. Patronek, *Hoarding of Animals: An Under-Recognized Public Health Problem in a Difficult-to-Study Population*, 114 PUB. HEALTH REP. 81 (Jan/Feb. 1999), *available at* http://www.tufts.edu/vet/cfa/hoarding/pubs/pubhlthrep.pdf.
17. *See, e.g.*, People v. Youngblood, 109 Cal.Rptr. 2d 776 (2001) (defendant was convicted of animal cruelty for keeping 92 cats in a single trailer, and the court found that her defense of keeping the cats to save them from euthanasia at animal control was not available under circumstances).
18. *See* Patronek, *Hoarding of Animals*, *supra* note 16.
19. *See generally* Hoarding of Animals Research Consortium *at* http://www.tufts.edu/vet/cfa/hoarding.
20. *See infra* Section IV.A, Forfeiture or Foster Care until Trial, Costs of Care in the Interim.

21. For definitions of animal fighting, *see, e.g.*, ARK. CODE ANN. § 5-62-120(1)(A)–(C) (2007) (bottom tier): "A person commits the offense of unlawful dog fighting in the first degree if he or she knowingly: (A) Promotes, engages in, or is employed at dog fighting; (B) Receives money for the admission of another person to a place kept for dog fighting; or (C) Sells, purchases, possesses, or trains a dog for dog fighting"; in California, it is illegal for "any person who, for amusement or gain, causes any bull, bear, or other animal, not including any dog, to fight with like kind of animal or creature, or causes any animal, including any dog, to fight with a different kind of animal or creature, or with any human being, or who, for amusement or gain, worries or injures any bull, bear, dog, or other animal, or causes any bull, bear, or other animal, not including any dog, to worry or injure each other, or any person who permits the same to be done on any premises under his or her charge or control, or any person who aids or abets the fighting or worrying of an animal or creature." CAL. PENAL CODE § 597b (2007) (top tier).
22. *See, e.g.*, OR. REV. STAT. § 167.310(3) (2007) (top tier): "'Good animal husbandry' includes, but is not limited to, the dehorning of cattle, the docking of horses, sheep or swine, and the castration or neutering of livestock, according to accepted practices of veterinary medicine or animal husbandry."
23. *See, e.g.*, CONN. GEN. STAT. § 53-247(b) (2007) (middle tier).
24. *See, e.g.*, FLA. STAT. ANN. § 828.125(3) (2007) (top tier).
25. *See, e.g.*, MO. ANN. STAT. § 578.182(2)(1) (2007) (bottom tier).
26. *See, e.g.*, IDAHO CODE ANN. § 25-3501a (2007) (bottom tier).
27. *See, e.g.*, IOWA CODE ANN. § 717B.1(1)(a) (2007) (middle tier).
28. *See, e.g.*, UTAH CODE ANN. § 76-9-301(11)(b)(i)–(ii) (2007) (bottom tier).
29. *See infra* Section IX.A., Expert Witness Database.
30. Larue v. State, 478 So. 2d 13 (Ala. App. Ct. 1985).
31. *See, e.g.*, U.S. v. Agurs, 427 U.S. 97 (1976).
32. *See, e.g.*, IDAHO CODE ANN. § 25-3520B (2007).
33. *See* Appendix C, Sample Forfeiture Petition.
34. C. LUKE, A. ARLUKE, & J. LEVIN, CRUELTY TO ANIMALS AND OTHER CRIMES: A STUDY BY THE MSPCA & NE. UNIV. (1997).
35. Guy R. Hodge & Randall Lockwood, *The Tangled Web of Animal Abuse: The Links between Cruelty to Animals and Human Violence*, HUMANE SOC'Y NEWS (Humane Soc'y of the U.S., Summer 1986).
36. Alan R. Felthous & Stephen R. Kellert, *Childhood Cruelty toward Animals among Criminals and Noncriminals*, 38(12) HUMAN RELATIONS (1985).
37. Elizabeth DeViney, Jeffrey Dickert & Randall Lockwood, *The Care of Pets within Child Abusing Families*, INT'L J. STUDY OF ANIMAL PROBLEMS (1983).
38. Frank Ascione, *Domestic Violence and Cruelty to Animals*, paper presented at the Fourth Int'l Conference on Family Violence, Durham, N.H. (July 24, 1995).

39. Michael Robin & Robert ten Bensel, *Pets and the Socialization of Children*, *in* PETS AND THE FAMILY (1985).
40. *See infra* Section VII.E.3, Veterinarians and Other Expert Witnesses.
41. *See infra* Section VII.E.4, Visual Aids for Trial.
42. 2 ANIMAL LAW 187 (Spring 1996).
43. *See infra* Section IV.B, The Link between Animal Abuse and Human Violence.
44. *See* Appendix F, Sample Verdict.
45. For a range of sentencing guidelines, *see, e.g.*, D.C. CODE ANN. § 22-1001(a) (2007) (bottom tier): a person faces imprisonment in jail not exceeding 180 days, or a fine not exceeding $250, or both if he "knowingly overdrives, overloads, drives when overloaded, overworks, tortures, torments, deprives of necessary sustenance, cruelly chains, cruelly beats or mutilates, any animal, or knowingly causes or procures any animal to be so overdriven, overloaded, driven when overloaded, overworked, tortured, tormented, deprived of necessary sustenance, cruelly chained, cruelly beaten, or mutilated, and whoever, having the charge or custody of any animal, either as owner or otherwise, knowingly inflicts unnecessary cruelty upon the same, or unnecessarily fails to provide the same with proper food, drink, air, light, space, veterinary care, shelter, or protection from the weather"; NEV. REV. STAT. § 574.100(2)(a)(1)(2) (2007) (middle tier): A first offender who overrides, tortures, injures, or abandons animals or fails to provide proper sustenance faces a sentence of "[i]mprisonment in the city or county jail or detention facility for not less than 2 days, but not more than 6 months," community service of "not less than 48 hours, but not more than 120 hours," and a fine of "not less than $200, but not more than $1,000."
46. *See, e.g.*, Commonwealth v. Bishop, 67 Mass. App. Ct. 1116 (2006) (defendant, who was convicted of animal cruelty and failing to provide a sanitary environment for his five dogs, was ordered to pay more than $60,000 for medical services provided for his dogs after they were taken from him).
47. *See, e.g.*, Humane Soc'y of the U.S., Animal Cruelty Laws: Where Does Your State Stand, *at* http://www.hsus.org/legislation_laws/state_legislation/animal_cruelty_laws_where_does_your_state_stand.html.
48. Pet-Abuse.Com, Animal Abuse Crime Database, http://www.pet-abuse.com/pages/cruelty_database.php.
49. Mich. State Univ. Coll. of Law, Animal Legal & Historical Ctr., http://www.animallaw.info.
50. *See also* Animal Cruelty Task Force of S. Ariz. *at* http://www.act-az.org.
51. *See* Animal Cruelty Laws, *supra* note 47.
52. *See* Appendix A, Sample Indictment.
53. *See* Blakely v. Washington, 542 U.S. 296 (2004).
54. *See* Appendix B, Sample Subpoena Duces Tecum.
55. *See infra* Section IX.A., Expert Witness Database.

CHAPTER 11

Expert Witnesses

KATHERINE C. BLOOMQUIST

I. Introduction

An expert witness is a witness who by virtue of education, training, skill, or experience is believed to have knowledge in a particular subject beyond that of the average person, sufficient that others may officially and legally rely upon the witness's specialized (scientific, technical or other) opinion about an evidence or fact issue within the scope of the witness's expertise.[1] Counsel may use an expert witness to support fact testimony, to teach the jurors scientific or technical principles, or to express an opinion. The purpose of this chapter is to discuss practical factors when selecting an expert for an animal litigation.

II. Choosing an Expert

Typically, expert opinions are most commonly sought to support or challenge causation and/or damages. First, counsel should consider whether any "experts" are already involved in the cases as fact witnesses. After thoroughly understanding the testimony of such a fact witness, counsel may consider whether the strength of the testimony will benefit from having the witness also provide an expert opinion, or whether to obtain an independent expert. Alternatively, it may be stronger to first obtain an independent expert opinion and then determine whether the "fact" expert witnesses already involved in the matter will willingly, or through deposition or cross-examination, agree with the independent expert's opinion. Second, consider the strength of the factual expert witnesses' qualifications and whether it benefits the case to have an additional independent expert.

A. The Expert's Qualifications

The exact nature of the expert testimony will help you determine what type of qualifications your expert needs. The following case illustrates the importance and strategy of choosing an expert who is qualified to testify to the subject at hand, as well as the use of fact witnesses as testifying experts.

In the case of *Gross v. Victoria Station*,[2] plaintiff Gross owned a breeding stallion and sport horse, "Traffic Secretary," that was boarded at defendant Victoria Station's stable. The horse escaped from its paddock, sustained lacerations, and became lame. The plaintiff claimed that as a result of the horse's injuries stemming from the escape, the horse would no longer be able to compete in the sport of eventing, which would cause lost breeding profits. In choosing an expert, the defendant secured an independent medical examination from a board-certified veterinarian that had years of experience specializing in lameness evaluations. This expert veterinarian was also well respected within the state of Minnesota. During the medical examination, the expert veterinarian found that the horse had a preexisting chronic right front lameness from its time racing on the track. Further discovery revealed records from the track that showed that the chronic right front lameness inhibited the horse's ability to perform during its time on the racetrack. The horse was retired from the track and entered the sport of eventing.

After eliciting the expert opinion, the defendant took the deposition of one of the treating veterinarians, and elicited the admission that the current lameness was more likely than not from the same problems exhibited on the track, and not the result of the escape injuries. The defendant then obtained affidavits from the plaintiff's two other treating veterinarians, who also opined consistently that the cause of the lameness was due to the preexisting right front lameness and was not a result of the escape. The treating veterinarians further opined that they agreed with the opinion of the defendant's independent expert veterinarian.

The defendant moved for summary judgment, citing to the testimony of all three of the plaintiff's treating veterinarians and the defendant's independent expert veterinarian. The defendant argued that all medical evidence showed that Traffic Secretary's escape from the pasture was unrelated to its current lameness. The plaintiff, in his response, attempted to argue that the medical evidence was irrelevant and that a trial should proceed on grounds of *res ipsa loquitur*. The trial court disagreed, and provided the plaintiff with more time to submit an affidavit from an expert. The plaintiff struggled to find an expert veterinarian to testify against the collective opinions of the veterinarians. Instead, the plaintiff submitted an affidavit from a conformation specialist who was certainly well qualified in her field of conformation, but was not a veterinarian. The defendant argued that the plaintiff's expert was not qualified to provide medical testimony on lameness. The trial court agreed, and granted the defendant's motion for summary judgment, finding that that the plaintiff had failed to offer any medical evidence that the defendant's employee's actions caused the lameness. More importantly, the trial court found that the conformation specialist was not qualified to issue an opinion on medical evidence as she had no "lameness training" or veterinary training.

The plaintiff appealed to the Minnesota Court of Appeals, and the decision was reversed.[3] The appellate court found that the plaintiff's expert was an "expert" within the meaning of the word. The defendant filed certiorari and appealed to the Minnesota Supreme Court. The Minnesota Supreme Court agreed with the trial court, citing that under Minnesota Rule of Evidence 702, an expert can be qualified by "knowledge, skill, experience, training, or education."[4] It continued that "the knowledge requirement may be satisfied by either formal education or sufficient occupational experience."[5] When reviewing the qualifications of the plaintiff's expert, the court ruled that although the conformation expert had a great deal of experience with horses, she was not an expert in equine lameness because she lacked special training or experience in that area.[6] Equine lameness is a subject that is not familiar to the average person, and for that reason, expert evidence is required for the plaintiff to prevail. Therefore, the supreme court reversed the judgment of the appellate court and affirmed the judgment of the trial court that the defendant wins.[7]

Proving causation in an animal litigation case frequently challenges the lawyer and the expert. Another case example, also on causation, illustrates the challenges of finding the right expert. In the case of *Henslee v. Farnam*,[8] the plaintiff sued Farnam in a product liability suit involving the product Equitrol, a feed-through fly-control product. Equitrol is intended to be top-dressed on feed, pass through a horse's system without absorption, land on the manure, and kill future fly larvae. The product contained the active ingredient of an organophosphate called tetrachlorovinphos, a cholinesterase inhibitor and neurotoxin with the trade name Rabon. Feed-through fly-control products containing Rabon are used in beef and dairy cattle and other livestock industries. Farnam advertised that Equitrol is designed to pass quickly through the horse's gastrointestinal tract without being digested, and that it is safe for all horses, including pregnant mares and lactating mares and their foals. The plaintiff alleged that the product was being absorbed, contrary to the defendant's representations, causing prematurity, abortions, and other physical harm to horses that ingested it.

In choosing experts, the plaintiff enlisted the help of the plaintiff's treating veterinarian to testify to the medical problems the horses had developed, as well as a professor of environmental toxicology that specialized in research on pesticides. The defendant elicited testimony of a toxicologist and other veterinarians to support its proposition that the product was not absorbed by the horses' gastrointestinal tract and did not cause harm to the horses.

Defendant Farnam challenged causation through summary judgment and *Daubert* hearings on the qualifications of the experts. The district court ruled that the plaintiff's experts were qualified to testify, and the case went to trial. The jury did not award damages, presumably finding that the plaintiff had not proven its case on causation.

The second case of a similar nature, *Wrather v. Farnam Cos.*, was filed in federal court in California with the same types of allegations and defenses, but yielded a different result.[9] In addition to using the testimony of three treating veterinarians and a professor of environment toxicology, the plaintiff retained a well-known, board-certified veterinarian, a specialist in the field of neonatal care. This veterinarian conducted a study on the effects of feeding Equitrol to a group of horses. The study revealed that the test horses exhibited a sharp drop in their whole-blood cholinesterase levels consistent with organophosphate poisoning. The study also revealed statistically significant differences in behavior between the horses on Equitrol and the control groups. In a series of behavioral tests, the horses on Equitrol exhibited heightened or intensified flight response. Defendant Farnam again challenged the plaintiff on *Daubert* grounds, both through summary judgment and motions in limine. The district court rejected the arguments, and all the experts were permitted to testify. The jury returned a verdict of $1,007,500 in favor of the plaintiffs.

These Equitrol cases underscore the importance of finding the right type of expert when causation is at issue. Presumably the added strength of the neonatal veterinary and his pilot study persuaded the jury to retain a verdict on a very novel scientific causation issue. Besides veterinarians, animal control officers, breeders, trainers, animal behaviorists, and veterinary behaviorists are all helpful to the trier of fact. Also remember that the expert you need may not be someone who is involved with animals on a daily basis. For example, if you can make an argument regarding emotional distress of a pet owner or the sentimental value of a pet, a human psychologist or psychiatrist may be required to give expert testimony regarding the human's pain and suffering. Be creative as to who may be needed to give the expert testimony that could help prove your case.

If your challenge is to determine the amount of damages incurred, a number of people may be qualified to give testimony, including appraisers, certified public accountants, trainers, veterinarians, and successful competitors. Your ultimate choice of expert may depend on the type of animal involved and the type of damages, whether it is the replacement cost of the animal, lost income due to the animal's injury, or increased costs for care of the animal. While most jurisdictions allow for property owners to provide testimony of the value of their property, which applies to animals, a more persuasive case is presented with the use of appraisers. If the claim is for lost economic damages of a breeding business, it is imperative that counsel select experts that have knowledge of the breeding industry as well as knowledge of the economics. Generally, counsel would want to select an economist to show lost profits of an animal breeding business, and counsel should expect a *Daubert* challenge on the "speculative nature of the damages." The expert or experts should be knowledgeable both as to the economics of the business and the nature of the animals and breeding industry.

Also consider that all animals are not the same. A veterinarian that may be well versed with dogs and cats may not have expertise with large animals. An equine veterinarian may have no experience with cattle. Similarly, exotic animals require specialists who deal with exotics. Keep in mind the type of animal involved when selecting an expert in animal litigation.

B. Practical Pointers in Selection and Use of an Expert

Counsel should also consider the particular expert's background and qualifications. Items to consider when selecting your expert include the following:

- The expert's general familiarity with the subject including education, degrees, and experience. Check to see that all credentials are in order and up to date.
- Determine which associations your expert is involved with and to what extent.
- Check for conflicts of interest.
- You should be prepared to educate the expert regarding the legal process. During your initial discussion with the expert, determine if the expert involved has any legal experience, whether testifying in a deposition or testifying in court. Because many "animal experts" have never seen the inside of a courtroom, they will naturally be less familiar with the rules of discovery, drafting an expert report, testifying through a deposition, and deadlines. Explain to the expert that there will be periods of intense activity to meet deadlines followed by lulls where there is little activity on the case.
- The expert's previous testifying experience is important. Check to see if your expert has testified only for plaintiffs or for defendants in litigation. Speak to other counsel who have utilized the expert or challenged the expert. Also see if your expert has ever been excluded from offering testimony in the past. It is also helpful to obtain testimony transcripts to evaluate the expert's presentation of his or her opinion. Finally, determine whether your expert has ever given contrary testimony that will affect the expert's credibility and reliability in the current litigation.
- Has your expert taken any positions publicly, either in writing or orally? Will those positions affect the expert's testimony?
- Always check your expert's criminal history and disciplinary record. Discreditation or disciplinary action will affect the expert's credibility.
- Is your expert able to effectively communicate his or her opinion to other people without resorting to terms that may be unfamiliar to other people? An expert who is unable to communicate to the average person will not be able to help present your case.
- Always check to see if your expert is available for the expected duration of the case. Does the expert have other professional

or family commitments that will interfere with his or her availability to testify? Does your expert have any health concerns or complications? Does your expert have any plans for vacations or other travel requirements during the time that you may need your expert to be available?
- In particular with animal experts, be very familiar with what associations they belong to and whether the association is considered "animal rights" or "animal welfare," given the possible impact that this may have on a jury.

III. Admissibility of Expert Witnesses

The primary rules to keep in mind when evaluating the admissibility of expert testimony are Federal Rules of Evidence 403 and 701–706:

> Rule 403: Exclusion of Relevant Evidence on Grounds of Prejudice, Confusion, or Waste of Time[10]
>
> Rule 701: Opinion Testimony by Lay Witnesses[11]
>
> Rule 702: Testimony by Experts[12]
>
> Rule 703: Bases of Opinion Testimony by Experts[13]
>
> Rule 704: Opinion on Ultimate Issue[14]
>
> Rule 705: Disclosure of Facts or Data Underlying Expert Opinion[15]
>
> Rule 706: Court Appointed Experts[16]

The Rules of Evidence of individual states are usually similar to the Federal Rules of Evidence, but you must check the rules applicable in each jurisdiction to determine the court's status on the admissibility of expert testimony. Also review the Federal Rules of Expert Disclosure, and the Local Rules of the Federal Court.

IV. Expert Witnesses and the Emerging Daubert *Standards*

A. *Daubert v. Merrell Dow Pharmaceuticals, Inc.*[17]

In this 1993 case, two minor children and their parents sued a pharmaceutical manufacturer alleging that the mother's prenatal ingestion of the drug Bendectin caused her children to be born with birth defects. Defendant Merrell Dow moved for summary judgment. The district court, utilizing the *Frye* standard, ruled that the expert testimony presented by the plaintiffs was inadmissible because of the types of studies performed by the experts in forming their opinions and the lack of peer review of the experts' studies, and granted the defendant's summary judgment motion.[18]

The Dauberts appealed, but the Ninth Circuit Court of Appeals affirmed the district court's ruling. The Dauberts appealed to the United States Supreme Court, which granted certiorari "in light of sharp divisions among the courts regarding the proper standard for the admission of expert testimony."[19] The primary issue before the Court was whether the adoption of Federal Rule of Evidence 702 eliminated the general acceptance test of *Frye* for the admission of scientific evidence.

The *Frye* test, or the "general acceptance test," resulted from the 1923 decision in *Frye v. U.S.*[20] regarding the admissibility of evidence from a precursor to the lie detector test and had been the standard for admissibility of expert testimony since then. In 1973, the Federal Rules of Evidence, which were adopted by Congress, took effect. Of particular importance in *Daubert*, Rule 702 states that "if scientific, technical, or other specialized knowledge will assist the trier of fact to understand the evidence or to determine a fact in issue, a witness qualified as an expert by knowledge, skill, experience, training, or education, may testify thereto in the form of an opinion or otherwise." The U.S. Supreme Court noted that the text of the rule does not state that "general acceptance" is an "absolute prerequisite to admissibility."[21] Thus, the Federal Rules of Evidence superseded *Frye v. U.S.*, and the Court reversed and remanded the Ninth Circuit's decision.[22]

In its discussion, the U.S. Supreme Court created a "gatekeeper" role for the trial judge in determining whether evidence is relevant and reliable, stating that under Rule 104(a), when scientific testimony is offered, the trial judge must determine "whether the expert is proposing to testify to (1) scientific knowledge that (2) will assist the trier of fact to understand or determine a fact in issue."[23] The U.S. Supreme Court also outlined a list of four factors the trial judge should consider when assessing if expert testimony could properly be applied to the facts of the case. The list was not intended to be all-inclusive or definitive and included:

1. Whether the theory or methods presented had been tested.
2. Whether the theory or methods have been subjected to peer review or publication.
3. The potential rate of error.
4. Whether the theory or method is generally accepted.[24]

The U.S. Supreme Court also advised trial judges to be mindful of the other applicable rules of evidence when evaluating the admissibility of expert testimony, including Rules 703, 706, and 403. In justifying its decision, the U.S. Supreme Court stated that shaky evidence, which may not have been admitted under *Frye*, can be, and should be, properly attacked through "vigorous cross-examination, presentation of contrary evidence, and careful instruction on the burden of proof."[25] It was also noted that the courtroom is designed to resolve legal disputes, not to test novel scientific theories.[26]

B. After *Daubert*

In light of the U.S. Supreme Court's ruling on *Daubert*, an expert must first be qualified to testify on the topic under Rule 702.[27] An expert can be qualified through "knowledge, skill, experience, training, *or* education" (emphasis added). The trial judge will determine whether a witness is a qualified expert under Rule 702, and an expert's qualifications are usually determined on a case-by-case basis.[28] Previously, an owner was sometimes considered qualified to testify about the value of an animal in question. However, since *Daubert*, an owner must be qualified as an expert in valuation in order to provide testimony on the value of damages.[29] Keep in mind, however, that even though the owner may be qualified as an expert, there may be a question of the credibility of the owner's testimony because the owner is an interested party in the case.

While it is usually not an issue, the next item to address is whether the expert's testimony is relevant. Testimony is relevant under Rule 702 if it will "assist the trier of fact" in understanding the issue at hand.

Finally, the expert's testimony must be reliable. Reliability usually does not focus on the expert's qualifications or conclusions, but rather on the methods used by the expert in forming his or her opinion. The rules allow for contradictory testimony and testimony from competing principles in the same field to be admitted as evidence.

The four factors outlined in *Daubert* of testing, peer review, rate of error, and general acceptance can be utilized by the trial judge in determining the reliability of an expert's opinion. It is important to remember, however, that the four factors are not exclusive and they may not be applicable to all cases. Other factors may be better utilized to analyze the reliability of expert testimony in certain cases.[30]

A court hearing, sometimes called a *Daubert* hearing, is usually held to address the relevance and reliability of an expert's testimony. The courts are not required to hold a hearing to comply with the standard set in *Daubert*, but the trial judges do have the "gatekeeper" role of making the initial assessment regarding the relevance and reliability, and ultimately admissibility, of an expert's testimony.[31]

1. General Electric Co. v. Joiner[32]

In light of its ruling in *Daubert*, the Supreme Court in *Joiner* addressed which standard of review should be exercised by appellate courts when the court reviews a decision to exclude expert testimony by a lower court. The Supreme Court held that the abuse of discretion standard, the standard applicable to the review of evidentiary rulings in general, was the proper standard by which to review a lower court's decision to admit or exclude expert scientific evidence.[33]

2. Kumho Tire Co. v. Carmichael[34]

One of the issues addressed by the Court in *Kumho* was whether *Daubert* applied only to scientific expert testimony and not to testimony from engineers or other experts who were not scientists. The Court held that *Daubert* assigned the "gatekeeping" role of the trial judge to testimony based upon "technical" and other "specialized" knowledge.[35] It further stated that the factors set out in *Daubert* to address the reliability of an expert's testimony do not apply in all cases and that other factors can, and should be, included.[36]

3. *Federal Rule of Evidence 702 Amendment in 2000*

In 2000, Rule 702 was amended to clarify the confusion that resulted after *Daubert*. The amended rule added three additional criteria to assist judges in determining the admissibility of expert testimony. The new rule states, "If scientific, technical, or other specialized knowledge will assist the trier of fact to understand the evidence or to determine a fact in issue, a witness qualified as an expert by knowledge, skill, experience, training, or education, may testify thereto in the form of an opinion or otherwise, if (1) the testimony is based upon sufficient facts or data, (2) the testimony is the product of reliable principles and methods, and (3) the witness has applied the principles and methods reliably to the facts of the case."

C. Applicability of *Daubert* to State Courts

While many state courts have adopted the *Daubert* standard regarding the admissibility of expert testimony, some states have rejected it in favor of retaining *Frye* or some other standard.[37]

V. Discovery of Experts

A. Applicable Rules

It is important to check the discovery rules that apply to each court's jurisdiction. State rules may differ from the federal rules regarding the discovery involving experts. Federal Rule of Civil Procedure 26(a)(2) provides that parties "must disclose to the other parties the identity of any witness it may use at trial to present evidence under Federal Rule of Evidence 702, 703, or 705." Rule 26 also states that a written report prepared and signed by the expert witness must accompany the disclosure of the expert's testimony and goes on to state that expert disclosures must happen in the order and at the times that the court orders in its scheduling order. The rule also gives a timeline for the disclosure of experts in the absence of any scheduling order by the court.[38]

B. Practical Pointers in Conducting Discovery When an Expert May Be Utilized

To depose an expert, counsel must essentially become an expert. While this may be a cliché, it has much truth. Counsel should utilize its expert in preparing the case from start to finish, including preparing for discovery and depositions. Obtain as much information on the expert prior to his or her deposition through Internet research, legal research, association research, and attorney and expert contacts. The following checklist may be of help in preparing for an expert deposition:

1. Personal information.
2. Education, including board certification, specializations, and licenses.
3. Employment: To avoid using too much costly deposition time in background, obtain as much personal information, education, and employment information from the expert's curriculum vitae, written disclosures, and discovery—unless the qualifications of the expert are a critical issue.
4. Oral presentations, classes taught, publications: If the publications were peer reviewed, inquire as to the comments, drafts, revisions, and rejections.
5. Research: Determine how the expert's research is initiated and who or what group is funding the research.
6. Past testimony: Secure past trial and deposition testimony transcripts prior to the deposition.

7. Retention as an expert: when, how, communications with whom? Obtain copies of correspondence between expert and client.
8. Opinion: assumptions made, any assistance by staff or third parties, data reviewed, data produced, medical notes (not just bills or invoices), methodology for arriving at opinion, literature supporting and opposing opinion. Any concerns regarding opinion? Other explanation for opinion?

Strategically, expert depositions may be approached as an opportunity to obtain admissions through cross-examination or to obtain information for trial through open-ended direct questioning. The benefit of the first approach may be an early settlement. However, if settlement does not occur, the cross-examination approach will tip counsel's hand as to its theme, which will allow opposing counsel and the expert to modify opinions and testimony prior to trial. Effective cross-examination at the deposition can lead to a limitation or exclusion of the expert's testimony, so preparation cannot be emphasized enough.

In preparing counsel's expert for deposition, the previous list may be useful as part of an outline. Even if a videotaped deposition is not noticed, it is helpful to practice the deposition with video analysis. In the animal litigation area, experts are not often as practiced or experienced in deposition or in court. Utilizing extra practice helps put the expert at ease about the process, and gives you a better idea as to how the expert may testify. In addition, the following points are good to cover with your expert:

- Ensure that the expert's curriculum vitae is up to date.
- Do not waive the reading and signing of the deposition transcript.
- Take breaks.
- Encourage the expert to avoid appearing defensive and to keep a calm demeanor. It will not help your client if the expert loses his or her temper during testimony.
- Advise the expert not to volunteer information, and to answer only the specific question asked. This can be very difficult for experts, particularly those in the field of education. However, it is imperative that the expert does not inadvertently provide information that is detrimental to your client's case.

Notes

1. If scientific, technical, or other specialized knowledge will assist the trier of fact to understand the evidence or to

> determine a fact in issue, a witness qualified as an expert by knowledge, skill, experience, training, or education, may testify thereto in the form of an opinion or otherwise, if (1) the testimony is based upon sufficient facts or data, (2) the testimony is the product of reliable principles and methods, and (3) the witness has applied the principles and methods reliably to the facts of the case.

FED. R. EVID. 702 (2009).

2. 578 N.W.2d 757 (Minn. 1998).
3. Gross v. Victoria Station, Nos. C4-97-477, 1997 WL 471388 (Minn. Ct. App., Aug. 19, 1997).
4. 578 N.W.2d at 761.
5. *Id.*
6. *Id.* at 762–763.
7. *Id.* at 762. *See also* Alpha Real Estate Co. of Rochester v. Delta Dental Plan of Minn., 664 N.W.2d 303, 310 (Minn. 2003) (stating that an appellate court shall give deference to the trial court's decisions regarding "issues arising during the course of the trial"); Teffeteller v. Univ. of Minn., 645 N.W.2d 420, 427 (Minn. 2002) (stating that appellate courts correctly apply a "very deferential standard" when reviewing a trial court's determination as to expert qualifications); Smeltzer v. Medtox Labs., 2006 WL 2095468 (D. Minn. 2006) (noting that expert testimony is required when a layperson could not possess well-founded knowledge on the subject and would instead be merely speculating); Sila v. Sears, Roebuck and Co., 2003 WL 22076550 (D. Minn. 2003) (holding that store sporting goods displays are not the type of issue that requires expert testimony); State v. Padua, 869 A.2d 192, 232, 273 Conn. 138, 200 (Conn. 2005) (distinguishing between a conclusion that is part of common knowledge and one that involves such "obscure and abstruse facts" such that a layperson would not possess well-founded knowledge as to the matter and therefore require expert testimony).
8. No. H-00-CV-2811 S.D. Tex. (Nov. 2002).
9. Santa Ana Civil No. 03-967JVS(RCx) (C.D. Cal. Mar. 25, 2004).
10.

> Although relevant, evidence may be excluded if its probative value is substantially outweighed by the danger of unfair prejudice, confusion of the issues, or misleading the jury, or by considerations of undue delay, waste of time, or needless presentation of cumulative evidence.

FED. R. EVID. 403.

11.

> If the witness is not testifying as an expert, the witness' testimony in the form of opinions or inferences is limited to those opinions or inferences which are (a) rationally based on the perception of the witness, (b) helpful to a clear

understanding of the witness' testimony or the determination of a fact in issue, and (c) not based on scientific, technical, or other specialized knowledge within the scope of Rule 702.

FED. R. EVID. 701.

12. See *supra* note 1.

13. The facts or data in the particular case upon which an expert bases an opinion or inference may be those perceived by or made known to the expert at or before the hearing. If of a type reasonably relied upon by experts in the particular field in forming opinions or inferences upon the subject, the facts or data need not be admissible in evidence in order for the opinion or inference to be admitted. Facts or data that are otherwise inadmissible shall not be disclosed to the jury by the proponent of the opinion or inference unless the court determines that their probative value in assisting the jury to evaluate the expert's opinion substantially outweighs their prejudicial effect.

FED. R. EVID. 703.

14. (a) Except as provided in subdivision (b), testimony in the form of an opinion or inference otherwise admissible is not objectionable because it embraces an ultimate issue to be decided by the trier of fact.

(b) No expert witness testifying with respect to the mental state or condition of a defendant in a criminal case may state an opinion or inference as to whether the defendant did or did not have the mental state or condition constituting an element of the crime charged or of a defense thereto. Such ultimate issues are matters for the trier of fact alone.

FED. R. EVID. 704.

15. The expert may testify in terms of opinion or inference and give reasons therefor without first testifying to the underlying facts or data, unless the court requires otherwise. The expert may in any event be required to disclose the underlying facts or data on cross-examination.

FED. R. EVID. 705.

16. (a) Appointment.—The court may on its own motion or on the motion of any party enter an order to show cause why

> expert witnesses should not be appointed, and may request the parties to submit nominations. The court may appoint any expert witnesses agreed upon by the parties, and may appoint expert witnesses of its own selection. An expert witness shall not be appointed by the court unless the witness consents to act. A witness so appointed shall be informed of the witness' duties by the court in writing, a copy of which shall be filed with the clerk, or at a conference in which the parties shall have opportunity to participate. A witness so appointed shall advise the parties of the witness' findings, if any; the witness' deposition may be taken by any party; and the witness may be called to testify by the court or any party. The witness shall be subject to cross-examination by each party, including a party calling the witness.
>
> (b) Compensation.—Expert witnesses so appointed are entitled to reasonable compensation in whatever sum the court may allow. The compensation thus fixed is payable from funds which may be provided by law in criminal cases and civil actions and proceedings involving just compensation under the fifth amendment. In other civil actions and proceedings the compensation shall be paid by the parties in such proportion and at such time as the court directs, and thereafter charged in like manner as other costs.
>
> (c) Disclosure of Appointment.—In the exercise of its discretion, the court may authorize disclosure to the jury of the fact that the court appointed the expert witness.
>
> (d) Parties' Experts of Own Selection.—Nothing in this rule limits the parties in calling expert witnesses of their own selection.

FED. R. EVID. 706.

17. 509 U.S. 579 (1993).
18. *Id*. at 583.
19. *Id*. at 585.
20. 293 F. 1013 (D.C. Cir., 1923).
21. 509 U.S. at 588.
22. *Id*. at 588–589.
23. *Id*. at 592. (quoting FED. R. EVID. 104(a).
24. *Id*. at 593–594.
25. *Id*. at 596.

26. *Id.* at 596–597.
27. *See* Berry v. City of Detroit, 25 F.3d 1342 (6th Cir. 1994); R.C. v. Commonwealth, 101 S.W.3d 897 (Ky. App. 2002).
28. *See* Bush v. Commonwealth, 839 S.W.2d 550 (Ky. 1992); Alaimo v. Racetrack at Evangeline Downs, Inc., 893 So. 2d 190 (La. App. 2005); Archibald v. Act III Arabians, 768 S.W.2d 827 (Tex. App. 1989); Restrepo v. New York, 146 N.Y. Misc. 2d 349 (N.Y. Ct. Cl. 1989); Guzowski v. Detroit Racing Assoc., Inc., 343 N.W.2d 536 (Mich. App. 1983); Lester v. Employers Mut. Liab. Ins. Co. of Wisc., 333 So. 2d 672 (La. App. 1976); Rombola v. Cosindas, 220 N.E.2d 919 (Mass. 1966).
29. *See* Lampley v. Webb, 1996 U.S. Dist. LEXIS 13376 (E.D. Pa. Sept. 12, 1996); Lester v. Employers Mut. Liab. Ins. Co. of Wisc., 333 So. 2d 672 (La. App. 1976).
30. *See* Advisory Committee's Notes to the 2000 Amendments to the Federal Rules of Evidence.
31. *See* Greenwell v. Boatright, 184 F.3d 492 (6th Cir. 1999).
32. 522 U.S. 136 (1997).
33. *Id.* at 141–142.
34. 526 U.S. 137 (1999).
35. *Id.* at 147.
36. *Id.* at 150–151.
37. *See* Goeb v. Tharaldson, 615 N.W.2d 800, 814 (Minn. 2000) (rejecting the *Daubert* standard in Minnesota and retaining instead the two-prong Frye-Mack test for admissibility of novel scientific evidence); Mitchell v. Commonwealth, 908 S.W.2d 100 (Ky. 1995) (adopting and incorporating the *Daubert* factors in Kentucky); Goodyear Tire & Rubber Co. v. Thompson, 11 S.W.3d 575 (Ky. 2000) (holding that the *Daubert* and *Mitchell* factors were properly considered by the trial court in determining admissibility of expert testimony); Courtaulds Fibers, Inc. v. Long, 779 So.2d 198 (Ala. 2000) (declining to adopt the *Daubert* standard and instead applying a "general acceptance" test).
38. Rule 26(a)(2)(c).

CHAPTER 12

Practical Considerations for Attorneys Handling Animal Law Cases

JULIE I. FERSHTMAN

Appendices

I. Introduction

Lawyers serving people with animal-related legal issues face unique challenges. On one hand, lawyers with this experience bring special compassion to their clients and a deep understanding of the importance of their legal matters. On the other hand, our clients' concerns will potentially come before a legal system that does not typically handle animal-related legal issues. Judges and counsel can, and often do, trivialize our clients' concerns. This requires special attention to the client at virtually all stages of the legal matter and special care and handling of the legal matter itself.

II. Unique Ethical Considerations

A. Rules of Ethics

All counsel are certainly mindful of Model Rule of Professional Conduct 3.1, which states: "A lawyer shall not bring or defend a proceeding, or assert or controvert an issue therein, unless there is a basis for doing so that is not frivolous." On the other hand, Rule 3.1 does provide that a lawyer may "offer good-faith argument for an extension, modification, or reversal of existing law."

Procedural rules within the applicable jurisdiction likely allow for penalties when counsel or a party file court documents and pleadings that are found to be frivolous, such as Federal Rule of Civil Procedure 11.[1] Although animal law practice sometimes warrants creative and novel approaches and theories, counsel should be especially mindful of these rules and their consequences. That is, what might seem completely warranted for the zealous representation of a client in need could potentially have adverse long-term consequences on the reputation of counsel.

B. Civility and Professionalism

It is widely believed that animal law is an emerging practice area that will find lawyers and firms more involved in these types of cases in the years ahead. More and more law schools now offer courses on Animal Law, and more lawyers have identified Animal Law among their areas of interest or areas of practice.[2]

At this stage, when animal law cases are not brought in great numbers and when animal law practitioners themselves are not well known, each lawyer handling these cases is essentially an ambassador for practitioners in the field. This is an opportunity to display civility and professionalism in all dealings with the court and opposing counsel. This is an opportunity to make sure that your court filings are properly supported, are timely submitted, and meet all ethical and legal requirements to avoid motions to strike or motions for sanctions. This is an opportunity to overcome stereotypes that animal law practitioners can be "fanatics" who are "out of touch" with reality. This is an opportunity to show that animal law cases are serious and not to be trivialized.

III. Evaluation of the Client's Goals and Expectations

Animal-related legal matters are charged with emotion. The strength of the human-animal bond is such that clients whose animals are the subject of a legal challenge are often very upset and want justice immediately—in a legal system that traditionally has little experience with animal-related matters. Make sure you understand your client's expectations and explain to the client as early as possible whether the expectations are achievable. For example, if your client seeks to close down the business of a kennel through litigation based on the negligent care of a boarded house pet, explain to your client whether the jurisdiction supports such damages and the likelihood that such a result can realistically be achieved.

A. Considerations of Economics

One of the realities for lawyers handling animal-related disputes is that damages are frequently not significant. For example, the client might have a beloved house pet who was injured while under the care of a kennel or a veterinarian. Even if the animal were to die, the common law in most jurisdictions would likely limit recovery to the animal's fair market value and possibly to incidental out-of-pocket costs. Under most circumstances, this amount is significantly less than the attorney's fee. Unless the jurisdiction is one that will account for and consider the "emotional distress" damage component, the potential recovery does not justify accepting the case under a standard contingency fee arrangement. (See Appendix A for a sample rejection letter to a potential client.)

Counsel have the extra challenge of managing client expectations. In accepting an animal-related matter, in considering methods to maximize recovery for the client, and in making decisions of effective litigation strategies, lawyers can consider the following issues.

1. Expense of Litigation Compared to Outcome

Clients are always concerned about the potential that their litigation expenses could exceed the amount at stake. The problem becomes even more apparent if the client insists on aggressive representation or if the matter requires extensive briefing and court appearances.

Counsel would be wise to discuss the likely cost up front with the potential client and seriously consider whether the matter should be accepted. If the proposed client insists that a "principle" justifies paying legal fees that far exceed the amount at stake, common sense holds that the "principle" will wear off as your fees grow, and you will be left with a disgruntled client.

2. Potential for Recovery of Legal Fees

The perception among many proposed clients is that the legal process is a "loser pay" system and that the lawyer's fees will be recovered by the opposing party at the end of the litigation. As attorneys, we know that this is rarely the case. Legal fees are recoverable in only four possible scenarios:

- An applicable statute governs the matter through which attorneys' fees are potentially recoverable (a few of these statutes are listed further in this section). These laws can include deceptive trade practice laws, consumer protection laws, civil rights laws, antitrust laws, and fair debt collection practice laws. Many basic animal-related disputes simply do not qualify.
- The parties had a contract that carefully and properly addresses attorneys' fees.
- An applicable court rule provides for attorneys' fees, typically as a sanction. Some court rules give judges the discretion to order one party to pay some or all of the other's legal fees and expenses if certain events occur, such as the violation of a valid court ruling.
- The court specifically found that the other party asserted a "frivolous" claim or defense in a lawsuit or has in some way acted in "bad faith" in a legal proceeding, and the judge has the power to punish the wrongdoer.

3. Potential for Opposing Party Being Insured

Counsel should consider the possibility that the opposing party is insured. On the positive side, if the defendant is insured for the matter involved, this will obviously increase the chance of successfully collecting a judgment. On the negative side, the insurance company's opposition to payment of a claim or payment of a settlement could significantly increase the chance that the matter will be aggressively defended.

Counsel for parties threatened with a claim or suit should advise their clients to confirm whether they have insurance coverage for a particular matter. Forwarding the claim or suit to the insurer for its evaluation purposes can be very important. If the matter is covered, or if the insurer has elected to defend it, the possibility exists that the company will seek to reassign it to its regular defense counsel servicing the area; potentially, the insurer might retain you to cover the defense at its expense.

4. Potential to Maximize Recovery by Invoking a Statute

Some state statutes provide potential treble damages, such as the Colorado Consumer Protection Act, which allows private citizens to bring suit and recover the amount of actual damages, $500, or three times the actual damages, whichever is greatest, together with the cost of reasonable attorneys' fees, if established by clear and convincing evidence that the person engaged in bad faith.[3]

5. Potential for Recovery of Emotional Distress Damages

A small, but potentially growing, number of jurisdictions have shown a willingness to allow animal owners to recover emotional distress damages in cases involving injury to or loss of an animal.[1] Counsel should consider whether the client has a claim for recovery of these damages, or whether a good-faith argument can be made successfully for the applicable jurisdiction to begin allowing such damages.

B. Practical Considerations

The mere fact that your client is embroiled in a legal dispute does not necessarily mean that immediate litigation is always the appropriate action. When your client insists on hiring you to pursue immediate litigation, certain other considerations deserve to be taken into account, as explored next.

1. Impact on Future Business Dealings

If the parties to a dispute, based on where they live or the nature of their business, will need to work together or do business together in the future, the dispute could be appropriate for an alternative to the litigation process, such as facilitation or mediation. These alternatives might have a greater chance of protecting the parties' continued business relationship.

2. *Negative Publicity*

An adverse judgment or verdict could be devastating to the reputation of a party to the litigation. Trial and appellate rulings on animal law matters can be newsworthy, for example, if a party recovers a particularly large sum of money or if a court creates novel case law.[5] Potential clients should be advised of the possibility of negative publicity and the fact that publicity cannot always be controlled. This fact might motivate the potential client to explore options to resolve the dispute or to keep it away from the litigation process and, by arrangement with the opposing party and its counsel, to bring the matter into a confidential dispute resolution mechanism, with an agreement of confidentiality.

3. *Potential for Counterclaims*

The litigation your client pursues could be met with a counterclaim directed against your client. This could force your client to fight two legal matters as well as impose on your client the burden of taking a defensive position on the counterclaim in addition to its offensive position in the principal claims. For this reason, before commencing litigation, discuss with your client whether grounds exist that could generate a counterclaim. For example, if your client seeks to bring a collection lawsuit for nonpayment of horse boarding fees, the filing of the litigation might prompt a counterclaim from the opposing party asserting that board payments were deliberately withheld because the stable materially breached the contract by providing substandard and negligent care of the boarded horse.

As a practical matter, counsel can evaluate whether the statute of limitations on the principal claim will exceed that of a counterclaim. This means, for example, that if your client seeks to bring a claim for nonpayment of animal boarding expenses, but the client is fearful that the client might defend itself by asserting a negligence case involving alleged injuries to the boarded animal, you can advise your client on the possibility of deferring litigation until the expiration of the negligence statute of limitations. That is, if the applicable state law imposes a six-year statute of limitations for claims involving breach of contract, but only a three-year statute of limitations on claims of negligence, it might be advisable for your client to wait until the negligence statute of limitations expires before initiating the breach of contract litigation. That way, a counter-claim for negligence would be time-barred while the collection action can proceed.

IV. Litigating on a Shoestring

Animal-related litigation can involve disputes with relatively small amounts at stake. Counsel seeking to reduce litigation expenses can consider a few options:

- Consider alternative dispute resolution (ADR), such as mediation, arbitration, or facilitation.
- To spare the expense of in-person depositions, utilize interrogatories and requests to admit as much as possible.
- Send well-written demand-for-settlement letters to the opposing party to encourage a settlement.

V. Fee Agreements

A carefully documented fee arrangement between counsel and client can serve several beneficial purposes. The written fee agreement starts the attorney-client relationship in a professional manner and helps prevent misunderstandings in the future. Additionally, the formalized fee arrangement could prevent fee-related disputes, grievances against the lawyer, and malpractice claims. Sample fee agreements for hourly fees as well as contingency fees are included in this chapter as Appendices B and C. Counsel developing their own fee agreement should make sure to check applicable ethical or other regulations.

A. Contingency

Before submitting retainer letters to your potential clients, pay particular attention to the applicable state ethical and other restrictions that might limit the contingency fee. These rules and restrictions might also establish whether the lawyer must refund retainers. See Appendix C for a sample contingency fee agreement.

B. Hourly

Setting your fee poses some challenges. If the economics are not significant in the matter, you might be persuaded to reduce your fee out of sincere interest in helping the client and easing the financial burden of the litigation. On the other hand, as a lawyer who might be especially experienced in handling animal law matters, you might believe yourself entitled to request a fee that is customarily charged by lawyers who have special expertise in certain unique areas of the law. While setting your fee, be aware of Model Rule of Professional Conduct 1.5(a) in regard to "reasonable fees."[6] See Appendix B for a sample retainer letter for an hourly fee arrangement.

C. Flat Fee

Flat fee arrangements could be desirable in certain animal law matters. Counsel might find these arrangements particularly risky in litigated matters, since the time and expense cannot always be predicted. By comparison, flat fee arrangements can be reasonable for routine transactional matters, such as the drafting of animal-related service contracts.

VI. Alternative Dispute Resolution

Alternative methods of dispute resolution (ADR) can be beneficial for clients. Not every dispute is suitable for an alternative to the legal system, however. Special consideration should be given to circumstances when ADR is more appropriate, such as

- Matters where amounts of money, rather than equitable or injunctive relief, are at issue
- Matters where the parties will likely do business together in the future
- Matters where the parties could have competing claims and counterclaims that involve an intensive evaluation of the facts, rather than merely issues of law
- Disputes that are required, by an enforceable contract, to be resolved through ADR
- Matters where the client is especially concerned about confidentiality
- Unique matters that could be better resolved by a tribunal with special expertise, if the arbitration can be handled by specially qualified, industry-oriented arbitrators

See Appendix D for a sample agreement to dismiss pending personal injury litigation and submit the dispute to arbitration.

VII. Settlements

Litigation attorneys are well aware of the fact that few cases ever proceed to trial. Rather, the overwhelming majority of cases are either settled or disposed of in some manner, such as dispositive motions. Counsel should carefully consider several factors in determining whether a case should be settled. A few factors are

- The extent to which the plaintiff has a compelling case of liability
- The strength of, or existence of, defenses by the defendant
- Credibility of the witnesses and parties
- Nature of the jurisdiction and how cases of the type at issue would be perceived
- The degree of damages and the ability to prove them
- Whether the jury will sympathize with the plaintiff or dislike the defendant
- Your ability to procure key witnesses and experts
- Overall litigation expense in taking the case through trial or even appeal
- Reputation of the assigned judge

It is foreseeable that counsel will need to prepare settlement agreements. When animal-related disputes are settled, the written agreements sometimes involve special provisions such as

- Possession and custody of the animal at issue in the dispute
- Possession of resulting offspring of the animal
- Future breeding rights (transferable or nontransferable)
- Obligation of a particular party to pay continuing expenses for the care and keeping of the animal until possession is transferred pursuant to the agreement
- Obligation of a particular party to procure or maintain appropriate insurance, such as mortality insurance and/or liability insurance
- Execution of breed registration papers

See Appendix E for a sample settlement agreement in a personal injury case.

APPENDIX A

Sample Letter Rejecting Potential Legal Matter

January 9, 2009
Mr. Burt Zealous
1234 Any Street
Yorktown, PA 78907

Re: Inability to Represent You in Your Dispute with Joe Defendant

Dear Mr. Zealous:

Thank you very much for contracting me this afternoon regarding your legal dispute with Joe Defendant and your interest in hiring me to represent you. Your confidence in my abilities is greatly appreciated.

I write to confirm our discussion. As we discussed today, it will not be possible for me to represent you in your matter. If you seek names of other possible attorneys to represent you in the matter with Mr. Defendant, you might want to contact the Pennsylvania Bar Association's Lawyer Referral Service. Its telephone number is: ______.

Please understand that your dispute with Mr. Defendant is likely governed by Pennsylvania's three-year statute of limitations for such disputes. Therefore, any litigation that you may bring against him should be filed by no later than _________.

Thank you, again, for keeping me in mind. Please consider contacting me on other unrelated matters in the future. I sincerely hope that your dispute with Mr. Defendant resolves itself to your satisfaction.

Sincerely,

George Grateful
PLANT & ANIMAL L.L.P.
Attorneys at Law
222 N. Smart, Suite 222
Intelligent, PA

APPENDIX B

Sample Retainer Agreement—Hourly Fee

[Date]

Best Friend
123 Trust Me Road
Honesty, IL 12345

Re: Retainer Letter—Dog Breeding and Sale Business

Dear Mr. Friend:

It was a pleasure speaking with you yesterday regarding your dog breeding and sale business. I look forward to working with you on this project.

As we discussed, Horse & Hound, L.L.P. requests all clients, new and existing, to execute its Engagement Letter. This Letter specifies the terms and conditions of our engagement and describes our responsibilities and the legal services we will perform for you.

1. **Engagement.** You are retaining this Firm for purposes of: ______
____
____
____
______________________, and any additional specific assignments (hereinafter "assigned matters"). The Firm will serve as your counsel in these specifically assigned matters until its engagement is terminated by you or this Firm or until the legal services have been fully performed and concluded.

2. **Scope of Legal Services to Be Performed.** As your counsel in these assigned matters, the Firm will perform the agreed upon services, including, but not limited to: ______________________________
______________________________.

3. **Compensation, Billing, and Expenses.** The Firm will charge you for services performed under this Letter agreement in accordance with the agreed hourly rate schedule which is $200/hour for Lawyer, unless otherwise agreed to in writing between you and Lawyer. A retainer in the

amount of $1,000 is required on or before March 31, 2009, from which billed time will be deducted until fully expended. Time will be accounted for in increments of one-tenth of an hour and invoices will reflect the time spent and a brief description of the services performed.

The Firm is authorized to incur, on your behalf, costs and expenses the Firm deems necessary to perform the legal services you assigned. In addition, you agree to pay or reimburse the Firm for these costs and out-of-pocket expenses incurred in connection with its work for you. The Firm may forward to you statements from vendors of $500.00 or more for direct payment by you. The Firm will bill you monthly for fees and expenses relating to its work, and you will pay each such billing within thirty (30) days of the invoice date.

4. Responsible Staff. Lawrence Lawyer will be responsible for Horse & Hound, L.L.P.'s relationship with you and should be contacted in the first instance concerning issues that pertain generally to that relationship. Mr. Lawyer will also be responsible for billing matters and will be primarily responsible for supervising the Firm's performance of services for you. Other lawyers in the Firm will be called upon only after conferring with you and your consent is obtained, except for occasional ministerial matters.

5. Conflicts of Interest. The Firm is not aware of any actual or potential conflicts of interest arising from its representation of you and the Firm's other clients. As conflicts of interest arise and are identified, the Firm will disclose them to you, and you and the Firm will work together to resolve them. While the Firm will have primary responsibility for monitoring and identifying conflicts of interest, you agree to assist the Firm in that regard.

6. Termination. You may terminate the Firm's engagement at any time and for any reason (or no reason). Upon termination, you will pay within ten (10) days the Firm's outstanding fees and expenses. Outstanding fees and expenses include both billed but unpaid invoices and unbilled time and expenses for services performed. You will give the Firm written notice of termination. Upon receipt of such notice, the Firm will stop performing services for you except with respect to those specific matters, if any, identified in the notice of termination or related correspondence. As to those specific matters only, the Firm will continue to represent you during a reasonable transition period until new counsel is engaged and the Firm is instructed to cease work on such matters.

The firm may terminate its engagement as your counsel at any time and for any reason, including but not limited to nonpayment or late payment of fees, to the extent permitted by the applicable rules of professional conduct. You will pay the Firm's outstanding fees and expenses within ten

(10) days of the effective date of such termination. Upon the termination of its engagement as counsel, the Firm will cooperate with you in the transfer of its responsibilities to successor counsel as directed by you.

7. Conclusion. We greatly appreciate the opportunity to work with you and provide legal services for you. If the terms and conditions set forth in this letter are satisfactory, please execute this letter and return an executed copy to the undersigned, keeping a copy in your file.

Horse & Hound, L.L.P. thanks you for your business. If there is any term of this Letter you would like to discuss, please do not hesitate to ask at any time.

Very truly yours,

HORSE & HOUND, L.L.P.
Lawrence Lawyer

Enclosures

The terms of the foregoing letter are agreed to and accepted as of March 31, 2009.

____

Best Friend

APPENDIX C

Sample Retainer Agreement—Contingency Fee

[Date]

Ms. Janet Hurt
789 Barking Ln.
Columbus, OH 78907

Re: Retainer Agreement—Matter Involving Alleged Personal Injury at Doghouse Kennels

Dear Ms. Hurt:

Thank you for hiring me to represent you in connection with the injury you sustained while picking up your dog at Doghouse Kennels on the evening of January 6, 2009.

Experience has taught me that the most successful attorney-client relationships are based on openness and a clear understanding of the role each party is to play. Therefore, I would like to confirm the terms of my engagement by you as your attorney in the above referenced matter, including the services I will perform, responsibilities, and compensation.

The services I will perform will be: (1) to evaluate all possible claims on your behalf for personal injuries and/or property damages against Doghouse Kennels; (2) to commence litigation against Doghouse Kennels on your behalf; and (3) to represent your interests in the litigation and keep you informed at all stages.

You hereby authorize me and/or my law firm to fully investigate your claim, and, should suit or other legal proceedings be filed on your behalf, to fully prepare for and prosecute the same. It is understood that neither one of us shall settle any claims without having first obtained the consent to such settlement of the other person.

We agree that any payment that I may receive for the services referred to in this letter agreement is entirely contingent upon my recovering for you, or on your behalf, money or property. For my professional services, you agree to pay me on a *contingency fee basis* through the following arrangement: (1) of any moneys recovered by me on your behalf through settlement, judgment, or otherwise, I shall receive thirty-three and ⅓ percent (33⅓%), and this amount shall be paid to or retained by me; and (2) the remainder shall be yours.

Despite the division of proceeds of a judgment or settlement, discussed above, we also understand and agree to the following:

First, you shall reimburse me for certain expenses and costs that are advanced by me and/or my office that are attributable to your matter, which could include, for example, significant long-distance telephone calls, telefaxes (40¢/page), photocopies (20¢/page), independent specialists or expert witnesses, accident reconstruction experts, overnight express mailings, and any other expense that my office fronts on your matter. If you are asked to pay any expenses described above, they shall be payable at the conclusion of the matter, and the amount of any recovery may be used to cover them. These expenses are not deducted from my one-third contingency attorney fee, discussed above, but shall be in addition to the fee.

Second, it is possible that deductions may need to be made for unpaid bills for doctors, hospitals, clinics, therapists, specialists, medical insurer/medical lien holders, and related items. Disbursement of such funds, if any, would need to be made directly to the doctor, hospital, or medical insurer/medical lien holder concerned.

Either of us may terminate this attorney-client relationship at any time and for any reason upon prior written notice to the other party. Should you desire in the future to change attorneys, you agree to reimburse me for all costs then expended and the agreed-upon percentage for any offer of settlement obtained at the time you may remove me from the matter. Or, if no offer of settlement has been made when our attorney-client relationship ends, then my office shall receive all costs expended plus one-half of the aforementioned percentages upon all monies subsequently obtained by you or any representative on your behalf. As your attorney in this matter, I will, of course, need to be kept abreast of all matters, and I will make sure that you are kept updated as much as possible.

Should any dispute occur between us arising out of this attorney-client relationship, we mutually agree to submit the dispute(s) to binding arbitration through the American Arbitration Association.

While I cannot guarantee successfully achieving your goals, I can assure you that I will, at all times, use my best efforts on your behalf.

Your business is greatly appreciated. If you should have any questions in regard to this letter or in regard to any aspect of this attorney-client relationship, please do not hesitate to contact me at any time.

Sincerely,

by:____________________________
Brenda Barrister

I HAVE READ THIS LETTER, APPROVE IT, AND AGREE TO ITS TERMS

Signed:____________________________
Janet Hurt
Dated: ____________________________

APPENDIX D

Sample Agreement to Arbitrate

Binding Arbitration Agreement

THIS BINDING ARBITRATION AGREEMENT (hereafter, "Agreement") is hereby stipulated and agreed to between JANE DOE and DON DOE (hereafter collectively, "Plaintiffs") and DAVE ROE and JEAN ROE (hereafter collectively, "Defendants") as follows:

A. On March 9, 2009, Plaintiff Jane Doe was injured by a stallion owned by the Roe Defendants at the Harper Valley PTA Horse Show (hereafter referred to as "the Incident");
B. The Plaintiffs have claimed personal injuries and loss of consortium against the Roe Defendants arising out of the Incident;
C. Plaintiffs have filed a lawsuit that is now pending in the Madison County, Montana, Circuit Court entitled: "*Jane Doe and Don Doe, Plaintiffs, v. Dave M. Roe and Jean Roe*," Case No. 09-12345 (hereafter referred to as "the Litigation"). The Litigation relates directly to the Incident and sets forth Plaintiffs' claims against the Defendants;
D. The Defendants have denied liability to the Plaintiffs, or either of them individually, and have asserted several defenses in the Litigation;
E. The Plaintiffs and the Defendants all agree to expedite the resolution of the disputed issues of liability and damages between them by submitting the Litigation (as to these parties, only) to binding arbitration subject to each of the following terms and conditions:

   1. The Plaintiffs will select the Plaintiffs' one (1) arbitrator. The Defendants will select the Defendants' one (1) arbitrator. The Plaintiffs and the Defendants will, together, agree upon the selection of the one (1) third, neutral arbitrator. No person shall sit as the neutral arbitrator who otherwise would be disqualified as a Circuit Court Judge trying this case;
   2. The Plaintiffs will pay the costs, expenses, and fees of Plaintiffs' arbitrator. The Defendants will pay the costs, expenses, and fees of the Defendants' arbitrator. The fee of the third, neutral arbitrator will be shared on a 50-50 basis between the Plaintiffs and the Defendants;

3. Attorneys' fees and fees to be paid to medical, lay, or expert witnesses are to be borne by the party that incurs them;
4. The parties will use their best efforts to commence the arbitration hearing by late June 2010;
5. The claims to be arbitrated shall be those set forth in the Plaintiffs' Complaint in the Litigation and the Defendants' Answer and Affirmative Defenses asserted in response;
6. The Court Rules governing admission of evidence will not be strictly followed in the arbitration hearing. Medical records and medical reports may be submitted to the arbitration panel without the necessity of deposing doctors or medical experts, producing records custodians, etc.;
7. Each party will provide the other party with arbitration summaries and documents intended to be used at the arbitration hearing no later than twenty-one (21) days prior to the date that the arbitration hearing is to commence. The arbitrators may consider all previous orders and decisions of the Madison County Circuit Court in the Litigation;
8. Either party may call any witnesses listed on the witness list of any party in the Litigation, or any other witnesses that both parties agree may be called. Plaintiffs and Defendants need not remain physically present at the arbitration proceedings, except when they are needed to testify;
9. The arbitrators shall determine the issues of liability and any allowable damages. They may not award to any prevailing party their witness fees, attorneys' fees, expenses of courts/arbitration, or related expenses, nor may they award to any party interest, costs, case evaluation sanctions, or offer of judgment sanctions. The decision, in writing, of any two (2) arbitrators will be binding;
10. The arbitrators shall be instructed to complete their deliberations and issue an arbitration award within fourteen (14) days from the date that the arbitration hearing is concluded and the proofs are closed. The arbitration award, if any, shall be rendered in the form of a single lump-sum amount in U.S. dollars that is expressed without any allocation as to past or future damages, allocation of fault as to any nonparty, reduction to present value, or mandatory structured settlement. The arbitrators' ruling shall set forth the general basis of their decision as to liability and damages, if any, but need not resemble a jury verdict form. The amount due, if any, to Plaintiffs as a result of the arbitration shall be fully

paid within thirty (30) days of the issuance of the arbitration award, except if either party pursues a postarbitration hearing motion to vacate the award pursuant to paragraph 12, below. Should a postarbitration motion to vacate the award be filed pursuant to paragraph 12, below, the amount due to Plaintiffs, if any, shall be fully paid within thirty (30) days of a final decision by a trial or appellate court of proper jurisdiction affirming the arbitration award;

11. The record of the arbitration hearing will be finalized at the close of the proofs. Postarbitration hearing motions will be allowed within thirty (30) days of the issuance of the arbitration award, only for grounds of fraud, lack of good faith, and arbitrator(s) exceeding their powers;
12. The decision of the arbitrators will represent a full and final award as to liability and damages between the Plaintiffs and the Defendants;
13. If a misarbitration (comparable to a mistrial) occurs for any reason, the subsequent arbitration hearing(s) will be subject to the same terms and conditions set forth in this Agreement;
14. Neither the amount of the arbitration award nor the identity of the parties will be disclosed by the parties or their attorneys to any persons or entities other than those necessary to finalize the conclusion of this matter and the disbursement of funds, if any, to the Plaintiffs;
15. Madison County, Montana, Case No.: 09-12345 may be dismissed as to the Plaintiffs and the Defendants, except that the court shall retain jurisdiction over this matter to enforce this agreement and resolve any disputes arising from the arbitration proceedings;
16. If Plaintiffs, or either of them individually, should die prior to the time that the arbitration hearing commences, their estates will continue as the Plaintiffs in this action;
17. Neither of the parties (nor any others acting on their behalf) will be liable for any interest, costs, attorneys' fees, mediation sanctions, or offer of judgment sanctions in consideration for this matter being placed into binding arbitration; and
18. This binding arbitration agreement may not be revoked.

Jane Doe, Plaintiff	Don Doe, Plaintiff
Dated: August __, 2009	August __, 2009

Dave Roe, Defendant
Dated: August __, 2009

Jean Roe, Defendant
August __, 2009

[counsel signatures underneath]

APPENDIX E

Sample Settlement Agreement

Settlement Agreement and Release

This SETTLEMENT AGREEMENT AND RELEASE (hereafter, "Agreement") is made and entered into as of this ___ day of ____________, 20__, by and between PAUL PLAINTIFF (hereafter, "PLAINTIFF") and DEFENDANT CORPORATION (hereafter, "DEFENDANT").

Defined Terms

A. "PLAINTIFF" shall mean PAUL S. PLAINTIFF and his heirs, personal representatives, successors, and assigns.
B. "DEFENDANT CORPORATION" shall mean, individually and collectively, DEFENDANT CORPORATION, a Delaware corporation, and its officers, directors, employees, and agents.
C. "LITIGATION" shall mean the case entitled "Paul S. Plaintiff v. Defendant Corporation, U.S. District Court, E.D. Pennsylvania, Case No.: 09-123456."
D. "CLAIMS" shall mean and include any and all claims, actions, causes of action, lawsuits, injuries, damages, judgments, verdicts, rights, counterclaims, demands, liabilities, legal fees and expenses, losses, costs, expenses, attachments, garnishments, liens, and compensation of any nature whatsoever, whether direct or derivative, in law or in equity, whether presently known or unknown, vested or contingent, suspected or unsuspected, foreseen or unforeseen, patent or latent, arising out of (or purporting to arise out of) the LITIGATION or relating to Pennsylvania common law or applicable state or Federal statutes, if any.

IT IS HEREBY AGREED by and among PLAINTIFF and DEFENDANT in sole consideration of the sum of FIFTY-FIVE THOUSAND AND 00/100 DOLLARS ($55,000):

A. RELEASE OF ALL CLAIMS AGAINST DEFENDANT. PLAINTIFF knowingly and voluntarily releases DEFENDANT from any and all CLAIMS that PLAINTIFF now holds or owns or may at any time have held or owned against DEFENDANT arising prior to the date of this Agreement, whether such claims arose or may arise under or by virtue of the laws of any jurisdiction, including without limitation, any and all claims, demands, and causes of action arising between the parties that were raised or could have been raised in the LITIGATION.

   DEFENDANT hereby knowingly and voluntarily releases PLAINTIFF from all CLAIMS that DEFENDANT now holds or owns or may at any time have held or owned against PLAINTIFF arising prior to the date of this Agreement, whether such claims arose or may arise under or by virtue of the laws of any jurisdiction, including without limitation, any and all claims, counterclaims, demands, and causes of action arising between the parties that were raised or could have been raised in the LITIGATION.

B. PAYMENT. Upon receipt of a fully executed copy of this Agreement, DEFENDANT, through its counsel, shall deliver to the attorney for PLAINTIFF a check in the amount of FIFTY-FIVE THOUSAND DOLLARS ($55,000) made payable to "Paul S. Plaintiff and Ann I. Mal, His Attorney." It is agreed that this amount shall constitute good and valuable consideration and shall be the sole consideration for this Agreement. It is agreed that this amount shall constitute good and valuable consideration and shall be the sole consideration for this Agreement.

C. NO ADMISSION OF LIABILITY. DEFENDANT denies that it engaged in any wrongful or unlawful conduct or is in any way liable for any claims asserted by PLAINTIFF in the LITIGATION. Neither the payment of any consideration or anything in this Agreement shall be construed an admission of any liability to PLAINTIFF.

D. STIPULATION FOR DISMISSAL OF SUBJECT LITIGATION. Upon the full execution of this Agreement, counsel for the parties shall promptly execute and file with the Court, a Stipulation and Order of Dismissal of the LITIGATION.

E. DISCHARGE OF ANY AND ALL LIENS. PLAINTIFF warrants that if any liens or encumbrances exist on the PLAINTIFF's claims against DEFENDANT, payment or satisfaction of any and all such liens that may now or hereafter exist shall be the sole responsibility of PLAINTIFF.

F. GOVERNING LAW. Pennsylvania law governs this Agreement.

G. SEVERABILITY. If any provision of this Agreement is found to be invalid or unenforceable, the remaining provisions shall continue in full force and effect without being impaired or invalidated in any way.

H. ENTIRE AGREEMENT. This Agreement is the entire agreement between the parties with respect to its subject matter and cancels and supersedes any prior agreements and negotiations. This Agreement can only be modified in writing signed by all parties.

I. BREACH/ATTORNEY FEES. If this Agreement is breached, the breaching party will pay the nonbreaching party's attorneys' fees and court costs.

J. ADVICE OF COUNSEL. PLAINTIFF has discussed this Agreement with and obtained advice from his legal counsel, Ann I. Mal, Esq. This Agreement is being signed voluntarily and of the PLAINTIFF's free act and deed.

The undersigned certifies that he has read and fully understands this Settlement Agreement and Release, and that he is signing it freely and voluntarily.

THIS IS A RELEASE—READ BEFORE SIGNING
by:______________________________
PAUL S. PLAINTIFF
[STATE-SPECIFIC NOTARY PUBLIC PORTION]

Notes

1. By presenting to the court a pleading, written motion, or other paper . . . an attorney or unrepresented party certifies that to the best of the person's knowledge, information, and belief, formed after an inquiry reasonable under the circumstances:

   (1) it is not being presented for any improper purpose, such as to harass, cause unnecessary delay, or needlessly increase the cost of litigation;

   (2) the claims, defenses, and other legal contentions are warranted by existing law or by a nonfrivolous argument

> for extending, modifying, or reversing existing law or for establishing new law;
>
> (3) the factual contentions have evidentiary support or, if specifically so identified, will likely have evidentiary support after a reasonable opportunity for further investigation or discovery; and
>
> (4) the denials of factual contentions are warranted on the evidence or, if specifically so identified, are reasonably based on belief or a lack of information.

FED. R. CIV. P. 11(b). FED. R. CIV. P. 11(c) allows a court to impose sanctions on a lawyer, firm, or party that violates this rule.

2. According to the ABA Tort Trial & Insurance Practice Section Animal Law Committee's brochure "Animal Law Committee" (2008), "Animal Law courses are offered at more than 90 American law schools."
3. COLO. REV. STAT. §§ 6-1-101 *et seq*.
4. *See, e.g.*, Burgess v. Taylor, 44 S.W.3d 806 (Ky. App. 2001); LaPorte v. Assoc. Indeps., 163 So. 2d 267 (Fla. 1964). For more information, see Chapter 9, Remedies in Animal-Related Litigation, and Chapter 2, Negligence and Tort Law.
5. For example, in Michigan on April 29, 1997, Wayne County, Michigan, Circuit Court Judge Kaye Tertzag in the case of *Murray v. Bill Wells Kennels and Robert James Turner* (Wayne County Cir. Ct. No. 95-536479-NO) issued a pretrial ruling that was particularly newsworthy. Judge Tertzag ordered that the plaintiff, who owned a dog, was entitled to recover emotional distress damages in her lawsuit against the defendant boarding kennel that was alleged to have given the dog negligent care leading to the dog's death. What made the trial court case unique was the fact that Michigan case law did not authorize the awarding of such damages. This ruling was broadly publicized.
6. Model Rule of Professional Conduct 1.5(a), to which many states have counterpart ethical rules, generally provides that a lawyer's fee shall be reasonable.

INDEX